SPSS 12 MADE SIMPLE

PAUL R. KINNEAR
COLIN D. GRAY

*Department of Psychology,
University of Aberdeen*

HOVE AND NEW YORK

First published 2004 by Psychology Press
27 Church Road, Hove, East Sussex BN3 2FA

Simultaneously published in the USA and Canada
by Psychology Press 270 Madison Avenue, New York NY 10016

Psychology Press is a part of the T&F Informa plc

Copyright © 2004 Psychology Press

Printed and bound in Great Britain by TJ International Ltd, Padstow, Cornwall, from pdf files supplied by the authors. Cover design by Hybert Design.

All rights reserved. No part of this book may be reprinted or reproduced or utilised in any form or by any electronic, mechanical, or other means, now known or hereafter invented, including photocopying and recording, or in any information storage or retrieval system, without permission in writing from the publishers.

This book is not sponsored or approved by SPSS, and any errors are in no way the responsibility of SPSS. SPSS is a registered trademark and the other product names are trademarks of SPSS Inc. SPSS Screen Images © SPSS Inc. SPSS UK Ltd, First Floor St Andrew's House, West Street, Woking, Surrey, GU21 1EB, UK.

Windows is a registered trademark of Microsoft Corporation. For further information, contact: Microsoft Corporation, One Microsoft Way, Redmond, WA 98052-6399, USA.

This publication has been produced with paper manufactured to strict environmental standards and with pulp derived from sustainable forests.

British Library Cataloguing in Publication Data

A catalogue record for this book is available from the British Library.

Library of Congress Cataloging-in-Publication Data

Kinnear, Paul R.
 SPSS 12 made simple / Paul R. Kinnear, Colin D. Gray.-- 1st ed.
     p. cm.
 Includes bibliographical references and index.
 ISBN 1-84169-524-6 (pbk.)
 1. SPSS (Computer file) 2. Social sciences--Statistical methods--Computer programs.
     I. Gray, Colin D. II. Title.

HA32.K553 2004
300'.285'555--dc22
                              2004012426

ISBN 1-84169-524-6

Contents

Preface x

CHAPTER 1   Choosing a statistical test *1*

1.1   INTRODUCTION *1*
1.2   CHOOSING A STATISTICAL TEST: SOME GUIDELINES *5*
1.3   SIGNIFICANCE OF DIFFERENCES *6*
  1.3.1   The design of the experiment: Independent versus related samples *6*
  1.3.2   Flow chart for selecting a suitable test for differences between averages *7*
  1.3.3   Two conditions: The t tests *8*
  1.3.4   Two conditions: Nonparametric tests *9*
1.4   ANALYSIS OF VARIANCE EXPERIMENTS *10*
  1.4.1   Between subjects and within subjects factors *10*
  1.4.2   Factorial designs: Between subjects and within subjects experiments *11*
  1.4.3   Mixed or split-plot factorial experiments *12*
  1.4.4   Flow chart for ANOVA *13*
  1.4.5   Analysing the results of one-factor experiments *13*
  1.4.6   Analysing the results of factorial experiments *15*
1.5   MEASURING STRENGTH OF ASSOCIATION BETWEEN VARIABLES *15*
  1.5.1   Flow chart for selecting a suitable test for association *15*
  1.5.2   Measuring association in nominal data: Contingency tables *16*
  1.5.3   Multiway contingency tables *16*
1.6   PREDICTING SCORES OR CATEGORY MEMBERSHIP *17*
  1.6.1   Flow chart for selecting the appropriate procedure for predicting a score or a category *17*
  1.6.2   Simple regression *18*
  1.6.3   Multiple regression *18*
  1.6.4   Predicting category membership: Discriminant analysis and logistic regression *18*
1.7   ONE-SAMPLE TESTS *18*
  1.7.1   Flow chart for selecting the appropriate one-sample test *19*
  1.7.2   Goodness-of-fit: Data in the form of measurements *19*
  1.7.3   Goodness-of-fit: Nominal data *20*
  1.7.4   Inferences about the mean of a single population *20*
  1.7.5   Nominal data: Testing a coin for fairness *20*
1.8   FINDING LATENT VARIABLES: FACTOR ANALYSIS *20*
1.9   A FINAL COMMENT *21*

CHAPTER 2 Getting started with SPSS 12 *22*

2.1 OUTLINE OF AN SPSS SESSION *22*
    2.1.1 Entering the data *22*
    2.1.2 Selecting the exploratory and statistical procedures *23*
    2.1.3 Examining the output *23*
    2.1.4 A simple experiment *23*
    2.1.5 Preparing data for SPSS *24*
2.2 OPENING SPSS *25*
2.3 THE SPSS DATA EDITOR *26*
    2.3.1 Working in Variable View *26*
    2.3.2 Working in Data View *31*
    2.3.3 Entering the data *32*
2.4 A STATISTICAL ANALYSIS *36*
    2.4.1 An example: Computing means *36*
    2.4.2 Keeping more than one application open *40*
2.5 CLOSING SPSS *40*
2.6 RESUMING WORK ON A SAVED DATA SET *41*
Exercise 1 Some simple operations with SPSS 12 *42*
Exercise 2 Questionnaire data *44*

CHAPTER 3 Editing and manipulating files *48*

3.1 MORE ABOUT THE SPSS DATA EDITOR *48*
    3.1.1 Working in Variable View *48*
    3.1.2 Working in Data View *55*
3.2 MORE ON THE SPSS VIEWER *58*
    3.2.1 Editing the output *58*
    3.2.2 More advanced editing *60*
    3.2.3 Tutorials in SPSS *64*
    3.3 SELECTING FROM AND MANIPULATING DATA FILES *64*
    3.3.1 Selecting cases *65*
    3.3.2 Aggregating data *67*
    3.3.3 Sorting data *69*
    3.3.4 Merging files *70*
    3.3.5 Transposing the rows and columns of a data set *74*
3.4 IMPORTING AND EXPORTING DATA *76*
    3.4.1 Importing data from other applications *76*
    3.4.2 Copying output *78*
3.5 PRINTING FROM SPSS *79*
    3.5.1 Printing output from the Viewer *79*
Exercise 3 Merging files – Adding cases & variables *89*
Appendix of files *93*

Contents v

CHAPTER 4   Exploring your data *95*

4.1   INTRODUCTION *95*
4.2   SOME USEFUL MENUS *96*
4.3   DESCRIBING DATA *97*
    4.3.1   Describing nominal and ordinal data *97*
    4.3.2   Describing measurements *103*
4.4   MANIPULATION OF THE DATA SET *115*
    4.4.1   Reducing and transforming data *115*
    4.4.2   The COMPUTE procedure *116*
    4.4.3   The RECODE and VISUAL BANDER procedures *122*
Exercise 4   Correcting and preparing your data *129*
Exercise 5   Preparing your data (continued) *132*

CHAPTER 5   Graphs and charts *134*

5.1   INTRODUCTION *134*
    5.1.1   Graphs and charts on SPSS *134*
    5.1.2   Viewing a chart *135*
5.2   BAR CHARTS *136*
5.3   ERROR BAR CHARTS *140*
5.4   PIE CHARTS *146*
5.5   LINE GRAPHS *149*
5.6   SCATTERPLOTS *150*
Exercise 6   Charts and graphs *153*
Exercise 7   Recoding data; selecting cases; line graph *156*

CHAPTER 6   Comparing averages: Two-sample and one-sample tests *159*

6.1   INTRODUCTION *159*
    6.1.1   SPSS procedures for two-sample tests *159*
    6.1.2   SPSS procedures for one-sample tests *160*
    6.1.3   Some general points about statistical tests *160*
    6.1.4   One tailed and two-tailed tests *162*
    6.1.5   Effect size *163*
6.2   PARAMETRIC METHODS: THE T TESTS *164*
    6.2.1   Assumptions underlying the independent-samples t test *164*
    6.2.2   An example of the use of the independent-samples t test *164*
    6.2.3   How to report the results of a statistical test *170*
    6.2.4   Demonstration of the effects of outliers and extreme scores in a small data set *171*
    6.2.5   The paired-samples (within subjects) t test *171*
6.3   EFFECT SIZE, POWER AND THE NUMBER OF PARTICIPANTS *175*
6.4   NONPARAMETRIC EQUIVALENTS OF THE T TESTS *179*
    6.4.1   Independent samples: Mann-Whitney test *179*
    6.4.2   Related samples: Wilcoxon, Sign and McNemar tests *182*
6.5   ONE-SAMPLE TESTS *184*

6.5.1 Goodness-of-fit: Data in the form of measurements (scale data) *185*
6.5.2 Goodness-of-fit: Nominal data *188*
6.5.3 Inferences about the mean of a single population *192*
Exercise 8 Comparing the averages of two independent samples of data *196*
Exercise 9 Comparing the averages of two related samples of data *200*
Exercise 10 One-sample tests *204*

CHAPTER 7 The one-factor between subjects experiment *207*

7.1 INTRODUCTION *207*
    7.1.1 Rationale of the ANOVA: The *F* test *207*
    7.1.2 Planned and post hoc comparisons *208*
    7.1.3 Effect size *208*
7.2 THE ONE-WAY ANOVA *210*
    7.2.1 An experiment on the efficacy of two mnemonic techniques *210*
    7.2.2 Procedure for the one-way ANOVA *211*
    7.2.3 Output for the one-way ANOVA *214*
    7.2.4 Other techniques *219*
7.3 NONPARAMETRIC TESTS *219*
    7.3.1 The Kruskal-Wallis test *219*
    7.3.2 Dichotomous data: The Chi-square test *221*
Exercise 11 One-factor between subjects ANOVA *222*

CHAPTER 8 Between subjects factorial experiments *226*

8.1 INTRODUCTION *226*
8.2 FACTORIAL ANOVA *229*
    8.2.1 Preparing the data for the factorial ANOVA *229*
    8.2.2 Exploring the data: Obtaining boxplots *230*
    8.2.3 Choosing a factorial ANOVA *231*
    8.2.4 Output for a factorial ANOVA *235*
8.3 EFFECT SIZE AND POWER IN FACTORIAL ANOVA *240*
8.4 EXPERIMENTS WITH MORE THAN TWO TREATMENT FACTORS *241*
Exercise 12 Between subjects factorial ANOVA (two-way ANOVA) *245*

CHAPTER 9 Within subjects experiments *248*

9.1 INTRODUCTION *248*
    9.1.1 Rationale of a within subjects experiment *248*
    9.1.2 Assumptions underlying the within subjects ANOVA *249*
    9.1.3 Effect size and power in within subjects ANOVA *249*
9.2 A ONE-FACTOR WITHIN SUBJECTS ANOVA *250*
    9.2.1 Entering the data *250*
    9.2.2 Exploring the data: Boxplots for within subjects factors *251*
    9.2.3 Running the within subjects ANOVA *252*
    9.2.4 Output for a one-factor within subjects ANOVA *256*
    9.2.5 Unplanned multiple comparisons: Bonferroni method *261*

Contents

9.3 NONPARAMETRIC TESTS FOR A ONE-FACTOR WITHIN SUBJECTS EXPERIMENT *261*
    9.3.1   The Friedman test for ordinal data *261*
    9.3.2   Cochran's Q test for nominal data *263*
9.4 THE TWO-FACTOR WITHIN SUBJECTS ANOVA *264*
    9.4.1   Preparing the data set *265*
    9.4.2   Running the two-factor within subjects ANOVA *266*
    9.4.3   Output for a two-factor within subjects ANOVA *269*
    9.4.4   Unplanned comparisons following a factorial within subjects experiment *273*
Exercise 13   One-factor within subjects (repeated measures) ANOVA *274*
Exercise 14   Two-factor within subjects ANOVA *276*

CHAPTER 10   Mixed factorial experiments *278*

10.1 INTRODUCTION *278*
    10.1.1   Rationale of a mixed factorial experiment *278*
10.2 THE TWO-FACTOR MIXED FACTORIAL ANOVA *279*
    10.2.1   Preparing the SPSS data set *279*
    10.2.2   Exploring the results: Boxplots *280*
    10.2.3   Running the ANOVA *281*
    10.2.4   Output for the two-factor mixed ANOVA *283*
10.3 THE THREE-FACTOR MIXED ANOVA *288*
    10.3.1   Two within subjects factors and one between subjects factor *288*
    10.3.2   One within subjects factor and two between subjects factors *289*
10.4 FURTHER ANALYSIS: SIMPLE EFFECTS AND MULTIPLE COMPARISONS *290*
Exercise 15   Mixed ANOVA (experiments with between and within subjects factors) *292*
Exercise 16   Mixed ANOVA: Three-factor experiment *294*

CHAPTER 11   Measuring statistical association *296*

11.1 INTRODUCTION *296*
    11.1.1   Statistical association between quantitative variables *296*
    11.1.2   Significance of a correlation and effect size *299*
11.2 CORRELATIONAL ANALYSIS WITH SPSS *299*
    11.2.1   Procedure for the Pearson correlation *302*
    11.2.2   Output for the Pearson correlation *303*
11.3 OTHER MEASURES OF ASSOCIATION *304*
    11.3.1   Measures of association strength for ordinal data *304*
    11.3.2   Measures of association strength for nominal data: The Crosstabs procedure *307*
    11.3.3   Finding the meaning of statistics in output tables *313*
Exercise 17   The Pearson correlation *315*
Exercise 18   Other measures of association *318*
Exercise 19   The analysis of nominal data *321*

CHAPTER 12 Regression *324*

12.1 INTRODUCTION *324*
    12.1.1 Simple, two-variable regression *324*
    12.1.2 Multiple regression *325*
    12.1.3 Residuals *325*
    12.1.4 The multiple correlation coefficient *325*
12.2 SIMPLE REGRESSION *325*
    12.2.1 Procedure for simple regression *326*
    12.2.2 Output for simple regression *329*
12.3 MULTIPLE REGRESSION *334*
    12.3.1 Procedure for simultaneous multiple regression *335*
    12.3.2 Procedure for stepwise multiple regression *339*
    12.3.3 The need for a substantive model of causation *342*
12.4 SCATTERPLOTS AND REGRESSION LINES *342*
Exercise 20 Simple, two-variable regression *347*
Exercise 21 Multiple regression *350*
Appendix to Exercise 21 – The data *352*

CHAPTER 13 Multiway frequency analysis *353*

13.1 INTRODUCTION *353*
    13.1.1 Comparison of loglinear analysis with ANOVA *354*
    13.1.2 Building a loglinear model *354*
13.2 TWO EXAMPLES OF A LOGLINEAR ANALYSES *355*
    13.2.1 First example: Exam success *355*
    13.2.2 Running a loglinear analysis for the Exam success data *357*
    13.2.3 Output for the Exam success loglinear analysis *359*
    13.2.4 Comparison with the total independence model *364*
    13.2.5 Second example: Gender and professed helpfulness *366*
    13.2.6 Running a loglinear analysis for the Gender data *368*
    13.2.7 Output for the Gender loglinear analysis *370*
Exercise 22 Loglinear analysis *372*

CHAPTER 14 Discriminant analysis and logistic regression *374*

14.1 INTRODUCTION *374*
    14.1.1 Discriminant analysis *375*
    14.1.2 Types of discriminant analysis *375*
    14.1.3 Stepwise discriminant analysis *375*
    14.1.4 Restrictive assumptions of discriminant analysis *376*
14.2 DISCRIMINANT ANALYSIS WITH SPSS *376*
    14.2.1 Preparing the data set *377*
    14.2.2 Exploring the data *377*
    14.2.3 Running discriminant analysis *378*
    14.2.4 Output for discriminant analysis *380*
    14.2.5 Predicting group membership *386*
14.3 BINARY LOGISTIC REGRESSION *387*

		14.3.1	Introduction *387*
		14.3.2	An example of a binary logistic regression with quantitative independent variables *389*
		14.3.3	The importance of exploring the data 390
		14.3.4	Preparing the data set *390*
		14.3.5	Running binary logistic regression *391*
		14.3.6	Output for binary logistic regression *393*
		14.3.7	Binary logistic regression with categorical independent variables *396*
		14.3.8	Output of binary logistic regression with categorical independent variables *398*
	14.4	MULTINOMIAL LOGISTIC REGRESSION *399*	
		14.4.1	Introduction *399*
		14.4.2	Running multinomial logistic regression *400*
		14.4.3	Output of multinomial logistic regression *402*
	14.5	SOME GENERAL POINTS *403*	

Appendix The data for logistic regression *404*
Exercise 23 Predicting category membership: Discriminant analysis and binary logistic regression *405*
Appendix to Exercise 23 – The data *408*

CHAPTER 15 Exploratory Factor analysis *409*

15.1	INTRODUCTION *409*		
	15.1.1	What are the 'factors' in factor analysis? *409*	
	15.1.2	Stages in a factor analysis *410*	
	15.1.3	The extraction of factors *411*	
	15.1.4	The rationale of rotation *411*	
	15.1.5	Confirmatory factor analysis and structural equation modelling *412*	
15.2	A FACTOR ANALYSIS OF DATA ON SIX VARIABLES *412*		
	15.2.1	Some technical terms *413*	
	15.2.2	Entering the data for a factor analysis *414*	
	15.2.3	The factor analysis procedure *414*	
	15.2.4	Output for factor analysis *417*	
15.3	USING SPSS CONTROL LANGUAGE *423*		
	15.3.1	The power of SPSS syntax: An example *423*	
	15.3.2	Using a correlation matrix as input for factor analysis *425*	
	15.3.3	Progressing with SPSS syntax *428*	

Exercise 24 Factor analysis *429*

Revision Exercises *431*

References *437*

Index *438*

Preface

SPSS 12 Made Simple is similar to our earlier books in assuming no previous knowledge of SPSS. Recent developments in SPSS, however, as well as the changing needs of the researcher, have necessitated a major revision.

In recent years, SPSS has produced a rapid succession of new releases. While some of these were relatively minor (though useful) improvements on the previous versions, others brought major changes. SPSS 10, in a radical new development, featured a Data Editor with two display modes: Variable View, in which the user named and specified the variables; and Data View, in which the data were entered. This excellent feature has been retained in subsequent releases. Release 12 brings further significant improvements. The restrictions on the naming of variables at the data entry stage have been greatly relaxed. Variable names can now be up to 64 characters in length. Moreover, although a variable name must still be a continuous string of characters (the first of which is a letter), there can now be a mixture of upper and lower case letters, as in *TimeOfDay*. The variable labels, which appear in SPSS output, are (within generous limits) largely free of restrictions.

SPSS 12 also features some major improvements in the quality of the graphics, as well as giving the user more editorial control over charts and displays. These advances, in combination with powerful facilities such as pivot tables, enable the SPSS user to produce graphs and tables of outstanding quality. SPSS 12 also retains interactive charts, a versatile and powerful facility capable of producing graphs (such as clustered bar charts with error bars) that are hybrids of the standard forms.

Over the years, our book has benefited from various kinds of input. The clarity of the text is continuously put to the test in the SPSS courses that we run for our students (undergraduate and postgraduate), from whom we receive valuable feedback. The frequent queries and problems sent to us by researchers have been another important factor in our decisions about coverage and emphasis. We have also been mindful of the recommendations of the current Publication Manual of the American Psychological Association and offer advice on the reporting of the results of statistical tests.

The gratifyingly positive response from researchers, students and instructors alike has confirmed the continuing need for an introductory text with illustrative examples and exercises for private or course study. Like its predecessors, this new book is the product of many years of experience in teaching data analysis with SPSS. We have found it helpful to use annotated screen snapshots of SPSS output, windows and dialog boxes to illustrate fine points of technique and these are used extensively throughout the book. The accompanying comments, together with worked examples and further exercises, clarify issues which, over the years, have arisen frequently during our SPSS practical classes and thesis supervision at the University of Aberdeen. As the title of our book indicates, the emphasis is upon practical data analysis rather than statistical theory, and a wide range of techniques are described.

Readers familiar with our previous books will notice some changes. The new edition's page size is smaller, which should make it easier for the reader to have the book sitting on the desktop beside the computer. We realise that, as time has gone by, the reader's requirements

Preface

have changed. Since nowadays everyone is familiar with the Windows environment, we have replaced the earlier chapter on Windows operations (formerly Chapter 2) with a new chapter, *Getting started with SPSS*, which is a guided tour of a typical SPSS session. Chapter 3, *More on editing and data entry*, includes new sections on aggregating data and merging files. Chapter 4, *Exploring your data*, has a section on the Visual Bander, a new Release 12 procedure, which recodes data with graphic representations of distributions. Chapter 5, *More graphs and charts*, includes, in addition to a detailed description of chart editing in SPSS 12, a new section on drawing bar graphs with error bars. Chapters 6 to 15, the statistical chapters, have been thoroughly revised and updated to exploit the capabilities of SPSS 12. Chapter 14, *Discriminant analysis and logistic regression*, now includes multinomial logistic regression, which is applicable when the dependent variables has more than two categories.

A major new feature of the statistical chapters is the inclusion of measures of effect size, reports of which are now required by many scientific publications, including all the American Psychological Association journals. We have also included a new section on power and sample size.

As before, the Exercises that immediately follow most chapters contain only chapter-specific material. The six Revision Exercises at the end of the book, on the other hand, require the reader to analyse a data set without the cueing that a chapter context would provide and are intended to help the reader to develop a sense of strategy in data analysis.

Throughout the preparation of this book, we have been most fortunate in having the advice, encouragement and SPSS expertise of John Lemon, Senior Computing Adviser at Aberdeen University's Directorate of Information Systems and Services. John read all the draft chapters and contributed many helpful comments and suggestions. We are also very grateful to Caroline Green, Senior Teaching Fellow, for her valuable observations on the Exercises and our students' progress with them in the practical classes. Our Departmental Computing Officer Martin Fraser has given us his unfailing support at every stage in the preparation of the book. Finally, we would like to express our gratitude to all those who, though too numerous to mention individually, have helped in various ways.

Colin Gray and Paul Kinnear

June, 2004.

CHAPTER 1

Choosing a statistical test

1.1 Introduction

1.2 Choosing a statistical test: Some guidelines

1.3 Significance of differences

1.4 Analysis of variance experiments

1.5 Measuring strength of association between variables

1.6 Predicting scores or category membership

1.7 One-sample tests

1.8 Finding latent variables: factor analysis

1.9 A final comment

1.1 INTRODUCTION

This book is intended for those working in disciplines in which the units of study (people, plants, coelacanths) vary with respect to what is being studied. It is therefore dangerous to generalise about all people, all animals, all trees, all coelacanths) on the basis of knowledge about only some of them. This is why researchers in such disciplines must make use of the methods of statistics.

An important concept here is that of a **sample**. A sample is a selection of observations (often assumed to be random) from a reference set, or **population**, of possible observations that might be made. By analogy with a lottery, it may be helpful to think of a population as the numbers being churned around in the barrel, and the sample as those actually drawn. Sampling implies **sampling variability**: samples from the same population can vary markedly in their characteristics. It follows that a random sample is not necessarily **representative**: it may have very different characteristics (e.g. mean and standard deviation) from those of the population from which it has been drawn.

When we carry out an experiment on reaction speed with 100 participants, we invariably do so because we want to make inferences about the reaction speeds of people in general: it is the **population** that is of primary interest, not the **sample**. But to make an inductive inference about all people on the basis of data from just **some** people is to risk a false conclusion.

Measures of characteristics of a sample (such as its mean and standard deviation) are known as **statistics**. The corresponding characteristics in the population are known as **parameters**. Our research question is invariably about parameters, not statistics. **Statistical inference** is a set of methods for making inductive (and hence fallible) inferences about parameters from the values of statistics.

We turn to the discipline of statistics when:
1. We want to describe and summarise the data as a whole;
2. We want to confirm that other researchers repeating our study would obtain a similar result.

It is in connection with 2. that the need for formal **statistical tests** arises. The researcher may see theoretically important patterns in a set of data. But are these merely the result of sampling variability or are they real patterns that would emerge if the project were to be repeated?

Statistical inference, being inductive, is subject to error. One aspect of statistical inference is the calculation of **estimates** of population parameters (e.g. the population mean) from the statistics of samples (the sample mean). The value of the sample mean is a **point estimate** of the population mean. But the sample mean may be wide of the mark as a point estimate. From the statistics of a sample, however, it is also possible to specify a range of values, known as a **confidence interval**, within which one can say, with a specified level of certainty, that the true population mean lies. A confidence interval is an **interval estimate** of a parameter.

Variables

A **variable** is a characteristic or property of a person, an object or a situation, comprising a set of different values or categories. Height is a variable, as are weight, blood type and gender. **Quantitative variables**, such as height, weight or age, are possessed in **degree** and so can be measured. Measurements express the degree to which a characteristic is possessed in terms of units (inches, pounds, kilograms) on an independent scale. In contrast, **qualitative** variables, such as sex, blood group or nationality, are possessed only in **kind**: they cannot be expressed in units. With qualitative variables, we can only make counts of the cases falling into the various categories, as when we might record that among an audience, there are 60 men and 40 women.

Types of data: Measurements, ordinal and nominal

The result of a research project is a set of **data**, that is, a body of information about the variables possessed by the humans, animals, trees, or whatever else is being studied. A set of data might contain information about people's heights, weights, attitudes, blood groups, ages, genders, and so on.

There are three main kinds of data:
1. **Measurements** (often known as **interval data**) are numbers expressing quantity as so-many units on an independent scale. (SPSS uses the term **scale** for such data.) Heights and weights are obvious examples. However, in the same category, it is usual to include performance scores, such as the number of times a participant hits a target, as well as IQs, responses to questionnaires and other psychometric data.

2. **Ordinal** data consist of ranks, assignments to ordered categories, or sequencing information. For example, if two judges give the same set of ten paintings ranks from *1* (for the best) to *10* (for the worst), the data set will consist of *10* pairs of ranks, one pair for each painting. If *100* participants in a research project are asked to rate, say, *30* objects by placing each object in one of five ordered categories, where *1* is *Very good* and *5* is *Very Bad*, the result will resemble *100* sets of ranks with **ties**, that is, with several objects sharing the same rank.
3. **Nominal** data relate to qualitative variables or attributes, such as gender or blood group, and are records of category membership. Nominal data are merely **labels**: they may take the form of numbers, but such numbers are arbitrary code numbers representing, say, the different blood groups. Any other numbers (as long as they are all different) would have served the purpose just as well.

While both measurements and ordinal data relate to quantitative variables, only in the former does each datum give quantitative information independently of the other data. Ranks mean nothing individually: they merely enable the reader to say that one individual has more or less of some variable than another individual with a different rank in the same data set.

Sometimes the term **categorical data** is used to denote either purely nominal assignments or assignments to ordered categories. This term straddles our distinction between types 2. and 3. above.

Hypotheses

Data are not gathered just for the sake of it. Research is driven by the desire to test a provisional supposition about nature known as a **hypothesis**. Often, a hypothesis states that there is a causal relationship between two variables: it is an assertion that the value of one variable, the **independent variable (IV)**, at least partially determines that of another, the **dependent variable (DV)**. For example, it might be hypothesised that ingestion of a certain drug improves skilled performance, in which case the IV is presence/absence of the drug, and the DV is task performance.

Univariate, bivariate and multivariate data sets

It is sometimes useful to classify data sets according to the number of DVs observed during the course of the investigation. If a data set consists of observations on only one variable (as when it contains people's heights), it is a **univariate** data set. If there are two variables (height and weight), it is a **bivariate** data set. If there are three or more variables (height, weight, reaction time, number of errors), it is a **multivariate** data set.

Experiments and quasi-experiments

An **experiment** is the collection of comparative data under controlled conditions. In a true experiment, the IV is **manipulated** by the investigator. For example, the drug effectiveness hypothesis could be tested by comparing the performance of a sample of people who have taken the drug with that of a comparison, or **control**, group who have not. (It is usual to improve the comparability of the two groups by presenting the controls with a **placebo**, that is, a neutral medium ideally identical with that in which the drug was presented to the **experimental** group.)

The IV is controlled by the investigator, and its values are determined **before the experiment is carried out**. This is achieved either by **random assignment** of the participants to the pre-set conditions or by deciding to test each participant under all conditions, if that is feasible. The DV, on the other hand, is **measured during the course of the investigation**.

In a true experiment, the IV, unlike gender, blood group, or nationality, is not an intrinsic property of the participants: the participants are assigned at random to the experimental or the control group. In other circumstances, however, the hypothesis might be that some aspect of a person's gender, nationality, religion or age group affects, say, their views on some issue. For example, do men and women have different views about violence on television? This hypothesis might be tested by interviewing some men and women and comparing their views. Here, the IV is gender, and the DV is attitude to violence. In this case, however, the participants have not been assigned to the categories making up the IV: the latter is an intrinsic property of the participant. Such **quasi-experiments** often produce results that are difficult to interpret unequivocally. The problem with quasi-experimental research is that the IV, being a **participant** (or **subject**) **variable**, is itself a whole package of other variables, some of which may not be under the control of the investigator. Some of the difficulties with quasi-experimental research can be overcome by following an appropriate sampling strategy. For example, in the gender-and-attitudes experiment, the men and women would be sampled from comparable social strata and similar age bands. But there is always the possibility that the effects of gender will be entangled, or **confounded**, with those of uncontrolled, **extraneous** variables.

Experimental versus correlational research

In true experiments and quasi-experiments, the IV is manipulated by the researcher, either directly, as in the former, or by sampling, as in the latter. In **correlational research**, the variables are recorded as they occur in the participants. For example, it might be hypothesised that cheerfulness (the DV) is promoted by exercise (the IV). One might test this hypothesis by asking participants in a study to rate themselves on cheerfulness and to say how often they take exercise. Here the problems of interpretation are multiplied. It may well turn out that the cheeriest people take the most exercise, the glummest take the least and moderately cheerful people lie somewhere in between. But both the putative IV (amount of exercise) and the putative DV (cheerfulness) may arise from a myriad other possible variables, including socioeconomic status, personality and physical type.

Implications for data analysis

Typically, the data from experiments and quasi-experiments are processed using statistical methods that are rather different from those used with data from correlational research. In the next section, we offer the reader some advice (together with some cautions and caveats) on choosing statistical tests.

1.2 CHOOSING A STATISTICAL TEST: SOME GUIDELINES

It is common for authors of statistical texts to offer advice on choosing statistical tests in the form of a flow chart, decision tree or similar diagram. The numerous schemes that have been proposed vary considerably, and sometimes contradict one another. The reason for the inconsistency is partly that most classifications tend to break down in certain circumstances. Moreover, in some situations, the correct choice has been hotly disputed.

On one matter at least, however, there is general agreement. **There is no such thing as a decision tree that will automatically lead the investigator to the correct choice of a statistical test in all circumstances.** Some of the later chapters contain illustrations of the penalties that a scheme-reliant approach can incur. At best, a decision tree can serve only as a rough guideline. Ultimately, a safe decision requires careful reflection upon one's own research aims and a **thorough preliminary exploration of the data**.

Considerations in choosing a statistical test

The choice of a statistical test depends upon:
1. The **research question**
2. The **plan**, or **design**, of the research
3. The **type of data** that you wish to analyse

This list is by no means comprehensive; nor do we intend to imply that any fixed ordering of these three considerations is appropriate in all situations. Moreover, a decision about one often has implications for the others.

The research question

We shall identify five basic research situations in which formal statistical tests can be applied (Figure 1). For each situation, the appropriate techniques will be discussed in the sections indicated in the figure.

The questions are as follows:
1. Is a difference (between averages) significant? For example, is resting heart rate the same before and after a fitness course? (Sections 1.3 and 1.4)
2. How strongly are variables associated? For example, do tall parents tend to have tall children? (Section 1.5)
3. Can scores on a target variable (or category membership, if the variable is qualitative) be predicted from data on other variables? For example, can university performance be predicted by scores on aptitude tests? (Section 1.6)
4. From a single sample of data, what can be said about the population? For example, if we know the vocabulary test scores of 100 children, what can we infer about the scores of the entire population of children in the same age group? (Section 1.7)
5. The user has a multivariate data set, perhaps people's scores on a battery of ability tests. Can these scores be accounted for (or classified) in terms

of a smaller number of hypothetical latent variables or **factors**? For example, can performance in a variety of intellectual pursuits be accounted for in terms of general intelligence? (Section 1.8)

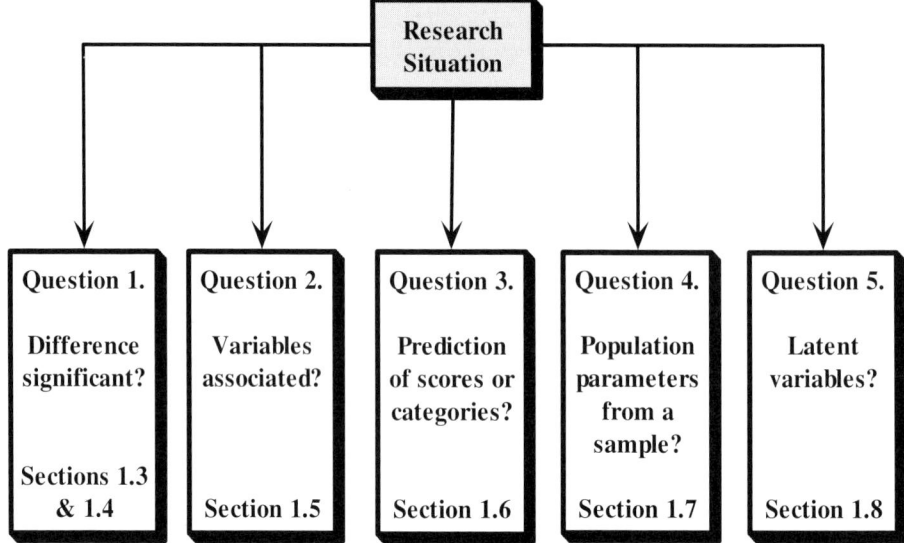

Figure 1. Five types of research situation

1.3 SIGNIFICANCE OF DIFFERENCES

The question of whether two means are significantly different is one that arises naturally in the context of experimental or quasi-experimental research, where the performance of the participants under different conditions is being compared.

Suppose that in a drug experiment, performance under two different conditions (experimental and control) has been measured and that the means have somewhat different values. This may seem to support the experimenter's hypothesis; but would a similar difference be found if the experiment were to be repeated? Here the researcher wishes to test the **statistical significance** of the difference, that is, to establish that the difference is too large to have been merely a chance occurrence.

1.3.1 The design of the experiment: Independent versus related samples

Of crucial importance in the choice of an appropriate statistical test is the question of whether the experiment would have resulted in **independent samples** or **related samples** of scores.

Independent samples

Suppose we select, say, *100* participants for an experiment and randomly assign half of them to an experimental condition and the rest to a control condition. With this procedure, the assignment of one person to a particular group has no effect upon the group to which another is assigned. The two **independent samples** of participants thus selected will produce two independent samples of scores. A useful criterion for deciding whether you have independent samples of data is that there must be **no basis for pairing the scores in one sample with those in the other**. An experiment in which independent samples of participants are tested under different conditions is known as a **between subjects experiment**.

Related samples

Suppose that each of fifty participants shoots ten times at a triangular target and ten times at a square target of the same area. For each target, each participant will have a score ranging from *0* (ten misses) to *10* (ten hits). As in the previous example, there will be two samples of *50* scores. This time, however, each score in either sample can be paired with the same participant's score with the other target. We have two **related samples** of scores, or a set of **paired data**. The scores in two related samples are likely to be substantially correlated, because the better shots will tend to have higher scores with either target than will the poorer shots. An experiment like this, in which each participant is tested under both (or all) conditions, is known as a **within subjects experiment**. Within subjects experiments are also said to have **repeated measures** on the IV (the shape of the target).

There are other ways of obtaining paired data. Suppose that in the current example, the participants were pairs of identical or fraternal twins: each participant shoots at only one target and their twin shoots at the other. This experiment will also result in two related samples of scores, because, as in the repeated measures experiment, there is a basis for pairing the data. Different statistical tests are appropriate for use with independent and related samples of data.

1.3.2 Flow chart for selecting a suitable test for differences between averages

Figure 2 outlines **some** of the considerations leading to a choice of a statistical test of the significance of differences between means (or frequencies, if one has nominal data). If there are more than two conditions or groups, an analysis of variance (ANOVA) may be applicable (see Section 1.4). In this section, we shall consider only the comparison between two groups or conditions, such as male versus female, or experimental group versus control group.

To use the chart, begin at the START box and consider how many conditions there are in the experiment. If there are two conditions, proceed down the chart to the next stage. The next questions are whether the samples are independent or related and whether the data are measurements, as opposed to nominal assignments. The appropriate test is then shown in the bottom box. If there are more than two conditions, an ANOVA should be considered and the flow chart in Figure 3 (see page 13) can be used to ascertain which ANOVA test might be appropriate.

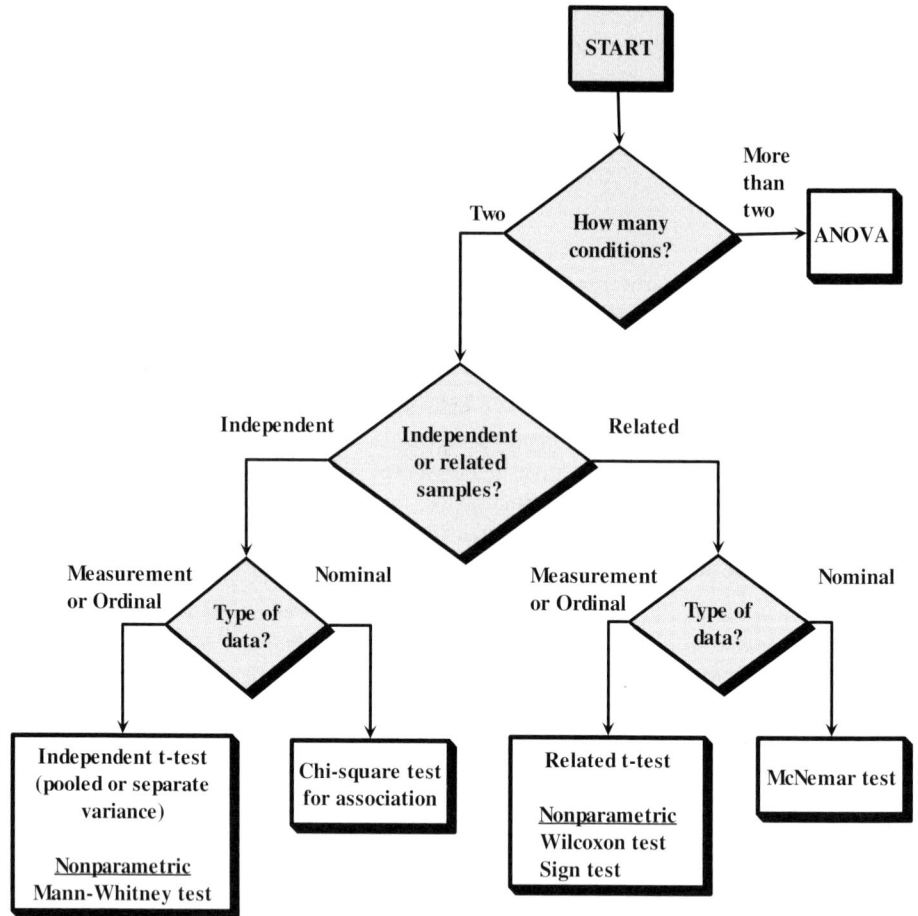

Figure 2. Flow chart showing the selection of a suitable test for differences between averages

1.3.3   Two conditions: The *t* tests

To compare the levels, or averages, of two *independent samples* of data in the form of measurements, the **independent-samples *t* test** is often appropriate (see Figure 2). This test and other *t* tests are fully described in Chapter 6.

See Chap. 6

In its original form, the independent-samples *t* test uses an average or **pooled** estimate of the supposedly constant population variance. For this reason, it is sometimes known as the **pooled *t* test**. Sometimes, however, the data may not conform to the requirements of the independent-samples *t* test. If the sample variances and/or sample sizes are markedly different, the **separate-variance *t* test** may be a safer choice or possibly resort to a nonparametric test as described in the next Section.

When one wishes to compare the means of two **related samples** of data, as when each participant in an experiment has been tested under both an experimental and a control condition, the **related samples *t* test** should be considered, or possibly (depending on the data distribution) a nonparametric test as described in the next Section.

1.3.4 Two conditions: Nonparametric tests

The *t* test is an example of a **parametric test**: that is, it is assumed that the data are samples from a population with a specified (in this case normal) distribution. Other tests, known as **nonparametric tests**, do not make specific assumptions about population distributions and are therefore also referred to as **distribution-free tests**.

There are circumstances in which a *t* test can give misleading results. This is especially likely to occur when the data set is small and there are some highly deviant scores, or **outliers**, which can inflate the values of the denominators of the *t* statistics.

Figure 2 identifies the nonparametric equivalents of the independent and related samples *t* tests. A nonparametric alternative to the independent-samples *t* test is the **Mann-Whitney U test**. Two nonparametric equivalents of the related-samples *t* test are the **Wilcoxon test** and the **Sign test**.

See Chap. 6

There has been much controversy about the use of nonparametric tests instead of *t* tests with some kinds of data. While some authors (e.g. Siegel & Castellan, 1988) strongly recommend the use of nonparametric tests, others, such as Howell (2002) emphasise the robustness of the parametric *t* tests to violations of their assumptions and the loss of power incurred by the use of the equivalent nonparametric tests. We suggest that, provided the data show no obvious contraindications, such as the presence of outliers, marked skewness or great disparity of variances (especially if the last is coupled with a large difference in sample size), a *t* test should generally be used. There are also circumstances in which the removal of outliers from the data set followed by another *t* test is a defensible procedure (e.g. very long reaction times that could be due to participants not being ready). Otherwise, a nonparametric equivalent should be considered. Data in the form of ratings are a grey area, and there has been considerable debate over whether they should be analysed with parametric or nonparametric tests. If, however, the data are measurements at the ordinal level in the first place, as with sets of ranks, or nominal data, a nonparametric test is the only possibility.

In a planned experiment, the data usually take the form of measurements on an independent scale with units. Occasionally, however, one might have a situation in which each participant attempts a task and either a pass or a fail is recorded. If so, a two-group experiment will yield two independent samples of **nominal data**. Here the research question is still one of the significance of

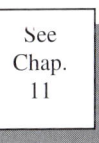
See Chap. 11

differences, albeit of differences between frequencies, rather than differences between means. With independent samples, a **chi-square test of association** will answer the question of whether the success rates in the two groups are significantly different.

Two correlated samples of dichotomous nominal data: The McNemar test

Suppose that, before they hear a debate on an issue, ten people are asked whether they are for or against the proposal. Afterwards, the same people are asked the same question again. This is a **within subjects experiment**, in which each participant is observed under two conditions: *Before* (an event) and *After*.

See Chap. 6

On each occasion of testing, a person's response is coded either as *0 (Against)* or *1 (For)*.

Since the same person produces two responses, we have a paired nominal data set, for which the **McNemar test** is appropriate if one wishes to claim that the debate has resulted in a change of opinion.

1.4 ANALYSIS OF VARIANCE EXPERIMENTS

The **analysis of variance (ANOVA)** is actually a whole set of techniques, each of which is based upon a model of how the data were generated and culminates in tests that are appropriate for that particular model only. It is therefore important to identify ANOVA experiments correctly, in order to choose the right tests. In this section, only some of the most common ANOVA experiments will be described. There are many others, which can be found in standard statistics textbooks such as Winer, Brown & Michels (1991).

In the ANOVA, a **factor** is a set of related conditions or categories. The conditions or categories making up a factor are known as its **levels**, even though, as in the qualitative factors of gender or blood group, there is no sense in which one category can be said to be 'higher' or 'lower' than the other. The terms **factor** and **level** are the equivalents, in the context of ANOVA, of the terms **independent variable** and **value**, respectively. A factor can be either a true independent variable or a participant characteristic, such as gender, that we 'manipulate' **statistically**, by sampling people from each of some set of categories. In ANOVA, participant variables are treated in exactly the same way as IVs that are directly manipulated by the experimenter.

1.4.1 Between subjects and within subjects factors

Some factors are **between subjects**: that is, the participant is tested under only one condition (i.e. at one level) of the factor. Gender is an obvious example. Other factors are **within subjects**, that is, the participant is tested under all the different conditions (levels) making up the factor. An experiment with a within subjects factor is also said to have **repeated measures** on that factor.

Returning to the simplest two-group drug experiment, in which the performance of an experimental (drug) group is compared with that of a control (placebo) group, we have one treatment factor (*Drug Condition*), comprising two conditions or levels: *Drug Present* and *Drug Absent*. Since different samples of participants perform under the different conditions, this is a **between subjects experiment**. Should the investigator wish to study the effectiveness of more than one drug, the performance of two or more groups of participants on different drugs could be compared with that of the controls. In that case, there would still be one treatment factor, but with three or more levels (see Table 1a).

Now suppose that another investigator wishes to test the hypothesis that words presented in the right visual hemifield are recognised more quickly than those presented in the left hemifield. Fifty participants are each presented with twenty words in the left and right hemifields and their median response times are recorded. In this experiment (as in the drug experiment), there is **one treatment factor** (in this example, *Hemifield of Presentation*) comprising two levels (conditions), *Left Field* and *Right Field*. But this time, the same participants perform under both conditions. This experiment is said to be of **within subjects** design, or to have **repeated measures on the Hemifield factor**.

In the general case of a one-factor, within subjects experiment, the factor would comprise three or more treatment conditions, or levels, and each participant would perform under all conditions. For example, to test the hypothesis that the accuracy with which a participant shoots at a target depends upon the shape of the target's perimeter, each participant might be tested with circular, square, triangular and diamond-shaped targets. Here the treatment factor *Shape of Target* would have four levels: *Circle*, *Square*, *Triangle* and *Diamond* (Table 1b).

Table 1. Between subjects and within subjects experiments in which there is one treatment factor with four levels

(a) A one-factor between subjects experiment

	Levels of the Drug factor			
	Control	Drug A	Drug B	Drug C
Participants	Group 1	Group 2	Group 3	Group 4

(b) A one-factor within subjects experiment

	Levels of the Shape factor			
	Circle	Square	Triangle	Diamond
Participants	The same participants perform with all four shapes			

1.4.2 Factorial designs: Between subjects and within subjects experiments

In addition to the effects of different drugs upon fresh participants, a researcher might also wish to investigate their effects upon those who have voluntarily gone without sleep for twenty-four hours. Accordingly, an experiment is designed as shown in Table 2, which shows two factors: *State* (*Fresh, Tired*); *Drug* (*Drug A, Drug B*). An experimental design with two or more factors is known as a **factorial** design.

Table 2. A two-factor factorial between subjects experiment

	Levels of the Drug factor	
Levels of the State factor	Drug A	Drug B
Fresh	Group 1	Group 2
Tired	Group 3	Group 4

Between subjects factorial experiments

Notice that, in Table 2, different samples of participants perform in the four combinations of the two treatment factors. Since each participant is tested only once, this type of experiment is said to be of **between subjects factorial** design. It can also be described as having **two factors with no repeated measures**. Factorial experiments are discussed in Chapter 8.

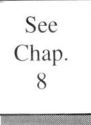

See Chap. 8

Within subjects factorial experiments

Table 3 shows another kind of factorial experiment.

Table 3. A two-factor factorial within subjects experiment				
Levels of the Shape factor:	\multicolumn{2}{c}{Triangle}	\multicolumn{2}{c}{Square}
Levels of the Colour factor:	Blue	Green	Blue	Green
Participants	\multicolumn{4}{c}{The same participants perform under all four combinations of shape and colour}

As before, there are two factors, which in this case are:
1. *Shape of Target* (*Triangle, Square*);
2. *Colour of Target* (*Blue, Green*).

This time, however, every participant is tested at both levels of each factor. This type of factorial design is known as a **within subjects factorial** experiment. Alternatively, the experiment in Table 3 can be said to have **repeated measures on both factors.** Within subjects experiments are discussed in Chapter 9.

See Chap. 9

1.4.3   Mixed or split-plot factorial experiments

Suppose that, in addition to the effects of target colour, the experimenter wishes to test the hypothesis that men and women differ in the colour of target with which they are more accurate (Table 4).

Table 4. A two-factor mixed factorial experiment with one between subjects factor (Gender) and one within subjects factor (Colour of Target)		
	\multicolumn{2}{c}{**Levels of the Colour of Target factor**}
Levels of the Gender factor	Red	Blue
Male	\multicolumn{2}{c}{Each participant is tested with red and blue targets}
Female	\multicolumn{2}{c}{Each participant is tested with red and blue targets}

Once again, there are two factors:
1. *Gender* (*Male, Female*);
2. *Colour of Target* (*Red, Blue*).

The first factor is between subjects; but the second factor is within subjects, because each participant shoots at both the red and the blue target. Factorial experiments with a mixture of between subjects and within subjects factors are known as **mixed** (or **split-plot**) factorial experiments. These are discussed in Chapter 10.

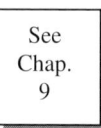
See Chap. 10

1.4.4 Flow chart for ANOVA

The between subjects, within subjects and mixed (or split-plot) factorial ANOVA are based upon different models of the data, and require different tests. The presence of a within subjects (or repeated measures) factor in an experiment results in the gathering of related (rather than independent) samples of data, which has important implications for the computation of the F ratios. Figure 3 offers some guidelines for the choice of the appropriate ANOVA or its nonparametric equivalent (if there is one).

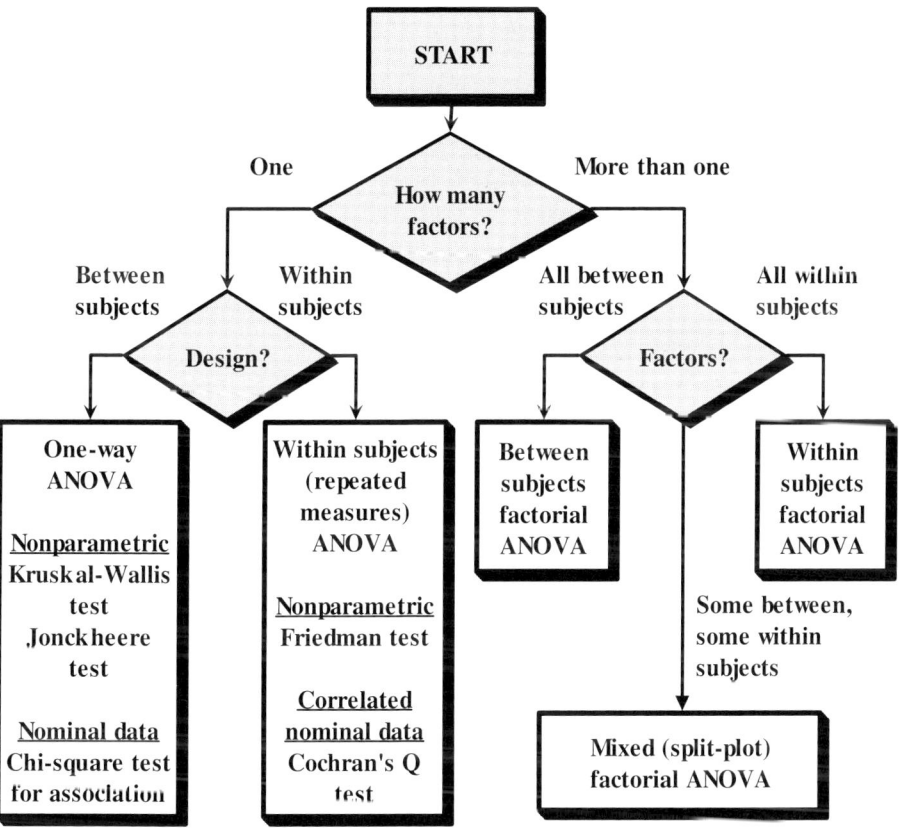

Figure 3. Flow chart for ANOVA experiments

To use the chart (Figure 3), begin at the START box and consider how many factors there are in the experiment. If there are two or more factors, work down the right-hand side of the chart. If there is just one factor, work down the left hand side.

1.4.5 Analysing the results of one-factor experiments

Figure 3 outlines the decisions leading to the correct choice of ANOVA model for an experiment with one factor. The **one-factor between subjects ANOVA** is often called the **one-way ANOVA** and is more fully described in Chapter 7. The **one-factor within subjects ANOVA** (sometimes called the **subjects by treatments** or **randomised blocks** ANOVA) is described in Chapter 9.

See Chaps. 7 & 9

The case of two conditions only: Equivalence of the t tests and ANOVA

The reader will have noticed that at the beginning of the section on ANOVA, the one-factor ANOVA was illustrated with the same simple two-condition experiments that were used to illustrate the use of the *t* tests. A natural question, therefore, is whether, in this special case, the independent and related *t* tests would lead to the same decision about the null hypothesis as would the one-way and within subjects ANOVA, respectively. In fact, they do.

An alternative to the one-way ANOVA: The Kruskal-Wallis k-sample test

So far, we have been considering the use of nonparametric alternatives to *t* tests. For data sets comprising more than two sets of measurements, however, there are also equivalent nonparametric tests. The **Kruskal-Wallis k-sample test** is equivalent to the one-way ANOVA: it is appropriate for independent samples of scores. The Kruskal-Wallis test is described in Chapter 7.

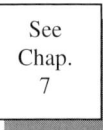

Independent samples of dichotomous nominal data

Suppose that a sample of participants is divided randomly into three equally-sized groups: two experimental groups (*Group A* and *Group B*) and a *Control* group. Each participant is tested with a criterion problem, a *1* being recorded if they pass, and a *0* if they fail. With the resulting nominal data set, a **chi-square test** for association can be used to test the null hypothesis that, in the population, there is no tendency for the problem to be solved more often in some conditions than in others (see Chapter 11).

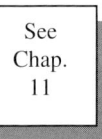

Correlated ordinal data: The Friedman test

Suppose that twenty people rank ten paintings in order of preference, each person assigning the ranks of 1 and 10 to their most preferred and least preferred painting, respectively. This operation will yield ten related samples of data, each sample comprising the ranks assigned to one painting by the twenty raters. Is there a tendency for some paintings to receive higher ranks than others? An appropriate test for use with this type of data is the **Friedman test**, which is considered more fully in Chapter 9.

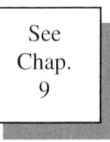

Three or more sets of correlated dichotomous nominal data: Cochran's Q test

Suppose that each person in an experiment is tested under all conditions, and that a *1* is recorded for a successful performance under a given condition and a *0* otherwise. This is a one-factor, within subjects experiment, which has produced related samples of nominal data. Figure 3 suggests that an appropriate test of the null hypothesis of no difference in performance among the conditions is **Cochran's Q test**, which is described in Chapter 9.

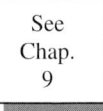

1.4.6 Analysing the results of factorial experiments

Figure 3 shows that for each of the three types of factorial experiment described here, there is a special ANOVA, which is appropriate for that kind of experiment only. The between subjects, within subjects and mixed ANOVA are described in Chapters 8, 9 and 10, respectively.

See Chaps. 8, 9 & 10

1.5 MEASURING STRENGTH OF ASSOCIATION BETWEEN VARIABLES

Do tall fathers tend to have tall sons, short fathers to have short sons and fathers of medium height to have sons of medium height? This question is one of a **statistical association** between the two variables *Father's Height* and *Son's Height*. To answer the question, you would need a data set comprising the heights of a substantial sample of fathers and those of their (first) sons.

1.5.1 Flow chart for selecting a suitable test for association

Figure 4 outlines the questions one needs to answer in order to make a decision about an appropriate measure of association.

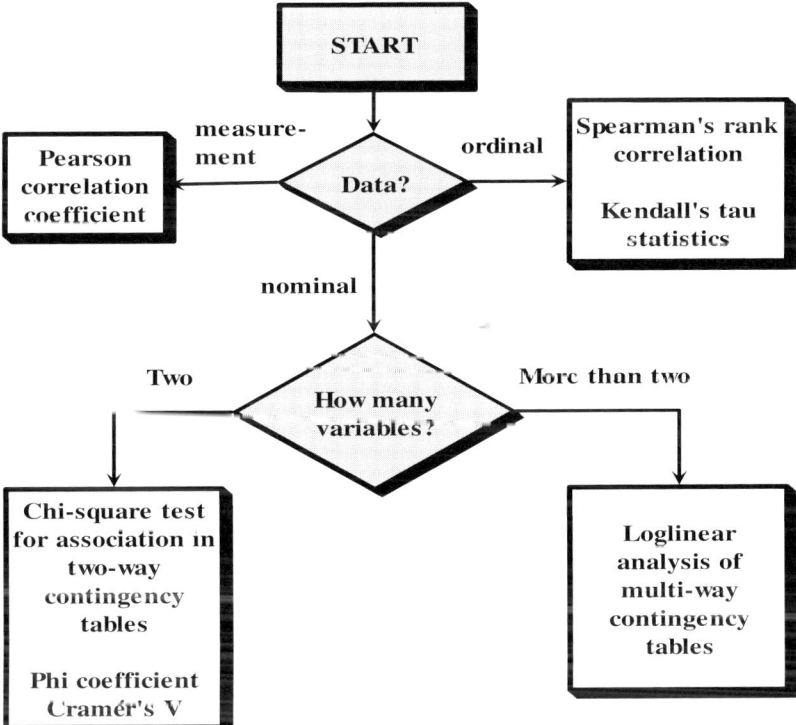

Figure 4. Flow chart showing measures of association

Begin at the START box and consider whether the data are measurements or ordinal. If the two variables are in the form of measurements, a **Pearson correlation** should be considered. However, as we shall see in Chapter 11, there are circumstances in which the Pearson correlation can be highly misleading. **It is essential to examine the data first before proceeding to obtain the correlation coefficient.**

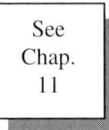

Measuring association in ordinal data

Now suppose we ask two judges to rank twenty paintings in order of preference. We shall have a data set consisting of twenty pairs of ranks. Do the judges agree? Again, our question is one of a statistical association. However, since the data are ordinal, a **rank correlation** is an appropriate statistic to use. There are two kinds of rank correlation: 1. **Spearman's rank correlation**; 2. the **Kendall tau** statistics. Both are considered more fully in Chapter 11.

1.5.2 Measuring association in nominal data: Contingency tables

Suppose that Fred claims to possess telepathic powers. Accordingly, in an experiment designed to test his claim, an experimenter tosses a coin 100 times, and Fred, seated behind a screen, states, on each occasion, whether the coin has turned up heads or tails. Table 5 presents the results of the experiment in what is known as a **contingency table**, an array designed to display the association (if any) between qualitative variables.

| | Table 5. A contingency table ||
| | Experimenter's toss ||
Fred's guess	Head (H)	Tail (T)
H	45	9
T	8	38

The presence of an association can be confirmed by using a **chi-square test** (see Chapter 11). Since the value of the chi-square statistic depends partly upon the sample size, it is unsuitable as a measure of the strength of association between two qualitative variables. Figure 4 names two statistics that measure strength of association between qualitative variables: **Cramér's V** and the **phi coefficient**. Both measures are discussed in Chapter 11.

1.5.3 Multi-way contingency tables

In the past three decades, there have been dramatic developments in the analysis of nominal data in the form of multi-way contingency tables. Previously, tables with three or more attributes were often 'collapsed' to produce two-way tables. The usual chi-square test could then be applied. Such 'collapsing', however, is fraught with risk, and the tests may give highly misleading results. The advent of modern **loglinear analysis** has made it possible to tease out the relationships among the attributes in a way that was not possible before (see Chapter 13).

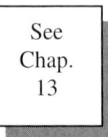

Choosing a statistical test 17

1.6 PREDICTING SCORES OR CATEGORY MEMBERSHIP

If there is an association between variables, it is natural to ask whether this can be exploited to predict scores on one variable from knowledge of those on another. Such prediction is indeed possible, and the methods by which this is achieved will be briefly reviewed in this section.

There are also circumstances in which one would wish to predict not scores on a target or criterion variable, but membership of a category of a qualitative variable. For example, it is of medical and actuarial interest to be able to assign individuals to an 'at risk' category on the basis of their smoking and drinking habits. Statistical techniques have been specially devised for this purpose also.

The purpose of the methods reviewed here is to predict a target, or **criterion** variable (the term **dependent variable** is also used in this context) from scores on other variables, known variously (depending on the context) as **regressors**, **predictors**, **independent variables**, and **covariates**. The predictors need not always be quantitative variables: qualitative variables, such as gender and blood group, are often included among the predictor variables in research of this kind.

1.6.1 Flow chart for selecting the appropriate procedure for predicting a score or a category

To use the flow chart (Figure 5) for selecting the appropriate prediction procedure, begin at the START box and consider whether the target variable is qualitative (e.g. a set of categories such as *Pass* and *Fail*) or quantitative (e.g. examination scores).

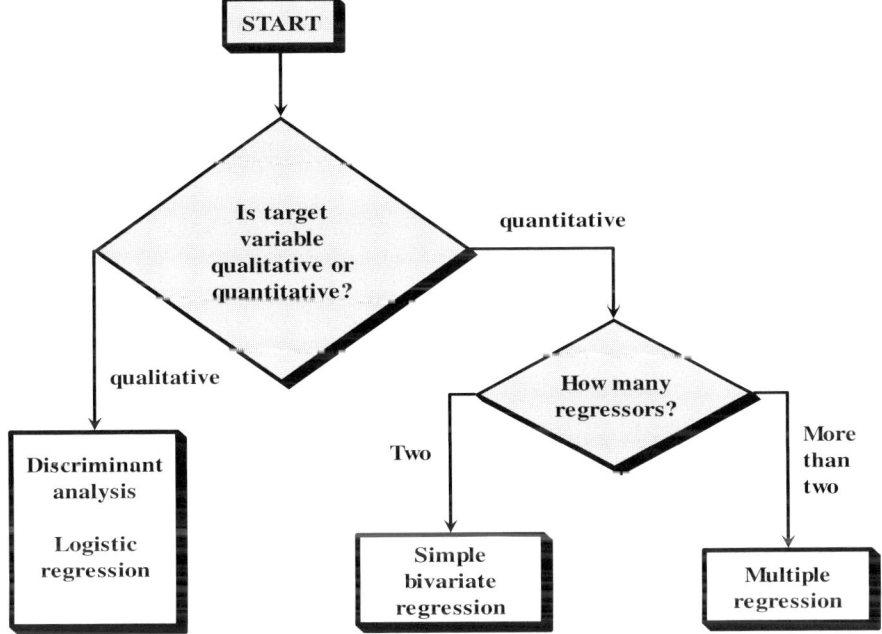

Figure 5. Flow chart showing procedures for prediction

Begin at the START box and consider the purpose of the test. If it is to test for goodness-of-fit, move down the left-hand side of the chart. If it is to estimate the population mean or its probable range, move down the right-hand side. The next consideration is the nature of the data: different types of data require different tests. If the target variable is quantitative, a **regression** method should be considered. In **simple regression**, there is one predictor; in **multiple regression**, there are two or more. Regression is the subject of Chapter 12. If the criterion variable is qualitative, the techniques of **discriminant analysis** and **logistic regression** should be considered. They are discussed in Chapter 14.

1.6.2 Simple regression

In some US universities, the authorities are interested in predicting students' grade point averages after a year of study from the scores they achieved on aptitude and intelligence tests when they matriculated.

Suppose that, given a student's verbal aptitude score at matriculation, we want to predict the same student's grade point average a year later. This is a problem in **simple regression**, and its solution is described in Chapter 12.

1.6.3 Multiple regression

A student's grade point average is associated not only with verbal aptitude, but also with numerical ability. Can grade point average be predicted even more accurately when both verbal ability and numerical ability are taken into account? This is a problem in **multiple regression**. If grade point average is correlated with both verbal and numerical aptitude, multiple regression will produce a more accurate prediction of a student's grade point average than will a simple regression upon either of the two regressors considered separately.

1.6.4 Predicting category membership: Discriminant analysis and logistic regression

Two statistical techniques designed to help the user make predictions of category membership are **discriminant analysis** and **logistic regression** (both are discussed in Chapter 14). In recent years, logistic regression, being a somewhat more robust technique than discriminant analysis, has become the preferred method.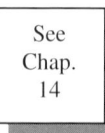

1.7 ONE-SAMPLE TESTS

Much psychological research involves the collection of two or more samples of data. This is by no means always true, however: sometimes the researcher draws a **single** sample of observations in order to study just **one** population.

The situations in which one might use a one-sample test are of two main kinds:
1. One may wish to compare a sample distribution with a hypothetical distribution, such as the normal. This is a question of **goodness-of-fit**.
2. One may wish to make inferences about the parameters of a single population from the statistics of a sample, either for the purpose of

Choosing a statistical test

ascertaining whether the sample is from a known population or estimating the parameters of an unknown population.

1.7.1 Flow chart for selecting the appropriate one-sample test

Figure 6 summarises the circumstances in which a researcher might make various kinds of one-sample tests. The tests reviewed in this section are more fully considered in Chapter 6.

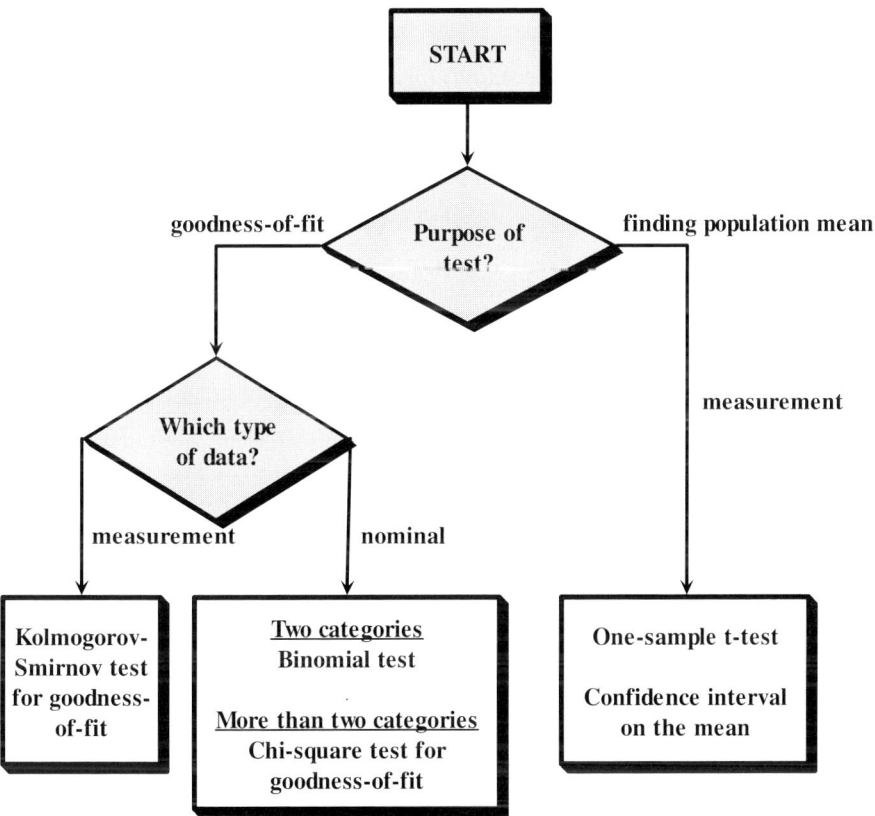

Figure 6. Flow chart of one-sample tests

Begin at the START box and consider the purpose of the test. If it is to test for goodness-of-fit, move down the left-hand side of the chart. If it is to estimate the population mean or its probable range, move down the right-hand side. The next consideration is the nature of the data: different types of data require different tests.

1.7.2 Goodness-of-fit: Data in the form of measurements

A question about a single population is often one of **goodness-of-fit**: has the sample been drawn from a population with a specified distribution shape? Suppose, for example, that one has a sample of measurements and wishes to ascertain whether these have been drawn from a normal population. Figure 6 shows that the **Kolmogorov-Smirnov test** is appropriate for this purpose.

See Chap. 6

1.7.3 Goodness-of-fit: Nominal data

Suppose a researcher wants to know whether 5-year-old children of a certain age show a preference for one of two toys (A or B). The choices of one hundred 5-year-olds are noted. Here the population comprises the choices (A or B) of 5-year-olds in general. Of the hundred children in the study, *60* choose toy A and *40* toy B. The null hypothesis states that the probability of choosing A (or B) is 0.5: more formally, it states that we have sampled *100* times from a Bernoulli population with $p = 0.5$. Does this theoretical distribution fit our data? Figure 6 indicates that a **binomial test** can be used to test this hypothesis.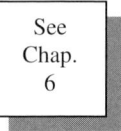

If, in the foregoing example, there were three or more toys to choose from, the **chi-square test for goodness-of-fit** can be used to test the null hypothesis that the children have no preference for any particular toy.

1.7.4 Inferences about the mean of a single population

Suppose we want to know whether the performance of a group of schoolchildren on a standardised test is typical of those in their age group. Figure 6 shows that a **one-sample *t* test** can be used to test the null hypothesis that the population mean has the putative 'population' value. Often, however, as when the researcher is working with a non-standardised test, it may not be possible to specify any null hypothesis. Suppose that a lecturer wishes to ascertain the typical reaction speed of first year university students within a certain age group. The lecturer may have data on, say, two hundred first year students; but the research question, being about the reaction speeds of first year students in general, concerns the population of reaction times. The sample mean is a **point estimate** of the unknown population mean. The *t* distribution can also be used to build a **confidence interval** around the sample mean, so that the researcher has a range of values within which the true population mean is likely to lie.

1.7.5 Nominal data: Testing a coin for fairness

When we toss a coin a large number of times to ascertain its fairness, we obtain a sample from the (infinite) population of such tosses. We might find that the coin turned up heads on 58 out of *100* tosses. Is the coin 'fair', that is, in the population, are the relative frequencies of heads and tails both 0.5?

The **binomial test** can be used to test the hypothesis that the population proportion is ½ (or, indeed, that it is any other specified proportion). A **confidence interval** can also be constructed on the sample proportion to give a range of values within which we can be confident that the true population proportion lies.

1.8 FINDING LATENT VARIABLES: FACTOR ANALYSIS

Suppose that *500* people are measured on twenty tests of ability. It is likely that if the correlations between each test and every other test are arrayed in a **correlation matrix (R)**, there will be substantial positive correlations among the tests in the battery.

Factor analysis (see Chapter 15) is a set of techniques which, on the basis of the correlations in an R matrix, classify all the tests in a battery in terms of relatively few underlying dimensions or **factors**. The reader will have noticed that the term **factor** has more than one meaning in statistics, because it has already occurred in the context of analysis of variance (ANOVA), where it denotes an independent variable that is manipulated either experimentally or statistically by the experimenter. Actually, the two meanings are not quite so disparate as might first be supposed. Arguably, the factors that emerge from factor analysis are also independent variables, since they contribute to performance on tests in the battery, which can therefore be regarded as dependent variables. However, the factors emerging from factor analysis can never be directly measured or controlled by the researcher: they are **latent** variables.

See Chap. 15

In **exploratory factor analysis**, the object is to find the minimum number of **factors** necessary to account for the correlations among the psychological tests. In **confirmatory factor analysis**, specified models are compared to see which gives the best account of the data.

1.9   A FINAL COMMENT

In this chapter, we have offered some advice about the circumstances in which one might consider using formal statistical tests to support the researcher's claim that what is true of a particular data set is likely to be true in the population. At this point, however, a word of warning is appropriate.

Formal tests, statistical models and their assumptions

The making of a formal statistical test of significance always presupposes the applicability of a statistical **model**, that is, an interpretation (usually in the form of an equation) of the data set as having been generated in a specified manner. The model underlying the one-sample t test, for example, assumes that the data are from a normal population. To some extent, statistical tests have been shown to be **robust** to moderate violations of the assumptions of the models upon which they are based, that is, the actual error rates are not markedly different from the nominal values. But there are limits to this robustness, and there are circumstances in which a result, declared by an incautious user to be significant beyond, say, the 0.05 level, may actually have been considerably more likely than that. There is no way of avoiding this pitfall other than by thoroughly exploring the data first (see Chapters 4 and 5) to ascertain their suitability for specified formal tests.

See Chaps. 4 & 5

CHAPTER 2

Getting started with SPSS 12

2.1 Outline of an SPSS session

2.2 Opening SPSS

2.3 The SPSS Data Editor

2.4 A statistical analysis

2.5 Closing SPSS

2.6 Resuming work on a saved data set

2.1 OUTLINE OF AN SPSS SESSION

There are three stages in the use of SPSS:
1. The data are entered into the **Data Editor**;
2. Descriptive and statistical procedures are selected from the **drop-down menus**;
3. The output is examined and edited in the **Output Viewer**.

2.1.1 Entering the data

There are several ways of placing data in the **Data Editor**. They can be typed in directly or read in from SPSS data files that have already been created. SPSS can also read data from files produced by other applications, such as EXCEL and STATISTICA, as well as text files.

Once the data are in the **Data Editor**, the user has available a wide variety of editorial functions. Not only can the data be amended in various ways, but also selections from the original set can be targeted for subsequent analysis.

In this chapter, we shall give considerable attention to the **Data Editor**, because it enables the user to control important features of the output (such as the labelling of variables) which can make the results of a statistical analysis easier to interpret.

The user can also access important editing functions from an array of **drop-down menus** at the top of the screen.

2.1.2 Selecting the exploratory and statistical procedures

It is also from the drop-down menus that the user selects statistical procedures. The user is advised to explore the data thoroughly before making any formal statistical tests. SPSS offers many graphical methods described in Chapters 4 and 5 of displaying a data set, which are of great assistance when you are getting to know your data.

2.1.3 Examining the output

The results of the analysis appear in the **SPSS Viewer**. In addition to the selection and trimming of items, the SPSS **Viewer** also offers facilities for more radical editing. The appearance of tables and other output can be dramatically transformed to tailor them to the purposes of the user.

From the SPSS **Viewer**, material can readily be transferred to files produced by other applications, such as Word, or printed out in hard copy.

2.1.4 A simple experiment

In this chapter, we shall illustrate the stages in a typical SPSS session by entering the results of a fictional experiment into the **Data Editor**, describing the data by choosing some statistics from the menu and examining the output. At this stage, we shall concentrate on the general procedure, leaving the details for later consideration.

Table 1 shows the results of an experiment designed to show the effects of a drug upon skilled performance.

Table 1. Results of an experiment designed to show whether a drug improves skilled performance

\multicolumn{8}{c}{Group}
\multicolumn{4}{c}{Placebo}	\multicolumn{4}{c}{Drug}
Case	Score	Case	Score	Case	Score	Case	Score
1	6	6	3	11	8	16	8
2	5	7	2	12	6	17	6
3	5	8	4	13	6	18	7
4	1	9	5	14	7	19	5
5	2	10	1	15	6	20	10

The experiment was of simple, two-group between subjects design, in which twenty participants attempted a test of skill. Ten participants (cases) were assigned at random to one of two conditions:
 1. A *Placebo* condition, in which the participant ingested a harmless saline solution;
 2. A *Drug* condition, in which the participant ingested a small dose of a drug.

The dependent variable was the participant's score on the skilled task. The independent variable was the condition to which the participant was assigned: *Drug* or *Placebo*. The experimental hypothesis was that the group that had been assigned to the *Drug* condition would outperform the group assigned to the *Placebo* condition.

We shall shortly show how these data can be placed in the **SPSS Data Editor** and the results summarised with a few statistics.

2.1.5 Preparing data for SPSS

The data shown in Table 1 are not in a form that the SPSS **Data Editor** will accept. In an SPSS data set, **each row must represent only one case** (equivalent terms are **'participant'** and **'subject'**) and each column represents a variable or characteristic on which that case has been measured. In other words, **each row of an SPSS data set must contain data on just one case or participant**. The data in Table 1 do not conform to this requirement: the first row of entries contains data from four different participants.

To make them suitable for analysis with SPSS, the data in Table 1 must be rearranged in a new format. In Table 2, the data in Table 1 have been re-tabulated, so that each row now contains data on only one participant.

Table 2. The data set of Table 1, recast in a form suitable for entry into SPSS

Participant	Condition	Participant's Score
1	1	6
2	1	5
3	1	5
4	1	1
5	1	2
6	1	3
7	1	2
8	1	4
9	1	5
10	1	1
11	2	8
12	2	6
13	2	6
14	2	7
15	2	6
16	2	8
17	2	6
18	2	7
19	2	5
20	2	10

In Table 2, the *Condition* variable identifies the group to which each participant belongs by means of an arbitrary code number, in this case *1* (for the *Placebo* condition) or *2* (for the

Drug condition). Unlike the numbers in the *Score* column, which express level of performance, the code numbers in the *Condition* column **serve merely as category labels**: the *Condition* variable is a special kind of **categorical variable** known as a **grouping variable** (see Chapter 1).

2.2 OPENING SPSS

There are several ways of beginning a session with SPSS, depending upon whether you intend to build a new file or access an old one. When SPSS is opened for the first time by clicking the SPSS icon, an introductory dialog box will appear with the title **SPSS 12.0 for Windows**.

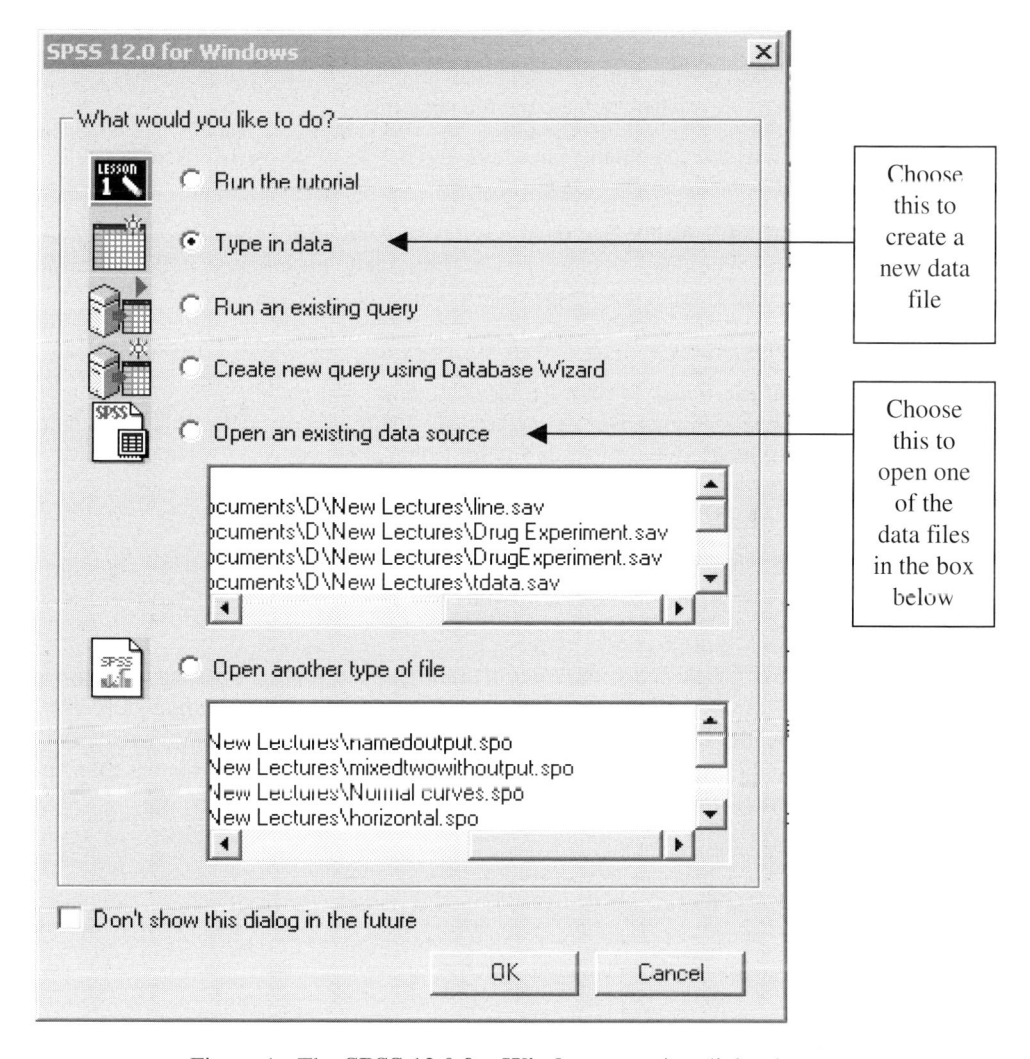

Figure 1. The **SPSS 12.0 for Windows** opening dialog box

Underneath the title is the question: *What would you like to do?* Make your choice by clicking one of the six small radio buttons and then **OK** (Figure 1). Here we shall assume that you wish to enter data for the first time, in which case click the button labelled **Type in data**. When you click **OK**, the **Data Editor** will appear on the screen.

At a later stage, you may wish to omit the introductory dialog box, in which case click the square labelled **Don't show this dialog in the future** in the bottom left corner of the dialog box.

2.3　THE SPSS DATA EDITOR

The SPSS **Data Editor** provides two alternative spreadsheet-like arrays:

1. **Data View**, into which the user can enter new data or (if an old file has been accessed) view whatever data the file contains;

2. **Variable View**, which contains the names and details of the variables in the data set.

When you are creating a file for the first time, it is advisable to lay the foundations in **Variable View** first, so that when you come to enter data in **Data View**, the columns in the spreadsheet will already have been labelled, reducing the risk of transcription errors.

A notational convention

In this book, we shall use *italics* to indicate variable names and values. We shall use a **bold** typeface for the names of menus, the names of dialog boxes and the items therein. Emboldening will also be used for emphasis and for technical terms.

2.3.1　Working in Variable View

When the **Data Editor** appears, you may find that you are in **Data View**. If so, click the tab labelled **Variable View** at the bottom left-hand side of the window and you will access **Variable View** (Figure 2).

When the **Data Editor** first appears, the caption in the title bar reads, '**Untitled – SPSS Data Editor**'. When you finish entering your data (or preferably during data entry as a protection against losing data should the system crash), you can supply a name for the file by selecting the **Save As...** item from the **File** drop-down menu and entering a suitable name in the **File Name** box. After you have done this, the title bar will display your new name for the file.

Getting started with SPSS 12   27

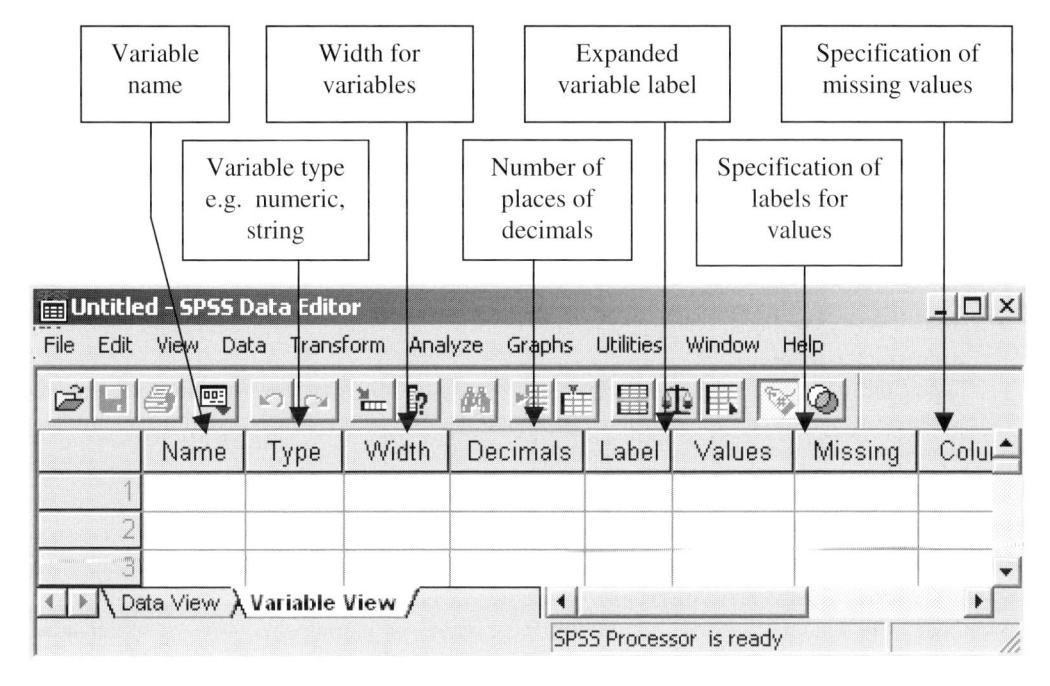

Figure 2. Variable View
(For this figure, some of the columns have been narrowed. All columns to the right of 'Missing', i.e., 'Columns', 'Align', and 'Measure', have been omitted.)

Notation for selecting from a menu

We shall adopt a notation for selecting items from a drop-down menu by which the sequence of selections is shown by indentation. For example, selection of the **Copy** item from the **Edit** drop-down menu will be written as
Edit
    Copy

*The **Name** and **Labels** columns*

Some of the column headings in **Variable View** (such as number of places of decimals) are self-explanatory. The **Name** and **Labels** columns, however, require some explanation. The **name** of a variable is a string of characters (normally letters and spaces but it can include digits) which will appear at the head of a column in **Data View**, but not in the output. In other words, a variable name is a convenient shortened name for use only within **Data View**. There is a set of rules for naming variables. This can readily be accessed by entering SPSS's **Help** menu and choosing
Help
    Topics
        Contents
             Variable names

The main message is that a variable name must be a **continuous** sequence (no spaces) of up to 64 characters (though long variable names are not recommended), **the first of which must be a letter**. It can be defined with any mixture of upper and lower case characters, and case is preserved for display purposes (e.g. *TimeofDay*). Although certain punctuation marks are permitted, it is simpler merely to remember to use letters and digits only.

Making entries in Variable View
- To name the variables *Case*, *Group* and *Score*, first check that there is a thickened border around the top leftmost cell (see Figure 2). If it is not there, move the cursor there and click with the mouse.
- Type *Case* and press the ↓ cursor key to move the highlighting down to the cell below to complete the entry of *Case* in the cell above. (Entry of information into a cell is only complete when the cursor is moved away by clicking on another cell.)
- Type *Group* into the second cell with a thickened border and press the ↓ key to move the highlighting down to the next row, completing the entry of *Group* in the cell above.
- Use the same procedure to enter the variable name *Score*.

SPSS will accept eight different **types** of variable, two of the most important being **numeric** (numerals with a decimal point) and **string** (e.g. names of participants, cities or other non-numerical material). Initially, some of the format specifications of a variable are set by default, and the pre-set values will be seen as soon as the variable name has been typed and control transferred from the **Name** cell. Unless you specify otherwise, **it will be assumed that the variable is of the numeric type.**

The number of places of decimals that will be displayed in **Data View** is pre-set at 2. Since the scores in Table 2 are all integers, it would be tedious to read entries such as *46.00*, *34.00* and *54.00*, as opposed to *46*, *34* and *54*. It is better to suppress the display of decimals in **Data View** by clicking on the **Decimals** column to obtain the following display

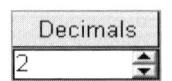

By clicking twice on the downward-pointing arrow, you can replace the number *2* already in the cell with zero (see Figure 3). Note that this countermanding of the default specification will apply **only to the variable concerned**. Rather than over-riding the default specifications piecemeal in this way, you can reset the decimal display to zero for every numeric variable in the data set by choosing
Edit
    Options…
        Data
and resetting the number of decimal places to zero. See Chapter 3 for details.

See Chapter 3

The **Label**, which should be a meaningful phrase, with spaces between the words, is the description of the variable that will appear **in the output**. In order to make the output as clear as possible, therefore, it is important to devise **meaningful** labels for all the variables in the data set. The labels shown in Figure 3, *Case Number* and *Experimental Condition*, are more informative than the corresponding variable names *Case* and *Group*, respectively, which are adequate for use within the **Data Editor**.

Getting started with SPSS 12

Figure 3. Part of **Variable View**, with entries specifying the names and details of the three variables

The **Values** column is for use with **grouping variables**. By clicking on **Values**, the user can supply a key to the meanings of the code numbers. In this case, the grouping variable is *Experimental Condition* and we can arbitrarily decide that *1* = *Placebo* and *2* = *Drug*. Click the first cell of the Values column to obtain the following display:

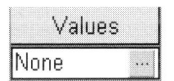

Note the grey area on the right with the three dots (…). Clicking this grey area will produce the **Values** dialog box (see Figure 4). Figure 4 (next page) shows how to fill in the **Values** dialog box so that, in the output, the code numbers *1* and *2* will be replaced by the more informative value labels *Placebo* and *Drug*, respectively. In addition, as you type 1 or 2 in **Data View**, the value labels will appear provided either **Value Labels** within the **View** drop-down menu is ticked or by clicking the icon in the toolbar.

*The **Width** column*

With string variables, the **Width** column controls the maximum length (in number of characters) of the string you will be allowed to enter when you are working in **Data View**. (The setting in Width has no effect upon the number of characters you can type in when working with a numeric variable.) The default setting for Width is *8*, but this can be changed by choosing
Edit
    Options
        Data
and changing the **Width** setting there. For more details, see Chapter 3. If a string is too long for the set width, you will find that you can no longer type in the excess letters in **Data View**.

See Chapter 3

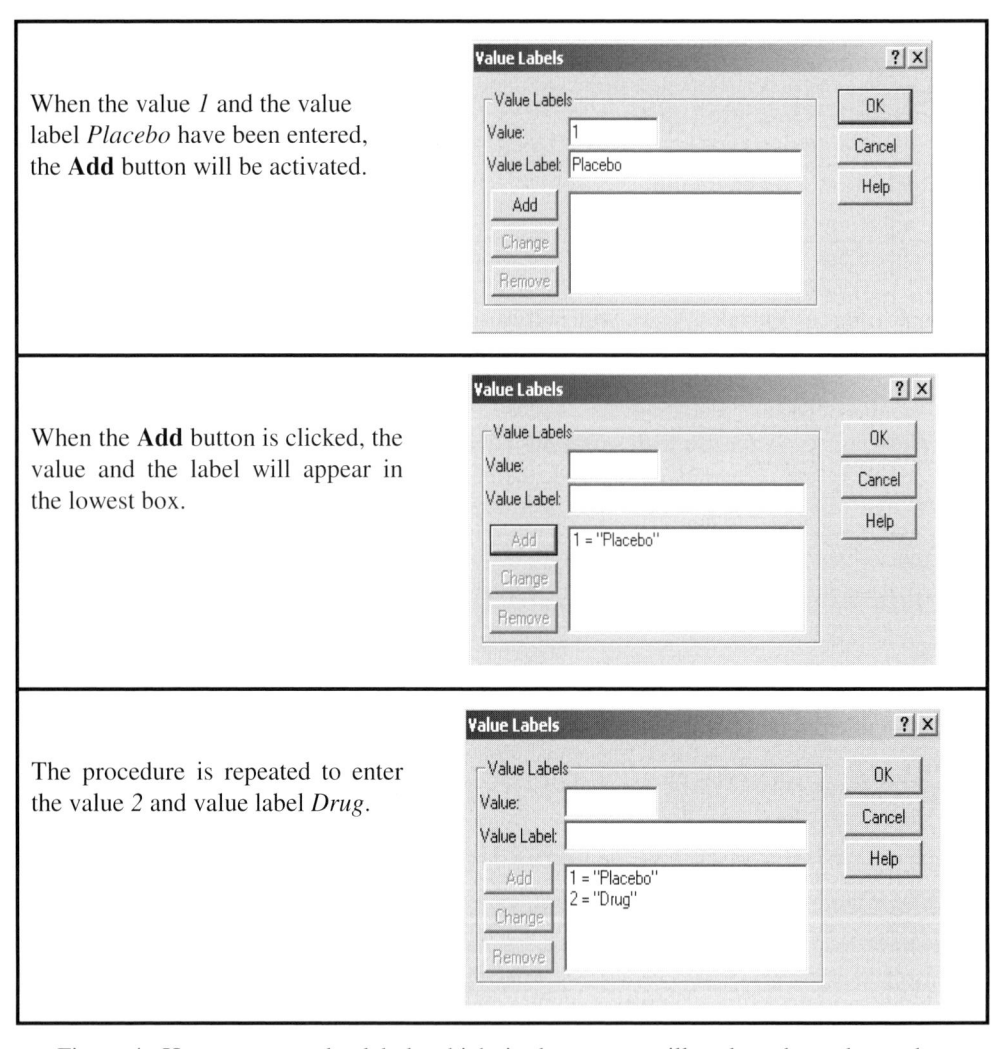

When the value *1* and the value label *Placebo* have been entered, the **Add** button will be activated.	
When the **Add** button is clicked, the value and the label will appear in the lowest box.	
The procedure is repeated to enter the value *2* and value label *Drug*.	

Figure 4. How to enter value labels which, in the output, will replace the code numbers making up a grouping variable

*The **Columns** column*

There is also, in **Variable View**, a column with the heading **Columns** (see Figure 2). The cells of this column display the actual widths, for all the variables in the data set, of the columns that will appear in **Data View**. Initially, the cells in **Columns** will show the same setting as the **Width** column: *8*. Were you to create a new numeric variable with a name whose length exceeded the preset width, only part of the name would be displayed in the **Name** column of **Variable View**. Moreover, in **Data View**, only part of the variable name would be visible at the head of the column for that variable.

To specify wider columns for a variable in **Data View** while working in **Variable View**, click the appropriate cell in **Columns** and adjust the setting there.

Copying settings

Values in the cells of **Variable View** can be copied and pasted to other cells using the standard Windows methods (see pp. 33–34). For example, having adjusted the **Columns** setting to, say, *15* characters for one variable of the data set, the new setting can be applied to other variables by copying and pasting the contents of the cell with the entry *15* into the cells for the other variables.

Modified settings can also be copied to **Columns** from the **Width** Column. Having adjusted an entry in the **Width** column to, say, *16*, the new setting can be copied and pasted into **Columns** in the usual way. The effect will be to widen the columns in **Data View** for the variables to which the new **Columns** setting has been copied.

2.3.2 Working in Data View

Once the appropriate specifications have been entered in **Variable View**, click the **Data View** tab at the bottom of the **Variable View** window to enter **Data View** (Figure 5). When **Data View** is accessed, the variable names *Case*, *Group* and *Score* will be seen at the heads of the first three columns as specified in **Variable View**. The default name *var*, which appears in the third, fourth and fifth columns, indicates that those columns have yet to be assigned to specified variables.

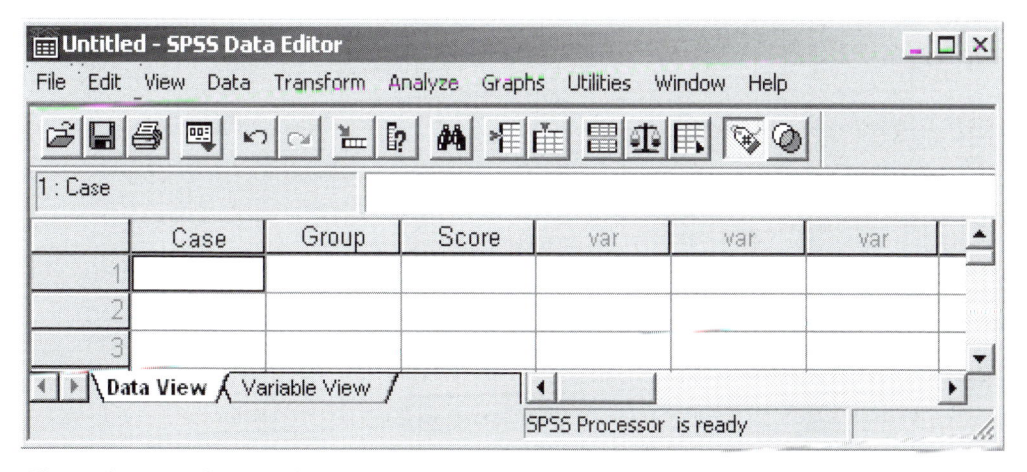

Figure 5. Part of **Data View**, showing the variable names *Case*, *Group* and *Score*. Control is located in the cell in the first row of the Case column, as shown by the thickened border of that cell and also the entry *1: Case* in the grey bar above the column headings

Running along the bottom of the **Data View** window is a horizontal band, in which various messages appear from time to time. When SPSS is accessed, the message reads: **SPSS Processor is ready**. The horizontal band is known as the **Status Bar**, because it reports not only whether SPSS is ready to begin, but also on the stage that a procedure has reached. If, for example, a large data set is being read from a file, progress is continually monitored, case by case, in the status bar.

2.3.3 Entering the data

The first variable, *Case*, represents the case number of the participants. Enter the number of each participant from *1* to *20*. The second variable *Group*, identifies the condition under which each participant performed the task: *1 = Placebo*; *2 = Drug*. Enter ten *1*'s into the first ten rows of the *Group* variable, followed by ten *2*'s. In the first ten cells of the *Score* column, enter the scores of the ten participants who performed the task under the *Placebo* condition, followed by those of the ten participants who performed under the *Drug* condition.

Figure 6 shows a section of **Data View**, in which the data in Table 1 have been entered.

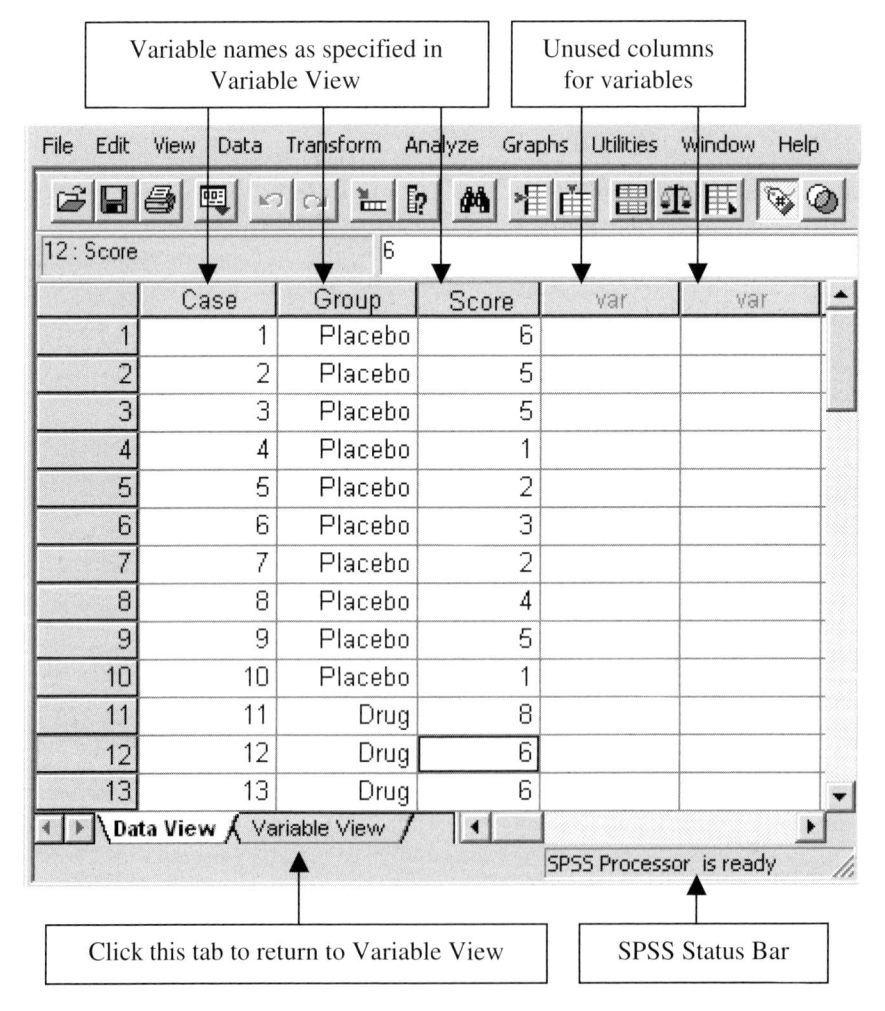

Figure 6. Part of **Data View** after the results in Table 1 have been entered.

Notice that in Figure 6, location of control is indicated by the thickened border of the cell in the 12th row of the second column. The value in this cell is 6. The contents of this cell are also displayed in a white area known as the **cell editor** just above the column headings. The value in the **cell editor** (and the cell itself) can be changed by clicking in the **cell editor**, selecting the present value, typing a new one and pressing ↵. The new value will appear in the grid.

Blocking, copying and pasting

Initially, only one cell in **Data View** is highlighted. However, it is possible to highlight a whole block of cells, or even an entire row or column. This **blocking** operation (when all the cells appear in **inverse video**, with the characters printed in white against a black background) is achieved either by clicking and dragging with the mouse or proceeding as follows:
- To **highlight a whole row or column**, click the grey box containing the row number or the column heading.
- To highlight a **block of cells within a row or column**, click on the first cell and (keeping the left button of the mouse pressed down) drag the pointer to the cell at the end of the block. The same result can be obtained by clicking the first cell in the block, pressing the **Shift** key and keeping it held down while using the appropriate cursor key (↑ or ↓) to move the highlighting along the entire block.

The blocking operation can be used to **copy the values in one column into another** or to **place them elsewhere in the same column**.
- Highlight a column of values that you wish to copy and then choose
  Edit
     Copy
- Next, highlight the cells of the target column and choose
  Edit
     Paste

The values in the source column will now appear in the target column. (Make sure that the number of highlighted target cells is equal to the number of cells copied.) For example, the successions of *1*'s and *2*'s identifying the *Placebo* and *Drug* conditions could have been entered as follows.
- Place the value *1* in the topmost cell of the *Group* column. Move the black rectangle away from the cell to complete the entry of the value and return the highlight to the cell, which will now contain the value *1*.
- Choose
  Edit
     Copy
  to store the value *1* in the clipboard.
- Highlight cells *2* to *10* and choose
  Edit
     Paste
  to place the value *1* in all the highlighted cells.

Using key combinations to copy and paste

Copying and pasting can also be carried out by using the key combinations **Ctrl + C** (that is, by holding the **Ctrl** key down while pressing C) and **Ctrl + V**, respectively.

Deletion of values

Whether you are working in **Variable View** or in **Data View**, entries can be removed by selecting the target items in the manner described above and pressing the **Delete** key.

Switching between Data View and Variable View

You can switch from one **Data Editor** display to the other at any point. While in **Data View**, for instance, you might want to return to **Variable View** to name further variables or add further details about existing ones. Just click the **Variable View** tab. When you have finished the new work in **Variable View**, click **Data View** to continue entering your data.

Creating more space for entries in Data View

While the widths of the columns in **Data View** can be controlled from **Variable View** in the manner described above, you can also control column width while working in **Data View**. To widen a column, click on the grey cell containing the variable name at the top of the column and click and drag the right-hand border to the right.

Displaying value labels in Data View

The values assigned to the numerical values of a grouping variable can be displayed in **Data View** by choosing
View
     Value Labels

See Figure 7.

Should the *Group* column in **Data View** not be sufficiently wide to show the value labels completely, create more space by placing the cursor in the grey cell at the head of the column containing the label *Group* and click and drag the right-hand border of the cell to the right.

Getting started with SPSS 12

The initial appearance of a section of **Data View**, showing the code numbers making up the grouping variable in the second data column.	9	9	1	5
	10	10	1	1
	11	11	2	8
	12	12	2	6
	13	13	2	6
	14	14	2	7

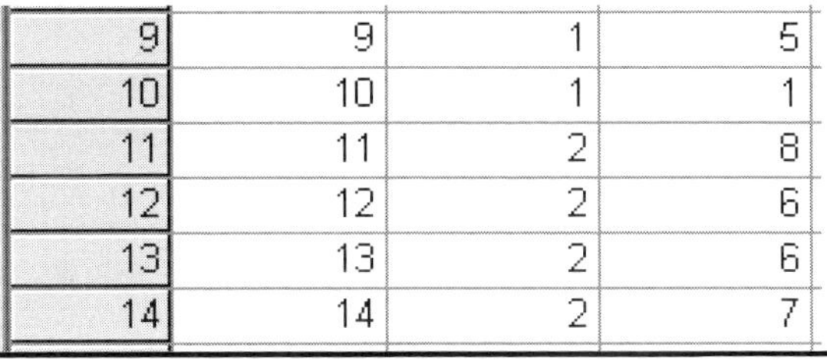

Activate **Value Labels** in the **View** menu or click the icon in the toolbar.

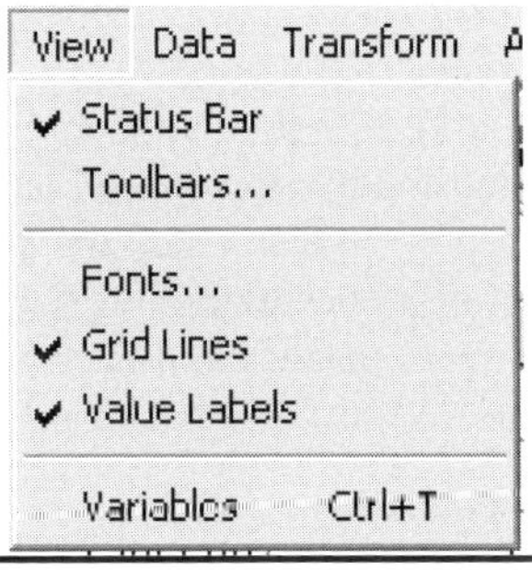

> View Data Transform
> ✔ Status Bar
>   Toolbars...
>   Fonts...
> ✔ Grid Lines
> ✔ Value Labels
>   Variables   Ctrl+T

The value labels for the grouping variable have now replaced the code numbers.	9	9	Placebo	5
	10	10	Placebo	1
	11	11	Drug	0
	12	12	Drug	6
	13	13	Drug	6
	14	14	Drug	7

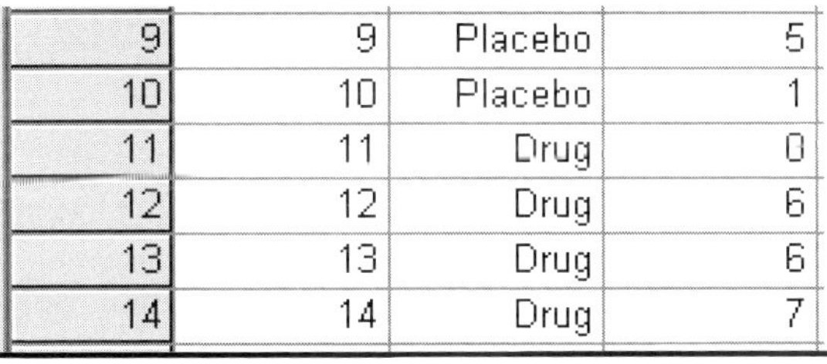

Figure 7. Displaying value labels in **Data View**

Using the display of values in the Data Editor as a guide when entering data

Having specified the variable type as *numeric* when in **Variable View**, you will find that **Data View** will accept, in the first instance, only numerical entries. You can arrange, however, for the first numerical entry, say *1*, to be displayed as the value label by choosing
View
    Value Label

Although you typed in *1*, you will now see the label *Placebo* in the cell. Moreover, you can copy and paste this label to the other nine cases in the *Placebo* group. When you come to the *Drug* group, however, you will need to type in *2* which, when you click another cell, will then appear as the value *Drug*. **Data View will not accept the word *Drug* typed in directly**. You can then copy and paste the second label to the remaining cases in the Drug group.

This procedure can be useful if, momentarily, as when your SPSS session has been interrupted, you have forgotten the number-label pairings you assigned in **Variable View**. It also helps you to avoid transcription errors when transferring your data from response sheets.

Saving the data file

When you finish entering your data (but preferably during data entry at intervals in case the system crashes), you can supply a name for the data file by choosing the **Save As...** item from the **File** drop-down menu, selecting an appropriate drive and/or folder and then entering a suitable name in the **File Name** box. After you have done this, the title bar will display your new name for the file. Note that if you do not do this, you will be prompted to supply a name for the data file when you wish to terminate your SPSS session and close down SPSS.

SPSS tutorials

For an animated step-by-step tutorial on entering data into SPSS, readers can work through the tutorial provided by SPSS. Click the **Help** drop-down menu, select **Tutorial** and then **Using the Data Editor**. The buttons in the right-hand bottom corner of each page of the tutorial enable the user to see the list of items (upward arrow) and to navigate forward and backward through the tutorial (right and left arrows).

2.4 A STATISTICAL ANALYSIS

2.4.1 An example: Computing means

In this section, we shall use SPSS to summarise the results of the experiment by obtaining some descriptive statistics such as the mean and standard deviation of the scores for each treatment group (Placebo and Drug).

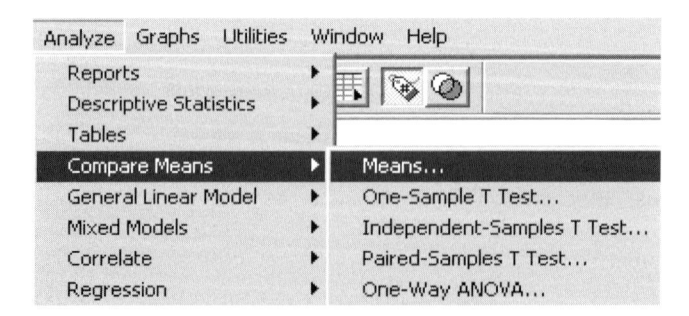

Figure 8. Finding the **Means** menu

- From the drop-down **Analyze** menu, choose
  Compare Means
      Means ....
  as shown in Figure 8.
- Click **Means...** to access the **Means** dialog box (Figure 9).

Initially, in the left-hand panel the variable names are obscured; but you can view the entire label by touching it with the screen pointer.

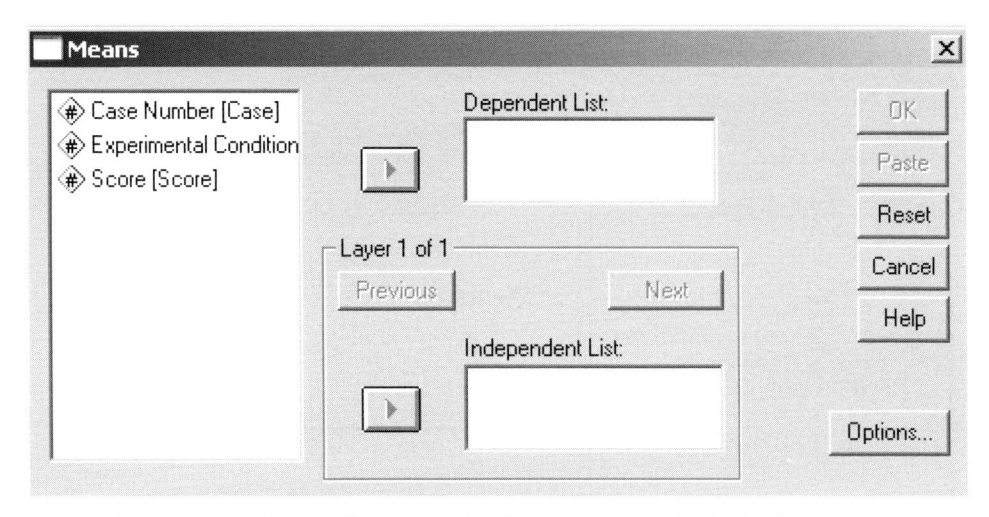

Figure 9. The **Means** dialog box showing the three variables in the data set

- Click on *Score* to highlight it and then on the arrow pointing to the **Dependent List** box. The variable name and label will then be transferred to the Dependent List box.
- In a similar manner transfer the variable *Experimental Condition* to the **Independent List** box (see Figure 10).

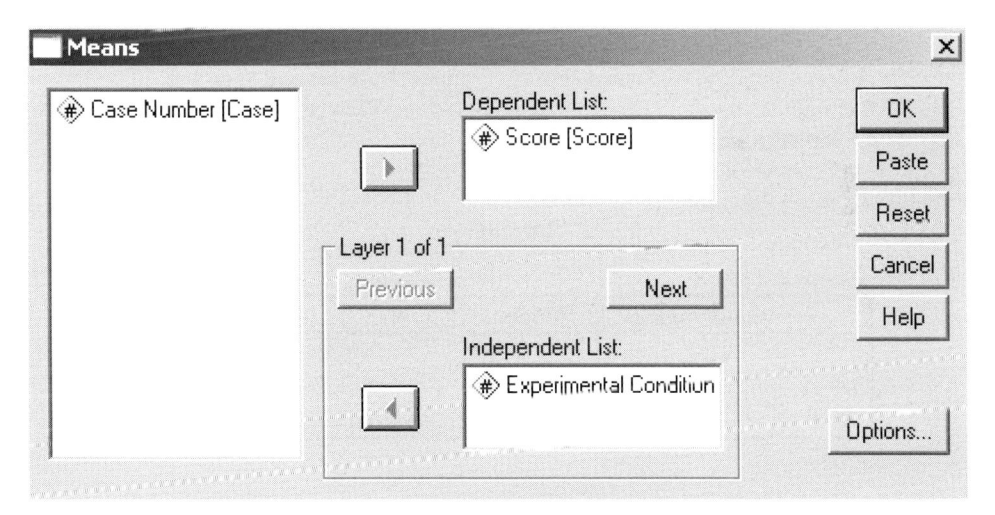

Figure 10. The completed **Means** dialog box for computing the mean scores for the two experimental conditions

Click **OK** to run the analysis. The results will appear in a new window called the **Output Viewer**, a section of which is shown in Output 1.

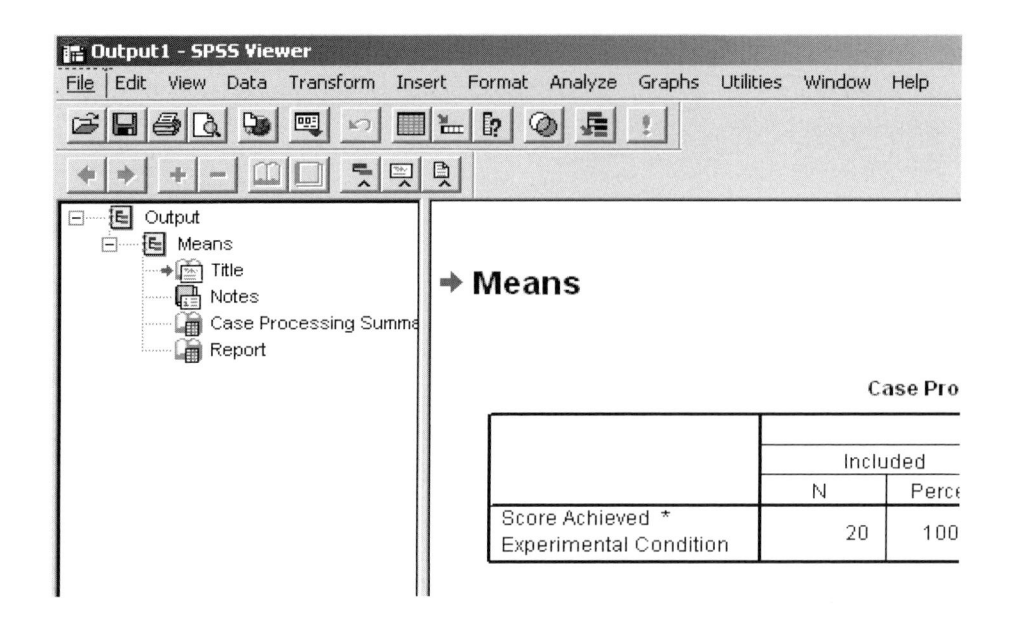

Output 1. Part of the **SPSS Viewer** window showing the list of output items in the left pane and the output tables in the right pane

The SPSS **Viewer** window is divided into two 'panes' by a vertical grey bar. The left pane shows the hierarchical organisation of the contents of the **Viewer**. The right pane contains the results of the statistical analysis and various other items. The contents of the **Viewer** on both sides of the bar can be edited.

Report

Score Achieved

Experimental Condition	Mean	N	Std. Deviation
Placebo	3.40	10	1.838
Drug	6.90	10	1.449
Total	5.15	20	2.412

Output 2. The **Report** table showing the mean, number of scores and standard deviation in each of the two groups

For the moment, however, the main item of interest is the **Report** (Output 2), which appears in the right pane. From the **Report**, it can be seen that the mean performance of those tested under the *Drug* condition was over twice the level of those tested under the *Placebo* condition.

Getting started with SPSS 12

It would seem, therefore, that the results of the experiment support the hypothesis. This, however, is insufficient: formal tests are necessary to confirm the appearance of the data. It should be noted, however, that before the researcher makes any formal statistical tests, the data should first be thoroughly explored. SPSS has an exploratory data analysis procedure, **Explore**, which offers a wide range of useful statistics. **Explore** can be run by choosing
Analyze
    Descriptive Statistics
        Explore....

> See Chapter 4

We shall consider **Explore** more fully in Chapter 4.

Editing the output in the Output Viewer

The **SPSS Viewer** offers powerful editing facilities, some of which can radically alter the appearance of a default table such as that shown in Output 2. Many of the tables in the output are **pivot tables**, that is, tables in which the columns and rows can be transposed and to which other radical alterations can be made.

Suppose, for example, like the editors of many scientific journals, you would prefer the experimental conditions *Placebo* and *Drug* to be column headings and the group means, standard deviations and *N*'s to be below them. If you double-click the **Report**, a hatched border will appear around the table (Output 3).

Report

Variables	Score Achieved ▼		
Experimental Condition	Mean	N	Std. Deviation
Placebo	3.40	10	1.838
Drug	6.90	10	1.449
Total	5.15	20	2.412

Output 3. An item which has been prepared for editing. On double-clicking the item, a hatched border appears around it

You will notice that, along the drop-down menus at the top of the **Viewer** window, a new menu, **Pivot**, has appeared.

Choose
- **Pivot**
    Transpose Rows and Columns (Figure 11).

The effect (see Output 4) is dramatic! The descriptive statistics now occupy the rows and the experimental conditions the columns.

The **Pivot** menu can be used to edit complex tables with three, four or more dimensions of classification. Such manipulation can be of great assistance in bringing out the most important features of your results.

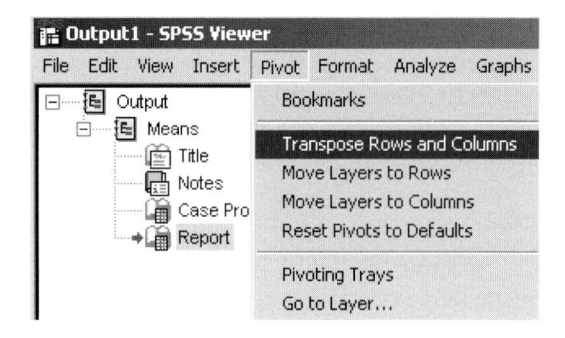

Figure 11. The **Pivot** drop-down menu with **Transpose Rows and Columns** selected

Report

Score Achieved

| | Experimental Condition |||
	Placebo	Drug	Total
Mean	3.40	6.90	5.15
N	10	10	20
Std. Deviation	1.838	1.449	2.412

Output 4. The transposed **Report** table

2.4.2 Keeping more than one application open

One useful feature of Windows is that the user can keep several applications open simultaneously. It is therefore quite possible to be writing a document in **Word** while at the same time running **SPSS** and importing output such as the **Report** in the previous section. If more than one application is open, the user can move from one to another by clicking on the appropriate button on the **Taskbar** (usually located at the foot of the screen). Alternatively, you can hold down the **Alt** key and press the **Tab** key repeatedly to cycle control through whatever applications may be open.

2.5 CLOSING SPSS

SPSS is closed by choosing **Exit** from the **File** menu. If you have not yet saved the data or the output at any point, a default dialog box will appear with the question: **Save contents of data editor to untitled?** or **Save contents of output viewer to Output 1?**. You must then click the **Yes**, **No** or **Cancel** button. If you choose **Yes**, you will be given a final opportunity to name the file you wish to save. Beware of saving unselected output files because they can become very large in terms of computer storage, especially if they contain graphics.

2.6 RESUMING WORK ON A SAVED DATA SET

There are several ways of resuming work on a saved data set. After opening SPSS and obtaining the introductory **SPSS 12 for Windows dialog box**, you can click the radio button **Open an existing data source** (Figure 1). A list of saved files with the extension *.sav* will appear in the upper **More Files** window. Select the appropriate file and click **OK**. The data file will then appear in **Data View**. Other kinds of file, such as SPSS output files, can be retrieved from the lower **More Files** window by clicking on the radio button labelled **Open another kind of file**.

While you in the **Data Editor**, it is always possible to access files by choosing **Open** from the **File** menu. A quicker method of accessing an SPSS data file is to double-click its icon. The data will immediately appear in **Data View**.

EXERCISE 1

Some simple operations with SPSS 12

Before you start

Before you begin the first exercise, make sure you have read Sections 2.1, 2.2 and 2.3.

An experiment on role models of aggression

In a study of the effects of adult models on the development of aggression, two groups of children were assessed on aggression after they had viewed the behaviour of either an aggressive or a neutral adult.

| Aggressive | 10 | 11 | 20 | 15 | 2 | 5 | 16 | 8 | 18 | 16 |
| Neutral | 9 | 9 | 12 | 8 | 10 | 2 | 7 | 10 | 11 | 9 |

Do these results support the hypothesis that aggressive role models promote aggressive behaviour?

Opening SPSS and preparing a data file

Open SPSS as described in Section 2.2. Click the radio button labelled **Type in data** and then **OK** to open the SPSS **Data Editor** (see Section 3). In order to compute means and other statistics, you could create two variables called *Neutral* and *Aggressive* and enter the scores in the appropriate columns. We suggest, however, that you proceed as in Section 2.1.5 and create a grouping variable, with some informative full label such as *Adult Behaviour*, and a shorter name, such as *Condition*, for use in the **Data Editor**. The full variable label for the dependent variable might be *Aggression Score* and the shorter name for the **Data Editor** could be *Score*.

Lay the foundations in **Variable View** first before typing in the data. Change the **Decimals** setting to zero to display only whole numbers in **Data View**. Decide on two arbitrary code numbers and value labels for the two conditions, such as *1 = Neutral* and *2 = Aggressive*. Enter these in the **Values** column, as described in Section 3.

Click the **Data View** tab to enter **Data View**. Try entering the data by copying and pasting, as described in Section 2.3. To see the value names as you are entering the data, click on **Value Labels** in the **View** menu.

We suggest that, early in the session, you save your work to a file with an informative name using
File
    Save As…

Computing the means and standard deviations

Obtain, in the manner described in Section 2.4.1, the means and standard deviations of the aggression scores for the children exposed to the neutral and aggressive adult models.

- **Which group has the higher mean?**

- **How does the size of the difference between the means compare with the standard deviations of the scores in the two groups?**

Pivoting the output table

Pivot the output table as described in Section 2.4.1 so that the headings *Neutral*, *Aggressive* and *Total* become those of columns rather than rows.

Closing SPSS

Close SPSS as described in Section 2.5.

EXERCISE 2

Questionnaire data

Introduction

Exercises 2 to 7 in this and later chapters are concerned with the preparation and entry of data into SPSS, and with various **exploratory data analysis (EDA)** procedures such as calculating descriptive statistics, drawing graphs, transforming and selecting data and so on. In this Exercise, the reader is asked to complete a short questionnaire and to enter the data from it into SPSS. In Exercise 3, your own data will be merged with a larger data set, consisting of the responses of *334* other people to the same questionnaire. Subsequently, the combined file will be used as the data set for the various EDA procedures described in later exercises.

A questionnaire

Please complete the questionnaire below by the writing in, on the table itself, the appropriate values or circling the appropriate options. It is sufficient to enter your age as a whole number of years. Enter your weight either, in traditional British units, as so-many stones plus so-many pounds (e.g. 8 in the upper box, 7 in the lower box if your weight is 8 stones 7 pounds) or, in metric units, as so-many kilos. Similarly, if you wish to give your height in British units, fill in two values, one for feet, the other for inches (e.g., 5 feet, 3 inches); whereas in metric units enter a single value, expressed to two places of decimals (1.52 metres).

What is your age?			Years	
What is your sex?	Male	1	Female	2
What is your Faculty of study?	Arts	1	Science	2
	Medicine	3	Other	4
What is your status?	Undergraduate	1	MSc postgraduate	2
	PhD postgraduate	3	Other	4
What is your approximate weight? Use British or metric measures					
		British units	Stones	
			Pounds	
		Metric units	Kilograms	

What is your approximate height? Use British or metric measures
British units — Feet ☐ Inches ☐
Metric units — Metres (include two decimal places) ☐
Do you smoke?   Yes 1   No 2
If so, how many a day? ☐

Having filled in the questionnaire in the usual way with pen or pencil, we are now going to ask you to do the same thing electronically, that is, by creating an SPSS file and entering your own data. The file will be saved for further use.

Opening SPSS

Log in to SPSS as described in Section 2.2. Select the radio button for **Type in data** from the opening **SPSS 12** window and click **OK**. If **Data View** appears first, click the **Variable View** tab to open **Variable View**.

Entering the data into the Data Editor

Data entry has two aspects:
1. Within **Variable View**, naming the variables and specifying their properties.
2. Within **Data View**, entering the data into the named columns representing the variables previously specified in **Variable View.**

Variable names, provided they conform to the rules for naming variables (Section 2.3.1), are normally a matter of individual preference. In this exercise, however, we have to take account of the fact that your data will later be merged with another (large) data set consisting of information from many people on the same variables. That operation requires that the corresponding variables in both data sets must have **exactly the same variable names**. It is also essential that you use the same **values** as in the larger data set (e.g. *1* for *Male*, *2* for *Female*). For this reason we ask you to use the following variable names and values:

CaseNo   (Add a variable label *Case number* - see below)
MyName   (Specify your name as a **string variable** - see below)
Age
Sex   (Enter the numerical values and their value labels: *1* for *Male*, *2* for *Female* - see below)
Faculty (Add values and value labels: *1* for *Arts*, *2* for *Science*, *3* for *Medicine*, *4* for *Other* - see below)
Status   (Add values and value labels: *1* for *Undergrad*, *2* for *MSc postgrad*, *3* for *PhD postgrad*, *4* for *Other* - see below)

Stones
Pounds
Kilos
Feet
Inches
Metres
Smoker   (Add values and value labels: *1* for *Yes*, *2* for *No* - see below)
NpDay   (Add the variable label *Number of Cigarettes per Day* - see below)

You will have noticed that the questionnaire did not ask for your name; nor indeed are names included in the large data set we shall be dealing with presently. Nevertheless, we ask you to include your name in the file you are building in order to clarify some aspects of file merging in SPSS.

In **Variable View**, enter all the variable names in the **Name** column, using the methods described in Section 2.3.1. In the **Type** column, retain **numeric** format (the default type) for all the variables except *Name* for which a **string** format (**alphanumeric**, or letters and numbers) will be used. In general, we recommend using the numeric format wherever possible: e.g. we prefer to enter qualitative variables such as gender, nationality or blood group as numeric grouping variables, taking care to **assign meaningful value labels** to the code numbers.

The string option for **Type** is selected by clicking anywhere in the corresponding cell of the **Type** column and then clicking the ellipsis (…) on the right to open the **Variable Type** dialog box. Select the **String** radio button and click **OK** to return to **Variable View**. You should also expand the column labelled **Width** to, say, *25* and copy and paste that value to **Columns** to allow your name to be entered in **Data View**.

While working in **Variable View**, use the **Values** column to assign value labels to the code numbers for *Sex, Faculty, Status* and *Smoker*. It is also useful to include a fuller description of any variable in the **Label** column, especially if the variable name is opaque (e.g. *Number of Cigarettes per Day* is clearer than *NpDay*).

The data are much easier to read if no decimals are displayed for any variable except *Metres* for which two decimal places will be required. Change the number in the **Decimals** column to *0* for all the variables except *Metres*, for which the default value *2* should be retained. Note that, for those respondents giving their weights or heights in British units, two SPSS variables will be allocated to each measure: *Stones* and *Pounds* for weight, and *Feet* and *Inches* for height. Those responding in metric units will enter their data in the *Kilos* and *Metres* variables. In Exercise 5, we shall be transforming British Units into metric units, so there is no need to worry about not knowing your metric measurements.

After specifying all the variables and their characteristics, click the **Data View** tab at the foot of **Variable View** to open **Data View** as described in Section 2.3.2. Enter your data along the first row, putting a *1* for your *Case*, typing in your name, age, a value for your sex, a value for your faculty and so on. If you do not smoke, do not enter anything in the *NpDay* column.

If you wish to enter your weight in stones plus pounds, enter values in the *Stones* and *Pounds* columns; otherwise enter a single value under *Kilos*. Similarly, if you want to enter your height in British units, enter values in the *Feet* and *Inches* columns; whereas a metric entry requires only a single value in the *Metres* column. If you have recorded your weight in pounds only, enter a *0* in the *Stones* column. If you have recorded your height in inches only, enter a *0* in the *Feet* column.

Saving the data

Once you have entered your data and checked them for accuracy, select
File
    Save As
to obtain the **Save Data As** dialog box.

You must now decide upon a suitable destination for your file (e.g. the computer's own hard disk C, a floppy disk in drive A, or a disk drive available on a networked system). We suggest you save your own data in a folder with a name such as *SPSS 12 Book Exercises data*, which you will have to create beforehand or by selecting the icon shown in the figure below and naming a new folder.

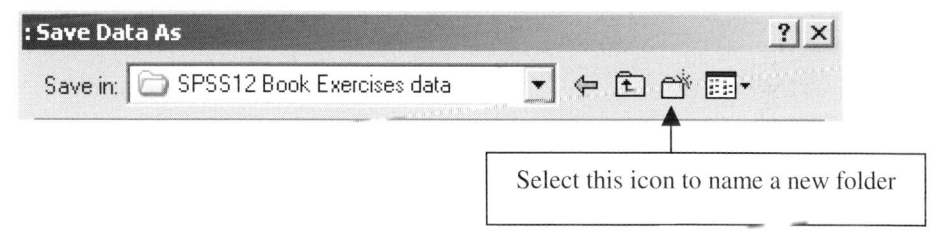

Select this icon to name a new folder

Choose **Save As** and, having made sure that *SPSS 12 Book Exercises data* is showing at the top of the dialog box, type the name *Ex2 Questionnaire Data* in the **File Name** box. Click **Save** to save your own questionnaire responses as the SPSS file *Ex2 Questionnaire Data*. You will be loading this file when you first open SPSS in the next Exercise.

Finishing the session

Close down SPSS and any other open windows before logging out of the computer.

CHAPTER 3

Editing and manipulating files

3.1   More about the SPSS Data Editor
3.2   More on the SPSS Viewer
3.3   Selecting from and manipulating files
3.4   Importing and exporting data
3.5   Printing from SPSS

3.1   MORE ABOUT THE SPSS DATA EDITOR

3.1.1   Working in Variable View

In Section 2.2, we introduced the **Data Editor**, with its two alternative displays, **Variable View** and **Data View**. Here we describe some additional features of **Variable View** (see Section 2.3.1).

> See Section 2.3.1

Inserting new variables among those already in Variable View

An additional variable can be inserted in **Variable View** by highlighting any row (click the grey cell on the left), and choosing
Data
>   **Insert Variable**

The new variable, with a default name such as VAR00004 (i.e. the next free name), will appear **above** the row that has been highlighted.

In **Data View,** the new variable will appear in a new column **to the left** of the variable that was highlighted in **Variable View**.

Editing and manipulating files 49

Rearranging the order of variables in Variable View

In Figure 1, is a section from **Variable View**, in which the top-to-bottom ordering of the variables determines their left-to-right order of appearance in **Data View**, which is *Case*, *Group*, then *Score*.

	Name	Type	Width	Decimals
1	Case	Numeric	8	0
2	Group	Numeric	8	0
3	Score	Numeric	8	0

Figure 1. The arrangement of the variables in **Variable View** determines their order of appearance in **Data View**

Suppose that you want to change the sequence of the variables in **Data View**: you want *Score* to appear to the left of *Group*. In **Variable View**, click the grey box to the left of the *Score* variable to highlight the whole row. Holding the left mouse button down, drag the screen pointer upwards. A red line will appear above the *Group* row. On releasing the mouse button, the variable *Score* will appear immediately under *Case* (Figure 2). In **Data View**, the variable *Score* will now appear to the left of the variable *Group*.

	Name	Type	Width	Decimals
1	Case	Numeric	8	0
2	Score	Numeric	8	0
3	Group	Numeric	8	0

Figure 2. The arrangement of variables after moving *Score* above *Group*

Large data sets: The advantages of numbering the cases

In the small data set we considered in Chapter 2, each row had a number and could be taken as representing one particular case or person. Suppose, however, that we had a much larger data set, containing thousands of cases. Suppose also that, from time to time, cases were to be removed from the data set or the data were sorted and re-sorted on different criteria. As a result, any particular row in the data set, say the 99th, may not always contain data on the same person throughout the exercise.

With a large data set like this, especially one that is continually changing, it is good practice to create, as the first variable, one with a name such as *Case*, which records each participant's original case number: 1, 2, ..., and so on. The advantage of doing this is that, even though a given person's data may occupy different rows at different points in the data-gathering exercise, the researcher always knows which data came from which person. Should the accuracy of the transcription of a participant's data into SPSS later be called into question, that person's data can always be identified and checked throughout the entire process of data entry.

Suppose you wish to add case numbers to a data set not currently containing such a variable. This is very conveniently done, especially when the data set is large, by using the **Compute Variable** procedure as follows:
- Ensure that the data file is present in the **Data Editor**.
- In **Variable View**, click on the grey cell to the left of the first row to highlight the entire row.
- Choose
  Data
      Insert Variable
  to create a new empty row above the original first row with the default variable name *VAR00001*.
- Remove the highlighting from the row by clicking elsewhere in the grid. Click on the **Name** cell and type in the variable name *Case*.
- Adjust the **Decimals** setting to zero.
- Enter the label *Case Number* in the **Label** column.
- Choose
  Transform
      Compute...
  to open the **Compute Variable** dialog box.
- Place the cursor in the **Target Variable** slot and enter the variable name *Case*.
- In the **Numeric Expression:** box on the right, type *$casenum* and click **OK** (Figure 3).
- Click the **Data View** tab to confirm that a new variable named *Case* has appeared, containing the counting numbers *1, 2, ...* .

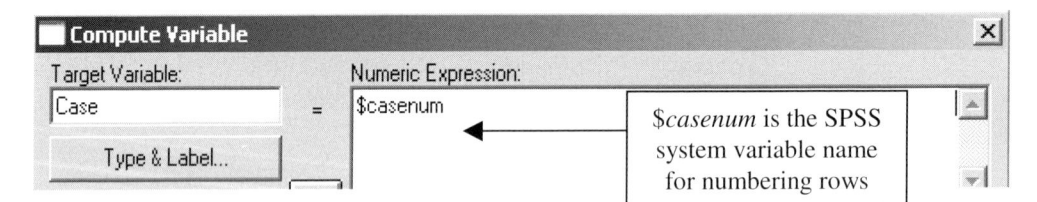

Figure 3. Part of the **Compute Variable** dialog box for generating case numbers

Note that this procedure cannot be used for creating case numbers in an empty data file. If it is desired to create case numbers before entering data, then dummy data must be entered (e.g. entering *1* in the first row of the variable *Case* and then copying it down for as many rows as the data set will need) before using *$casenum* in the **Compute Variable** procedure.

Changing the global default number of decimal places and maximum width for string variables using the Edit menu

The default settings for variable width and the number of places of decimals are *8* and *2*, respectively. If you wish to enter several new variables and display them all as whole numbers (integers), choose
Edit
    Options
        Data

Editing and manipulating files 51

and change the pre-set values. Figure 4 shows the **Options** dialog box.

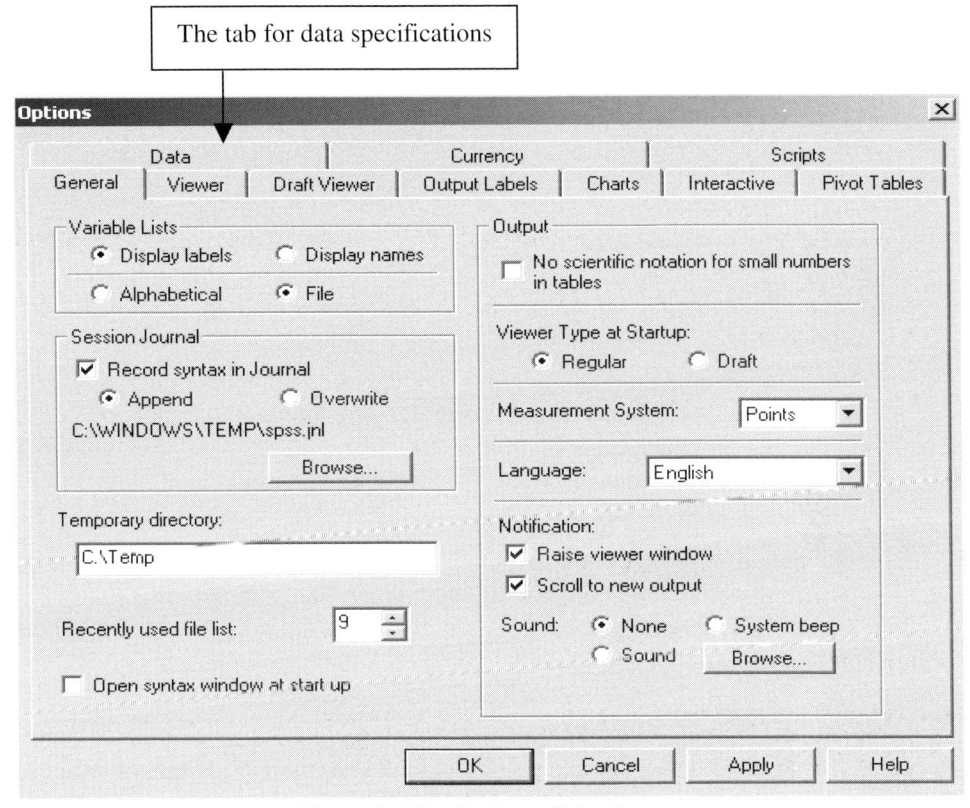

Figure 4. The **Options** dialog box

- Click the tab labelled **Data**. In the new dialog box is an area headed **Display Format for New Numeric Variables** (Figure 5), in which both the width and number of decimal places can be amended.
- In the box containing the number of **Decimal Places**, click the downward arrow on the right until *0* appears. Click **OK** and the **Options d**ialog box will close. The changes you have specified will apply only to any **new** numeric variables that you may create. You will find that, even after amending the default settings in **Options**, the appearance of numerical data already in **Data View** is unchanged.
- At the foot of the **Data** dialog box, is a button labelled **Apply**, which is activated when you change the settings. The purpose of the **Apply** button is to register the changes you have made **without closing the dialog box**. You can then click other tabs and make whatever changes you wish to make in those before leaving **Options**.

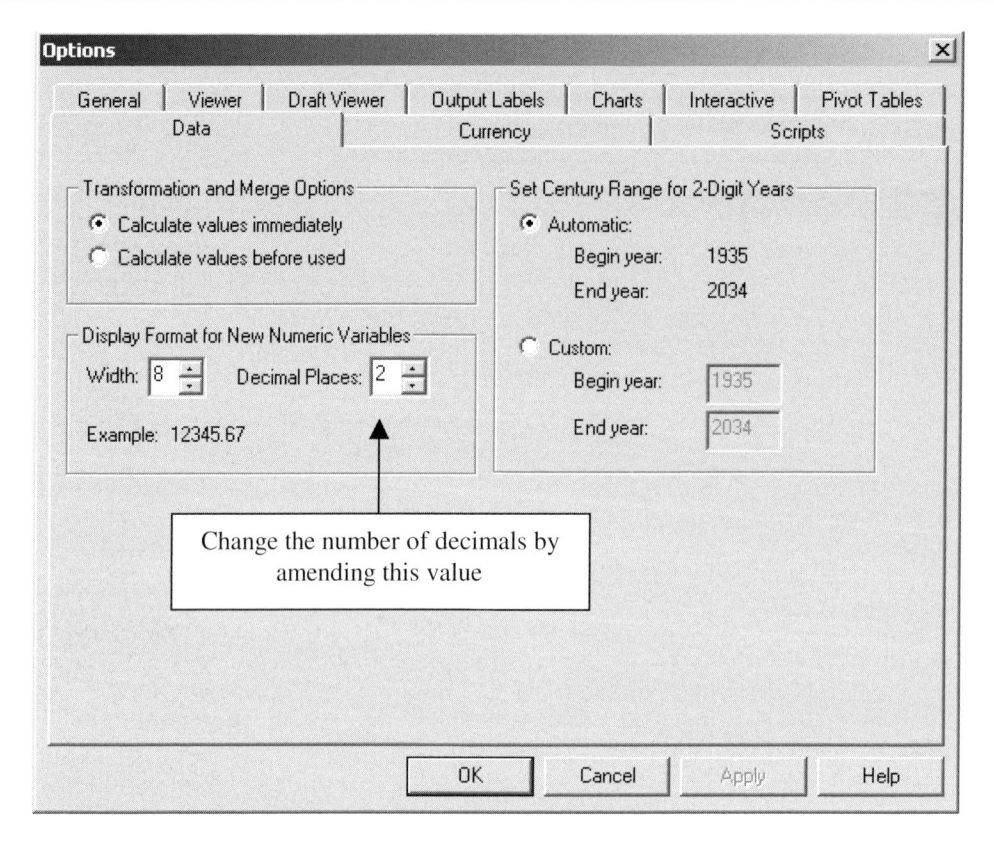

Figure 5. The **Options** dialog box showing the panel for adjusting the **Display Format for New Numeric Variables**

If you are working on a networked computer where the software and settings are held on a central server, any changes you may make by changing the entries in **Options** may apply only for the duration of your own session: when you log off, the system will restore the original default values.

*Changing the type of variable (the **Type** column)*

In **Variable View**, there is a column headed **Type**. The **Type** column specifies the general form that an entry for a particular variable will take when it appears in the data set. By default, the variable type is assumed to be **numeric**, but seven other types can be specified in SPSS.

A **string** is a sequence of characters, such as a person's name, which is treated as a qualitative variable (not as a numeric variable) by the system. Had we entered, in the variable *Name*, the names of all the participants taking part in the drug experiment, *Name* would have been a **string variable**.

To create a string variable, proceed as follows:
- After typing in the name of the variable, highlight the cell in the **Type** column thus

Editing and manipulating files

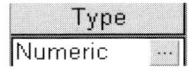

- Click the grey area with the three dots to the right of **Numeric** to open the **Variable Type** dialog box (Figure 6).

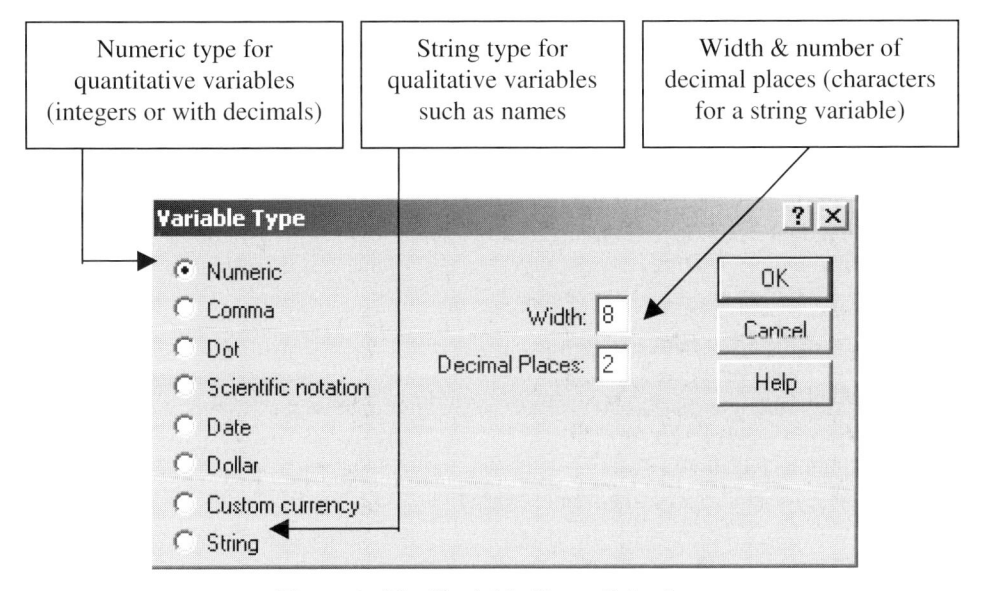

Figure 6. The **Variable Type** dialog box

- In the dialog box is a list of eight variable types, each with a radio button. Initially, the **Numeric** button will be marked.
- Descriptions of the different types of variable will be found by clicking the **Help** button in the dialog box.
- Click the **String** radio button at the foot of the list. The **Width** and **Decimal Places** boxes will immediately be replaced by a box labelled **Characters**.
- Change the default value 8 in the **Characters** box to some larger number such as 20 to accommodate the longest likely name. Do this by moving the cursor into the number box, selecting the 8 and typing in 20.
- Click **OK**. In **Variable View**, the variable type *String* will now appear in the **Type** column and the cell for the *Name* variable in the **Width** column will now show 20.
- Click the **Width** column and copy the specifications either by choosing **Copy** from the **Edit** menu or with the key combination **Ctrl + C**.
- Click on **Columns** and paste the new **Width** specification (20) there either by choosing **Paste** from the **Edit** menu or with the key combination **Ctrl + V**. The effect of this move will be to make sufficient space available in **Data View** to see the longest name in the data set. Alternatively, in **Data View**, the right-hand edge of the box containing the variable *Name* can be dragged to the right by holding down the left mouse button and dragging it as far as desired.

*Missing values (the **Missing** column)*

SPSS assumes that all data sets are complete (i.e. that the cells in every row and every column have something in them). The user, however, may not have entries for every case on every variable in the data set (e.g. a participant's age might not have been recorded). Such missing entries are marked by SPSS with what is known as a **system-missing** value, which is indicated in the **Data Editor** by a full stop. SPSS will exclude system-missing values from its calculations of means, standard deviations and other statistics.

It may be, however, that for some purposes the user wishes SPSS to treat certain responses actually present in the data set as missing data. For example, suppose that, in an examination, some candidates either walked out the moment they saw the paper or, having attempted at least some of the examination, earned only a nominal mark (say 20% or less) from the examiner. In either case, you might wish to treat the candidate's response as a missing value, but for some purposes you might want to retain information about the relative frequencies of the two responses in the output. In SPSS terminology, the user wants certain responses to be treated as **user-missing** values (as opposed to **system-missing** values).

Suppose you want SPSS to treat as missing:
1. Any marks between *0* and *20*;
2. Cases where the candidate walked out without giving any written response at all.

A walk-out could be coded as an arbitrary, but salient, number, such as *-9*: the negative sign helps the number to stand out as impossible mark.

To define such user-missing values:

- In **Variable View**, move the cursor to the **Missing** column and click on the appropriate cell for the variable concerned.
- Click the grey area with the ellipsis to the right of **None** to open the **Missing Values** dialog box.
- Initially, the **No missing values** radio button is marked. The three text boxes underneath give the user the opportunity to specify up to three **Discrete Missing Values**, referred to in SPSS as *missing (1)*, *missing (2)*, and *missing (3)*. These may either be numerical, as with a grouping variable, or short string variables (up to 8 characters in length), but they must be consistent with the original variable type. In the case of a string variable, the procedure is case sensitive. The other options in the dialog box are for scale (quantitative) variables: the user may define a missing value as one falling within a specified range, or one that falls either within a specified range or within a specified category.
- Click the **Range plus one discrete missing value** button. Enter the values *0* and *20* into the **Low** and **High** boxes, respectively, and *-9* into the **Discrete value** box. The completed dialog box is shown in Figure 7.
- Click **OK** and the values will appear in the **Missing** column cell.

As with the attributes of number of decimals places and width, missing value specifications can be copied to other variables by pasting them into the appropriate cells.

Editing and manipulating files 55

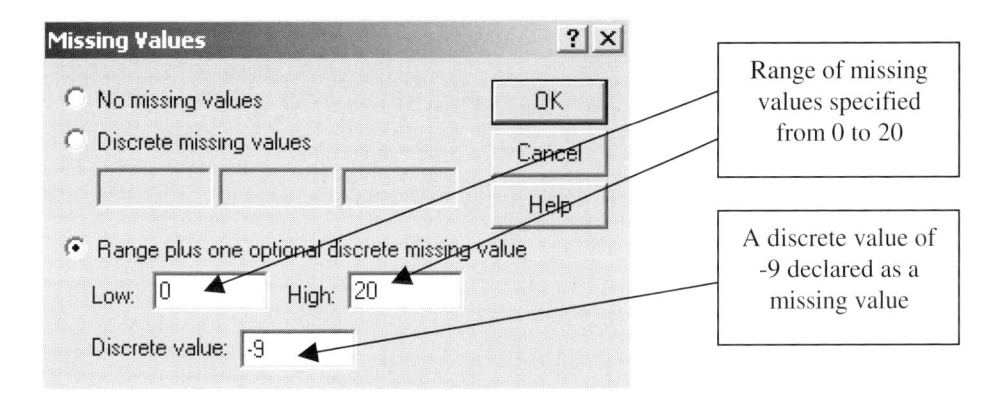

Figure 7. The completed **Missing Values** dialog box showing a range of missing values between *0* and *20* and a discrete value of *-9*

*Data alignment (the **Align** column)*

In **Data View**, by default, numbers are right-aligned and strings are left-aligned. These settings can be changed by clicking on the appropriate cell in the **Align** column and choosing **Left**, **Right** or **Center**.

*Measurement level (the **Measure** column)*

The default measurement level is **Scale** for numeric variables and **Nominal** for **String** variables. (Although a grouping variable refers to a set of qualitative categories, its representation in SPSS is still numeric, because it is a set of code numbers for the groups or conditions.) In some chart-drawing procedures, however, it is necessary to specify whether the measurement is nominal or ordinal.

3.1.2   Working in Data View

In Sections 2.3.2 and 2.3.3, the entry of data in **Data View** was briefly considered. Here we shall describe some additional features of **Data View**.

Reading in SPSS files

See Sections 2.3.2 & 2.3.3

- When the opening SPSS window appears, select **Open an existing data source**.
- Select the appropriate file. (If you are working on a networked computer, you may have to click **More files ...** and locate the file or folder containing the file.)
- Click **OK** to load the data file into **Data View**.

Alternatively, one of the following methods can be used:

- Click the radio button of the opening SPSS window labelled **Type in data** and then **OK** to bring **Data View** to the screen. Select
    File
        Open
            Data

to show the **Open File** dialog box. The target file can then be specified.
- If SPSS has not yet been opened, you can use the Windows **Find** menu or **My Computer** to locate the file, which should open when double-clicked. SPSS will automatically open with the data loaded in **Data View** and the specifications in **Variable View**. While data are being read into **Data View** from a file, the hour-glass will appear and messages will appear in the **Status Bar** at various stages in the operation. The message **SPSS Processor is ready** signals the end of the reading process.

Entering data into Data View before specifying variables in Variable View

Although we strongly recommend that you lay the foundations in **Variable View** before actually entering the data in **Data View**, it is possible to begin immediately to enter data into **Data View**. It is also possible to copy blocks of data directly into **Data View**, which can be useful when you are importing data from another application which does not have one of the many data formats recognised by SPSS. The details of the variables can be added in **Variable View** later.

Choose
File
 New
to create an empty SPSS data file. Enter **Data View** and type the value *23* into the cell in the second row of the fourth column. **Data View** will now appear as in Figure 8.

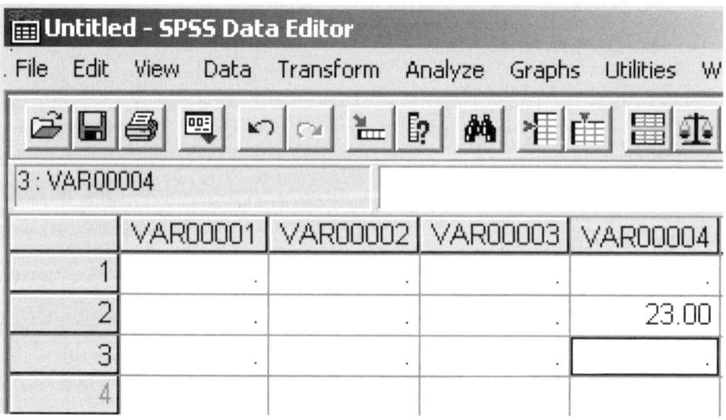

Figure 8. The appearance of **Data View** after entering a datum without previously naming variables in **Variable View**

The fourth variable has now been given the default name *VAR00004*. Notice that SPSS has assumed that we have a 2 × 4 matrix of data and filled in the blank cells with the system-missing symbol. Should you type values into cells to the right of the fourth column, more default variable names will appear as SPSS expands the supposed data matrix to include the new column and row. If you click on a cell underneath the lowest row of dots, more rows of dots will appear, the lowest of which contains the cell you have just clicked.

To assign meaningful names and labels to the default variables visible in **Data View**, switch to **Variable View** and assign the specifications there. You can either enter **Variable View** in the usual way by clicking the **Variable View** tab at the bottom of **Data View** or double-click the default heading of the variable you wish to name. Either way, when you enter **Variable View**, you will see that the default variable names have been entered there. In other words, the two display modes of the **Data Editor** are interchangeable in the order in which they are completed.

Inserting additional variables while working in Data View

To add a new variable **to the right of those already in Data View**, you have only to type a value into a cell to the right of the present matrix of data. To add a new column **between two of those within the present data set**,
- Highlight the variable **to the right of** the intended position of the new variable.
- Choose
  Data
     Insert Variable
  to create a new, empty, variable to the left of the variable you have highlighted.

Rearranging the variables in Data View

Suppose that in **Data View**, the order of the variables is *Case*, *Group* and *Score*, and you want to change the order to *Case*, *Score* and *Group*. We recommend that you do this in **Variable View** (see Section 3.1.1), but the following procedure works in **Data View**.
- Create a new, empty variable to the left of *Group* in the manner described above.
- Click on the grey cell at the head of the *Score* column to highlight the whole column.
- Choose
  Edit
     Cut
  to remove the *Score* variable and place it in the clipboard.
- Click the grey cell at the head of the new, empty variable to highlight the whole column
- Use **Edit** and **Paste** to move the *Score* variable including its data and definitions into its new position to the left of *Group*.

Adding new cases

Columns can be lengthened by choosing
Data
   Insert cases
which will have the effect of adding new empty rows underneath the existing columns.

There are occasions, however, when you may want to place rows for additional cases in the middle of the data set. Suppose that, in the drug experiment, you want to add data on an additional participant who has been tested under the *Placebo* condition. Proceed as follows.
- Click the grey cell on the left of the row of data **above** which you want to insert the new case. (This will be the row of data for the first participant who performed under the Drug condition.) The row will now be highlighted.

- Choose
  Data
    Insert Cases
  to create a new empty row above the one you highlighted.

You can now type in the data from the additional placebo participant.

3.2 MORE ON THE SPSS VIEWER

We described the **SPSS Viewer** in part of Section 2.4.1 and how the output can be edited. The **Viewer** consists of two panes (see Output 1 in Chapter 2), the widths of which can be adjusted by clicking and dragging the vertical bar separating them. The left pane lists the items of output in order of their appearance in the right pane, each item having an icon and a title.

See Section 2.4.1

The icon shows whether the item is visible in the right pane (open-book icon) or invisible (closed-book icon). By double-clicking the icon, the item can be made visible or invisible in the right pane, where all actual output is presented. The output can also be rearranged by moving the appropriate icons around in the left pane by clicking and dragging them. A single click on an item in the left pane will bring the item into view in the right pane. Unwanted items in the output can be deleted by highlighting them in the left pane and pressing the **Delete** key. In this book, only selections from the right pane will normally be reproduced.

In Section 2.4.1 we tabulated the results of the Drug experiment using the **Compare Means** procedure. Here (see Output 1) we have added a column of medians by clicking **Options…** in the **Means** dialog box and transferring **Median** from the **Statistics** panel to the **Cell Statistics** panel. (It is often a good idea, when exploring data, to compare means with medians: if they have similar values, symmetrical distributions are suggested. Here, however, the medians have been included merely to demonstrate some editing in the **Viewer**.)

Report

Score Achieved

Experimental Condition	Mean	N	Std. Deviation	Median
Placebo	3.40	10	1.838	3.50
Drug	6.90	10	1.449	6.50
Total	5.15	20	2.412	5.50

Output 1. Output from **Compare Means** procedure, with means, sample sizes, standard deviations and medians

3.2.1 Editing the output

In Section 2.4.1, we demonstrated that the output in the **SPSS Viewer** could be edited by showing the effect of a pivoting procedure. Here we consider some more ways of improving the appearance of the output.

Editing and manipulating files

To edit an item, say a table, in the **Viewer**, double-click it. The table will now be surrounded by a hatched box indicating that you are now in the **Viewer**'s editor. Once a selected item has been surrounded by a hatched box, the following changes can be made:

- To **widen or narrow columns**, move the cursor on to a vertical line in the table and click and drag the line to the left or the right.
- **Items** can be **deleted** by highlighting them and pressing the **Delete** key.
- **Whole columns or rows** can be **deleted** by highlighting them and pressing the **Delete** key (see below for details).
- **Text** can sometimes be altered by double-clicking an item and deleting letters or typing in new ones.
- If values are listed, it is possible to re-specify the number of decimal places shown by highlighting the numbers concerned in a block, pressing the **right-hand** mouse button, selecting **Cell Properties...** and changing the specification in the **Cell Properties** dialog box.

For example, suppose that, in the **Report** table (Output 1), we want to dispense with the third row (*Total*) containing the statistics of all twenty scores in the data set considered as a single group and also the column of **Medians**.
- Click the left cell in the bottom row.
- Press the **Ctrl** button and, keeping it pressed, click the other cells in the *Total* row and the mumbers in the *Median* column. The **Report** table will now appear as in Output 2.

Report

Variables	Score Achieved			
Experimental Condition	Mean	N	Std. Deviation	Median
Placebo	3.40	10	1.838	3.50
Drug	6.90	10	1.449	6.50
Total	5.15	20	2.412	5.50

Output 2. Highlighting material to be deleted

- Press the **Delete** key to remove the bottom row and the rightmost column.
- Click outside the shaded border to leave the **Editor**. The **Report** table will now appear as in Output 3.

Report

Score Achieved

Experimental Condition	Mean	N	Std. Deviation
Placebo	3.40	10	1.838
Drug	6.90	10	1.449

Output 3. The edited **Report** table after removing the *Total* row and *Median* column

3.2.2 More advanced editing

The **Data Editor** offers even more powerful editing facilities, some of which can radically alter the appearance of a default table such as the **Report** table we have been editing. Many of the tables in the output are **pivot tables**, that is, tables in which the columns and rows can be transposed and to which other radical alterations can be made. In Chapter 2, we showed how, by choosing

Pivot
   Transpose Rows and Columns

we could change the rows of the default **Report** table into columns and vice versa (see Section 2.4.1). Here we illustrate the manipulation of a three-way table of means.

> See Section 2.4.1

A three-way table of means

It is well known that generally females are better at recalling verbal material and males are better at recalling graphic material. An experiment was carried out recalling verbal or graphic items after either a short, medium or long period of inspection of the items. Male and female participants were each divided into six subgroups looking at verbal or graphic items for the three inspection times. Coding variables for *Sex*, *Task*, and *InspectionTime* were named in **Variable View** along with *Score* for the number of items recalled. Corresponding **Labels** were specified as *Sex*, *Type of Task*, *Inspection Time* and *Number of Items Recalled*. The **Mean** procedure with *Number of Items Recalled* entered in the **Dependent List** and each of *Sex*, *Type of Task* and *Inspection Time* entered as layers in the **Independent List** generated Output 4 when only **Mean** was selected for the **Cell Statistics** box within **Options**. The rows for Total have been edited out of Output 4 for simplicity.

Report

Mean

Sex	Type of Task	Inspection Time	Number of Items Recalled
Male	Verbal	Short	4.00
		Medium	5.00
		Long	5.00
	Graphic	Short	2.67
		Medium	3.67
		Long	4.00
Female	Verbal	Short	5.33
		Medium	5.67
		Long	6.33
	Graphic	Short	1.67
		Medium	2.33
		Long	3.33

Output 4. The output from the **Mean** procedure

Editing and manipulating files

It is possible to effect a simple transposition of all the rows in Output 4 into columns and vice versa by choosing **Transposing rows and Columns** from the **Pivot** menu. There is little to be gained from this, however, because of the complexity of the table. To improve the clarity of the table, we want to select individual variables for transposition. This finer control is achieved by using the **Pivoting Trays** procedure.

After highlighting the **Report** table (Output 4) by double-clicking anywhere within in, choose
Pivot
   Pivoting Trays
to obtain the **Pivoting Trays1** display shown in Figure 9.

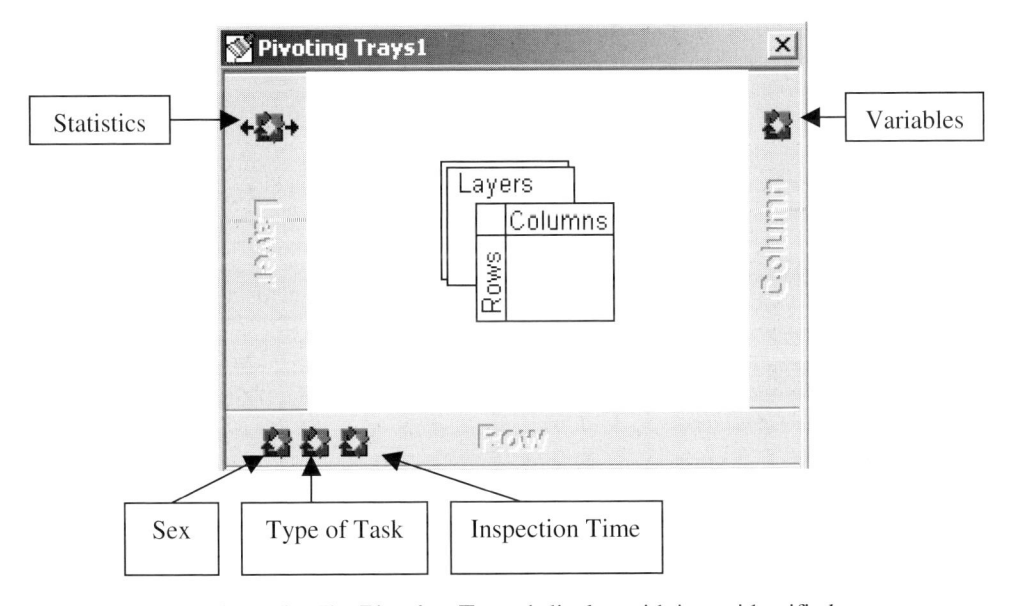

Figure 9. The **Pivoting Trays1** display with icons identified

The icons in the grey borders represent the dimensions of the table, the identity of which can be seen by placing the screen pointer on the icon. The best way to see how the pivoting trays work is to click and drag the icons to other grey borders in the display and observe the resulting changes in the table of means.

From left to right, the three icons in the bottom **Row** border represent the variables *Sex*, *Type of Task* and *Inspection Time* respectively, which is the order in which these three dimensions appear in the table. This order can be changed by clicking and dragging the three icons to different positions. For example, if we click and drag the present rightmost icon (*Inspection Time*) to the left of the other two icons, that dimension will now appear in the leftmost position in the table (Output 5).

Report

Mean

Inspection Time	Sex	Type of Task	Number of Items Recalled
Short	Male	Verbal	4.00
		Graphic	2.67
	Female	Verbal	5.33
		Graphic	1.67
Medium	Male	Verbal	5.00
		Graphic	3.67
	Female	Verbal	5.67
		Graphic	2.33
Long	Male	Verbal	5.00
		Graphic	4.00
	Female	Verbal	6.33
		Graphic	3.33

Output 5. The appearance of the table after the order of the icons in the **Rows** margin of the pivoting trays has been changed (compare with Output 4)

In Outputs 4 and 5, the labels of the three factors in the experiment are all in rows. Should we wish to retain the levels of *Sex* and *Type of Task* in rows, but move those of *Inspection Time* into columns, we need only click and drag the icons for *Inspection Time* from the grey margin labelled **Row** to the right-hand grey margin labelled **Column** (Figure 10).

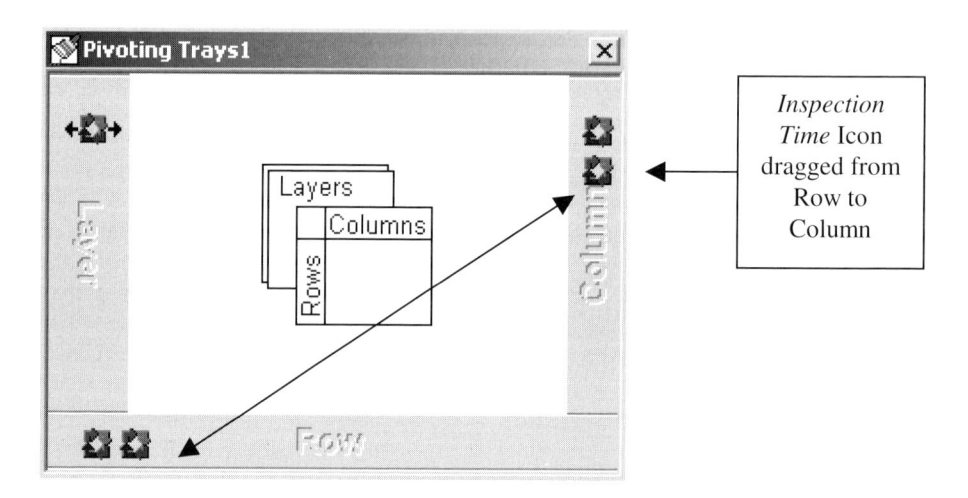

Figure 10. The *Inspection Time* icon has been dragged to the **Column** margin

Editing and manipulating files

The effect of this manipulation is that, whereas the two types of *Sex* and *Type of Task* will appear in rows as before, the three levels of *Inspection Time* now appear at the heads of three columns (Output 6).

Report

Mean

		Number of Items Recalled		
		Inspection Time		
Sex	Type of Task	Short	Medium	Long
Male	Verbal	4.00	5.00	5.00
	Graphic	2.67	3.67	4.00
Female	Verbal	5.33	5.67	6.33
	Graphic	1.67	2.33	3.33

Output 6. Edited table in which *Inspection Time* has been transposed to columns

The left grey margin of the pivot tray is labelled **Layer**. A **layer** is a tabulation at one particular level of another factor. In the tables we have looked at so far, all the dimensions have been shown. Suppose, however, that we want to view the two-way table of means for *Type of Task* and *Inspection Time* for each level of *Sex*. Simply click and drag the *Sex* icon from the grey **Rows** margin of the pivot tray to the **Layer** margin (Figure 11). The table will now appear as in Output 7.

Icon for *Sex* dragged from Row to Layer

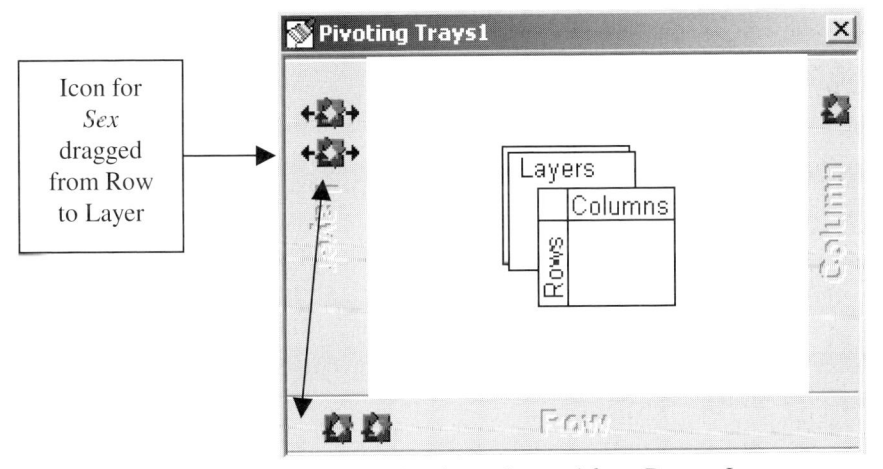

Figure 11. The *Sex* icon has been dragged from Row to Layer

We can see the means for *Type of Task* and *Inspection Time* only for the Male level of Sex. To see the means for Female, simply click on the arrow to the right of Male and select Female

Report		
Statistics	Mean	
Sex	Male	

Type of Task	Inspection Time	Number of Items Recalled
Verbal	Short	4.00
	Medium	5.00
	Long	5.00
Graphic	Short	2.67
	Medium	3.67
	Long	4.00

Output 7. A layered table, in which the means for *Type of Task* and *Inspection Time* are displayed at only one level of *Sex*. The means for Female can be seen by clicking the arrow to the right of Male and selecting Female

3.2.3 Tutorials in SPSS

The SPSS package now includes some excellent tutorials on various aspects of the system, including the use of the **Viewer** and the manipulation of pivot tables.

To access a tutorial choose:
Help
    Tutorial

and double-click to open the tutorial menu. The buttons in the right-hand bottom corner of each page of the tutorial enable the user to see the list of items (upward arrow) and to navigate forward and backward through the tutorial (right and left arrows).

3.3 SELECTING FROM AND MANIPULATING DATA FILES

So far, the emphasis has been upon the construction of a complete data set, the saving of that set to a file on disk, and its retrieval from storage. There are occasions, however, on which the user will want to operate selectively on the data. It may be, for instance, that only some of the cases in a data set are of interest (those contributed by the participants in one category alone, perhaps); or the user may wish to exclude participants with outlying values on specified variables. In this section, some of these more specialised manoeuvres will be described.

Transformation and recoding of data will be discussed in Chapter 4.

3.3.1 Selecting cases

Let us assume that, in **Data View**, we have the results of the Drug experiment. In the original data set, there were two variables: *Experimental Condition* and *Score Achieved*. Suppose, however, that a *Gender* variable has been added, where *1 = Male* and *2 = Female*, and that we want to examine the data from the female participants only.

- Choose
  Data
      Select Cases…
  to obtain the **Select Cases** dialog box (see Figure 12).
- Initially, the **All cases** radio button is marked. Click the **Select Cases: If** button and complete the **Select Cases: If** dialog box as shown in Figure 13.
- Return to the **Select Cases** dialog box and click **OK** to select only the female participants for analysis.

A section of **Data View** is shown in Figure 14. Another column, headed *filter_$*, has now appeared, containing the entries *Not Selected* and *Selected*. Note that, although the name *filter_$* will appear in subsequent dialog boxes, it should not be selected as a variable for analysis because it will only report the number of selected cases.

The row numbers of the unselected cases (the males) have been marked with an oblique bar. This is a useful indicator of **case selection status.** The status bar (if enabled at the foot of **Data View**) will carry the message **Filter On**. Any further analyses of the data set will exclude cases where *Gender = 1*.

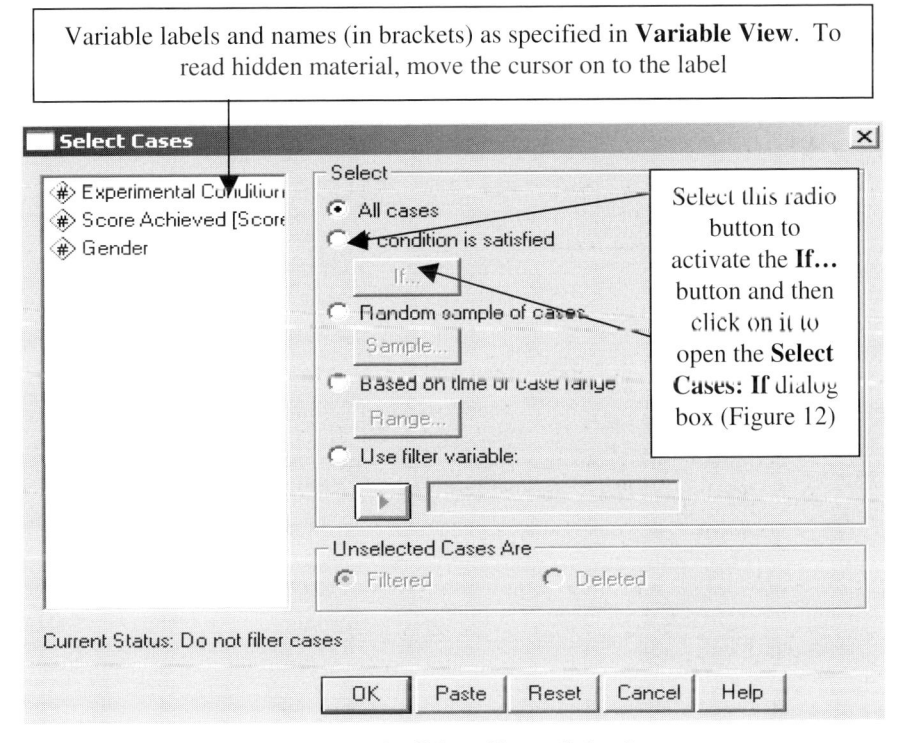

Figure 12. The **Select Cases** dialog box

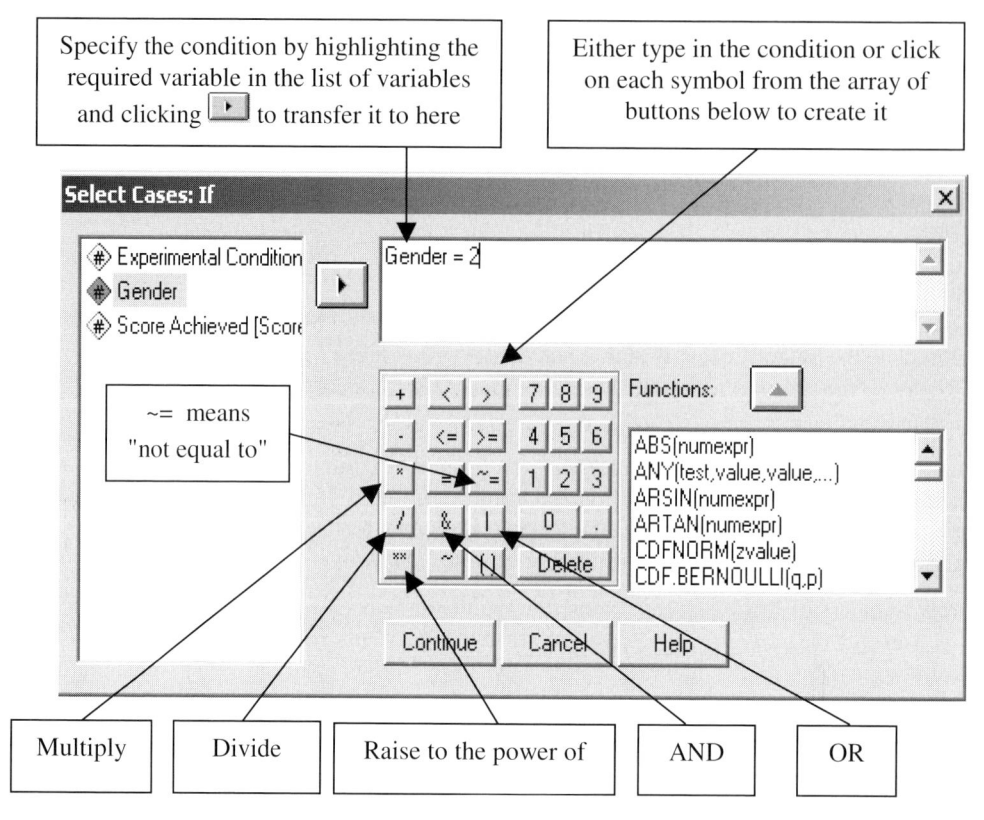

Specify the condition by highlighting the required variable in the list of variables and clicking ▶ to transfer it to here

Either type in the condition or click on each symbol from the array of buttons below to create it

~= means "not equal to"

Multiply

Divide

Raise to the power of

AND

OR

Figure 13. The **Select Cases: If** dialog box with the expression for excluding group 1 from the variable group

The oblique bars shows deselected cases

Case	Group	Gender	Score	filter_$
1	Placebo	Male	6	Not Selected
2	Placebo	Female	5	Selected
3	Placebo	Male	5	Not Selected
4	Placebo	Female	1	Selected
5	Placebo	Male	2	Not Selected
6	Placebo	Female	3	Selected
7	Placebo	Male	2	Not Selected
8	Placebo	Female	4	Selected
9	Placebo	Male	5	Not Selected
10	Placebo	Female	1	Selected
11	Drug	Male	8	Not Selected
12	Drug	Female	6	Selected
13	Drug	Male	6	Not Selected

Figure 14. **Data View**, showing that only the scores of the female participants will be included in the analysis

Editing and manipulating files 67

Case selection can be **cancelled** as follows:
- From the **Data menu**, choose **Select Cases** and (in the **Select Cases** dialog box) click **All cases**.
- Click **OK**.

3.3.2 Aggregating data

In a School of Business Studies, students take a selection of five courses each. (There is a degree of choice, so that different students may take somewhat different selections of courses.) On the basis of their performance, the students are marked on a percentage scale. We shall be concerned with the marks of ten of the students, whose marks on the five courses they took are contained in the SPSS data file *Students marks* and reproduced in the Appendix to this Chapter on p93. Figure 15 is a section of **Data View**, showing some of their marks.

	Student	Course	Mark
1	Anne	Accountancy	80
2	Rebecca	Accountancy	78
3	Susan	Accountancy	87
4	Anne	Computing	49
5	Fred	Computing	55
6	Rebecca	Computing	65
7	Susan	Computing	56
8	Anne	German	40
9	Fred	German	72
10	Jim	German	73

Figure 15. Part of the file *Students marks* in **Data View**

*Finding course averages: The **Aggregate** procedure*

Suppose we want to find the mean mark for each of the courses that were taken. SPSS's **Aggregate** procedure groups cases according to the nominal variable specified (e.g. *Course*) and then aggregates the values of the quantitative variable specified (e.g. *Mark*). Various options are available for how the aggregation is done (e.g. mean, median, percentage above a specified value). We shall use the **Aggregate** procedure to group the marks according to course and calculate the mean mark for each course.

Choose
Data
    Aggregate…
to obtain the **Aggregate Data** dialog box (Figure 16).

In the **Aggregate Data** dialog box, the **Break Variable** is the variable on the basis of which the marks are to be grouped (i.e. *Course*). The **Aggregate Variable** is the mark that a student received (i.e. *Mark*). In case of unintentional actions, it is wiser to create a new data file rather than replace the working data file. This is done by clicking the radio button **Create new data file** in the bottom left corner of the dialog box. Click **File…** and specify a folder and file name for saving the results of the **Aggregate** procedure (e.g. *Course Mean Marks*) – see Figure 17 for the completed dialog box.

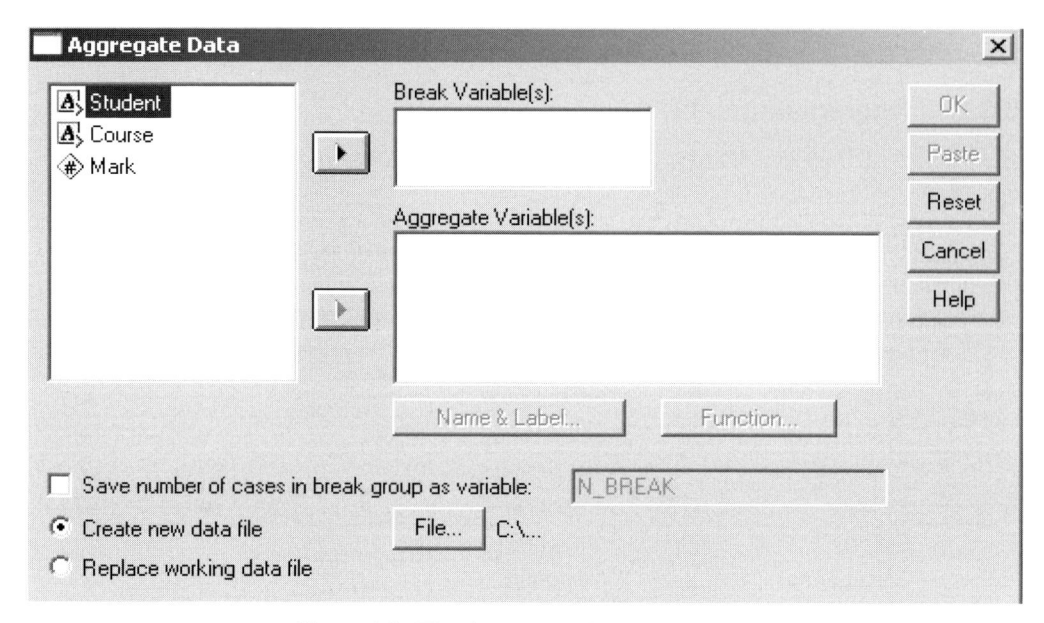

Figure 16. The **Aggregate Data** dialog box

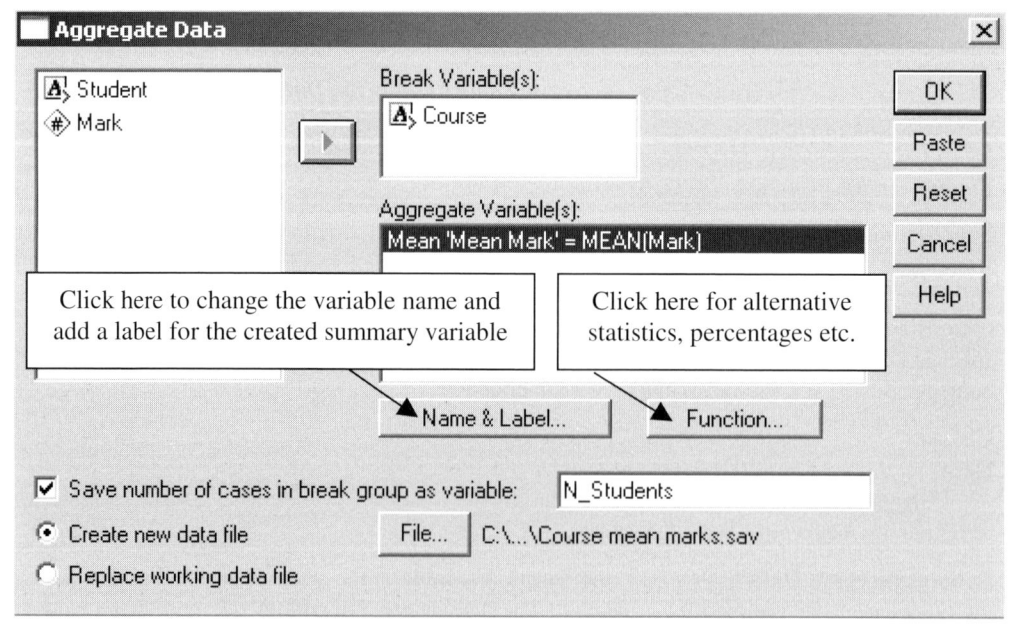

Figure 17. The completed **Aggregate Data** dialog box. The results of the aggregation (*Mean*) will be saved in the file *Course average marks* and the count of cases in the variable *N_Students*

Editing and manipulating files 69

Notice that in the **Aggregate Variable(s)** panel is the expression Mark = MEAN(Mark). Unless otherwise instructed, SPSS will calculate the mean mark for each course. You can choose another statistic (such as the Median) by clicking on the **Function...** button and changing the specification. You can also change the variable name and specify a variable label by clicking **Name & Label...** and completing the dialog box. Here the variable has been named as *Mean* with a label *Mean Mark*.

Since the students had a degree of choice and some courses were more popular than others, the means calculated by the **Aggregate** procedure are based on varying sample sizes. It is therefore wise to request the inclusion of sample sizes by marking the small box labelled **Save number of cases in break group as variable** and changing the variable name to a more meaningful one such as *N-Students*. Click **OK**.

To see the results of the aggregation, you need to open the new data file *Course average marks* (Figure 18), which shows the mean mark (*Mean*) awarded to the students taking each of the courses that were selected and the size of the sample of marks from which the mean was calculated in the column *N_Students*.

	Course	Mean	N_Students
1	Accountancy	81.67	3
2	Computing	56.25	4
3	German	67.50	4
4	Graphics	57.43	7
5	Law	82.88	8
6	Management	50.43	7
7	Mathematics	63.67	6
8	Politics	51.00	5
9	Spanish	57.33	3
10	Statistics	67.33	3

Figure 18. Mean mark on each of the courses together with the number of students who took each course

3.3.3 Sorting data

Suppose that, in order to appraise the courses, you want to list them in order of the mean marks the students achieved.

- With the data file *Course mean marks* in the **Data Editor**, choose
  Data
    Sort Cases...
  to obtain the **Sort Cases** dialog box. Figure 19 shows the completed dialog box.
- Since you will probably want the marks to be arranged with the highest at the top and the lowest at the bottom, we have marked the **Descending** button in **Sort Order**. (Note, however, that in **file merging** – see below – the sort order must be the same as the file to be merged.)
- Click **OK** to see the mean marks listed in descending order of magnitude (Figure 20).

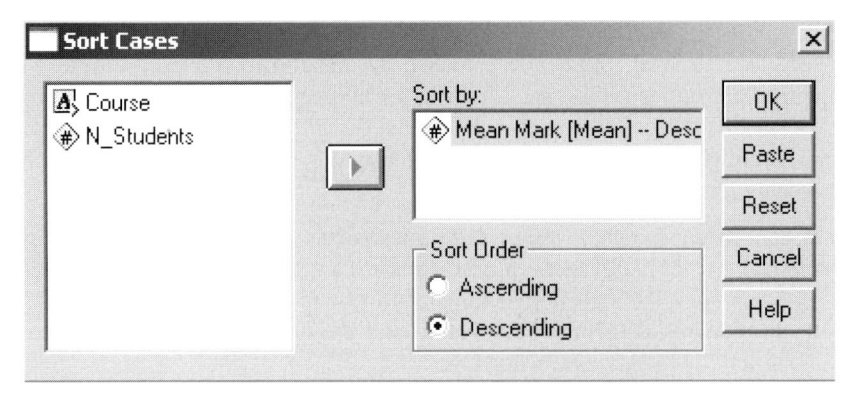

Figure 19. The completed **Sort Cases** dialog box

	Course	Mean	N_Students
1	Law	82.88	8
2	Accountancy	81.67	3
3	German	67.50	4
4	Statistics	67.33	3
5	Mathematics	63.67	6
6	Graphics	57.43	7
7	Spanish	57.33	3
8	Computing	56.25	4
9	Politics	51.00	5
10	Management	50.43	7

Figure 20. Results of the sorting procedure. The courses are now listed in descending order of their mean marks

3.3.4 Merging files

SPSS offers a powerful procedure known as **file merging**, which enables the user to import data into a file known as the **working file** from an **external** file. The **File Merge** procedure has two principal uses:
1. You can use it to import extra data (i.e., more cases) on **the same set of variables**.
2. You can use it to import data on **extra variables** that are not already in the working file.

*Using **Merge Files** to import more cases of the same variables from an external file*

In Chapter 2, an experiment was described in which the skilled performance of ten people who had ingested a small quantity of a supposedly performance-enhancing drug was compared with the performance of a placebo group of the same size. The scores of the twenty participants were stored in a file named *Drug Experiment*. Suppose, however, twenty more participants

Editing and manipulating files

were to be tested under exactly the same conditions (ten under the *Placebo* condition and ten under the *Drug* condition) and the new data stored in a file named *Drug more data*.

The **Merge Files** procedure can be used to import the new data from the file *Drug more data* into the file *Drug Experiment*, so that, instead of having ten scores for each condition we shall have twenty. The success of this type of file-merging operation requires that **the specifications for the two variables must be exactly the same in both files**. Before attempting the following exercise, check both files in **Variable View** to make sure that the specifications (name, width, type, values) of the variables *Case*, *Group* and *Score* are identical.

Ensure that the file containing the original data *Drug Experiment* is in the **Data Editor**. Then
- Choose
  Data
     Merge Files
        Add Cases …
  to obtain the **Add Cases: Read File** directory box.
- Select the file *Drug more data* from the directory box and click **Open** to obtain the **Add Cases from …** dialog box (Figure 21).

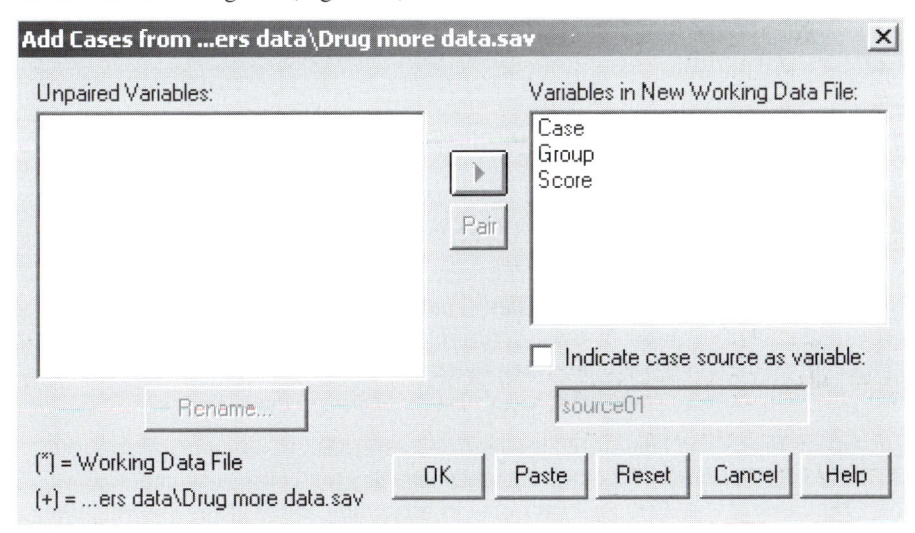

Figure 21. The **Add Cases from …** dialog box

- Since both data files contain only the variables *Case*, *Group* and *Score*, the right-hand panel headed **Variables in New Working Data File:** contains *Case*, *Group* and *Score* and no variable names appear in the left-hand panel headed **Unpaired Variables**. Had the external file contained an extra variable, variables or a variable specification did not match between the two files, its name or their names would have appeared in the left-hand panel.
- Click **OK** to obtain the merged file, a section of which is shown in Figure 22.

	Case	Group	Score
18	18	Drug	7
19	19	Drug	5
20	20	Drug	10
21	1	Placebo	5
22	2	Placebo	3
23	3	Placebo	6

Figure 22. A section of the merged file showing the first three cases from the file *Drug more data* added on beneath the last three cases from the file *Drug Experiment*

*Using **Merge Files** to add extra variables*

Suppose you wished to add the mean mark for the courses (using the means created by the **Aggregate** procedure in Section 3.4.2 and stored in the file *Course mean marks*) to the table of Students' Marks in the data file *Students marks* so that the students could compare their marks with the mean for their course. This can be done by the procedure **Merge Files Add Variables…**. What we are trying to do, in effect, is to look up in the *Course mean mark* file (Figure 18), the means for all the courses and assign the appropriate mean to each student taking a particular course in the original file *Students marks*. The **Merge Files** procedure uses the common variable (in this case *Course*) as a **key variable**. When matches for cases (in this example *Course*, not students) are found in the external file, the corresponding entries for the target variable *Mean* are imported into the working file.

In the terminology of SPSS, the external file *Course mean marks* is to be used as a **lookup file**, or **keyed table**. We also want **Merge Files** to use the cases of the **key variable** (i.e. *Course*) in the working file, not those in the external file, since there could be (though not in our example) courses there that were not taken by any of the students we are studying. We want matches only with those courses that are specified in the file *Students Marks*.

The success of this second kind of file-merging operation has two essential prerequisites:
1. The **specifications of the key variable** must be exactly the same in both files.
2. The cases in both files must be sorted **in ascending order of the key variable**.

In our example, *Students marks* has been sorted in alphabetic order of the *Course* name but the file of *Course mean marks* has not. Thus the first step is to do this by
- Open the file *Course mean marks* in **Data Editor**.
- Sort the cases by selecting
  Data
    Sort Cases…
  and transferring the variable name *Course* to the **Sort by** box.
- Click **OK** and then save the sorted data file using **Save As…** to *Course mean marks sorted*.

Now the **Merge Files** procedure can be started.
- Ensure that the data file *Students marks* is in the **Data Editor**.
- Choose

Editing and manipulating files

    Data
      Merge Files
        Add Variables…

to obtain the **Add Variables: Read File** directory box.

- Select the required file (here it is *Course mean marks sorted*) and click the **Open** button to obtain the **Add Variables from …** dialog box (Figure 23).

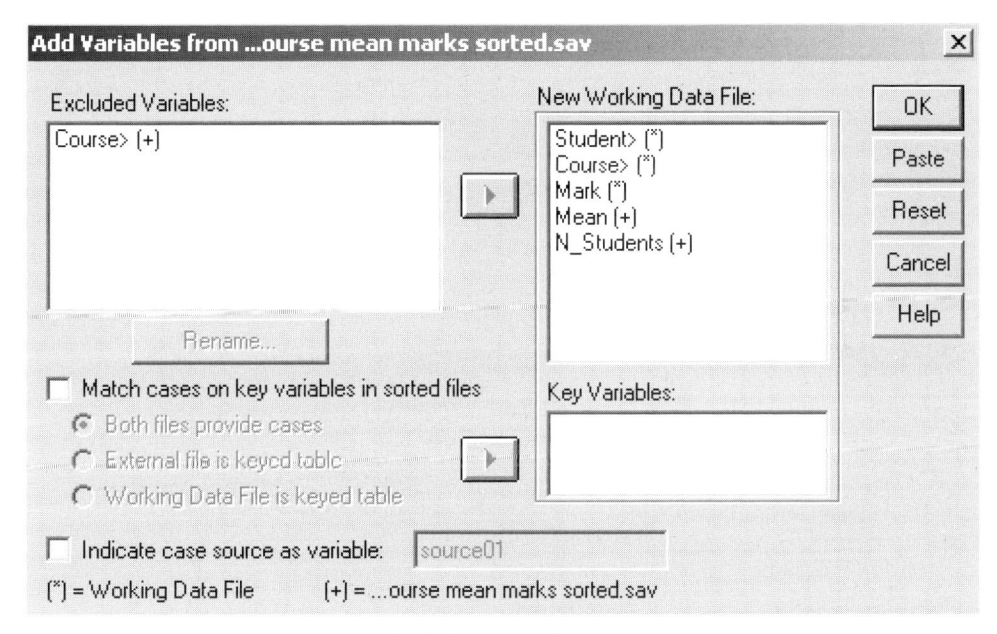

Figure 23. The **Add Variables from …** dialog box

Notice that, for the moment, the common variable *Course* appears in the left-hand panel as an **Excluded Variable**. However, we are going to use *Course* as a **key variable** and use the external file *Course mean marks sorted* as a **look up file** or **keyed table** to import the means for each course associated with those cases of the variable *Course* that **File Merge** finds in the working data file *Students marks*. We also want to reject the variable *N_Students* from the final data file.

Proceed as follows.
- Click **Match cases on key variables in sorted files**.
- Mark the button labelled **External file is keyed table**.
- Transfer *Course* to the **Key Variables** box.
- Click *N_Students* in the **New Working Data File** panel to highlight it and then click on the arrow to transfer it to the **Excluded Variables** panel on the left. The completed dialog box is shown in Figure 24.

Click **OK** to run the file merge. A section of the merged file is shown in Figure 25.

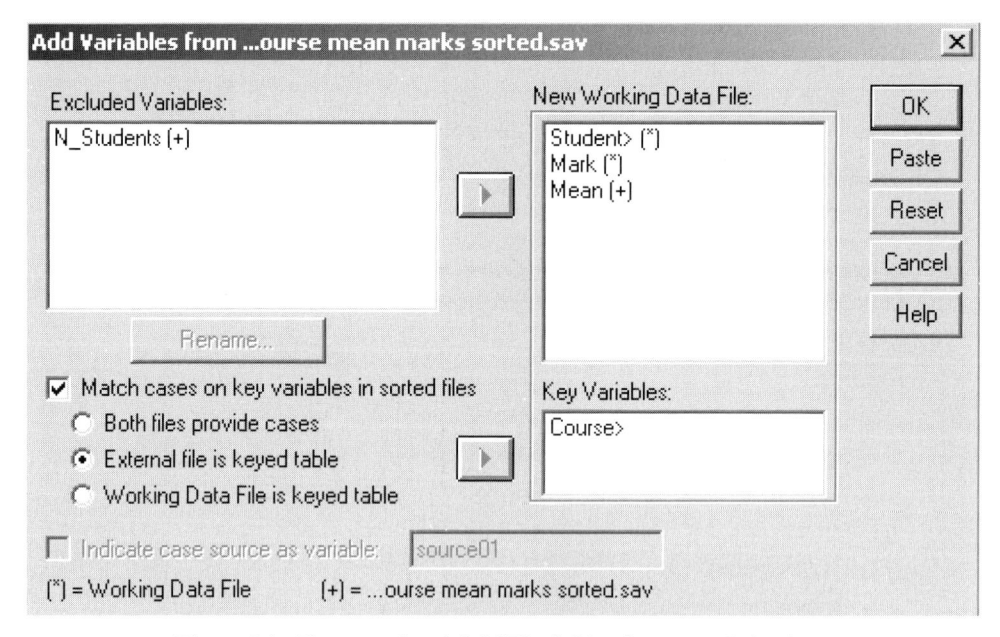

Figure 24. The completed **Add Variables from ...** dialog box

	Student	Course	Mark	Mean
1	Anne	Accountancy	80	81.67
2	Rebecca	Accountancy	78	81.67
3	Susan	Accountancy	87	81.67
4	Anne	Computing	49	56.25
5	Fred	Computing	55	56.25
6	Rebecca	Computing	65	56.25
7	Susan	Computing	56	56.25
8	Anne	German	40	67.50
9	Fred	German	72	67.50
10	Jim	German	73	67.50

Figure 25. Part of the merged file, in which the means of the courses have been 'looked up' in the external file *Course mean marks sorted* and added to the file *Students marks*

3.3.5 Transposing the rows and columns of a data set

In an experiment on time estimation, a researcher asks nine participants to make five verbal estimates of each of seven time intervals ranging from 10 to 40 seconds in duration. Each participant, therefore, makes a total of thirty-five judgements.

In the data set shown in Figure 26, the cases represent particular time intervals. For some purposes, such as averaging judgements across participants, we might wish to transform this data set to one in which each row represents a participant and each column represents a time interval.

Editing and manipulating files

	Interval	Amy	Fred	Joe	Stephen
1	10	8	120	7	8
2	10	6	10	9	7
3	10	5	20	6	10
4	10	7	5	8	9
5	10	5	10	6	11
6	15	15	25	10	13
7	15	6	8	9	12
8	15	14	12	10	12
9	15	7	8	12	12
10	15	14	10	12	15
11	20	20	60	15	18
12	20	10	18	14	15

Figure 26. A section of **Data View**, showing verbal estimates of the time intervals specified by the first variable, *Interval*

- Choose
  Data
    Transpose…
  to view the **Transpose** dialog box (Figure 27).

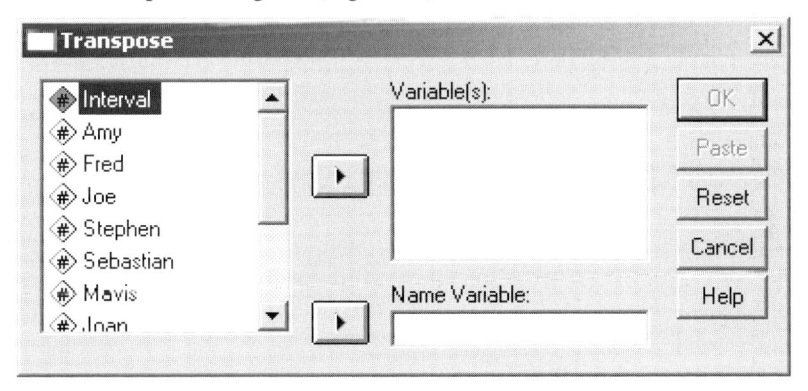

Figure 27. The **Transpose** dialog box

- Select all the variables and transfer them to the **Variable(s)** box on the right by clicking the central black arrow.
- Click **OK** to view the transposed matrix (Figure 28).

It can be seen from Figure 28 that SPSS has created a new variable *CASE_LBL* containing not only the names of the participants but also the *Interval* variable. The row containing the Interval variable should now be deleted and the default names *var001*, *var002*, … replaced (in **Variable View**) with names such as *Ten1*, *Ten2*, …, *Fifteen1*, *Fifteen2*, … remembering that SPSS will not allow duplication of variable names. In addition, the first variable CASE LBL should be renamed *Name*. Part of the final transformed data set is shown in Figure 29.

	CASE_LBL	var001	var002	var003	var004
1	Interval	10	10	10	10
2	Amy	8	6	5	7
3	Fred	120	10	20	5
4	Joe	7	9	6	8
5	Stephen	8	7	10	9
6	Sebastian	6	5	7	6

Figure 28. The transposed data set, in which the data from the participants are now contained in rows

	Name	Ten1	Ten2	Ten3	Ten4	Ten5	Fifteen1	Fifteen2
1	Amy	8	6	5	7	5	15	6
2	Fred	120	10	20	5	10	25	8
3	Joe	7	9	6	8	6	10	9
4	Stephen	8	7	10	9	11	13	12
5	Sebastian	6	5	7	6	5	9	9
6	Mavis	10	8	10	8	10	15	10

Figure 29. Part of the transformed data set in which the columns and rows of the original data set have been transposed

3.4 IMPORTING AND EXPORTING DATA

It is possible to import data into SPSS from other applications or platforms such as Microsoft EXCEL and SPSS for Macintosh. SPSS can also read ASCII tab-delimited or comma-delimited files, with values separated by tabulation symbols or fixed format files with variables recorded in the same column locations for each case. It is also possible to export SPSS data and output into other applications such as word processors and spreadsheets.

3.4.1 Importing data from other applications

Importing EXCEL files

When importing files from EXCEL, the following points should be observed:
1. If the first row of the EXCEL file does not contain variable/column names or data, then the material may not be read into SPSS properly. Either delete blank rows or amend the **Range** in SPSS's **Opening Excel Data Source** dialog box after selecting the EXCEL file to be read.
2. Dates must be formatted as *DD-MMM-YYYY.
3. It may be necessary to have a number of attempts to ensure a satisfactory import. For example, some file types may need changing (e.g. from **String** to **Numeric**) within **Variable View**.

Editing and manipulating files 77

To import the EXCEL file named *test1.xls*, which is stored in the author's folder *SPSS 12 data*:
- Choose
  File
    Open
        Data…
  to obtain the **Open File** dialog box.
- Select the appropriate **Look in** folder (Figure 30).

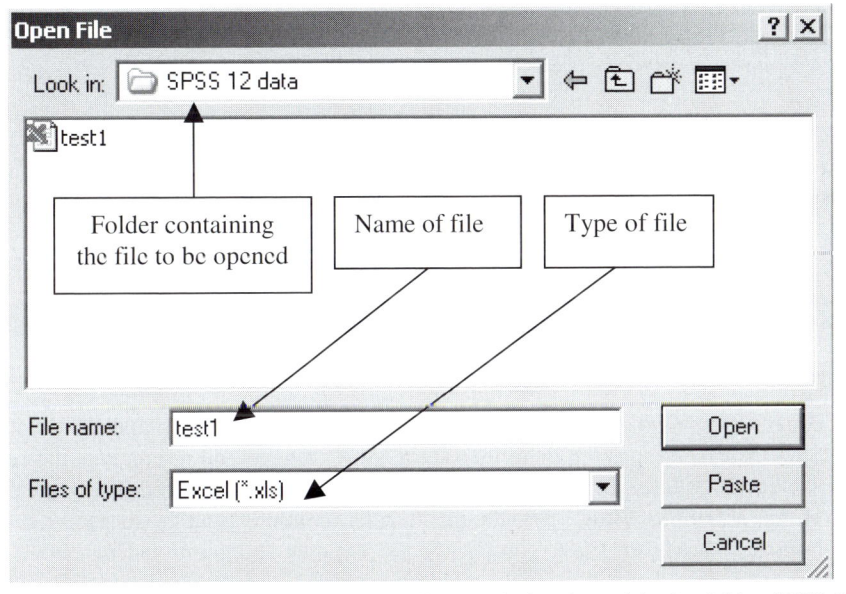

Figure 30. The **Open File** dialog box with the file *test1.xls* selected in the folder *SPSS 12 data*

- Click the directory of file types in the **Files of type:** box and highlight **Excel (*.xls)**.
- A list of files with the *.xls* extension will then appear in the white panel above. Click the appropriate file and its name will appear in the **File name:** box.
- Click **Open** to open the **Opening File Options** dialog box (Figure 31). Activate the **Read variable names** check box to transfer the EXCEL variable names into the SPSS **Data Editor**.

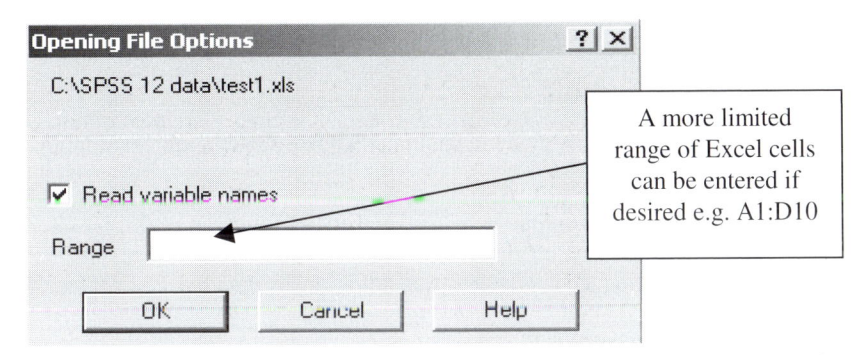

Figure 31. The **Opening File Options** dialog box with **Read variable names** selected

- If an error message appears stating that SPSS cannot load an EXCEL worksheet, it may be necessary to return to EXCEL and re-save the file in the format of a different version of EXCEL, to copy and paste columns of data directly into SPSS **Data View**, or to re-format the cells.
- Click **OK** to transfer the file into SPSS. **Variable View** will list the variable names and their types, and **Data View** will show the transferred data and variable names (Figure 32). It may be necessary to change variable types in **Variable View**.
- The file can then be saved as an SPSS data file.

	A	B	C	D
1	Name	Sex	Age	Score
2	Brown, G	m	25	87
3	Green, F	m	18	78
4	Mason, P	f	23	100
5	Sampson, G	m	24	67
6	Winston, P	f	20	50

	name	sex	age	score
1	Brown, G	m	25.00	87.00
2	Green, F	m	18.00	78.00
3	Mason, P	f	23.00	100.00
4	Sampson, G	m	24.00	67.00
5	Winston, P	f	20.00	50.00

Figure 32. Transfer of an EXCEL file (left) to SPSS (right)

It is also possible to copy columns of data from an EXCEL file by highlighting the data (but not the column headings), selecting **Copy** from EXCEL's **Edit** menu and then, with **Paste** from SPSS's **Edit** menu, pasting them into **Data View**. (Again, do not include the cell at the head of the SPSS column in the selection.) The variables can then be named in the usual manner within **Variable View**. Should the EXCEL columns contain strings (e.g. names), make sure that, in **Variable View**, you change the **Type** of variable to **String** before pasting. Other types of file can be transferred in a similar manner.

Exporting data from SPSS to EXCEL

The **Save As** procedure allows you to save an SPSS file (or a selection of data) as an EXCEL file. The procedure is entirely straightforward.

SPSS data can also be prepared for export to another application or platform by saving it to a wide range of formats, including **SPSS portable (*.por)**. Full details of importing and exporting files are available in SPSS's **Help** facility.

3.4.2 Copying output

The optimal procedures for copying items in the **Viewer** differ slightly for tables and graphics.

To **copy a table**, proceed as follows:
- Ensure that the table of output in SPSS **Viewer** has a box around it by clicking the cursor anywhere within the table or graphic. If you wish to copy more than one table, then ensure that all the desired tables are boxed by holding down the **Ctrl** key whilst clicking on each table in turn.
- Click **Copy** in the **Edit** menu.

- Switch to the word processor and ensure that the cursor is located at the intended insertion point.
- Select **Paste Special…** in the word processor's **Edit** menu and then **Formatted Text (RTF)** if it is desired to edit or format the table within the word processor.
- Alternatively, select **Paste Special…** in the word processor's **Edit** menu and then **Picture.** The picture can be repositioned and resized within the word processor but it cannot be edited. However the quality of the image is higher than it is when **Paste** is used.

To **copy a graphic**, proceed as follows:
- Ensure that the graphic in the SPSS **Viewer** has a box around it by clicking the cursor anywhere within it. If you wish to copy more than one graphic, ensure that all the desired graphics are boxed by holding down the **Ctrl** key whilst clicking on each chart or graph in turn.
- Click **Copy** in the **Edit** menu.
- Switch to the word processor and ensure that the cursor is located at the insertion point.
- Click **Paste Special…** and select **Picture (Enhanced Metafile)**. The item can then be centred, enlarged or reduced by clicking it so that it acquires a box around it with the usual Windows tabs. To centre the box, click and drag it to the desired position. To enlarge or reduce the size of the graphic, drag one of the tabs in the appropriate direction.

3.5 PRINTING FROM SPSS

It is possible to make extensive use of SPSS without ever printing out either the contents of the **Viewer** or the data in the **Data Editor**. Both data and output can easily be backed up electronically by saving to disk; and important SPSS output is easily exported to the document you actually want to print out. Moreover, SPSS output can be extremely extensive and indiscriminate printing can be very wasteful. In the worst scenario, an inept printing operation could result in dozens of sheets of paper, with a single line of print on each. There are, nevertheless, occasions on which it is both useful and necessary to print out selected items in the **Viewer** window or even a hard copy of the raw data. In this section, we offer some suggestions to help you control and improve printed output from SPSS.

There are differences between printing output from the **SPSS Viewer** and printing data from the **Data Editor**. In either case, however, problems can arise if there has been insufficient editorial control.

3.5.1 Printing output from the Viewer

We shall illustrate some aspects of printing from the **Viewer** with the data from the drug experiment. Suppose that, having entered the data into the **Data Editor**, we run the **Means** procedure, with requests for several optional extras such as medians, range statistics, measures of effect size and one-way ANOVAs to increase the extent of the output.

We strongly recommend that, before you print any output, you should make full use of the **Viewer**'s editing facilities to **remove all irrelevant material**. When using SPSS, one invariably requests output which, at the end of the day, proves to be superfluous. Moreover, as we have seen, radical changes in tables and other output can be made (and great economies in space) by using the **Viewer**'s powerful editing facilities. Since some of the output tables can be very wide, unnecessary columns can be removed. Some pivoting may help not only to make a table more readable but also more manageable for a printing operation.

For some kinds of material, it is better to use **landscape** orientation for the sheet, that is, have the shorter side vertical, rather than the more usual **portrait** orientation. It is easy to make such a specification while working in the **Viewer** before printing anything out. To clarify a batch of printed output, we also recommend that you add explanatory captions, such as *Output for the Drug Experiment*. Otherwise, it is only too easy to accumulate pages of SPSS output, the purpose of which becomes increasingly unclear as time passes. All these things can easily be done while you are working in the **Viewer**. Often, however, even after you have edited and severely pruned the **Viewer**'s contents, you will only be interested in printing out a **selection** of the items.

Using Print Preview

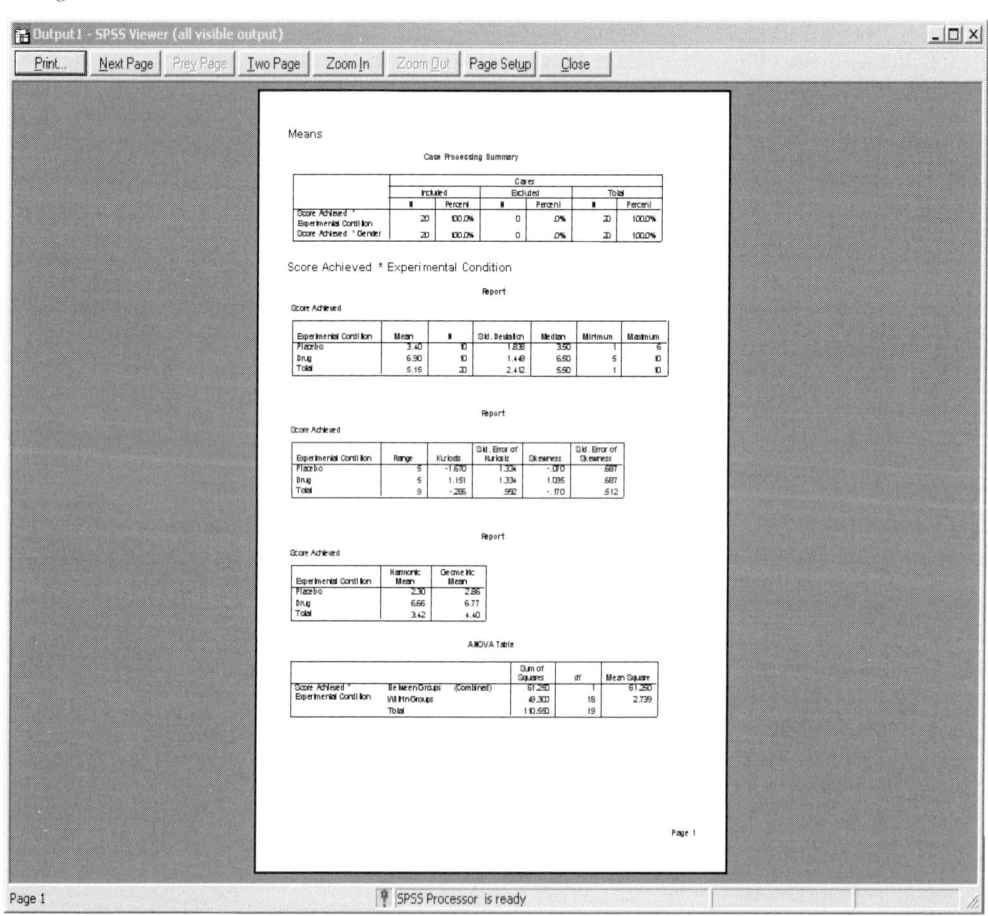

Figure 33. The **Viewer (all visible output)** dialog box for viewing page content when printing from the SPSS **Viewer**

- To ascertain the content of each page of the output that will be printed before any selection of items has been made, choose
  File
     Print Preview...
  to view the content of the first page in the **Viewer (all visible output) box** (Figure 33).

The contents of the other pages can be viewed by pressing the **PgDn** key as often as you need. Alternatively, you can click on the **Next Page** button in the row of buttons at the top of the dialog box. You will see that, when no item has been selected, the output extends to several pages.

Selecting items for printing

There are two ways of selecting items: you can click the item's icon in the left pane of the **Viewer**; or you can click the item itself in the right pane. Either way, a rectangle with a single continuous border will appear around the item or items concerned. It is, perhaps, easier to click on the items in the right pane directly to make it immediately clear what has been selected.

Try selecting any item in the **Viewer** and choose **Print Preview**, to see the **SPSS Viewer (selected output)** window, which will display only the item you have selected. If you return to the **Print** dialog box, you will see that the **Selection** radio button in the **Print range** panel has now been activated. Were you to click **OK** at this point, only the selected item would be printed.

To select two or more items, click the first and, pressing the **Ctrl** key and keeping it held down, click the other items that you wish to select. (You will also need to hold down the **Ctrl** key if you are clicking icons in the left pane to achieve a multiple selection.) The items need not be adjacent. If you now choose **Print Preview**, you will see that it shows only the items you have selected, and it is only those items that will actually be printed.

Deleting items from the Viewer

Items are removed from the **Viewer** by selecting them and pressing the **Delete** button. After a multiple selection, pressing the **Delete** button will remove all the selected items.

Re-arranging the items in the Viewer

Items can be rearranged very simply by clicking and dragging them in the left-hand pane, a red arrow showing where the item will be relocated as you drag. Alternatively items in the right-hand pane can be cut and pasted in the usual manner by selecting the item, choosing **Cut** from the **Edit** menu, moving the cursor to the desired new position and choosing **Paste** from the **Edit** menu. Key combinations of **Ctrl + X** for cutting and **Ctrl + V** for pasting can also be used.

Creating page breaks

You can also exert some control over the appearance of the output in the **Viewer** by creating a **page break** between items that clearly belong to different categories.

- Click the item above which you want to create a page break.
- Choose
  Insert
    Page Break
- Return to the **Viewer** and click outside the selection rectangle to cancel the selection.

If you now return to **Print Preview**, you will see that a page break has been created and the item you selected is now at the top of a fresh page. Used in conjunction with re-ordering, page breaks can help you to sort the items in the **Viewer**. Bear in mind, however, that creating page breaks always increases the number of sheets of paper in the printed output.

Using Page Setup

Click on the **Page Setup** button at the top of the **Print Preview** dialog box to enter the **Page Setup** dialog box (Figure 34).

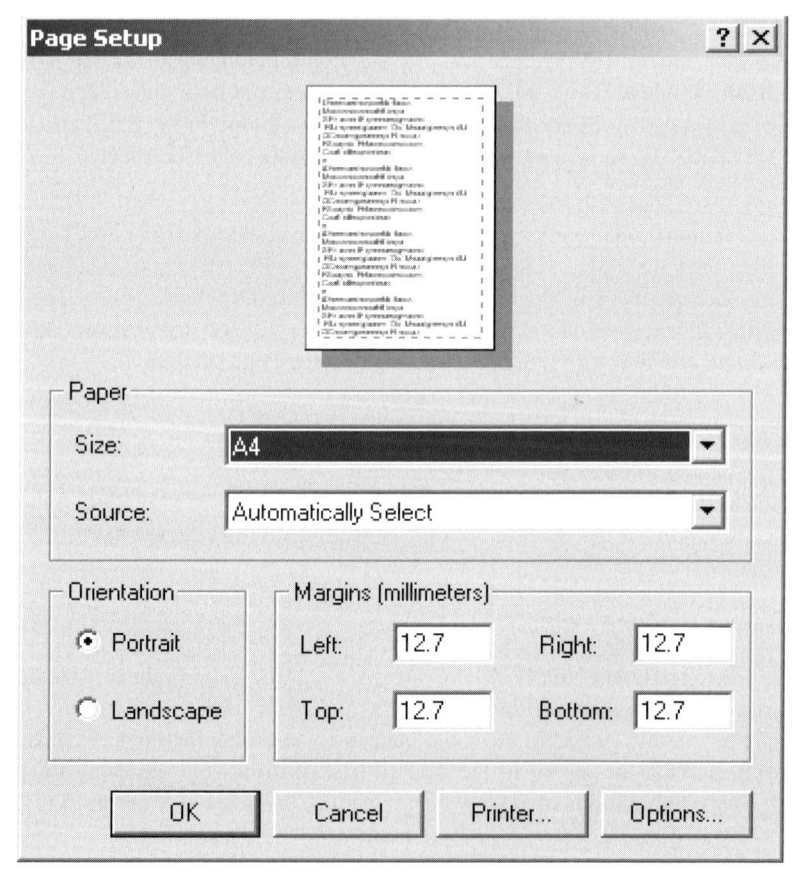

Figure 34. The **Page Setup** dialog box

In the **Orientation** panel, is the radio button for changing from **Portrait** to **Landscape** orientation. Sometimes, for printing purposes, the landscape orientation can accommodate particularly wide tables that will not fit in portrait orientation.

Click the **Options...** button to enter the **Page Setup: Options** dialog box (Figure 35).

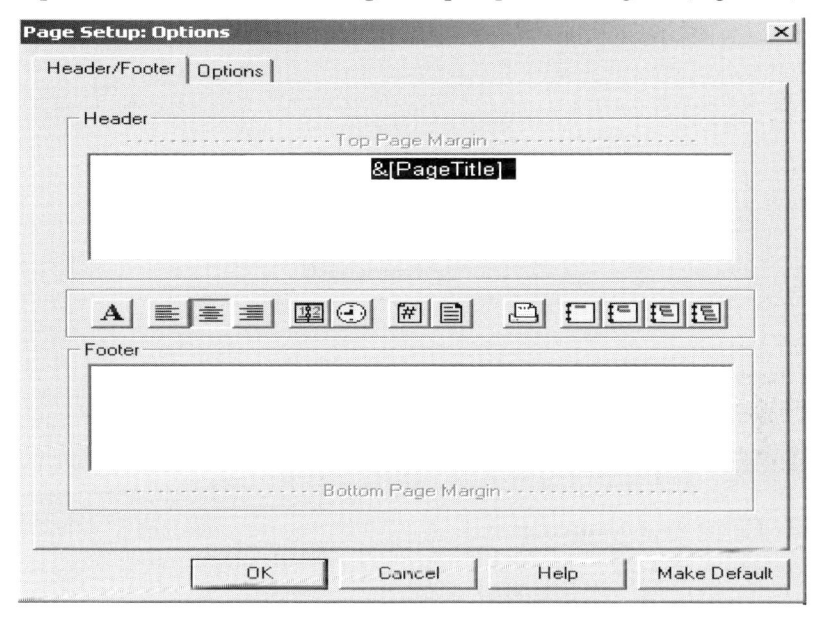

Figure 35. The **Page Setup: Options** dialog box

In the **Header/Footer** tab, you can immediately type in a meaningful title for the output that you wish to select for printing, such as *Results of the drug experiment*. You can specify the position of the title (left, central or right) by clicking on the appropriate button from the selection underneath the **Header** box (see Figure 36).

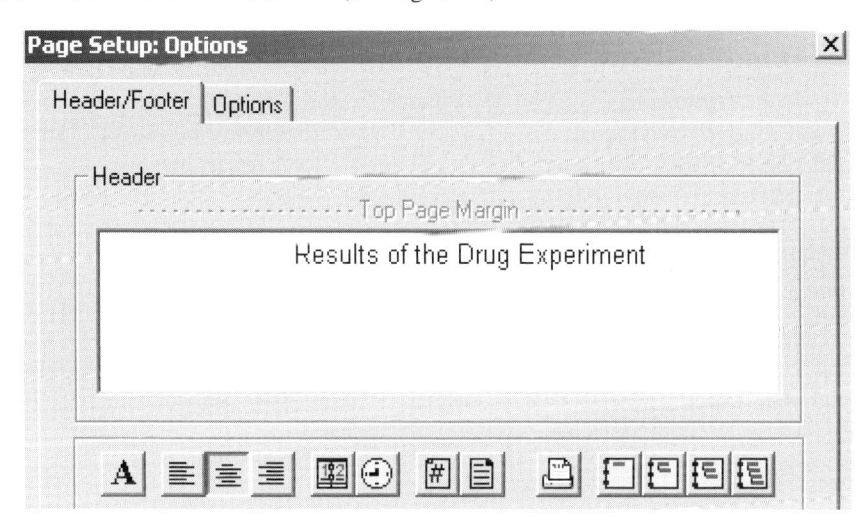

Figure 36. Writing a caption for the selected output. The middle positioning button has been clicked, indicating that the caption will be in a central position on the page

By selecting your new caption and clicking the **A** button, you can also choose an appropriate font, such as a large size of Ariel Bold, to make the title more impressive (see Figure 37). Should inspection of the **Viewer** show that you have chosen too large a font size, you can return to **Page Setup: Options** and request a smaller font.

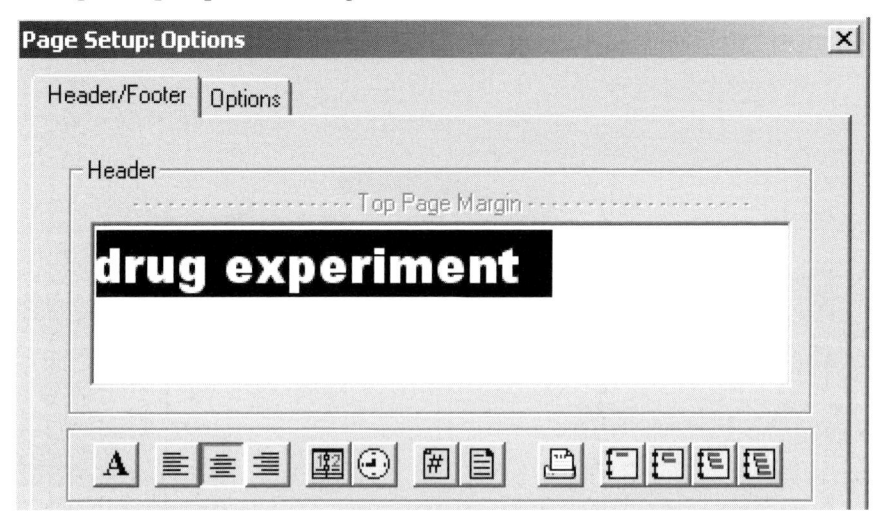

Figure 37. Part of **Page Setup: Options**, showing (in reverse video) the font that you have selected for the title of the printed output

Note that when, having made such specifications, you return to the **Viewer**, you will not see the caption you have just added – you will have to choose **Print preview** to see it again. The caption will, nevertheless, be printed out when you return to the **Print** dialog box and click **OK**.

Changing the spacing between items in the printed output

By clicking on the **Options** tab, you can also change the spacing between items in the **Viewer**. The effects of re-specifying the number of spaces between items will be obvious in the **SPSS Viewer (all visible output) window**. When you return to the **Viewer**, however, the items will appear with their original spacing.

Centralising items in the Viewer

You can centralise the position of a printed item by clicking it in the **Viewer** and pressing **Ctrl + E**. In the **Viewer** itself, the only effect will be the appearance of the symbol |▪| to the left of the selected item, which will remain in its original position in the **Viewer** window. In **Print preview**, however, the item will appear centralised and that is the way it will be printed.

Resizing tables for printed output

The situation can arise in which a table, even after much pruning and pivoting, is still too large to print without breaking it up. In such cases, parts of the table will be printed one beneath the other. It is possible, however, to shrink an entire table so that it remains unbroken. First double-click the item to produce the shaded border.

Choose
Format
    Table Properties

to produce the **Table Properties** dialog box (Figure 38), in which you can request that a particularly wide or long table must be accommodated on the page without being broken up.

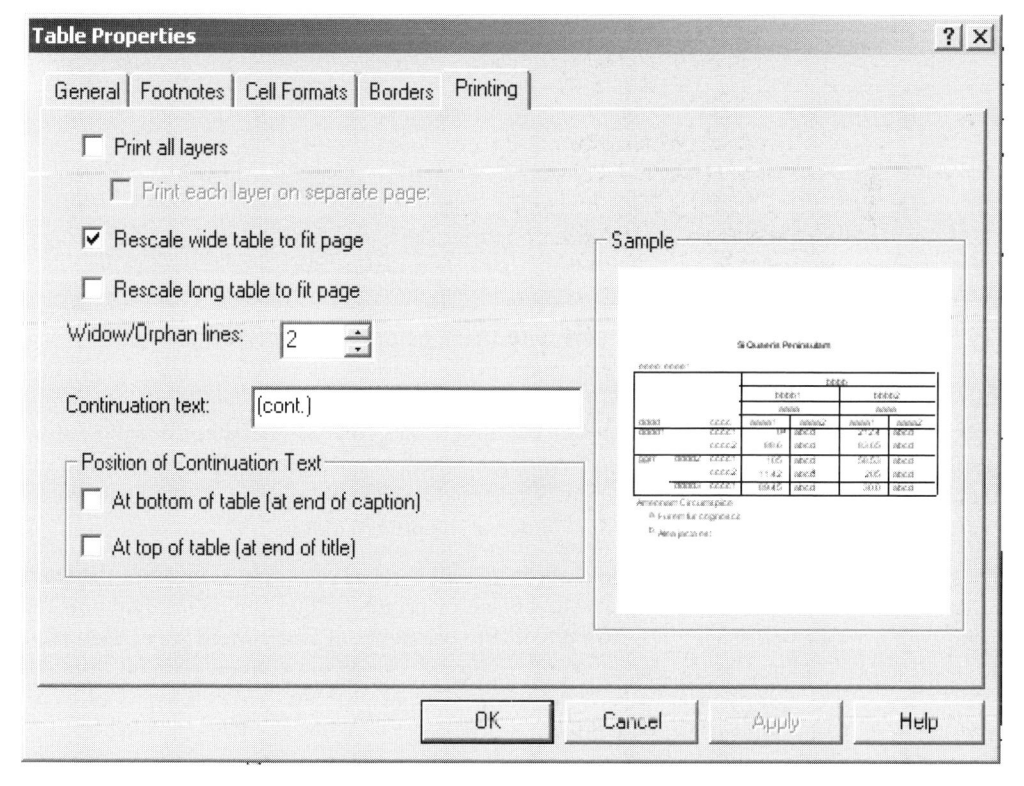

Figure 38. The **Table Properties** dialog box. The table in the editor can be re-scaled by marking the appropriate radio button

*The Viewer's **Print** dialog box*
- Access the **Viewer's Print** dialog box (Figure 39) by choosing
File
    Print...

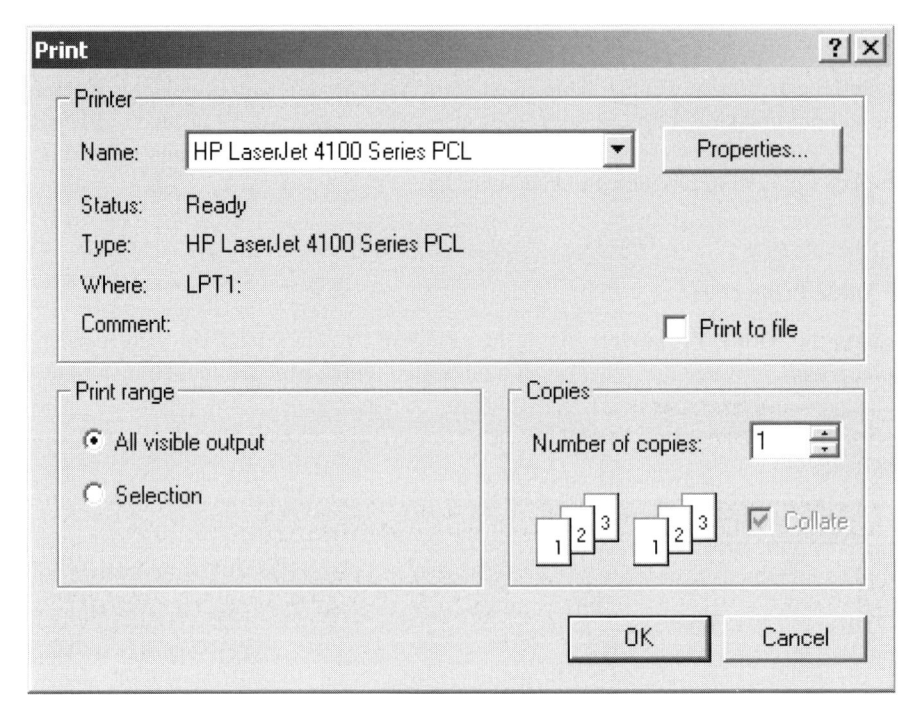

Figure 39. The **Print** dialog box for printing output from the **SPSS Viewer**

Note the **Print Range** section in the lower left area of the box. By default, the radio button labelled **All** is active, which means that pressing **OK** will result in the **entire contents** of the **Viewer** being printed out indiscriminately. The default setting of copies is *1*, but obviously an increase in that value to *2* will double the volume of the printed output.

This **Print** dialog box differs from the dialog you will receive when you print from the **Data Editor**, in which you would be offered the choice of printing either the entire output or the pages within a specified range. It is also possible to print out only the current page. However, no page range is offered in the dialog shown in Figure 39. When you are printing from the **SPSS Viewer**, the radio button marked **Selection** will only become active when a selection from the items in the **Viewer** has been made.

Printing from the Data Editor

It is possible to print out raw data from **Data View**. There are, however, several problems with this approach. Most notably, if there are too many variables to fit on to one page of printed output and hundreds of cases, it can be difficult to keep track of the output. It sometimes helps to add dummy columns, each cell of which contains a single numerical value, but this can be quite tedious.

To print only selected parts of the data set, use the click-and-drag method to define the target sections by highlighting them to display the material in reverse video. This requires a little practice; but it will be found that when the screen pointer touches the lower border of the window, the latter will scroll down to extend the blackened area to the desired extent. If the pointer touches the right border, the window will scroll to the right across the **Data Editor**. When the **Print** dialog box (Figure 39) appears, the marker will now be on **Selection** (the lowest radio button). Click **OK** to obtain a hard copy of the selected areas.

Using the Viewer to print data

An alternative way of obtaining a hard copy of the raw data is to print the data from the **Viewer**.
- Choose
  Analyze
    Reports
      Case Summaries...
to obtain the **Summarise Cases** dialog box, a completed example of which is shown in Figure 40.

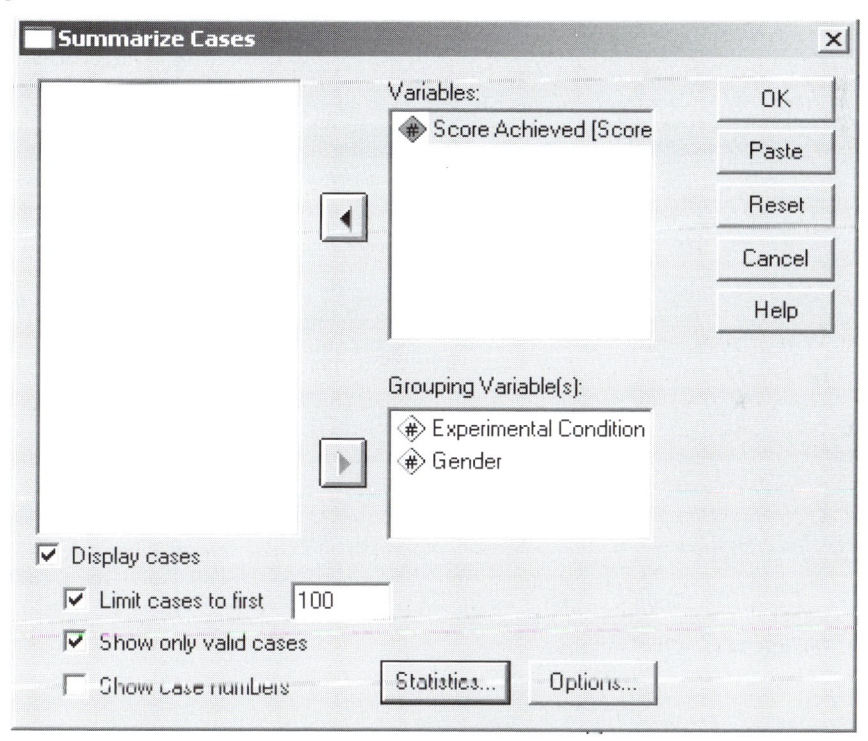

Figure 40. The completed **Summarize Cases** dialog box

The **Case Summaries** output for the data from the drug experiment is shown in Figure 41. In such a case summary, the precise conditions under which a score was achieved are made quite clear, which is why we prefer to use this method of printing raw data.

Case Summaries[a]

						Score Achieved
Experimental Condition	Placebo	Gender	Male	1		6
				2		5
				3		2
				4		2
				5		5
				Total	N	5
			Female	1		5
				2		1
				3		3
				4		4
				5		1
				Total	N	5
			Total	N		10
	Drug	Gender	Male	1		8
				2		6
				3		6
				4		6
				5		5
				Total	N	5
			Female	1		6
				2		7
				3		8
				4		7
				5		10
				Total	N	5
			Total	N		10
	Total	N				20

a. Limited to first 100 cases.

Figure 41. The **Case Summaries** of the data from the drug experiment

EXERCISE 3

Merging files – Adding cases & variables

This Exercise shows you how to open a saved file and how to merge your data with other files. The relevant sections are 2.6 (resuming work on a saved data set), 3.1.2 (reading in SPSS files) and 3.3.4 (merging files).

Opening your saved file in SPSS

Log in to SPSS as described in Section 2.2. Open the file that you saved under the name *Ex2 Questionnaire Data* from the previous Exercise. Select the radio button **Open an existing data source** in the SPSS opening window and highlight the filename. It may be necessary, especially in a networked computer, to select the **More Files...** option and select another disk drive or folder. Alternatively, select the **Type in data** radio button to open **Data View**, choose **File**, click **Open**, and finally **Data** to open the **Open File** selection box. Change the **Look in:** selection to the folder and/or disk drive where the file has been stored, click the filename so that it appears in the **Filename** box, and then **Open**. Your file should appear in **Data View**, where part of your own data might appear as follows:

	CaseNo	MyName	Age	Sex	Faculty	Status	Stones	Pounds
1	1	Alan Brown	25	1	1	1	14	0

Locating the larger data set

The file containing the large data set with which you are going to merge your own data is to be found at the following WWW address:

http://www.abdn.ac.uk/psychology/materials/spss.shtml

in the file labelled *Ex3 Questionnaire data* within the section *Release 12*. If this file has not already been downloaded on to a file server or hard disk drive for easier access, enter WWW and save the file to a more convenient place such as your hard disk drive. (In order to see the appropriate icons for accessing WWW, minimise the SPSS window by clicking the icon in the top right-hand corner.)

Merging your data with the larger data set

To carry out the file merge, select
Data
    Merge Files
        Add Cases

to obtain the **Add Cases: Read File** selection box, which prompts you to specify the file (the large data set) from which you want to merge other cases with your own. Locate the file *Ex3 Questionnaire Data* and click it. You should now see the **Add Cases: Read File** dialog box, with *Ex3 Questionnaire Data* in the **File Name:** box. Click **Open**. A new dialog box labelled **Add Cases from**, together with the full name of the data file, will appear.

If you have entered the correct variable names in your own data file, the **Add Cases from** dialog box should show just one variable name *(MyName)* in the **Unpaired Variables:** box and all the other variable names should be in the **Variables in New Working Data File:** box (see Figure 1). A match will not be found for your variable *MyName*, because the large data set does not contain the names of the participants.

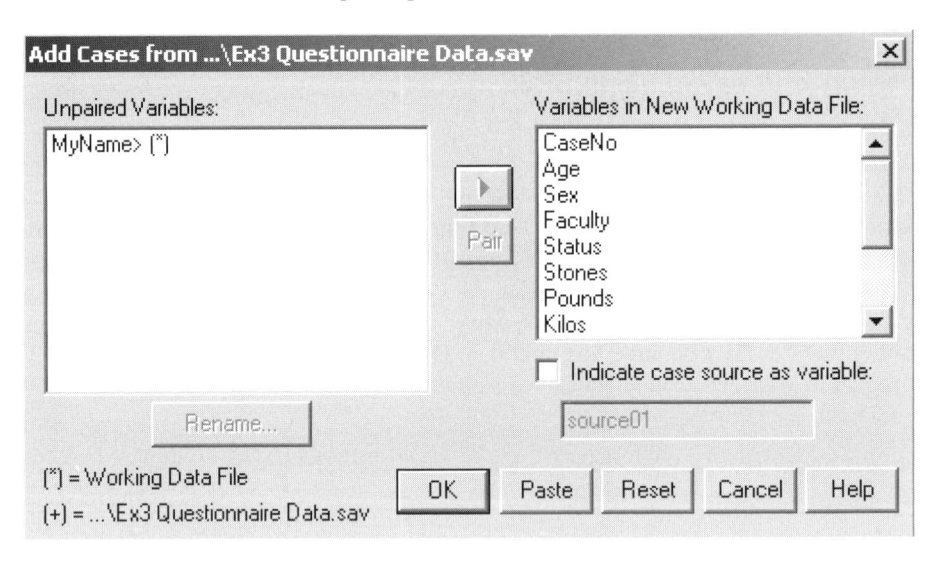

Figure 1. The **Add Cases from** dialog box showing the names of Unpaired Variables (here there is just one, *MyName*) and corresponding names from both files (Variables in New Working Data File)

Suppose, however, there had been a mismatch between one of the variable names you had typed into **Data View** and the name of the corresponding variable in the large data set. Suppose that, when you were building *Ex2 Questionnaire Data*, you had typed *Ages* instead of *Age*. The variables *Ages* and *Age* would both have appeared in the **Unpaired Variables:** box. You would have then had to select *Ages* and click **Rename** to obtain another dialog box, allowing you to rename it as *Age*. The correct variable name *Age* would then be transferred to the list in **Variables in the New Working Data File**.

Click **OK** to merge the files. The first few variables in the first two lines of the merged data set might appear as follows:

	CaseNo	Age	Sex	Faculty	Status	Stones	Pounds
1	1	25	1	1	1	14	0
2	1	23	1	1	1	11	0

Editing and manipulating files

Notice that the same case number appears in the first two rows. Since your own case is being added to the *334* cases already in the data set, change your case number to *335*.

Clearly, since yours is the 335th case, you want your own data to appear below the others in **Data View**. To rearrange the cases in ascending order of magnitude, choose

Data
    Sort Cases...

to see the **Sort Cases** dialog box. Transfer *CaseNo* to the **Sort By** panel on the right and click **OK**.

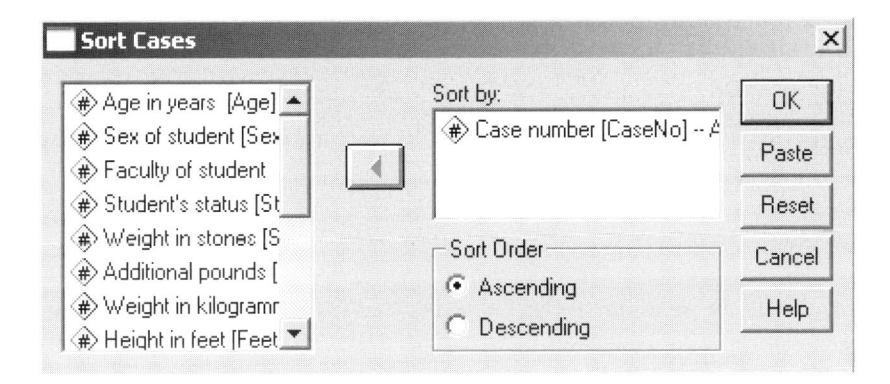

You will now find that your own data occupy the bottom row in **Data View**.

Save the merged file as *Merged Questionnaire Data*.

A warning

In the large data set, the *Faculty* variable was of the numeric type, with values assigned as follows:

1 = Arts, *2* = Science, *3* = Medicine, *4* = Other.

Suppose that you had inadvertently assigned *1* to *Science* and *2* to *Arts*, instead of the other way round, and that as a science student, you had recorded a *1* in your own data set. SPSS will not warn you of the discrepancy. Instead, it will adopt your convention throughout the merged data set and all those people who recorded *1*s in the larger original data set will now be recorded as scientists, not arts students. You can confirm this by choosing Value Labels from the View menu. All those previously recorded as science students will now be recorded as arts students and vice versa.

When two files are being merged, it is the value assignments **in the first file** that determine those for the entire merged file, even when, as in the present example, the former contains only a single case.

Another file-merging exercise: Adding extra variables to a file

In Section 3.3.2, we described the use of the **Aggregate** procedure to create a file showing the average marks of students who had taken various courses at a business school. Open the

Students marks file from the website specified earlier or enter it from the Appendix on the next page. Follow the **Aggregate** procedure described in Section 3.3.2 to obtain the course averages and the numbers of students taking the courses. Save the new information to a file named *Course average marks*.

Also available from the website or from the Appendix is the *Assignment* file which contains the courses to which the lecturers at the business school were assigned. The aim of this Exercise is to add, to the file containing the course averages, the names of the lecturers who were assigned to those courses. The link between the course averages and the lecturers can be made with the **Merge Files** procedure, using *Assignment* as a lookup file to obtain the names of the lecturers who gave the courses listed in *Course average marks*.

- Open *Course average marks*.
- Choose
  Data
    Sort Cases ...
- Fill in the **Sort Cases** dialog box, specifying that you are sorting by *Course*. Keep the sorting order as Ascending. Click **OK**.
- Save the sorted file as *Course average marks*.

(It would normally be necessary to check that the other file being used for the merging of data also had its entries in the variable *Course* arranged alphabetically and if not, to use a **Sort Cases...** procedure to do so. In this case, the file *Assignment* already has its *Course* entries arranged alphabetically.)

- Choose
  Data
    Merge Files
      Add Variables...
- In the **Add Variables: Read File** dialog box, choose *Assignment* and click **Open**.
- In the **Add Variables from...** dialog box, click the selection box **Match cases on key variables in sorted files** and then click the **External file is keyed table** radio button.
- Transfer *Course* from the **Excluded Variables** box to the **Key Variables** box.
- Click **OK**.

Look at the resulting data file and notice the new column headed *Lecturer*. This shows that the lecturer's name has been paired with each course and the average mark that those students taking the course received.

- **Which of Tom Fielding's courses has the highest average mark and what is the average mark for that course?**

Finishing the session

Close down SPSS and any other windows before logging out.

Appendix of files

File of Students marks

Student	Course	Mark	Student	Course	Mark
Anne	Accountancy	80	Rebecca	Law	85
Rebecca	Accountancy	78	Susan	Law	91
Susan	Accountancy	87	Fred	Management	70
Anne	Computing	49	Jim	Management	57
Fred	Computing	55	Joe	Management	53
Rebecca	Computing	65	John	Management	41
Susan	Computing	56	Kevin	Management	45
Anne	German	40	Rebecca	Management	43
Fred	German	72	Sebastian	Management	44
Jim	German	73	Jim	Mathematics	66
Susan	German	85	Joe	Mathematics	60
Anne	Graphics	58	John	Mathematics	68
Fred	Graphics	54	Kevin	Mathematics	71
Jim	Graphics	65	Mary	Mathematics	56
Joe	Graphics	55	Sebastian	Mathematics	61
Kevin	Graphics	58	Joe	Politics	62
Mary	Graphics	50	John	Politics	45
Rebecca	Graphics	62	Kevin	Politics	49
Anne	Law	93	Mary	Politics	56
Fred	Law	88	Sebastian	Politics	43
Jim	Law	89	John	Spanish	62
Joe	Law	91	Mary	Spanish	57
John	Law	43	Sebastian	Spanish	53
Kevin	Law	83	Mary	Statistics	70
Rebecca	Law	85	Sebastian	Statistics	62

File of Assignment of Lecturers to Courses

Lecturer	Course
EvelynBrown	Accountancy
TimRice	Book Keeping
DavidJones	Computing
EvelynBrown	German
JoanSmith	Graphics
TimRice	Investment Management
SarahAlbert	Law
TomFielding	Management
EvelynBrown	Mathematics
TomFielding	Politics
TomFielding	Spanish
TimRice	Spreadsheets
EvelynBrown	Statistics
JoanSmith	The Internet
JoanSmith	Web Management

CHAPTER 4

Exploring your data

4.1   Introduction

4.2   Some useful menus

4.3   Describing data

4.4   Manipulation of the data set

4.1   INTRODUCTION

In recent years, statisticians have devised a set of statistical methods specially designed for the purpose of examining a data set. Together, they are known as **Exploratory Data Analysis (EDA)**. (For a readable account of EDA, see Howell, 2002). EDA has now found its way into all good statistical computing packages, including SPSS.

Suppose we have a set of measurements, say the heights in centimetres of a group of children. There are usually three things we want to know about such a data set:

1. The general **level**, or **average value**, of their heights;
2. The **dispersion** of height, i.e. the degree to which the individual scores tend to **vary** around or **deviate** from the average, as opposed to clustering closely around it;
3. The **distribution shape**, i.e. the relative frequencies with which heights are to be found in various regions of the total range of the variable.

We assume that the reader is familiar with the most common measures of level (the **mean**, the **median** and the **mode**) and of dispersion (the **standard deviation** and **quantile range** statistics). We also assume familiarity with terms relating to the distribution of the data set, such as **skewness**, **bimodality** and so on.

Different statistics are appropriate for data of different types: there is little point in finding the mean of a set of ranks, for example, because the resulting average would depend solely upon the number of people (or objects) in the sample. Should the reader be a little rusty on such matters, we strongly recommend reading the relevant chapters of a good textbook on the topic. However before embarking on EDA, it is vital to check the integrity of the data in case there have been date entry errors (e.g. typing 100 instead of 10). This can be done using the same procedures as for EDA.

The influence of outliers and asymmetry of distribution

Statistics such as the mean and standard deviation are intended to express, in a single number, some characteristic of the data set as a whole: the former is intended to express the **average**, that is, the general level, typical value, or **central tendency**, of a set of scores; the latter is a measure of their **spread**, or **dispersion**. There are circumstances, however, in which the mean and standard deviation are poor measures of central tendency and dispersion. This can occur when the distribution is markedly skewed, or when extreme cases known as **outliers** exert undue **leverage** upon the values of these statistics.

4.2 SOME USEFUL MENUS

The most important procedures for exploring data are to be found in the **Analyze** and **Graphs** menus. A powerful and complex system such as SPSS can often offer many different approaches to a problem in data analysis. Similar graphics, for instance, can be produced by procedures on either the **Analyze** or the **Graphs** menus. Descriptive statistics are available on several different procedures.

In the **Analyze** menu are **Reports**, **Descriptive Statistics**, **Tables** and **Compare Means**. When the **Reports** or **Descriptive Statistics** are highlighted, the submenus shown in Figure 1 appear.

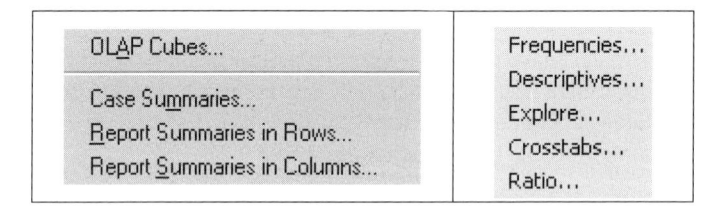

Figure 1. The submenus of **Reports** and **Descriptive Statistics**

The **Reports** submenu (left side of Figure 1) provides facilities for calculating various descriptive statistics of selected quantitative variables subdivided by categories of specified grouping variables. The **OLAP Cubes** (Online Analytical Processing) procedure initially outputs the selected statistics for selected quantitative variables summed across *all* categories of the grouping variables. The initial **OLAP Cubes** table in the output, however, is a pivot table, double-clicking on which brings the **Pivot** menu to view. You can then specify particular categories and combinations of categories by clicking tabs at the top of the table in the usual way (see Chapter 3). The desired combination will then appear as a layer of a multi-way table. As with all pivot tables, the appearance of **OLAP Cubes** can be improved by using the **Viewer**'s editing facilities.

Exploring your data

In Chapter 3, we saw that **Case Summaries** provide very useful summaries of data sets, including the raw data themselves. This is ideal for printed records.

The output for **Row Summaries in Rows** or **Report Summaries in Columns** is not tabulated in boxes, is printed in less clear font and is rather difficult to read.

The **Descriptive Statistics** submenu (right side of Figure 1) includes **Frequencies**, **Descriptives**, **Explore**, **Crosstabs and Ratio**. All are highly recommended and will be described and illustrated in later sections of this Chapter.

The **Tables** submenu (left side of Figure 2) enables the user to display output in attractive tables, which can be pasted directly into reports of experiments or surveys. The **Basic Tables** and **Tables of Frequencies** procedures are particularly useful.

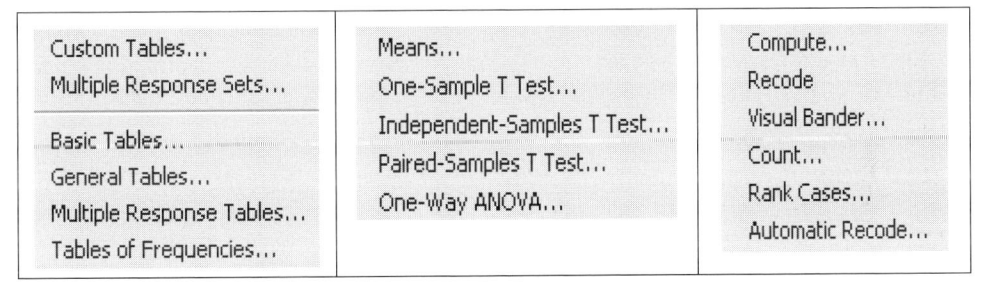

Custom Tables...	Means...	Compute...
Multiple Response Sets...	One-Sample T Test...	Recode
Basic Tables...	Independent-Samples T Test...	Visual Bander...
General Tables...	Paired-Samples T Test...	Count...
Multiple Response Tables...	One-Way ANOVA...	Rank Cases...
Tables of Frequencies...		Automatic Recode...

Figure 2. The submenus of **Tables**, **Compare Means** and **Transform**

The **Compare Means** submenu (middle of Figure 2) contains just one item of relevance to exploring data, namely **Means**. This title is misleading because the procedure can only be used for listing the means of variables subdivided by categories of grouping variables: there must be at least one grouping variable present in your data set for the procedure to work. To obtain the means of ungrouped scores, you must turn to **Reports**, **Tables**, or to **Descriptives**, which is found in the **Descriptive Statistics** menu.

The items in the **Graphs** menu will form the material in Chapter 5, although we shall meet some of them in this Chapter, since they are options in several of the other exploratory procedures.

Finally, in the **Transform** menu (right of Figure 2) there are several useful procedures, some of which will be described and illustrated at the end of this Chapter.

4.3 DESCRIBING DATA

To illustrate the data-descriptive procedures, we shall make use of a medical-actuarial data set comprising *Case*, two quantitative variables, *Weight* and *Height*, and two qualitative variables, *Sex* and *Bloodtype*. Table 1 shows the data set already entered in **Data View** (*Case* has been omitted from the Table for clarity).

4.3.1 Describing nominal and ordinal data

Suppose we want to know the frequencies of cases in the categories in the two grouping variables *Sex* and *Bloodtype*. We might also want a graphical display of these frequencies, such as a **bar chart** or **pie chart**. For measurements such as heights or weights, a **histogram** is a useful graph. There are several ways of obtaining such displays.

Table 1. The Blood Group, Sex, Height and Weight data in **Data View**

	Bloodtype	Sex	Height	Weight		Bloodtype	Sex	Height	Weight
1	Group O	Male	178	75	17	Group O	Female	163	60
2	Group O	Male	196	100	18	Group O	Female	142	51
3	Group A	Male	145	60	19	Group A	Female	150	55
4	Group O	Male	170	71	20	Group O	Female	165	64
5	Group B	Male	180	80	21	Group A	Female	160	53
6	Group O	Male	175	69	22	Group O	Female	175	50
7	Group AB	Male	185	78	23	Group O	Female	182	72
8	Group A	Male	190	90	24	Group B	Female	169	65
9	Group O	Male	183	70	25	Group O	Female	162	62
10	Group B	Male	182	85	26	Group B	Female	182	80
11	Group A	Male	170	72	27	Group O	Female	165	67
12	Group O	Male	160	77	28	Group A	Female	171	50
13	Group O	Male	170	95	29	Group O	Female	146	55
14	Group AB	Male	172	68	30	Group AB	Female	151	48
15	Group B	Male	190	120	31	Group O	Female	164	59
16	Group O	Male	180	75	32	Group B	Female	176	71

General Tables or **Tables of Frequencies** (on the **Tables** menu), and **Crosstabs** (on the **Descriptive Statistics** menu) all provide a convenient two-way contingency table (e.g. rows representing blood groups and columns representing sexes) but **Crosstabs** also supplies a column of totals and statistics such as **chi-square** and various **correlation coefficients**. **Frequencies** (in **Descriptive Statistics**) gives frequency distributions for both nominal and ordinal data, as well as percentages and cumulative percentages. There are options for selecting graphics such as bar charts, pie charts and histograms.

To obtain a table of frequencies with percentages:
- Choose
  Analyze
  　　Tables
  　　　　Tables of Frequencies…
  to open the **Table of Frequencies** dialog box.
- Transfer the variable name *Blood Group* to the **Frequencies** box and *Gender* to the **Subgroups In each Table** box.
- Click the **Statistics** button and select **Display** in the **Percents** tick box. Click **Continue**.
- Click **OK**.

Exploring your data

The completed Table of Frequencies dialog box is shown in Figure 3 and the output in Output 1.

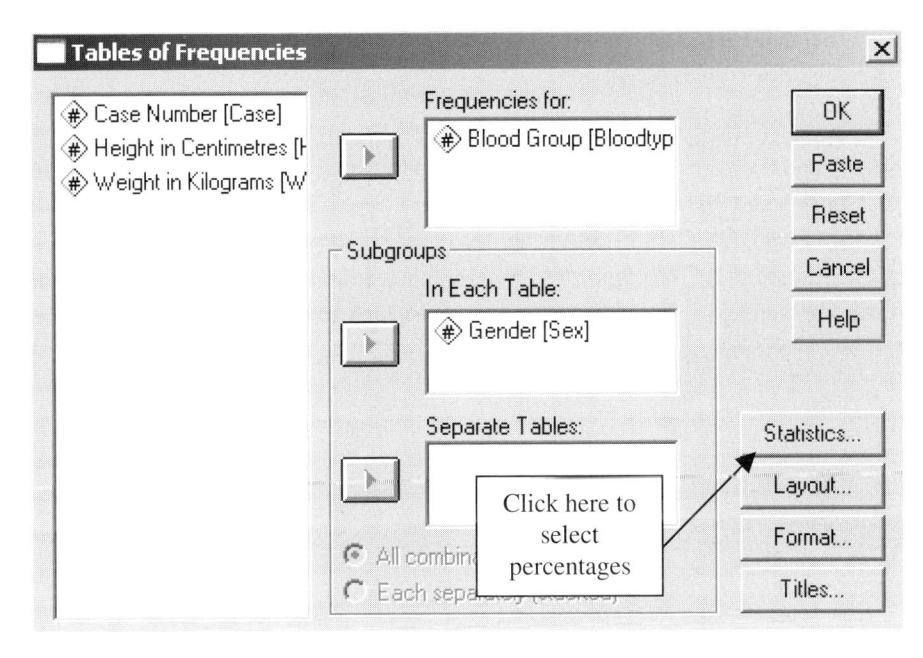

Figure 3. The **Table of Frequencies** dialog box for frequencies and percents of Blood Group and Gender

	Gender			
	Male		Female	
	Blood Group		Blood Group	
	Count	%	Count	%
Group A	3	18.8%	3	18.8%
Group B	3	18.8%	3	18.8%
Group AB	2	12.5%	1	6.3%
Group O	8	50.0%	9	56.3%

Output 1. Frequencies and percents of Blood Group for each Gender

Tables such as that shown in Output 1 quickly show whether the data have been entered correctly by comparing the blood group counts with those in the original data set. Checks should also be conducted on the other variables (e.g. checking the minimum and maximum heights by using the **Descriptives** procedure for *Height* as shown in Section 4.3.2). A height of over 200 cm or under 100 cm would merit a scrutiny of the data in **Data View** for a possible transcription error.

The following procedure offers not only frequencies but also charts.

- Choose
  Analyze
    Descriptive Statistics
      Frequencies…
  to open the **Frequencies** dialog box.
- Follow the steps shown in Figure 4.
- Click **Charts** to obtain the **Frequencies: Charts** dialog box (Figure 5) and select the **Bar Chart(s)** radio button. There is also the choice of frequencies or percentages for the y axis in the **Chart Values** box.
- Click **Continue** to return to **Frequencies** and then **OK** to run the procedure.

List of remaining variable labels and names

List of variables for which **Frequencies** output is to be generated; the names are transferred by highlighting them in the left-hand box and clicking

For more statistics, click here to open the **Frequencies: Statistics** dialog box

Click here to open the **Frequencies: Charts** dialog box for selecting particular charts and diagrams

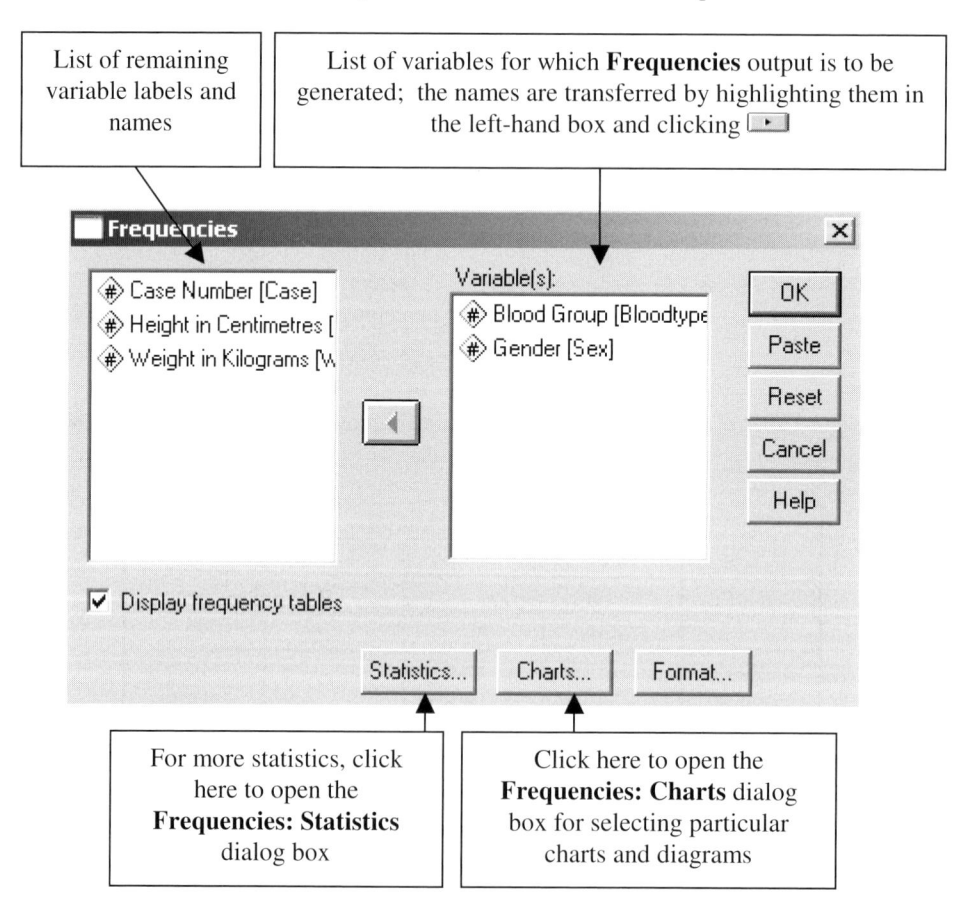

Figure 4. The **Frequencies** dialog box for Blood Group and Gender

Exploring your data

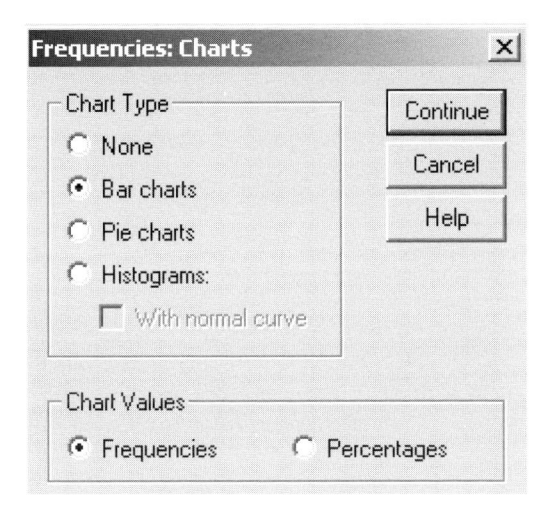

Figure 5. The **Frequencies: Charts** dialog box with **Bar charts** selected

The output consists of a couple of tables (Output 2) and the bar chart for Blood Group is shown in Output 3 (the bar chart for Gender has been omitted). Note that the bar chart can also be requested directly with the **Bar** procedure in the **Graphs** menu. It is possible to edit the bar chart to centre or change the axis labels, the title, the shading of the boxes and other aspects of the graph; more details about editing graphics will be given in the next chapter.

Blood Group

		Frequency	Percent	Valid Percent	Cumulative Percent
Valid	Group A	6	18.8	18.8	18.8
	Group B	6	18.8	18.8	37.5
	Group AB	3	9.4	9.4	46.9
	Group O	17	53.1	53.1	100.0
	Total	32	100.0	100.0	

Gender

		Frequency	Percent	Valid Percent	Cumulative Percent
Valid	Male	16	50.0	50.0	50.0
	Female	16	50.0	50.0	100.0
	Total	32	100.0	100.0	

Output 2. Frequency listings for Blood Group and Gender

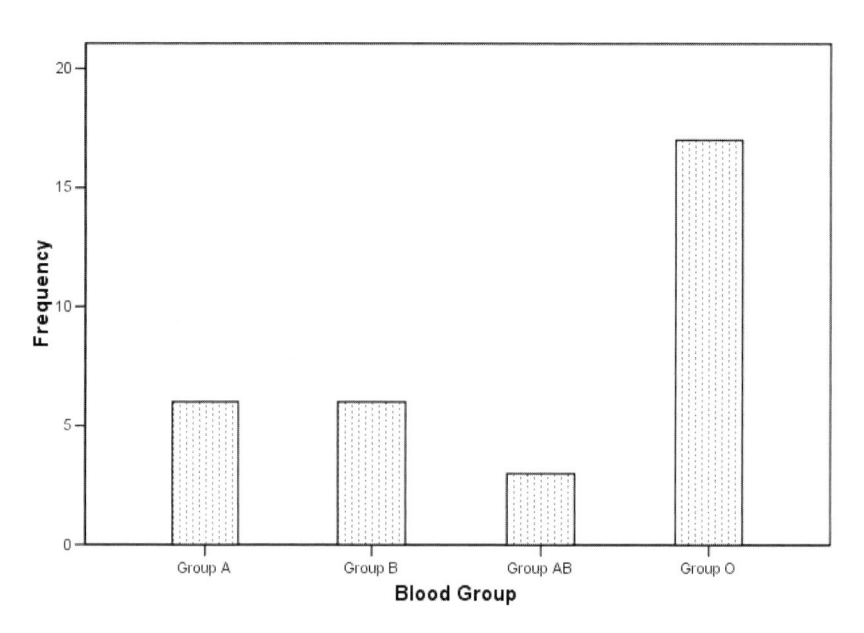

Output 3. Bar Chart for Blood Group

- Contingency tables can also be obtained with several procedures. **Crosstabs** generates contingency tables from nominal or ordinal data. Here we illustrate its use with Blood Group and Gender.

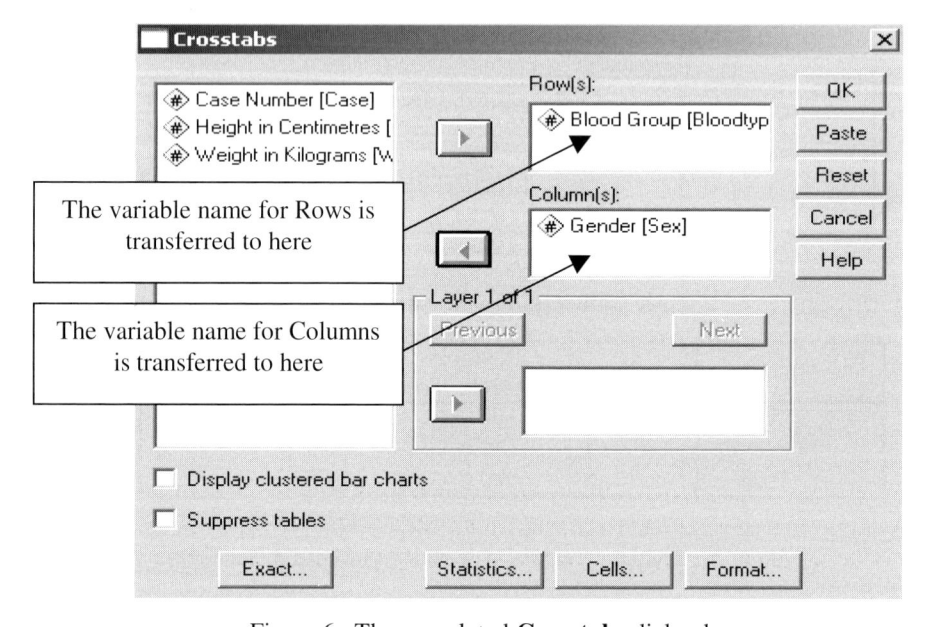

Figure 6. The completed **Crosstabs** dialog box

- Choose
  Analyze
  Descriptive Statistics
  Crosstabs...
  to open the **Crosstabs** dialog box.
- Transfer the variable names as shown in Figure 6 and click **OK**.

If one of the variables has more than about four categories, it is better to use it for **Rows** rather than **Columns**, otherwise the output will be too wide for printing on a single page. In this example, a narrower table is produced if Blood Group is nominated for **Rows**.

The output is shown in Output 4.

Blood Group * Gender Crosstabulation

Count

		Male	Female	Total
Blood Group	Group A	3	3	6
	Group B	3	3	6
	Group AB	2	1	3
	Group O	8	9	17
Total		16	16	32

Output 4. Contingency table from **Crosstabs** for Gender and Blood Group

Crosstabs is only applicable to contingency tables. It should be requested only for nominal or ordinal data (i.e. categories or ranks) and not for measurements such as heights or scores unless they have been recoded into categories (e.g. tall; medium; short).

4.3.2 Describing measurements

There are many procedures for describing and exploring data in the form of measurements.

Exploring variables without subdivision into categories of grouping variables

The most basic procedure is **Basic Tables** within the **Table** menu.
- Choose
  Analyze
  Tables
  Basic Tables ...
  to open the **Basic Tables** dialog box.
- Transfer the desired variable names to the **Summaries** box.
- The default statistic is the mean. Others can be selected by clicking the **Statistics** button and selecting **Mean, Median** and **Standard Deviation**, for example. Click **Continue**.
- Click **OK**.

The completed dialog box is shown in Figure 7 and the output in Output 5.

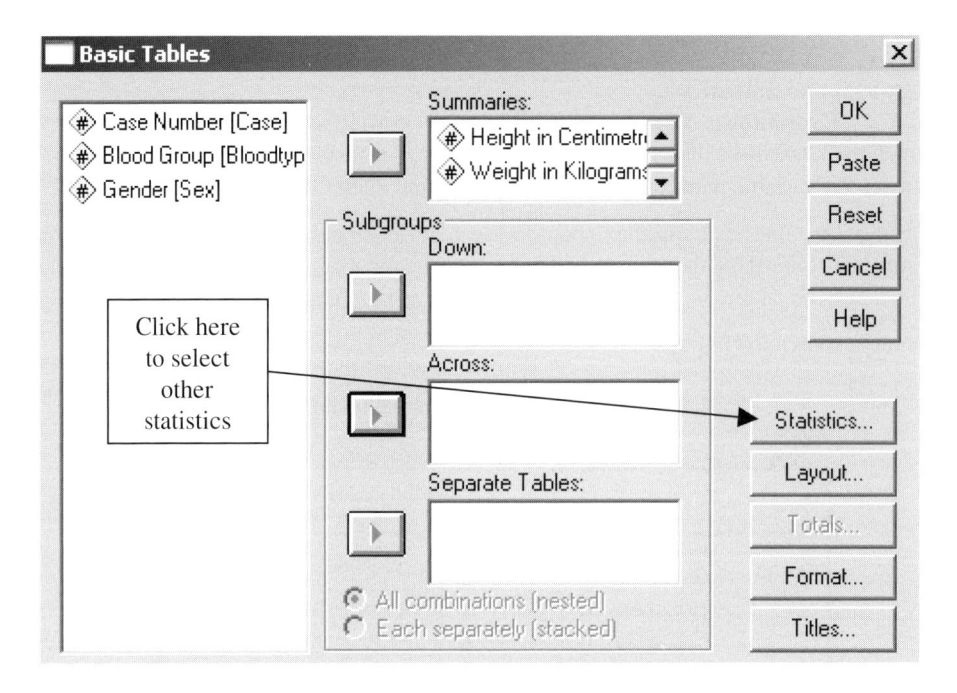

Figure 7. The **Basic Tables** dialog box with Height and Weight selected

	Mean	Median	Std Deviation
Height in Centimetres	170	171	14
Weight in Kilograms	70	70	16

Output 5. Output from **Basic Tables** showing the mean, median and standard deviation of Height and Weight

A similar output can be obtained using **Descriptives** in the **Descriptives Statistics** menu.
- Choose
  Analyze
    Descriptive Statistics
        Descriptives...
  to open the **Descriptives** dialog box.
- Transfer the variable names as shown in Figure 8 and click **OK**.

Exploring your data 105

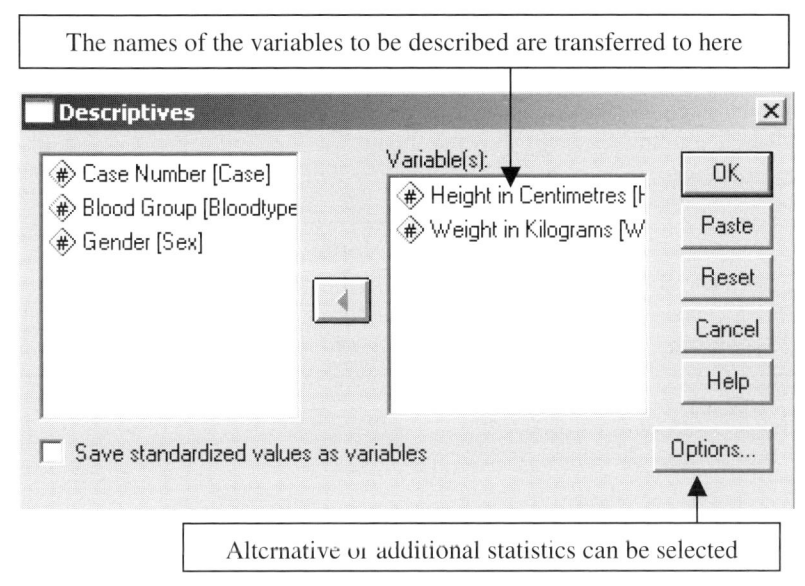

The names of the variables to be described are transferred to here

Figure 8. The completed **Descriptives** dialog box

Alternative or additional statistics can be selected

The output is shown below in Output 6.

Descriptive Statistics

	N	Minimum	Maximum	Mean	Std. Deviation
Height in Centimetres	32	142	196	170.28	13.68
Weight in Kilograms	32	48	120	70.22	15.93
Valid N (listwise)	32				

Output 6. Descriptive statistics for Height and Weight

To obtain percentiles (e.g. quartiles), or to draw various graphics such as boxplots, stem-and-leaf tables or histograms, the appropriate procedures are **Frequencies** and **Explore**.

The next example illustrates the use of **Frequencies** to draw a histogram, compute some descriptive statistics, and display some percentile values for the variable *Height*. Proceed as follows:
- Choose
  Analyze
    Descriptive Statistics
      Frequencies…
- In the **Frequencies** dialog box (Figure 4), enter the variable name Height in Centimetres into the **Variables** box. Check that the **Display frequency tables** checkbox is not showing ✓ , otherwise a full frequency table will be listed. For a large data set, this table could be huge.

- Click **Charts** to open the **Frequencies: Charts** dialog box (Figure 5).
- In the **Chart Type** box, click the **Histograms** radio button, and mark the **With normal curve** box by clicking that also. Click **Continue**.
- Back in the **Frequencies** dialog box, click **Statistics** to open the **Frequencies: Statistics** dialog box and follow the steps shown in Figure 9.
- Click **Continue** to get back to the **Frequencies** dialog box and click **OK**.

Quartiles specifies the 25th, 50th and 75th percentiles

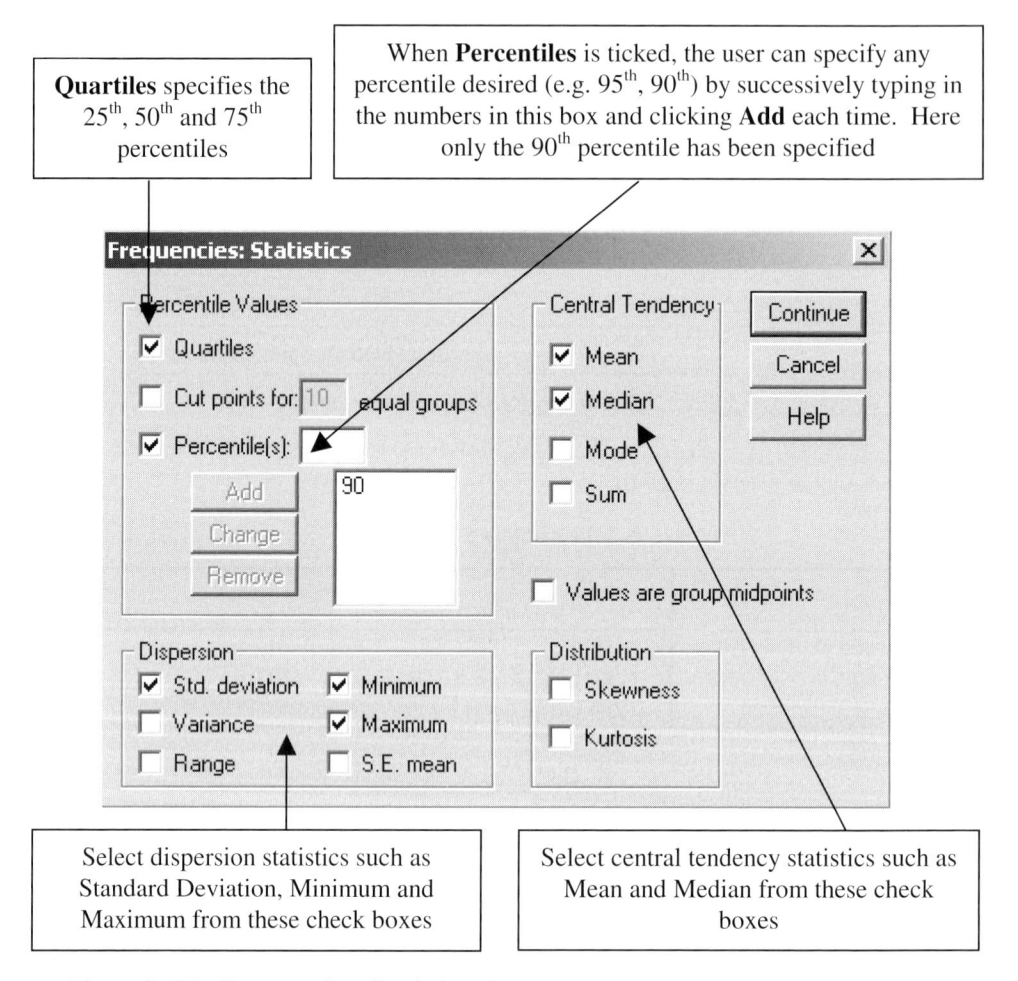

When **Percentiles** is ticked, the user can specify any percentile desired (e.g. 95th, 90th) by successively typing in the numbers in this box and clicking **Add** each time. Here only the 90th percentile has been specified

Select dispersion statistics such as Standard Deviation, Minimum and Maximum from these check boxes

Select central tendency statistics such as Mean and Median from these check boxes

Figure 9. The **Frequencies: Statistics** dialog box with various statistics selected

The statistical output is shown in Output 7 and the edited histogram in Output 8.

Statistics

Height in Centimetres

N	Valid	32
	Missing	0
Mean		170.28
Median		170.50
Std. Deviation		13.68
Minimum		142
Maximum		196
Percentiles	25	162.25
	50	170.50
	75	181.50
	90	188.50

The three quartiles requested by ticking the **Quartiles** box

The 90th percentile requested by ticking the **Percentiles** box and specifying 90

Output 7. The requested percentiles and descriptive statistics for Height

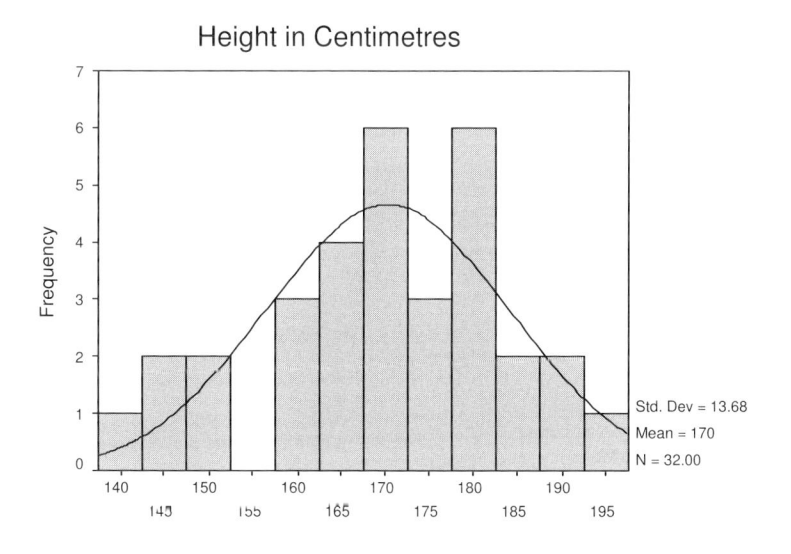

Height in Centimetres

Std. Dev = 13.68
Mean = 170
N = 32.00

Output 8. Histogram and superimposed normal curve of the distribution of Height

Explore also produces stem and-leaf displays and boxplots (see below).

Exploring variables with subdivision into categories of grouping variables

When the user wishes to explore quantitative variables subdivided by categories of grouping variables (e.g. the heights of men and women), several procedures are available including **Basic Tables**, **Explore** in the **Descriptive Statistics**, and **Means** in the **Compare Means** menu. There is also the option of a one-way analysis of variance. Note especially that **Means** cannot be used for variables that have not been grouped by another variable: for such variables, **Descriptives** must be used instead. **Explore** in the **Descriptive Statistics** menu contains a large variety of graphs and displays (which are also available directly from the **Graphs** drop-down menu), as well as a variety of statistics.

The first example uses the **Basic Tables** procedure (see Figure 7); but this time the variable name *Blood Group* is transferred to the **Subgroups Down** box and *Gender* to the **Subgroups Across** box. We have selected **Count**, **Mean**, and **Standard Deviation** from the Statistics option box. The output is shown in Output 9.

			Gender					
			Male			Female		
			Count	Mean	Std Deviation	Count	Mean	Std Deviation
Blood Group	Group A	Height in Centimetres	3	168.3	22.5	3	160.3	10.5
		Weight in Kilograms	3	74.0	15.1	3	52.7	2.5
	Group B	Height in Centimetres	3	184.0	5.3	3	175.7	6.5
		Weight in Kilograms	3	95.0	21.8	3	72.0	7.5
	Group AB	Height in Centimetres	2	178.5	9.2	1	160.3	.
		Weight in Kilograms	2	73.0	7.1	1	160.3	.
	Group O	Height in Centimetres	8	176.5	10.7	9	162.7	12.5
		Weight in Kilograms	8	79.0	11.8	9	60.0	7.2

Output 9. Output from **Basic Tables** showing statistics for Height and Weight across Blood Group and Gender

The next example shows the use of **Means** to compute statistics such as the mean and standard deviation when one variable has been grouped by categories of another (e.g. height grouped by gender). Proceed as follows:
- Choose
    Analyze
        Compare Means
            Means...
    to open the **Means** dialog box (the completed version is shown in Figure 10).
- Follow the steps in Figure 10 and click **OK**.

Exploring your data

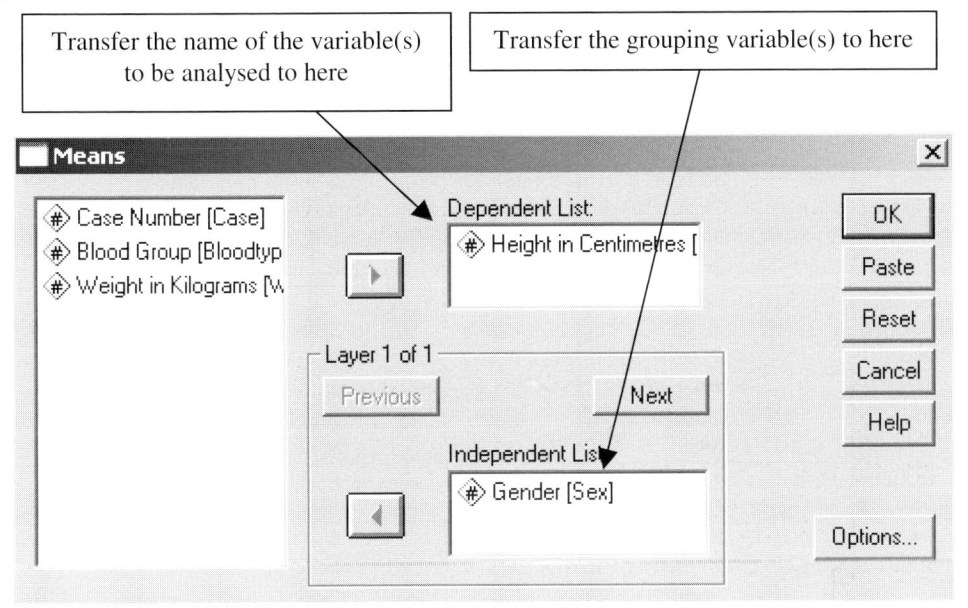

Figure 10. The **Means** dialog box for Height categorised by Gender

The output is listed in Output 10. The **Means** procedure has computed statistics such as the mean and standard deviation for the male and female participants separately.

Height in Centimetres

Gender	Mean	N	Std. Deviation
Male	176.63	16	12.46
Female	163.94	16	12.06
Total	170.28	32	13.68

Output 10. The mean Height for each level of Gender requested with Means

Breaking down the data with two or more classificatory variables: Layering

In Figure 10, notice the centrally located box containing two sub-dialog buttons **Previous** and **Next,** as well as the caption **Layer 1 of 1.** Here a **layer** is a qualitative variable, such as *Sex*. If you click **Next**, you can add another qualitative variable such as Blood Group [*Bloodtype*], so that the data are classified thus**:**

1st Layer	*Sex*	Male	Female
2nd Layer	*Bloodtype*	A AB B O	A AB B O

The output tabulates the mean Height, N and standard deviation for all combinations of Gender and Blood Group as shown in Output 11. Note that if you had not clicked on **Next** before adding the second classificatory variable, the output would have consisted of Height by

Gender and Height by Blood Group separately (i.e. only a single layer would have been used for each analysis).

Height in Centimetres

Gender	Blood Group	Mean	N	Std. Deviation
Male	Group A	168.33	3	22.55
	Group B	184.00	3	5.29
	Group AB	178.50	2	9.19
	Group O	176.50	8	10.66
	Total	176.63	16	12.46
Female	Group A	160.33	3	10.50
	Group B	175.67	3	6.51
	Group AB	151.00	1	.
	Group O	162.67	9	12.47
	Total	163.94	16	12.06
Total	Group A	164.33	6	16.33
	Group B	179.83	6	7.00
	Group AB	169.33	3	17.16
	Group O	169.18	17	13.35
	Total	170.28	32	13.68

Output 11. The use of layering to compute the mean Height, N and standard deviation for all combinations of Gender and Blood Group

Explore (in the **Descriptive Statistics** menu) can be regarded as a general exploratory data analysis (EDA) procedure. **Explore** offers many of the facilities already illustrated with other procedures, and (like **Means** and **Compare Means**) allows quantitative variables to be subdivided by the categories of a qualitative variable such as gender. If, for example, a data set contains the heights of 50 men and 50 women collected into a column headed *Height* and (in another column) code numbers making up the grouping variable *Sex*, the procedure **Explore** will produce statistical summaries, graphs and displays either for the 100 height measurements considered as a single group, or the heights of males or females (or both) considered separately.

A useful first step in the analysis of data is to obtain a picture of the data set as a whole. **Explore** offers three kinds of graphs and displays:
    1. Histograms;
    2. Stem-and-leaf displays;
    3. Boxplots.

Readers unfamiliar with these can find, in Howell (2002), clear descriptions of histograms on pp. 19–20, of stem-and-leaf displays on pp. 21–23 and of boxplots on pp. 57–60.

The basis of all three types of graph is a table called a **frequency distribution**, which sets out either (in the case of nominal data) the categories comprising a qualitative variable and gives the frequency of observations in each category or (with measurements) divides the total range of values into arbitrary **class intervals** and gives the frequency of measurements that fall within each interval, that is, have values between the upper and lower **bounds** of the interval concerned. With data on height recorded in centimetres, for example, the total range could be

Exploring your data 111

divided into the class intervals (140–149, 150–159, 160–169, ...), and the frequency distribution would give the **frequencies** of heights within each of these ranges.

A **bar graph** (SPSS calls this a 'bar chart': see Output 3) is suitable for qualitative (nominal) data, such as the numbers of people in a sample belonging to the various blood groups. In a bar graph, the bars are separated to clarify the fact that the horizontal axis contains no scale of measurement; in fact, the order of the bars in Output 3 is arbitrary, since the Group AB bar could as well have followed the Group A bar. A **histogram** (see Output 8), on the other hand, is appropriate for measurements. Here the class intervals are stepped out along the horizontal axis and above each interval a bar is drawn whose height represents the number of people whose measurements fell within that interval. *In a histogram, as compared with a bar graph, the bars touch one another.*

To use the **Explore** procedure:
- Choose
  Analyze
   Descriptive Statistics
    Explore...
  to open the **Explore** dialog box.
- Follow the steps shown in Figure 11.

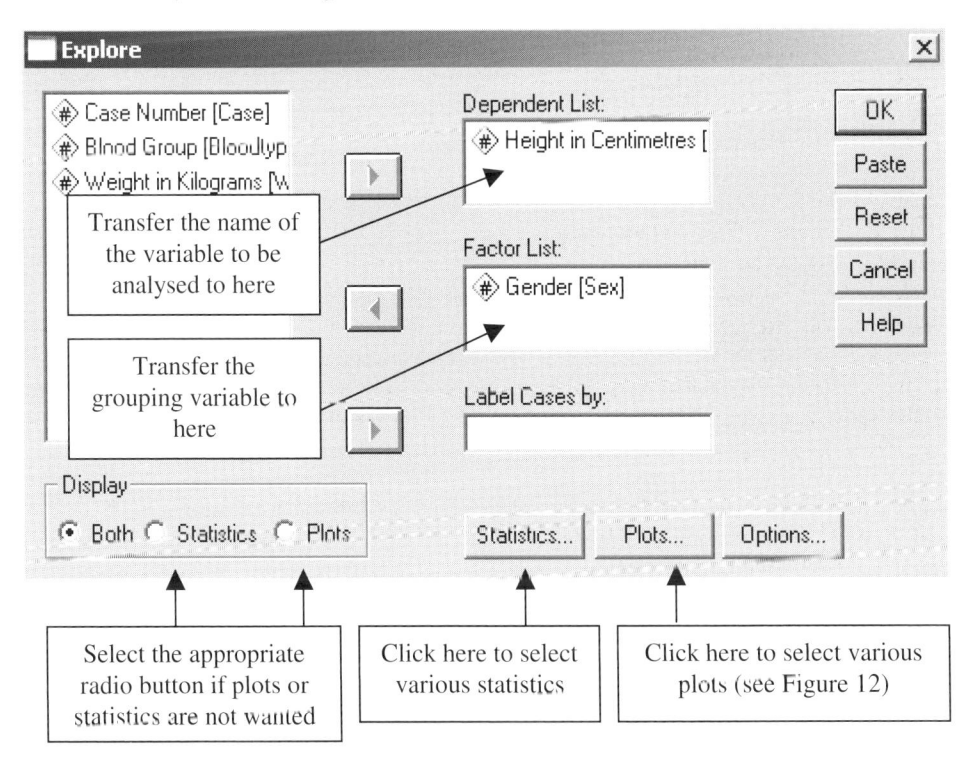

Figure 11. The **Explore** dialog box for Height categorised by Gender

- If there is a variable identifying the cases (e.g. *Case*), then click *Case* and ▶ to transfer it to the **Label Cases by** box. Outliers or extreme cases (these will be explained later) are

identified in boxplots by their row numbers by default or by the identifier in the variable entered in the **Label Cases by** box.
- Click **Plots** to open the **Explore: Plots** dialog box and follow the steps shown in Figure 12. The default setting for the **Boxplots** is a side-by-side plot for each level of the factor (i.e. *Female* and *Male*). For **Descriptive**, the options are **Stem-and-leaf** and **Histogram**. Since we have seen the histogram earlier, we shall click **Stem-and-leaf** only.
- Click **Continue** and then **OK**.

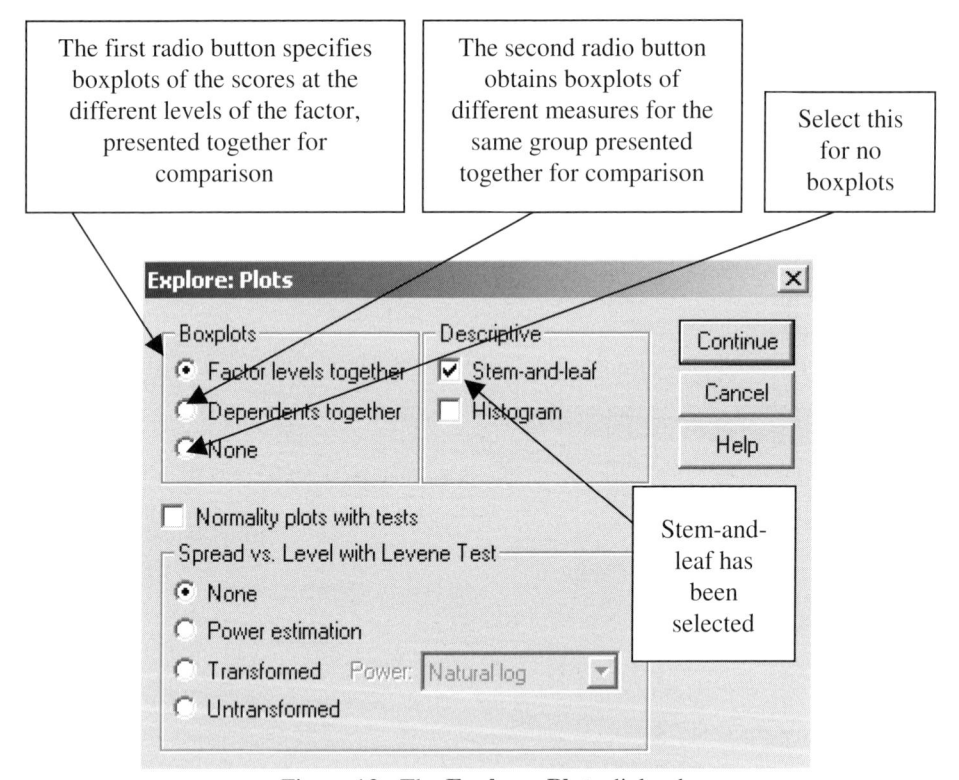

Figure 12. The **Explore: Plots** dialog box

Should you wish to have boxplots of two dependent variables side-by-side at each level of a classificatory variable (such as gender, or blood group), both dependent variables must be entered into the **Dependent List** box, and (in the **Boxplots** dialog box) the **Dependents together** radio button must be selected. In the present example, of course, it would have made no sense to plot boxplots of *Height* and *Weight* side-by-side at each level of *Sex*, since height and weight measurements have quite different scales.

The tables and the boxplots are shown in Outputs 12 and 13.

The descriptive statistics and stem-and-leaf display of *Height* for Males (one of the levels of *Sex*) is shown in Output 12; the output for Females is not shown. In the **stem-and-leaf display**, the central column of numbers (16, 16, 17, 17, ..., 19), which is the **stem**, represents the leading digit or digits (here they are hundreds and tens of centimetres). The numbers in the column headed **Leaf** are the final digits (centimetres). Each stem denotes the lower bound of

Exploring your data

the class interval: for example, the first number, 16, represents the lower bound of the class interval from 160 to 164, the second 16 from 165 to 169, the first 17 from 170 to 174 and so on. The column headed **Frequency** lists the number of cases on each stem. In stem 18, for example, there are four cases with heights between 180 and 184 centimetres. They are 180, 180, 182 and 183, since the leaves are listed as 0, 0, 2, 3. In addition, there is one case with a height between 185 and 189, namely 185. The display also shows extreme cases: there is one value equal to or less than 145. The stem-and-leaf display is very useful for displaying small data sets, but becomes ponderous for large sets, for which the histogram is more suitable.

Descriptives

Gender				Statistic	Std. Error
Height in Centimetres	Male	Mean		176.63	3.12
		95% Confidence Interval for Mean	Lower Bound	169.98	
			Upper Bound	183.27	
		5% Trimmed Mean		177.31	
		Median		179.00	
		Variance		155.32	
		Std. Deviation		12.46	
		Minimum		145.00	
		Maximum		196.00	176.63
		Range		51.00	169.98
		Interquartile Range		14.50	183.27
		Skewness		-.95	177.31
		Kurtosis		1.64	179.00

```
Height in Centimetres Stem-and-Leaf Plot for
SEX= Male

 Frequency     Stem &  Leaf

     1.00 Extremes    (=<145)
     1.00         16 . 0
      .00         16 .
     4.00         17 . 0002
     2.00         17 . 58
     4.00         18 . 0023
     1.00         18 . 5
     2.00         19 . 00
     1.00         19 . 6

 Stem width:        10
 Each leaf:       1 case(s)
```

Output 12. Descriptive statistics, and stem and-leaf display for Height categorised by Gender (only the output for Males shown here)

Output 13 shows the **boxplots** of the heights of the male and female cases plotted side by side, for comparison. The structure of a boxplot is shown in Table 2. The box itself represents that portion of the distribution falling between the 25th and 75th percentiles, i.e. the **lower** and **upper quartiles** (in EDA terminology these are known as **hinges**). The xth percentile is the value below which x% of the distribution lies, so 50% of the heights lie between the 25th and 75th percentiles. The thick horizontal line across the interior of the box represents the median.

The vertical lines outside the box, which are known as **whiskers**, connect the largest and smallest values that are not outliers or extreme cases.

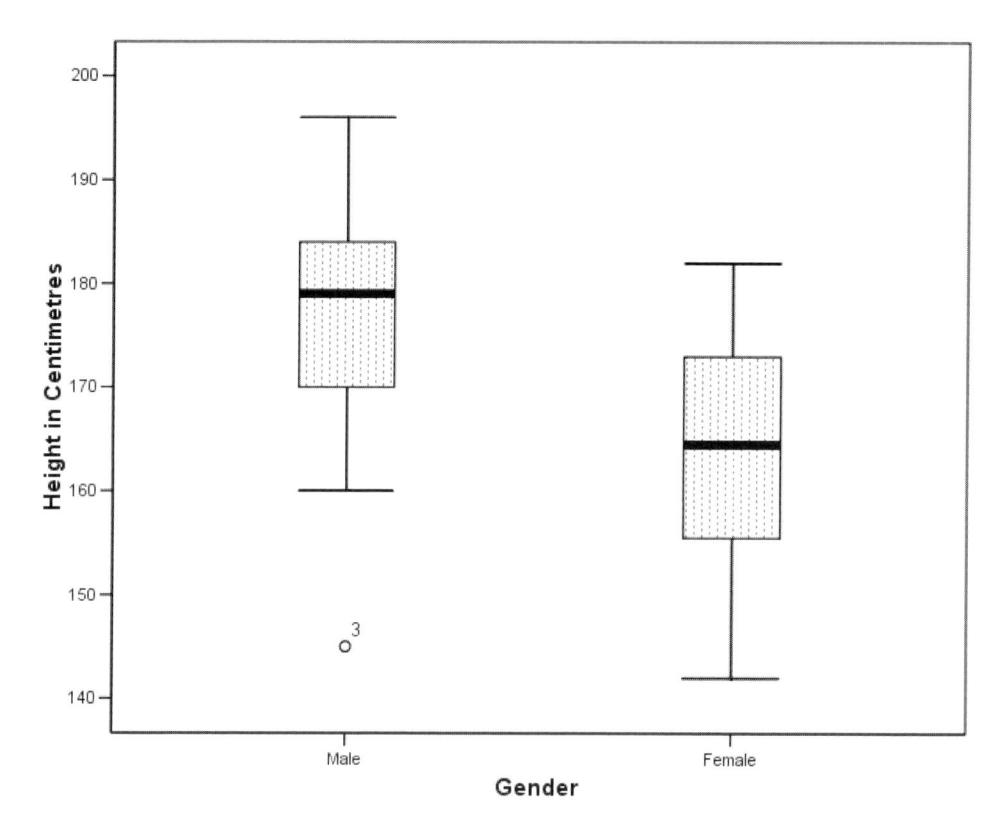

Output 13. Boxplots of Height categorised by Gender

Output 13 shows one **outlier** but no **extreme cases**. An **outlier** (o) is defined as a value more than 1.5 box-lengths away from the box, and an **extreme case** (*) as more than 3 box-lengths away from the box. The number(s) alongside o and * are the case number(s). The case numbers are either the row numbers in **Data View** by default, or the identifiers from the variable entered in the **Label Cases by** box.

Skewness is indicated by an eccentric location of the median in the box. Notice that the distribution of heights for females is much more symmetric than that for males. The o^3 under the Male boxplot in Output 13 indicates the existence of an outlier and that it is the value for the case in row 3. This value (145cm) is well below the average height for males and its presence is also noted in the stem-and-leaf display in Output 12.

Boxplots are particularly useful for identifying outliers and extreme cases in data sets, and can be requested directly by choosing
Graphs
    Boxplot....

Exploring your data 115

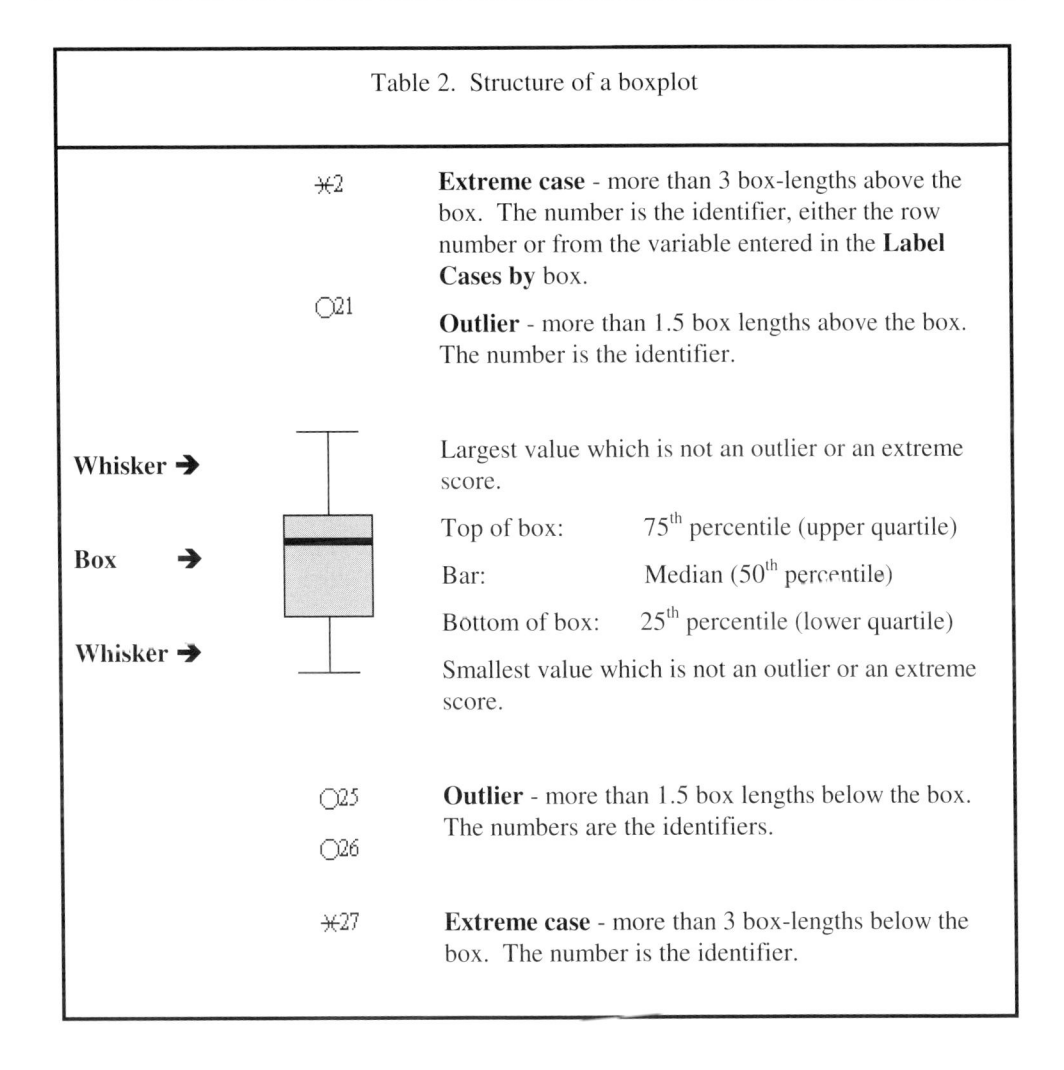

	Table 2. Structure of a boxplot
✳2	**Extreme case** - more than 3 box-lengths above the box. The number is the identifier, either the row number or from the variable entered in the **Label Cases by** box.
○21	**Outlier** - more than 1.5 box lengths above the box. The number is the identifier.
Whisker ➔	Largest value which is not an outlier or an extreme score.
Box ➔	Top of box: 75th percentile (upper quartile) Bar: Median (50th percentile) Bottom of box: 25th percentile (lower quartile)
Whisker ➔	Smallest value which is not an outlier or an extreme score.
○25 ○26	**Outlier** - more than 1.5 box lengths below the box. The numbers are the identifiers.
✳27	**Extreme case** - more than 3 box-lengths below the box. The number is the identifier.

4.4 MANIPULATION OF THE DATA SET

4.4.1 Reducing and transforming data

After a data set has been entered into SPSS, it may be necessary to modify it in certain ways. For example, an exploratory data analysis may have revealed that one or two extreme cases have exerted undue leverage upon the values of statistics such as the mean and standard deviation. One approach to this problem is to de-select the extreme cases and repeat the analysis with the remaining scores (cf. Tabachnick & Fidell, 2001). Any exclusions, however, should be mentioned in the experimental report. Cases can be dropped from the analysis by using the **Select Cases** command (Section 3.3.1).

Sometimes, in order to satisfy the distribution requirements for the use of a particular statistic, it may be necessary to **transform** the values of a variable. For example, a distribution of response latencies is often **positively skewed,** i.e. it has a long tail to the right; whereas the distribution of the logarithms of the raw scores is more symmetrical. Transformations are easily implemented with the **Compute** procedure (Section 4.4.2).

Finally, it is sometimes convenient to combine or alter the categories that make up a qualitative or ordinal variable. This is achieved with the **Recode** procedure, which can construct a new variable with the new category assignments (Section 4.4.3).

4.4.2 The COMPUTE procedure

Transforming the data

The **Compute** procedure was used in Chapter 3 to number the cases in a data set. **Compute** can also be used to calculate many different kinds of transformations of the original data set. New variables of transformed data can be created or the values of existing variables can be replaced by the transformed values. We do not recommend the second approach, because the original values for the variable cannot then be recovered. The **Compute** procedure also allows transformation of subsets of the original data set that have been specified by logical conditions.

Output 14 shows a histogram of the response latencies of fifty people. Typically, such data show a positively skewed distribution, with a long tail to the right. For the purposes of statistical testing, the investigator might want to transform the original data to make the distribution more symmetrical. Such normalisation can often be achieved by taking the logarithms, square roots, reciprocals and other functions of the original scores. These transformations, however, have different effects upon distribution shape, as the following exercise will demonstrate. We shall begin by using the **Compute** procedure to calculate the natural logarithms of the raw data.

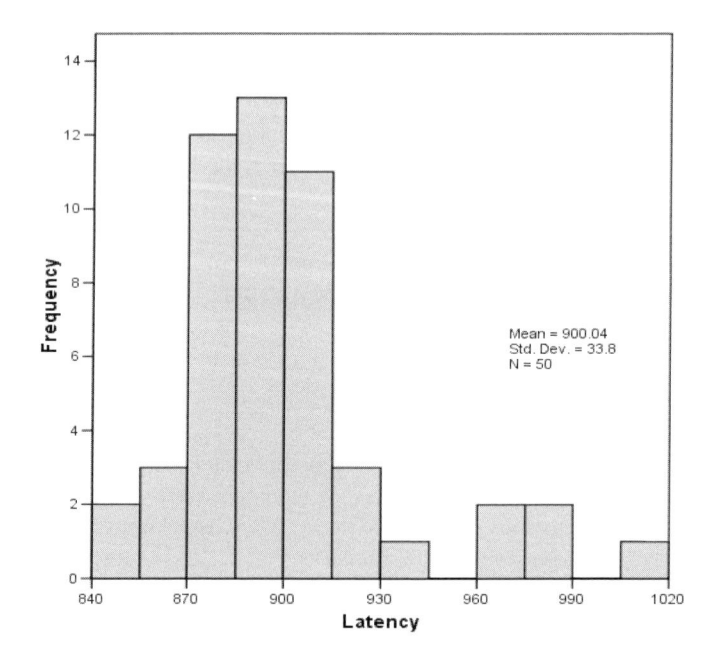

Output 14. Histogram of the response latencies of 50 people

Exploring your data 117

Assuming the data set is present in the **Data Editor**,
- Choose
  **Transform
      Compute…**
  to open the **Compute Variable** dialog box (the completed version is shown in Figure 13).
- Click in the **Target Variable** box at top left and type the name *LogLtncy*.
- Scroll down through the **Functions:** box on the right to find the natural logarithm function **LN(Numexpr)**. Click on it and then ▲ to paste it into the **Numeric Expression** box where it will appear as **LN[?]**.
- In the list of variables in the lower left panel, click *Latency* and ▶ to make this variable the argument of the log function (i.e. *Latency* replaces ?). The expression **LN[Latency]** will now appear in the **Numeric Expression** box (see Figure 13).
- Click **OK**.

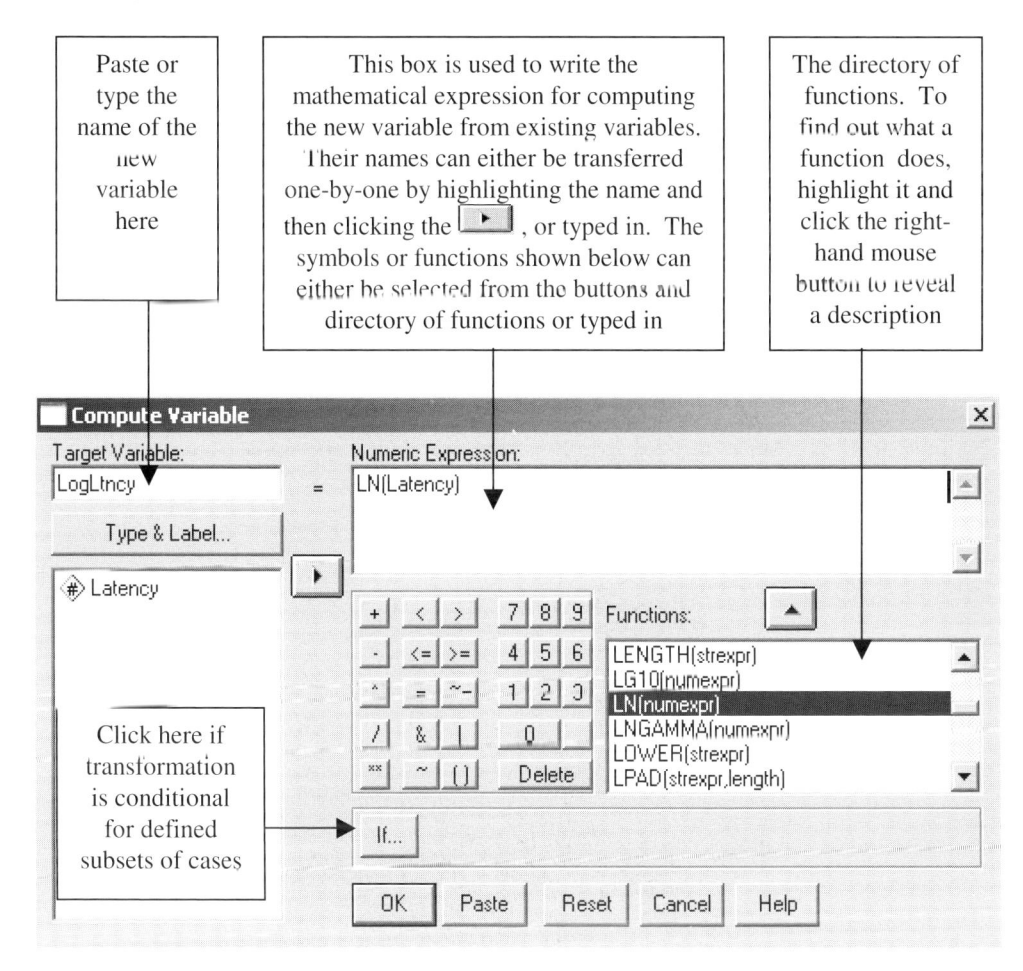

| Paste or type the name of the new variable here | This box is used to write the mathematical expression for computing the new variable from existing variables. Their names can either be transferred one-by-one by highlighting the name and then clicking the ▶, or typed in. The symbols or functions shown below can either be selected from the buttons and directory of functions or typed in | The directory of functions. To find out what a function does, highlight it and click the right-hand mouse button to reveal a description |

Figure 13. The completed **Compute Variable** dialog box for computing the natural logarithm of *Latency*

A new column *LgLtncy*, containing the natural logs of the values of *Latencies*, will appear in **Data View**. You may wish to add a label (e.g. Log of Latency) for this new variable and to change the number of decimal places – see Section 2.3.1. A setting of two decimal places works well in this example; but with a reciprocal transformation (see below), four places of decimals would be required. Output 15 shows the histogram of the logs of the original latencies. The transformation has clearly reduced the skewness of the distribution.

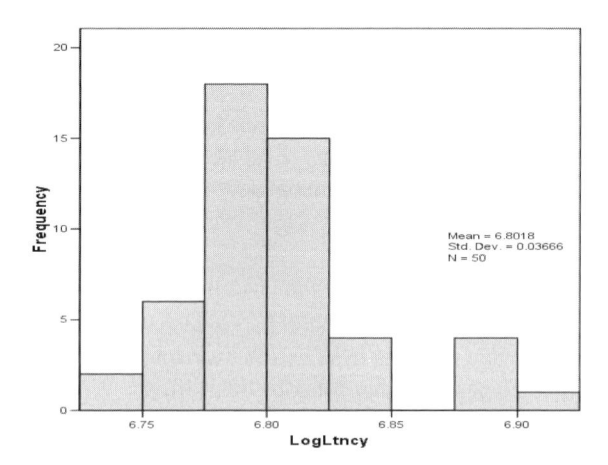

Output 15. Histogram showing the distribution of the natural logs of the response latencies. The distribution is more symmetrical than that of the untransformed values of Latency

Other functions produce even more striking transformations of the original data. The reciprocal transformation (1/x), for example, produces the distribution pictured in Output 16. This time, there is a tail to the left, indicating that this is an inappropriate transformation for these data.

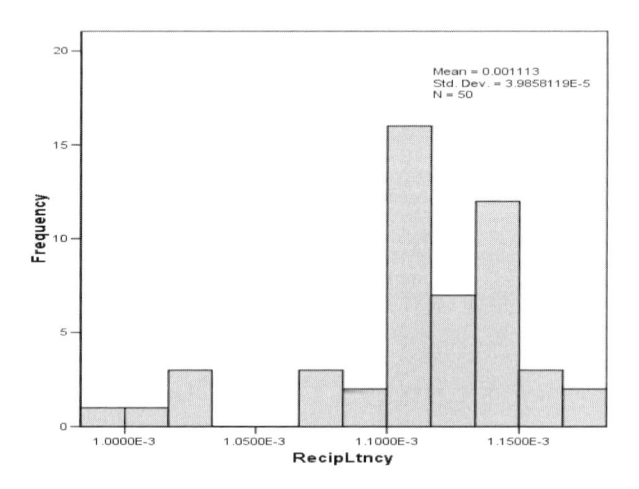

Output 16. The distribution of a reciprocal (1/x) transformation of the response latencies. This distribution is negatively skewed, with a tail to the left

Exploring your data 119

Using Compute to obtain functions of several variables

Compute can also be used to combine values of variables. Suppose you have a data set comprising the marks of schoolchildren in their French, German and Spanish examinations. You might be interested in averaging each child's score over the three examinations.

One way of doing this is to write your own numerical expression in the **Numerical Expression** box of the **Compute Variable** dialog box (e.g. name the new variable *MeanMark* and enter the expression *(French + German + Spanish)/3*. Should any child not have taken all three examinations, however, the mean would not be calculated and a system-missing mark would appear in **Data View** instead.

Another way is to paste the **MEAN** function from the **Functions** list into the **Numerical Expression** box and transfer the variable names French, German and Spanish into the pasted function taking care to have a comma between each name and to ensure that ? is no longer present (e.g. **MEAN**(French, German, Spanish)). Should a child's mark be missing, the mean of the other two marks will be calculated. The function MEAN, therefore, calculates the mean from whatever valid values may be present. Only if a child has sat none of the three examinations, will a system-missing value of the mean be recorded.

Figure 14 is a section of **Data View** comparing the results of using these two ways, *MeanbyDiv* for the first way and *MEAN* for the second way.

ChildsN	French	German	Spanish	MeanbyDiv	MEAN
Fred	67	78	23	56.00	56.00
Mary	50	50	.	.	50.00
John	.	.	.	.	.
Peter	0	50	50	33.33	33.33
Amy	0	.	.	.	.00
Jack	23	.	.	.	23.00

Figure 14. Two ways to computing the means of three variables

It can be seen from Figure 14 that the add-then-divide way only works when there are marks on all three examinations. It fails with Mary, John, Amy and Jack. The MEAN way fails to produce a result only with John, who did not sit any of the examinations. The MEAN function also makes a clear distinction between zeros and missing values: Mary correctly receives the mean of 50 and 50 (50); whereas Peter correctly receives the mean of 0, 50 and 50 (33.33). Jack correctly receives a mean of 23 even though he sat only one examination.

Conditional computations

A medical researcher has gathered some data on the drinking and substance intake of patients. Figure 15 shows a section from **Data View**, in which *0 = No Abuse and 1 = Abuse*.

	Patient	Alcohol	Substances
1	Sarah	No Abuse	No Abuse
2	Alan	Abuse	No Abuse
3	Jim	No Abuse	Abuse
4	Joe	Abuse	Abuse

Figure 15. A section of the data set for substance abuse in patients

The researcher wants to create a third variable, *Addict*, with values as follows:
    0 for patients with No Abuse on both variables
    1 for patients with Abuse on *Alcohol* but No Abuse on *Substances*
    2 for patients with No Abuse on *Alcohol* but Abuse on *Substances*
    3 for patients with Abuse on both variables.

The problem can be solved in several ways. We could begin by letting *Addict* = *Alcohol* + *Substances* + *1*. We could then instruct the **Compute** routine to proceed as follows. If either *(Alcohol = Substances = 0)* or *(Alcohol = 1 and Substances = 0)*, subtract *1* from *Addict*. This will solve the problem, because the remaining combinations would fail to meet either condition and no subtraction would take place.

- Choose
Transform
    Compute
to access the **Compute Variable** dialog box.
- Type *Addict* into the **Target Variable** box.
- Transfer the variable names *Alcohol* and *Substances* to the **Numeric Expression** box and create the expression *Alcohol* + *Substances* + *1* (see Figure 16).
- Click **OK**.

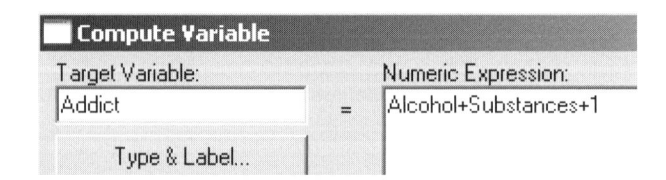

Figure 16. Part of the **Compute Variable** dialog box for computing values for the new variable Addict

The values of *Addict* will then appear in **Data View** as shown in Figure 17.

	Patient	Alcohol	Substances	Addict
1	Sarah	0	0	1
2	Alan	1	0	2
3	Jim	0	1	2
4	Joe	1	1	3

Figure 17. **Data View** showing the newly computed variable Addict

Exploring your data

These values for *Addict* are correct except for Sarah and Alan who should have a value of *0* and *1* respectively. We therefore have to modify the computation of these values of *Addict* by subtracting *1* from the total when both variables have *0*, or if *Alcohol = 1* and *Substances = 0*. This is done by constructing a conditional expression in the **Compute Variable: If Cases** dialog box.

- Return to the **Compute Variable** dialog box and change the Numeric Expression entry to *Addict – 1*.
- Click the **If...** button to open the **Compute Variable: If Cases** dialog box.
- Click the radio button labelled **Include if Case satisfies condition:**
- In the box on the right enter the expression:
  (Alcohol = 0 & Substance = 0) | (Alcohol = 1 & Substances = 0).
  The symbol **&** means **AND** and the symbol | means **OR** in this logical expression. Care must be taken with inserting brackets in the conditional expression to ensure the logical operators **AND** and **OR** operate appropriately.
- The top part of the completed dialog box will appear as in Figure 18.

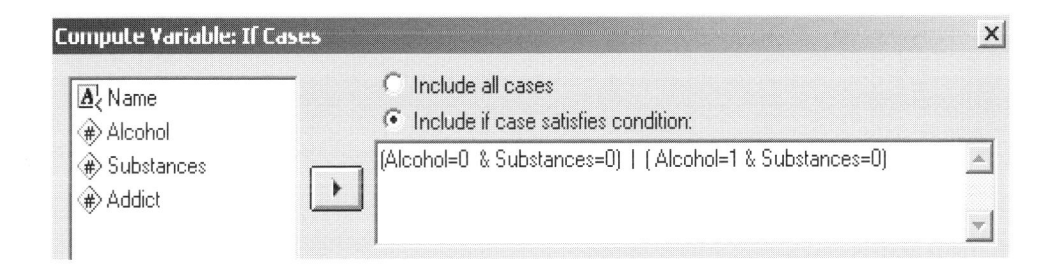

Figure 18. Top part of the **Compute Variables: If Cases** dialog box with the specially written conditional expression

- Click **Continue** to return to the **Compute Variable** dialog box.
- Click OK to compute the altered values of *Addict*.

The entries in **Data View** will now appear as shown in Figure 19.

	Patient	Alcohol	Substances	Addict
1	Sarah	0	0	0
2	Alan	1	0	1
3	Jim	0	1	2
4	Joe	1	1	3

Figure 19. The desired values for Addict after using a conditional expression in the **Compute Variable** dialog box

An alternative method would be to compute *Addict = Alcohol*10 + Substances* and then use the **Recode** procedure (next Section) to recode the resulting set of values.

4.4.3 The RECODE and VISUAL BANDER procedures

We have seen that the **Compute** procedure operates upon one or more of the variables in the data set, so that there will be as many values in the transformed variable as there were in the original variable. Sometimes, however, rather than wanting a transformation that will systematically change all the values of a variable, the user may want to assign relatively few code numbers to values that fall within specified ranges of the variable.

For example, suppose we have a set of 18 children's examination marks on a scale from 0 to 100 (Table 3). We shall recode these into three bands: 0-49 as Fail; 50-74 as Pass; 75-100 as Good. This can easily be done by using either of two other procedures on the **Transform** menu: the **Recode** procedure or the **Visual Bander** procedure.

		Table 3. Children's examination marks			
Child	Mark	Child	Mark	Child	Mark
1	62	7	70	13	50
2	51	8	40	14	50
3	40	9	63	15	42
4	68	10	81	16	65
5	38	11	62	17	30
6	40	12	78	18	71

*Using the **Recode** procedure*

Enter the data into **Data View** in variables named *Case* and *Marks* and then:
- Choose
  Transform
  >   **Recode...**
  and click **Into Different Variables** to open the **Recode into Different Variables** dialog box (Figure 20). Just as in the case of the **Compute** procedure, it is possible to change the values in the same variable to the recoded values but we recommend placing the recoded values in a new variable, perhaps *Grade*.
- Click *Marks* and ▶ to paste the name into the **Numeric Variable→Output Variable** box.
- Type the name of the output variable *Grade* into the **Name** box and click **Change** to insert the name into the **Numeric Variable→Output Variable** box (Figure 20).
- Click the **Old and New Values** box to open the **Recode into Different Variables: Old and New Values** dialog box (the completed dialog box is shown in Figure 21).
- Follow the steps in Figure 21 for defining the old and new values. These will categorise all exam marks less than 50 as *Fail,* 50-74 as *Pass* and 75 and over as *Good.*
- Click **Continue** and **OK**.

Exploring your data 123

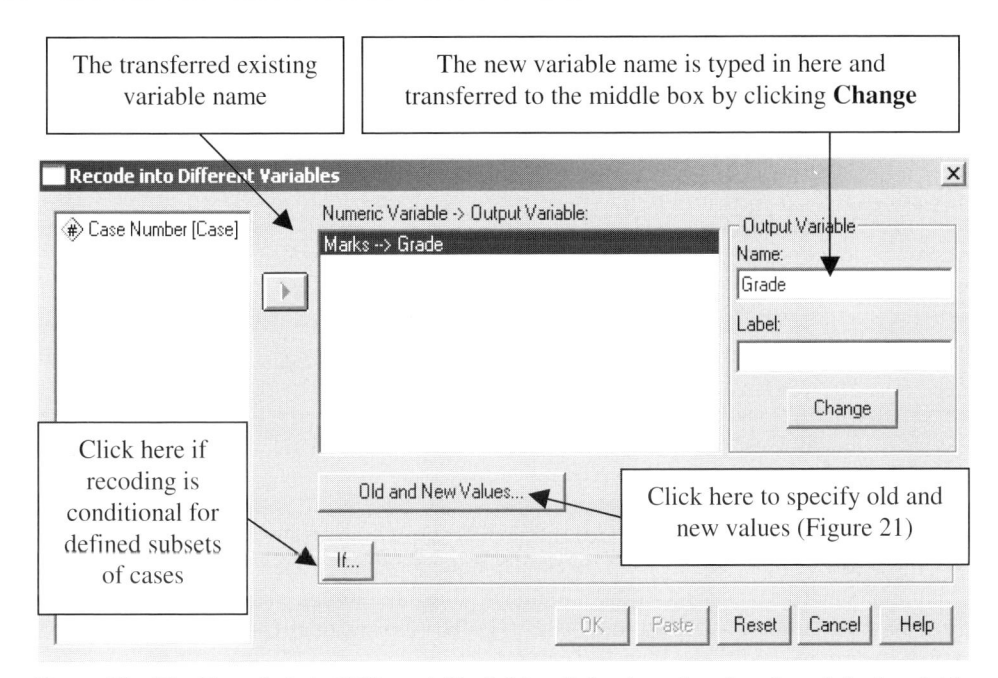

Figure 20. The **Recode into Different Variables** dialog box showing the original variable and the one to which the recoded values will be placed

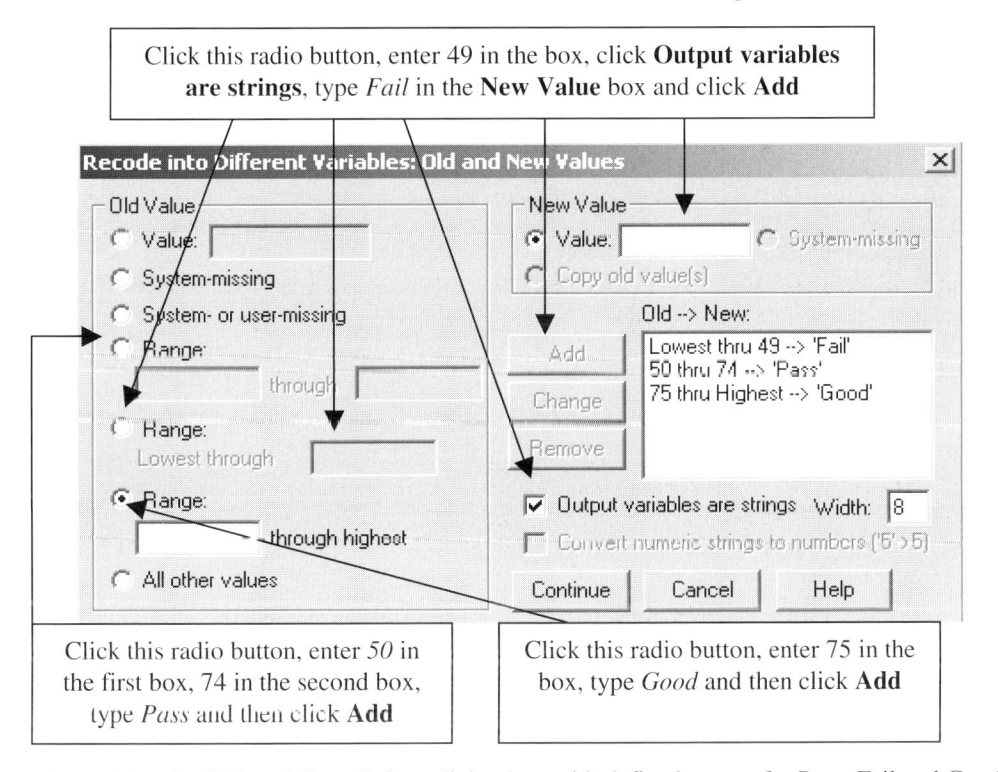

Figure 21. The **Old and New Values** dialog box with defined ranges for Pass, Fail and Good

A new string variable *Grade* containing the recoded labels *Pass*, *Fail* and *Good* will appear in **Data View** (Figure 22).

	Case	Marks	Grade
8	8	40	Fail
9	9	63	Pass
10	10	81	Good
11	11	62	Pass
12	12	78	Good

Figure 22. Part of **Data View** showing the new string variable *Grade* with the labels Pass, Fail and Good

Using the Visual Bander

The **Visual Bander** procedure provides many different ways of categorising variables on the basis of cut-off values, equal-width intervals, equal-percentile intervals or on means and selected standard deviation intervals. We shall illustrate its use with the medical data by categorising the height data into three bands: (1) tall (greater than 180 cm); (2) intermediate (160 to 180 cm); (3) short (less than 160 cm).

- Choose
  Transform
    Visual Bander
  to open the **Visual Bander** dialog box.
- Select *Height in Centimetres* and click on arrowhead to transfer the variable name to the **Variables to Band** box (Figure 23).

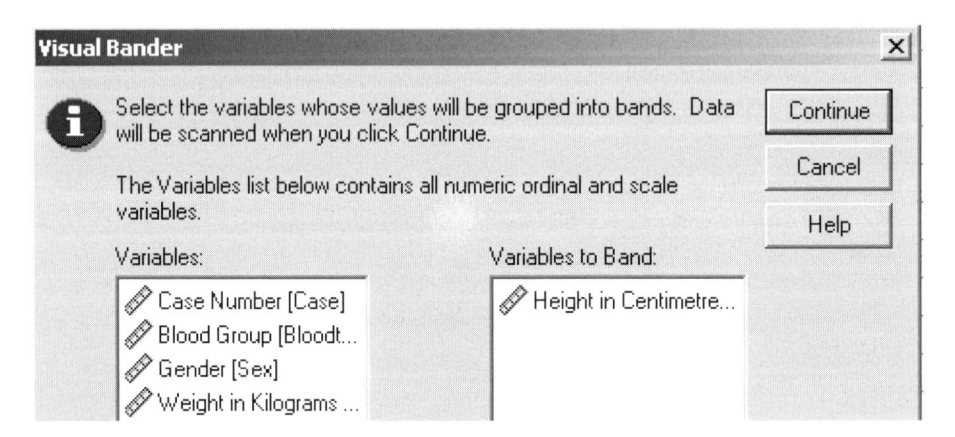

Figure 23. The upper part of the **Visual Bander** dialog box

- Click **Continue** to open the next dialog box.
- Click *Height in Centimetres* in the **Scanned Variable List** box to show the histogram of heights (Figure 24).

Exploring your data

- Enter *160* in the first **Value** cell (it overwrites HIGH) and *Short* in the first **Label** cell. Click the lower radio button **Excluded (<)** to indicate that the category *Short* is greater than 160 cm. Had we defined the category as "160 and less", then the default radio button **Included (<=)** would apply.

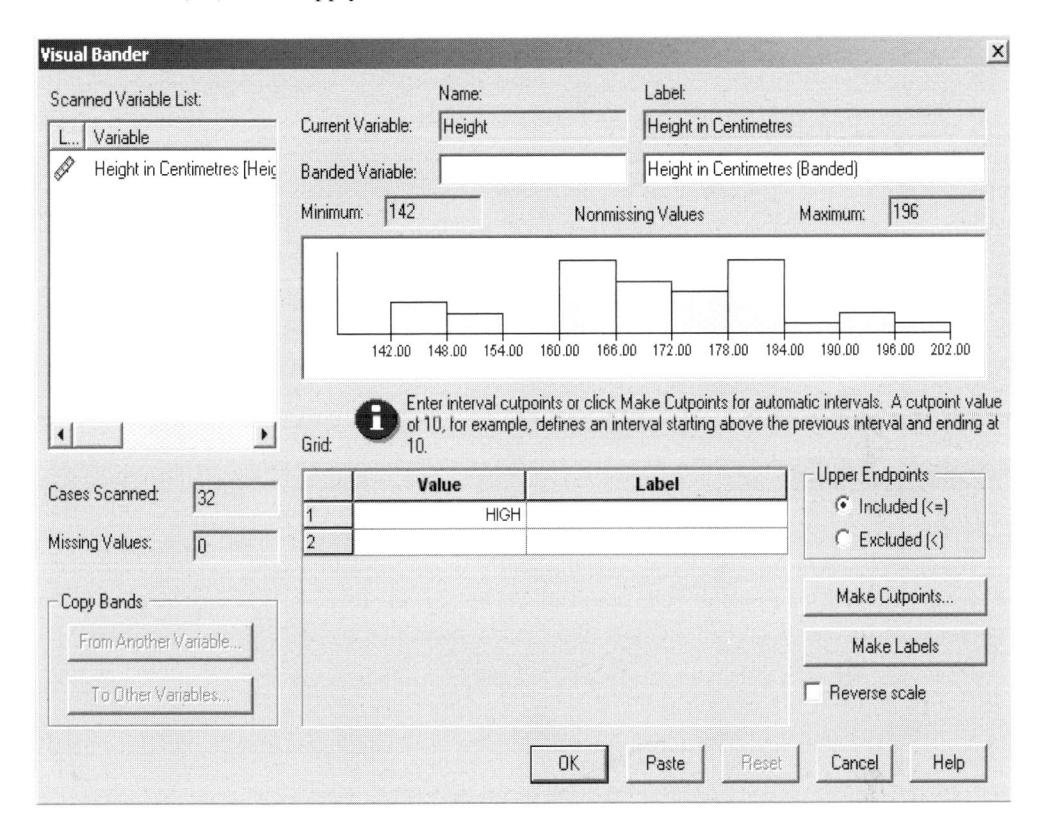

Figure 24. The histogram of Height is shown after clicking on the variable name

- Enter *180* in the second **Value** cell and *Medium* in the second **Label** cell.
- Enter *220* (any value beyond the tallest value would suffice) in the third **Value** cell and *Tall* in the third **Label** cell.
- Enter a variable name such as observing the usual rules for naming variables (e.g. *HeightBands*) in the **Banded Variable** cell (Figure 25).
- Click **OK**.

Notice that as each cutpoint is entered, its position is drawn into the histogram above as soon as the cursor is moved to another cell. If desired, the cursor can be positioned over one of these lines and moved left or right by clicking and dragging. The new variable *HeightBands* is shown in Figure 28.

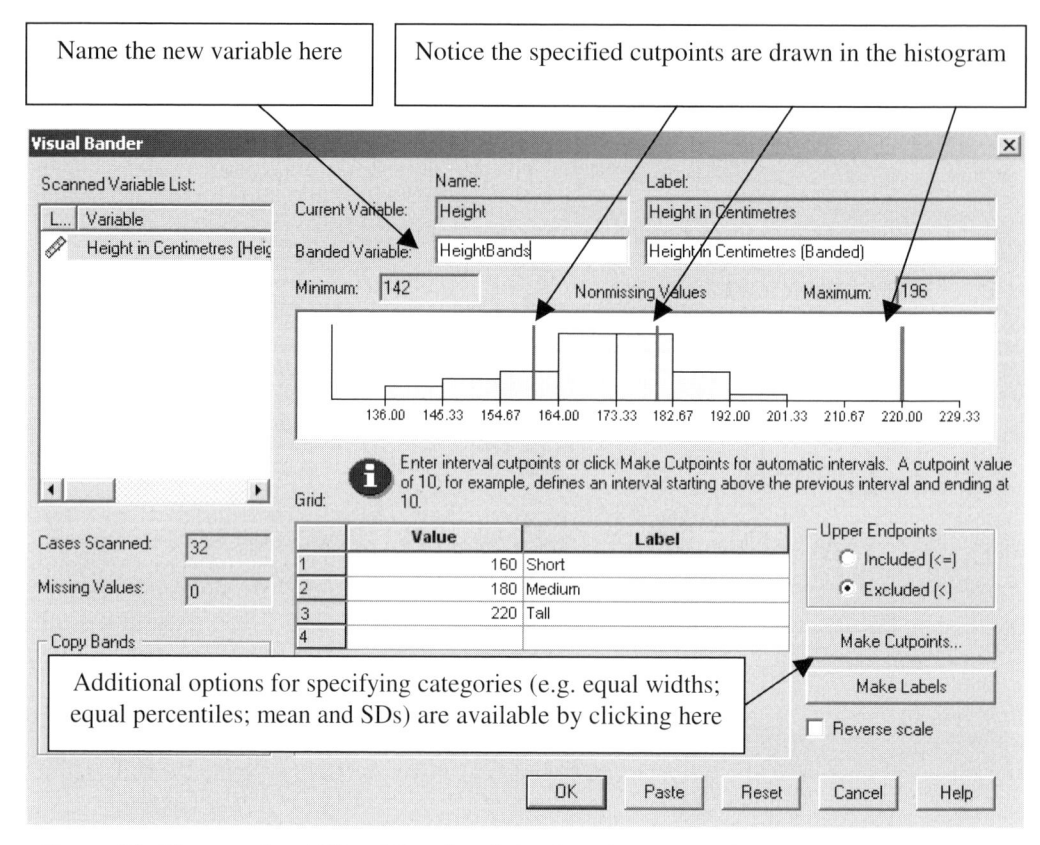

Figure 25. The completed **Visual Bander** dialog box for categorising Height into three bands

To split the heights into equal percentiles (i.e. <25th percentile, 25-50th percentile, 50-75th percentile and >75th percentile), proceed as follows:
- Follow the steps of the previous example but instead of entering values and labels, click **Make Cutpoints** and enter *3* into the **Number of Cutpoints** (Figure 26) i.e. one less than the number of intervals. SPSS will automatically show *25* in the **Width%** box below.
- Click **Apply**, fill in suitable labels in the usual place (Figure 27).
- Enter a new variable name (e.g. *HeightPercentiles*) in the **Banded Variable** box.
- Click **OK**.

The new variable *HeightPercentiles* is shown in Figure 28.

Exploring your data 127

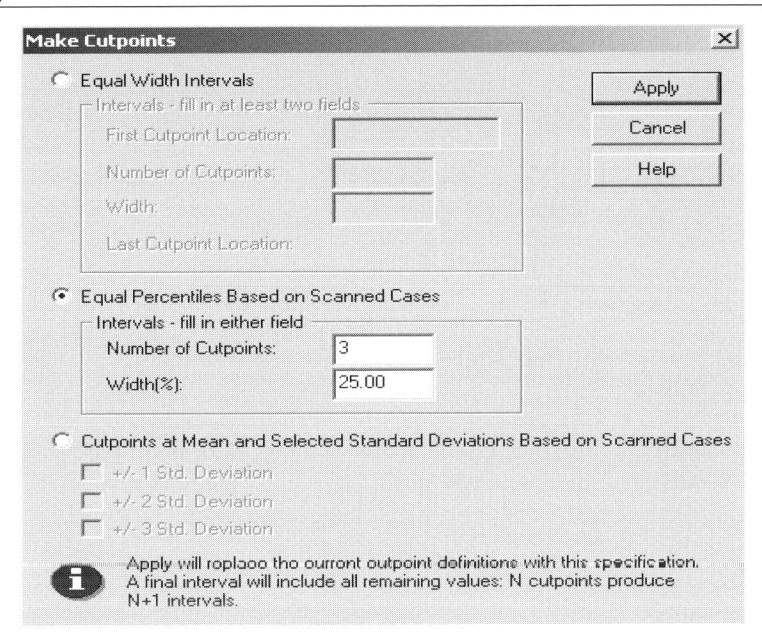

Figure 26. The completed **Make Cutpoints** dialog box for creating four equal percentile bands

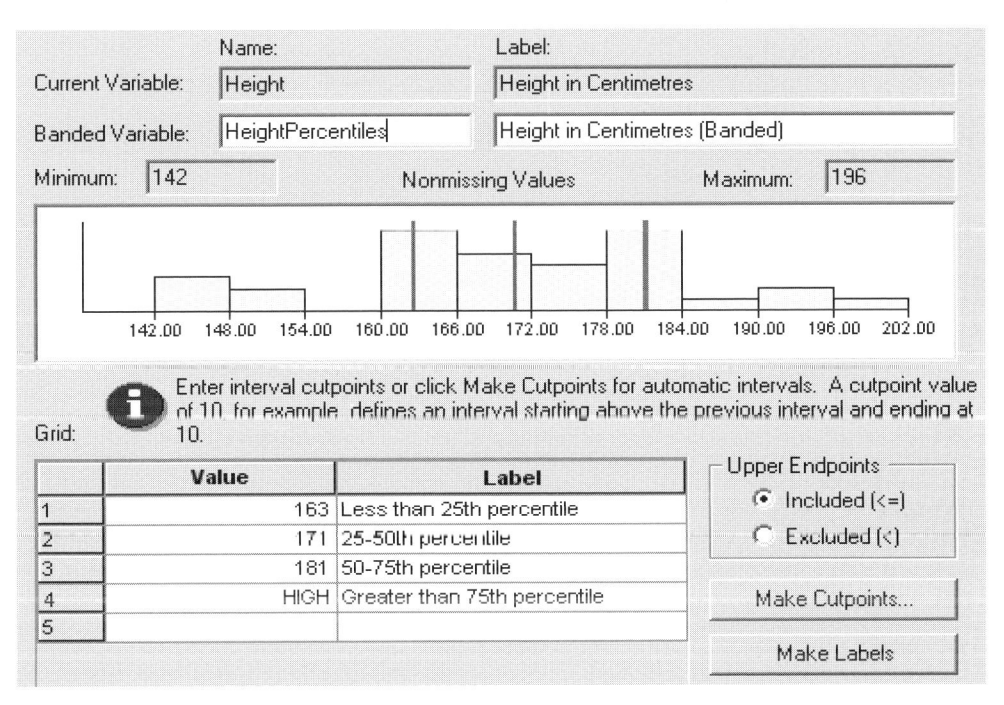

Figure 27. The **Visual Bander** dialog box with new variable name (*HeightPercentiles*) and labels for the percentile bands. The values were entered automatically by SPSS and are shown on the histogram above

	Bloodtype	Sex	Height	Weight	HeightBands	HeightPercentiles
1	Group O	Male	178	75	Medium	50-75th percentile
2	Group O	Male	196	100	Tall	Greater than 75th percentile
3	Group A	Male	145	60	Short	Less than 25th percentile
4	Group O	Male	170	71	Medium	25-50th percentile
5	Group B	Male	180	80	Tall	50-75th percentile
6	Group O	Male	175	69	Medium	50-75th percentile

Figure 28. The new variables *HeightBands* and *HeightPercentiles* created by **Visual Bander**

Exploring your data 129

EXERCISE 4

Correcting and preparing your data

This Exercise explores the data in your saved file of merged data (see Exercise 3), consisting of the responses of 335 people (including yourself) to a questionnaire.

Opening SPSS

Open SPSS in the usual way, selecting the data file *Merged Questionnaire Data* which was saved in the previous Exercise. Ensure that the value labels (e.g. Female) are visible in **Data View** (if not, choose **Value Labels** in the **View** drop-down menu or click the **Labels** icon in the toolbar).

Describing categorical data: Obtaining a frequency distribution

Use
Analyze
    Descriptive Statistics
        Frequencies… procedure described in **4.3.1** to obtain a frequency listing for the variable *Smoker*. In the **Frequencies** dialog box, click **Charts…** . In the **Frequencies: Charts** dialog box, select **Bar Chart(s)**.

Inspect the frequency table in the **SPSS Viewer**. Is the information in the table what you expected? Before taking any steps to remedy the situation, inspect the bar chart as well.

The bar chart

You will notice immediately that, although the variable *Smoker* was supposed to consist only of Yes and No responses, the horizontal axis of the bar chart also shows a bar for 3. There is obviously an error in the data set. Look at the frequency table again. It shows that the 335 cases that were processed included an entry of 3. There is also one missing value labelled *System*. In **Data View**, this will be represented by a full stop. Return to **Data View** by clicking the name of your merged file in the **Task Bar** at the foot of the screen.

In **Data View**, you will see that for the variable *Smoker*, Case 10 has a *3* and Case 14 has no value. The *3* in Case 10 should obviously be a *2*, since there is no entry in *NpDay*. In Case 14, the person is recorded as smoking 5 cigarettes per day, so the missing value should be replaced by *1* (Yes). Such transcription errors are common when one is preparing large data sets, which is why it is so important to screen your data before carrying out any analysis. Sometimes it is more convenient to find suspicious values by highlighting the appropriate variable in **Data View** and selecting
Edit
    Find…
You then enter the suspect value (in this case *3*) in the **Find what** box and click **Find Next**.

To remedy the two transcription errors that you have found, click *3* for Case 10 to get `3 ▼`, click the arrow and select *No* from the choice of options. Do the same for Case 14, but select *Yes* from the choice of options.

Save the corrected data file, using the **Save As** item within the **File** drop-down menu, to a new file name *Questionnaire Data (corrected)* so that you do not confuse it with the uncorrected data file *Merged Questionnaire Data*.

Now re-run the **Frequencies** procedure and notice the differences in the output. Your data-screening operation has detected and rectified two errors in the original data set.

Obtaining a bar chart from the Graphs menu

You can obtain a bar chart directly, without any additional statistics, by selecting
Graphs
     Bar ...
to obtain the **Bar Charts** dialog box. The default settings, i.e., **Simple** and **Summaries for Groups of Cases**, are fine for present purposes.

- Click **Define** to open the **Define Simple Bar: Summaries for Groups of Cases** dialog box. Check that in the **Bars Represent** box, the **N of cases** option is selected. Enter the variable name *Smoker* in the **Category Axis** box.
- Click **OK** to obtain the bar chart.

Editing a bar chart

Now try to edit the bar chart in the **Viewer**. (There will be more on editing graphs in Chapter 5.) Initially, bar charts (and other graphics) appear in colour on the screen. A coloured screen image, however, does not print well in black and white. To make the image suitable for black-and-white printing, some editing is necessary. Proceed as follows.

- Double-click anywhere on the bar chart to open the **Chart Editor** window. To edit any part of the figure, you must select that part of the screen figure and double-click it to open the editing dialog box. At the same time, the item(s) will show a purple colour or appear within a purple frame. So double-click one of the bars to see the **Properties** dialog box or alternatively right click to open the **Properties** dialog box.
- Click the **Fill & Border** tab at the top. Click **Fill** and select the desired colour (e.g. a light grey). If you click **Apply**, you can preview the result in the chart and change to another colour if desired. Once you are satisfied with the change, click **Close**. You can also change the fill pattern by clicking the **Pattern** box at the bottom left of the **Color** panel.

It is possible to control many other features of charts and graphs with the **Chart Editor**. For example, by double-clicking an axis, a dialog box will appear enabling you to label the axis and position the label either centrally or to right or left (use the **Justification** selection). You can also change other aspects of the screen figure, such as the spacing of bars and boxes in graphs. (Select the **Bar Options** tab in the **Properties** dialog box.)

There are many other adjustments that can be made; but the way forward is to try some more editing yourself.

When you have finished editing the graph, return to **SPSS Viewer** by clicking `×` in the top right-hand corner. (You can also leave the Chart Editor by choosing **File** and **Close**.) To save your edited chart, ensure that it has a box around it; if not, click anywhere within the bar chart and a box will appear. Then select

File
 Save

to obtain a directory dialog box for selecting the disk drive and folder for the file.

Try printing out your chart, following the instructions in Section 3.5.

Describing categorical data: Cross-tabulation

The next part of the Exercise is to produce some contingency tables, using the **Crosstabs** procedure (Section 4.3.1). A cross-tabulation is a table showing the frequency of observations in each combination of two categorical variables. Cross-tabulate the *Sex* and *Faculty* of the cases in your merged data set as follows:

Choose
Analyze
 Descriptive Statistics
  Crosstabs

to open the **Crosstabs** dialog box. Enter one of the variables into the **Row(s)** box by clicking its name and then on [▸]. Enter the other variable into the **Column(s)** box. Click **OK**. From an inspection of the output answer the following question:

- **How many females are in the Faculty of Medicine?**

You can re-arrange this table by using the **Pivot** procedure (see Section 3.2.2). Double-click on the table so that a hashed box surrounds it. Select the **Pivot** drop-down menu, then **Pivoting Trays**. Experiment with the data by interchanging the variables among the **Layer**, **Column** and **Row** borders. (Do this by clicking and dragging the variables between the borders in the **Pivoting Trays1** box.)

If you want to save the cross-tabulation output, click the second sub-table containing the cross-tabulation and then **Save**. Complete the dialog box.

Finishing the session

Close down SPSS and any other windows before logging out.

EXERCISE 5

Preparing your Data (continued)

Opening SPSS

For this Exercise, you should have available the corrected merged data set that you corrected in the course of the previous Exercise and saved as *Questionnaire Data (corrected)*. Open SPSS with this data set in the usual way.

Describing interval data

The next part of the Exercise is to explore the *Age* variable by tabulating a range of statistics and drawing a histogram with a superimposed normal curve.

Choose
Analyze
    Descriptive Statistics
        Frequencies…
to see the **Frequencies** dialog box. Transfer *Age* to the *Variables* box.

Click **Statistics…** to see the **Frequencies: Statistics** dialog box. Choose Quartiles, Mean, Median, Std. Deviation, Range, Minimum and Maximum. Click **Continue**.

Back in the **Frequencies** dialog box, turn off **Display Frequency Tables**.

Now choose
Charts
    Histograms
and click the **With Normal Curve** option. Click **Continue** to return to the **Frequencies** dialog box.

- **Edit the histogram to make it suitable for black-and-white printing**
- **Print the histogram**.

Manipulation of the data set – transforming variables

It is sometimes useful to change the data set in some way. For instance, in the current data set, some people have entered their weight in stones and pounds, others in kilograms. Likewise, some people may have entered their height in feet and inches (or just inches), others in metres. In order to have useful data on weight and height, you must use the same units of measurement. In this Exercise we shall adopt metric units (kilograms and metres). This will necessitate converting any other measurements into metric measurements. Use the **Compute** procedure (Section 4.4.2) by selecting
Transform
    Compute …

to see the **Compute Variable** dialog box. In the **Target Variable** box, type the name of the variable (*Kilos*) which contains the kilograms data. In the **Numeric Expression** box, enter the conversion function: entering **(Stones*14 + Pounds)** * **0.453** to convert pounds to kilograms. (One pound is 0.453 kilograms and stones convert to pounds by multiplying by 14.) Note that, in computing, the symbol * is used for multiplication. Do not click **OK** yet!

There remains one further problem: what about those cases whose weight is already in *Kilos* and do not have any values in the *Stones* and *Pounds* variables? If the formula above were to be immediately applied, these people would end up with no values in the *Kilos* column.

To convert only the cases with stones and pounds measurements, you must select the **If** box in the **Compute Variable** dialog box, then the **Include if case satisfies condition** box and enter the following expression **stones > 0** which tells the program to calculate the kilograms if the entry in *Stones* is nonzero. Select **Continue** and then **OK**.

You will receive a message which asks **Change existing variable?**. Select the **OK** option. Now the program will calculate all the missing *Kilos* data and enter them in the data set. Check that it has done this. Save the file using the **Save As** option, giving the amended file a new name (e.g. *Metric Data*). This ensures that you still have a copy of the old file, in case you have made any mistakes in calculation and you wish to retrieve the old data at some future time. (It is often regarded as a safer procedure to recode data into a new variable since it allows one to check that the correct recoding procedure has been requested. This has not been done here because we need to preserve the values in *kilos* already present for some cases.)

Now do a similar conversion for the height data, converting feet and inches to metres. To do this you will need to know that there are 12 inches in a foot and 1 inch is 0.0254 metres. Work out a conversion factor with this in mind. Remember to change the condition to **Feet >0**. When you have converted the height data, save the file again, this time by simply clicking **Save** rather than **Save As** since you have already nominated *Metric Data* as the new file.

Describing interval data – means of cases categorised by a grouping variable

You can obtain a table of means for one variable at different categories (or combinations) of another variable (or variables). Use the **Means** procedure described in Section 4.3.2 to obtain a two-way table of means for *Metres* by *Sex*. Then use the same procedure to obtain a three-way table of *Kilos* by *Sex* by *Faculty*. (Look carefully at Section 4.3.2 to see how to layer the variables, using **Next**, to produce the three-way table.)

- **Print the output of this exercise.**

Finishing the session

Close down SPSS and any other windows before logging out of the computer.

CHAPTER 5

Graphs and charts

5.1   Introduction
5.2   Bar charts
5.3   Error bar charts
5.4   Pie charts
5.5   Line graphs
5.6   Scatterplots

5.1   INTRODUCTION

SPSS offers a wide range of graphs and charts. We shall first consider some general points about graph-drawing in SPSS. It is worth noting that the most elaborate charts do not necessarily bring out the results of an investigation in the clearest way. Three-dimensional effects, for example, though they may be aesthetically attractive, can obscure the very point that you are trying to bring out.

5.1.1   Graphs and charts on SPSS

There are several different ways of producing graphs with SPSS. There is a selection of procedures on the **Graphs** menu. But graphs are options in procedures in other menus as well. For instance, there is a **Charts** option in the **Frequencies** procedure. These are **standard** charts; although they can be customised to a considerable extent. The appearance of graphs can be controlled to an even greater extent as **interactive charts**, which are available on the **Interactive** (or **I-graph**) submenu. We shall use the **Interactive** (or **I-graph**) system only to produce a **bar chart with error bars**, a graph which is not available in the standard **Error Bar** procedure.

For best results, the data set should be prepared beforehand. It's easier to change variable names and labels in **Variable View** first. If there are missing data, specify beforehand whether they should be included in the chart. Missing data can be excluded from graphs by turning off the **Display groups defined by missing values** box in the **Options** dialog box.

Once you are in a chart procedure, it's often easier to add a title first, rather than at the editing stage after the chart has been produced. (Note, however, that for **boxplots**, titles can only be added at the editing stage.)

When completing a dialog box for a graph, you can often leave some boxes unchecked. For example, with a large data set, the **Label Cases by** option can clutter the output with too many labels. The acid test of whether enough information has been specified in a dialog box is whether the **OK** button is enabled: if it isn't, more information is needed.

5.1.2 Viewing a chart

A chart in the Viewer may occasionally disappear from the screen. You can recall it by clicking its icon in the left-hand pane of the Viewer. If you are working in another window, you can restore the chart by selecting it from the **Window** menu at the top of the screen.

You can make a chart narrower by clicking it and dragging the right-hand handle of the surrounding frame leftwards. If you wish to change the aspect ratio of **all** charts to make them narrower, select
Edit
    Options
        Charts
and amend the value in the **Chart Aspect Ratio** box. The default value is *1.25*, but if you change that to, say, *1*, graphs and charts will appear narrower.

Unwanted images use up memory. Bear in mind that images can always be recreated from saved data files. Save only those that you need at the moment.

Once a dialog box for a chart has been completed, the **command syntax** (see Chapter 15) can be saved to a file from which the (unedited) graph can be generated at any time in the future. Graphs that have been edited can be stored as **chart templates** for future use. Chart templates are very useful for generating whole sets of similar graphs for analogous tables of data, such as those at different layers of a multi-way table.

Editing charts

SPSS provides a special **Chart Editor** for graphic material. (There is another editor for **interactive graphs**.) The **Chart Editor** allows a wide range of changes to be made to a graph or chart; though proficiency takes practice. Enter the **Chart Editor** by double-clicking anywhere in the image. A single click will draw a single frame around the image. After double-clicking, the original image is shaded and a copy of it is shown in the **Chart Editor**.

The **Chart Editor** allows the user to change text, colours, type of graphic, title, axis ticks and labels, and other features. Many of these changes are made by double-clicking the item in the chart and completing dialogs.

For black-and-white printing, it is usually best to use the **Chart Editor** to remove the colours and replace them with patterns. Alternatively, the default setting for charts can be changed from cycling through colour to cycling through patterns. To do this
- Choose
Edit
    Options...
and select the **Charts** tab in the **Options** dialog box.
- Within the **Style Cycle Preference** selection panel, select **Cycle through patterns only**.

- Click **Fills...** and select whichever pattern you wish for **Simple Charts** and delete the empty pattern box in **Grouped Charts** by clicking the radio button for **Grouped Charts**, selecting the empty box pattern and clicking **Remove**. Click **Continue**.
- Click **Apply** and then **OK**.

This change will only apply for the current session if your computer is part of a networked system.

5.2 BAR CHARTS

Simple bar charts

Output 1 shows a **simple bar chart** summarising the results of the drug experiment (see Table 1 in Section 2.1.4).

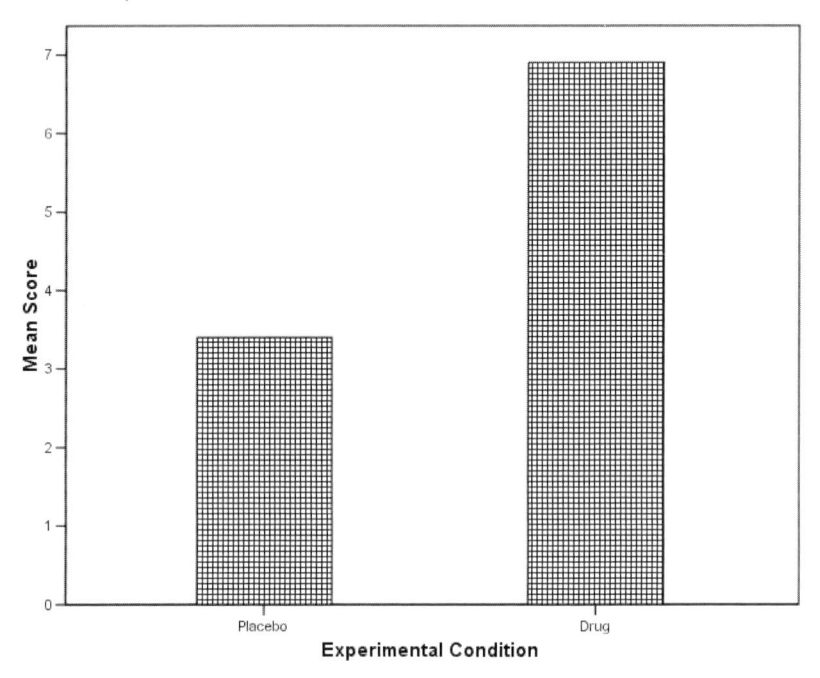

Output 1. A simple bar chart with Experimental Condition as the category variable

A simple bar chart shows only a single categorical variable, in this case the Experimental Condition under which the participants in the study performed.

Clustered bar charts

A **clustered bar chart** shows two variables. On the horizontal axis, is the categorical variable (in the present study *Experimental Condition*). In addition, however, the data in each category are subdivided according to a second, **cluster** variable. Output 2 shows a clustered bar chart

Graphs and charts

summarising the results of the drug experiment. On the horizontal axis, as before, is the independent variable *Experimental Condition*. In addition, the variable *Gender* has been used to cluster the data under the separate *Placebo* and *Drug* conditions.

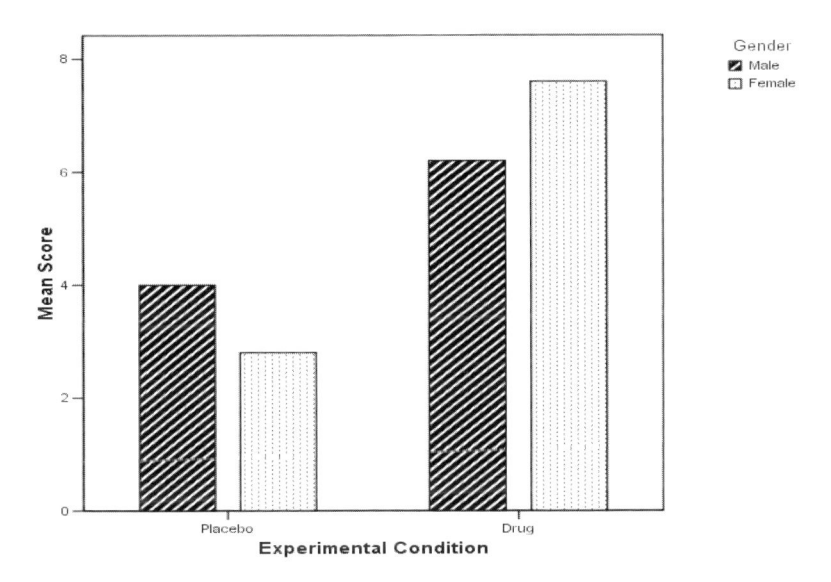

Output 2. A clustered bar chart, with Experimental Condition as the categorical variable and Gender as the cluster variable

To obtain such a clustered bar graph, proceed as follows.

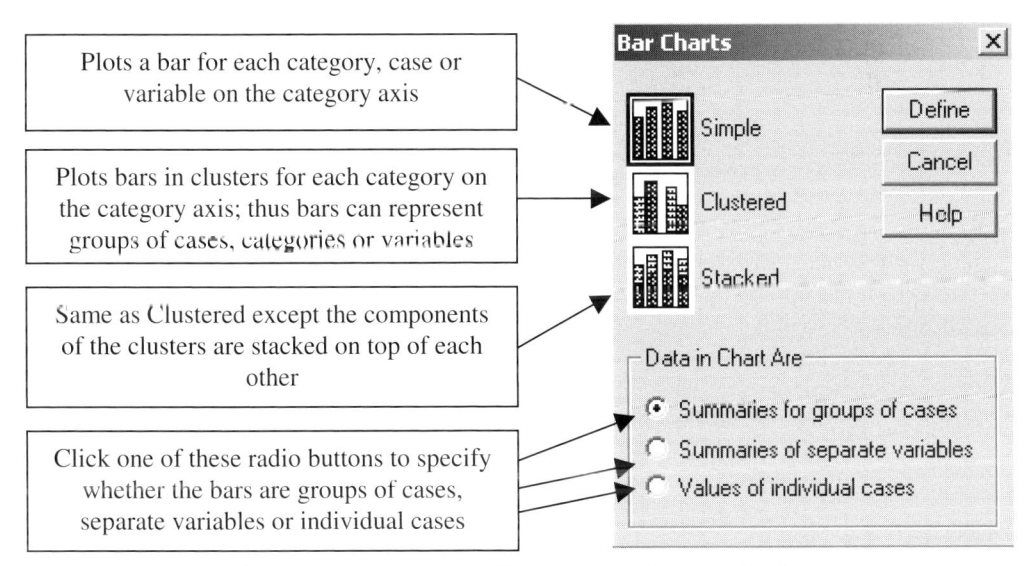

Figure 1. The **Bar Charts** dialog box with **Clustered** and **Summaries for groups of cases** selected

- Choose
  Graphs
      Bar...
  to obtain the **Bar Charts** dialog box (Figure 1).
- Choose **Clustered** by clicking the middle diagram to get the black border (which, initially, will be round the **Simple** option) to move down to the **Clustered** diagram.
- Click **Define** to obtain another dialog box with the rather ponderous caption: **Define Clustered Bar: Summaries for Groups of Cases** (the completed dialog box is shown in Figure 2).
- Transfer the variable names as shown in Figure 2.

[Dialog box: **Define Clustered Bar: Summaries for Groups of Cases**

- Case Number [Case]
- Bars Represent:
  - N of cases
  - % of cases
  - Cum. n of cases
  - Cum. % of cases
  - Other summary function
    - Variable: MEAN(Score)
    - Change Summary...
- Category Axis: Experimental Conditio
- Define Clusters by: Gender
- Template: Use chart specifications from: File...
- Buttons: OK, Paste, Reset, Cancel, Help, Titles..., Options...

Annotation: Click **Other summary function** radio button and then transfer *Score* to here]

The variable name *Experimental Condition* has been transferred to the **Category Axis** box in order to plot a cluster of bars for each condition respectively

The variable name *Gender* has been transferred to the **Define Clusters by** box to specify the components of the clusters

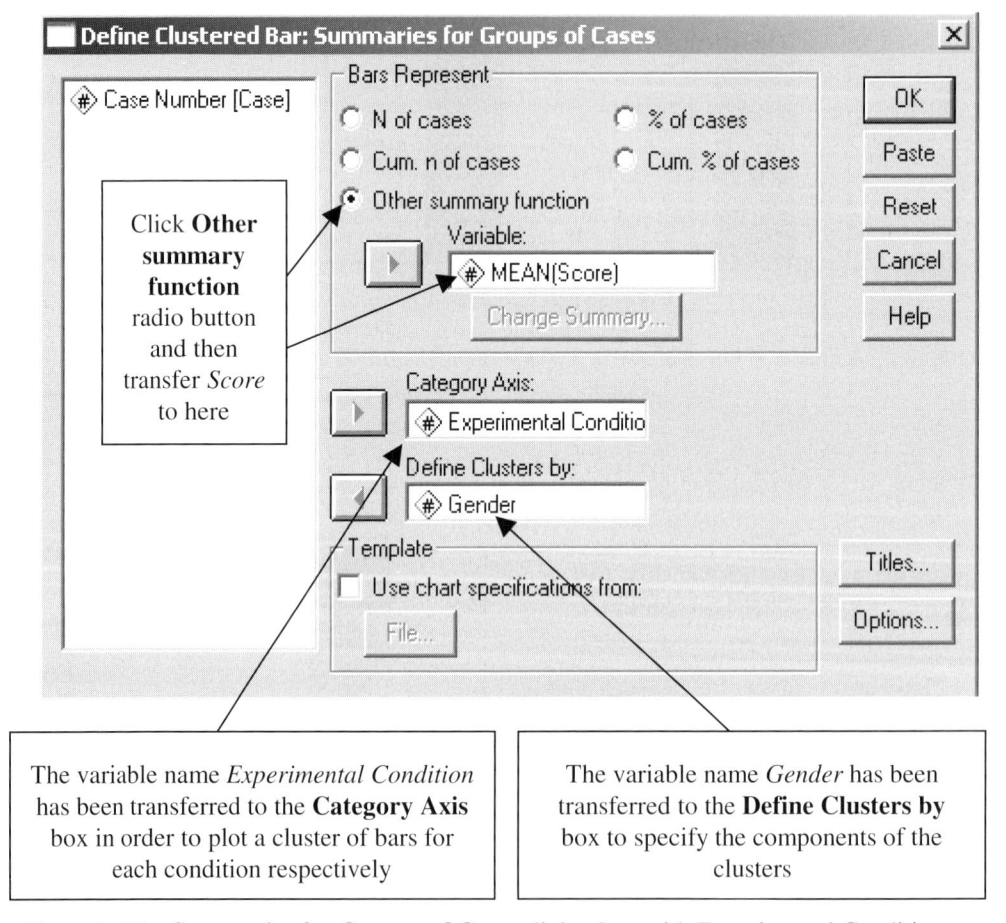

Figure 2. The **Summaries for Groups of Cases** dialog box with Experimental Condition as the categorical variabled and Gender as the cluster variable

- Click **OK** to obtain a clustered bar chart similar to that shown in Output 2.
- If the chart is to be printed in black and white, it is best to use the **Chart Editor** to change the colours of the graph to shades of grey. In fact, we have found it most effective to change the fill colour to white and mark the bars with distinguishing fill patterns.

- Alternatively changing the default **Chart** options to **Cycle through patterns only** as described in Section 5.1.2 renders editing unnecessary.

Editing a bar chart

- Double-click the chart to open the **Chart Editor**.
- To change, say, the bars representing *Males*, click within the *Gender* key the identification for Male. All the bars representing males will then appear with a purple frame.
- Double-click any of the purple-framed bars or right click to open the **Properties** dialog box (top section shown in Figure 3).
- To change the colour and fill of the bars, click the **Fill & Border** tab to open a dialog box for selecting fill colours, border colours and fill patterns.
- To change the fill colour, click the **Fill** box and then select a colour from the right-hand palette of colours, white and black.
- To change the fill pattern, click the **Pattern** box and select a fill.
- Click **Apply** to make these changes in the chart without leaving the editor.
- The bar width and the gaps between the clusters of bars can be changed by clicking the **Bar Options** tab and moving the sliders or changing the numbers in the % boxes.
- The variable bars can be rearranged by clicking the **Variables** tab, selecting the variable to be moved, pressing the right-hand mouse button, and then selecting the move to be made. For example, you can see what the chart would look like if the clustering was done by *Experimental Condition* rather than by *Gender*.
- Other changes can also be made, such as alterations to the axis labels and the bar identification key.

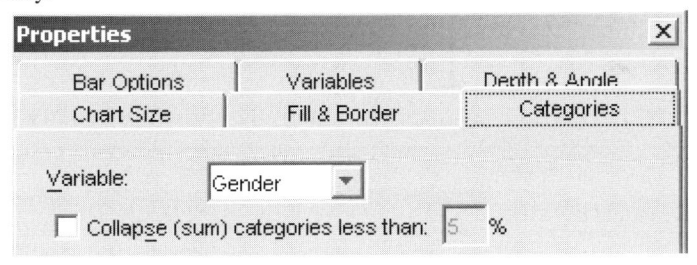

Figure 3. The top section of the chart **Properties** dialog box showing the various tabs

SPSS offers helpful tutorials on editing charts. You can access these by clicking
Help
    Tutorial
and then double-clicking each of
Tutorials
    Creating and Editing Charts

The usual buttons in the right-hand bottom corner of each page of the tutorial enable the user to see the list of items (upward arrow) and to navigate forward and backward through the tutorial (right and left arrows).

5.3 ERROR BAR CHARTS

An alternative to a bar graph is an **Error Bar chart**, in which the mean of the scores in a particular category is represented by a single point and the spread (confidence interval for the mean, multiples of the standard deviation or multiples of the standard error of the mean – the user can choose between these) is represented by a vertical line (T-bar or whiskers) passing through the point. Output 3 is a clustered error bar chart summarising the results of the drug experiment.

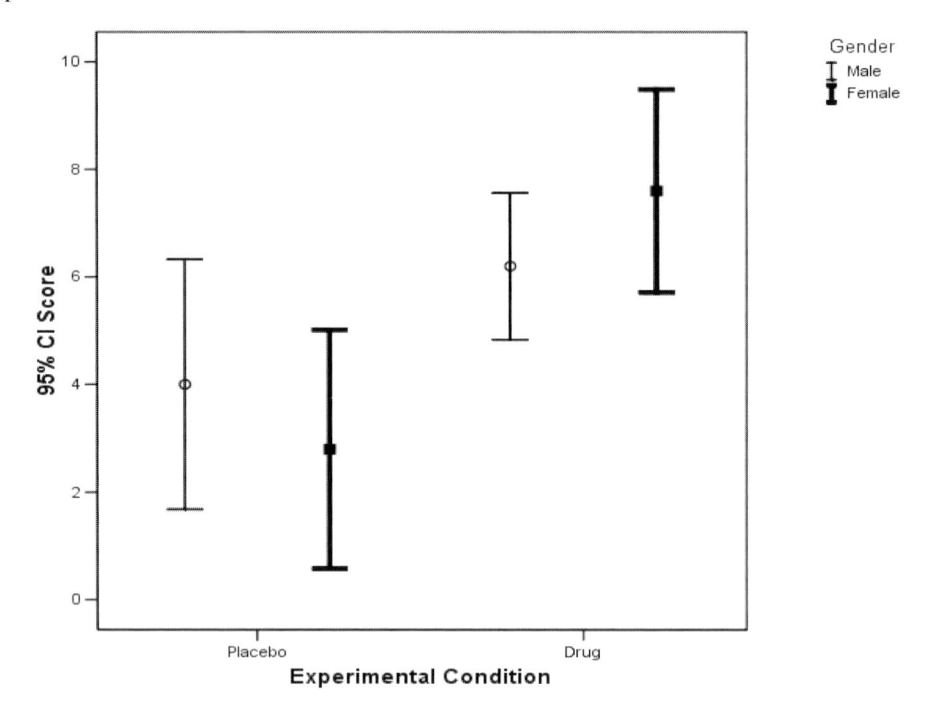

Output 3. A clustered error bar chart with Experimental Condition as the category variable and Gender as the cluster variable

To produce an error bar chart choose
Graphs
    Error Bar…
to open the **Error Bar** dialog box and complete it exactly as if you were ordering a clustered bar chart.

You will notice that in Output 3, there are no lines linking the error bars. This is entirely appropriate, since the bars represent qualitatively distinct categories. In other circumstances, however, as when the categories are ordered, it may be desirable to join up the points (when there are more than two) with interpolation lines. This is easily achieved by clicking the means to highlight them when in the **Chart Editor** and selecting the **Add interpolation line** icon from the **Chart Editor** toolbar.

Clustered bar charts with error bars

SPSS's interactive graphing procedure can also be used to produce more complex graphs, such as clustered bar charts with error bars. This hybrid of bar charts and error bar charts is common in the literature. Output 4 shows such a graph of the results of the drug experiment.

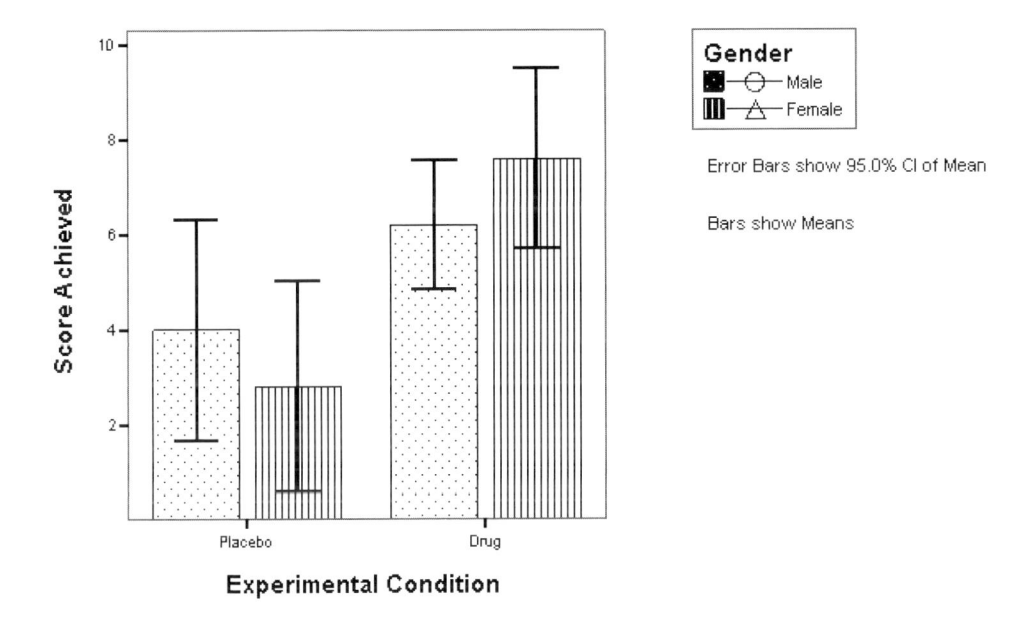

Output 4. A clustered bar chart with error bars

To produce a clustered bar chart with errors bars, you will have to use the **I-graph** system.
- Choose
  Graphs
    Interactive
      Bar
  to see the **Create Chart** dialog box, which is completed as shown in Figure 5. In **I-graph**, the variable names are transferred by clicking and dragging them from the panel on the left.
- After transferring *Experimental Condition* to the **X Axis** box, right-mouse click the variable name and select **Categorical** from the choice. This will ensure a neater form of graph.
- Note especially that *Gender* has been transferred to the **Style** rather than the **Color** box in the **Legend Variables** panel in order to create the bar fill patterns in Output 4. If you wish the bars to be coloured, transfer *Gender* to the **Color** box instead.
- When *Gender* is transferred, a warning box will appear (Figure 4). Click **Convert** to make the variable categorical. Check that the display to the right shows **Cluster**: if it shows **Stack**, click the arrow on the right and select **Cluster**.

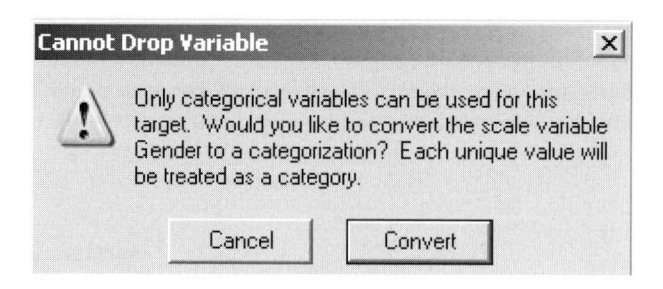

Figure 4. Warning box to ensure that the clustering variable is categorical. Click **Convert**

- Click the **Error Bars** tab at the top of the **Create Bar Chart** dialog box (Figure 6) and ensure that there is a tick in the **Display Error Bars** check box. You can also select **Standard Deviation** or **Standard Error of Mean** instead of **Confidence Interval for Mean** if preferred. The slider or the number box allow you to change the **CI percentage** or the **number of SDs** desired.
- Click **OK** to run the procedure.

The chart will appear in colour in the **Viewer**, with the error bars partially obscured.

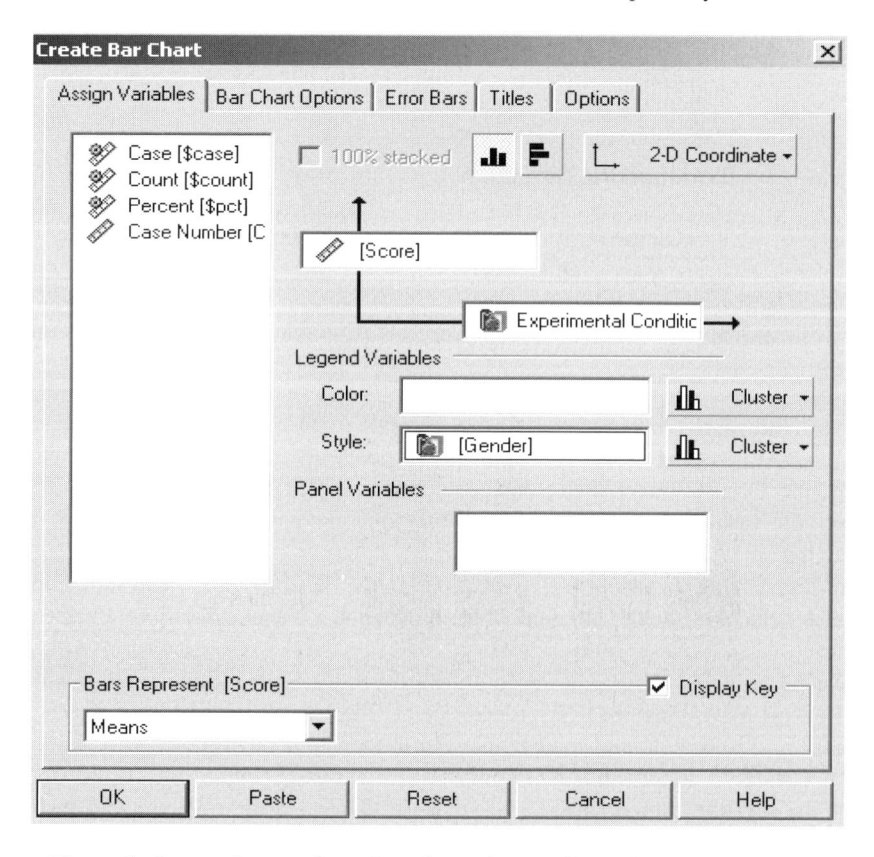

Figure 5. Interactive graph settings for a clustered bar chart with error bars

Graphs and charts 143

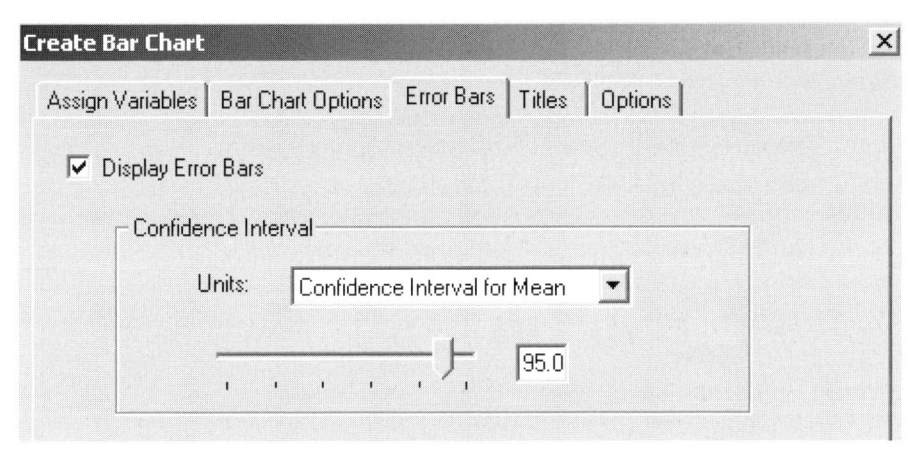

Figure 6. Top part of the **Create Bar Chart** dialog box with **Display Error Bars** check box ticked and **95% Confidence Interval for Mean** selected

- Double-click the image to enter the **Interactive Graph** editor (Figure 7).

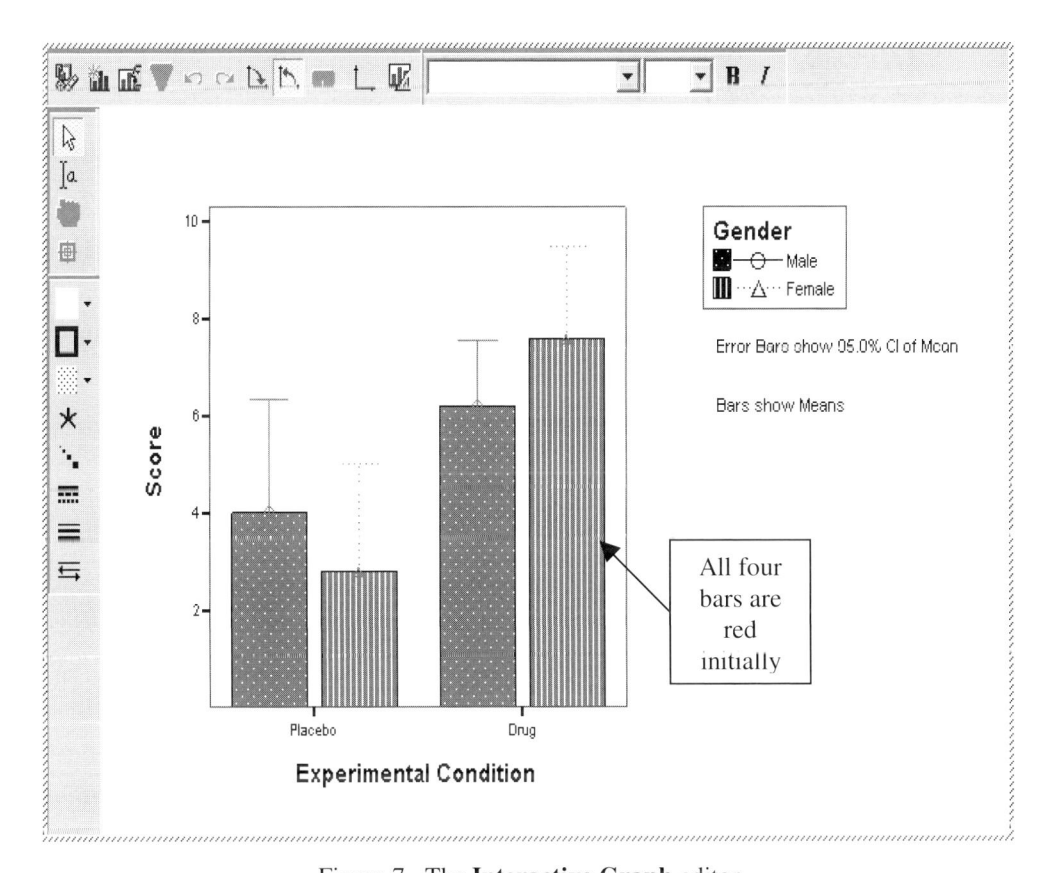

Figure 7. The **Interactive Graph** editor

- To change the appearance of the large bars so as to make the lower halves of the error bars visible, double-click anywhere within the large bars to open the **Bars** dialog box (Figure 8).

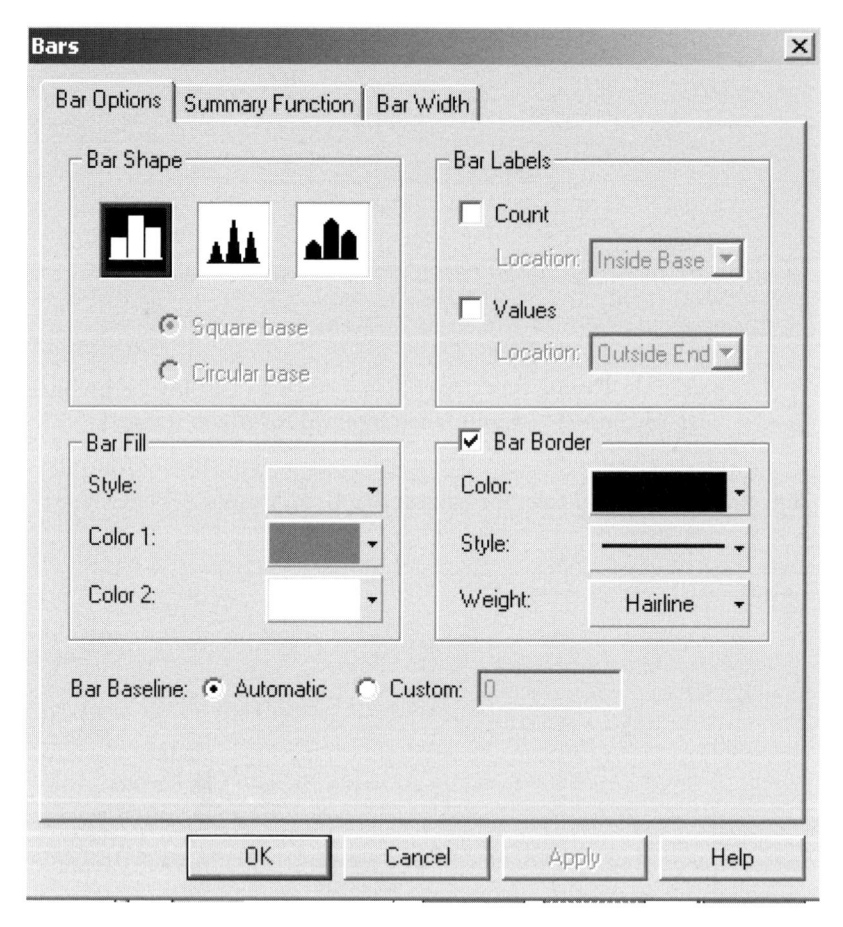

Figure 8. The **Bars** dialog box for changing the shape, colour and width of bars

- Click the patch of colour (initially it is red) in the box to the right of **Color 1** to open a colour selection panel. We recommend the selection of white. Click the **Apply** button and observe what happens to the bars (you may require to slide the dialog box to one side to see the chart underneath). To retain the appearance of the patterned fill, click the panel to the right of **Color 2**, select black, click **Apply** and observe that the patterned fills re-appear.
- To make the bars narrower, select the **Bar Width** tab and adjust the **Bar Width** slider (or change the value in the box). Do not adjust the **Cluster Width** else the error bars will no longer be central to the bars.
- To make the error bars more visible, we recommend changing them all to solid lines and making them thicker. Click on any of the error bars to open the **Error Bar** dialog box (Figure 9). Click the **Color** panel in the **Error Bar Style** panel and change it from its initial red to black. Click the **Weight** panel and select **1½ pt**. Click off the **Display**

Symbol check box to remove the symbol representing the means. Click the **Width** tab and change the width to **20%**. Finally click **OK**.

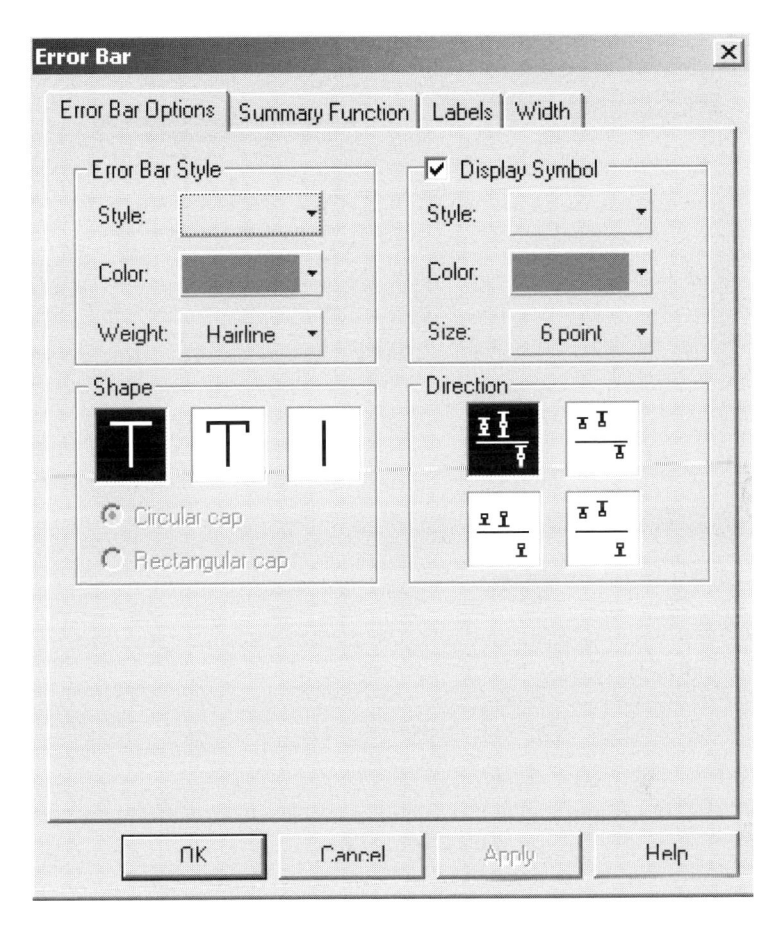

Figure 9. The **Error Bar** dialog box for changing the appearance of the error bars

- Finally to make all the error bars into solid lines, double-click anywhere within the Gender legend box (top right of Figure 8) to open the **Style Legend** dialog box (Figure 10). Select the **Line** tab and click on the line to be changed (here it is Female). Select the new style to be adopted from the **Line Styles** panel (e.g. the solid line) and click **OK**.

In Output 4, the error bars were clearly visible against the grey and white patterned bars representing the means as the result of all these editing changes in the **I-graph Chart Editor**.

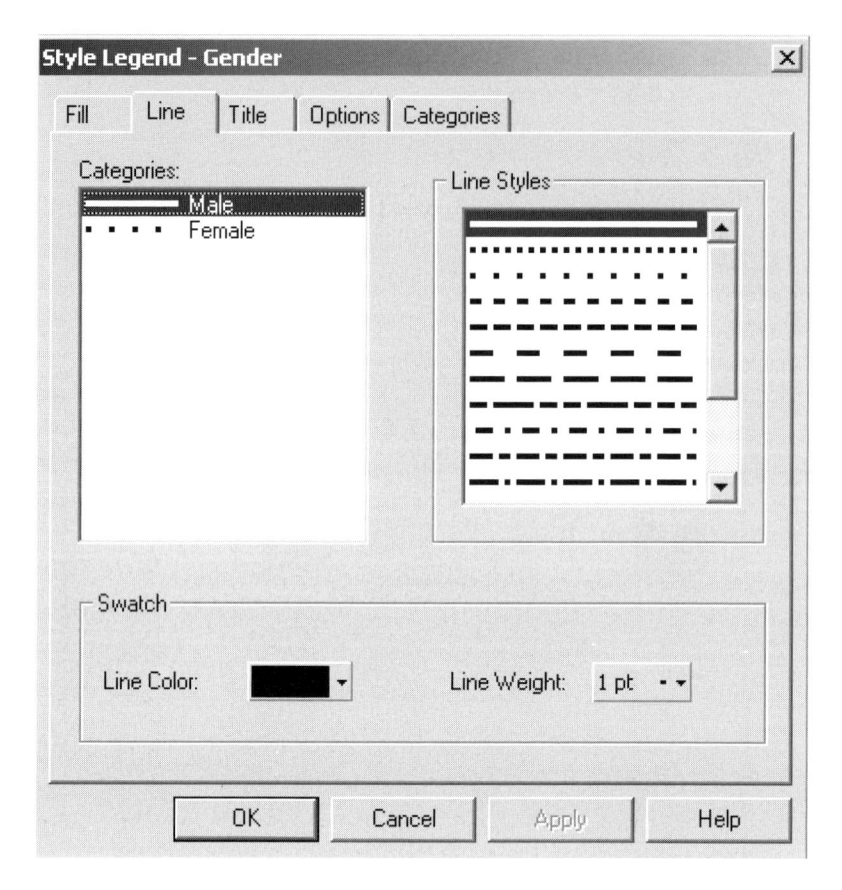

Figure 10. The **Style Legend** dialog box enabling changes to be made to the appearances of the error bar lines

5.4 PIE CHARTS

The **pie chart** is an alternative to a bar graph which provides a picturesque display of the frequency distribution of a qualitative variable. It is a particularly valuable kind of graph for displaying the relative frequencies of the same set of categories over time or for bringing out the varying compositions of two things.

To illustrate the production of a pie chart, we shall use the medical data set of data on blood group, gender, height and weight.

To draw a pie chart of the categories within *Blood Group*:
- Choose
    Graphs
        Pie…
    to open the **Pie Charts** dialog box (not reproduced here).
- Click **Define** to open the **Define Pie: Summaries for Groups of Cases** dialog box (the completed version is shown in Figure 11).

Graphs and charts

> Transfer the variable name Blood Group here in order to define the categories of the slices

> Specify what the slices are to represent (here it is the percentage of cases)

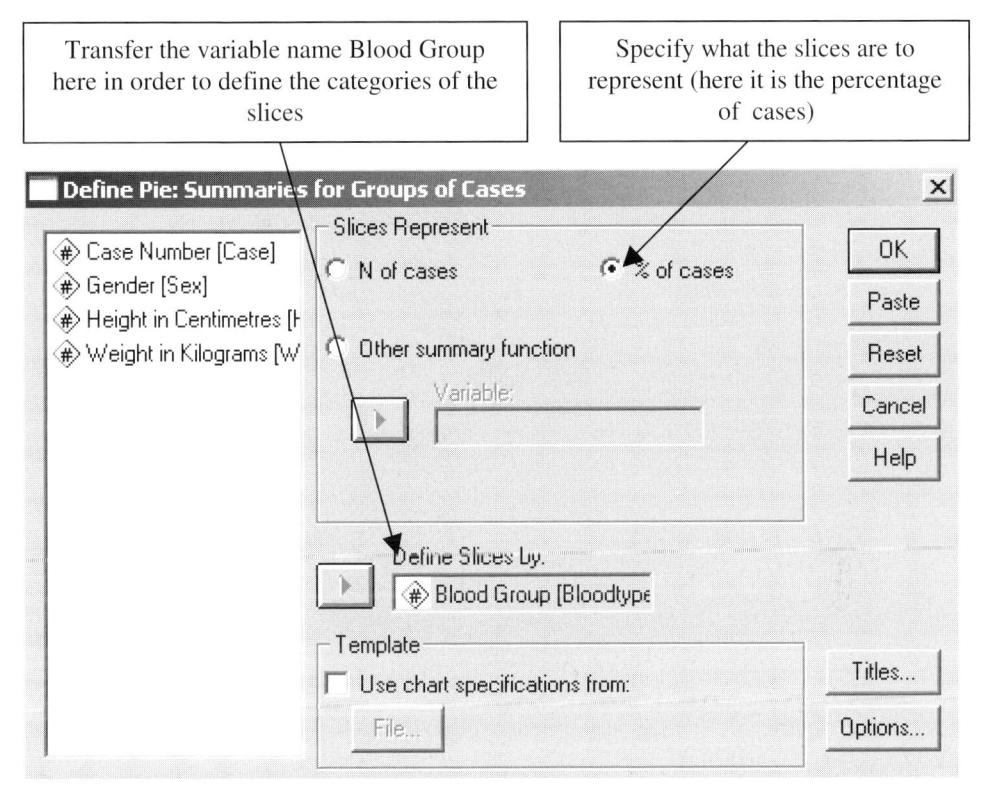

Figure 11. The **Summaries for Groups of Cases** dialog box with Blood Group selected as the variable defining the slices.

- Click Blood Group and on ▶ to paste the name into the **Define Slices by** box.
- Click **% of cases** so that the slices represent percentages rather than the values of N.
- Finally, it is desirable to have a title: click **Titles** and type the desired title into the box (e.g. *Blood Group Distribution*), click **Continue** and then **OK** to draw the pie chart, an edited version of which is shown in Output 5.

The pie chart in Output 5 has been edited by changing the colours to grey or white, and adding some patterns in the **Fill** dialog box. Alternatively, it would not require editing if the option described in Section 5.1.2 is adopted for cycling through patterns rather than through colours. It is also possible to rotate the pie if it is desired to bring a particular slice to the top. Slices can have labels within them rather than in a key and can be 'exploded' i.e. moved out a little from the circle for emphasis (Output 6).

> See Section 5.1.2

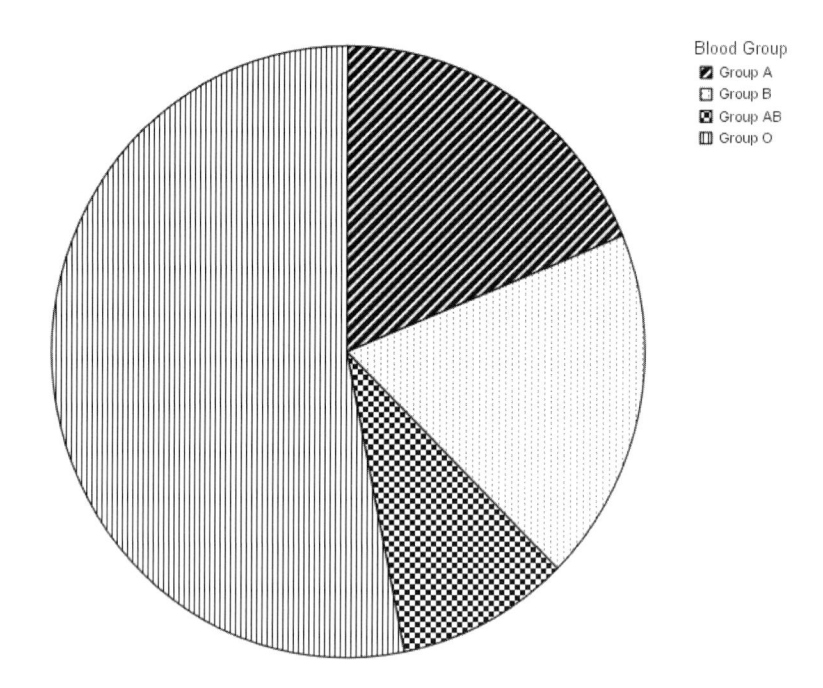

Output 5. The edited Pie Chart of the distribution of Blood Group

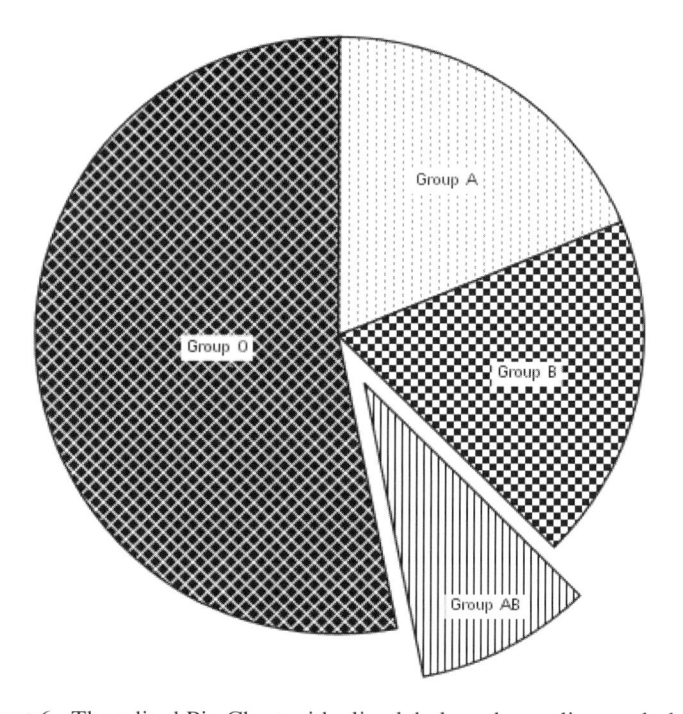

Output 6. The edited Pie Chart with slice labels and one slice exploded

5.5 LINE GRAPHS

Suppose that, in our analysis of the medical data, we want to produce a **line graph** of mean weight against height. Along the horizontal axis, the total range of heights is divided into fixed intervals. Above the mid point of each interval is plotted the mean of the weights of people whose heights fall within the interval and adjacent points are joined by straight lines. The total range of heights of the participants is split into, say, five intervals by using the **Visual Bander** procedure (see Section 4.4.3) to create a new variable *HeightBands* consisting of the intervals <155, 156-165, 166-175, 176-185, >185. Specify the upper limits (155, 165, 175, 185, 210) in the **Value** cells and the intervals in the **Label** cells.

See Section 4.4.3

- Choose
  Graphs
     Line...
  and completing the **Line Charts** (choose **Simple** and click **Define**) and the **Define Simple Line: Summaries for Groups of Cases** dialog boxes (Figure 12).

To specify a summary statistic for the line graph, click **Other summary function** radio button, highlight the relevant variable, and transfer the variable name to the **Variable** box

The default statistic is MEAN. A different statistic can be specified by clicking the **Change Summary...** box and making a selection from the **Summary Function** dialog box

Transfer the variable name of the variable defining the values of the x-axis of the line to here

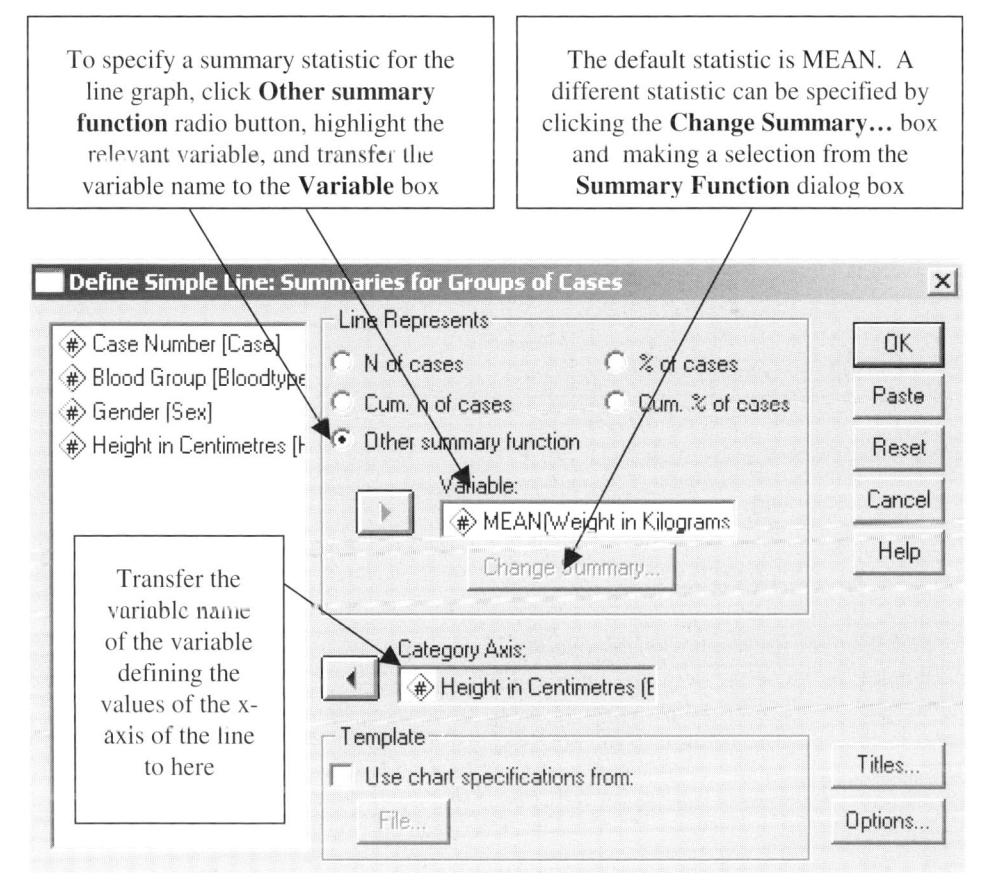

Figure 12. The **Summaries for Groups of Cases** dialog box for mean Weight categorised by ranges of Height in Centimetres (Banded)

The edited line graph is shown in Output 7. The editing operations included the following:

1. Remove *(Banded)* from the X-axis label. Double-click the label so that it is surrounded with a purple frame and click the cursor within the frame: You can now add or delete sections of the label.

2. Insert the filled circles for the means by clicking on the line to highlight it (it changes to purple) and then clicking on the **Show Line Markers** icon (third icon from the right in the top toolbar). Initially unfilled circles will appear: These can be made solid by clicking on them and changing **Fill** to black in the **Marker** box.

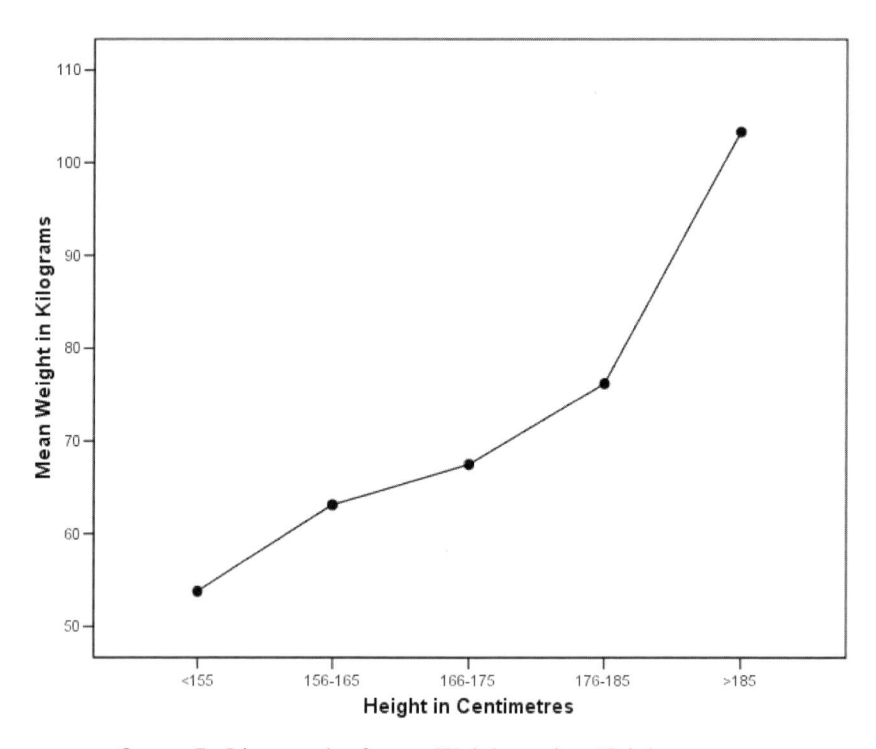

Output 7. Line graph of mean Weight against Height category

5.6 SCATTERPLOTS

Another diagram for displaying the relationship between two variables is the **scatterplot,** in which the scales of values of the two variables (such as height and weight) are set out on the horizontal and vertical axis and each person is represented as a point whose co-ordinates are his or her particular height and weight. A scatterplot should always be plotted and examined before a correlation coefficient is calculated (Chapter 11) or a regression analysis is carried out (Chapter 12).

See Chaps. 11 & 12

Graphs and charts

To obtain the scatterplot of weight against height:
- Choose
  Graphs
      Scatter...
  to open the **Scatterplot** dialog box (not shown here).
- Click **Define** to open the **Simple Scatterplot** dialog box.
- Transfer the variable names as shown in Figure 13.
- Click **OK**.

The output is shown in Output 8.

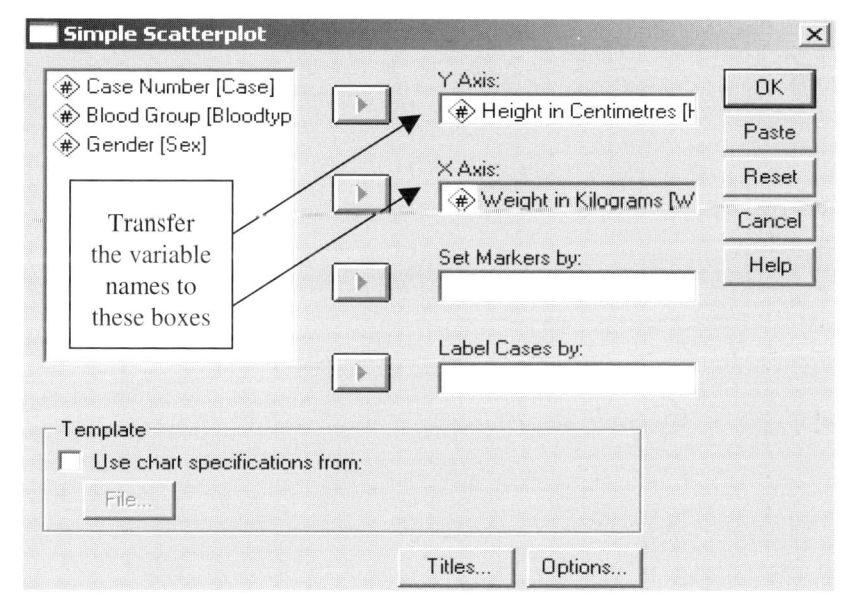

Figure 13   The **Simple Scatterplot** dialog box. A scatterplot of Height against Weight has been specified

Inspection of the scatterplot shows that the line graph in Output 7, although bringing out a clear positive relationship between height and weight when average weights are considered, masks considerable individual variability. The heights of people of around 50 kg in weight range from just over 140 cm to 175 cm in height.

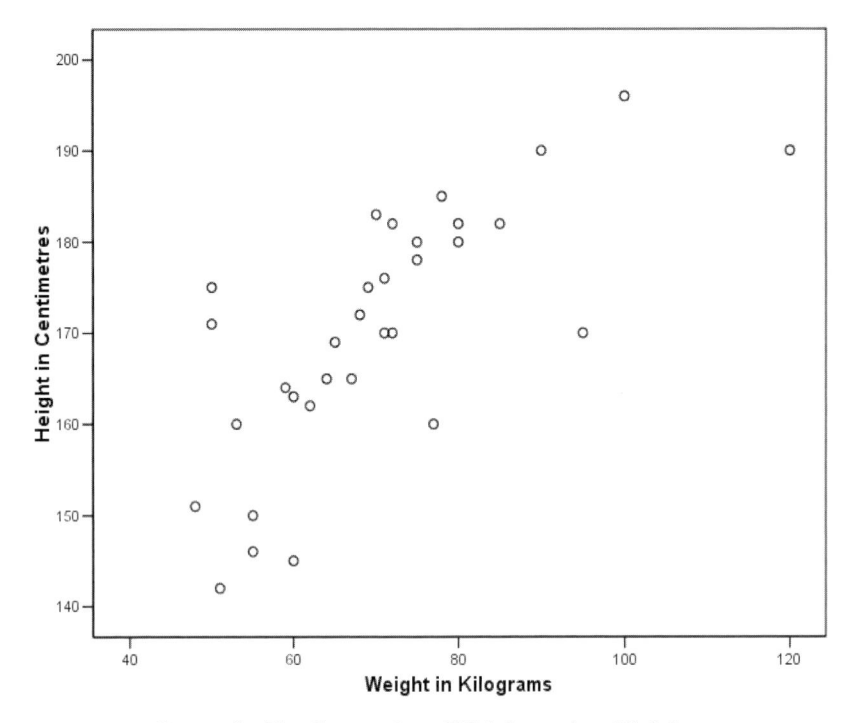

Output 8. The Scatterplot of Height against Weight

EXERCISE 6

Charts and graphs

Opening SPSS

Open the data file *Metric Data* which you saved in the previous Exercise.

Charts and graphs

1) Stem-and-leaf plot and boxplot

Use the **Explore** procedure (Section 4.3.2) to produce stem-and-leaf plots and boxplots of *Metres* categorised by *Sex*. Once you are in the **Explore** dialog box, remember to click the **Plots** radio button at the bottom left to suppress the Statistics output. Click **Plots...**, ensure that **Stem-and-leaf** has been selected (if not, click the check-box) and return to the **Explore** dialog box by clicking **Continue**. Enter the variable name *Case* into the **Label Cases by...** box.

The **stem-and-leaf plot** provides more information about the original data than does a histogram. As in a histogram, the length of each row corresponds to the number of cases that fall into a particular interval. However, the stem-and-leaf plot represents each case with a numeric value that corresponds to the actual observed value. This is done by dividing observed values into two components – the leading digit or digits, called the **stem**, and a trailing digit, called the **leaf**. For example, the value 64 would have a stem of 6 and a leaf of 4. In the case of heights in metres, the stems are the metres expressed to the first decimal place, the leaves are the second decimal place. Thus the **modal** height (i.e. the most frequent height) for males is shown with a stem of 17 (1.7 metres), the leaves being the second decimal place. If there are too many 'leaves' for one stem, the stem is repeated in further rows.

The **boxplot** is another type of display, which is more fully explained in Section 4.3.2. The central box spans 50% of the cases (those between the upper and lower quartiles) and the extensions (**whiskers**) cover the remaining cases, excluding **outliers** (shown as o's) or **extreme scores** (shown as asterisks).

- **Prepare the boxplot for printing in black-and-white, and print the Output.**
- **Within the female group, which stem contains the most leaves?**

Examine the boxplot for males and note the case numbers of the outliers so that you can check their actual heights in the data set. To locate a specific case in the data set, select

Data
> **Go to Case ...**

to obtain the **Go to Case** dialog box. You then enter the required case number and click **OK**.

- Write down the actual heights of the males identified as outliers on the box plots.

2) Bar charts

Draw a bar chart of *Kilos* and *Metres* by *Sex* using the **Bar** procedure on the **Graphs** menu.

Choose
Graphs
> **Bar**
>> **Clustered**

and select the radio button for **Summaries of Separate Variables** in the **Data in Chart Are** box. Click **Define** and enter *Kilos* and *Metres* into the **Bars Represent** box and *Sex* into the **Category Axis** box.

- Study the chart produced. Does this seem a sensible graphic representation of the height and weight variables? If not, why not? You do not need to print the chart, but make a note of why the representation is not appropriate and suggest a better way of displaying the mean heights and weights of subjects split by sex.

The take-home message is that SPSS may produce the graph that you ask for, but the end result may not be a sensible representation of the data. It may be helpful to draw a rough sketch of what you expect the graph to look like before requesting SPSS to produce it.

Plot a new bar chart of the mean number of cigarettes smoked (*NpDay*) categorised by *Sex* and by *Faculty*. Do this by choosing
Graphs
> **Bar**
>> **Clustered**

and select the radio button for **Summaries for groups of cases** in the **Data in Chart Are** box (this is the default selection). Click **Define** and then click **Other summary function** within the **Bars Represent** box. Then enter *NpDay* into the **Variable** box (it will appear as **MEAN(Number of cigarettes per day [NpDay])**), *Sex* in the **Category Axis** box, and *Faculty* in the **Define Clusters by** box. Click the **Options...** button and check the radio button marked **Display groups defined by missing values**. Click **Continue** and then **OK** to run the procedure.

In the **SPSS Viewer** window you should see a bar chart arranged by sex, with each cluster consisting of bars representing the three Faculties and Missing (apparently no female in the Missing category smokes).

Now specify a chart with four clusters (Faculties) of two (sex) instead of two clusters (sex) of four (Faculties). This can be done by returning to the dialog box and changing *Sex* and *Faculty* around.

Try changing the colours into black-and-white **Fill Patterns**. This is a two-stage procedure involving changing each colour to white and then selecting a different fill pattern for each. Follow the steps described at the end of Section 5.2.

Add a title by choosing
Chart
   Title...

and entering a title into the **Title 1:** box. Change the justification to **Centre**.

Finally return the edited barchart to the **SPSS Viewer** by closing the **Chart Editor** (by clicking ⊠ in the top right-hand corner). Try printing the edited barchart from the **SPSS Viewer**.

Pie chart

Draw a pie chart (see Section 5.4) for the *Status* variable and give the chart a title, including your **own** name in the title (e.g. Pie Chart of Status produced by Mary Smith) by selecting
Graphs
   Pie...
to open the **Pie Charts** dialog box.

To show the count in each slice (or perhaps the percentage), proceed as follows:
- Double-click near the pie chart to open the **Chart Editor** window.
- Click on one of the pie slices to highlight them with a purple frame.
- Select the fifth icon from the right on the top toolbar (bars with label boxes in them and called **Show Data Labels**) or alternatively click the **Chart** drop-down menu and select **Show Data Labels** to open the **Properties** dialog box.
- The count (number of cases) will now appear in each slice. Click **Close** to close the **Properties** dialog box.

To show percentages and category of *Status* in each slice, proceed as follows:
- Return to the **Properties** dialog box and select the **Data Value Labels** tab at the top of the **Properties** dialog box.
- Delete **Count** from the **Contents** box by highlighting it and clicking the red X on the right. It will move to the **Available** box. Then select **Percent** from the **Available** box and click on the green arrow to move it to the **Contents** box. Do the same with *Status*. Click **Apply**. You can then delete the **Status** key and thereby save space.

Try the following:
- **Edit the chart to make it suitable for black-and-white printing.**

Return the edited pie chart to SPSS Viewer by closing the Chart Editor in the usual way.
- **Print the pie chart.**

Finishing the session

Close down SPSS and any other windows before logging out of the computer.

EXERCISE 7

Recoding data; selecting cases; line graph

Aim

This Exercise shows you how to recode data, select cases and draw a line graph.

Opening SPSS

Open SPSS with the data file *Metric Data* saved in an earlier Exercise.

Recoding data

Sometimes you may wish to recode values or categories within a variable (e.g. you might want to combine more than one value or category into a single new value or category). Suppose that you are not particularly interested in whether people are doing a MSc degree or a PhD degree, but just want to know whether they are postgraduates. You can change the data set to give you this information, either within the original variable, *status*, or by creating a new variable containing the recoded information.

In this session you are going to use a new variable, since this retains the original variable *status* for checking that the recoding has been done correctly. It also maintains the original values in the data set.

Use the **Recode** (Section 4.4.3) procedure to recode the status codes *MSc Postgrad* and *PhD Postgrad* (i.e. categories 2 and 3) into a new category 1 and the codes *Undergrad* and *Other* (i.e. categories 1 and 4) into a new category 2.

You will need to follow the section carefully. The **Recode** procedure creates a new variable which you are asked to name: we suggest *NewStatus*. To do this, you will have to choose the **Recode into Different Variables** option within the **Recode** procedure.

- Choose
  Transform
   Recode
    Into Different Variables
  to open the **Recode into Different Variables** dialog box.
- Highlight Attendee's Status and click ▶ to transfer it into the **Input Variable → Output Variable** box.
- Type *NewStatus* in the **Name** box within the **Output Variable** box and click **Change**. The new variable name *NewStatus* will now appear alongside *Status*.
- You might also type *New Status* into the **Output Variable Label** box as a label for the new variable *NewStatus*.

- Click **Old and New Values** and then fill in the corresponding values in the **Value** box of **Old Value** and in the **Value** box of **New Value**, clicking **Add** each time. The following should then appear in the right-hand box: 1 → 2, 2 → 1, 3 → 1, 4 → 2.
- Finally click **Continue** and **OK**.

When you have followed this procedure, check that you have the new variable at the far right of your data set. Now you should clarify the values by adding suitable labels. To do this, switch to **Variable View** and then click **None** in the cell in the **Values** column for the row of the new variable *NewStatus*.

When the grey box with three dots appears, click it to open the **Values Labels** dialog box. Complete this box in the usual way by assigning *Postgrad* to value 1 and *Others* to value 2, and finally click **OK**. To see whether this has worked, switch to **Data View** and check the data for the new variable *NewStatus*.

Save the data file again.

Now use the **Visual Bander** procedure to recode the heights of people as Tall, Medium or Short.
- Click **Visual Bander** in the **Transform** drop-down menu, transfer the variable *Height in metres* to the **Variables to Band** box by highlighting *Height in metres* and clicking on the arrow. Click **Continue**.
- When the **Visual Bander** dialog box re-appears, click the variable name *Height in metres* in the **Scanned Variable List** box. A histogram will now appear on the right.
- Name the new variable in the **Banded Variable** box as *HeightBands*.
- Enter the following values and labels into **Value** and **Label** cells: 1.70 Short; 1.80 Medium; 2.10 Tall. By accepting the default **Included (<=)** in **Upper Endpoints**, Short is defined as 1.70m or less, Medium as 1.71m to 1.80m, and Tall as 1.81 to 2.10m. The value of 2.10m is arbitrary; any value greater than the tallest person would suffice. Re-read the end of Section 4.4.3 for extra help.
- Click **OK**.

Check your data to make certain that they have all been classified in the manner that you planned.

Pie chart

Produce a pie chart with a title showing what percentages of the cases are tall, medium or short. Edit the pie chart to show the percentage for each slice (see Exercise 6 if you need to refresh your memory).

- **Edit the pie chart to prepare it for black-and-white printing. Print the pie chart.**

Select cases

It is also useful to be able to select the cases you want to analyse. Suppose, for example, that you wished to consider only the data relating to females. Use **Select Cases** (Section 3.3.1) to specify that only the female cases will be analysed.

Now suppose that, since smoking is said to suppress appetite, you wanted to see whether female smokers were lighter in weight than non-smokers. Use the **Compare Means** (Section

4.3.2) procedure to do this. Remember the **Dependent** variable will be *Kilos* and the **Independent** variable *Smoker*.

- **Print the Report table produced. Note that as a result of the Select Cases procedure you have just followed, this table will apply to the female respondents only.**

- **Are there any differences between the smokers and the non-smokers? Comment briefly on any differences you find. (When you think about this, bear in mind the difference in size between the smoking and non-smoking groups.)**

Line graph

A **line graph** is suitable when there is an interval or ordinal scale for one of the variables with not more than about ten values. When the scale is nominal, a bar chart is preferable. Now that you have an ordinal scale of height with three values in the variable *HeightBands*, you can draw a line graph of *Sex* against *HeightBands*.

First, however, the selection of females in the previous section must be reversed by returning to the **Select Cases** dialog box and clicking the **All cases** radio button.

- Choose
  Graphs
    Line
      Multiple
        Summaries for groups of cases
  to open the **Define Multiple Line: Summaries for Groups of Cases** dialog box.
- Insert the variable *HeightBands* into the **Category Axis** box and *Sex* into the **Define Lines by** box.
- Click **Options** and deselect **Display groups defined by missing values** (this stops the missing data for height being plotted). Click **Continue**.
- Select the **% of cases** radio button in the **Lines represent** box.
- Click **OK** to plot the lines.

A two-line graph should then appear, one line for Male and one line for Female, with the points on the abscissa labelled Short, Medium and Tall. Click the chart to enter **Chart Editor** and delete **(Banded)** from the x-axis label by clicking on it so that it is highlighted with a purple border and then move the cursor in and delete the appropriate section. In order to differentiate the sexes clearly in the printed graph, change one of the lines to a discontinuous line by clicking on one of the lines and then selecting a different **Style** from the choice in the **Lines** dialog box. You can change the colour within the same dialog box. Click **Apply** and **Close**. You may also wish to show the markers for the different categories, in which case, select the third icon from the top right toolbar (**Show Line Markers**). If you wish to change the style of the markers, double-click on one of them to open the **Properties** dialog box. There the type, size and colour can be altered.

Finishing the session

Close down SPSS and any other windows before logging out of the computer.

CHAPTER 6

Comparing averages: Two-sample and one-sample tests

6.1 Introduction

6.2 Parametric methods: The t tests

6.3 Effect size, number of participants and power

6.4 Nonparametric equivalents of the *t* tests

6.5 One-sample tests

6.1 INTRODUCTION

In Chapter 1 (Section 1.2), five types of research situation were identified. In the first, the researcher has **two samples** of scores and wants to know whether the difference between sample averages is significant. Here a **two-sample test** is appropriate. As an aid to choosing an appropriate test, we offered a provisional decision chart (Chapter 1, Figure 2), the important proviso being that the data must meet the requirements of the statistical model upon which the test is based.

See Section 1.2

The first question in the flow chart concerns the number of groups or conditions. This chapter is partly concerned with the use of SPSS to carry out the tests recommended by the chart when there are only two conditions. In the fifth research situation described in Chapter 1, the researcher has only a single sample of scores, on the basis of which he or she wishes either to make an inference about the mean of the population or decide whether the distribution of the sample is sufficiently well fitted by a theoretical distribution (Chapter 1, Figure 6). This chapter will also describe the use of SPSS to make appropriate **one-sample tests** in such situations.

6.1.1 SPSS procedures for two-sample tests

Table 1 shows the SPSS menus and submenus for various two-sample tests. The left half of Table 1 identifies **parametric tests**, which make assumptions about population distributions and parameters. The right half of the table identifies **non-parametric tests**, which make fewer assumptions. Each half of the table is subdivided according to whether the samples are independent or related. (Incidentally, SPSS refers to related samples as **paired samples** in the case of the *t* test, but as **related samples** in the context of nonparametric tests.)

Table 1. Comparing the averages of two samples: The SPSS menus

Research situation		Research situation	
Populations assumed to have normal distributions and equal variances		No specific assumptions about the population distributions	
Independent samples	Paired samples	Independent samples	Related samples
Names of the SPSS procedures		**Names of the SPSS procedures**	
Compare Means		Nonparametric Tests	
Independent-Samples T Test…	Paired-Samples T Test…	2 Independent Samples…	2 Related Samples…

6.1.2   SPSS procedures for one-sample tests

Table 2 shows the SPSS menus and submenus for various one-sample tests. The left side of the table shows the one-sample *t* test; the right side lists some non-parametric tests.

Table 2. One-sample tests: Parametric and nonparametric tests in the SPSS **Analyze** and **Nonparametric Tests** procedures, respectively

Parametric tests	**Nonparametric tests**		
SPSS procedures	**SPSS procedures**		
Analyze	Nonparametric Tests		
↓	↓	↓	↓
Compare Means (One-Sample T Test…)	Chi-Square…	Binomial…	1-Sample K-S*…

↓ indicates that the item below is part of the submenu of the item above
* Kolmogorov-Smirnov Test

6.1.3   Some general points about statistical tests

A **statistical hypothesis** is a statement about the parameters or distribution of one or more populations. In Chapter 2, we described an experiment designed to show that a certain drug enhances skilled performance. The **scientific hypothesis** was that, in the population, the mean scores of the *Drug* and *Placebo* groups are different. Since the mean performance of the *Drug* group was considerably higher than that of the *Placebo* group, the scientific hypothesis seemed to be supported. Nevertheless, since we only have samples from the populations concerned, it is decidedly risky to come to definite conclusions. The methods of statistical inference enable the researcher to come to tentative conclusions about populations, though since these are inferences (and therefore error-prone), it is necessary to attach measures of confidence that they are correct.

In traditional hypothesis testing, it is not the scientific hypothesis that is tested directly, but its negation, which is known as the **null hypothesis**. In the drug experiment, the null hypothesis is that, in the population, there is **no difference** in the mean scores under the *Drug* and *Placebo* conditions. The null hypothesis is tested by gathering data and obtaining the value of a **test statistic**, such as t or F. A test statistic can only function as such if it has a **known sampling distribution**, that is, we can state the probability of obtaining values within a specified range.

In **significance testing**, a small, fixed probability known as a **significance level** is decided upon before the data are gathered. Conventionally, the significance level is set at .05 or .01 (.05 is more common). Next, a **critical region** is chosen, that is, a range of atypical values for the test statistic such that the probability of a value in the range is equal to the significance level. The critical region is taken to lie in one or both **tails** of the distribution, where values would be least commonly found if the null hypothesis is true. If the value of the test statistic falls within the critical region, the result is said to be **significant** and hence to justify rejection of the null hypothesis.

The **p-value** of a test statistic is the probability, under the null hypothesis, of obtaining a value at least as extreme as the one obtained. A statistical test shows **significance** if the p-value is less than the significance level.

A **confidence interval** is a range of values calculated around the value of a statistic such as the mean or the difference between means which, under the null hypothesis, will include the true parameter value μ or $(\mu_1 - \mu_2)$ in a specified percentage of samples. (In a test of the difference between means, the null hypothesis usually states that in the population, the mean difference is zero.) The **95% confidence interval** $\bar{X} \pm t_{.025} \times s_{\bar{X}}$ includes μ in 95% of samples.

Think of a confidence interval as a hoop one is trying to throw over a post from a distance of several feet. Each sample (and confidence interval) is one throw. The **95% confidence interval** is a hoop wide enough to fall over the post on 95% of occasions. The **99% confidence interval** is considerably wider and will fall over the post on 99% of tosses (samplings). If the 95% confidence interval fails to include the hypothetical mean or difference between means under the null hypothesis, the result is statistically significant beyond the .05 level.

If the value of a test statistic such as t falls within the critical region under the null hypothesis, the confidence interval will also fail to include the hypothetical population mean. **The two criteria for significance are exactly equivalent.** Later, however, we shall see that a confidence interval can tell us more than can a t-value and a p-value. In fact, some journal editors now insist that reports of statistical tests include confidence intervals.

Returning to the drug experiment, if our test rejects the null hypothesis of quality of means in the population, we regard this as evidence for the scientific hypothesis that the drug affects performance.

There are problems with significance testing as we have described it. We shall touch upon some of these later in the chapter.

6.1.4 One-tailed and two-tailed tests

Suppose that two supposedly equivalent forms of a test, A and B, have been prepared and that 50 people take each of them. A large difference between the mean scores in either direction (A > B or B > A) is evidence against the null hypothesis that in the population there is no difference between the means for A and B. If the significance level is set at .05, the critical region is divided equally between the two tails of the sampling distribution of the test statistic, that is, the top .025 and bottom .025 of the distribution. When the critical region is distributed symmetrically in this way, we are said to be making a **two-tailed test.**

Often, however, the experimental hypothesis specifies the direction of the difference: Group A, say, is expected to perform better than Group B. The negation of this **directional** hypothesis is the null hypothesis that Group A is **not** better than Group B, including the possibility that it may be worse. Some argue that, since only a large difference **in favour of Group A** will count as evidence against the null hypothesis, the entire region of rejection can be located entirely in the upper tail of the distribution: that is, we can reject the null hypothesis if the value of the test statistic falls in the top .05 of the distribution, rather than the top .025. If we follow this approach, we are said to be making a **one-tailed test**. Clearly, if you obtain a difference in the expected direction, you are twice as likely to reject the null hypothesis on a one-tailed test as you are on a two-tailed test.

The difficulty with being prepared to reject the null hypothesis when you obtain a less extreme result in the expected direction is that, were the direction of the difference to be opposite to that predicted, however large that difference might be, you would still have to accept the null hypothesis: otherwise your critical region would be 5% + 2.5% = 7.5% of the distribution, which is arguably too high. For this reason, some are opposed to the use of one-tailed tests. By default, SPSS gives the results of two-tailed tests of significance in the output.

Journal editors have varying views about one-tailed and two-tailed tests. Their decision in a particular case is likely to depend partly upon non-statistical considerations, such as the cogency of the scientific hypothesis. It makes a difference whether a specified directional difference is predicted from a well-argued scientific hypothesis, as opposed to an indiscriminate process of frantic, theoretically unmotivated *ex post facto* data-snooping in the hope of finding 'significance' somewhere in the data. When reporting the results of the test, all the researcher can do is to provide full information about the statistics, the p-values and whether they are 2-tailed or 1-tailed.

6.1.5 Effect size

An important consideration when you plan to test the significance of, say, a difference between two means for significance is the size of the effect. For the simple two-group between subjects experiment, Cohen (1988) has suggested as a measure of effect size the statistic d, where

$$d = \frac{\mu_1 - \mu_2}{\sigma}$$

Cohen's measure thus expresses the difference, in the population, between the means as so-many standard deviations. In practice, the parameters μ_1, μ_2 and σ would be estimated from the means of the two samples and an estimate of the supposedly homogeneous population standard deviation. Suppose, for example, that in a drug experiment, the group who had ingested the drug had a mean score of 12, whereas the controls had a mean score of 10. The average standard deviation of the scores in the two groups was 2. According to Cohen's measure, the strength of the effect is (12–10)/2 = 1.

On the basis of a study of a considerable body of published literature, Cohen (1988) has suggested a categorisation of effect size as follows.

Effect size (d)	Size of Effect
0.2 to 0.5	Small
0.5 to 0.8	Medium
>0.8	Large

The drug experiment, therefore, found that the drug had a 'large' effect upon performance.

Cohen's measure d is much used in **meta-analysis**, which is the combination of statistics from several independent studies with a view to integrating all the evidence into a coherent body of empirical knowledge.

Many journal editors now insist that reports of the results of statistical tests should include measures of effect size as well as the statistics, the p-value and the confidence interval. As Keppel & Wickens (2004) observe, however, a variety of measures of effect strength are reported in the literature (p.167). Moreover, since some of these measures do not take sampling error into account, they tend to overestimate the strength of the effect in the population. A common measure of effect strength, for example, especially in analysis of variance (ANOVA), is the statistic **eta-squared** η^2. However, since η^2 does not allow for shrinkage arising from sampling error, it produces higher estimates of effect strength than does another statistic **estimated omega-squared** $\hat{\omega}^2$, which takes shrinkage into account. Both statistics are estimates of the same theoretical effect strength ω^2, which is defined in terms of parameters, not statistics. Keppel and Wickens recommend the $\hat{\omega}^2$ measure, rather than η^2, for measuring effect size in ANOVA.

It is therefore important, when reporting effect sizes, to make it quite clear which of the several available measures you have used. Most of them can readily be converted to any of the others (see Keppel & Wickens, 2004; Chapter 8).

6.2 PARAMETRIC METHODS: THE T TESTS

If you are not familiar with the *t* test, we strongly recommend that you read the relevant sections of a good statistical text (e.g. Gravetter & Wallnau, 2000; Chapters 9-11 give a lucid account).

6.2.1 Assumptions underlying the independent-samples *t* test

With independent samples, the *t* statistic is calculated by dividing the difference between the sample means by an estimate of the standard deviation of the distribution of differences, which is known as the **standard error of the difference**. Should the sample variances have similar values, it is common practice to work with a pooled estimate of the supposedly constant population variance. The term **pooled *t* test** is used when the sample variances are averaged like this. If the variances are markedly disparate, the pooled estimate is not used and a **separate variance t test** is made. The precise value of *t* needed for significance depends upon the **degrees of freedom** of the distribution, which in turn depends upon the sizes of the samples in the experiment; but a value of *t* greater than or equal to 2 is usually significant, unless the samples are very small.

The model underlying a *t* test assumes that the data have been derived from normal distributions with equal variance. Computer simulations, however, have shown that even with moderate violations of these assumptions, one may still safely proceed with a *t* test, provided the samples are not too small, do not contain outliers (atypical scores), and are of equal (or nearly equal) size. **There are, however, situations in which even the separate-variance *t* test can give a highly misleading result (see below).**

6.2.2 An example of the use of the independent-samples *t* test

In an experiment on lateralisation of cortical function, twenty participants are each assigned to one of two groups, one group performing a recognition task with material presented in the left visual field, the other a similar task with material presented in the right visual field. The dependent variable is response latency. The results are shown in Table 3.
- In **Variable View**, name the variables as *Case* for the case number, *Field* for the grouping (independent) variable, and *RecogTime* for the dependent variable.
- In the **Label** column, add the labels *Case Number*, *Visual Field* and *Word Recognition Time*.
- In the **Values** column, define the values and their labels for the variable *Field* as follows: *1 = Left Field, 2 = Right Field*.
- Open **Data View** and type in the case number, the value for *Field* and recognition time for each participant.

Table 3. Recognition times of those presented with words either in the left or the right visual field

Case	Left Field
1	500
2	513
3	300
4	561
5	483
6	502
7	539
8	467
9	420
10	480

Case	Right Field
11	392
12	445
13	271
14	523
15	421
16	489
17	501
18	388
19	411
20	467

Exploring the data

Before running the *t* test, it is important to check the data for anomalies such as extreme values or skewed distributions. Such considerations are particularly important with small data sets such as this one. Since this data set contains a grouping variable, the **Explore** procedure (Chapter 4, Section 4.3.2) is appropriate.

See Section 4.3.2

- Choose
  Analyze
     Descriptive Statistics
        Explore…
  to open the **Explore** dialog box (see Chapter 4, Figure 11).
- Transfer the dependent variable *Word Recognition Time* in the left-hand box to the **Dependent List:** box. Transfer the grouping variable *Visual Field* to the **Factor List:** box.
- Click **Plots…** to open the **Explore: Plots** dialog box, deselect the **Stem-and-leaf** check box and select the **Histogram** check box. Click **Continue** to return to the **Explore** dialog box.
- Click **OK** to run the **Explore** procedure.

The output is extensive. In Output 1, the *Left Field* boxplot shows an extreme value of 300 ms for case 3 ('*3 means, 'Case 3 is an extreme value'). In Output 2, which shows histograms of the same distributions, the same extreme value appears as the isolated left-hand box in the Left Field histogram. Another score, 271 ms for Case 13, appears as the isolated left-hand box in the *Right Field* histogram, though it is not flagged as an outlier in the boxplot.

See Table 2, Chap. 4

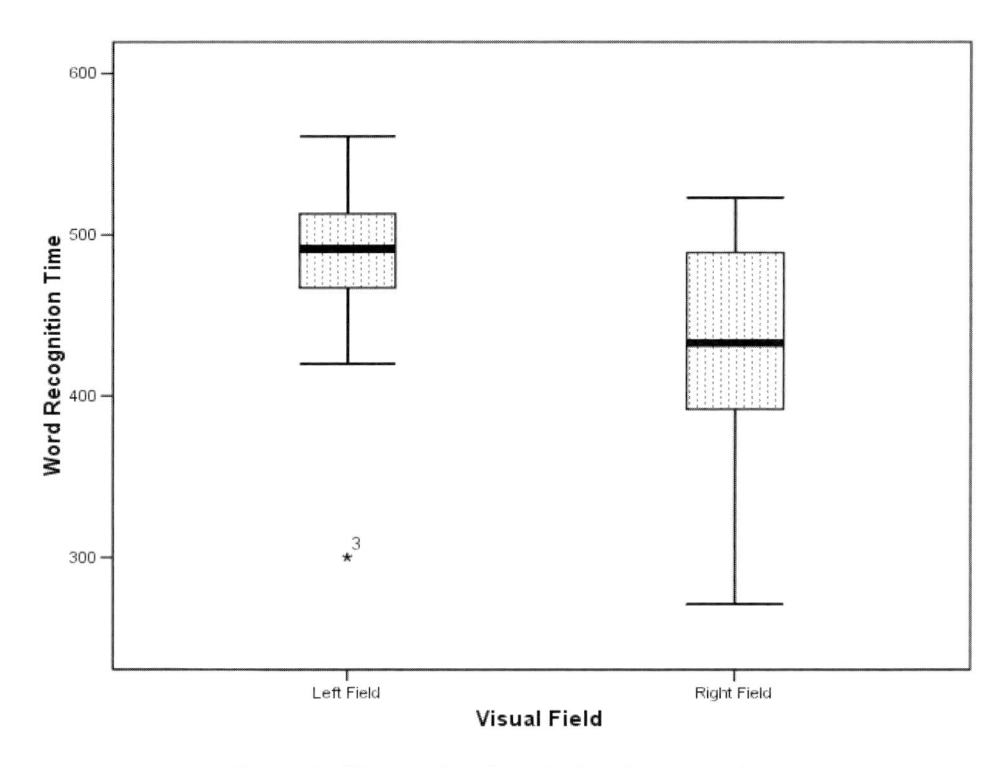

Output 1. The boxplots from the **Explore** procedure

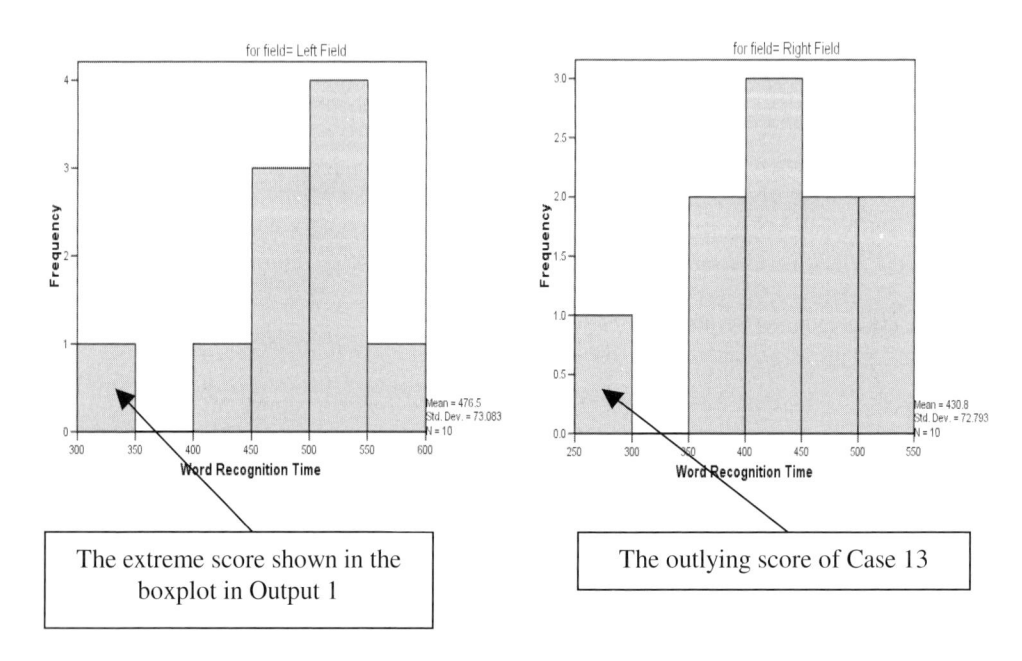

The extreme score shown in the boxplot in Output 1

The outlying score of Case 13

Output 2. The histograms from the **Explore** procedure

Comparing averages: two-sample and one-sample tests

With such a small sample, the presence of the markedly atypical scores of Cases 3 and 13 is likely to exert undue leverage on the values of the statistics summarising the data set. We shall therefore de-select Cases 3 and 13 before running the *t* test. This is easily done using the **Select Cases** procedure described in Chapter 3, Section 3.3.1.

See Section 3.3.1

- Choose
  **Data
  Select Cases…**
  to open the **Select Cases** dialog box (see Chapter 3, Figure 12).
- Click the **If condition is satisfied** radio button and then **If…** to open the **Select Cases: If** dialog box.
- Transfer *Word Recognition Time* to the conditional statement box. Type in an expression such as >300 to select all times greater than 300 ms. Click **Continue** to return to the **Select Cases** dialog box.
- Click **OK**.

Inspection of the data in **Data View** will show that cases 3 and 13 have been de-selected. Now we can continue with the *t* test.

Running the t test
- Choose
  **Analyze
  Compare Means
  Independent-Samples T Test …**
  to open the **Independent-Samples T Test** dialog box (Figure 1).

Transfer the variable name to the **Test Variable(s)** box

Transfer the grouping variable name to the **Grouping Variable** box

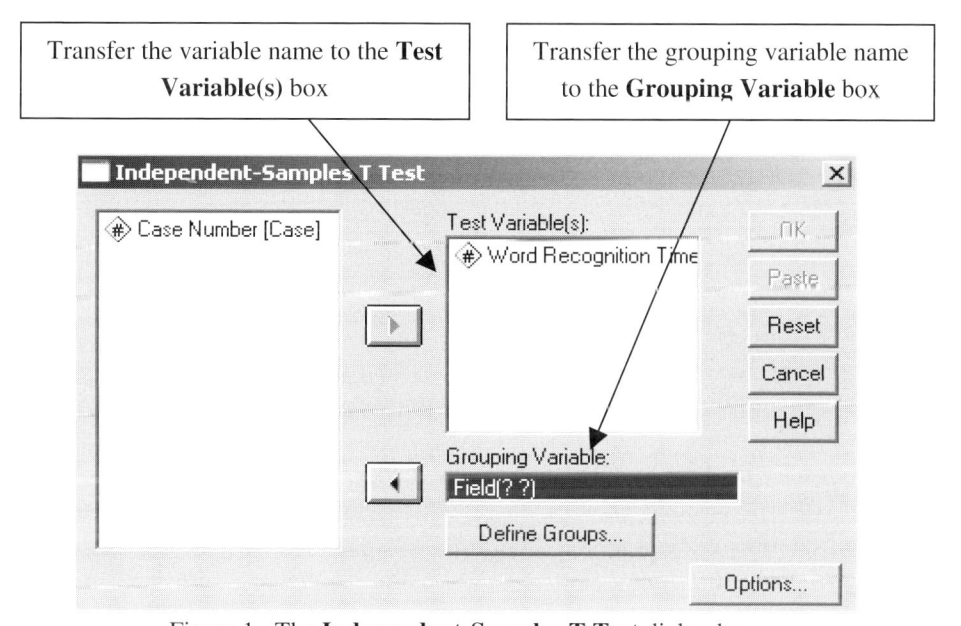

Figure 1. The **Independent-Samples T Test** dialog box

- Transfer the dependent variable *Word Recognition Time* to the **Test Variable(s)** box. Transfer the grouping variable *Visual Field* to the **Grouping Variable** box. At this point the **Grouping Variable** box will appear with **Field [? ?]** as shown in Figure 1.
- Define the values of the groups by clicking **Define Groups** to obtain the **Define Groups dialog box** (Figure 2).

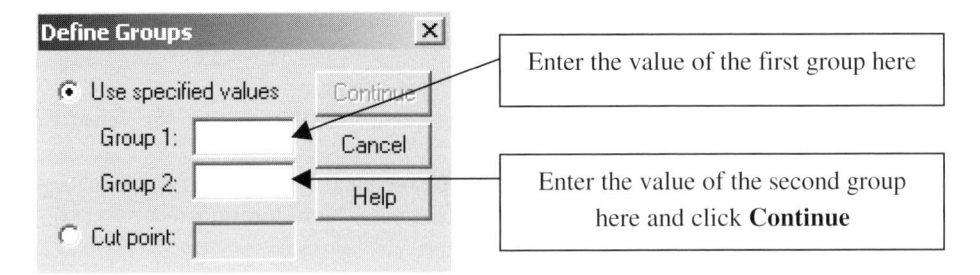

Figure 2. The **Define Groups** dialog box before defining the values of the two groups

- Type the value *1* into the **Group 1** box and the value *2* into the **Group 2** box, and click **Continue**. The values 1, 2 will then appear in brackets after *field* in the **Grouping Variable** box:

- Click **OK** to run the *t* test.

Early in the output, is a table (Output 3), **Group Statistics**, listing some statistics of the two samples, including the means (496.11 and 448.56). The two means are certainly different; but is this difference significant?

Group Statistics

	Visual Field	N	Mean	Std. Deviation	Std. Error Mean
Word Recognition Time	Left Field	9.00	496.11	41.01	13.67
	Right Field	9.00	448.56	49.14	16.38

Output 3. Summary table of group statistics

The answer to this question is shown in Output 4, **Independent Samples Test**, which tabulates the value of *t* and its p-value, **Sig. (2-tailed)**. Also given are the **95% Confidence Interval of the Difference** for both the **Equal variances assumed** and the **Equal variance not assumed** situations. These are the results of the pooled and separate variance *t* tests, respectively.

Notice **Levene's Test for Equality of Variances**, which is a test for homogeneity of variance. Provided Levene's test is **not significant** (p > 0.05), the variances can be assumed to be homogeneous and the **Equal Variances** line of values for the *t* test can be used. (This is the **pooled *t* test** mentioned earlier.)

Independent Samples Test

		Levene's Test for Equality of Variances		t-test for Equality of Means						
		F	Sig.	t	df	Sig. (2-tailed)	Mean Difference	Std. Error Difference	95% Confidence Interval of the Difference Lower	Upper
Word Recognition Time	Equal variances assumed	1.00	.33	2.23	16.00	.04	47.56	21.33	2.33	92.78
	Equal variances not assumed			2.23	15.50	.04	47.56	21.33	2.21	92.90

Levene's statistic has a p-value for F greater than 0.05 (F is not significant). Therefore assume equal variances

The t value (df =16) is 2.23. The two-tail p-value is 0.04. The p-value for a one-tail test is therefore 0.02 (t is significant at the 5% level)

The mean difference is 47.56

The 95% confidence interval (2.33 to 92.78) does not include 0. On a two-tailed test, the result is significant at the 5% level

Output 4. T test output for **Independent Samples**

In summary:
- If p > 0.05, the homogeneity of variance assumption is tenable, and the equal-variance (pooled) *t* test (**Equal variances assumed**) can be used.
- If p < 0.05, the homogeneity of variance assumption has been violated and the separate variance *t* test (**Equal variances not assumed**) is used.

The reader will have observed that in this example, both the p-values and t-values for **Equal variance assumed** and **Equal variance not assumed** are identical. That would not have been the case had the variances been heterogeneous: the two *t* tests can lead to different decisions about the null hypothesis. In this example, the **Levene Test** is not significant (p > 0.05), so the *t* value calculated with the pooled variance estimate (**Equal variances assumed**) is appropriate.

The most important result is that the value of *t* (df = 16) is 2.23, with a two-tail p-value, **Sig. (2 tailed)** of 0.04. (For a one-tailed test, we would halve this value to obtain a p-value of 0.02 (2%): *t* is significant at the 5% level.) The *t* test rejects the null hypothesis and so confirms the scientific hypothesis that words presented in the right visual field will be more quickly recognised than those in the left visual field.

Note carefully that the value in the **Sig.** column in Output 4 is the **p-value**, not the **significance level** (which is set beforehand at .05 – sometimes .01). With a non-significant result, the p-value would be high, perhaps .6 or .7. This high value would appear in the **Sig.** column, even though the test has not shown significance.

The **95% Confidence Interval of the Difference** is 2.33 to 93.78 which does not include 0, the value under the null hypothesis. Had the lower value been negative, the result of the two-tailed *t* test would not have been significant.

The **effect size** (see Section 6.1.4) for a two-sample (between subjects) experiment is

$$d = \frac{\mu_1 - \mu_2}{\sigma}$$

Here we have to use estimates of these values. In the numerator, we place the difference between the sample means (47.56). We obtain a pooled estimate of the supposedly constant population standard deviation using

$$s = \sqrt{\frac{(n_1 - 1) \times s_1^2 + (n_2 - 1) \times s_2^2}{n_1 + n_2 - 2}}$$

Thus

$$s = \sqrt{\frac{8 \times 41.01^2 + 8 \times 49.14^2}{16}} = 45.26$$

and so our estimate of effect strength is

$$d = \frac{47.56}{45.26} = 1.05$$

In Cohen's classification of effect size, this is a **large** effect.

6.2.3 How to report the results of a statistical test

The 2001 Publication Manual of the American Psychological Association (APA) recommends that when reporting a statistical result, you should, in general, '…include sufficient information to allow the reader to fully understand the analysis conducted and possible alternative explanations for the results of these analyses' (p.138).

In particular, with the value of a statistic such as t, you should include degrees of freedom (with other statistics, the number of observations is given), the p-value and a statement about the significance (or insignificance) of the result. Some editors would expect you to include the confidence interval as well, and a statement of the size of the effect giving, for example, the value of Cohen's *d* statistic.

The report of a statistical test should be preceded by a brief statement of the results, including relevant statistics such as the mean and standard deviation. Your report of the result of the *t* test would look something like this:

> As predicted, those presented with words in their right hemifield (M = 448.56; SD = 49.14) showed shorter latencies than those presented with words in their left hemifield (M = 496.11; SD = 41.01). The difference is significant beyond the .05 level: t (16) = 2.23; p = .04. The 95% confidence interval on the difference

Comparing averages: two-sample and one-sample tests   171

between means is (2.33, 92.78), which excludes zero. Cohen's d = 1.07, a 'large' effect in his classification of effect size (Cohen, 1988).

6.2.4 Demonstration of the effects of outliers and extreme scores in a small data set

Recall that the *t* test we have described was run on a data set with two outliers removed. You might wish to re-run the test on the complete data set (Table 3). You would find that the value of *t* now fails to reach significance: t(18) = 1.41; p = .797. Cohen's d = .63. The 95% confidence interval is (−22.83, 114.23), which comfortably includes zero.

The *t* test fails to show significance because the two low scores have the effect of increasing the standard error of the difference (the denominator of *t*) from 21.33 to 32.62, thereby reducing the value of *t*. In small data sets such as this, the presence of an outlying pair of scores, even one showing a difference in the same direction as the others, can have the effect of increasing the denominator of the *t* statistic more than the numerator and so reduce the value of *t* to insignificance. The inflation of the denominator derives from the vulnerability of the standard deviation to the leverage exerted by outliers. The elements of the variance (and standard deviation) are the **squares** of deviations from the mean, and large deviations thus continue to have a disproportionate influence, even after the square root operation has been carried out.

6.2.5 The paired-samples (within subjects) *t* test

In an experiment on lateralisation of cortical functioning, a participant looks at a central spot on a computer screen and is told to press a key on recognition of a word that may appear on either side of the spot.

Table 4. Paired data: Median word recognition times in milliseconds for words in the left and right visual fields

Case	Left Field	Right Field
1	323	304
2	512	493
3	502	491
4	385	365
5	453	426
6	343	320
7	543	523
8	440	442
9	682	580
10	590	564

The experimental hypothesis is that words presented in the right visual field will be more quickly recognised than those in the left visual field, because the former are processed by the left cerebral hemisphere, which is thought to be more proficient with verbal information. For each participant, the median response time to forty words in both the right and the left visual fields is recorded, as indicated in Table 4.

Prepare the data file from the paired data in Table 4 as follows:
- Using the techniques described in Chapter 2 (Section 2.3), open **Variable View** and name the variables *Case*, *LeftField* and *RightField*. Add fuller labels, such as *Case Number, Left Visual Field* and *Right Visual Field*.
- Now switch to **Data View** (which will show the variable names) and enter the data.

See Section 2.3

Notice that, since in this example, the same participants perform under both the *Left Field* and the *Right Field* conditions, there is no grouping variable.

Exploring the data

To check for anomalies in the data before running the *t* test, construct a scatterplot. Choose the **Scatter** procedure on the **Graphs** menu (Chapter 5, Section 5.6). In the **Simple Scatterplot** dialog box, enter *Left Visual Field* in the **Y Axis** box and *Right Visual Field* in the **X Axis** box. The scatterplot is shown in Output 5.

See Section 5.6

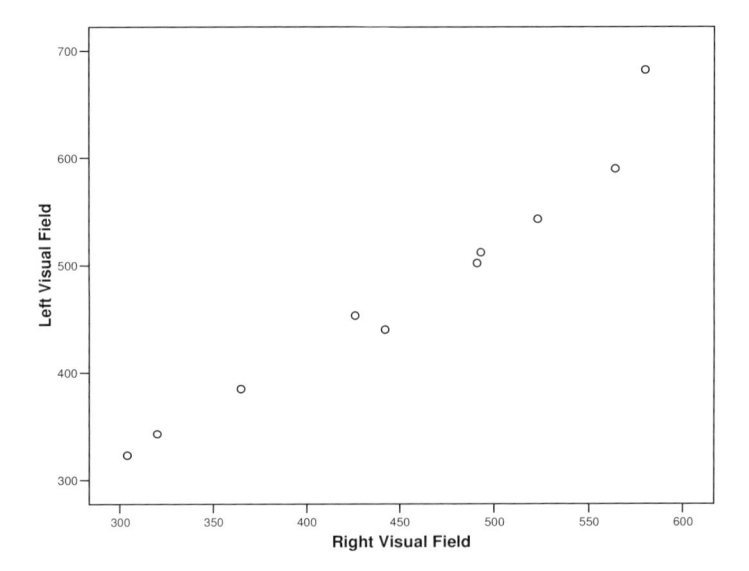

Output 5. The scatterplot of Left Visual Field against Right Visual Field

No outlier appears in the scatterplot. When outliers are present, the user can either consider removing them or choose a nonparametric method such as the **Sign test** or the **Wilcoxon matched pairs test**. The former is completely immune to the influence of outliers; the latter is much more resistant than the *t* test. Should there be no contraindications against the use of the *t* test, however, the parametric *t* test is preferable to a nonparametric test because the latter would incur the penalty of a loss of **power** (see below).

Comparing averages: two-sample and one-sample tests 173

Running the t test

Proceed as follows:
- Choose
  Analyze (see Figure 3)
    Compare Means
       Paired-Samples T Test ...
  to open the **Paired-Samples T Test** dialog box (the completed version is shown in Figure 4).
- Transfer the variable names to the **Paired Variables** box as described in Figure 4.
- Click **OK**.

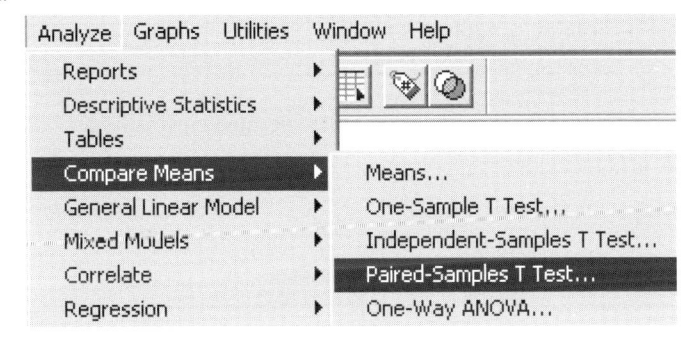

Figure 3. The **Compare Means** menu

Highlight the variables to be paired (the highlighted variable names will appear in the **Current Selections** box), then click ▶ to transfer the pair to the **Paired Variables** box

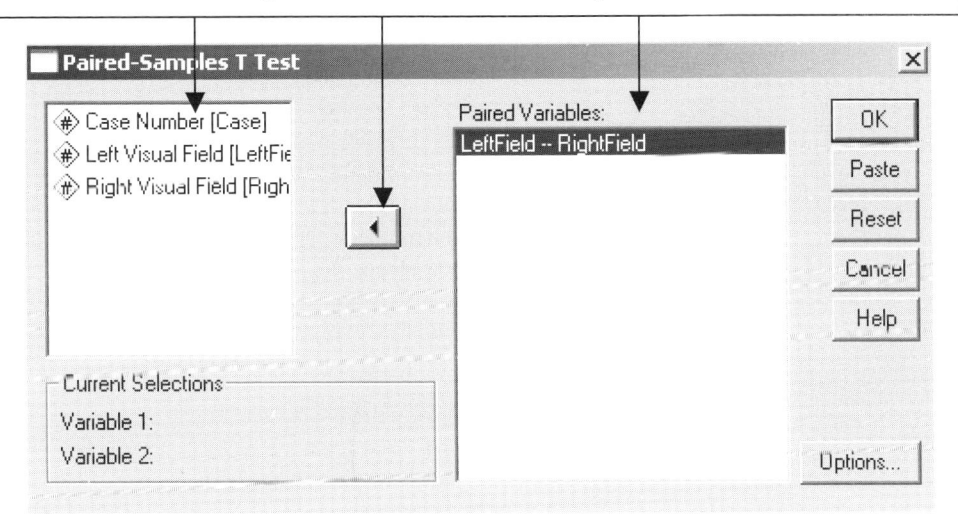

Figure 4. The **Paired-Samples T Test** dialog box for pairing Left and Right Visual Fields

Since it is possible to run *t* tests on several pairs of variables at the same time, the output specifies the **Pair** under consideration in each sub-table. In this example, there is only one pair. The upper part of Output 6, **Paired Samples Statistics**, tabulates the statistics for each variable. The second output table (lower part of Output 6), **Paired Samples Correlations,** gives the value of the correlation coefficient, which is 0.97.

Paired Samples Statistics

		Mean	N	Std. Deviation	Std. Error Mean
Pair 1	Left Visual Field	477.30	10	112.09	35.45
	Right Visual Field	450.80	10	97.09	30.70

Paired Samples Correlations

		N	Correlation	Sig.
Pair 1	Left Visual Field & Right Visual Field	10	.97	.00

Output 6. Paired samples statistics and correlations

The final table (Output 7), **Paired Samples Test,** shows various statistics and their p-values.

Paired Samples Test

	Paired Differences					t	df	Sig. (2-tailed)
	Mean	Std. Deviation	Std. Error Mean	95% Confidence Interval of the Difference				
				Lower	Upper			
Left Visual Field - Right Visual Field	26.50	27.81	8.80	6.60	46.40	3.01	9	.015

- The mean difference between pairs of values
- The SD of the differences between pairs of values
- The 95% confidence interval does not include the null hypothesis mean of 0. Hence the result is significant beyond the 5% level
- The value of t for 9 df is 3.01, with a two-tail p-value of 0.015

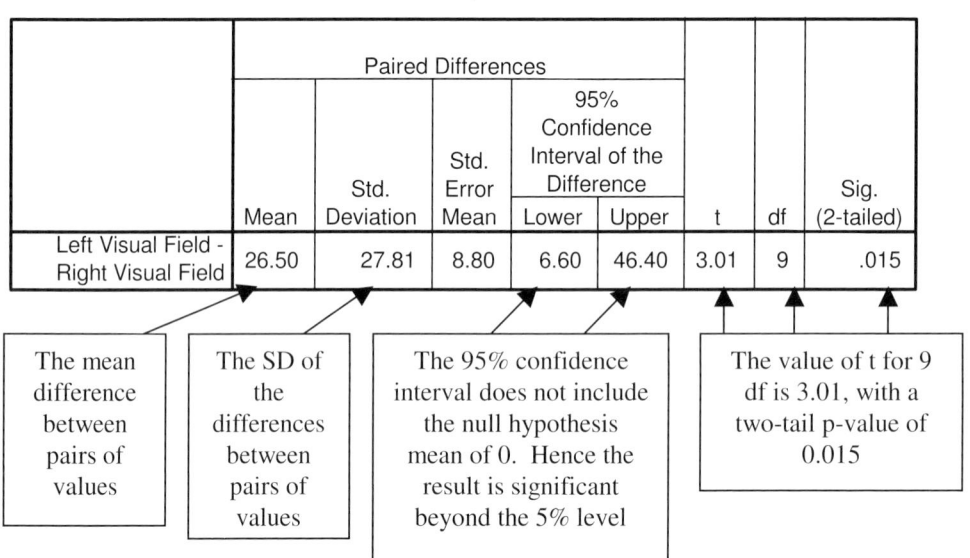

Output 7. T test output for paired samples

Ouput 7 presents statistics of the distribution of differences between the paired scores (**Paired Differences**), the **95% confidence Interval of the Difference**, the value of *t*, its degrees of freedom and its p-value **Sig. (2-tailed)**. We see that the value of *t* (on 9 degrees of freedom) is *3.01*, and that the p-value, *Sig. (2-tailed),* is 0.015. The result of the *t* test is significant beyond the .05 level. The 95% confidence interval on the difference between means is (6.60, 46.40), which excludes zero, the value under the null hypothesis.

The **effect size** (see Section 6.1.5) is $d = \dfrac{\mu_1 - \mu_2}{\sigma_{X_1 - X_2}}$

where $\sigma_{X_1 - X_2}$ is the standard deviation of the difference scores from the two populations. Here we have to use estimates of these population values, that is, 26.50 for the difference between means and 27.81 for the standard deviation of the difference scores. These are the first two entries in Output 7. Thus

$$d = \frac{26.50}{27.81} = 0.95$$

In Cohen's Table, this would be a **Large** effect.

Report of the results of the t test

We can report the results of the test as follows.

> The mean response latency for the Left Visual Field (M = 477.30, SD = 112.09) was greater than the mean for the Right Visual Field (M = 450.80, SD = 97.09). A related-samples *t* test showed significance beyond the .05 level: t(9) = 3.01; p = .015(two-tailed). The 95% confidence interval was (6.60, 46.40), which does not include the value of zero specified by the null hypothesis. Cohen's d = .95, which is a large effect.

6.3 EFFECT SIZE, POWER AND THE NUMBER OF PARTICIPANTS

Problems with significance testing

There are problems with significance testing as we have described it. A statistical test may show significance, with a p-value much smaller than .05, and yet the result may be trivial – even misleading. Suppose a manufacturer of matches claims that the mean length of their matches is 4 cm. A quality control inspector selects a sample of 900 matches and finds that the sample mean is 3.98 cm and the standard deviation is 0.15 cm (i.e. 1.5 mm). A one-sample *t* test of the null hypothesis that the population mean is 4 cm shows that t (899) is given by

$$t = \frac{3.98 - 4}{0.15 / \sqrt{900}} = 4.0$$

The corresponding p-value is 0.0000685 (2-tailed), which is significant beyond the .01 level. The difference of .02 between the claimed mean (4 cm) and the sample mean (3.98 cm) is very small. The standard error of the mean, however, which is given by σ/√n, is very small indeed with such a large *n*. In fact, the null hypothesis can **always** be rejected, provided the sample is large enough. This is the rationale for the dictum that you **cannot prove the null hypothesis**. The eminent statistician, Sir Ronald Fisher, took the view that while significance implied that the null hypothesis was false, an insignificant result did not allow the researcher to accept the null hypothesis.

The 95% confidence interval on the mean is (3.970187 cm, 3.989813 cm). This tells the true story, because even the lower limit of the confidence interval is 4 cm to one decimal place. What the manufacturer is really claiming is that the mean length of the matches is 4 cm to the nearest millimetre (0.1 cm), a claim which the data have shown to be substantially correct. Statistical 'significance', therefore, does not demonstrate the existence of a **substantial** difference.

The alternative hypothesis

Critics of significance testing have pointed out that its advocates, in focusing exclusively upon the null hypothesis, failed to acknowledge that in order to specify a critical region of values that will lead to rejection of the null hypothesis, attention must be paid to the **alternative hypothesis (H_1)**, that is, the statistical equivalent of the scientific hypothesis. Otherwise, there is no basis for claiming that the critical region should lie in the tails of the distribution of the test statistic, as opposed to a narrower band of more frequently occurring values anywhere else within the range of possible values.

In the system of Neyman and Pearson, the problem of hypothesis testing was re-conceived in terms of a choice or decision between the **null hypothesis (H_0)** and the **alternative hypothesis (H_1)**, against which H_0 is tested. Since in Neyman-Pearson hypothesis-testing we have the option of accepting H_0 as well as rejecting it, two kinds of error are possible:
1. We may reject the null hypothesis when it is true, thus making a **Type I error**.
2. We may accept the null hypothesis when it is false, thus making a **Type II error**.

The **probability of a Type I error** is denoted by the Greek symbol **alpha α**, which is the significance level (.05 or .01). The **probability of a Type II error** is denoted by the Greek symbol **beta β**. The **Power (P)** of a statistical test is the probability that the null hypothesis, if false, will be rejected. Since, in Neyman-Pearson hypothesis-testing, one must either accept or reject the null hypothesis and the two events are complementary (i.e. they exhaust the possibilities), the power of a statistical test is 1 − (Type II error rate) i.e. **P = 1 − β**. The decisions made in hypothesis testing are set out in Table 5.

Table 5. Correct decisions and errors in hypothesis testing: Type I and Type II errors and power (P)

		Experimenter's Decision	
		Accept H_0	**Accept H_1**
State of Nature	H_0 is true	Correct decision	**Type I error** Probability = α
	H_1 is true	**Type II error** Probability = β	Correct decision Power P = 1 − β

Figure 5 shows the relationships among the Type I and Type II error rates and power for a one-sample test of the null hypothesis (H_0) that the mean of a population has a specified value (μ_0) against the alternative hypothesis (H_1) that the population mean is μ_1. The test statistic is the sample mean and the curves are the sampling distributions of the mean under H_0 and H_1.

Since the test is one-tailed, the entire critical region is located in the upper tail of the sampling distribution of the mean. With a two-tailed test, values in the critical region would have a probability of α /2 under H_0.

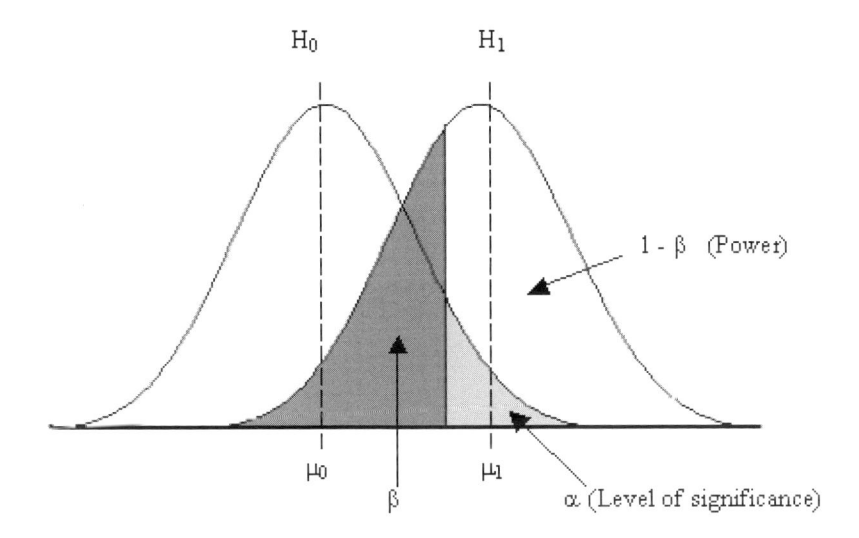

Figure 5. Relations among Type I and Type II error rates and power

There are no simple relationships between the **Type I error rate (α)** on the one hand and the **Type II error rate (β)** and **power (P)** on the other. It is clear from Figure 5, however, that, other things being equal, adopting a smaller significance level (say .01 instead of .05) will reduce the power of the test. Another factor affecting power, however, is the difference between the mean under H_0 and the mean under the alternative hypothesis H_1: the greater the difference, the lower the β-rate and the greater the power.

It is also clear from Figure 5 that a factor in the power of a test is the degree of overlap between the sampling distributions under the null and alternative hypotheses: the less the overlap, the greater the power. Since the standard deviation of the sampling distribution of the mean is $\sigma/\sqrt{n}$, the degree of overlap will be reduced (and the power of the test increased) by increasing the sample size.

Among the other factors affecting the power of a test are the type of test (parametric or nonparametric), the design of the experiment (within subjects or between subjects) and the degree of discrepancy between the sizes of the samples in the case of between subjects experiments.

Our example of the lengths of matches, which demonstrated a misleading result with a test that was much too powerful, is quite unrepresentative of the situation in many areas of research, in which there is often a shortage, rather than a surplus, of data. Cohen (1962, 1988) drew attention to the low power of the tests used on the data from many of the experiments reported in the literature, a state of affairs arising from a general tendency to test too few participants. It is generally agreed that the power of a test should be at least 0.8, and in many reported studies the power is much lower than this.

Power, however, is not the only consideration. Since P depends upon the difference between the means under the null and alternative hypotheses, we must decide upon the smallest difference that we would wish a test to show to be significant on 80% of occasions.

How many participants shall I need in my experiment?

Several authors, such as Clark-Carter (1997), have published tables giving the power that will be achieved by using different numbers of participants, given that one is hoping to reveal an effect of a minimum specified size, as measured by Cohen's statistic *d* and other measures of effect size.

For example, suppose that you plan to carry out an experiment comparing the performance of a group of participants who have taken a supposedly performance-enhancing drug with that of a placebo group. You wish to make a *t* test that will reveal an effect of medium size and achieve a power of 0.8. According to Table A15.2 on p.607 of Clark-Carter's book, if you wish to achieve a power of 0.8 on a between subjects *t* test for an effect size of 0.5, you will need to test 60 participants in each group, that is, a total of 120 participants. Clark-Carter provides a useful selection of tables giving the sample sizes necessary to achieve specified power levels in a variety of commonly used statistical tests.

Returning to the example of the matches, our manufacturer is really claiming that their matches are 4 cm to the nearest millimetre (0.1cm). We know, from the statistics of the previous large sample, that, in the population, the standard deviation is close to 0.15cm. We want to make a test that will reject the null hypothesis with an effect size of (0.1/0.15) = 0.7 which, according to Cohen's classification, is an effect of medium size. From Table A15.3 (Clark-Carter, p.609), we shall require a sample size of 14 to achieve a power of 0.8. The sample mean is 3.98 cm, giving t(13) = 0.50; p = .6254 (two-tailed). Should the inspector only be interested in the possibility that the matches are shorter than 4 cm, a one-tailed test may be justified and the one-sided p-value is .3127. In either case, we can accept the null hypothesis and regard the manufacturer's claim as confirmed.

The same tables can also be used to determine the power of a test for a specified sample size. In the example of the matches, the power of a one-sample *t* test to reject the null hypothesis with an effect size of 0.7 when n = 900 is, according to Clark-Carter's Table A15.3, 0.9999, that is, very close to unity.

Useful software

Some useful programs for determining the sample size necessary to achieve specified levels of power for different effect sizes are now available. One of these, GPOWER (Erdfelder, Faul & Buchner, 1996), is available on the Internet and its use is free. You can obtain information about GPOWER (and many other aspects of effect size and power analysis) by using a internet search engine such as Google. You can download GPOWER into your own computer. Keppel & Wickens used GPOWER to construct a table (Keppel & Wickens, 2004: Table 8.1, p.173) showing the sample sizes necessary for a range of combinations of power, effect size and values of estimated omega-squared $\hat{\omega}^2$. If this table is used to estimate sample size, the values obtained will be similar to those given in Clark-Carter's tables.

6.4 NONPARAMETRIC EQUIVALENTS OF THE T TESTS

When there are serious violations of the assumptions of the *t* test, nonparametric tests can be used instead. They should not be used as a matter of course, however, because should the data meet the requirements of the *t* test, the comparable nonparametric test may lack the power to reject the null hypothesis, should that be false, especially if the data are less plentiful than one would wish. It is best, therefore, to consider the parametric test first, resorting to the nonparametric alternative only if the data seriously violate the requirements and no justification can be found for removing extreme scores or outliers.

SPSS offers a wide selection of nonparametric tests in the **Nonparametric Tests** submenu of **Analyze**. The **Mann-Whitney** test is an alternative to the independent samples *t* test; the **Sign** and **Wilcoxon** tests are nonparametric counterparts of the paired samples *t* test. Most nonparametric methods use statistics, such as the median, that are resistant to outliers and skewness. In the tests described here, H_0 states that, in the population, the two **medians** are equal.

'Asymptotic' p-values

With large samples, several of the most common nonparametric test statistics have sampling distributions approximating to known continuous distributions and the approximation is close enough to provide serviceable estimates of p-values. (The term **asymptotic** means that the approximation becomes ever closer as the sample size grows larger.) With small samples, however, the approximation can be much poorer. And yet, it is in precisely those circumstances in which we would consider using nonparametric tests (i.e. with small samples, or samples with outliers and skewed distributions) that we can place least reliance on the approximate p-values.

Fortunately, with the usual reports of the approximate, **asymptotic** p-values, SPSS also provides **exact** p-values. We recommend that you report the **exact** p-values for nonparametric tests, rather than the **asymptotic** p-values.

6.4.1 Independent samples: Mann-Whitney test

Here we will use the original data set shown in Table 3, rather than the set after removal of the two outliers which we used for the *t* test. With the data in **Data View**,
- Choose
  Analyze
    Nonparametric Tests
      Independent Samples ...
  to obtain the **Two-Independent-Samples** dialog box (Figure 6).
- Transfer the **test variable** (which, in this procedure, is SPSS's term for the **dependent variable**) *Word Recognition Time* to the **Test Variable List** box. Transfer the grouping variable *Visual Field* to the **Grouping Variable** box. Click **Define Groups** and add the group numbers *1* and *2* in the usual way (Figure 6).

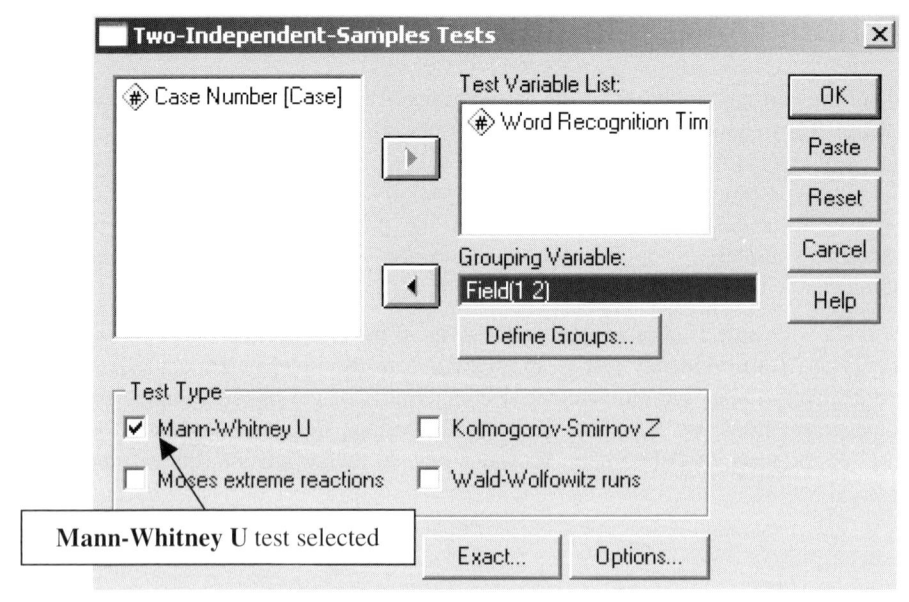

Figure 6. The **Two-Independent-Samples** dialog box for Word Recognition Time categorised by Visual Field with the **Mann-Whitney U** Test selected

- Click the **Exact…** button to see the **Exact Tests** dialog box and activate the **Exact** radio button (see Figure 7).
- Click **Continue** to return to the **Two-Independent-Samples Tests** dialog box. Return to the **Two-Independent-Samples Tests** dialog box and then **OK** to run the test.

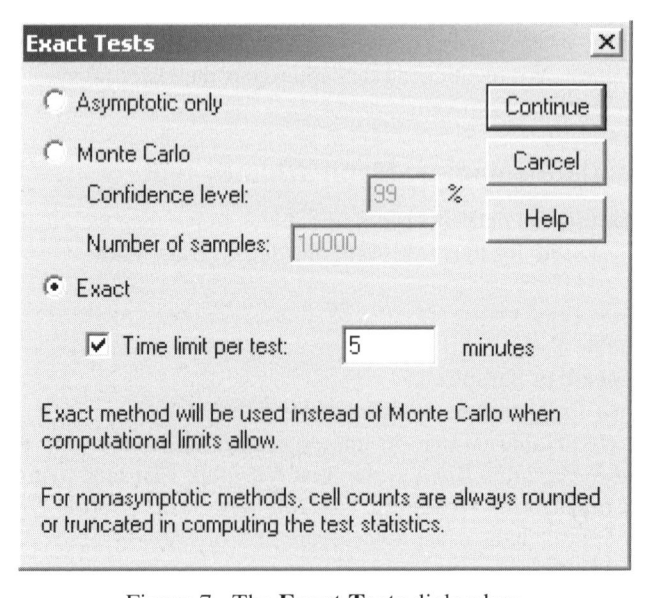

Figure 7. The **Exact Tests** dialog box

The first table (Output 8) in the output, **Ranks**, tabulates the sums of ranks for the Left and Right Fields.

Ranks

	Visual Field	N	Mean Rank	Sum of Ranks
Word Recognition Time	Left Field	10	12.65	126.50
	Right Field	10	8.35	83.50
	Total	20		

Output 8. The table of ranks for the **Mann-Whitney test**

In the process of determining the value of the test statistic U, all the scores in the data set are ranked in order of magnitude, after which the means of the ranks of the scores in each of the two groups are calculated. In Output 8, you can see that the mean rank of the scores obtained under the *Right Field* condition is markedly less than that of the scores obtained under the *Left Field* condition. Nevertheless, as we shall see, this difference is insufficient for the test to achieve significance.

Test Statistics[b]

	Word Recognition Time
Mann-Whitney U	28.500
Wilcoxon W	83.500
Z	-1.626
Asymp. Sig. (2-tailed)	.104
Exact Sig. [2*(1-tailed Sig.)]	.105[a]
Exact Sig. (2-tailed)	.110
Exact Sig. (1-tailed)	.055
Point Probability	.004

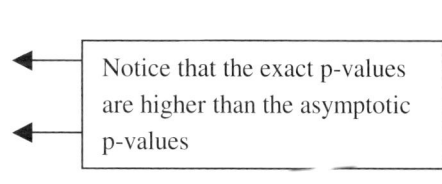

Notice that the exact p-values are higher than the asymptotic p-values

a. Not corrected for ties.
b. Grouping Variable: Visual Field

Output 9. The output for the **Mann-Whitney test**

From Output 9, we see from the exact p-values that the **Mann-Whitney** tests fails to show significance on either a one-tailed or a two-tailed test. Were you to rely upon the results of this statistical test alone, you would have to conclude that the scientific hypothesis that words presented in the right visual field will be more easily recognised than those in the left visual field has not been confirmed by these data.

Your report of the results of the **Mann-Whitney U test** would run along the following lines

> Although the mean response time for words presented to the right visual field (M = 440.56 ms, SD = 49.14 ms) was less than the mean response time for

words presented to the left visual field (M = 496.11 ms, SD = 41.01 ms), a Mann-Whitney U test failed to show significance: U = 28.5; exact p = .110 (two-tailed).

In view of the strongly directional nature of the scientific hypothesis, you may feel that a one-tailed test is justified, in which case you might report the result as follows:

Although the mean response time for words presented to the right visual field (M = 448.56 ms, SD = 49.14 ms) was less than the mean response time for words presented to the left visual field (M = 496.11 ms, SD = 41.01 ms), a Mann-Whitney U test failed to show significance beyond the .05 level: U = 28.5; exact p = .055 (one-tailed).

We have already seen that with small data sets, in which there are extreme scores and outliers, parametric statistical tests such as the *t* test can produce misleading results. This is also true of nonparametric tests. Despite its greater robustness to the influence of outliers and extreme scores, the **Mann-Whitney test** still fails to show significance, despite the obvious pattern in the data. It is certainly not immune to the influence of disorderly data, particularly when the samples are small. You might wish to run the test with the reduced data set used for the *t* test.

6.4.2 Related samples: Wilcoxon, Sign and McNemar tests

With the data from Table 4 in the **Data Editor**,
- Choose
  Analyze
  > **Nonparametric Tests**
  >> **Related Samples ...**

to obtain the **Two-Related-Samples Tests** dialog box (Figure 8).

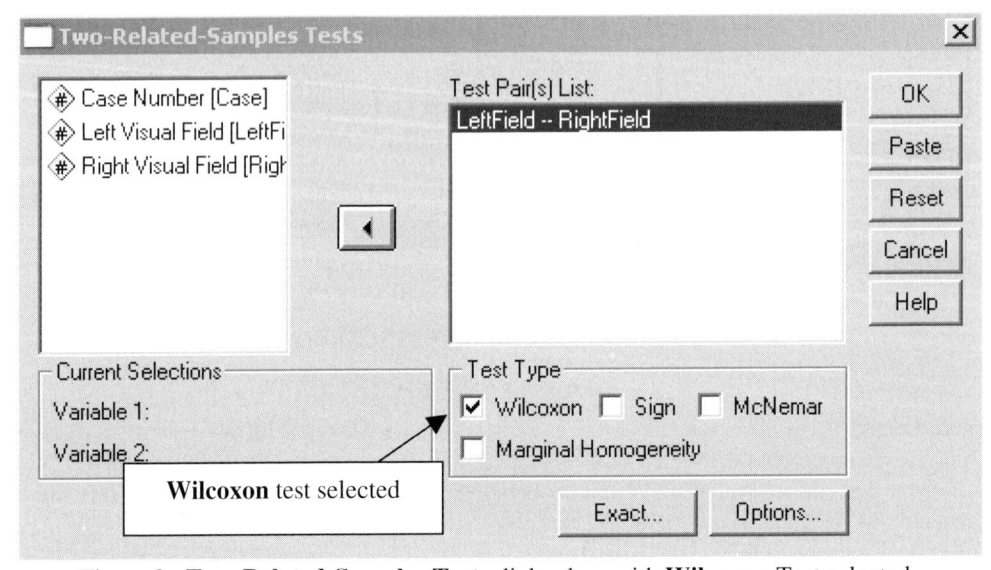

Figure 8. **Two-Related-Samples Tests** dialog box with **Wilcoxon** Test selected

- Transfer the variable names *Left Visual Field* and *Right Visual Field* to the **Test Pair(s) List:** box, where they will appear joined by dashes as shown.

- As when making the Mann-Whitney test, click **Exact...** to see the **Exact Tests** dialog box and mark the **Exact** radio button.
- Click the **Options...** button to see the **Two-Related-Samples: Options** dialog box and choose **Descriptive**.
- Click **Continue** to return to the **Two-Related-Samples Tests** dialog box and click **OK** to run the procedure.

The first table in the output (Output 10) gives the means and standard deviations of the scores obtained under the *Left Visual Field* and *Right Visual Field* conditions.

Descriptive Statistics

	N	Mean	Std. Deviation	Minimum	Maximum
Left Visual Field	10	477.30	112.091	323	682
Right Visual Field	10	450.80	97.085	304	580

Output 10. Table showing the means and standard deviations of the scores obtained under the Left Visual Field and Right Visual Field conditions

In the **Wilcoxon test**, each participant's score under the *Right Visual Field* condition is paired with the same person's score under the *Left Visual Field* condition. A set of difference scores is obtained by consistently subtracting the *Left Visual Field* score in each pair from the *Right Visual Field* score. Output 11 shows that in 9 out of 10 cases, the Left Visual Field score was greater. The differences are then ranked in order of their absolute values (that is, ignoring their signs). The test statistic *W* is the smaller sum of ranks of the same sign: in this case, *1*.

Ranks

		N	Mean Rank	Sum of Ranks
Right Visual Field - Left Visual Field	Negative Ranks	9[a]	6.00	54.00
	Positive Ranks	1[b]	1.00	1.00
	Ties	0[c]		
	Total	10		

[a]. Right Visual Field < Left Visual Field
[b]. Right Visual Field > Left Visual Field
[c]. Left Visual Field = Right Visual Field

Output 11. Table of ranks for the **Wilcoxon test**. Note that W is the smaller of the two Sums of Ranks so W = 1

The third table (Output 12), **Test Statistics**, gives the exact two-tailed and one-tailed p-values for the statistic W (for **Wilcoxon**). Clearly the test has shown significance beyond the .01 level.

Test Statistics[b]

	Right Visual Field - Left Visual Field
Z	-2.705[a]
Asymp. Sig. (2-tailed)	.007
Exact Sig. (2-tailed)	.004
Exact Sig. (1-tailed)	.002
Point Probability	.001

a. Based on positive ranks.

b. Wilcoxon Signed Ranks Test

Output 12. The output for the Wilcoxon test

In Output 12, the statistic Z is the basis of the asymptotic p-value. Your report of the results of this test would run along the following lines:

> A Wilcoxon matched-pairs, signed ranks test showed that the difference between the median response time for words presented in the left visual field (M = 477.3 ms, SD = 112.09 ms) and the right visual field (M = 450.80; SD = 97.09) was significant beyond the .01 level: exact p = .004 (two-tailed). The sums of ranks were 54 and 1 for the negative and positive ranks, respectively, therefore W = 1.

Other non-parametric alternatives to the paired t test

Although the **Wilcoxon test** assumes neither normality nor homogeneity of variance, it does assume that the two samples are from populations with the same distribution shape. It is therefore also vulnerable to the influences of outliers – though not to nearly the same extent as the *t* test. The **Sign test**, which is even more robust than the Wilcoxon, can be requested by clicking its check box (report its result by quoting the p-value in the **Exact Sig. (2-tailed)** row). The **McNemar test** is applicable to paired qualitative data.

6.5 ONE-SAMPLE TESTS

In Section 1.7 of Chapter 1, two situations were identified in which a researcher might wish to make a one-sample test:
1. You may wish to compare a sample distribution with a hypothetical distribution, such as the normal distribution. On this basis, you would hope to claim that your data are (approximately) normally distributed. In technical terms, this is a question of **goodness-of-fit**.
2. You may wish to make **inferences about the parameters of a single population from the statistics of a sample**, either for the purpose of ascertaining whether the sample is from a known population or estimating the parameters of an unknown population. For example, if you have the heights of

Comparing averages: two-sample and one-sample tests   185

a hundred children in a certain age group, what can be said about the **typical** height of children in that age group?

The scope of goodness-of-fit tests extends far beyond ascertaining normality of distribution. With nominal data, for example, goodness-of-fit tests can be used to confirm the existence of preferences among a range of choices, or the fairness of a coin or a die.

So far in this chapter, we have been concerned with comparisons between the means of two samples. Yet, as we shall see presently, in the case of paired data, a one-sample test can be used to make such a comparison. In fact, the *t* **test for two related samples** that we described earlier in this chapter is actually a special case of a **one-sample *t* test**.

6.5.1   Goodness-of-fit: Data in the form of measurements (scale data)

A researcher has a sample of measurements (say the heights of 100 people) and wishes to ascertain whether these have been drawn from a normal population. Testing for normality of distribution is one of the commonest applications of a goodness-of-fit test. The **Kolmogorov-Smirnov test** is appropriate for this purpose.

The histograms of the relative frequencies of some variables such as height and IQ are bell-shaped, indicating that they have an approximately normal distribution. The area under such a curve between two points on the horizontal axis represents the probability of a value within that particular range. In the distribution of IQ, the mean (which lies under the highest point of the curve) is 100 and the standard deviation is 15. The probability of an IQ in the range from 100 to 115, that is between the mean and a value one standard deviation above the mean, is approximately 0.3. This probability is the area under the curve between the uprights on the values 100 and 115 on the horizontal axis.

The **cumulative probability** of any particular value in a distribution is the probability of obtaining a value less than or equal to that value. For example, the cumulative probability of an IQ of 100 is 0.5, because in a symmetrical distribution, the mean splits the population (and the total area under the curve) into two equal parts. If we construct a table giving the cumulative probabilities of the IQs in the range from, say 40 to 140 in steps of ten units, and plot a histogram, we shall have a picture of the **cumulative distribution** of the IQ variable. The cumulative normal distribution is not bell-shaped, but has the shape of a flattened S, rising slowly at first, accelerating as the mean is approached, decelerating as the mean is passed, and eventually flattening out at the upper end of the distribution.

Table 6. Fifty IQ scores sampled from a normal population with $\mu=100$ and $\sigma = 15$

104.6	101.1	122.5	116.5	87.7	105.9	71.7	107.4	92.4	107.3
76.4	90.5	98.6	99.3	118.5	85.7	118.5	107.1	81.8	104.3
91.4	90.7	128.7	118.7	103.7	123.0	102.7	95.3	105.0	70.7
100.3	100.0	117.1	135.1	111.0	90.8	81.8	103.1	112.1	116.8
84.4	96.4	120.6	92.1	118.3	93.7	112.3	100.9	88.7	104.5

The **Kolmogorov-Smirnov test** for goodness-of-fit compares the cumulative probabilities of values in your data set with the cumulative probabilities of the same values in a specified theoretical distribution. If the discrepancy is sufficiently great, the test indicates that your data are not well fitted by the theoretical distribution. The **Kolmogorov-Smirnov statistic** D is the greatest difference in cumulative probabilities across the entire range of values. If its value exceeds a cut-off level, the null hypothesis that your sample is from the specified population is rejected. Table 6 shows some fictitious IQ data that were selected randomly by SPSS from a normal population with a mean of 100 and a standard deviation of 15.

To test the distribution for goodness-of-fit to a normal distribution, use the **Kolmogorov-Smirnov test**.

- In **Variable View**, name a variable *IQ* (assign the label *Intelligence Quotient*). Enter the data in **Data View**.
- Choose
  Analyze
      Nonparametric Tests
          1-Sample K-S...
  to obtain the dialog box for the **One-Sample Kolmogorov-Smirnov Test** dialog box (Figure 9).

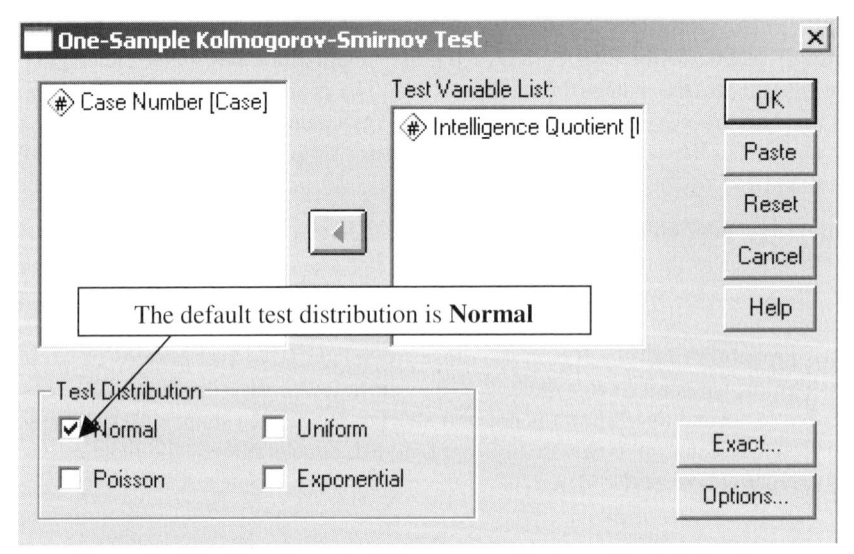

Figure 9. The **One-Sample Kolmogorov-Smirnov Test** dialog box

- Transfer *Intelligence Quotient* to the **Test Variable List** box and notice that the default **Normal** checkbox has been selected.
- Click **Exact...** to see the **Exact Tests** dialog box and choose **Exact**. Click **Continue** to return to the **One-Sample Kolmogorov-Smirnov Test** dialog box.
- Click **Options...** to see the **One-Sample K-S: Options** dialog box and choose **Descriptive** and **Quartiles**. Click **Continue** to return to the **One-Sample Kolmogorov-Smirnov Test** dialog box.
- Click **OK**.

Output 13 shows the **Descriptive Statistics** that we requested from **Options**. (Since the original table was rather wide, we used the **Transpose Rows and Columns** procedure on the Pivot menu.)

Descriptive Statistics

		Intelligence Quotient
N		50
Mean		102.1982
Std. Deviation		14.55456
Minimum		70.71
Maximum		135.12
Percentiles	25th	91.2939
	50th (Median)	102.9535
	75th	113.3954

Output 13. The descriptive statistics of the fifty IQ scores

Output 14 shows the results of the test of goodness-of-fit.

One-Sample Kolmogorov-Smirnov Test

		Intelligence Quotient
N		50
Normal Parameters [a,b]	Mean	102.1982
	Std. Deviation	14.55456
Most Extreme Differences	Absolute	.077
	Positive	.058
	Negative	-.077
Kolmogorov-Smirnov Z		.548
Asymp. Sig. (2-tailed)		.925
Exact Sig. (2-tailed)		.989
Point Probability		.000

a. Test distribution is Normal.
b. Calculated from data.

Output 14. Results of the **Kolmogorov-Smirnov test** of goodness-of-fit

The 'differences' referred to in Output 14 are the differences between the cumulative probabilities for various sample values and the corresponding cumulative probabilities assuming a normal distribution. The absolute value of the largest difference (D) is 0.077. We see that the exact p-value of D (two-tailed) is .989. The null hypothesis of normality of distribution is accepted. That is exactly what you would expect, because we know that the data set has indeed been drawn from a normal population.

We write the result as follows:

> A one-sample Kolmogorov-Smirnov test of goodness-of-fit provided no evidence against the null hypothesis that the sample has been drawn from a normal population: D = .077; exact p = .989 (two-tailed).

6.5.2 Goodness-of-fit: Nominal data

Dichotomous nominal data
Suppose a researcher wants to know whether 5-year-old children of a certain age show a preference for one of two toys (A or B). The choices of one hundred 5-year-olds are noted. Of the hundred children in the study, 60 choose toy A and 40 toy B. As another example, suppose that, in order to determine whether a coin is 'fair' (that is, heads and tails are equally likely to occur), we toss a coin 100 times, and find that the coin turns up heads on 58 tosses.

In both examples, the null hypothesis states that the probability of choosing A (or B) on each trial is 0.5. The term **Bernoulli trials** is used to denote a series of events or experiments with the following properties:
1. The outcomes of every trial can be divided into the same two dichotomous categories, one of which can be regarded as a 'success', the other as a 'failure'.
2. The outcomes of the trials are independent.
3. The probability of a 'success' is the same on all trials.

Note that 1. does not imply that there are only two outcomes, only that we can divide the outcomes into two categories. Suppose that a candidate sitting a multiple-choice examination with six alternatives per question were to choose the answer by rolling a die each time. In that case, although there are six outcomes per question, they can be classified dichotomously into *Pass* (with a probability of 1/6) and *Fail* (with a probability of 5/6).

Where, as in the foregoing examples, we have Bernoulli trials, the **Binomial test** can be used to test the null hypothesis that the probability of a success on any trial has a specified value. In the case of coin-tossing, that specified probability will usually be *0.5*. The binomial test, however, can be used to test the hypothesis that the population proportion has **any** specified value.

To illustrate the binomial test, we shall use our first example of the children's choices between two toys. Of the 100 five-year-olds studied, 60 chose toy A and 40 chose toy B. Proceed as follows:
- Assign code numbers to the two choices, say *1* to toy A and *2* to toy B.
- In **Variable View**, name a variable *Toy* and assign the values 1 to Toy A and 2 to Toy B.
- Name a second variable *Frequency* for the number of choices.
- Enter the data in **Data View**.
- In order to ensure that the two choices will be weighted by their frequencies of occurrence, select **Weight Cases…** in the **Data** menu to obtain the **Weight Cases** dialog box, select the **Weight Cases by** radio button, transfer *Frequency* to the **Frequency Variable** box, and click **OK**.

- Select
  Analyze
  Nonparametric Tests
  Binomial ...
  to open the **Binomial Test** dialog box (Figure 10).
- Transfer *Toy* to the **Test Variable List**. Notice the small **Test Proportion** box on the right, containing the default value *0.5*. This is appropriate for the present test, because if the experiment was conducted properly and the children had no preference, the probability of each choice is *0.5*. In other situations, however, that would not be the case, as when a candidate is guessing the correct answers to the questions in a multiple-choice examination, in which case, if there were four choices, the **Test Proportion** would be 0.25. The **Weight Cases** procedure ensures that the two choices will be weighted by their frequencies of occurrence.
- Click **Exact...** to see the **Exact Tests** dialog box and choose **Exact**. Click **Continue** to return to the **Binomial Test** dialog box.
- Click **OK** to run the Binomial test.

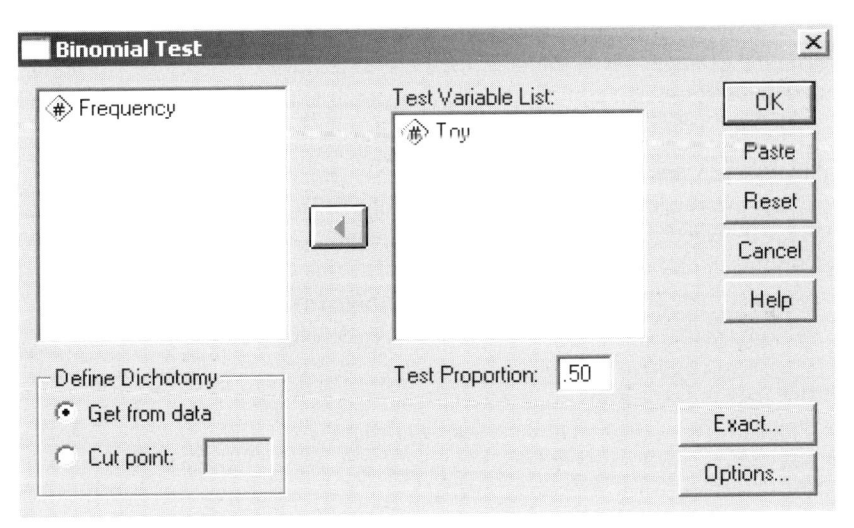

Figure 10. The **Binomial Test** dialog box with *toy* selected for the **Test Variable List**

The output is shown in Output 15.

Binomial Test

		Category	N	Observed Prop.	Test Prop.	Asymp. Sig. (2-tailed)	Exact Sig. (2-tailed)
Toy	Group 1	Toy A	60	.60	.50	.057[a]	.057
	Group 2	Toy B	40	.40			
	Total		100	1.00			

a. Based on Z Approximation.

p-value is 0.057 (i.e. the result is not significant)

Output 15. The output for the **Binomial Test**

The important item here is the rightmost entry, headed **Exact Sig (2-tailed)**. Since this p-value exceeds 0.05 (in fact, it is almost 0.06), the null hypothesis is accepted. The result of the test is written as follows:

> Although more children (60%) chose toy A than toy B (40%), a binomial test failed to reject the hypothesis that there is no preference: p = .057 (two-tailed).

Small numbers of trials: Omitting the Weight Cases procedure

Should we have only the outcomes of a few Bernoulli trials, as when a coin is tossed twenty times, it is easier to enter the result of each toss directly, rather than aggregate the data and use the **Weight Cases** procedure. In **Variable View**, name one variable *toss* with two values (1 is a Head, 2 a Tail), enter the data in **Data View**, and complete the **Binomial Test** dialog box by transferring the variable name *Toss* to the **Test Variable List:** box.

Goodness-of-fit test with three or more categories

If, to extend the example of toy preferences, there were three or more toys to choose from, the **Chi-square goodness-of-fit test** can be used to test the null hypothesis that all three toys are equally attractive to children.

Suppose that there were three toys, A, B and C. Of 90 children tested, the numbers choosing the three toys were 20, 41 and 29, respectively. This is the distribution of observed frequencies. If there is no preference in the population, we should expect that 30 children would choose each of the three toys. How well does this theoretical **uniform distribution** fit the observed distribution? The **Chi-square goodness-of-fit test** is run as follows:

- In **Variable View** define the variables *Preference* and *Frequency*, the former with three levels: *1* for *A*, *2* for *B*, *3* for *C*.
- Enter the data in **Data View**.
- Use **Weight Cases...** to weight the values in *Frequency*.
- Choose
  Analyze
      Nonparametric Tests
          Chi-Square...
  to open the **Chi-Square Test** dialog box (Figure 11).
- Transfer the variable name *Preference* to the **Test Variable List:** box.
- Click **Exact...** to see the **Exact Test** dialog box and choose **Exact**. Click **Continue** to return to the **Chi-Square Test** dialog box.
- Click **OK**.

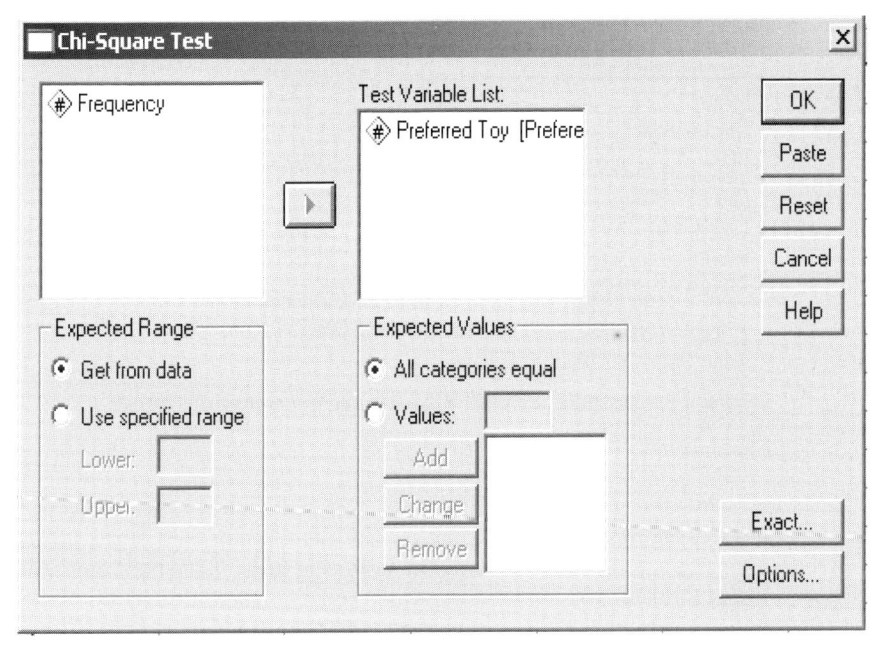

Figure 11. The **Chi-Square Test** dialog box with Preferred Toy transferred to the **Test Variable List** box

The first table (Output 16) in the output shows the observed and expected frequencies. Any transcription errors will immediately be apparent here. Notice that the expected frequencies are 30 for each choice, because if there is no preference, the three choices are equally likely, and we should have approximately equal numbers of children choosing A, B and C.

TOY

	Observed N	Expected N	Residual
A	20	30.0	-10.0
B	41	30.0	11.0
C	29	30.0	-1.0
Total	90		

Output 16. The observed and expected frequencies

The next table (Output 17) presents the results of the Chi-square goodness-of-fit test.

Test Statistics

	Preferred Toy
Chi-Square a	7.400
df	2
Asymp. Sig.	.025
Exact Sig.	.026
Point Probability	.003

a. 0 cells (.0%) have expected frequencies less than 5. The minimum expected cell frequency is 30.0.

Output 17. The output for the **Chi-square goodness-of-fit test**

Output 16 showed marked discrepancies between the expected and observed frequencies, and it is not surprising that the **Exact Sig.** (i.e. the p-value) in Output 17 is small (.026). The report of the results of this test would run along the following lines. (The bracketed value with the chi-square symbol is the degrees of freedom, which is the number of categories minus one.)

> Inspection of the frequency distribution shows that twice as many children (41) chose Toy B as chose Toy A (20). Approximately the expected number (29) preferred Toy C. A chi-square test of the null hypothesis that the three toys were equally attractive to the children showed significance beyond the .05 level: $\chi^2(2) = 7.4$; exact $p = .026$.

The interpretation of the results of this test requires care. The experimenter may have had theoretical reason to expect that Toy B would be preferred to the other toys. All the chi-square test has shown, however, is that the hypothesis of no preference is untenable. We have not demonstrated that any one toy was preferred significantly more (or less) than either of the others. Had the purpose of the investigation been to show that Toy B was preferable to the other two, a better analytic strategy would have been to dichotomise a child's choice as either *B* or *NotB*. This can be done by preparing a fresh data set with 49 for *B* and 41 for *NotB*. A binomial test would test the null hypothesis that the number of children choosing B exceeded the expected value. In the **Binomial Test** dialog box, the **Test Proportion** would be set at 1/3 = .33. The binomial test shows significance beyond the .05 level: p = .01. This result does support the scientific hypothesis that Toy B is preferred to either of the other two toys.

6.5.3 Inferences about the mean of a single population

The mean and standard deviation of the 50 IQ scores in Table 6 (Section 6.5.1) are 102.2 and 14.6 respectively. (You can confirm this with **Descriptives...** in **Descriptive Statistics** submenu in the **Analyze** menu.) What can we infer about the population mean?

On the sample mean, a **95% confidence interval** can be constructed, that is, a range of values centred on the sample mean which will include the population mean in 95% of samples. To do this (assuming the data have already been entered in a variable named *IQ* in **Data View**):

- Choose
  Analyze
  > **Descriptive Statistics**
  > > **Explore…**

  to obtain the **Explore** dialog box.
- Transfer the variable name Intelligence Quotient (*IQ*) to the **Dependent List** box.
- If you click **Statistics…** (not the **Statistics** radio button), you will obtain the **Explore: Statistics** subdialog box, in which it can be seen that the **Descriptives** check box has been selected, and a **Confidence Interval for Mean** with *95* in the *%* box has already been specified by default. (The user may wish to specify a higher confidence level, such as 99%.)
- Click **Continue** to return to the **Explore** dialog box.
- Click **OK**.

An edited version of the output is shown in Output 18. The output gives the sample **Mean** as *102.15* and the **95% Confidence Interval for Mean** as extending from *98.020* to *106.288*. Not surprisingly, the actual population mean (*100*) lies within this range since, as we have seen, the data were actually generated by commanding SPSS to select 50 scores from a normal population with a mean of *100* and a standard deviation of *15*. Note, incidentally, that, because of sampling error, the sample mean is not *exactly 100*.

Descriptives

			Statistic	Std. Error
Intelligence Quotient	Mean		102.154	2.0571
	95% Confidence Interval for Mean	Lower Bound	98.020	
		Upper Bound	106.288	

Output 18. The mean and the 95% Confidence Interval for Mean

Using a confidence interval to test a hypothesis about the mean of a single population

A hypothesis about the mean of a single population can be tested by constructing a confidence interval on the sample mean. If the hypothetical mean value lies outside the confidence interval, the null hypothesis can be rejected beyond the .05 level (for the 95% confidence interval) and the .01 level (for the 99% confidence interval). In the present case, the null hypothesis that the population mean IQ is 100 must be accepted, which is the correct decision.

Using a one-sample t test to test a hypothesis about the mean of a single population

We have claimed that the fifty IQ scores are a random sample from a normal population with a mean of 100 and a standard deviation of 15. We have seen that one way of testing this hypothesis is to construct a 95% confidence interval on the mean and reject the hypothesis if the sample mean falls outside this interval.

Another approach is to make a **one-sample *t* test** of the null hypothesis that the mean is 100.

To do so:

- Choose
  Analyze
     Compare Means
        One-Sample T Test...
  to open the **One-Sample T Test** dialog box (Figure 12).
- Transfer the variable name *IQ* to the **Test Variable(s):** box and type 100 (the null hypothesis value for the mean) into the **Test Value:** box.
- Click **OK**.

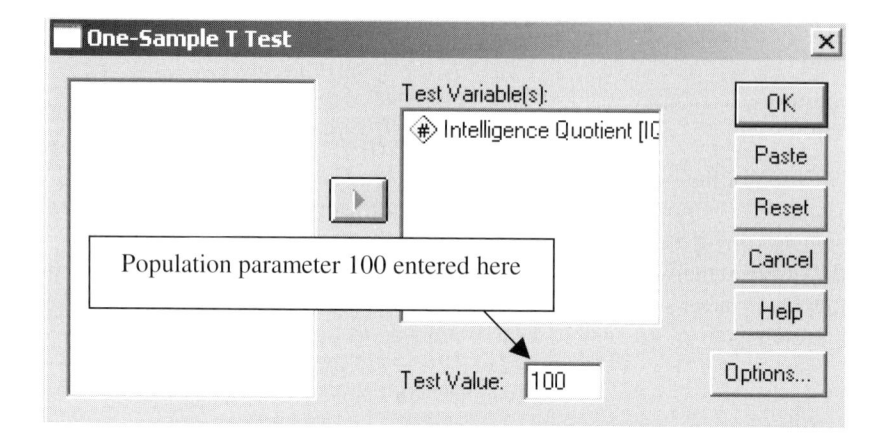

Figure 12. The **One-Sample T Test** dialog box with IQ transferred to the **Test Variable(s)** box and *100* entered for the **Test Value**

The first table in the output (Output 19), **One-Sample Statistics**, tabulates some descriptive statistics.

One-Sample Statistics

	N	Mean	Std. Deviation	Std. Error Mean
Intelligence Quotient	50	102.15	14.55	2.06

Output 19. The descriptive statistics table

The second table (Output 20) includes the *t* **test** results and the **95% Confidence Interval**. It can be seen from the table that the null hypothesis must be accepted.

The **effect size** (see Section 6.1.5) here is simply the difference between the population means divided by the standard deviation of the population of the defined population i.e.

$$d = \frac{\mu_1 - \mu_0}{\sigma}$$

We have to resort to using the sample value of the mean as the best estimate of the population value and the standard deviation calculated from the sample as the best estimate of σ. Thus

$$d = \frac{2.15}{14.55} = 0.15$$

In Cohen's Table, this is less than the lowest value for a **Small** effect, thereby confirming the non-significance of the result.

One-Sample Test

	\multicolumn{5}{c}{Test Value = 100}
	t	df	Sig. (2-tailed)	Mean Difference	95% Confidence Interval of the Difference
					Lower / Upper
Intelligence Quotient	1.05	49	.30	2.15	-1.98 / 6.29

With t = 1.05 and df = 49, the p-value of 0.30 shows that the observed mean difference is not statistically significant assuming μ = 100

The 95% confidence interval from -1.98 to 6.29 includes the population mean difference of 0. Thus the observed mean difference is not significant

Output 20. The output for the one-sample *t* test

This result is written as

> The mean intelligence quotient (M = 102.15, SD = 14.55) was greater than the population value of 100. A one-sample *t* test showed that this was not significant: t (49) = 1.05; p = .30 (two-tailed). The 95% confidence interval of the difference was (-1.98, 6.29), which includes the population mean difference of zero specified by the null hypthesis. Cohen's d = 0.15, which is a small effect.

The related t test as a special case of the one-sample t test

Earlier we said that a related-samples *t* test was a special case of a one-sample *t* test. From a set of paired data, we can obtain a single column of differences by consistently subtracting, say the scores on the right from those on the left. The null hypothesis states that, in the population, the mean of these **difference scores** is zero. If we enter the differences as the Test Variable in the One-Sample T Test dialog box enter *0* in the **Test Value** box, and run the test, we shall obtain exactly the same result as we would have done if we had run a related-samples *t* test on the two columns in the original data set.

EXERCISE 8

Comparing the averages of two independent samples of data

Aim

The previous Exercises have used data from a questionnaire. The next few Exercises will be based on data from experiments designed to test experimental hypotheses. In real experiments, of course, a larger number of participants would have been used.

Before you start

Before proceeding with this Exercise, we suggest you read Chapter 6 carefully. In this Exercise, we shall be making an **independent samples *t* test** (Section 6.2.2). In Exercise 9, we shall be making a **paired-samples *t* test** (Section 6.2.5). Finally in Exercise 10, we shall be making **one-sample tests** (Section 6.5).

An investigation of the effects of a drug upon performance

The data we are going to explore in this Exercise might have been produced by the following project. A team of investigators has good reason to believe that a small dosage of a certain drug changes the speed with which people can make decisions. They decide to try to confirm this by carrying out an experiment in which the decision times of 14 people who have taken the drug are compared with those of a control group of 14 other people who have performed the task under a placebo condition. The experimenters expect that the average decision time of the experimental group will differ from that of the placebo group. The results are shown in Table 1.

Table 1. Decision times of the experimental and placebo groups in the drug experiment

\multicolumn{4}{c	}{DRUG GROUP}	\multicolumn{4}{c}{PLACEBO GROUP}
Case	Time	Case	Time	Case	Time	Case	Time
1	390	8	425	15	446	22	440
2	494	9	421	16	749	23	471
3	386	10	407	17	599	24	501
4	323	11	386	18	460	25	492
5	660	12	550	19	390	26	392
6	406	13	470	20	477	27	578
7	345	14	393	21	556	28	398

Opening SPSS

In the opening window of SPSS, select the **Type in data** radio button. If **Data View** appears first, click the tab **Variable View** to open **Variable View**.

Constructing the SPSS data set

Construct the data set as described in Section 3.1. In **Variable View**, the first variable, *Case*, will represent the participants. The second is the grouping variable (i.e. the type of treatment – drug or placebo). Call the grouping variable *Condition* and label the values: *1 = Drug; 2 = Placebo*. Label the variable *Experimental Condition*. The third variable, which can be named *Score*, contains all the participants' scores on the dependent variable. Notice that the *Score* variable includes the scores for **both** treatments. The grouping variable *Condition* is needed to enable the computer to identify the group to which a score belongs. Since there are no decimals in the data, ensure that the values in the **Decimals** column are all *0*.

Click the **Data View** tab and enter the data of Table 1 into **Data View** in the manner described in Section 3.1.2. When the data have been entered, save them to a file with a name such as *Drugs*.

Exploring the data

The first step is always to examine the data set to see whether there are any odd features.

We shall want a table of means and standard deviations, together with indicators of distribution shape such as histograms and boxplots. The statistics for the subgroups are most easily obtained with the **Means** procedure. (The plots are obtained with the **Explore** procedure.) Follow the instructions in Section 4.3.2, remembering that the dependent variable name is *Score* and the independent variable name is *Condition*.

- **Write down the values of the means and standard deviations. Do these statistics appear to support the scientific hypothesis?**

(Note that the **Means** procedure requires the presence of a grouping variable in the data set. Should the mean and standard deviation of a set of ungrouped data be required, use the **Descriptives** procedure.)

Graphical displays of the data

To draw the boxplots, proceed as described in Section 4.3.2. The dependent variable is *Score*, the factor is *Condition*, and the **Labels Cases by** is *Case*. (This choice labels any outliers or extreme scores in the boxplots with the number of the case, which is more useful than the default row number, especially if some cases have been deselected.) Remember to click the **Plots** radio button in the **Display** section of the **Explore** dialog box, thus turning off the **Both** radio button and ensuring that the descriptive statistics tables are omitted. Click **Plots**, deselect the **Stem-and-leaf** check box and select **Histogram** check box. Click **Continue** and finally **OK**.

The output in **SPSS Viewer** begins with the usual **Case Processing Summary** listing the number of valid cases in each group. Then it shows **Boxplots** and **Histograms** for the two groups. The boxplots show two outliers with the identifying numbers of the participants concerned (because you specified the participants' numbers in the **Label Cases by** box in the **Explore** dialog box).

When there is a marked discrepancy between the mean and median of a set of scores, the distribution is probably skewed or otherwise asymmetrical. Atypical scores, or **outliers** can also pull the value of the mean away from that of the median. Read Section 4.3.2 carefully for an explanation of SPSS's boxplot displays.

- **Identify any outliers by means of their identifiers, which are numbers in the variable *case*. State their values.**

Printing the output

If you want a hard copy of the output, follow the procedure described in Section 3.5. The precise details will depend upon your local set-up.

The independent samples *t* test

Run an independent samples *t* test on the full data set as described in Section 6.2.2 but do not remove any outliers at this stage.

Output for the independent samples *t* test

Guidance on how to interpret the output is given in Section 6.2.2. We suggest you study that section and try to answer the following questions.

- **On the basis of the Levene test p-value, which row of the *t* test results will you use?**

- **Write down the value of t and its tail probability. Is the p-value evidence against the null hypothesis? Remember that if the result is sufficiently unlikely (i.e. $p < 0.05$) under the null hypothesis, it is regarded as evidence against the null hypothesis and hence in favour of the experimental hypothesis.**

- **Write down your interpretation of the result of the test: has the *t* test confirmed the pattern shown by the means of the two groups?**

- **If the hypothesis had been one-tailed (e.g. that decision times of the experimental group will tend to be shorter than those of the control group), then the appropriate p-value would be obtained by dividing the two-tailed p-value by 2. What would be the one-tailed p-value in that case?**

A nonparametric equivalent of the independent samples *t* test: The Mann-Whitney U test

The running of the **Mann-Whitney** test on SPSS is described in Section 6.4.1. Run the procedure as described in that section.

Output for the Mann-Whitney test

The output gives the values of the statistics U and W (the W statistic belongs to a test by Wilcoxon which is the exact equivalent of the Mann-Whitney), followed by a standard normal deviate score Z and a 2-tailed probability value corrected for ties. An exact 2-tailed probability value not corrected for ties concludes the table. If the p-value is less than 0.05, the null hypothesis can be rejected and the groups declared to differ significantly.

- **Write down the results of the Mann-Whitney test, including the value of U and its p-value. State whether the result is significant and whether the Mann-Whitney test confirms the result of the *t* test. In what circumstances might you expect the p-values of U and t to differ?**

Printing the output

To obtain a hard copy of the output, proceed as described in Section 3.5.

Re-running the tests after deselecting the two outliers

Deselect the two outliers using the **Select Cases...** procedure (see Section 3.3.1) by entering score <600 in the **Select Cases** dialog box. Then re-run the *t* test and the Mann-Whitney test.

- **Write down the new value of t and its p-value (assuming a two-tail test). Is the conclusion different from what it was with the complete data set?**

- **Write down the results of the Mann-Whitney test (assuming a two-tail test), including the value of U and its p-value. Is the conclusion different from what it was with the complete data set?**

- **Write down your interpretation of the effects on each test of eliminating the outliers.**

Finishing the session

Close down SPSS and any other windows before logging out of the computer.

EXERCISE 9

Comparing the averages of two related samples of data

Before you start

The methods described in the previous Exercise, (the **independent samples *t* test** and the **Mann-Whitney** test), are appropriate for data from a between subjects experiment, that is, one with independent samples of participants in the two groups. Suppose, however, that the data had come from an experiment in which the same participants had been tested under both the experimental and control conditions. Such a within subjects experiment would yield a set of paired (or related) data. In this Exercise, we shall consider some methods for comparing the averages of the scores obtained under the experimental and control conditions when we have a set of paired data (SPSS calls such sets **paired samples**), rather than independent samples. Before proceeding with this exercise, the reader should review the material in Section 6.2.5.

THE PAIRED-SAMPLES T TEST

An experiment on hemispherical specialisation

In an experiment investigating the relative ease with which words presented in the left and right visual fields were recognised, participants were instructed to fixate a spot in the centre of the field. They were told that, after a short interval, a word would appear to the left or the right of the spot and they were to press a key as soon as they recognised it. In the trials that followed, each word was presented an equal number of times in each field, though the order of presentation of the words was, of course, randomised. From the results, a table of median decision times was constructed from the participants' reactions to presentations of 40 words in each of the two visual fields (Table 1).

Table 1. Median decision times for words presented to the right and left visual fields

Case	Right visual field	Left visual field	Case	Right visual field	Left visual field
1	323	324	8	439	442
2	493	512	9	682	683
3	502	503	10	703	998
4	376	385	11	598	600
5	428	453	12	456	462
6	343	345	13	653	704
7	523	543	14	652	653

Comparing averages: two-sample and one-sample tests

The question is whether these data support the experimental hypothesis that there is a difference between the response times for words in the left and right visual fields? Before proceeding with this Exercise, we suggest you read Section 6.2.5, which describes the procedure for a paired-samples *t* test.

Opening SPSS

In the opening window of SPSS, select the **Type in data** radio button. If **Data View** appears first, click the tab labelled **Variable View** to open **Variable View**.

Preparing the SPSS data set

In the data set for the independent samples *t* test, one of the variables must be a grouping variable, showing which participants performed under which conditions. With the paired-samples *t* test, however, there are no groups, so no coding variable is needed.

After naming a variable *Case*, name two more variables: *RVF* with the label *Right Visual Field* in the **Label** column, and *LVF* with the label *Left Visual Field* in the **Label** column. Since there are no decimals in the data, ensure that the values in the **Decimals** column are all 0.

Select **Data View** and enter the data in the usual way, as described in Section 3.1.2.

Exploring the data

As always, it is wise to explore the data, rather than automatically pressing ahead with a formal test. Use **Scatter** in the **Graphs** menu for a *Left Visual Field* against *Right Visual Field*. From inspection of the scatterplot, it is quite clear that there is a glaringly obvious outlier. It is instructive to ascertain the effect of its presence upon the results of the *t* test, in comparison with the nonparametric **Wilcoxon** and **Sign** tests.

Running the paired-samples *t* test

Run the **paired-samples *t* test** by following the procedure described in Section 6.2.5.

Output for the paired-samples *t* test

From the details given in the *t* test output, it is clear that there are contraindications against the use of the paired-samples *t* test for the data in the present experiment. There is marked discrepancy between the standard deviations of the scores obtained under the *Right Visual Field* and *Left Visual Field* conditions, which arises from the presence of an outlier, which showed up dramatically in the scatterplot.

- Write down the value of *t* and its p-value. Is *t* significant? Write down, in terms of the research hypothesis, the meaning of this result.

What has happened here? You should find the *t* test result puzzling to say the least. You might find another clue by examining the distribution of differences between the scores. Use **Compute** to calculate a difference between *Left Visual Field* and *Right Visual Field*, putting the answer in a variable called *Differences*.

- **What do you notice about the values in *Differences*? Is there a discernible pattern? (What about the directions of the differences?) Relate this to the scientific hypothesis.**

NONPARAMETRIC ALTERNATIVES TO THE PAIRED-SAMPLES T TEST

The Wilcoxon matched pairs test

Now carry out the **Wilcoxon matched pairs** test, following the procedure described in Section 6.4.2.

- **Write down the value of the statistic and its p-value. Compare the p-value with that for the *t* test. Do the results of the test support the scientific hypothesis?**

The Sign test

This test is based very simply on how many positive and negative differences there are between pairs of data, assuming that the value of one variable is consistently subtracted from the value of the other. It is a straightforward application of the **binomial test** to paired data, such as the results of the visual field experiment above. To merely record the signs (rather than the magnitudes) of the differences between the times for the left and right visual fields is certainly to lose a considerable amount of information.

When paired data show no contraindications for using a parametric test, the *t* **test** is preferable to the **Sign test** because the latter would incur a needless sacrifice of statistical power. The great advantage of the **Sign test** is its robustness to the influence of outliers and no assumptions about bivariate normality in the original paired data. The procedure is very similar to that for the **Wilcoxon test** except that within the **Test Type** box, the **Wilcoxon** check box should be clicked off and the **Sign** check box clicked on. Click **OK** to run the test.

- **Write down the results of the Sign test, including the p-value. Is the result significant? Compare this with the result of the paired samples *t* test and explain any discrepancy.**

Eliminating the outliers

When there are contraindications for the *t* **test**, the use of a nonparametric test is not the only alternative available. Another approach is to consider the possibility of deselecting some of the data. In the present set of paired data, there is one difference between scores value in the variable *Differences* that is much larger than all the others. This may have arisen because *Case 10* had special difficulty in recognising words in the left visual field. At any rate, that participant's performance is quite atypical, and certainly calls into question the claim that he or she was drawn from the same population as the others. It is instructive to re-analyse the data after excluding the scores of *Case 10*. This is done by using the **Select Cases** procedure (Section 3.3.1). Follow the procedure described in that section to eliminate *Case 10* from the data. (Hint: give the instruction to select cases if *case* ~= 10. The sign ~= means "not equal to".)

Now re-run the **paired-samples *t* test**, and run both the **Wilcoxon** and the **Sign** test on the reduced data set. Examine the new output.

- **Write down the value of t and its tail probability. Write down your interpretation of this new result. Similarly give the statistics and their p-values for the Sign and Wilcoxon tests. Explain your findings.**

Finishing the session

Close down SPSS and any other windows before logging out of the computer.

EXERCISE 10

One-sample tests

Before you start

Before beginning this Exercise, the reader should study Section 6.5.

The Kolmogorov-Smirnov test for goodness-of-fit

A researcher wishes to ascertain whether response latencies have been drawn from a normal population. The **Kolmogorov-Smirnov test** is an appropriate goodness-of-fit test for this purpose. Table 1 shows the decision-making response latencies of fifty young adults.

Table 1. Response latencies of fifty young adults (ms)

910	1013	921	895	879	906	892	902	902	858
874	900	894	872	909	878	935	878	849	969
879	926	877	861	876	906	897	860	887	968
896	905	876	906	928	899	899	899	889	903
977	900	899	892	986	891	881	879	850	874

Name a variable *Latency* and enter the data. Draw a histogram of the distribution, along with a normal curve using

Analyze
> **Descriptive Statistics**
>> **Frequencies…**

to open the **Frequencies** dialog box. Click **Charts…** and select **Histograms**, together with the checkbox **With normal curve**. Return to the **Frequencies** dialog box by clicking **Continue** and ensure that the tick in **Display frequency tables** has been turned off. Finally click **OK**.

- From inspection of the histogram, would you expect the Kolmogorov-Smirnov test to accept or reject the null hypothesis of normality of distribution?

- If the normal curve were a good fit, where would you expect most of the area under the bars to lie?

Run a **Kolmogorov-Smirnov** test for goodness-of-fit on the data in Table 1, as described in Section 6.5.1.

- Write out the result of the Kolmogorov-Smirnov test.

- Is the result what you had expected?

Nominal data: The binomial test

A die is rolled ten times, during which 6 sixes turn up. Have we grounds for suspecting that the die is unfair? Note that the probability of obtaining a six from the roll of a die is 1/6 (0.17). This is the null hypothesis value to enter as the **Test Proportion** in the **Binomial Test** dialog box (see Section 6.5.2).

Use the procedure described in Section 6.5.2 to enter the data but now define the grouping variable as *Die* with the values *1* for *Six* and *2* for *Not Six*. Remember to apply **Weight Cases…** to the second variable *Freq* and to change the value of **Test Proportion** in the **Binomial Test** dialog box.

- Write out the result of the binomial test.
- Do we have grounds for suspecting that the die is unfair?

Nominal data: The chi-square test for goodness-of-fit

One hundred 5-year-old children are asked which of five toys they prefer. Their choices are as in Table 2.

Table 2. Toy preference

Toy A	Toy B	Toy C	Toy D	Toy E
40	25	15	15	5

Is there evidence that some toys are preferred to others?

The data are entered as in Section 6.5.2, but with five categories here instead of three. Remember to apply **Weight Cases…** to the second variable *Freq*.

- Write down the result of the chi-square test for goodness-of-fit.
- Referring to this result, write down your answer to the research question. What is the null hypothesis here? What does falsification of the null hypothesis imply?

The one sample *t* test

Table 3 contains the heights of fifty 18-year-old female college students, measured in the year 2000.

Table 3. Heights of female college students (cms)									
162	157	166	157	168	177	168	166	168	166
168	166	161	158	162	167	175	161	171	173
166	178	177	174	178	166	159	175	168	168
166	167	163	173	166	172	166	177	171	168
156	166	165	172	168	162	163	160	169	170

Past records, which ended in 1910, showed that over the previous decade, the mean height of women in the same college was 160 cms. No data on spread (or dispersion) are available. Do the present data suggest that women going to this college are taller (or shorter) nowadays?

The directional question of whether today's college women are taller than their predecessors can be approached by making a **One sample *t* test** (see Section 6.5.3) on the data of Table 3. Enter the data into a variable such as *Height*.
Choose
Analyze
> **Compare Means**
>> **One-Sample T Test...**

to obtain the **One-Sample T Test** dialog box. For the **Test Value**, enter the value *160*. Click **OK** to run the test.

- **Write out the result of the one-sample *t* test.**
- **Does the result of the test indicate that today's college women are taller?**

Finishing the session

Close down SPSS and any other windows before logging out of the computer.

CHAPTER 7

The one-factor between subjects experiment

7.1   Introduction

7.2   The one-way ANOVA

7.3   Nonparametric tests

7.1   INTRODUCTION

7.1.1   Rationale of the ANOVA: The F test

In Chapter 6, we saw that if two groups of participants perform a task under different conditions, an independent samples t-test can be used to test the null hypothesis (H_0) of equality of the two population means. If the test shows significance, we reject H_0 and conclude that there is a difference between the two population means.

The same null hypothesis, however, can also be tested by using one of the set of techniques known as **analysis of variance** (**ANOVA** for short). Despite its name, the ANOVA, like the t-test, is concerned with the testing of hypotheses about **means**. In fact, if the ANOVA and the (pooled) t-test are applied to the data from a simple, two-group experiment, the tests will give the same result: if the t-test shows the difference between the means to be significant, then so will the ANOVA and vice versa.

The ANOVA, however, is more versatile than the t-test. Suppose that in an investigation of the effects of mnemonic training upon recall, three groups of subjects are tested:
1. A group trained in Mnemonic Method A;
2. A group trained in Mnemonic Method B;
3. An untrained Control group, who were asked only to memorise the material.

Does mnemonic training have any effect? The null hypothesis is the negation of this possibility: it states that, in the population, the mean amounts recalled are the same under the three conditions. The t-test cannot test this hypothesis. The **one-way ANOVA**, however, can test the null hypothesis that all three population means are equal.

A lucid account of the one-factor between subjects (one-way) ANOVA is given in Gravetter & Wallnau (2000), Chapter 13. Basically, the rationale is this. A group mean is an estimate of people's typical level of performance under one condition. Suppose that mnemonic groups A and B easily outperformed the control group: in other words, there is high variability **between (i.e. among) groups**. Some of this variability between means, however, arises from sampling error, which we shall need to estimate. The sampling error of the mean can be estimated from the spread of the scores in each group around their group mean. The **ANOVA F statistic** is calculated by dividing an estimate of the **between groups** variance by an estimate of the **within groups** variance:

$$F = \frac{\text{variance between}}{\text{variance within}}$$

Although the between groups variance estimate is found from the values of the group (treatment) means, its value reflects not only population differences among the group means, but also sampling error. The within groups estimate is simply the average of the variances of the scores in the different groups and so does not reflect differences between groups. It is, in fact, a pooled estimate of the supposedly constant population variance of the scores at all levels of the single treatment factor.

If there are substantial differences in the population among the treatment means, the numerator of F (and therefore the value of F itself) will be inflated and the null hypothesis is likely to be rejected. If, on the other hand, there are no differences in the population, both the numerator and denominator of F reflect only sampling error. In that case, they will usually have similar values, giving a value of F close to unity. A high value of F, therefore, is evidence against the null hypothesis of equality of all three population means.

There remains a problem. If H_0 states that all the means are equal, the alternative hypothesis is simply that they are not all equal. If the ANOVA F test is significant, we can conclude there is at least one difference **somewhere** among the means; but we cannot claim that the mean for any particular group is significantly different from the mean of any other group. Further analysis is necessary to confirm whatever differences there may be among the individual treatment means.

7.1.2 Planned and post hoc comparisons

The question of exactly how one should proceed after finding a significant F test is not a simple one, and an adequate treatment of it earns an extensive chapter in many statistical texts (e.g. Gravetter & Wallnau, 2000; Howell, 2002). It is important to distinguish between those comparisons that were **planned** before the data were actually gathered, and those that are made as part of the inevitable process of unplanned **data-snooping** that takes place after the results have been obtained. Planned comparisons are often known as **a priori** comparisons; unplanned comparisons are known as **post hoc** comparisons. It is possible to do either kind of comparison with SPSS.

Effect size

In the context of ANOVA, effect size is conceived as the proportion of the total variability among the scores that can be explained by manipulation of the treatment factor: that is,

$$\text{Effect size} = \frac{\text{Explained variability}}{\text{Total variability}}$$

The oldest measure of effect size is the statistic η^2 (**eta squared**), which is also known as the **correlation ratio**.

For the one-way ANOVA, the value of η^2 is given by the following formula:

$$\eta^2 = \frac{SS_{treatment}}{SS_{total}} = \frac{SS_{between}}{SS_{total}}$$

where SS represented the total "sum of squares" for the various subscripts shown.

We can also obtain the value of η^2 directly from the value of the F ratio with the equivalent formula:

$$\eta^2 = \frac{(g-1)F}{(g-1)F + g(n-1)}$$

where g is the number of groups and n is number of participants in each group.

The following table shows how η^2 compares with Cohen's classification of **effect size**.

Table 1. Cohen's d statistic, eta-squared and effect size		
Cohen's d statistic	η^2	**Cohen's effect size**
0.2	.01	Small
0.3	.02	
0.4	.04	
0.5	.06	Medium
0.6	.08	
0.7	.11	
0.8	.14	Large
0.9	.17	
1.0	.20	
1.1	.23	
1.2	.27	
1.3	.30	
1.4	.33	
1.5	.36	
1.6	.39	
1.7	.42	
1.8	.45	
1.9	.47	
2.0	.50	

Cohen's labels for **effect size** were intended as a very tentative classification: nowhere does he specify precise ranges of d for 'small', 'medium' and 'large' effects. An **effect size** of .25, for example, would be a 'smallish' effect (Welkowitz, Ewen & Cohen, 1982; p.228). Presumably d = .7 would qualify as 'largish' and d = .6 as 'middling'. Anything from .8 upwards would come clearly into the 'large' category.

The statistic η^2 tends to overestimate the effect size in the population. A measure of effect size that corrects this positive bias is $\hat{\omega}^2$ (estimated omega squared), which is given by

$$\hat{\omega}^2 = \frac{SS_{between} - (g-1)MS_{within}}{SS_{total} + MS_{within}}$$

where g is the number of groups. The value of $\hat{\omega}^2$ can also be found from the value of F thus:

$$\hat{\omega}^2 = \frac{(g-1)(F-1)}{(g-1)(F-1) + N}$$

where $N = gn$, the total number of participants (Keppel & Wickens, 2004; p.164).

How many participants shall I need?

In the next section, we shall consider the ANOVA of some data from a between subjects experiment in which three groups of participants recall material under three different conditions. How many participants shall we need if we wish to find an effect of medium size with a power of .8?

Clark-Carter (1997) provides a series of tables for use with ANOVA designs, each table giving the sample sizes necessary to achieve specified power levels for a range of effect sizes. Each table is applicable to an ANOVA source with a fixed number of degrees of freedom. Since our single treatment factor has three conditions, the degrees of freedom for that factor is 2. Table A15.5, p621, is appropriate for "Treatment df = 2".

Entering Table A15.5 at the column headed $\eta^2 = .059$ (the nearest value to .06 for a medium-sized effect) and choosing the row with the nearest value of power to .8 (namely .79), we find that n = 50 for that row. We shall therefore need a total of 150 participants for the three conditions in our experiment.

7.2   THE ONE-WAY ANOVA

7.2.1   An experiment on the efficacy of two mnemonic techniques

Suppose that the recall of material by two groups of participants, each trained in a different mnemonic method (*Mnemonic A* or *Mnemonic B*), is compared with that of a group of untrained controls. The results are shown in Table 2.

Table 2. The numbers of words recalled by participants using different mnemonic training methods									
Control Group	3	5	3	2	4	6	9	3	8	10
Mnemonic A	10	8	15	9	11	16	17	17	7	10
Mnemonic B	20	15	14	15	17	10	8	11	18	19

As with drug experiment, we shall need two variables:
1. A grouping variable *Group* identifying the condition under which a score was achieved;
2. A variable *Score* containing all the scores in the data set.

This time, however, the grouping variable will consist of three values (one for each mnemonic method, the third for the controls). You might assign the values thus: *1 = Control; 2 = Mnemonic A; 3 = Mnemonic B*. The following sections will be clearer if you prepare the data set in **Variable View** and **Data View** before reading these sections so that you can run the procedures in SPSS as they are described.

Exploring the data

Before embarking on the ANOVA, it is important to check the data for anomalies such as extreme values or skewed distributions. This can be done with the **Explore** command (see Chapter 4, Section 4.3.2) for the independent samples t-test, or more simply with the **Boxplot...** command in the **Graphs** menu. The boxplots are shown in Output 1 where it can be seen that the data set has no extreme values or outliers. The eccentric positions of the median lines in the *Control* and *Mnemonic A* boxes, however, indicate that the scores in those groups have skewed distributions. We can proceed with the ANOVA, however, without deselecting any cases.

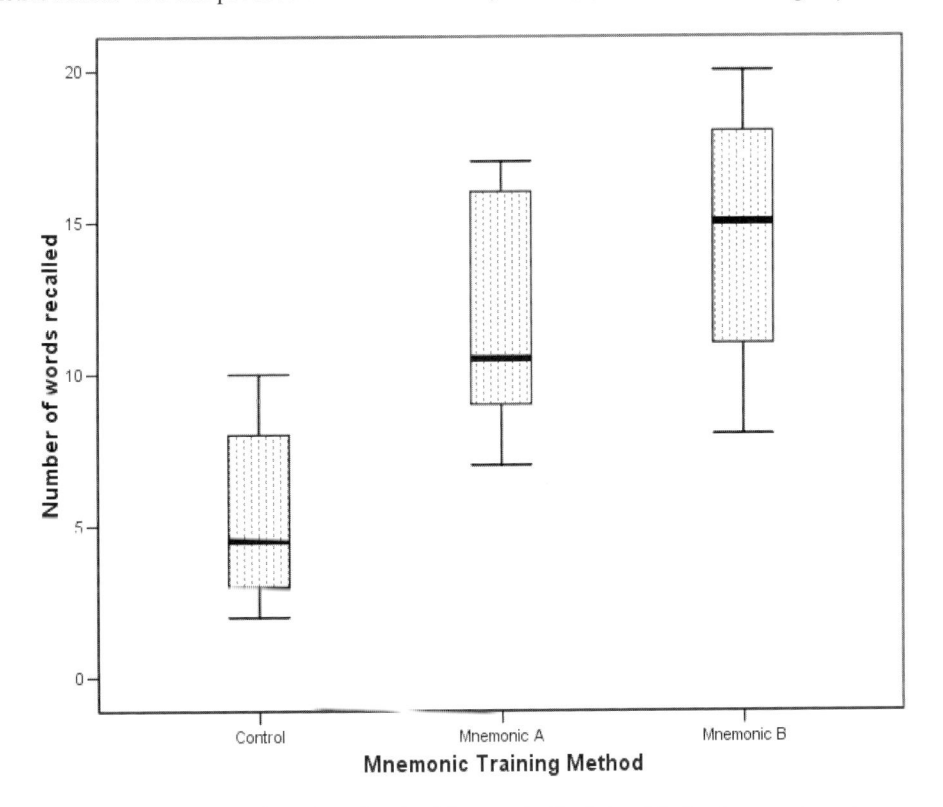

See Section 4.3.2

Output 1. The boxplots for the Mnemonic Training Methods experiment

7.2.2 Procedure for the one-way ANOVA

The one-way analysis of variance is selected by proceeding as follows:

- Choose
  Analyze
     General Linear Model (see Figure 1)
        Univariate…
  to open the **Univariate** dialog box (the completed box is shown in Figure 2).
- Transfer the variable names as shown in Figure 2.

Should the user not want to use all the levels in a grouping variable, it would be necessary to invoke the **Select Cases** command to identify the levels for the analysis.

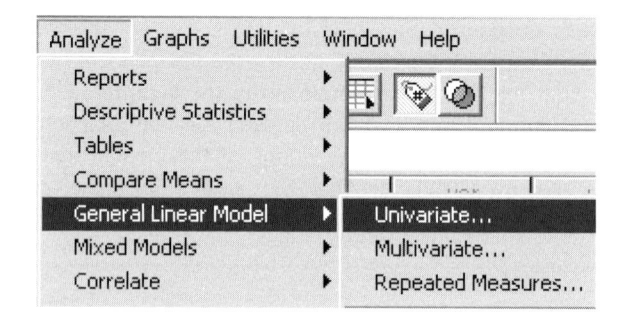

Figure 1. The **General Linear Model** menu in **Analyze**

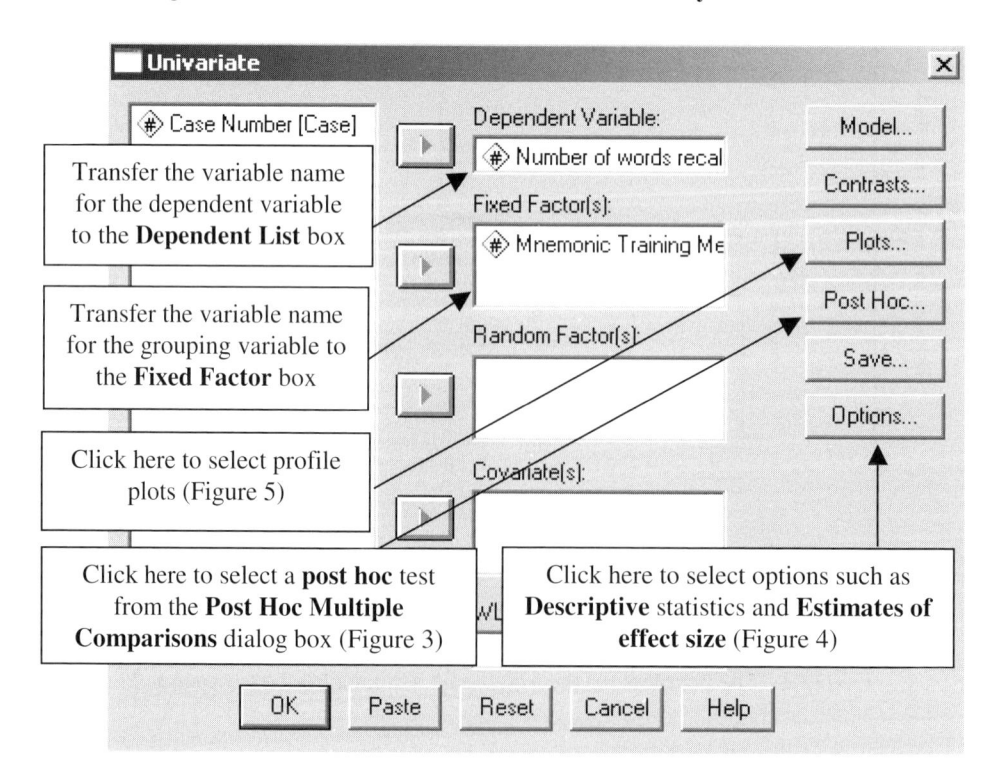

Figure 2. The **Univariate** dialog box with *Number of words recalled* as the dependent variable and *Mnemonic Training Method* as the independent variable

The one factor between subjects experiment

- Unplanned multiple pairwise comparisons among the means can be requested by clicking the **Post Hoc...** button to obtain the **Univariate: Post Hoc Multiple Comparisons for Observed Means** dialog box (Figure 3). Transfer the variable name *Group* to the **Post Hoc Tests for** box, click the check box opposite **Tukey** and finally the **Continue** button.

Figure 3. The **Post Hoc Multiple Comparisons** dialog box with **Tukey** selected

- **Descriptive statistics, Estimates of effect size** and **Homogeneity tests** (i.e. Levene's test) can be obtained by clicking **Options** to obtain the **Univariate: Options** dialog box (Figure 4), clicking the appropriate check boxes and finally the **Continue** button.

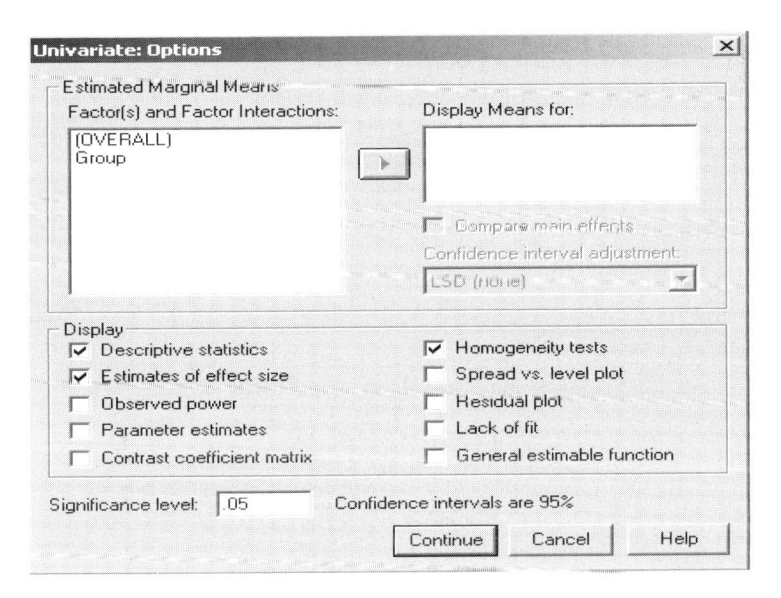

Figure 4. The **Options** dialog box with **Descriptive statistics, Estimates of effect size** and **Homogeneity tests** selected

- Click **Plots...** to open the **Univariate: Profile Plots** dialog box (Figure 5). Transfer the variable name *Group* to the **Horizontal Axis** box and click on the activated **Add** button to transfer the name *Group* to the **Plots** box below. Click **Continue** to return to the **Univariate** dialog box.
- Finally click **OK** to run the analysis.

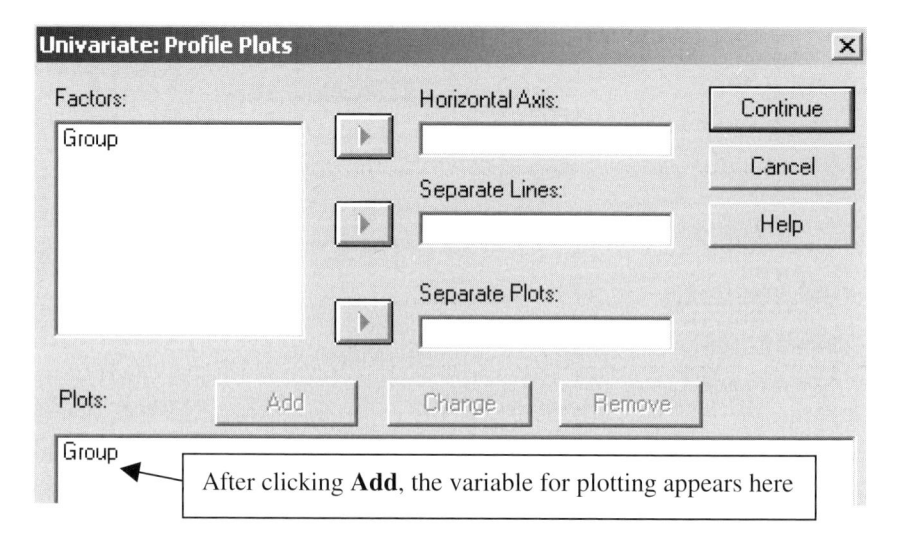

Figure 5. The top part of the **Profile Plots** dialog box with *Group* selected for plotting

7.2.3 Output for the one-way ANOVA

Descriptive statistics

Output 2 shows the specifications of the independent variable *Mnemonic Training Method*.

Between-Subjects Factors

		Value Label	N
Mnemonic Training Method	1	Control	10
	2	Mnemonic A	10
	3	Mnemonic B	10

Output 2. Specification of the levels of the between-subjects factor

Check this table, to make sure that SPSS agrees that the factor has three levels and 10 participants are tested at each level. Transcription errors can be spotted here.

Output 3 tabulates the requested **Descriptive statistics** and the **Levene's Test for Equality of Variance**.

Descriptive Statistics

Dependent Variable: Number of words recalled

Mnemonic	Mean	Std. Deviation	N
Control	5.30	2.830	10
Mnemonic A	12.00	3.859	10
Mnemonic B	14.70	4.001	10
Total	10.67	5.313	30

Levene's Test of Equality of Error Variances

Dependent Variable: Number of words recalled

F	df1	df2	Sig.
1.013	2	27	.377

Tests the null hypothesis that the error variance of the dependent variable is equal across groups.

The p-value (Sig.) for the **Levene F Statistic** is 0.377 (not significant). Thus there is no evidence for heterogeneity of variance

Output 3. The requested descriptive statistics and homogeneity test

The non-significance of the **Levene Statistic** for the **Test of Homogeneity of Variances** indicates that the assumption of homogeneity of variance is tenable.

The profile plot of means

The requested profile plot of the means is shown in Output 4.

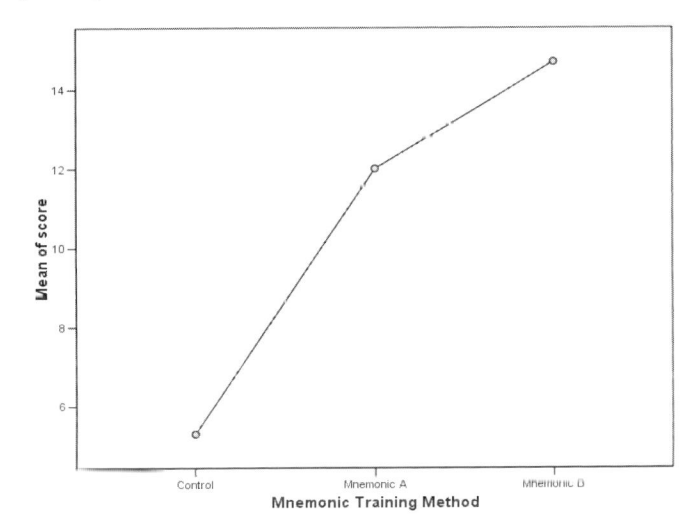

Output 4. The plot of the means

The ANOVA summary table

The summary table for the one-way ANOVA is shown in Output 5.

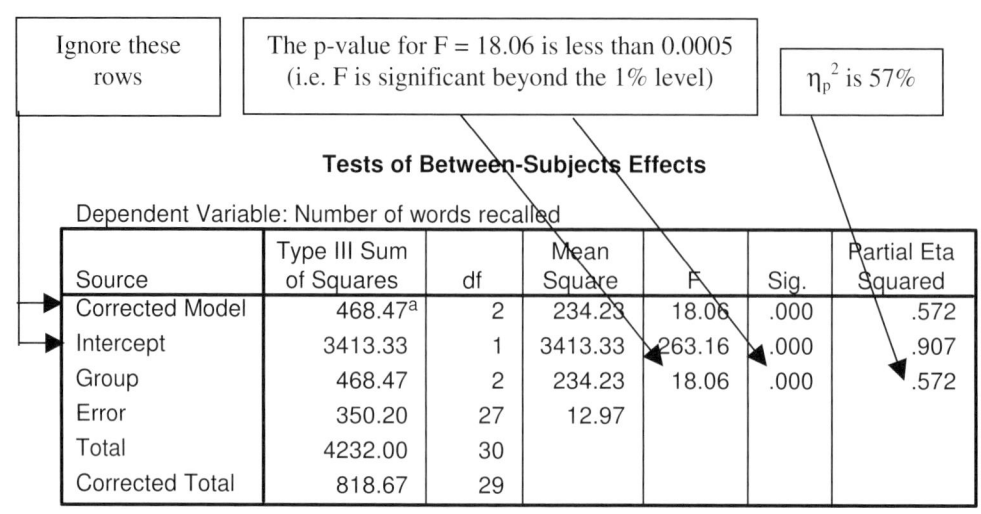

Tests of Between-Subjects Effects

Dependent Variable: Number of words recalled

Source	Type III Sum of Squares	df	Mean Square	F	Sig.	Partial Eta Squared
Corrected Model	468.47[a]	2	234.23	18.06	.000	.572
Intercept	3413.33	1	3413.33	263.16	.000	.907
Group	468.47	2	234.23	18.06	.000	.572
Error	350.20	27	12.97			
Total	4232.00	30				
Corrected Total	818.67	29				

a. R Squared = .572 (Adjusted R Squared = .541)

Annotations:
- Ignore these rows (Corrected Model, Intercept)
- The p-value for F = 18.06 is less than 0.0005 (i.e. F is significant beyond the 1% level)
- η_p^2 is 57%

Output 5. The **Summary Table** for ANOVA with F and η_p^2

Some terms in Output 5 may be unfamiliar. The terms **Corrected Model** and **Intercept** refer to the regression method that was used to run the ANOVA and need not concern us. The term **Type III Sum of Squares** need not concern us either.

By using the methods described in Chapter 3, the default table was edited to remove all unnecessary information. The number of decimal places was reduced to two by double-clicking the whole table so that it showed a hashed border, highlighting the appropriate column of numbers so that they were shown in inverse video, clicking the right-hand mouse button to show a menu, selecting the item **Cell Properties…**, selecting in the **Format** box the item *#.#*, changing the number of decimals shown in the **Decimals** box to 2, and finally clicking **OK**. The edited table is shown in Output 6.

Tests of Between-Subjects Effects

Dependent Variable: Number of words recalled

Source	Sums of Squares	df	Mean Square	F	Sig.	Partial Eta Squared
Group	468.47	2	234.23	18.06	.000	.572
Error	350.20	27	12.97			
Corrected Total	818.67	29				

Output 6. The edited **ANOVA summary table**

The p-value (**Sig.**) for the F ratio of 18.06 is listed as .000, which means that it is less than .0005. Therefore, H_0 is rejected. Note that in a scientific paper, it is not acceptable to write, 'p = .000'. Write the p-value as: $p < .0005$.

Notice the column headed **Partial Eta Squared**, which is denoted by η_p^2. In the one-way ANOVA, the value of this statistic is simply that of η^2 as we defined it earlier:

$$\eta_p^2 = \frac{SS_{between}}{SS_{between} + SS_{within}} = \frac{SS_{group}}{SS_{group} + SS_{error}} = \frac{468.47}{468.47 + 350.20} = 0.572$$

Clearly using a mnemonic strategy has been shown to have a large effect upon recall.

It is instructive to calculate the value of $\hat{\omega}^2$, a more conservative estimate of effect strength. It is easier to calculate $\hat{\omega}^2$ from the F ratio thus:

$$\hat{\omega}^2 = \frac{(g-1)(F-1)}{(g-1)(F-1)+N} = \frac{2(18.06-1)}{2(18.06-1)+30} = 0.532$$

As expected, this estimate of effect strength is slightly lower than η_p^2.

We suggest that your report of the results of the ANOVA might run along the following lines:

> The mean scores under the Mnemonic A (M = 12.00, SD = 3.859) and Mnemonic B (M = 14.70, SD = 4.001) conditions were higher than the mean score for the control group (M = 5.30, SD = 2.830). The one-way ANOVA showed F to be significant beyond the .01 level: F(2, 27) = 18.06; p <.0005. Partial eta squared = .572.

Notice the manner in which the value of F is reported. The bracketed numbers are the degrees of freedom of the between subjects and within subjects (error) mean squares.

Unplanned multiple comparisons with Tukey's HSD test

The results of the **Tukey** test are tabulated in Outputs 7 and 8.

Output 7 lists the differences between means **Mean Difference (I-J)**, their standard errors, p-values (**Sig.**) and **95% Confidence Interval** for each pair. Inspection of the p values shows that the Control group differs significantly (p < 0.05) from both Mnemonic A and Mnemonic B groups but mnemonic A does not differ significantly from Mnemonic B (p > 0.05).

This is more clearly shown by Output 8, in which the groups are divided into homogeneous subsets, thus showing which means do *not* differ from one another (i.e. the members within each subset). Here the *Control* group, whose mean score differs significantly from *Mnemonic A* and from *Mnemonic B*, is in a separate subset from the other two groups, which do not differ significantly from one another.

Multiple Comparisons

Dependent Variable: Number of words recalled
Tukey HSD

(I) Mnemonic Training Method	(J) Mnemonic Training Method	Mean Difference (I-J)	Std. Error	Sig.	95% Confidence Interval Lower Bound	95% Confidence Interval Upper Bound
Control	Mnemonic A	-6.70*	1.61	.00	-10.69	-2.71
	Mnemonic B	-9.40*	1.61	.00	-13.39	-5.41
Mnemonic A	Control	6.70*	1.61	.00	2.71	10.69
	Mnemonic B	-2.70	1.61	.23	-6.69	1.29
Mnemonic B	Control	9.40*	1.61	.00	5.41	13.39
	Mnemonic A	2.70	1.61	.23	-1.29	6.69

*. The mean difference is significant at the .05 level.

These differences are significant since the p-value is less than 0.01

These differences are not significant since the p-value is greater than 0.05

Output 7. The **Tukey test** output

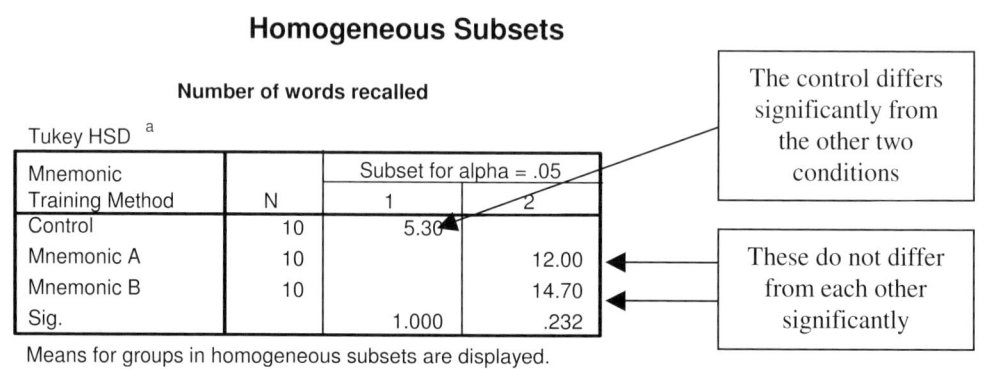

Homogeneous Subsets

Number of words recalled

Tukey HSD [a]

Mnemonic Training Method	N	Subset for alpha = .05 — 1	Subset for alpha = .05 — 2
Control	10	5.30	
Mnemonic A	10		12.00
Mnemonic B	10		14.70
Sig.		1.000	.232

Means for groups in homogeneous subsets are displayed.
a. Uses Harmonic Mean Sample Size = 10.000.

The control differs significantly from the other two conditions

These do not differ from each other significantly

Output 8. The homogeneous subsets from **Tukey's test**

The rationale of **Tukey's HSD** test is that if the treatment means are arranged in order of magnitude, and the smallest is subtracted from the largest, the probability of obtaining a large difference increases with the size of the array of means. For a pairwise difference to achieve significance on the Tukey test, it must exceed a **critical difference (CD)**, which is given by the formula

$$CD = q_{critical}\sqrt{\frac{MS_{error}}{n}}$$

where $q_{critical}$ is the critical value of a special statistic known as the **Studentized Range Statistic q**. (A table of critical values for *q* is given in Howell, 2002; pp. 744 – 745, Appendix q.) The MS_{error} is the mean square for the error term of the one-way ANOVA, and n is the number of scores in each treatment group.

The **Univariate: Post Hoc Multiple Comparisons** dialog box (Figure 4) listed several other tests for making unplanned comparisons. There is a discussion of various *post hoc* tests in Howell (2002), Chapter 12.

7.2.4 Other techniques

SPSS will run **planned comparisons** and (where the independent variable is quantitative) a **trend analysis**. These techniques are described in texts such as Howell (2002) and Keppel & Wickens (2004). We shall not consider them further here.

7.3 NONPARAMETRIC TESTS

Should the data be unsuitable for ANOVA (as when there is marked heterogeneity of variance, or the data are highly skewed), one should consider using **nonparametric** tests, which assume neither homogeneity of variance nor a normal distribution. With inherently ordinal data, the parametric ANOVA cannot be used in any case (see Chapter 5).

7.3.1 The Kruskal-Wallis test

The nonparametric equivalent of the one-way (between subjects) ANOVA is the **Kruskal-Wallis Test**. To run this test, proceed as follows:
- Choose
  Analyze
    Nonparametric Tests
      K Independent Samples… (Figure 6)
  to open the **Tests for Several Independent Samples** dialog box (the completed version is shown in Figure 7).

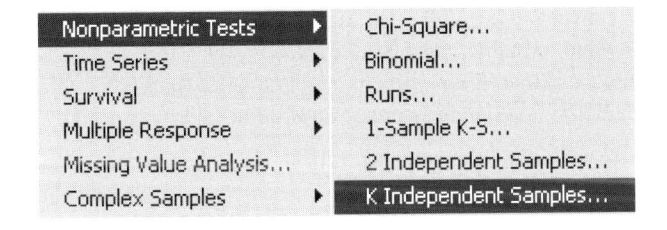

Figure 6. Part of the **Analyze** menu showing **Nonparametric Tests** and its submenu with **K Independent Samples** selected

- Transfer the variable names and define the range of the grouping variable as shown in Figure 7.
- Since the **Exact** tests can take some time, we shall content ourselves with the **asymptotic** p-value.
- Click **OK**.

> Transfer the variable name for the dependent variable to the **Test Variable List** box

> Transfer the variable name for the grouping variable to the **Grouping Variable** box

> When the grouping variable name is first transferred, the **Define Range...** button will highlight. Click it to open the **Define Range** dialog box. Enter 1 in the **Minimum** box and 3 in the **Maximum** box, then click **Continue**.

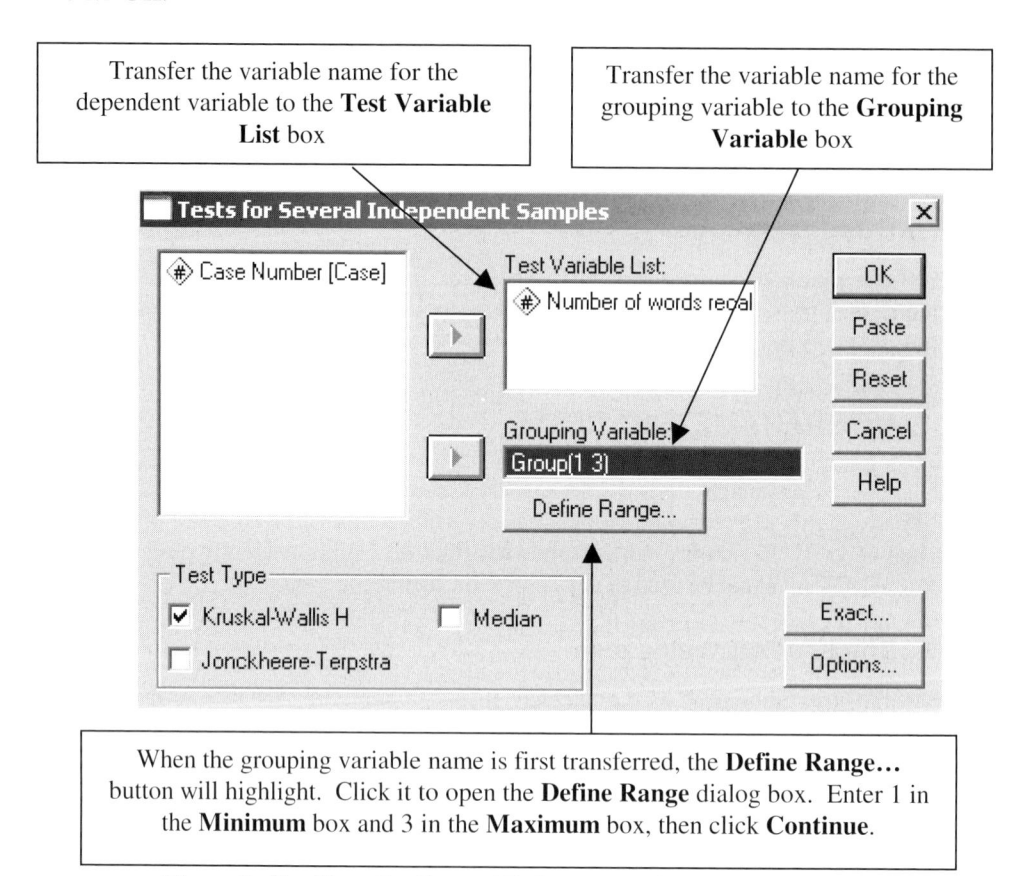

Figure 7. The **Tests for Several Independent Samples** dialog box

The test results are shown in Output 9. The first subtable, **Ranks**, tabulates the mean rank for each group. The second subtable, **Test Statistics**, lists the value of Chi-Square, its df and its p-value (**Asymp. Sig.**). Since the p-value is much smaller than 0.01, the Kruskal-Wallis test agrees with the parametric test that the three groups do not perform equally well. We can write this result as:

> The mean rank under the Mnemonic A condition is 17.8 and Mnemonic B condition is 22.10 compared with 6.60 for the control group. The Kruskal-Wallis chi-square test is significant beyond the .01 level: χ^2 (2) = 16.63; p < .005.

Kruskal-Wallis Test

Ranks

	Mnemonic Training Method	N	Mean Rank
Number of words recalled	Control	10	6.60
	Mnemonic A	10	17.80
	Mnemonic B	10	22.10
	Total	30	

Test Statistics[a,b]

	Number of words recalled
Chi-Square	16.63
df	2.00
Asymp. Sig.	.00

The p-value associated with a Chi-square value of 16.63 is less than 0.005 (i.e. the test is significant at the 1% level)

a. Kruskal Wallis Test
b. Grouping Variable: Mnemonic Training Method

Output 9. The Kruskal-Wallis One-Way ANOVA output

7.3.2 Dichotomous data: The Chi-square test

If three groups of participants attempt a problem under different conditions, and it is noted whether each individual managed to solve it, the result will be a set of nominal data. With such a data set, the **chi-square test** can be used to test the null hypothesis that, in the population, there is no tendency for the problem to be solved more often in some conditions than in others. The procedure is described in Chapter 11.

EXERCISE 11

One-factor between subjects ANOVA

Before you start

We suggest that you review the material in Chapter 7 before working through this practical exercise.

The purpose of a one-factor between subjects ANOVA

In one-factor between subjects ANOVA, the **F ratio** compares the spread among the treatment means with the (supposedly uniform) spread of the scores within groups about their group means. The purpose of this exercise is to help clarify the rationale of the F ratio by showing how its value is affected by various manipulations of some (or all) of the data. Before proceeding with this exercise, we ask you to suppose that a one-factor ANOVA has been carried out upon a set of data and yields an F value of, say, 7.23. Now suppose we were to multiply every score in the experimental results by a constant, say 10. What would happen to the value of F: would it still be 7.23? Or would it increase? Or decrease?

We also invite you to speculate upon the effect that adding a constant (say 10) to all the scores in just one of the groups would have upon F: suppose, for example, we were to add 10 to all the scores in the group with the largest mean. Would F stay the same, increase or decrease in value? Would the effect be the same if the constant were added to the scores of the group with the smallest mean?

As a first approach to answering these questions, we shall carry out a **one-factor ANOVA** on a set of data. Then we shall see what happens to the value of F when the data are transformed as described in the previous paragraphs.

Some data

Suppose a researcher is interested in how well non-Chinese-speaking students can learn Chinese characters using different kinds of mnemonic. Independent groups of participants are tested under three conditions: *No Mnemonic*, *Mnemonic 1* and *Mnemonic 2*. The dependent variable is the number of Chinese characters that are correctly recalled. The data are shown in Table 1.

Table 1. Results of a completely randomised experiment on the effects of different mnemonic systems upon recall of logographic characters										
No Mnemonic (10 control subjects)	4	6	4	3	5	7	10	4	9	11
Mnemonic 1 (10 subjects trained in Mnemonic 1)	11	9	16	10	12	17	18	16	8	11
Mnemonic 2 (10 subjects trained in Mnemonic 2)	21	16	15	16	18	11	9	12	19	20

Opening SPSS

Open SPSS and select the **Type in data** radio button in the opening window. If **Data View** appears first, click the **Variable View** tab to open **Variable View**.

Construction of the SPSS data set

Rearrange the data of Table 1 into a form suitable for analysis by SPSS by following the procedure described in Section 7.2.1. In **Variable View**, name the variables *Case*, *Group*, *Score*, remembering to change the value in the **Decimals** column to 0 each time. The variable *Group* will need appropriate values and value labels specified in the **Values** column. It is also recommended that variable labels should be entered in the **Label** column e.g. *Case Number*, *Training Condition*.

Switch to **Data View** and enter the data. The easiest way of entering the case numbers is to wait until all the other data have been entered. Then access **Compute** and enter *Case* as the **Target Variable** and *$casenum* as the **Numeric Expression**. All the case numbers will automatically appear in the *Case* column of **Data View**.

Save the data set to a file such as *Ex11 Mnemonics*.

Exploring the data

As always, we recommend a preliminary exploration of the data set before any formal testing is carried out, in case there have been any data entry errors or contraindications for using ANOVA. As in Exercise 8, use the **Means** procedure for descriptive statistics and **Explore** for checks on the distributions of the scores within the groups. (Remember to click the **Plots** radio button to suppress the **Statistics** output. This will save you from being swamped with superfluous statistics).

The output for **Means** begins with a **Case Processing Summary** table, followed by a table labelled **Report** listing the means, number of cases (N) and standard deviations for the three groups. After that, side-by-side boxplots appear.

- Examine the Output for the Means procedure. Do the means appear to differ? Are the standard deviations similar in value?

The output for **Explore** begins with a **Case Processing Summary** table, followed by the stem-and-leaf displays for the three groups. The final item shows the side-by-side boxplots.

- Do the boxplots suggest any anomalies in the distributions of the data in any of the three groups? Write a statement assessing the suitability of the data for ANOVA.

Procedure for the one-way ANOVA

The procedure for the one-way ANOVA is described in detail in Section 7.2.2. Remember to click the **Post Hoc...** button, select **Tukey** and click **Continue** to return to the **Univariate** dialog box. This is because if the ANOVA F-ratio is significant, you will want to know which pairs of means differ significantly.

Click **OK** to run the ANOVA and the multiple comparisons procedure.

Output for the one-way ANOVA

Examine the ANOVA Summary Table.

- Write down the value of F and its associated p-value. Is F significant? What are the implications of this result for the experimental hypothesis? What was the null hypothesis? What does the falsity of the null hypothesis imply?

Look at the table of **Multiple Comparisons**.

- Construct your own table showing clearly which pairs of levels are significantly different and which are not.

RE-ANALYSIS OF TRANSFORMED DATA SETS

In this section, we return to the question of the effects of transforming the data upon the ANOVA statistics.

1) Multiplying every score by a constant

We recommend that whenever you have occasion to transform the values of a variable in an original SPSS data set, you should construct a new target variable, rather than change (perhaps irreversibly) the original data. Use the **Compute** procedure (Section 4.4.2) to multiply each value in the data set by a factor of 10. Follow the instructions in that section, choosing, for the target variable, a mnemonic name such as *AllByTen*. Now change the **One-way ANOVA** dialog box so that the dependent variable is *AllByTen* instead of *Score* and click **OK** to run the analysis.

- Write down the value of F and its associated p-value. Is F significant? What are the implications of this result for the experimental hypothesis?

In the output, you will see that both the between groups and within groups variance estimates have increased by a factor of 100. It is easy to show algebraically that when each of a set of scores is multiplied by a constant, the new variance is the old variance times the square of the constant. Since, however, the factors of 100 in the numerator and denominator of the F ratio cancel out, the value of the F ratio remains unchanged.

2) Adding a constant to the scores in only one group

This time, we want a dependent variable that contains, for two of the three groups, the original scores. In the third (Mnemonic 2) group, however, every score must be increased by 10. First use **Compute** to copy the values in *Score* to a new target variable *NewScore*. Use **Compute** again to add *10* to the numbers in this new variable **only when the grouping variable has the value 3**. To do this, type *NewScore* into the **Target Variable** box and *NewScore +10* in the **Numeric Expression** box. Click **If** to open the **Compute Variable: If Cases** dialog box. Transfer the grouping variable name *Group* into the box and add the expression *=3*. Click **Continue** and **OK** to run the procedure. In **Data View**, check that the values in *NewScore* for the third group have changed but the rest have their original values. Now re-run the **one-way ANOVA**, using *NewScore* as the dependent variable.

- Write down the value of F and its associated p-value. Is F significant? What are the implications of this result for the experimental hypothesis?

You will see that the effect of adding a constant of *10* to all scores in the *Mnemonic 2* group has no effect at all upon the within groups variance estimate. Adding the same constant to all the scores in a set has no effect upon the spread of the scores – it merely shifts the mean. The between groups mean square, however, computed from the values of the treatment means alone, has increased considerably. The within groups mean square, on the other hand, is the average of the variance estimates of the scores within groups and is quite independent of the spread among the group means. Consequently, it is quite possible to change the value of the former without affecting that of the latter and vice versa. The effect of increasing the mean of the third group is to increase the spread of the three treatment means. This increases the value of $MS_{between}$ while leaving MS_{within} unaltered. The result is an increase in F.

Finishing the session

Close down SPSS and any other windows before logging out of the network.

CHAPTER 8

Between subjects factorial experiments

8.1   Introduction

8.2   Factorial ANOVA

8.3   Effect size and power in factorial ANOVA

8.4   Experiments with more than two treatment factors

8.1   INTRODUCTION

Experiments with two or more factors are known as **factorial** experiments. In the simplest case, there is a different sample of participants for each possible combination of conditions. This arrangement is known as a **between subjects** (or **completely randomised**) factorial experiment.

Suppose that a researcher has been commissioned to investigate the effects upon simulated driving performance of two new anti-hay fever drugs, A and B. It is suspected that at least one of the drugs may have different effects upon fresh and tired drivers, and the firm developing the drugs needs to ensure that neither has an adverse effect upon driving performance.

The researcher decides to carry out a two-factor factorial experiment, in which the factors are:
1. **Drug Treatment**, with levels **Placebo, Drug A** and **Drug B**;
2. **Alertness**, with levels **Fresh** and **Tired.**

All participants are asked to take a flavoured drink which contains either (in the **Drug A** and **Drug B** conditions) a small quantity of the drug or (in the control or **Placebo** condition) no drug. Half the participants are tested immediately on rising; the others are tested after twenty hours of sleep deprivation. A different sample of ten participants is tested under each of the six treatment combinations: (Fresh, Placebo); (Fresh, Drug A); (Fresh, Drug B); (Tired, Placebo); (Tired, Drug A); (Tired, Drug B).

Notice that in this experiment, each level of either factor is to be found in combination with every level of the other. The two factors are said to **cross**. There are experiments in which the factors do not cross: that is, not all combinations of conditions (or groups) are present, but they will not be considered in this book. The two-factor between subjects factorial experiment can be represented as a table in which each row or column represents a particular level of one of the treatment factors, and a **cell** of the table (i.e. a single rectangle in the grid) represents one particular treatment **combination** (Table 1). In Table 1, the cell on the bottom right represents the combination (Tired, Drug B). The Group 6 participants were tested under that treatment combination.

Table 1. A completely randomised, two-factor factorial experiment on the effects of two factors upon simulated driving performance

Levels of the Alertness factor:	Levels of the Drug Treatment factor:		
	Placebo	Drug A	Drug B
Fresh	Group 1	Group 2	Group 3
Tired	Group 4	Group 5	Group 6

The mean scores of the participants are shown in Table 2. The row and column means, which are known as **marginal means**, are the mean scores at each level of either factor considered separately, ignoring the other factor in the classification.

Table 2. Mean scores achieved by the participants in the drugs experiment

	Placebo	Drug A	Drug B	*Means*
Fresh	21.0	12.0	22.0	18.3
Tired	10.0	18.0	16.0	14.7
Means	15.5	15.0	19.0	16.5

Main effects and interactions

In a two-factor experiment, two kinds of treatment effects are possible:
1. **Main effects**;
2. An **interaction**.

The marginal column means in Table 2 represent the mean scores of the participants who were tested at each level of the Drug Treatment factor, ignoring the other experimental factor, Alertness. Similarly, the marginal row means in Table 2 represent the mean scores of the fresh and tired participants, ignoring the Drug Treatment factor. Should at least one of the differences among the means for the three levels of the Drug Treatment factor be sufficiently great as to indicate a difference in the population, the Drug Treatment factor is said to have a **main effect**. Similarly, a large difference between the two row means would indicate that the Alertness factor also has a main effect. Since Table 2 shows that there are indeed marked differences among both row and column marginal means, there may be main effects of both factors.

Turning now to the cell means in Table 2, another striking feature of the results emerges. If we look at the fresh participants only, we see a sharp dip in performance with Drug A: that is, a dose of this drug actually has an adverse effect upon the performance of fresh participants. Drug B, on the other hand, has no such effect: the mean performance of the participants under that condition is much the same as that of the placebo group. The corresponding means for the tired participants show a different pattern. Under Drug A, their performance is almost as good as that of the fresh placebo group. Drug B also appears to improve the performance of sleep-deprived participants. It would appear, therefore, that the researcher's suspicions were well founded: Drug A may improve the performance of tired drivers; but it seems to have an adverse effect upon fresh drivers.

Definition of an interaction

The effect of one treatment factor (such as Alertness) at one particular level of another factor (e.g. on the Drug A participants only) is known as a **simple main effect**. From inspection of Table 2, it would appear that the Alertness factor has different simple main effects at different levels of the Drug Treatment factor: its effect is diminished with Drug B and actually reversed with Drug A. When the simple main effects of one treatment factor are not homogeneous at all levels of another, the two factors are said to **interact**. An interaction between two factors, such as Drug Treatment and Alertness, is indicated by a multiplication sign thus: Drug Treatment × Alertness. The results of the experiment, therefore, suggest the presence of a Drug Treatment × Alertness interaction.

The interaction pattern that we have just described can be pictured graphically, as plots of the cell means for the Fresh and the Tired participants against Drug Treatment (see Figure 1). In the present example, the Fresh participants' performance profile is V-shaped, plunging under the Drug A condition. The Tired participants' profile, on the other hand, rises to higher levels under both the Drug A and Drug B conditions. The presence of an interaction is indicated by **profile heterogeneity** across the levels of one of the factors, that is, by **non-parallel profiles.** This is certainly the case with the profiles across the three Drug Treatment conditions of the Fresh and Tired participants in the present experiment.

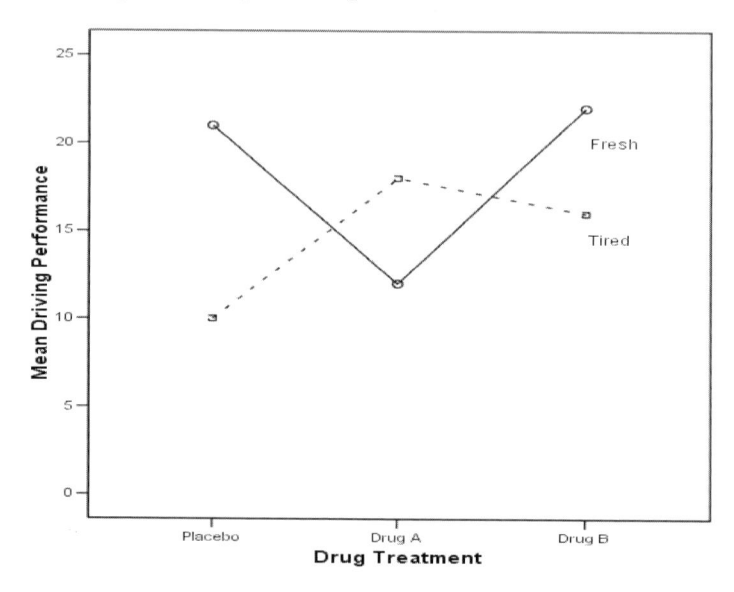

Figure 1. A pattern of cell means suggestive of an interaction

Main effects and interactions are independent: it is quite possible to obtain significant main effects without any significant interaction between the factors; it is also possible to have significant interactions without any significant main effects. The appearance of the profiles in

Figure 1, however, is affected partly by the presence of main effects, as well as any interaction that might be present. It is non-parallelism of the profiles, rather than their separation or slope, which indicates an interaction.

8.2 FACTORIAL ANOVA

The rationale of the factorial ANOVA tests for the presence of main effects and interactions is simply and lucidly described in Gravetter & Wallnau (2000; Chapter 15). If you are unfamiliar with such ANOVA terms as **sum of squares**, **mean square** and **degrees of freedom**, we urge you to read their earlier ANOVA chapters as well.

The analysis of variance of data from a factorial experiment offers tests not only for the presence of a main effect of each factor considered separately, but also for interactions between (or among) the factors.

Table 3 shows the raw data from the two-factor factorial **Drug Treatment** × **Alertness** experiment.

Table 3. Results of the Drug Treatment × Alertness factorial experiment				
Levels of the Alertness factor:	**Levels of the Drug Treatment factor:**		
	Placebo	**A**	**B**
Fresh	24 25 13 22 16 23 18 19 24 26	18 8 9 14 16 15 6 9 8 17	27 14 19 29 27 23 19 17 20 25
Tired	13 12 14 16 17 13 4 3 2 6	21 24 22 23 20 13 11 17 13 16	21 11 14 22 19 9 14 11 21 18

8.2.1 Preparing the data for the factorial ANOVA

Since there are two factors, two **grouping variables** will be required to specify the treatment combination under which each score was achieved. If the grouping variables are *Alertness* and *Drug*, and performance in the driving simulator is *DrivePerf*, the data file will consist of a column for case numbers, two for the grouping variables, and a fourth for *DrivePerf*.

Proceed as follows:

- In **Variable View**, use the **Name** column to create the four named variables, as described in Chapter 2, Section 2.3.
- In the **Decimals** column, change the values to *0* to display whole numbers.
- In the **Label** column, enter informative variable labels, such as *Case Number, Alertness, Drug Treatment,* and *Driving Performance*.
- In the **Values** column, add values and labels for the grouping variables, such as *1* and *2* (with labels *Fresh* and *Tired*, respectively) for the variable *Alertness* and *1, 2,* and *3* (with labels *Placebo, Drug A,* and *Drug B*, respectively) for the variable *Drug*.
- Enter **Data View**. To display the labels for the values entered for the grouping variables, check the View menu to make sure that **Value Labels** is ticked.

See Section 2.3

230   Chapter 8

Part of the completed data set is shown in Figure 2. Note that the values for the grouping variables *Alertness* and *Drug Treatment* have been replaced by their corresponding labels. For example, in case 28, the value *1* has been replaced by *Fresh* and *2* has been replaced by *Drug B*. Likewise, in case 31, the value *2* has been replaced by *Tired* and *1* by *Placebo*.

Case	Alertness	Drug	DrivingPerf
27	Fresh	Drug B	19
28	Fresh	Drug B	17
29	Fresh	Drug B	20
30	Fresh	Drug B	25
31	Tired	Placebo	13
32	Tired	Placebo	12
33	Tired	Placebo	14
34	Tired	Placebo	16

Figure 2. Part of **Data View** showing some of the data from Table 3

8.2.2   Exploring the data: Obtaining boxplots

Before running the ANOVA, it is important to explore the data to check for any problems with the distributions.

To obtain the boxplots under each of the six treatment combinations, proceed as follows:
* Choose
   Graphs
      Boxplot…
   to open the **Boxplot** dialog box.

Transfer the variable name for the dependent variable to the **Variable** box

Transfer the variable name for the category axis to the **Category Axis** box

Transfer the variable name for defining the clusters to the **Define Clusters by** box

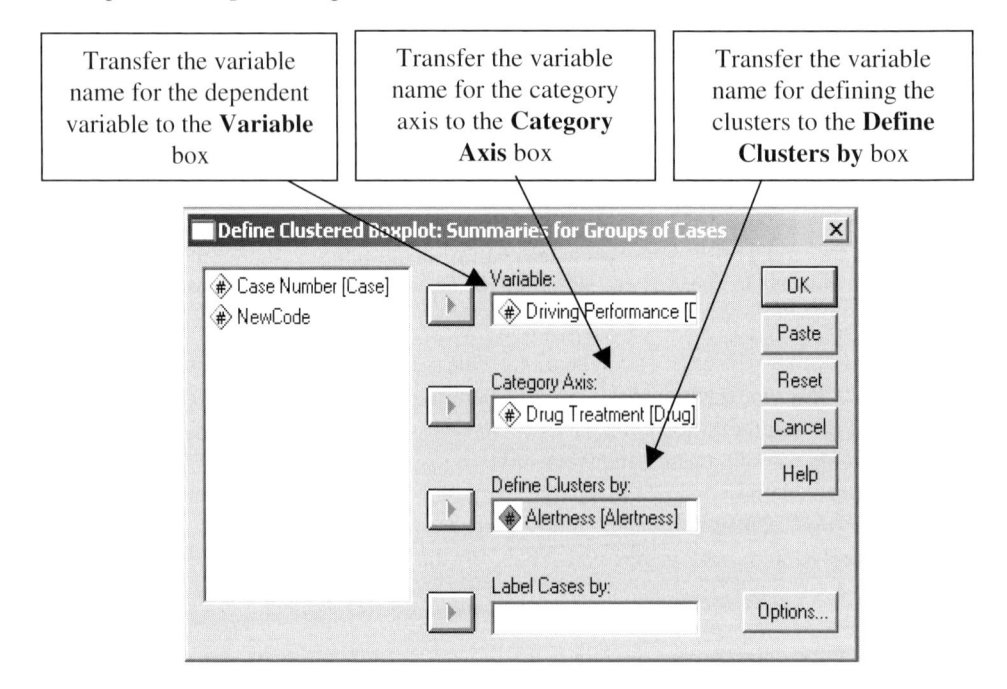

Figure 3. The **Define Clustered Boxplot: Summaries for Groups of Cases** dialog box

Between subjects factorial experiments

- Select **Clustered** by clicking the icon. Click **Define** to open the **Define Clustered Boxplot: Summaries for Groups of Cases** dialog box.
- Transfer the variable names as shown in Figure 3.
- Click **OK**.

The edited boxplots are shown in Output 1.

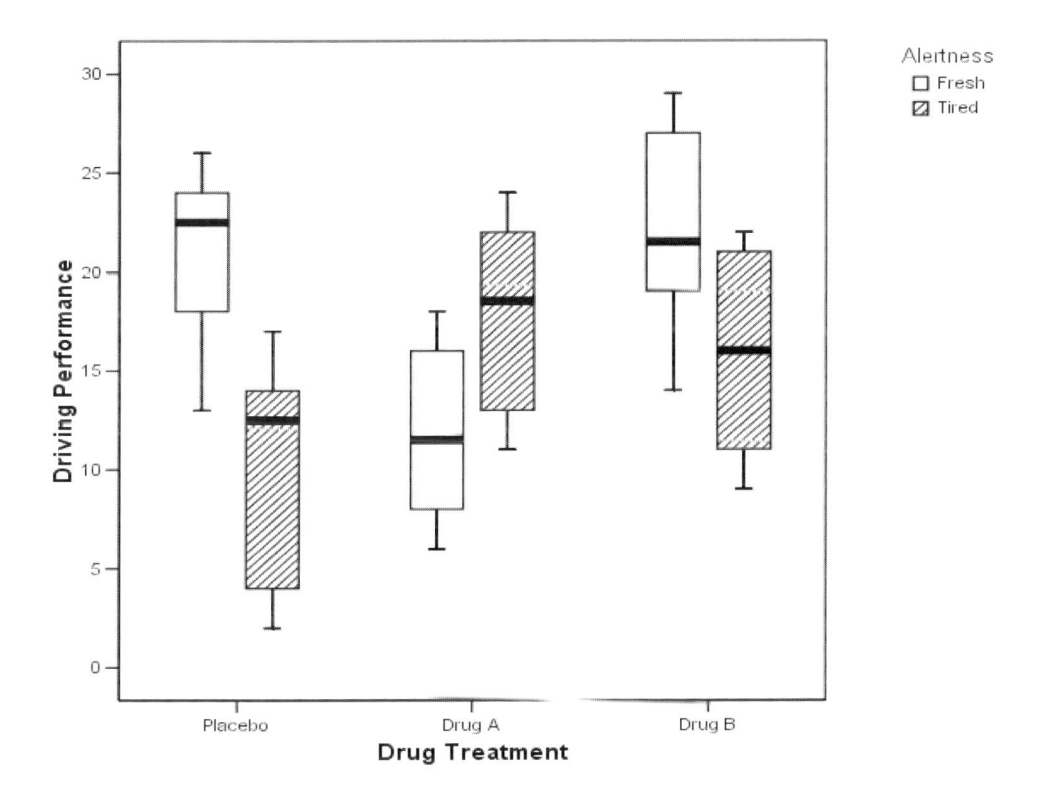

Output 1. Boxplots clustered for *Alertness* at each level of *Drug Treatment*

These boxplots show no extreme cases, which would have been flagged with an asterisk. (See Chapter 4, Table 2, for details of the structure of a boxplot.) None of the distributions is markedly skewed. There is therefore no need to remove any cases or apply a transformation to make the distribution more symmetrical. We can safely proceed with the ANOVA.

> See Table 2 in Chap. 4

8.2.3 Choosing a factorial ANOVA

In SPSS, a factorial ANOVA is run by choosing from the **General Linear Model (GLM)** menu (Figure 4).

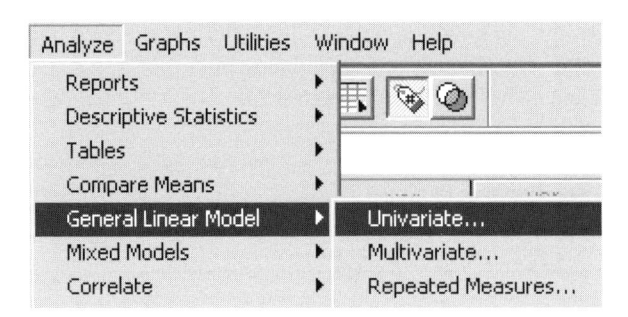

Figure 4. The **General Linear Model** menu leading to **Univariate**

For a between subjects factorial ANOVA, we must choose the **Univariate** option, bearing in mind that, although there are two independent variables (factors), namely, *Drug Treatment* and *Alertness*, there is only one dependent variable, *Driving Performance*.
- To run a factorial ANOVA on the results of the Drugs and Driving experiment, choose
  Analyze
  > **General Linear Model**
  > > **Univariate...**

  to open the **Univariate** dialog box.
- Transfer the variables in the usual manner. The **Dependent Variable** is *Driving Performance* and the **Fixed Factor(s)** (see below for an explanation) are the grouping variables *Alertness* and *Drug Treatment*. The completed dialog box is shown in Figure 5.

WLS Weight

The **WLS Weight** box in Figure 5 is used for identifying a variable containing weights for weighted least-squares analysis. We do not consider this type of analysis in this book.

Factors with Fixed and Random effects

The box labelled **Random Factor(s)** in Figure 5 is used only if the levels of a factor are a random sample of possible levels. In practice, this is rare, and most treatment factors have **fixed effects**. In the present example, *Alertness* and *Drug Treatment* are fixed effects factors.

Covariates

A **covariate** is a variable which, although not of direct interest in the investigation, could be expected to correlate (or **co-vary**) with the dependent variable. For example, suppose that our participants all belonged to an organisation which collected their IQ scores. It would be interesting to know whether the mean IQs of the various experimental groups were similar in value, otherwise, genuine treatment effects could be confounded with differences in intelligence. There are techniques known as **Analysis of Covariance (ANCOVA)** that essentially remove the effects of covariates and perform ANOVA on a 'purified' data set. The advantage is often a reduction of 'data noise' and a resulting increase in the power of the ANOVA tests. To run an ANCOVA, transfer the name(s) of the covariate(s) into the covariate box.

Between subjects factorial experiments

Transfer the variable name for the dependent variable to the **Dependent Variable** box

Transfer the variable names of the grouping variables to the **Fixed Factor(s)** box

For random factor grouping variables (most grouping variables are not random factors)

This box is used for a covariate (a variable such as IQ that might predict the dependent variable but is not of direct interest to the investigator)

Click here to open the **Plots...** dialog box (see Figure 6)

Click here to open the **Post Hoc...** dialog box (see Figure 7)

Click here to select **Descriptive statistics, Estimates of effect size** and **Homogeneity tests** check boxes

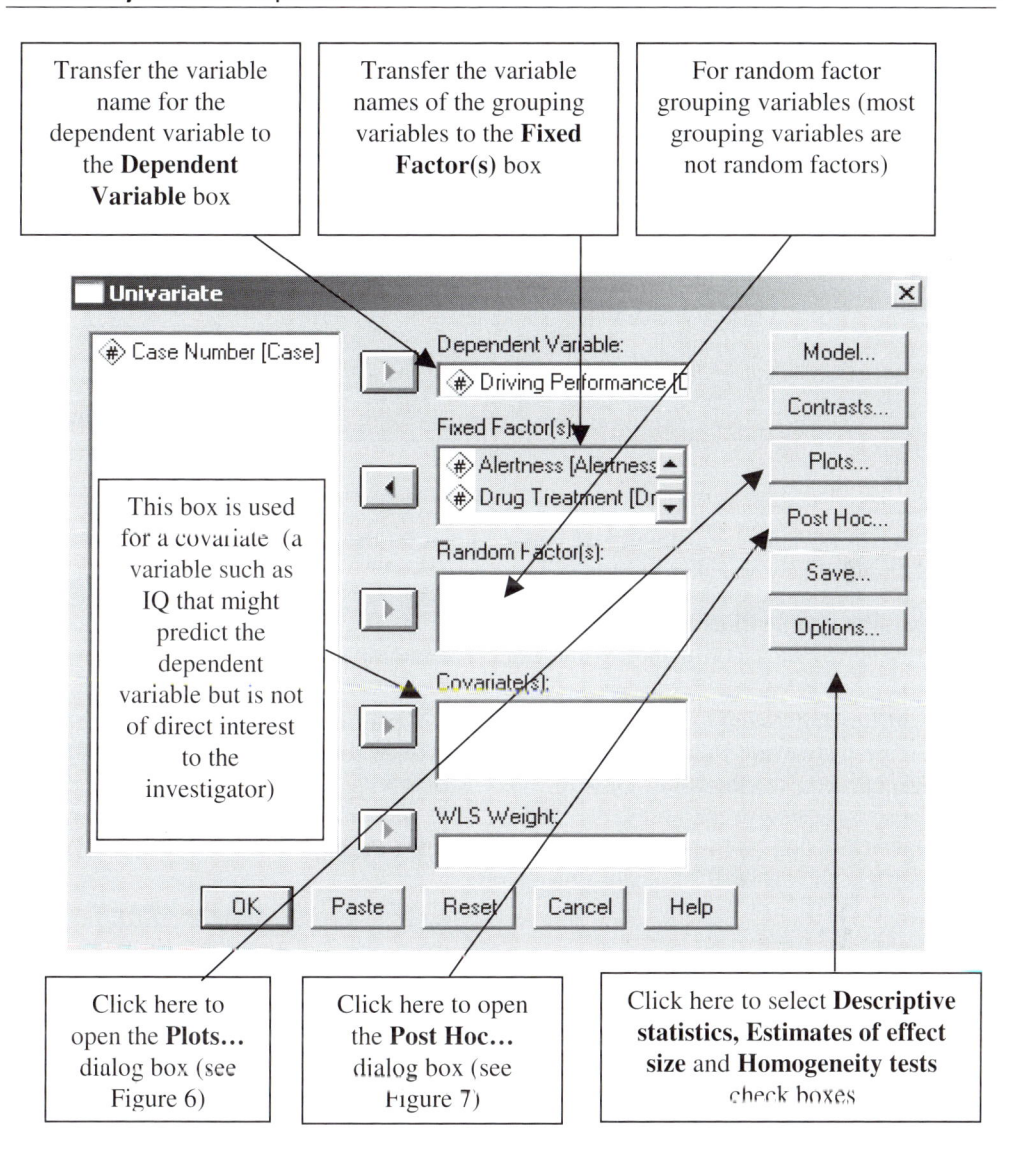

Figure 5. The completed **Univariate** dialog box

- Various optional additions to the output can be selected. To obtain a table of means and standard deviations for each level and each combination of levels of the factors, click **Options...** and select the **Descriptive statistics** check box. Click also the check box for **Estimates of effect size** (the meaning of effect size is described in Section 8.3). Click **Continue** to return to the **Univariate** dialog box.
- To obtain a profile plot of the means, click **Plots...** to open the **Univariate: Profile Plots** dialog box. Select *Drug* for the **Horizontal Axis** box and *Alertness* for the **Separate Lines** box. Click **Add** to add the plot to the **Plots** list i.e. Drug*Alertness (see the dialog box in Figure 6). Click **Continue** to return to the **Univariate** dialog box.

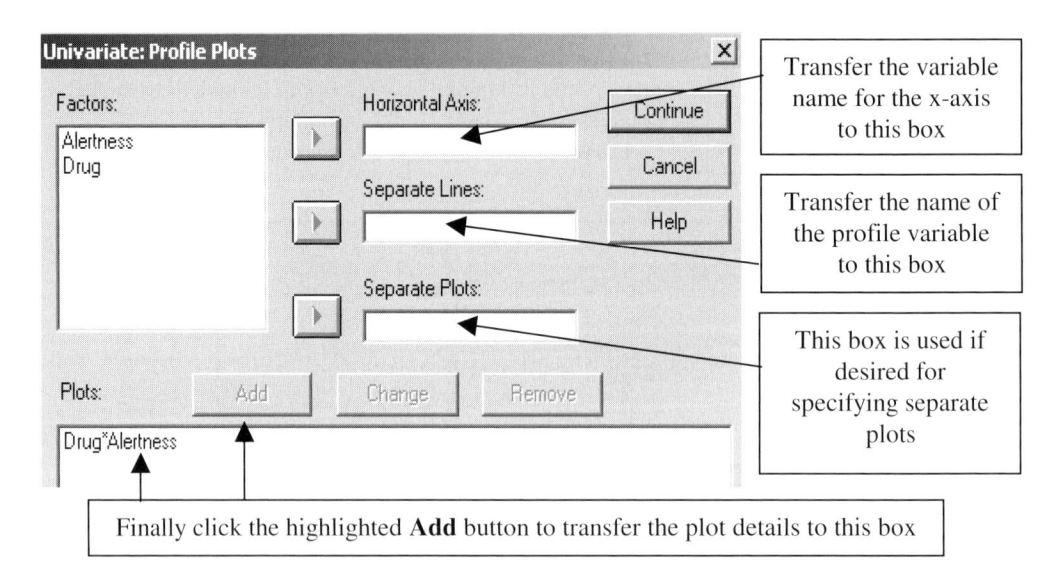

Figure 6. The **Profile Plots** dialog box for plotting Drug*Alertness i.e. plotting Drug along the horizontal axis with the separate lines representing the levels of Alertness

- To obtain paired comparisons among either set of marginal means, click **Post Hoc...** to open the **Univariate Post Hoc Multiple Comparisons for Observed Means** dialog box. Select *Drug* for the **Post Hoc Tests for** box (there is no point in running a post hoc test for *Alertness* because it has only two levels) and click the check box for **Tukey**. The completed dialog box is shown in Figure 7. Click **Continue** to return to the **Univariate** dialog box and then **OK** to run the procedure.

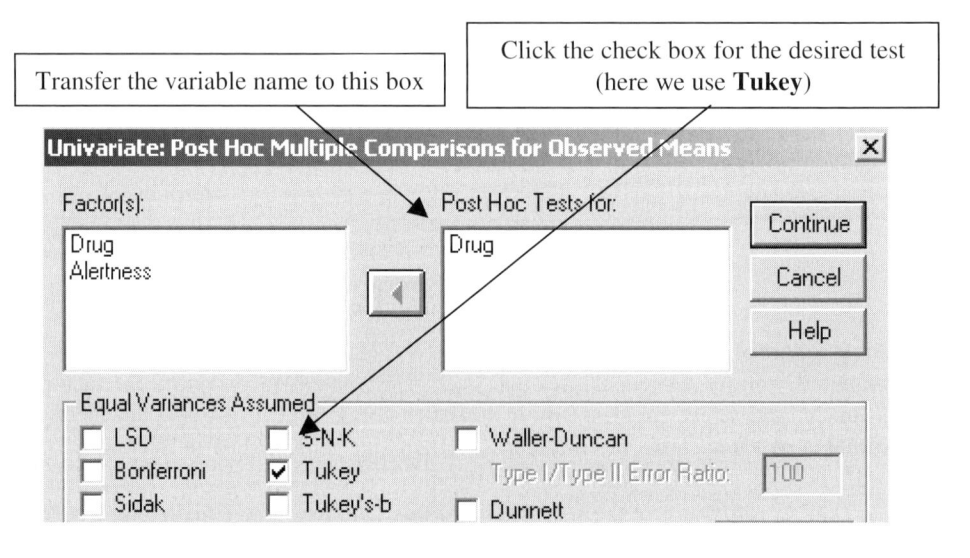

Figure 7. Part of the completed **Post Hoc** dialog box for Drug using the Tukey test

8.2.4 Output for a factorial ANOVA

The results are shown in Output Listings 2-5. The table in Output 2, **Between Subjects Factors**, summarises the factor names and level labels, together with the number of cases at each level.

Between-Subjects Factors

		Value Label	N
Alertness	1	Fresh	30
	2	Tired	30
Drug Treatment	1	Placebo	20
	2	Drug A	20
	3	Drug B	20

Output 2. The table of Between-Subjects Factors

Output 3 is the table of descriptive statistics requested from **Options…** .

Descriptive Statistics

Dependent Variable: Driving Performance

Alertness	Drug Treatment	Mean	Std. Deviation	N
Fresh	Placebo	21.00	4.29	10
	Drug A	12.00	4.42	10
	Drug B	22.00	4.94	10
	Total	18.33	6.35	30
Tired	Placebo	10.00	5.66	10
	Drug A	18.00	4.64	10
	Drug B	16.00	4.78	10
	Total	14.67	5.97	30
Total	Placebo	15.50	7.47	20
	Drug A	15.00	5.38	20
	Drug B	19.00	5.65	20
	Total	16.50	6.38	60

Output 3. The table of descriptive statistics

The table in Output 4, **Tests of Between-Subjects Effects**, is the ANOVA summary table, which tabulates the sources of variation, their **Sums of Squares**, degrees of freedom (**df**), mean squares, **F** ratios and p-values (**Sig.**). Note that, in the between subjects factorial ANOVA, each F ratio is the Mean Square for the source divided by the Error Mean Square (23.15). The final column **Partial Eta Squared** is the estimate of effect size (explained in Section 8.3).

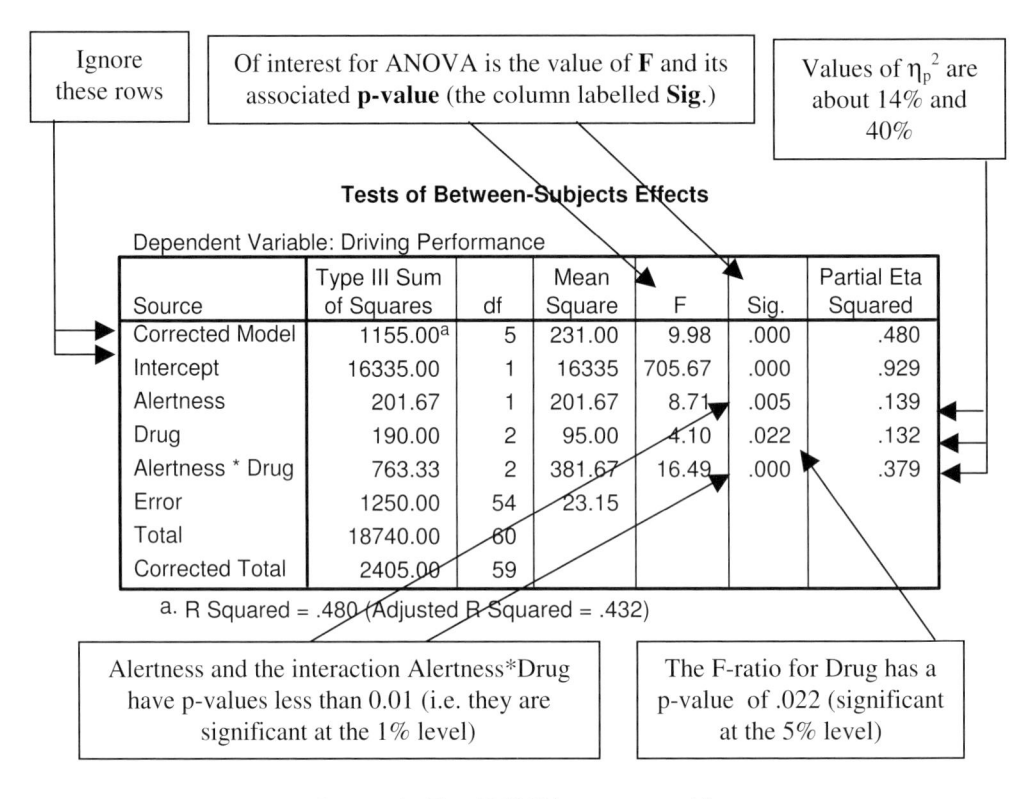

Tests of Between-Subjects Effects

Dependent Variable: Driving Performance

Source	Type III Sum of Squares	df	Mean Square	F	Sig.	Partial Eta Squared
Corrected Model	1155.00[a]	5	231.00	9.98	.000	.480
Intercept	16335.00	1	16335	705.67	.000	.929
Alertness	201.67	1	201.67	8.71	.005	.139
Drug	190.00	2	95.00	4.10	.022	.132
Alertness * Drug	763.33	2	381.67	16.49	.000	.379
Error	1250.00	54	23.15			
Total	18740.00	60				
Corrected Total	2405.00	59				

a. R Squared = .480 (Adjusted R Squared = .432)

Ignore these rows

Of interest for ANOVA is the value of **F** and its associated **p-value** (the column labelled **Sig.**)

Values of η_p^2 are about 14% and 40%

Alertness and the interaction Alertness*Drug have p-values less than 0.01 (i.e. they are significant at the 1% level)

The F-ratio for Drug has a p-value of .022 (significant at the 5% level)

Output 4. The ANOVA summary table

This table was edited in **SPSS Viewer** to reduce three decimal places to two. This was done by double-clicking the whole table so that it showed a hashed border, highlighting the five columns of numbers so that they were shown in inverse video, clicking the right-hand mouse button to show a menu, selecting the item **Cell Properties...**, selecting in the **Format** box the item **#.#**, changing the number of decimals shown in the **Decimals** box to 2, and finally clicking **OK**.

The terms **Corrected Model** and **Intercept** refer to the regression method used to carry out the ANOVA and can be ignored. The three rows **Alertness, Drug** and **Alertness*Drug** are of most interest, since these report tests for the two main effects and the interaction. Note the **Sig.** (i.e. p-value, or tail probability) for each F ratio. There are significant main effects for both the *Alertness* and *Drug* factors: the former is significant beyond the 0.01 level, the latter beyond the 0.05 level, but not beyond the 0.01 level. In addition to main effects of both treatment factors, there is a significant interaction. The p-value is given as *.000*, which means that it is less than *0.0005*. **Write p < .0005, not .000**. Clearly, the *Drug* factor has different effects upon Fresh and Tired participants. To ascertain the nature of these effects, however, we shall need to examine the pattern of the treatment means more closely.

These results should be reported by specifying the name of the factor followed by the value of the F ratio (with the df of the numerator and denominator separated by a comma in brackets) the p-value, and the value of partial eta squared e.g.

The mean Driving Performance scores for the Fresh and Tired conditions (Alertness factor) differed significantly beyond the .01 level: $F(1, 54) = 8.71$; $p = .005$. Partial eta squared = .139 representing a large effect. The mean Driving Performance scores for the two Drug conditions and the Placebo condition (Drug Treatment factor) differed significantly at the 5% level: $F(2, 54) = 4.10$; $p = .022$. Partial eta squared = .132 representing a large effect. The mean Driving Performance scores for the interaction of Alertness and Drug differed significantly beyond the .01 level: $F(2, 54) = 16.49$; $p < .0005$. Partial eta squared = .379 representing a large effect.

Optional post hoc test

The optional **Tukey** Post Hoc test results for the factor Drug Treatment are shown in Outputs 5 & 6. It can be seen that Drugs A and B differ significantly from one another, but neither differs significantly from Placebo.

Multiple Comparisons

Dependent Variable: Driving Performance
Tukey HSD

(I) Drug Treatment	(J) Drug Treatment	Mean Difference (I-J)	Std. Error	Sig.
Placebo	Drug A	.50	1.52	.942
	Drug B	-3.50	1.52	.064
Drug A	Placebo	-.50	1.52	.942
	Drug B	-4.00*	1.52	.029
Drug B	Placebo	3.50	1.52	.064
	Drug A	4.00*	1.52	.029

Based on observed means.
*. The mean difference is significant at the .05 level.

> The only difference with a p-value (**Sig**.) less than 0.05 is Drug A and Drug B. Note these rows are highlighted with *

Output 5. Multiple pairwise comparisons with the Tukey Post Hoc test for the Drug Treatment factor

Driving Performance

Tukey HSD [a,b]

Drug Treatment	N	Subset 1	Subset 2
Drug A	20	15.00	
Placebo	20	15.50	15.50
Drug B	20		19.00
Sig.		.942	.064

Means for groups in homogeneous subsets are displayed.
Based on Type III Sum of Squares
The error term is Mean Square(Error) = 23.148.
  a. Uses Harmonic Mean Sample Size = 20.000.
  b. Alpha = .05.

Levels within a column do not differ significantly. The only levels in different columns are Drug A and Drug B which therefore do differ significantly

Output 6. The homogeneous subsets from the Tukey Post Hoc test for the Drug Treatment factor

The optional profile plot is shown in Output 7 (this is a repeat of Figure 1). It has been edited in **SPSS Viewer** to change coloured lines to black, to change one of the lines into dashes, and to represent the means as black discs.

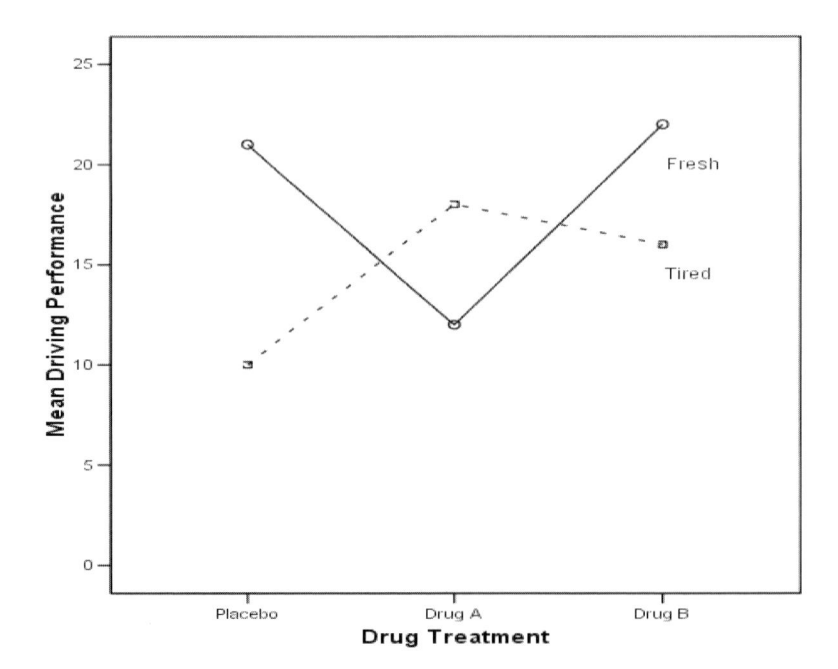

Output 7. Profile plots of Alertness across the levels of the Drug Treatment factor

The graph shows several important results:
1. Fresh participants given a Placebo score more highly than Tired participants.
2. Drug A causes a deterioration in the performance of Fresh participants but enhances the performance of Tired participants.
3. Drug B, while slightly enhancing performance for Fresh participants, also enhances the performance of Tired participants; though not to the same extent as Drug A.

Notice that the most interesting results from this experiment are to be found in the analysis of the cell means following the discovery of a significant interaction between the two factors Drug Treatment and Alertness. As is so often the case in factorial experiments, the presence of an interaction draws attention away from main effects (which, as we have seen, are apparent from considerations of the marginal means). In the present example, it is of relatively little interest to learn that the mean level of performance of drugged participants is somewhat higher than that of undrugged participants, because the three Drug profiles are so disparate; nor is it surprising to find that Fresh participants outperform tired ones.

Often, having made a preliminary graphical exploration of the cell means, the user will wish to make some unplanned pairwise comparisons among selected cell means to confirm the patterns evident in the graph. For example, Output 7 suggests that the simple fact of tiredness led to a deterioration in performance. That would be confirmed should a comparison between the means for the combination (Placebo, Fresh) and (Placebo, Tired) prove significant. To confirm that Drug A actually has deleterious effect upon the performance of Fresh participants, we should need to find a significant difference between the means for the (Fresh, Placebo) and (Fresh, Drug A) conditions. It is possible, too, that the apparent enhancement by Drug B of the performance of Fresh participants may not be significant. That would be confirmed by a non-significant difference between the means for conditions (Placebo, Fresh) and (Drug B, Fresh).

Since the Alertness factor comprises only two conditions, the answer to the question of whether tiredness alone produces a significant decrement in performance is answered by a test for a **simple main effect** of Alertness at the Placebo level of the Drug Treatment factor. Tests for simple main effects are available using SPSS, but the user must know the syntax of the SPSS control language. Another approach is to perform an ANOVA only upon the data at the level of the qualifying factor concerned. If we go back to **Data View**, select the data only from the Placebo condition using the **Select Cases** procedure in the **Data** menu and request a one-way ANOVA with Alertness as the single factor, we shall find that

$$F(1, 18) = 23.99; \ p = .0001.$$

This confirms the simple main effect of Alertness at the Placebo level of the Drug Treatment factor and hence that the difference between the means for the (Placebo, Fresh) and (Placebo, Tired) conditions is indeed significant.

Some of the other questions mentioned can only be answered by directly making pairwise comparisons between specified treatment means. Since many such comparisons are possible, it is necessary to protect against inflation of the *per family* type I error rate by using a conservative method such as the **Tukey** test.

8.3 EFFECT SIZE AND POWER IN FACTORIAL ANOVA

It is now expected that a statement of the result of a statistical test will be accompanied by a statistic showing the size of the effect of the independent variable upon on the dependent variable. In the case of ANOVA, one purely descriptive measure of effect size is **eta-squared (η^2)** which is the proportion of variance in the dependent variable accounted for by differences in the levels of the independent variable. In the case of the one-way ANOVA, η^2 is defined as follows:

See Section 7.1.3

$$\eta^2 = \frac{SS_{treatment}}{SS_{total}} = \frac{SS_{between}}{SS_{total}}$$

In the two-factor ANOVA with treatment factors Factor 1 and Factor 2, there are three between subjects sources of variance: two main effect sources and the interaction. For Factor 1, the **complete η^2** is defined as follows:

$$\eta^2 = \frac{SS_{F1}}{SS_{total}} = \frac{SS_{F1}}{SS_{F1} + SS_{F2} + SS_{F1 \times F2} + SS_{within}}$$

Some authors prefer an alternative form of η^2, called **partial η^2** or η_p^2 in which the variance of the sums of squares for a particular effect is expressed as a proportion, not of the total sum of squares, but of the sum of squares of that effect plus the error sum of squares:

$$\eta_p^2 = \frac{SS_{treatment}}{SS_{treatment} + SS_{error}}$$

SPSS provides this statistic (**Estimates of effect size**) as an option within the **Options...** dialog box. The choice between the **complete** η^2 and **partial** η^2 statistics will depend upon the experiment and purpose of the investigation (see Keppel & Wickens, 2004; p. 235). Both fail to allow for sampling error. Two measures which do take sampling error into account are **complete omega squared (ω^2)** and **partial omega squared (ω_p^2)** – see Keppel & Wickens, 2004; pp. 232 – 233.

As before, the interpretation of these measures is conventional. Clark-Carter (1997) recommends that we consider 0.01 as a small effect, 0.06 as a medium effect and 0.14 as a large effect. Interpolating among these values, we suggest the following:

Effect size (η_p^2)	Size of Effect
<0.01 (<1%)	Small
0.01 to 0.10 (1-10%)	Medium
>0.10 (>10%)	Large

How many participants shall I need for a between subjects factorial ANOVA?

For simplicity, we shall be working with a very small fictitious data set, specially prepared to illustrate certain types of results. In a real research situation, we should have to test many more participants to achieve tests of sufficient power. But how many people would we need to test?

Clark-Carter (1997) provides a series of tables for use with ANOVA experiments, each table giving the sample sizes necessary to achieve specified power levels for a range of effect sizes. Each table is applicable to an ANOVA source with a fixed number of degrees of freedom, irrespective of whether the source is a main effect or an interaction. Where an experiment has two or more factors, however, it is necessary to distinguish between the sample size n (the number of participants tested under each combination of conditions) and the value for n given in the table. In factorial ANOVA, the error degrees of freedom and the tabled value (which we now refer to as n') are related as follows:

$$n' = \frac{\text{error df}}{\text{treatment df} + 1} + 1 \qquad (1)$$

Since the sample size n is a term in the error degrees of freedom, the value of n can easily be obtained from n' by using the following formula:

$$n = \frac{(\text{treatment df} + 1)(n' - 1)}{(\text{number of treatment combinations})} + 1 \qquad (2)$$

Returning to our planned two-factor factorial experiment on Drugs and Driving, what is the sample size n that would be needed to achieve a power of .80 to reject the null hypothesis in the presence of an effect of 'medium' size ($\eta^2 = .06$)? Considering the Drug Treatment factor, $df = 2$. Consulting Table A15.5 in Clark-Carter's book (1997; p.621), we find that $n = n' = 50$.

Substituting in formula (2), we have $n = \frac{3 \times 49}{6} + 1 = 25.5$ (i.e. 26) which means that we shall require a total of $6 \times 26 = 156$ participants for the experiment.

8.4 EXPERIMENTS WITH MORE THAN TWO TREATMENT FACTORS

SPSS can readily be used to analyse data from more complex factorial experiments, with three or more treatment factors. We should warn the reader, however, that experiments with more than three factors should be avoided, because interpretation of complex interactions involving four or more factors is often extremely difficult. Here we illustrate how easily an analysis of a three factor ANOVA can be run with SPSS. Suppose the driving simulation data had included *sex* as an additional factor, as shown in Table 4.

Table 4. Results of a three-way factorial experiment

Levels of the Alertness factor:	Levels of the Sex factor:	Levels of the Drug Treatment factor:		
		Placebo	A	B
Fresh	Male	24 25 13 22 16	18 8 9 14 16	27 14 19 29 27
Fresh	Female	23 18 19 24 26	15 6 9 8 17	23 19 17 20 25
Tired	Male	13 12 14 16 17	21 24 22 23 20	21 11 14 22 19
Tired	Female	13 4 3 2 6	13 11 17 13 16	9 14 11 21 18

The data set in **Data View** would now have to include three grouping variables (*Alertness*, *Sex*, and *Drug*), as well as a column for the dependent variable *DrivingPerf*. Figure 8 shows a section of **Data View** with the new grouping variable *Sex* added.

	Case	Alertness	Drug	DrivingPerf	Sex
1	1	Fresh	Placebo	24	Male
2	2	Fresh	Placebo	25	Male
3	3	Fresh	Placebo	13	Male
4	4	Fresh	Placebo	22	Male
5	5	Fresh	Placebo	16	Male
6	6	Fresh	Placebo	23	Female
7	7	Fresh	Placebo	18	Female
8	8	Fresh	Placebo	19	Female
9	9	Fresh	Placebo	24	Female
10	10	Fresh	Placebo	26	Female

Figure 8. Part of **Data View** showing some of the data in Table 4

To run the three-factor ANOVA, proceed as follows:
- Open the **General Linear Model - Univariate** dialog box and complete it as in Figure 5, but adding variable *Sex* to the **Fixed Factor(s)** box.
- Select the optional **Descriptive statistics** and **Estimates of effect size** check boxes from **Options...** and the **Tukey Post Hoc** test for *Drug* from **Post Hoc...**, clicking **Continue** each time to return to the **Univariate** dialog box.
- To obtain a profile plot of the means, click **Plots...** to open the **Univariate: Profile Plots** dialog box. Select *Drug* for the **Horizontal Axis** box, *Alertness* for the **Separate Lines** box and *Sex* for the **Separate Plots** box. Click **Add** to add the plot to the **Plots** list and then **Continue** to return to the **Univariate** dialog box.
- Click **OK**.

The first table in the output lists the number of cases for each level of the variables (Output 8).

Between-Subjects Factors

		Value Label	N
Alertness	1	Fresh	30
	2	Tired	30
Drug Treatment	1	Placebo	20
	2	Drug A	20
	3	Drug B	20
Sex	1	Male	30
	2	Female	30

Output 8. The table of Between-Subjects Factors

The next table in the output (not reproduced here) shows the descriptive statistics requested in the **Options...** dialog box.

With three factors, the ANOVA summary table (Output 9) is considerably longer than in the two-factor case. As before, there are main effects. This time, however, there are three different main effects, one for each of the three factors in the experiment. In the two-factor experiment, there can be only one two-way interaction; but in the three-factor experiment, there are three and here all are significant except Drug*Sex.

Moreover, in the three-factor table a new interaction appears, Alertness * Drug * Sex. This is known as a **three-way**, or **three-factor interaction**. A three-factor interaction is said to occur when there is heterogeneity of the interaction between two factors across the levels of a third. These results are reported as follows:

> The mean Driving Performance scores for the Fresh and Tired conditions (Alertness factor) differed significantly beyond the .01 level: $F(1, 48) = 11.49$; $p = .001$. Partial eta squared = .193 representing a large effect.
>
> The mean Driving Performance scores for the two Drug conditions and the Placebo condition (Drug Treatment factor) differed significantly beyond the .01 level: $F(2, 48) = 5.41$; $p = .008$. Partial eta squared = .184 representing a large effect.
>
> The mean Driving Performance scores for Males and Females (Sex factor) differed significantly beyond the .01 level: $F(1, 48) = 11.49$; $p = .001$. Partial eta squared = .193 representing a large effect.
>
> The mean Driving Performance scores for the interaction of Alertness and Drug differed significantly beyond the .01 level: $F(2, 48) = 21.75$; $p < .0005$. Partial eta squared = .475 representing a large effect.
>
> The mean Driving Performance scores for the interaction of Alertness and Sex differed significantly at the 5% level: $F(1, 48) = 7.02$; $p < .011$. Partial eta squared = .128 representing a large effect.
>
> The mean Driving Performance scores did not differ significantly for the interaction of Drug and Sex: $F(2, 48) = .43$; $p = .656$, and for the interaction of Alertness, Drug and Sex: $F(2, 48) = 1.93$; $p = .156$.

In conclusion, in addition to the significant main effects and interaction noted in Output 4, there are now also a significant main effect *sex* and a significant interaction of *sex* and *alert*.

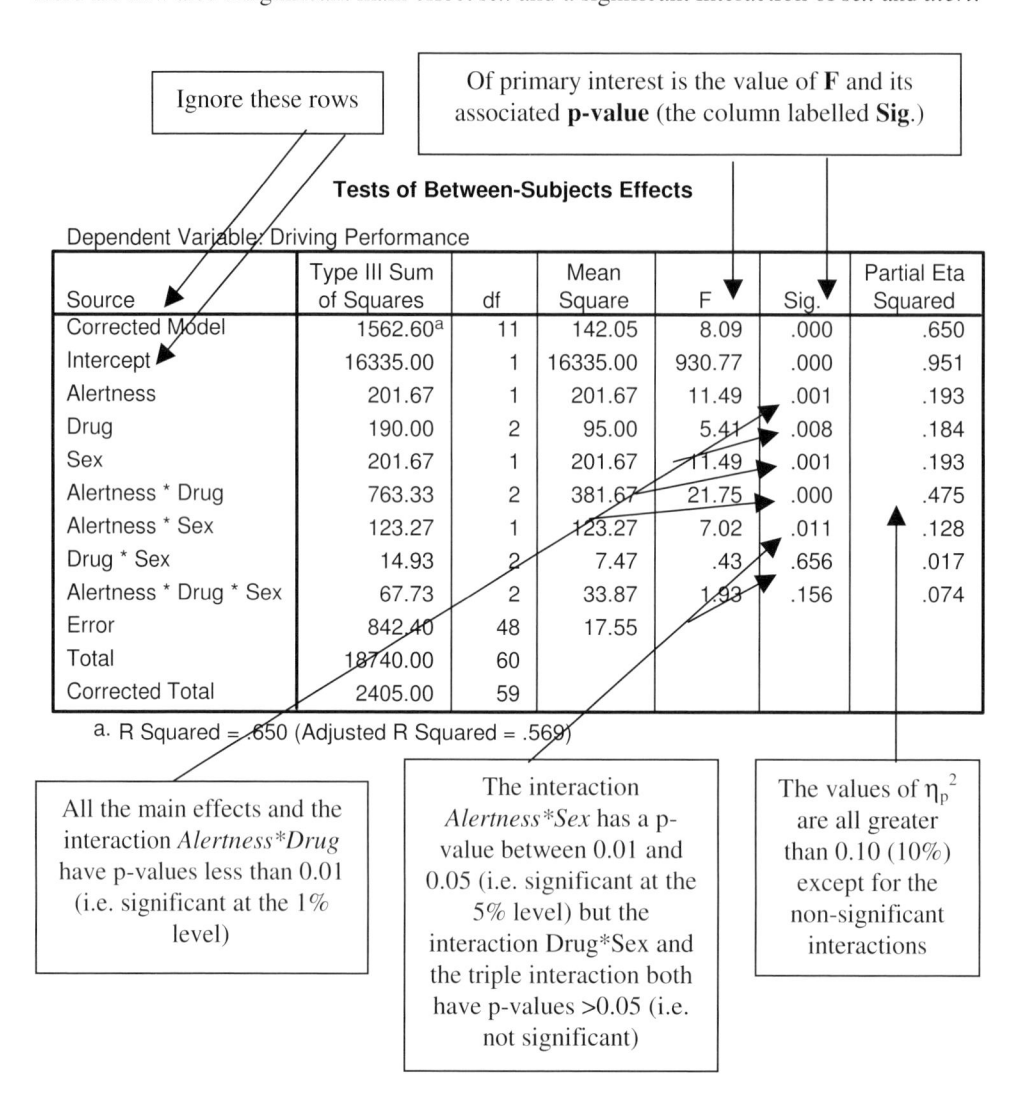

Tests of Between-Subjects Effects

Dependent Variable: Driving Performance

Source	Type III Sum of Squares	df	Mean Square	F	Sig.	Partial Eta Squared
Corrected Model	1562.60[a]	11	142.05	8.09	.000	.650
Intercept	16335.00	1	16335.00	930.77	.000	.951
Alertness	201.67	1	201.67	11.49	.001	.193
Drug	190.00	2	95.00	5.41	.008	.184
Sex	201.67	1	201.67	11.49	.001	.193
Alertness * Drug	763.33	2	381.67	21.75	.000	.475
Alertness * Sex	123.27	1	123.27	7.02	.011	.128
Drug * Sex	14.93	2	7.47	.43	.656	.017
Alertness * Drug * Sex	67.73	2	33.87	1.93	.156	.074
Error	842.40	48	17.55			
Total	18740.00	60				
Corrected Total	2405.00	59				

a. R Squared = .650 (Adjusted R Squared = .569)

Boxed annotations:
- Ignore these rows (pointing to Corrected Model and Intercept)
- Of primary interest is the value of **F** and its associated **p-value** (the column labelled **Sig.**)
- All the main effects and the interaction *Alertness*Drug* have p-values less than 0.01 (i.e. significant at the 1% level)
- The interaction *Alertness*Sex* has a p-value between 0.01 and 0.05 (i.e. significant at the 5% level) but the interaction Drug*Sex and the triple interaction both have p-values >0.05 (i.e. not significant)
- The values of η_p^2 are all greater than 0.10 (10%) except for the non-significant interactions

Output 9. The three-way factorial ANOVA summary table

Finally tables for the **Post Hoc Tests** and the **Profile Plots** (one for Males and one for Females) will be given in **SPSS Viewer**.

EXERCISE 12

Between subjects factorial ANOVA (two-way ANOVA)

Before you start

Before proceeding with this practical, please read Chapter 8. The following exercise assumes a knowledge of the standard **factorial ANOVA** terminology.

An experiment on the memories of chess players

'Must have a marvellous memory!'. This is something often said of a good chess player; but do good chess players necessarily have better short-term memories than those who are mediocre? To find out, a psychologist tested chess players at three levels of proficiency on their ability to reconstruct board positions they had just been shown. Some of the positions used were from real games selected from tournaments; but others were merely random placings of the same pieces. The psychologist predicted that whereas the better players would show superior reconstructions of real board positions, this superiority would disappear when they tried to reproduce random placements. The dependent variable in this experiment was a participant's *score* on reconstruction. There were two independent variables (factors):
    1.   Competence   (Novice, Average, Good).
    2.   Position   (Real, Random).

An important feature of the design of this experiment was that a different sample of participants performed under each of the six treatment combinations: that is, each group of players at a given level was subdivided into those reconstructing Real positions and those reconstructing Random positions.

What the psychologist is predicting is that, when performance is averaged over Random and Real positions, the better players will achieve higher performance means; but this will turn out to be because of their superior recall of Real board positions only, and the beginners will be just as good at reconstructing Random positions. The **two-factor ANOVA**, therefore, should show a significant interaction between the factors of Competence and Position, as well as (possibly) a main effect of Competence. The latter might be expected to arise because the better players' much superior performance in reconstructing real board positions pulls up the mean value of their performance over both Real and Random positions, even though they may not excel beginners on the Random task.

The results of the experiment are shown in Table 1.

Table 1. Results of the experiment on the reconstruction of positions by chess players

Posit-ion	Novice					Competence Average					Good				
Real	38	39	42	40	40	65	58	70	61	62	88	95	86	89	89
	42	37	38	40	38	58	63	66	62	65	88	90	85	92	86
Rand-om	50	53	40	41	36	50	40	43	37	38	41	40	50	42	41
	42	44	46	44	45	42	44	38	37	43	43	46	41	44	45

Opening SPSS

Open SPSS and select the **Type in data** radio button in the opening window. If **Data View** opens first, click the **Variable View** tab to open **Variable View**.

Preparing the SPSS data set

Recast the data of Table 1 into a form suitable for entry into SPSS along the lines of the description in Section 8.2.1. You will need a variable for cases (there are 60 participants) as well as two grouping variables, *Competence* and *Position*, with appropriate values and value labels specified in the **Values** column, and one dependent variable, *Score*. Ensure that the values in the **Decimals** column have been reduced to 0. We also recommend you to use the **Label** column to assign fuller labels to the variables: e.g. Case Number, Competence, Position of Pieces. Switch to **Data View** and enter the data, leaving the values for *case* until last, when you can use **Compute** to enter them automatically, making *case* the **Target Variable** and *$casenum* the **Numeric Expression**.

As always, save the data set with a suitable name.

Exploring the data

Before proceeding with the ANOVA, it is important to explore the data. Look at the boxplots (see Section 8.2.2) using
Graphs
    Boxplot....
to open the **Boxplot** dialog box.

- What do you notice about the distribution of data among the three levels of Competence and between the two levels of Position?

Although means can be requested in the dialog box for the ANOVA, it is recommended to include the calculation of the means at the exploration of data stage. Do this using the **Means** command (see Section 4.3.2) and layering the two classificatory variables *Competence* and *Position*.

- What do you notice about the values of the means for the two levels of Position across the three levels of Competence?

Procedure for the two-way ANOVA

Choose
Analyze
    General Linear Model
        Univariate...

to open the **Univariate** dialog box. Then complete the dialog box as described in Section 8.2.3, specifying a plot of the means using the **Plots...** dialog box, selecting **Descriptive statistics** and **Estimates of effect size** using the **Options...** dialog box, and a **Tukey** Post Hoc test for *Competence* (ignore *Position* since it has only two levels) using the **Post Hoc...** dialog box.

Output for the two-way ANOVA

Tables listing the levels of the factors and descriptive statistics will appear first. The ANOVA summary table gives F ratios for the main effects of *Competence* and *Position* and also for the interaction between the two factors.

- **Write down the values of *F* (and the associated p-values) and the values of Partial Eta Squared (the measure of effect size) for the main effect and interaction tests. Do these results confirm your predictions from inspection of the output from the Means procedure? Relate these results to the experimental hypothesis about the short-term memory of chess players. Are the effect sizes large, medium or small?**

Post hoc comparisons among the levels of competence

Inspect the output for the post hoc comparisons of the levels of competence.

- **Construct your own table showing clearly which pairs of levels are significantly different and which (if any) are not.**

Graph of cell means

Inspect the graph.

- **What do you conclude from the plot?**

Finishing the session

Close down SPSS and any other windows before logging out of the computer.

CHAPTER 9

Within subjects experiments

9.1 Introduction

9.2 A one-factor within subjects ANOVA

9.3 Nonparametric tests for a one-factor within subjects experiment

9.4 The two-factor within subjects ANOVA

9.1 INTRODUCTION

9.1.1 Rationale of a within subjects experiment

A potential problem with between subjects experiments (Chapters 7 & 8) is that if there are large individual differences in performance, searching for a meaningful pattern in the data can be like trying to listen to a radio programme against a loud background crackle of interference. For example, in the Mnemonic Training Method experiment described in Chapter 7, some of the scores obtained by participants in the control condition may well be higher than those of participants who were trained to use a mnemonic. There are some people who, if asked to read through a long list, could, **without any training at all**, reproduce most of the items accurately; whereas others, even after training, would recall very few items. Individual differences, therefore, can introduce considerable **noise** into the data from between subjects experiments.

In the **within subjects experiment** (see Chapter 1), each participant is tested at all levels of every treatment factor in the experiment. Each participant, therefore, serves as his or her own control, making it possible, in the within subjects ANOVA, to remove the variance associated with individual differences in overall ability and make a more powerful *F* test.

Another drawback with the between subjects experiment is that it is wasteful of participants: if the experimental procedure is a short one, a participant may spend more time travelling to and from the place of testing than actually performing the experiment. The within subjects experiment allows the researcher to make fuller use of the participant's time and trouble.

In summary, therefore, the within subjects experiment has two advantages over the between subjects experiment:
   1. It cuts down data noise.
   2. It makes more efficient use of time and resources.

The within subjects experiment, however, also has disadvantages, which in some circumstances can outweigh considerations of convenience and the maximisation of the signal-to-noise ratio.

Where participants are tested on not one but several tasks, their performance on the later tasks may improve through a **practice effect**. Practice effects, however, are only one type of **carry-over**, or **order effect**. Not all carry-over effects are positive: e.g., recall of the items in a list is vulnerable to interference from items in previous lists (proactive interference). In within subjects experiments, carry-over effects are potential **extraneous variables**, whose effects may be confounded with those of the treatment factor.

The possibility of confounding carry-over effects is reduced by the procedure known as **counterbalancing**, in which the order of the conditions making up a within subjects factor is varied from participant to participant, in the hope that carry-over effects will balance out across conditions. Counterbalancing is not always sensible, however, as in the mnemonics experiment, where (as we have seen) it would make little sense to have the control condition coming last. Such matters must be considered carefully before opting for a within subjects experiment.

9.1.2 Assumptions underlying the within subjects ANOVA

A statistical test always assumes that the data have been generated in a certain manner, as specified by a statistical **model**, and so have certain properties. For example, the ANOVA for between subjects experiments (Chapters 7 and 8) requires that there must be homogeneity of variance from group to group. The model for the within subjects ANOVA makes additional specifications, over and above those made by the between groups models. The most important of these is that the covariances among the scores at the various levels of the within subjects factor are homogeneous. (A covariance, like the Pearson correlation, is a measure of the degree of statistical association between two variables.) This requirement is known as the assumption of **homogeneity of covariance** (or **sphericity**). If this assumption is violated, the true type I error rate (i.e. the probability of rejecting H_0 when it is true) may be inflated.

SPSS tests for homogeneity of covariance with the **Mauchly sphericity test**. Should the data fail the sphericity test (i.e. p-value < 0.05), the ANOVA F test can be modified to make it more *conservative* (less likely to reject the null hypothesis). SPSS offers three such tests, varying in their degree of conservativeness: the **Greenhouse-Geisser**, the **Huynh-Feldt**, and the **Lower-bound**. All three tests reduce the degrees of freedom of the numerator and the denominator of the F ratio, thus increasing the value of F required for significance.

9.1.3 Effect size and power in within subjects ANOVA

As with the between subjects ANOVA, SPSS provides, as a measure of the size of the effect of an independent variable, the statistic known as **partial eta-squared** η_p^2, where $\eta_p^2 = \frac{SS_{treatment}}{SS_{treatment} + SS_{error}}$. Remember (Section 8.3) that Clark-Carter (1997) recommends that we consider 0.01 as a small effect, 0.06 as a medium effect and 0.14 as a large effect. Interpolating among these values, we suggest the following classification:

See Section 8.3

Effect size (η_p^2)	Size of Effect
<0.01 (<1%)	Small
0.01 to 0.10 (1-10%)	Medium
>0.10 (>10%)	Large

For a given number of data points, a within subjects ANOVA can (provided the assumptions of the underlying model are met) make tests of greater power than those of a between subjects ANOVA with the same numbers of factors and levels. Clark-Carter (1997; p.254) suggests that approximate guidelines on sample size and power for within subjects experiments can be obtained by using the procedures he describes for between subjects ANOVAs.

9.2 A ONE-FACTOR WITHIN SUBJECTS ANOVA

Suppose that in an experiment on aesthetics, each participant was asked to produce three pictures of the same object, using just one of three different materials for any one picture: Crayons, Paintbrushes or Felt-tip pens.

The dependent variable was the average rating, on the aesthetic dimension of pleasingness, that a picture received from a panel of judges. The independent variable was the type of implement used to produce the picture. Since the participants would certainly vary in artistic ability, it was decided to use a within subjects experiment to reduce the potential noisiness of the data. (In an attempt to neutralise carry-over effects, the order in which the three implements were used was counterbalanced across participants.) The data are shown in Table 1.

Table 1. Results of a one-factor within subjects experiment

Case	Levels of factor: Implement		
	Crayon	Paintbrush	Felt-tip
1	10	12	14
2	18	10	16
3	20	15	16
4	12	10	12
5	19	20	21
6	25	22	20
7	18	16	17
8	22	18	18
9	17	14	12
10	23	20	18

9.2.1 Entering the data

Since the participants have not been divided into groups, no grouping variable is required for entry of these data into the SPSS Data Editor. In **Variable View**, using the procedures described in Section 2.3, define the variables *Case*, *Crayon*, *Paintbrush*, and *FeltTip*. Using the **Label** column, expand the variable

See Section 2.3

names to *Case Number*, *Crayon Pencil*, *Paintbrush* and *Felt-tip Pen*. Set the number of decimal places displayed to zero. In **Data View**, enter the data from Table 1 into the first four (pre-labelled) columns.

9.2.2 Exploring the data: Boxplots for within subjects factors

To draw boxplots of the data at the various levels of a within subjects factor, select
Graphs
    Boxplot...
to open the **Boxplot** dialog box (Figure 1).

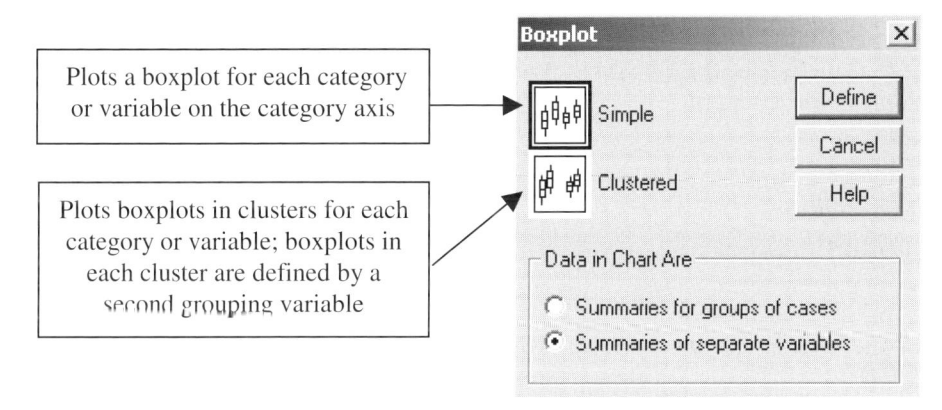

Plots a boxplot for each category or variable on the category axis

Plots boxplots in clusters for each category or variable; boxplots in each cluster are defined by a second grouping variable

Figure 1. The **Boxplot** dialog box with **Summaries of separate variables** selected

- In the **Data in Chart Are** box, activate the **Summaries of separate variables** radio button. Click the **Define** button (Figure 1) to open the **Define Simple Boxplot: Summaries of Separate Variables** dialog box (the completed version is shown in Figure 2).
- Transfer the variable names to the **Boxes Represent** box as shown in Figure 2.
- Click **OK** to obtain the boxplots (the edited version is shown in Output 1). (Editing is described in Chapter 5, Section 5.1.2.)

See Section 5.1.2

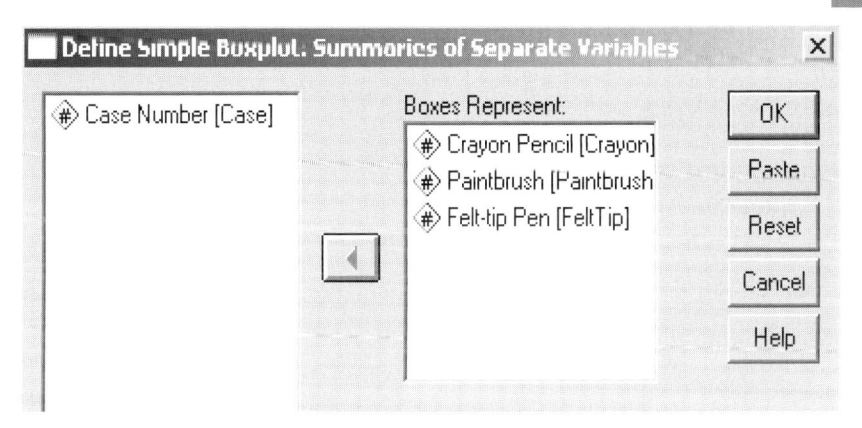

Figure 2. The **Summaries of Separate Variables** dialog box with the three variables selected

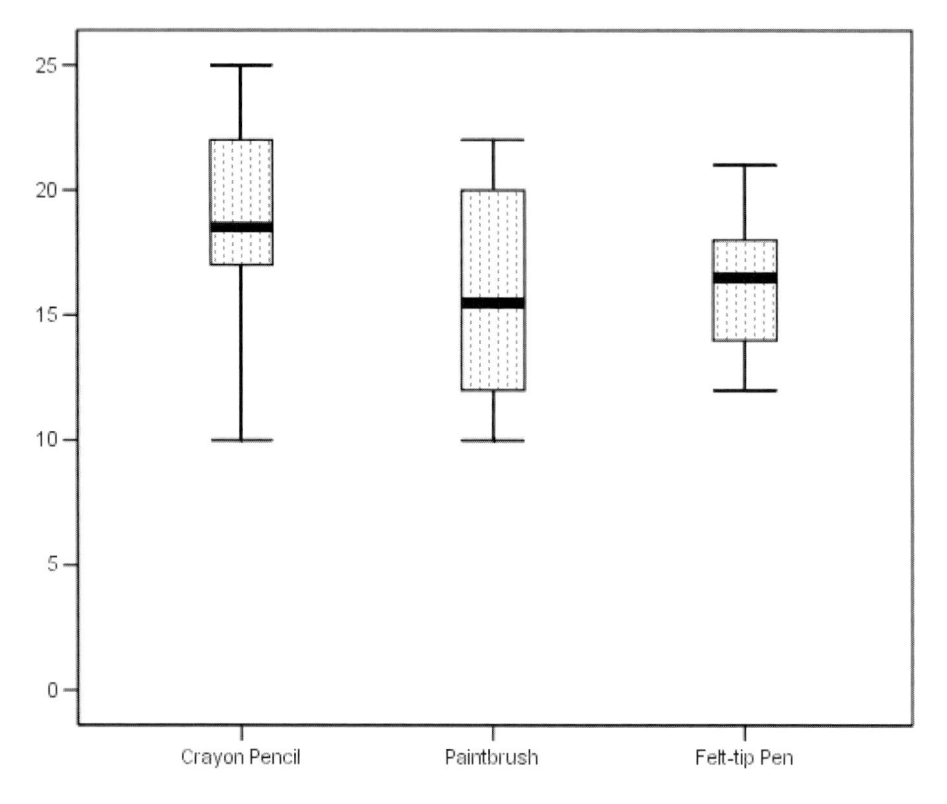

Output 1. Boxplots of the data for the three types of drawing implement

The boxplots reveal no extreme cases (which would have been flagged by * - see Table 2 in Section 4.3.2 for details of the structure of a boxplot). None of the distributions is markedly skewed. There is therefore no need to remove any cases or apply any transformation to symmetrise the distribution. We can carry on with the ANOVA.

See Table 2 in Section 4.3.2

9.2.3 Running the within subjects ANOVA

The within subjects ANOVA is selected as follows:
- Choose
    Analyze
        General Linear Model
            Repeated Measures... (Figure 3)
    to open the **Repeated Measures Define Factor(s)** dialog box (Figure 4).

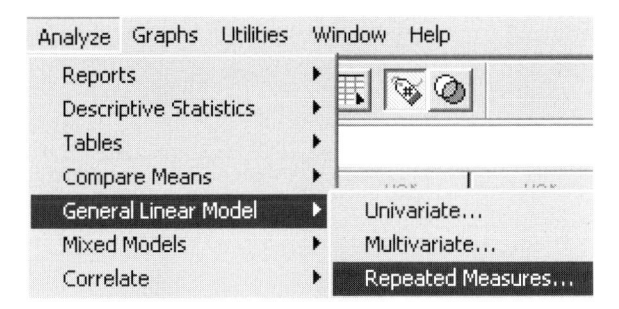

Figure 3. The **General Linear Model** menu

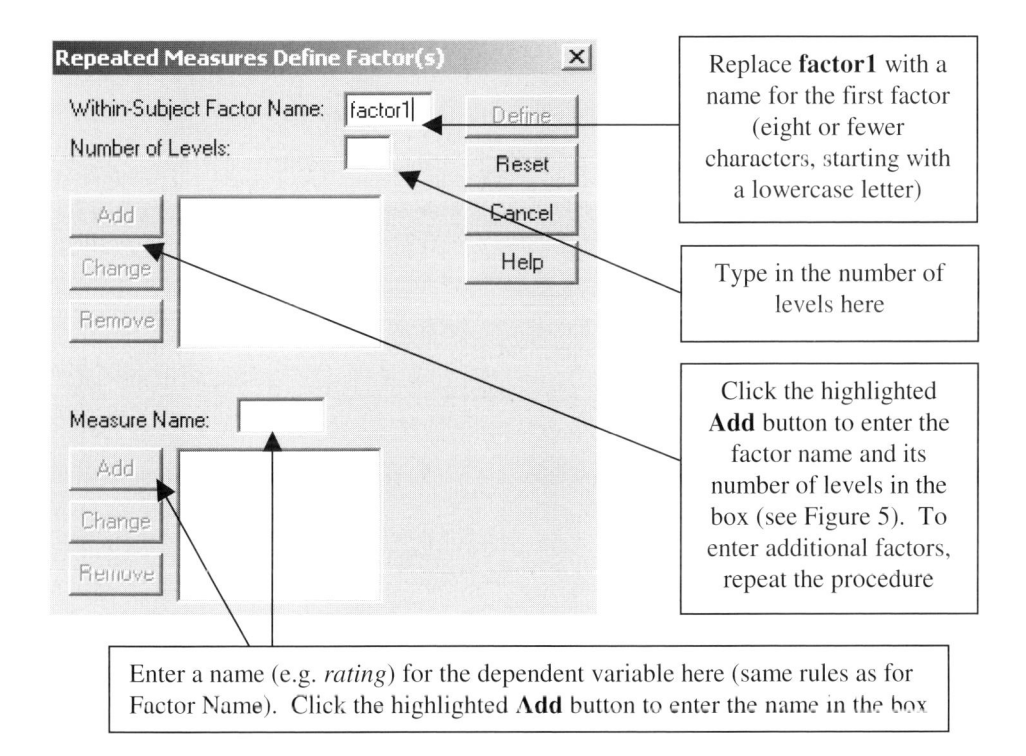

Figure 4. The **Repeated Measures Define Factor(s)** dialog box

- Follow the steps described in Figure 4 to obtain the situation shown in Figure 5.
- Click **Define** to return to the **Repeated Measures ANOVA** dialog box (the upper half of which is shown in Figure 6).

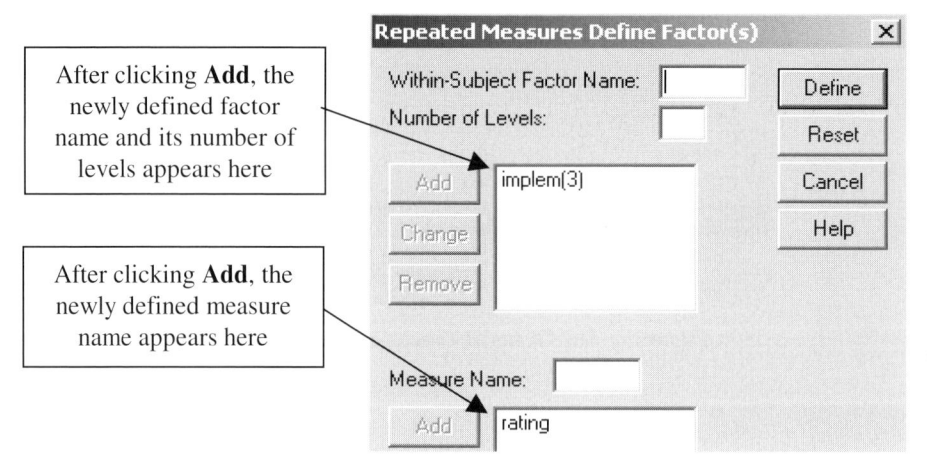

Figure 5. The **Define Factor(s)** dialog box for the factor *implem* and the measure *rating*

- You will see that the uppermost variable name has been highlighted. Highlight the variables *Crayon*, *Paintbrush* and *FeltTip* by clicking-and-dragging the cursor down over them and clicking ▶ to transfer all three into the **Within Subjects Variables [implem]** box. The question marks will be replaced by the variable names as shown in Figure 7.

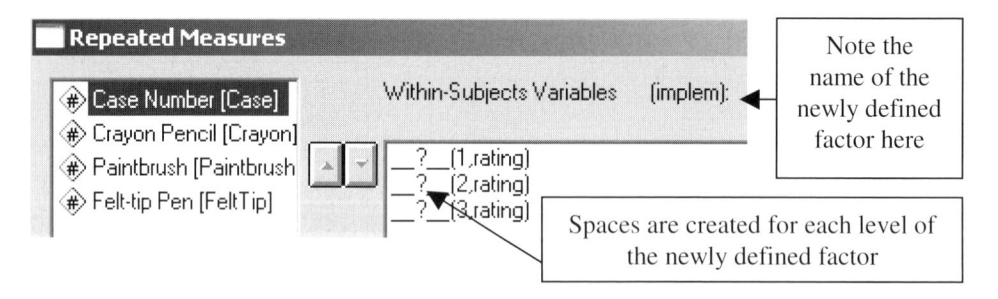

Figure 6. The upper half of the **Repeated Measures** dialog box after defining the **Within-Subjects Variables** factor as *implem* with three levels

Within subjects experiments

[Annotation: The variable names for each level of the factor *implem* are displayed here]

[Dialog box: Repeated Measures
- Case Number [Case]
- Within-Subjects Variables (implem): Crayon(1,rating), Paintbrush(2,rating), FeltTip(3,rating)
- Between-Subjects Factor(s)
- Buttons: OK, Paste, Reset, Cancel, Help
- Bottom buttons: Model..., Contrasts..., Plots..., Post Hoc..., Save..., Options...]

[Annotation: Click here to open the **Profile Plots** dialog box (Figure 8)]

[Annotation: This option is not available for within subjects factors]

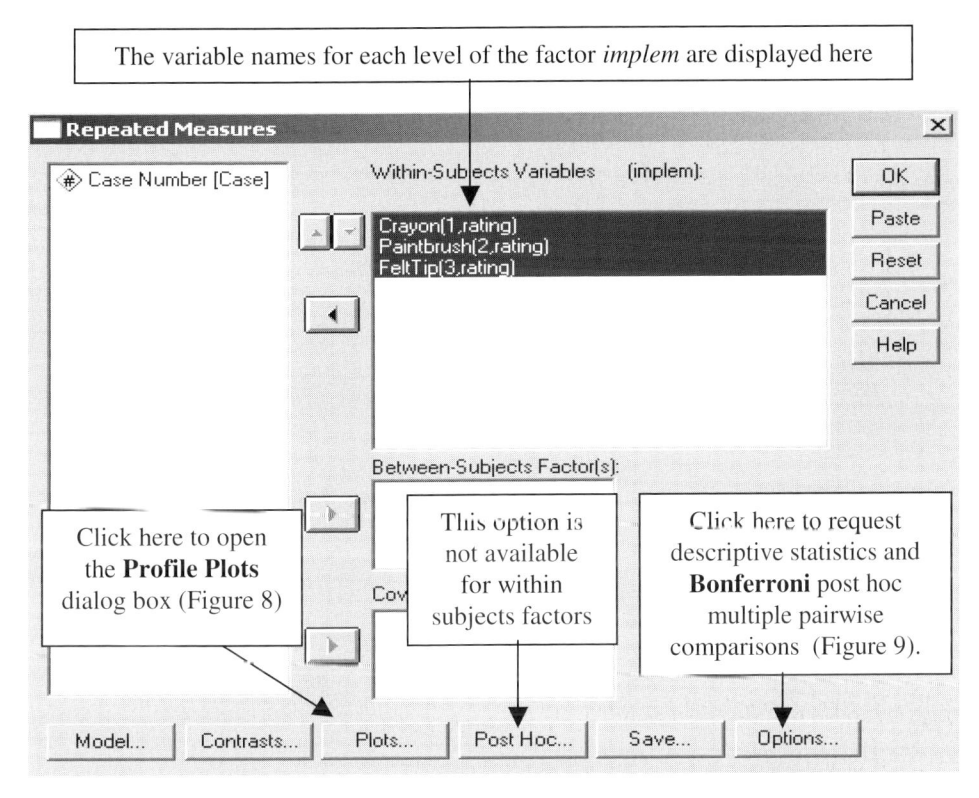

[Annotation: Click here to request descriptive statistics and **Bonferroni** post hoc multiple pairwise comparisons (Figure 9).]

Figure 7. The completed **Repeated Measures** dialog box

- There are some useful options with a repeated measures ANOVA. For example, you can obtain a profile plot of the levels of the within subjects factor by clicking **Plots...** and following the steps shown in Figure 8. Click **Continue** to return to the original dialog box.

[Annotation: To obtain a profile plot, transfer the factor name to this box]

[Annotation: Click **Add** to transfer the factor name to this box]

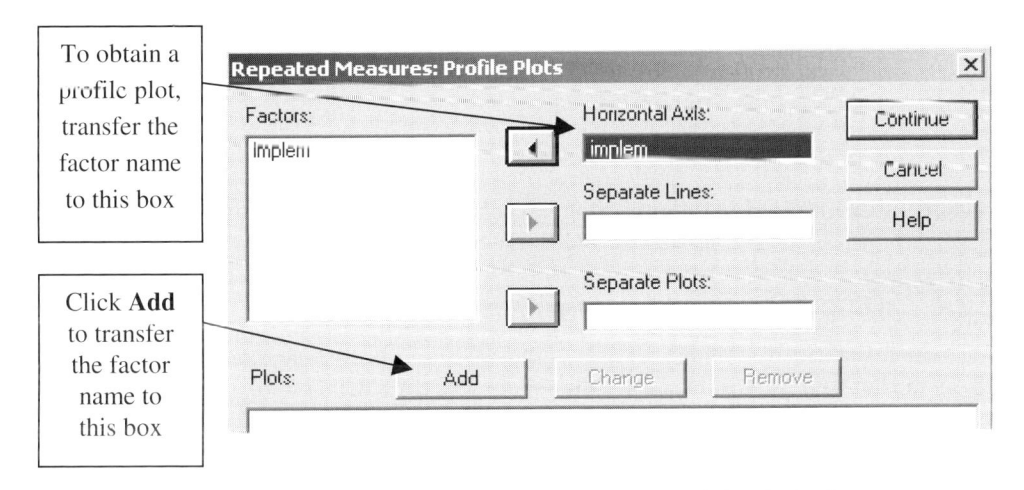

[Dialog box: Repeated Measures: Profile Plots
- Factors: implem
- Horizontal Axis: implem
- Separate Lines:
- Separate Plots:
- Plots: Add, Change, Remove
- Buttons: Continue, Cancel, Help]

Figure 8. The **Profile Plots** dialog box for a plot at each level of a factor

256   Chapter 9

- A table of **descriptive statistics, estimates of effect size** and a table of **Bonferroni adjusted pairwise comparisons** among the levels of the within subjects factor are requested by clicking **Options…** in the **Repeated Measures** dialog box and following the steps shown in Figure 9. Click **Continue** to return to the original dialog box.
- Click **OK** to run the procedure.

Transfer the name of the factor to this box

To request Bonferroni comparisons, click the check box for **Compare main effects**. Select **Bonferroni** in the **Confidence interval adjustment** window

Click the **Descriptive statistics** and **Estimates of effect size** check boxes to request a table of descriptive statistics and values of η_p^2

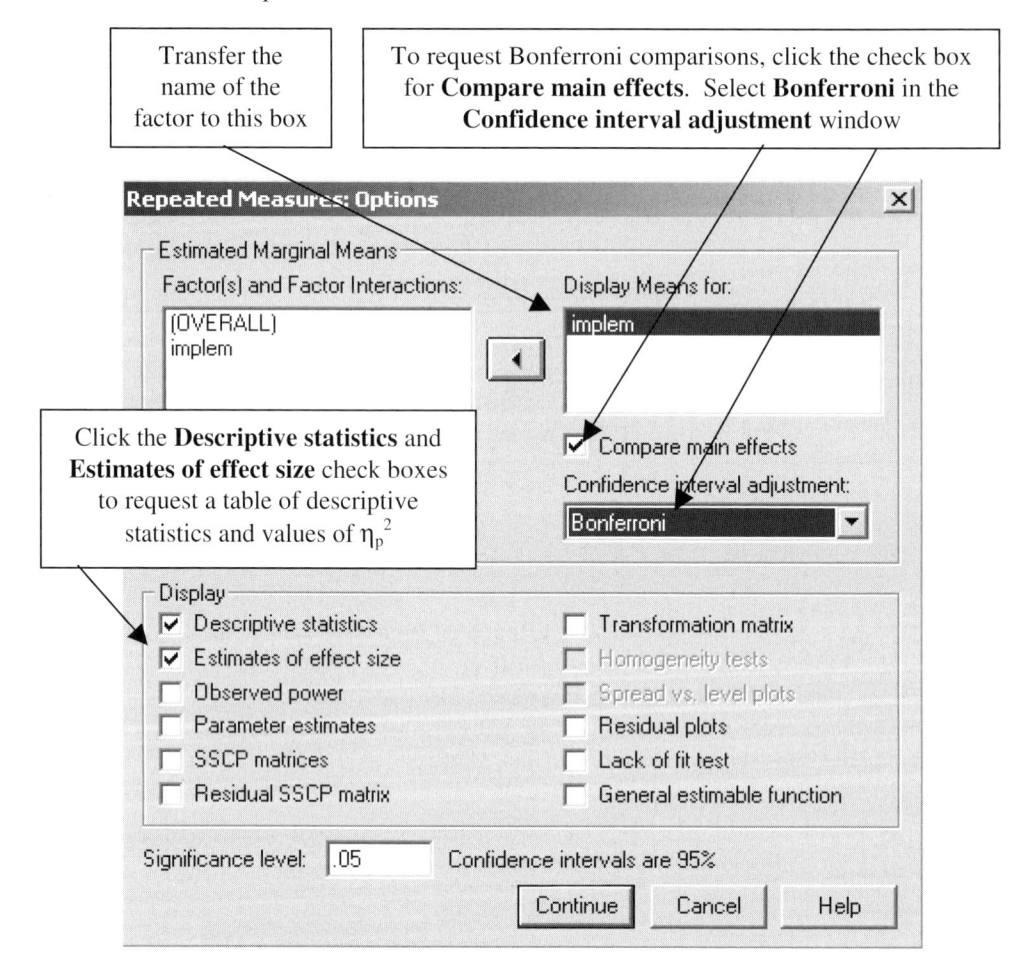

Figure 9. The completed **Options** dialog box requesting **Descriptive statistics, Estimates of effect size** and **Bonferroni** comparisons

9.2.4 Output for a one-factor within subjects ANOVA

The output is extensive, but not all of it is required for a within subjects ANOVA. Output 2 shows the left-hand pane of the **SPSS Viewer**, in which are itemised the various subtables that appear in the right-hand pane. Three of the tables should be deleted immediately by highlighting each in turn and pressing the **Delete** key on the keyboard: **Multivariate Tests**; **Tests of Within-Subjects Contrasts**; **Tests of Between-Subjects Effects** (in this example, there are no between subjects factors). The **Multivariate Tests** in **Estimated Marginal Means** can also be deleted.

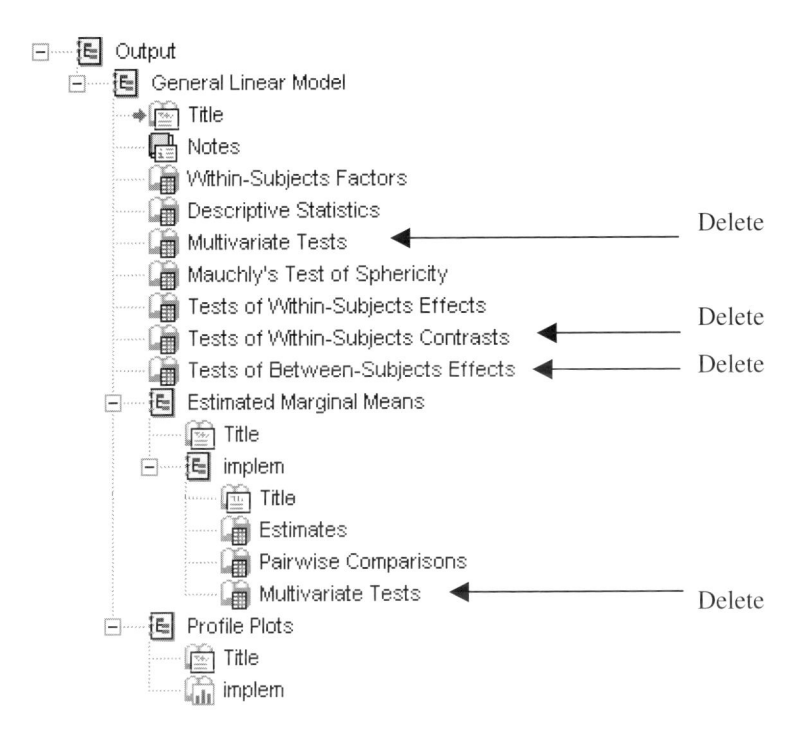

```
Output
    General Linear Model
        Title
        Notes
        Within-Subjects Factors
        Descriptive Statistics
        Multivariate Tests          ←——————— Delete
        Mauchly's Test of Sphericity
        Tests of Within-Subjects Effects      Delete
        Tests of Within-Subjects Contrasts  ←——— Delete
        Tests of Between-Subjects Effects   ←——— Delete
        Estimated Marginal Means
            Title
            implem
                Title
                Estimates
                Pairwise Comparisons
                Multivariate Tests   ←——————— Delete
        Profile Plots
            Title
            implem
```

Output 2. The left-hand pane of the **SPSS Viewer** for the Repeated Measures (within subjects) analysis

Output 3 shows the **TItle**, the **Within-Subjects Factors** list for the measure *rating* and the specially requested **Descriptive Statistics** table.

Within-Subjects Factors

Measure: rating

implem	Dependent Variable
1	Crayon
2	Paintbrush
3	FeltTip

Descriptive Statistics

	Mean	Std. Deviation	N
Crayon Pencil	18.40	4.648	10
Paintbrush	15.70	4.270	10
Felt-tip Pen	16.40	3.062	10

Output 3. The **Within-Subjects Factors** list and **Descriptive Statistics** table

Output 4 reports the result of the **Mauchly's Test of Sphericity**, a test for homogeneity of covariance (see Section 9.1). There are two possible results. If the p-value (**Sig.**) is greater than .05, the null hypothesis of homogeneity of covariance (sphericity) is accepted. If the p-value is less than .05, the null hypothesis of homogeneity of covariance is rejected. The result of Mauchly's Test indicates how we should read the final ANOVA summary table.

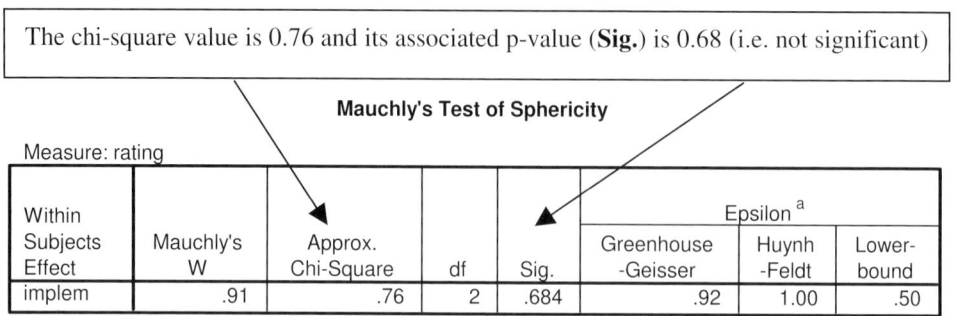

The chi-square value is 0.76 and its associated p-value (**Sig.**) is 0.68 (i.e. not significant)

Mauchly's Test of Sphericity

Measure: rating

Within Subjects Effect	Mauchly's W	Approx. Chi-Square	df	Sig.	Epsilon [a] Greenhouse-Geisser	Huynh-Feldt	Lower-bound
implem	.91	.76	2	.684	.92	1.00	.50

Tests the null hypothesis that the error covariance matrix of the orthonormalized transformed dependent variables is proportional to an identity matrix.

a. May be used to adjust the degrees of freedom for the averaged tests of significance. Corrected tests are displayed in the Tests of Within-Subjects Effects table.

Output 4. Mauchly's Test of Sphericity and values of epsilon for conservative ANOVA *F* tests

The ANOVA summary table (Output 5) shows the results of four *F* tests of the null hypothesis that, in the population, pictures produced by all three implements are equally pleasing.

Tests of Within-Subjects Effects

Measure: rating

Source		Type III Sum of Squares	df	Mean Square	F	Sig.	Partial Eta Squared
implem	Sphericity Assumed	39.27	2	19.63	4.86	.021	.351
	Greenhouse-Geisser	39.27	1.83	21.41	4.86	.024	.351
	Huynh-Feldt	39.27	1.83	19.63	4.86	.021	.351
	Lower-bound	39.27	1.83	39.27	4.86	.055	.351
Error(implem)	Sphericity Assumed	72.73	18	4.04			
	Greenhouse-Geisser	72.73	16.50	4.41			
	Huynh-Feldt	72.73	18.00	4.04			
	Lower-bound	72.73	9.00	8.08			

Since the Mauchly result was not significant, the **Sphericity Assumed** rows apply. The other rows could be deleted in the Output Viewer

For F = 4.86 with a p-value (**Sig.**) of 0.02, the factor is significant at the 5% level

The value of η_p^2 is 35% (i.e. a large effect size)

Output 5. The ANOVA summary table for the within-subjects effects

The results of the tests are given in separated rows, labelled **Sphericity Assumed**, **Greenhouse-Geisser**, **Huynh-Feldt** and **Lower-Bound**. In the lower part of the table, the same row labels are used for the error terms of the four F statistics reported in the top half of the table. Each F ratio was obtained by dividing the treatment mean square in its row by the error mean square in the row of the same name in the lower half of the table. If Mauchly's Test does not show significance, we can read, in the ANOVA summary table, only the rows labelled **Sphericity Assumed**. If Mauchly's Test does show significance, we suggest that, in the ANOVA summary table, you read the rows labelled **Greenhouse-Geisser**.

The conservative test only makes a difference when:
1. There is heterogeneity of covariance (i.e. Mauchly's Test is significant);
2. The F with unadjusted degrees of freedom (i.e. the values shown in the Sphericity Assumed rows) is barely significant beyond the 0.05 level.

Should F have a low tail probability (say p<0.01), the null hypothesis can be safely rejected without making a conservative test. In the present case, Mauchly's Test gives a p-value of 0.68, so there is no evidence of heterogeneity of covariance. The usual ANOVA *F* test can therefore be used.

The main result in Output 5 is the value of **F** and its associated p-value (**Sig.**) for the within subjects factor *implem*. This table has been edited to reduce the number of decimal places to two in some of the columns and to narrow some of the columns.

In the case of the factor *implem*, note that the p-value for F in the **Sphericity Assumed** row is *0.021*: that is, the obtained value of F is significant beyond the five per cent (.05) level, but not beyond the 0.01 level. We can therefore conclude that the type of implement used does affect the ratings that a painting receives. We can write this result as:

> The mean scores for the three types of writing implement differed significantly at the 5% level: F(2, 18) = 4.86; p = .021   Partial eta squared = .351 representing a large effect.

The value of 18 for the error df can be seen in the row labelled **Error (implem) Sphericity Assumed**. In the present case, there was no need to make a conservative *F* test because Mauchly's Test was not significant. It is apparent from the **Sig.** column that *in this particular example* the conservative tests make no difference to the result of the ANOVA *F* test.

The next table (Output 6) shows the pairwise comparisons adjusted according to the **Bonferroni** method (see Section 9.2.5).

See Section 9.2.5

Pairwise Comparisons

Measure: rating

(I) implem	(J) implem	Mean Difference (I-J)	Std. Error	Sig.^{a}	95% Confidence Interval for Difference^a Lower Bound	Upper Bound
1	2	2.70*	.90	.044	.07	5.33
	3	2.00	1.01	.238	-.97	4.97
2	1	-2.70*	.90	.044	-5.33	-.07
	3	-.70	.78	1.000	-2.97	1.57
3	1	-2.00	1.01	.238	-4.97	.97
	2	.70	.78	1.000	-1.57	2.97

Based on estimated marginal means
*. The mean difference is significant at the .05 level.
a. Adjustment for multiple comparisons: Bonferroni.

Only one comparison has a p-value (**Sig.**) less than 0.05

Output 6. The Bonferroni adjusted pairwise comparisons among the levels of the within subjects factor *implem* for the measure *rating*

The requested profile plot is shown in Output 7, which is an edited version of the default plot, adjusted to include zero on the vertical scale. The default plot, with only a small section of the scale on the vertical axis, makes the differences among the means look enormous.

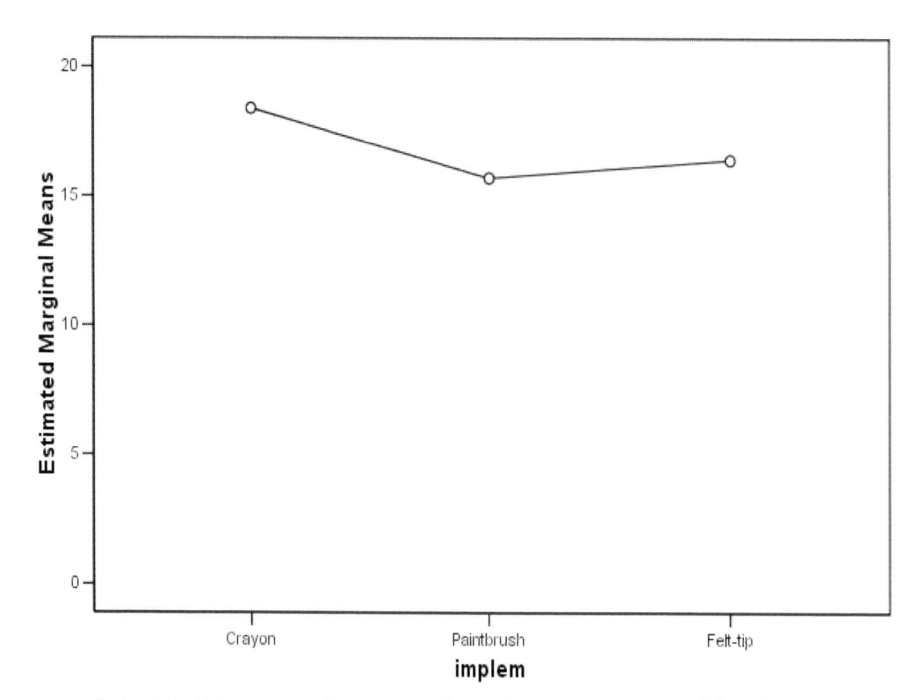

Output 7. The plot of the mean ratings for the three types of implement

9.2.5 Unplanned multiple comparisons: Bonferroni method

There is some doubt as to whether, following significant main effects of within subjects factors, the **Tukey test** affords sufficient protection against inflation of the *per family* type I error rate. Other methods, therefore, have been recommended. In Section 7.1.2, we distinguished between planned and unplanned tests. Suppose it is planned to make exactly *c* pairwise comparisons among a set of treatment means resulting from a one-factor experiment. It is desired to keep the *per family* error rate at 0.05. In the **Bonferroni method**, ordinary t-tests are used for the pairwise comparisons, but the *per family* error rate is divided by the number of planned comparisons. To achieve significance, therefore, each t-test must show significance beyond (sometimes well beyond) the 0.05 level.

The **Bonferroni method**, although primarily intended for the making of planned comparisons, can also be used to make *unplanned* pairwise multiple comparisons among a set of *k* treatment means following a one-factor ANOVA. In this case, however, the *per family* type I error rate must be divided by the number of possible pairs (*c*) that can be drawn from an array of *k* means, which is given by

$$c = \frac{k!}{2!(k-2)!}$$

where the symbol ! means **factorial** (e.g. 4! is $4 \times 3 \times 2 \times 1 = 24$). In the present example, the ANOVA has shown a significant main effect of the Implement factor. Here the number of treatment means (*k*) = 3, so *c* = 3. The **Bonferroni t-tests**, therefore, will have to show significance beyond the 0.05/3 = 0.02 level, approximately. The p-values (**Sig.**) given in Output 5 are the usual within subjects t-test p-values multiplied by 3 to reflect this adjustment for multiple comparisons.

9.3 NONPARAMETRIC TESTS FOR A ONE-FACTOR WITHIN SUBJECTS EXPERIMENT

As with the one-factor completely randomised experiment, nonparametric methods are available for the analysis of ordinal and nominal data.

9.3.1 The Friedman test for ordinal data

Suppose that six people rank five objects in order of 'pleasingness'. Their decisions might appear as in Table 2.

If we assume that the highest rank is given to the most pleasing object, it would appear, from inspection of Table 2, that Object 3 is more pleasing to most of the raters than is Object 1. Since, however, the numbers in Table 2 are not independent measurements but ranks, the one-factor within subjects ANOVA cannot be used here. The Friedman test is suitable for such ordinal data. In **Variable View**, name the variables *Object1, Object2, ... Object5* (with no spaces before the digits). In **Data View**, enter the data in the usual way.

Table 2. Six people's ranks of five objects in order of 'pleasingness'

	Object 1	Object 2	Object 3	Object 4	Object 5
Person 1	2	1	5	4	3
Person 2	1	2	5	4	3
Person 3	1	3	4	2	5
Person 4	2	1	3	5	4
Person 5	2	1	5	4	3
Person 6	1	2	5	3	4

To run the Friedman test:
- Choose
  Analyze
    Nonparametric Tests
      K Related Samples...
  to obtain the **Tests for Several Related Samples** dialog box (Figure 10).

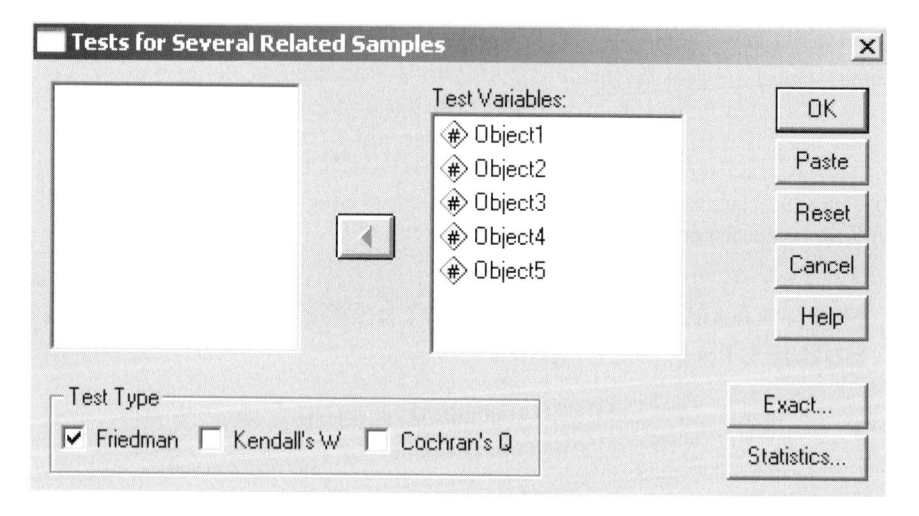

Figure 10. The **Tests for Several Related Samples** dialog box with the **Friedman** Test selected

- In the panel on the left, will appear a list of the variables. This list should include the items *Object1*, *Object2*, ..., *Object5*, which will contain the numbers shown in Table 2. Simply transfer these names to the **Test Variables:** box in the usual way. Make sure the **Friedman** check box has been ticked.
- Click the **Exact...** button to see the **Exact Tests** dialog box and activate the **Exact** radio button. Click **Continue** and then **OK**.

The **Friedman Test** results are shown in Output 8.

Within subjects experiments

Friedman Test

Ranks

	Mean Rank
OBJECT1	1.50
OBJECT2	1.67
OBJECT3	4.50
OBJECT4	3.67
OBJECT5	3.67

Test Statistics [a]

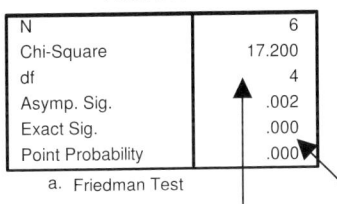

N	6
Chi-Square	17.200
df	4
Asymp. Sig.	.002
Exact Sig.	.000
Point Probability	.000

a. Friedman Test

The chi-square value 17.2 has a p-value (**Exact Sig.**) of <.0005 (which is significant beyond the 1% level)

Output 8. Friedman test results

Clearly the rankings differ significantly across the objects since the p-value is less than 0.01. We can write this result as:

$$\chi^2 (4) = 17.2; p < 0.01.$$

9.3.2 Cochran's Q test for nominal data

Suppose that six children are asked to imagine they were in five different situations and had to choose between Course of Action A (coded *0*) and B (coded *1*). The results might appear as in Table 3. From inspection of Table 3, it would seem that Course of Action B (i.e. cells containing *1*) is chosen more often in some scenarios than in others. A suitable confirmatory test is **Cochran's Q** test, which was designed for use with related samples of dichotomous nominal data.

Table 3. Courses of action chosen by six children in five scenarios

	Scene 1	Scene 2	Scene 3	Scene 4	Scene 5
Child 1	0	0	1	1	1
Child 2	0	1	0	1	1
Child 3	1	1	1	1	1
Child 4	0	0	0	1	0
Child 5	0	0	0	0	0
Child 6	0	0	0	1	1

To run Cochran's Q test:
- Bring the **Test for Several Related Samples** dialog box to the screen (see previous section and Figure 10), click off the **Friedman** check box and click the **Cochran** check box.
- Click the **Exact...** button to see the **Exact Tests** dialog box and activate the **Exact** radio button. Click **Continue** and then **OK**.

The results are shown in Output 9.

Cochran Test

Frequencies

	Value 0	Value 1
SCENE1	5	1
SCENE2	4	2
SCENE3	4	2
SCENE4	1	5
SCENE5	2	4

Test Statistics

N	6
Cochran's Q	9.818[a]
df	4
Asymp. Sig.	.044
Exact Sig.	.042
Point Probability	.030

a. 0 is treated as a success.

The Q value 9.818 has a p-value (**Exact Sig.**) of 0.042 (which is significant at the 5% level)

Output 9. Cochran test results

It is clear that the same course of action is not taken in all five scenarios:

Cochran Q = 9.82; df = 4; p = .042.

Note that, as always, we must be cautious in our statement of the implications of statistical significance. We can reject the null hypothesis that there is, in the population, no difference among the five scenarios, confirming the variation among the scenarios apparent in Table 3. We cannot, however, conclude from this that the difference between any two particular scenarios is also significant. Further pairwise post hoc comparisons could be made by using the **Sign Test**, controlling the **Type I error rate** with the **Bonferroni** procedure previously described.

9.4 THE TWO-FACTOR WITHIN SUBJECTS ANOVA

An experiment is designed to investigate the detection of certain theoretically important patterns presented on a screen. The patterns vary in shape and solidity. The dependent variable (DV) is the Number of Errors made in responding to the pattern, and the two factors Shape (Circle, Square, or Triangle) and Solidity (Outline or Solid) are the independent variables (IVs). The experimenter suspects that a shape's solidity affects whether it is perceived more readily than another shape. The same sample of participants is used for all the possible treatment combinations: that is, there are two within subjects (repeated measures) factors in the experiment. The results are shown in Table 4.

Within subjects experiments

Table 4. Results of a two-factor within subjects experiment

SHAPE:- SOLIDITY:-	Circle		Square		Triangle	
	Solid	Outline	Solid	Outline	Solid	Outline
Participant						
1	4	2	2	8	7	5
2	3	6	2	6	8	9
3	2	10	2	5	5	3
4	1	8	5	5	2	9
5	4	6	4	5	5	10
6	3	6	4	6	9	12
7	7	12	2	6	4	8
8	6	10	9	5	0	10
9	4	5	7	6	8	12
10	2	12	12	8	10	12

Extra care is needed when entering data from experiments with two or more within subjects factors. It is essential to ensure that SPSS understands which data were obtained under which combination of factors. In the present example, there are six data for each participant, each datum being a score achieved under a different combination of the two factors. We can name the data variables as *CircleSolid*, *CircleOutline*, *SquareSolid*, *SquareOutline*, *TriangleSolid* and *TriangleOutline*, representing all possible combinations of the shape and solidity factors. Such systematic, from-left-to-right naming not only helps to avoid transcription errors at the data entry stage, but also prevents incorrect responses when you are in the **Repeated-Measures Define Variable(s)** dialog box and are naming the within subjects factors.

9.4.1 Preparing the data set

The first four rows of data in **Data View** appear as in Figure 11.

Case	CircleSolid	CircleOutline	SquareSolid	SquareOutline	TriangleSolid	TriangleOutline
1	4	2	2	0	7	5
2	3	6	2	6	8	9
3	2	10	2	5	5	3
4	1	8	5	5	2	9

Figure 11. Part of **Data View** for the two factor within subjects ANOVA

Note that the left-to-right ordering of the variable names is exactly the order in which they appeared in the original table of results (Table 4).

9.4.2 Running the two-factor within subjects ANOVA

- Select
  Analyze
  General Linear Model
  Repeated Measures...
  and complete the various dialog boxes by analogy with the one-factor example, defining a second within subjects (repeated measures) factor and the dependent measure as *errors*.

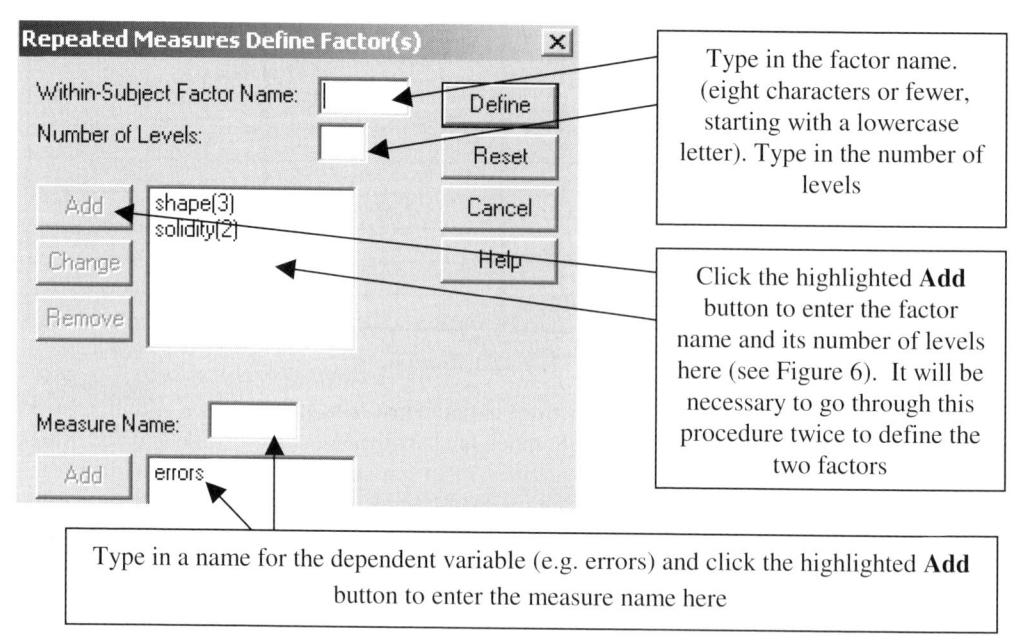

[Dialog box: **Repeated Measures Define Factor(s)** with Within-Subject Factor Name, Number of Levels, showing shape(3) and solidity(2) entered, Measure Name with "errors" entered, and Define/Reset/Cancel/Help buttons.]

Annotations:
- Type in the factor name. (eight characters or fewer, starting with a lowercase letter). Type in the number of levels
- Click the highlighted **Add** button to enter the factor name and its number of levels here (see Figure 6). It will be necessary to go through this procedure twice to define the two factors
- Type in a name for the dependent variable (e.g. errors) and click the highlighted **Add** button to enter the measure name here

Figure 12. The **Repeated Measures Define Factor(s)** dialog box with two factors and their numbers of levels defined as well as a name for the dependent variable

- The completed **Repeated Measures Define Factor(s)** dialog box, with the two within subjects factor names *shape* and *solidity*, is shown in Figure 12 together with a measure name *errors*. (This is the name of the dependent variable in the study.)
- After **Define** has been clicked, the **Repeated Measures** dialog box appears with the six variables listed in alphabetical order on the left. (The top half is reproduced in Figure 13.)

Within subjects experiments 267

> Note the names of the newly defined factors here

> Spaces are created for each combination of levels of the two factors. Care must be taken in transferring the appropriate variable names to each space

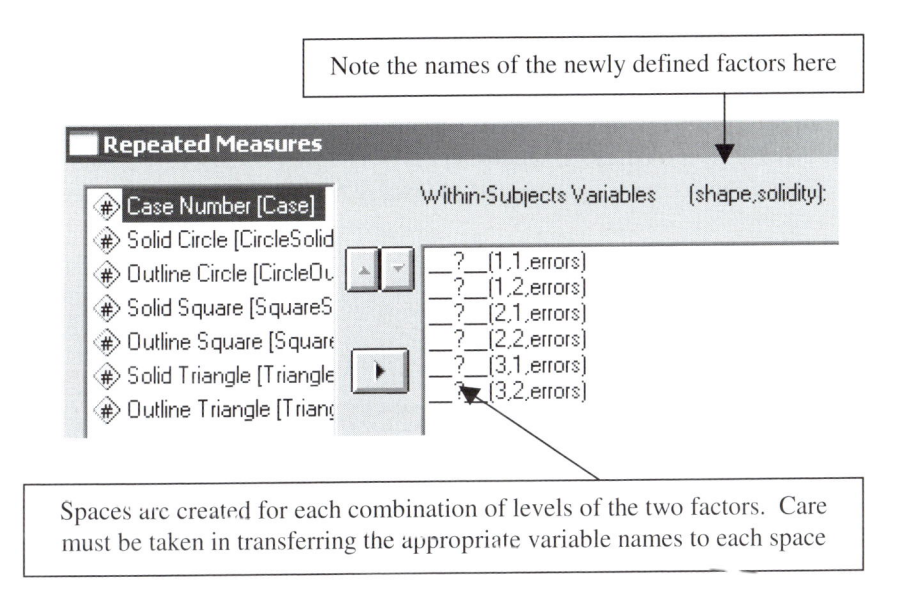

Figure 13. The top half of the **Repeated Measures** dialog box for two factors *shape* and *solidity* before transferring the variable names

On the right, in the box labelled **Within-Subjects Variables [shape, solidity]**, appears a list of the various combinations of the code numbers representing the levels of each of the two treatment factors. It will be noticed that, as one reads down the list, the first number in each pair changes more slowly than the second. When there is more than one within subjects factor, it is inadvisable immediately to transfer the variable names in a block from the left-hand box to the **Within-Subjects Variables** box by a click-and-drag operation, as in the one-factor situation. First, check that the downward order of the variable names in the left-hand panel matches the order of the names in **Variable View** (or **Data View**).

Table 5. Numbering of levels in within subjects variables

Shape Factor	Shape 1 (Circle)		Shape 2 (Square)		Shape 3 (Triangle)	
Solidity Factor	Solidity 1 (Solid)	Solidity 2 (Outline)	Solidity 1 (Solid)	Solidity 2 (Outline)	Solidity 1 (Solid)	Solidity 2 (Outline)
Variable name	*Circle Solid*	*Circle Outline*	*Square Solid*	*Square Outline*	*Triangle Solid*	*Triangle Outline*

Should your experiment be more complex, with more levels in the factors, it is safer to transfer the variables to the **Within-Subjects Variables** slots one at a time, noting the numbers in the square brackets and referring to the names of the newly defined within subjects factors (in this case *shape* and *solidity*) inside the square brackets in the caption above the **Within-Subjects Variables** box.

A table such as Table 5 clarifies the numbering of the levels of within subjects factors. Thus the variable *CircleSolid* is [shape 1, solidity 1] i.e. [1,1], *CircleOutline* is [1,2] and so on.

- The top half of the completed **Repeated Measures ANOVA** dialog box is shown in Figure 14.

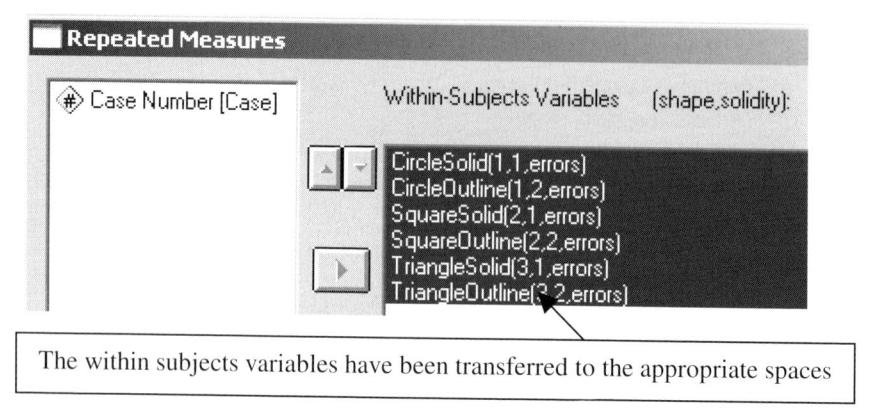

Figure 14. The **Within-Subjects Variables** section of the **Repeated Measures** dialog box after transferring the variable names

- There are some useful options associated with a repeated measures ANOVA. Request a profile plot of the levels of one of the factors across the levels of the other factor by clicking **Plots...** and following the steps shown in Figure 15. Click **Continue** to return to the original dialog box.

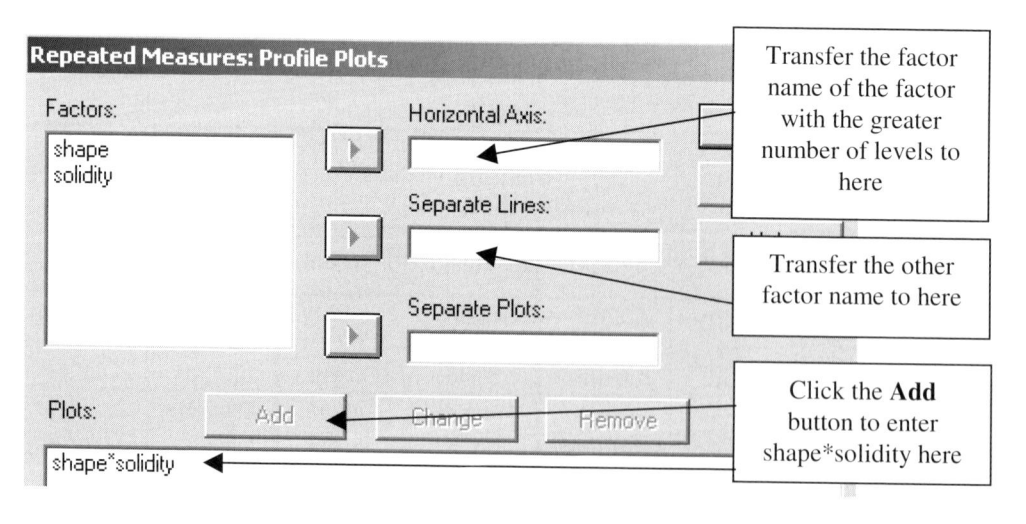

Figure 15. Part of the **Profile Plots** dialog box for requesting a profile plot shape*solidity

Within subjects experiments

- A table of **descriptive statistics**, **estimates of effect sizes** and a table of post hoc **Bonferroni pairwise comparisons** among the levels of within subjects factors with more than two levels are requested by clicking the **Options...** button in the **Repeated Measures** dialog box and following the steps shown in Figure 16. Click **Continue** to return to the original dialog box and then **OK**.

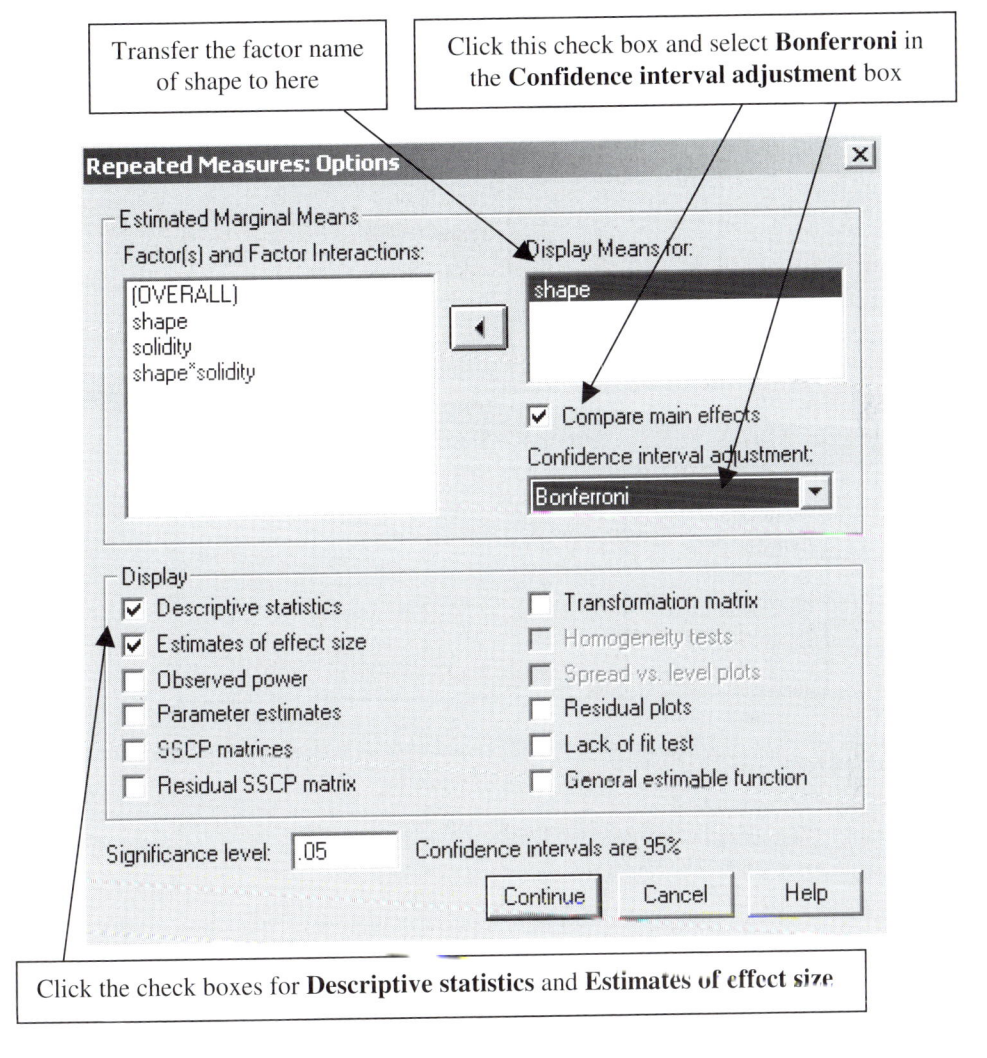

Figure 16. The completed **Options** dialog box for requesting **Descriptive statistics**, **Estimates of effect size** and **Bonferroni** comparisons among the levels of shape

9.4.3 Output for a two-factor within subjects ANOVA

As in the case of the one-factor within subjects ANOVA, the output is extensive, and not all of it is required. You can make life easier by pruning some items and removing others altogether. Three of the subtables in the left-hand pane of the **SPSS Viewer** can be immediately deleted by highlighting each in turn and then pressing the **Delete** key on the keyboard: **Multivariate Tests**; **Tests of Within-Subjects Contrasts**; **Tests of Between-Subjects Effects** (in this example, there are no between subjects factors).

See Output 2 in Section 9.2.4

Output 10 shows the **Title**, **Within-Subjects Factors** list and the specially requested **Descriptive Statistics** table.

Within-Subjects Factors

Measure: errors

shape	solidity	Dependent Variable
1	1	CircleSolid
	2	CircleOutline
2	1	SquareSolid
	2	SquareOutline
3	1	TriangleSolid
	2	TriangleOutline

Descriptive Statistics

	Mean	Std. Deviation	N
Solid Circle	3.60	1.838	10
Outline Circle	7.70	3.268	10
Solid Square	4.90	3.446	10
Outline Square	6.00	1.155	10
Solid Triangle	5.80	3.190	10
Outline Triangle	9.00	3.018	10

Output 10. The **Within-Subjects Factors** list and **Descriptive Statistics** table

The next table (Output 11) reports the result of the **Mauchly's Test of Sphericity** for homogeneity of covariance (see Section 9.3).

The table is more extensive than that in Output 4, because there are two factors. Notice that the test is not applied when a factor has only two levels, as in the case of *solidity*. The test is not significant (i.e. there is no evidence of heterogeneity of covariance) for either *shape* or the interaction of *shape* and *solidity*, so the significance levels in the rows labelled **Sphericity Assumed** can be accepted. You should now remove from the ANOVA table the rows giving the results of the various conservative *F* tests.

Within subjects experiments

> The Chi-square values and their p-values (**Sig.**) showing that none is significant. Note that the test does not apply to factors with only two levels (e.g. *solidity*)

Mauchly's Test of Sphericity [b]

Measure: errors

Within Subjects Effect	Mauchly's W	Approx. Chi-Square	df	Sig.	Epsilon[a] Greenhouse-Geisser	Huynh-Feldt	Lower-bound
shape	.67	3.25	2	.197	.75	.87	.50
solidity	1.00	.00	0	.	1.00	1.00	1.00
shape * solidity	.90	.82	2	.663	.91	1.00	.50

Tests the null hypothesis that the error covariance matrix of the orthonormalized transformed dependent variables is proportional to an identity matrix.

a. May be used to adjust the degrees of freedom for the averaged tests of significance. Corrected tests are displayed in the Tests of Within-Subjects Effects table.

b. Design: Intercept
Within Subjects Design: shape+solidity+shape*solidity

Output 11. **Mauchly's Test of Sphericity** and more conservative statistics for *shape* and for the interaction of *shape* and *solidity*

The edited ANOVA summary table (minus the rows with the conservative tests and the words Sphericity Assumed) for the within subjects factors *shape* and *solidity*, and their interaction is shown in Output 12. Notice that, in contrast with a two-factor between subjects ANOVA, there are three error terms, one for each main effect and one for the interaction.

Tests of Within-Subjects Effects

Measure: errors

Source	Type III Sum of Squares	df	Mean Square	F	Sig.	Partial Eta Squared
shape	46.03	2	23.02	2.98	.076	.249
Error(shape)	138.97	18	7.72			
solidity	117.60	1	117.60	54.56	.000	.858
Error(solidity)	19.40	9	2.16			
shape * solidity	23.70	2	11.85	1.41	.270	.135
Error(shape*solidity)	151.30	18	8.41			

> The factor *solidity* has **F** = 54.56 with a p-value (**Sig.**) less than 0.0005 (i.e. F is significant beyond the 1% level)

> The main effect of the factor *shape* and the interaction *shape*solidity* have small values of **F** with p-values greater than 0.05 and are therefore not significant

Output 12. The edited ANOVA summary table for the within subjects factors and their interaction

Output 12 shows that the factor *shape* has no significant main effect, since the p-value for F in the column headed **Sig.** is greater than 0.05. We can write this result as follows:

> There was no significant effect of the Shape factor: F(2, 18) = 2.98; p = .076.

The factor *Solidity* is also significant, since its p-value is less than 0.01 (the output value 0.000 means that the p-value is less than .0005). We can write this result as:

> The Solidity factor had a main effect that was significant beyond the 1% level: F(1, 9) = 54.56; p = <.0005. Partial eta squared = .858. This is a large effect.

Finally, there was no significant *shape*solidity* interaction: F(2, 18) = 1.41; p = .270.

Since the factor *shape* is not significant, the **Bonferroni pairwise comparisons** table should be ignored.

The edited profile plot is shown in Output 13. An interaction is indicated when the profiles cross one another, diverge or converge. Obviously the slight difference in profile here is insufficient for a statistically significant interaction.

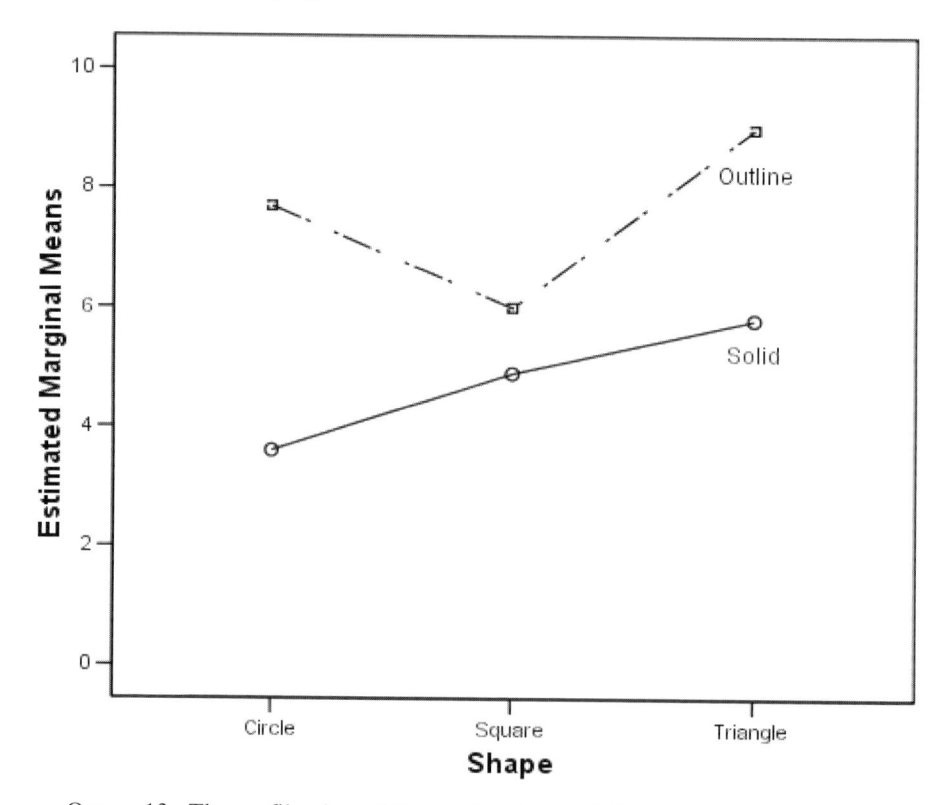

Output 13. The profile plots of the two levels of solidity across the three shapes

In conclusion, Output 12 shows that only the *Solidity* factor has a significant effect: the other factor, *Shape* and its interaction with *Solidity*, are not significant.

9.4.4 Unplanned comparisons following a factorial within subjects experiment

In the example we have just considered, the question of unplanned multiple comparisons does not arise, because
1. There is no interaction.
2. The sole significant main effect involves a factor (*Solidity*) with only two levels, implying that the two means must be significantly different.

Had there been a significant interaction, however, the approach already described in the context of the one-factor within subjects experiment would also have been applicable here.

The problem with the **Bonferroni test** is that even with only six cells, it is very difficult to get a difference sufficiently large to be significant. With six cells, $c = 15$ and each t-test has to have a p-value of 0.003 or less to be deemed significant. There is, therefore, a case to be made for testing initially for **simple main effects** of the principal experimental factor of interest at various levels of the other factor. A significant simple main effect may justify defining the comparison family more narrowly and improves the chances of finding significant differences. As in a between subjects factorial experiment, a simple main effect of a factor can be computed by carrying out a one-way ANOVA upon the data at only one level of the other factor. In the case of a within subjects factorial experiment, however, the data at different levels of either factor are not independent. It is wise, therefore, to adopt a stricter criterion for significance of a simple main effect in such cases, by applying the **Bonferroni** criterion and setting the significance level for each simple effect test at 0.05 divided by the number of tests (for simple main effects) that will be made.

EXERCISE 13

One-factor within subjects (repeated measures) ANOVA

Before you start

Before proceeding with this Exercise, we suggest that you study Chapter 9.

A comparison of the efficacy of statistical packages

Table 1 shows the results of an experiment in which the dependent variable was the time taken for ten participants to perform a statistical analysis using three statistical computer packages Pack1, Pack2 and Pack3. During the course of the experiment, each participant used every package and the order of use was counterbalanced across participants.

Table 1. Times taken by participants to carry out an analysis with different computing packages

Case	Pack1	Pack2	Pack3	Case	Pack1	Pack2	Pack3
1	12	15	18	6	10	12	14
2	18	21	19	7	18	17	21
3	15	16	15	8	18	17	21
4	21	26	32	9	23	27	30
5	19	23	22	10	17	25	21

Opening SPSS

Open SPSS and select the **Type in data** radio button in the opening window. If **Data View** appears first, click the **Variable View** tab to open **Variable View**.

Preparing the SPSS data set

Prepare the SPSS data set as described in Section 9.2.1. Since there is just one group of participants, there is no grouping variable. Add suitable variable labels in the **Label** column such as Case Number, Package 1, Package 2, Package 3. Remember to save the data set as a data file with a suitable filename.

Exploring the data

Use the methods described in Section 9.2.3 to check for any distribution problems. Remember that outliers represented by O are not as problematic as extreme values represented by *.

Procedure for the within subjects (repeated measures) ANOVA

The within subjects ANOVA (SPSS refers to it as Repeated Measures) is selected by choosing:
Analyze
    General Linear Model
        Repeated Measures...

to open the **Repeated Measures Define Factor(s)** dialog box. Follow the procedure described in Section 9.2.3. Remember to click **Plots...** and complete the **Repeated Measures: Profile Plots** dialog box by transferring *package* to the **Horizontal Axis:** box, clicking **Add** and then **Continue** to return to the original dialog box.

Output for the within subjects (repeated measures) ANOVA

Section 9.2.4 offers some guidelines for the interpretation of the output. First, there is a **Table of Within-Subjects Factors**, which lists the levels of the *package* factor. Then there is a table of **Multivariate Tests**, which can be deleted by clicking its icon in the left-hand pane of the **SPSS Viewer** and pressing the **Delete** key. Next comes **Mauchly's Test of Sphericity**. Check that the result does not show significance. If not, you need only read the row labelled **Sphericity Assumed** in the **Table of Within-Subjects Effects** below, in which case you should delete the other rows by double-clicking anywhere in the table, highlighting the material to be deleted and pressing the **Delete** key. The remaining two tables can be ignored.

- What is the value of the F ratio and its associated p-value (tail probability) for the *package* factor? Is F significant? What are the implications for the experimental hypothesis?

Inspect the **Profile Plots** showing the means of the three packages.

- Is the appearance of the plot consistent with the finding from the ANOVA that there is a significant main effect?

Finally with reference to Section 9.2.4, use the Bonferroni method to ascertain which pairs of statistical packages are significantly different.

- List which packages differ significantly.

Finishing the session

Close down SPSS and any other windows before logging out of the computer.

EXERCISE 14

Two-factor within subjects ANOVA

Before you start

We suggest that you read Section 9.4 before proceeding. In this Exercise, we consider the ANOVA of within subjects factorial experiments, that is, experiments with repeated measures on all factors.

A two-factor within subjects experiment

An experiment is carried out to investigate the effects of two factors upon the recognition of symbols briefly presented on a screen, as measured by the number of correct identifications over a fixed number of trials. The factors are Symbol (with levels Digit, Lower Case, and Upper Case) and Font (with levels Gothic and Roman). Each of the six participants in the experiment is tested under all six combinations of the two treatment factors. The results are shown in Table 1.

Table 1. Results of a two-factor within subjects experiment

Case	Digit Gothic	Digit Roman	Lower Case Gothic	Lower Case Roman	Upper Case Gothic	Upper Case Roman
1	2	6	18	3	20	5
2	4	9	20	6	18	2
3	3	10	15	2	21	3
4	1	12	10	9	25	10
5	5	8	13	8	20	8
6	6	10	14	10	16	6

Opening SPSS

Open SPSS and select the **Type in data** radio button in the opening window. If **Data View** appears first, click the **Variable View** tab to open **Variable View**.

Preparing the SPSS data set

In **Variable View**, define the variables as described in Section 9.4, assigning the variable names systematically, as in DigitGothic, DigitRoman, LowerGothic, LowerRoman, UpperGothic, UpperRoman. For clarity, it is recommended that self-explanatory labels such as Gothic digits, Roman digits, Gothic lowercase, and so on, be assigned by making appropriate entries in the **Label** column of **Variable View**. Enter the data into **Data View**, under the appropriate pre-headed columns. Ensure that the values in the **Decimals** column are all *0*.

Exploring the data

Obtain boxplots to check the distributions.

Running the two-factor within subjects ANOVA

To run the ANOVA, select
Analyze
> **General Linear Model**
>> **Repeated Measures...**

and complete the various dialog boxes following the procedure described in Section 9.4. Remember to click **Plots...** and complete the **Repeated Measures: Profile Plots** dialog box by transferring *symbol* to the **Horizontal Axis:** box and *font* to the **Separate Lines:** box, clicking **Add** and finally **Continue**, to return to the **Repeated Measures** dialog box.

Output for the two-factor within subjects experiment

The output for the two-factor repeated measures ANOVA is explained in Section 9.4. Remove the unnecessary tables at the beginning.

Next comes a table of **Mauchly's Test of Sphericity**. Check carefully to see whether there is evidence of non-sphericity. The main table of interest is the **Tests of Within-Subjects Effects**. For each factor and interaction, read the row **Sphericity Assumed** if the relevant Mauchly test is not significant; otherwise read the **Greenhouse-Geisser** row. If none of the Sphericity tests is significant, you should delete the conservative tests rows by double-clicking anywhere in the table, highlighting the material to be deleted and pressing the **Delete** key. The remaining two tables can be ignored.

- **Give the F ratio and p-value for each factor and the interaction. Interpret these results in terms of the aims of the study.**

Finally inspect the **Profile Plots**.

- **Describe the plot and comment on whether it confirms the various ANOVA results.**

Finishing the session

Close down SPSS and any other windows before logging out of the computer.

CHAPTER 10

Mixed factorial experiments

10.1   Introduction

10.2   The two-factor mixed factorial ANOVA

10.3   The three-factor mixed ANOVA

10.4   Further analysis: Simple effects and multiple comparisons

10.1   INTRODUCTION

10.1.1   Rationale of a mixed factorial experiment

Suppose that a researcher designs an experiment to explore the hypothesis that engineering students, because of their training in two-dimensional representation of three-dimensional structures, have a more strongly developed sense of shape and symmetry than do psychology students.

Three theoretically important shapes are presented on a monitor screen to samples of Psychology and Engineering students under sub-optimal conditions. The dependent variable, which we shall call *Naming*, is the number of shapes correctly identified. The results of the experiment are shown in Table 1.

It can be seen from Table 1 that there were two factors in this experiment:
1. Student Category, with levels Psychology and Engineering;
2. Shape, with levels Triangle, Square and Rectangle.

Since each participant was tested with all three shapes, Shape is a within subjects factor. Student Category, however, is a between subjects factor. It is very common for factorial designs to have within subjects (repeated measures) factors on *some* (but not *all*) of their treatment factors. Since such experiments have a mixture of between subjects and within subjects factors, they are often said to be of **mixed** design. A common alternative term is **split-plot**, which reflects the agronomic context in which this type of experiment was originally used.

Table 1. Results of a two-factor mixed factorial experiment with one within subjects factor and one between subjects factor

Levels of the Student Category factor:	Case	Levels of the Shape factor:		
		Triangle	Square	Rectangle
Psychology	1	2	12	7
	2	8	10	9
	3	4	15	3
	4	6	9	7
	5	9	13	8
	6	7	14	8
Engineering	7	13	3	35
	8	21	4	30
	9	26	10	35
	10	22	8	30
	11	20	9	28
	12	19	8	27

10.2 THE TWO-FACTOR MIXED FACTORIAL ANOVA

In Chapter 9, we saw that the within subjects ANOVA is run by using the **Repeated Measures** procedure in the **General Linear Model** menu. The mixed ANOVA is also run with the **Repeated Measures** procedure.

See Chap. 9

10.2.1 Preparing the SPSS data set

In Table 1, we chose to represent the experimental design with the levels of the within subjects factor arrayed horizontally and those of the between subjects factor stacked vertically, with Engineering under Psychology. We did so because this arrangement corresponds to the way in which the results must appear in **Data View**.

As always, the first column of **Data View** will contain the case numbers. The second column will contain a single grouping variable *Category* representing the *Psychologists* (*1*) and the *Engineers* (*2*). The third, fourth and fifth columns will contain the results at the three levels of the *Shape* factor (i.e. *Triangle*, *Square*, and *Rectangle*).

Using the techniques described in Chapter 2, Section 2.3, enter **Variable View** and name five variables: *Case*, *Category* (the grouping variable), *Triangle*, *Square*, and *Rectangle*. Use the **Label** column to assign more meaningful variable names (*Case Number, Category of Student*) and the **Values** column to assign labels to the numerical values of the grouping variable *Category* (*1* = *Psychology Student*, *2* = *Engineering Student*). Ensure that the **Decimals** column is set at *0* for each variable.

See Section 2.3

Click the **Data View** tab and enter the data into **Data View** (Figure 1). If values rather than labels appear in the variable category, enter the **View** menu and click **Value Labels**.

Case	Category	Triangle	Square	Rectangle
1	Psychology Student	2	12	7
2	Psychology Student	8	10	9
3	Psychology Student	4	15	3
4	Psychology Student	6	9	7
5	Psychology Student	9	13	8
6	Psychology Student	7	14	8
7	Engineering Student	13	3	35
8	Engineering Student	21	4	30
9	Engineering Student	26	10	35
10	Engineering Student	22	8	30
11	Engineering Student	20	9	28
12	Engineering Student	19	8	27

Figure 1. The data from Table 1 in **Data View**

10.2.2 Exploring the results: Boxplots

As usual, the first step is to explore the data set. The boxplot was described in Section 4.3.2. Here, however, the **clustered boxplot** (which clusters the levels of the within subjects factor at different levels of the between subjects variable) is appropriate.

To obtain a clustered boxplot, proceed as follows:
- Click
  Graphs
    Boxplot…
  to open the **Boxplot** dialog box.
- Select the **Clustered** option and (within the **Data in Chart Are** section) the **Summaries of separate variables** radio button. Click **Define** to enter the **Define Clustered Boxplot: Summaries of Separate Variables** dialog box.
- Transfer the variable names *Triangle, Square* and *Rectangle* to the **Boxes Represent** box and the variable name *Category of Student* to the **Category Axis:** box.
- Click **OK**.

The edited boxplot is shown in Output 1.

Notice the extreme score (case 3) for the number of rectangles identified by a Psychology student and the outlier (case 7) for the number of triangles identified by an Engineering student. In a real research situation, it might have been worth eliminating the two deviant scores, but here we shall work with the entire data set. Sometimes extreme scores are errors (i.e. values have been entered into the data file incorrectly) but they can also be genuine, though atypical, data.

Mixed factorial experiments

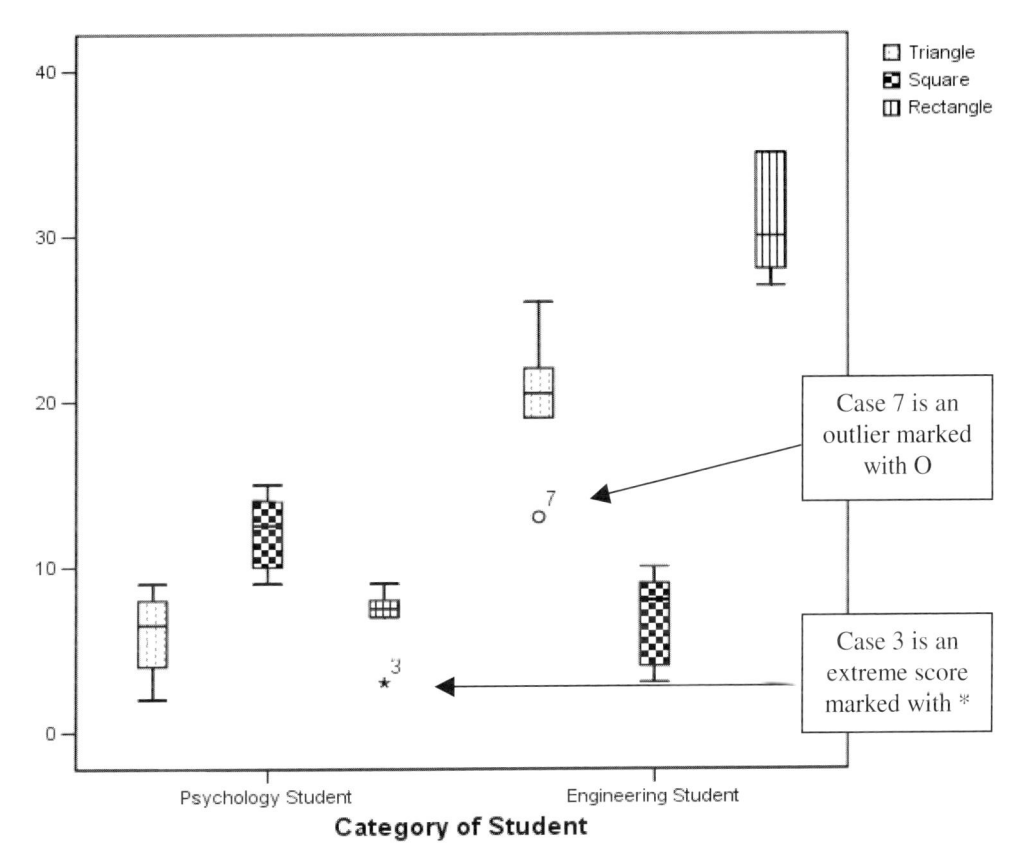

Output 1. Edited boxplots of the three shapes for each student category

10.2.3 Running the ANOVA

- Select
  Analyze
    General Linear Model
      Repeated Measures...
  to open the **Repeated Measures Define Factor(s)** dialog box. (The completed version is shown in Figure 2.)
- In the **Within-Subject Factor Name** box, delete *factor1* and type a generic name (such as *shape*) for the repeated measures factor. This name must not be that of any of the three levels making up the factor and must also conform to the rules governing the assignment of variable names. In the **Number of Levels** box, type the number of levels (*3*) making up the repeated measures factor. Click **Add** and, in the lowest box in Figure 2, the entry *shape(3)* will appear. As the **Measure Name**, enter *Naming*, which is the name of the dependent variable.

[Figure: Repeated Measures Define Factor(s) dialog box. Annotations: "A factor named *shape* with 3 levels has been defined" pointing to shape(3); "A measure name of *naming* has been added" pointing to the Measure Name field containing "naming".]

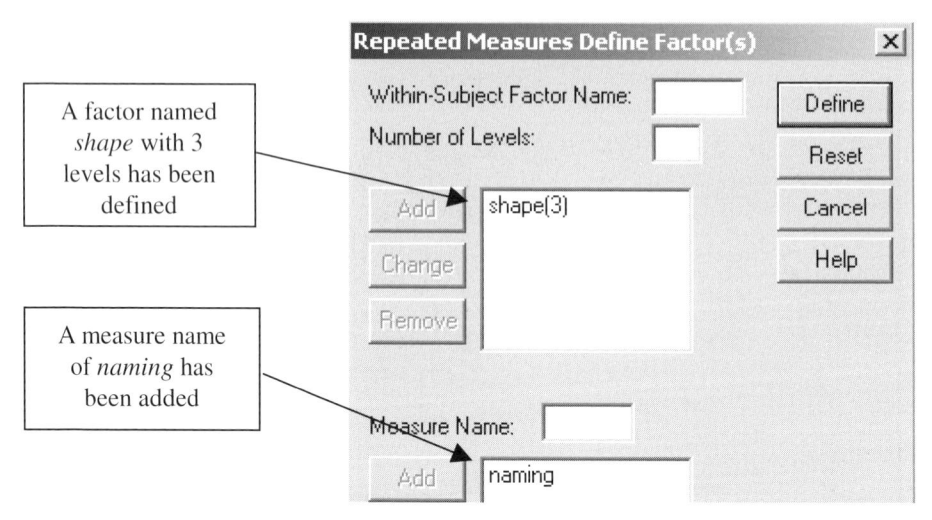

Figure 2. The **Repeated Measures Define Factor(s)** for three levels of *shape*

- Click **Define** to open the **Repeated Measures ANOVA** dialog box.
- Transfer the variable names *Rectangle, Square, Triangle* to the **Within-Subjects Variables** box as shown in Figure 3.
- The new element is the presence of the between subjects factor *Category of Student*. Transfer its name to the **Between-Subjects Factor(s)** box as shown in Figure 3.
- You should also request a number of useful additional options. A profile plot of the levels of the within subjects factor *shape* for each level of the between subjects variable *category* is requested by clicking **Plots...** and following the steps shown in Figure 15 in Chapter 9. Click **Continue** to return to the **Repeated Measures** dialog box. [See Section 9.4.2]
- A table of **descriptive statistics**, **estimates of effect size** and a table of **Bonferroni adjusted pairwise comparisons** among the levels of the within subjects factor *shape* are requested by clicking **Options...** and following the steps shown in Figure 16 in Chapter 9. Click **Continue** to return to the **Repeated Measures** dialog box.
- Had there been more than two levels in the between subjects variable *Category*, a Tukey post-hoc test could have been requested by clicking **Post Hoc...**, transferring the variable name category to the **Post Hoc Tests for** box, and clicking the **Tukey** check box. Click **Continue** to return to the original dialog box.
- Click **OK** to run the ANOVA.

Mixed factorial experiments

[Screenshot of SPSS Repeated Measures dialog box with annotations:]

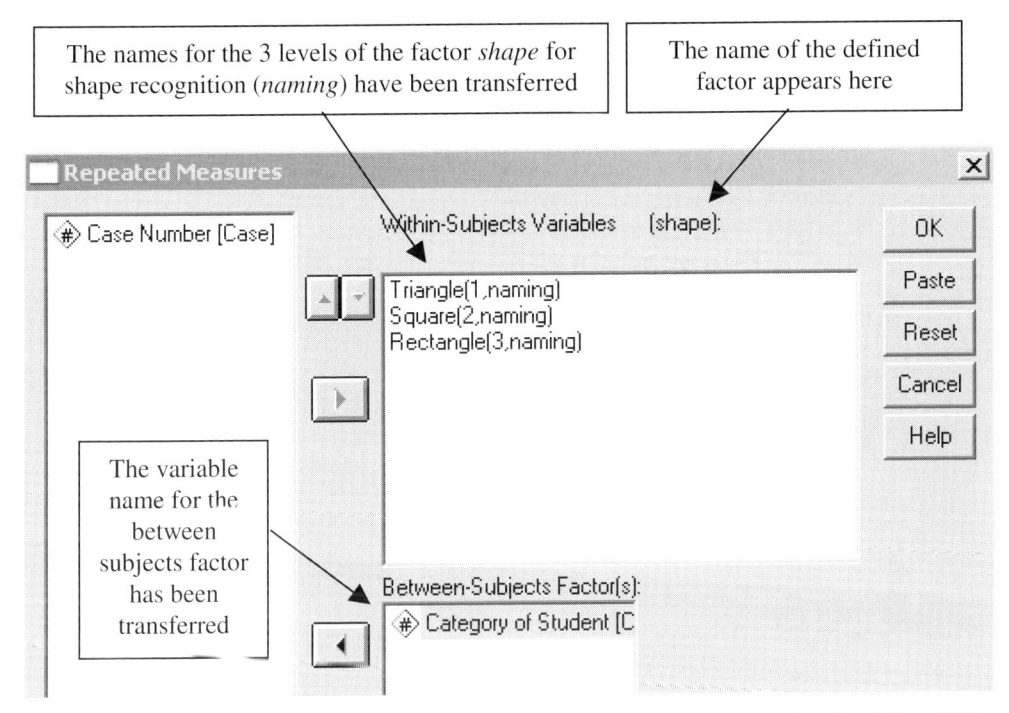

- "The names for the 3 levels of the factor *shape* for shape recognition (*naming*) have been transferred" — pointing to Within-Subjects Variables (shape): Triangle(1,naming), Square(2,naming), Rectangle(3,naming)
- "The name of the defined factor appears here" — pointing to (shape)
- "The variable name for the between subjects factor has been transferred" — pointing to Between-Subjects Factor(s): Category of Student [C

Figure 3. Part of the **Repeated Measures** dialog box showing the three levels of the within subjects factor *shape* and the between subjects factor *category*

10.2.4 Output for the two-factor mixed ANOVA

Output 2 shows the left-hand pane of the **SPSS Viewer** listing the various items appearing in the right-hand pane. Two items, **Multivariate Tests** and **Tests of Within-Subjects Contrasts**, can be deleted immediately by highlighting each in turn and pressing the **Delete** key on the keyboard. In the **Estimated Marginal Means** section, the **Multivariate Tests** table can also be deleted.

```
⊟ → 📄 General Linear Model
     📄 Title
     📄 Notes
     📄 Within-Subjects Factors
     📄 Between-Subjects Factors
     📄 Descriptive Statistics
     📄 Multivariate Tests          ←——————————— Delete
     📄 Mauchly's Test of Sphericity
     📄 Tests of Within-Subjects Effects
     📄 Tests of Within-Subjects Contrasts  ←——— Delete
     📄 Tests of Between-Subjects Effects
   ⊟ 📄 Estimated Marginal Means
        📄 Title
      ⊟ 📄 shape
           📄 Title
           📄 Estimates
           📄 Pairwise Comparisons
           📄 Multivariate Tests   ←——————————— Delete
   ⊟ 📄 Profile Plots
        📄 Title
        📄 shape * Category of Student
```

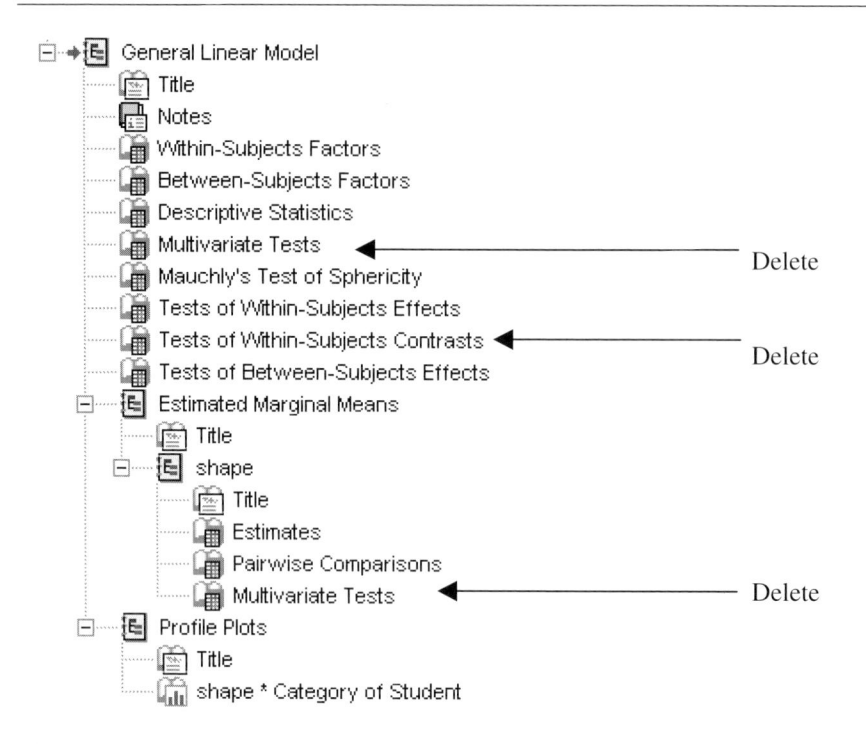

Output 2. The left-hand pane of **SPSS Viewer** listing the output items for the mixed ANOVA

Output 3 shows the two SPSS tables identifying the levels of the Within-Subjects factors and the levels of the Between-Subjects factors.

Within-Subjects Factors

Measure: naming

shape	Dependent Variable
1	Triangle
2	Square
3	Rectangle

Between-Subjects Factors

		Value Label	N
Category of Student	1	Psychology Student	6
	2	Engineering Student	6

Output 3. The **Within-Subjects Factors** list of levels and the **Between-Subjects Factors** list of levels

Output 4 shows the table of descriptive statistics requested in **Options**. Inspection of the means shows different profiles across the factor *shape* for the two student categories.

Descriptive Statistics

	Category of Student	Mean	Std. Deviation	N
Triangle	Psychology Student	6.00	2.61	6
	Engineering Student	20.17	4.26	6
	Total	13.08	8.13	12
Square	Psychology Student	12.17	2.32	6
	Engineering Student	7.00	2.83	6
	Total	9.58	3.65	12
Rectangle	Psychology Student	7.00	2.10	6
	Engineering Student	30.83	3.43	6
	Total	18.92	12.74	12

Output 4. The optional table of **Descriptive Statistics**

The next table, in Output 5, reports the result of the **Mauchly's Test of Sphericity** for homogeneity of covariance. (Section 9.2.4 describes the correct procedure when the Mauchly statistic is significant.) [See Section 9.2.4]

In the present case, the **Mauchly** statistic has a p-value of 0.63, so there is no evidence of heterogeneity of covariance. The usual (Sphericity Assumed) F test can therefore be used. You should simplify that ANOVA table (below) accordingly by removing the information about the conservative F tests.

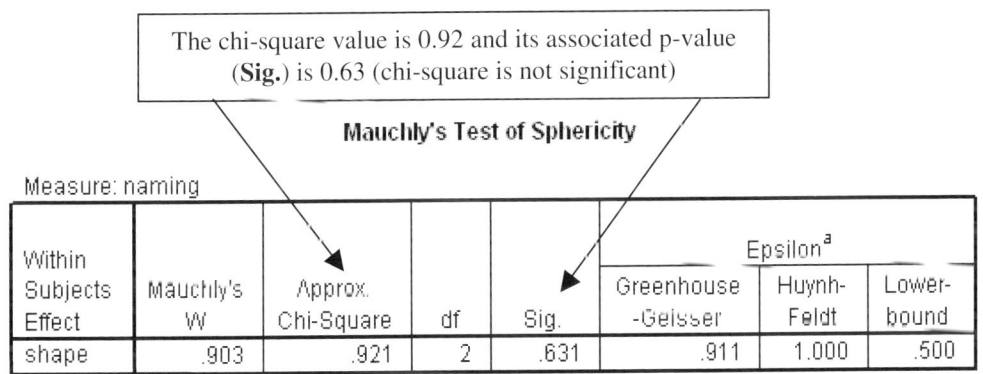

The chi-square value is 0.92 and its associated p-value (**Sig.**) is 0.63 (chi-square is not significant)

Mauchly's Test of Sphericity

Measure: naming

Within Subjects Effect	Mauchly's W	Approx. Chi-Square	df	Sig.	Greenhouse-Geisser	Huynh-Feldt	Lower-bound
shape	.903	.921	2	.631	.911	1.000	.500

Epsilon[a]

Tests the null hypothesis that the error covariance matrix of the orthonormalized transformed dependent variables is proportional to an identity matrix.

a. May be used to adjust the degrees of freedom for the averaged tests of significance. Corrected tests are displayed in the Tests of Within-Subjects Effects table.

Output 5. **Mauchly's Test of Sphericity** and values of **Epsilon** for more conservative tests

Tests for within subjects and interaction effects

Output 6 (edited to remove the conservative tests) shows the ANOVA summary table for the within subjects factor *shape* and the *category by shape* interaction.

Tests of Within-Subjects Effects

Measure: naming

Source	Type III Sum of Squares	df	Mean Square	F	Sig.	Partial Eta Squared
shape	533.56	2	266.78	32.62	.000	.765
shape * Category	1308.22	2	654.11	79.99	.000	.889
Error(shape)	163.56	20	8.18			

Both the factor *shape* and the interaction *shape*Category* have p-values (**Sig.**) less than 0.01 (significant at the 1% level)

Output 6. The edited ANOVA summary table for the within-subjects factor *shape* and its interaction with the between-subjects factor *category*

Note that the factor *Shape* is significant beyond the 1 per cent level: the p-value (**Sig.**) 0.000 is less than 0.0005. **Write p < .0005, not .000**. This result would be reported as:

> The mean scores for the three shapes differed significantly beyond the 1% level: $F(2, 20) = 32.62$; $p < 0.0005$. Partial eta squared = .765 representing a large effect.

The interaction *Category × Shape* is also significant beyond the 1% level: the p-value is less than 0.0005. This result would be reported as:

> There was a significant interaction between *Category* and *Shape*: $F(2, 20) = 79.99$; $p < 0.0005$. Partial eta squared = .889 representing a large effect.

Test for between subjects effects

Output 7 shows the ANOVA summary table for the between subjects factor *Category*.

Ignore the terms **Intercept** and **Type III**: these refer to the regression that was used to perform the analysis. With a p-value (**Sig.**) of less than 0.0005, there is clearly a significant difference in performance between the two groups of students. This result would be reported as:

> The mean scores for the categories of student differed significantly at the 1% level: $F(1,10) = 98.95$; $p < 0.0005$. Partial eta squared = .908 representing a large effect.

The ANOVA strongly confirms the patterns discernible in Table 2: the *Shape* and *Category* factors both have significant main effects; the interaction between the factors is also significant.

Tests of Between-Subjects Effects

Measure: naming
Transformed Variable: Average

Source	Type III Sum of Squares	df	Mean Square	F	Sig.	Partial Eta Squared
Intercept	6916.69	1	6916.69	634.88	.000	.984
Category	1078.03	1	1078.03	98.95	.000	.908
Error	108.94	10	10.89			

The p-value (**Sig.**) for *Category* is less than 0.0005 (significant at the 1% level)

Output 7. The ANOVA summary table for the between-subjects factor *category*

Bonferroni Pairwise Comparisons for the within subjects factor

Output 8 shows the pairwise comparisons requested in **Options**.

Pairwise Comparisons

Measure: naming

(I) shape	(J) shape	Mean Difference (I-J)	Std. Error	Sig.[a]	95% Confidence Interval for Difference[a] Lower Bound	Upper Bound
1	2	3.50*	.97	.015	.71	6.29
	3	-5.83*	1.22	.002	-9.34	-2.32
2	1	-3.50*	.97	.015	-6.29	-.71
	3	-9.33*	1.28	.000	-13.02	-5.65
3	1	5.83*	1.22	.002	2.32	9.34
	2	9.33*	1.28	.000	5.65	13.02

Based on estimated marginal means
*. The mean difference is significant at the .05 level.
a. Adjustment for multiple comparisons: Bonferroni.

Differences significant at the .01 level.   Difference significant at the 5% level

Output 8. The **Bonferroni pairwise comparisons** for the factor *shape*

Profile plot

The requested profile plot is shown (edited) in Output 9.

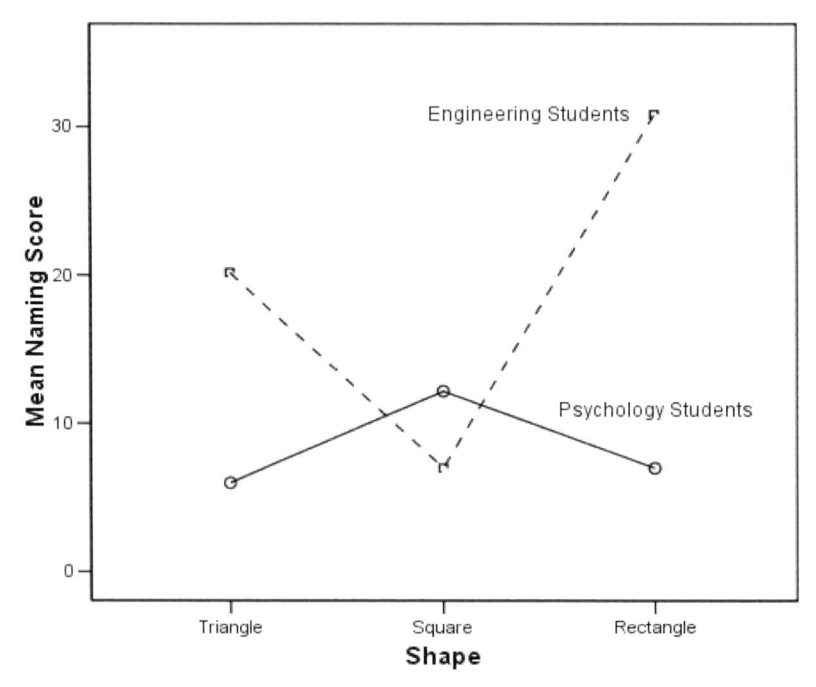

[Figure: Plot showing Mean Naming Score vs Shape (Triangle, Square, Rectangle) for Engineering Students and Psychology Students]

Output 9. The factor Shape performance profiles for each student category

The plot confirms the pattern of the boxplots in Output 1. With squares, the Psychology students improved, while the Engineering students slumped.

10.3 THE THREE-FACTOR MIXED ANOVA

The procedures described in Section 10.2 can readily be extended to the analysis of data from mixed factorial experiments with three treatment factors. There are two possible mixed three-factor factorial experiments:
1. Two within subjects factors and one between subjects factor;
2. One within subjects factor and two between subjects factors.

10.3.1 Two within subjects factors and one between subjects factor

Suppose that to the experiment described in Section 10.2, we were to add an additional within subjects factor, such as Solidity (of the shape), with two levels, Solid or Outline. The participants (either Psychology or Engineering students) now have to try to recognise both Solid and Outline Triangles, Squares, and Rectangles. Since there are six combinations of the Shape and Solidity factors, we shall need to have six variables in **Data View** to contain all the scores. Prepare the named columns systematically in **Variable View** by taking the first level of one factor (say, Shape) and combining it in turn with each of the levels of the second factor (Solidity), and then doing the same with the second and third levels of the first factor. The top part of **Data View** might appear as in Figure 4.

Mixed factorial experiments

Case	Category	Triangle Solid	Triangle Outline	Square Solid	Square Outline	Rectangle Solid	Rectangle Outline
1	Psychology Student	13	15	12	23	12	14

Figure 4. The variable names for a three-factor mixed factorial experiment with two within subjects factors

Care must be taken when transferring variable names within the **Repeated Measures** dialog box. The danger is that the names in **Data View** (and hence in the list in the left-hand box of the **Repeated Measures** dialog box) may not be in the required sequence. (The order of the defined factors, and hence the correct sequence of variable names, is shown in square brackets above the box.) It may be necessary to transfer the variable names one at a time to the **Within-Subjects Variables** box to ensure that the variable names are correctly placed in the slots provided. The upper part of the completed dialog box is shown in Figure 5.

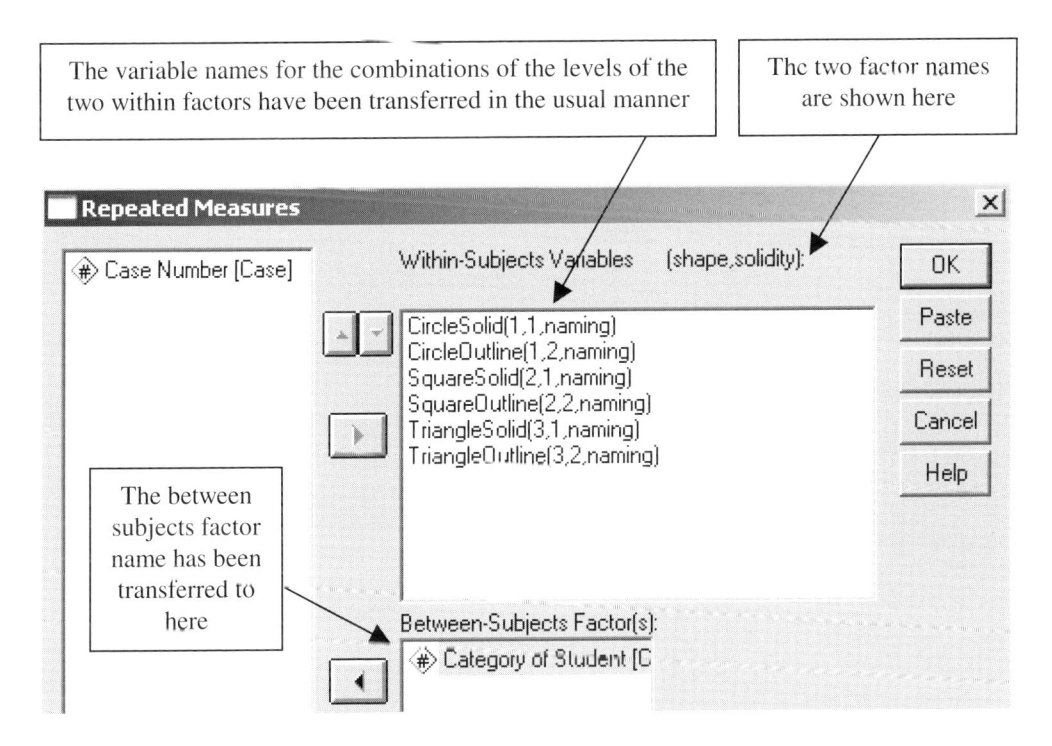

Figure 5. The upper part of the **Repeated Measures** dialog box for a three-factor mixed factorial experiment, with two within subjects factors and one between subjects factor

10.3.2 One within subjects factor and two between subjects factors

Suppose the experiment described in Section 10.2 were to have an additional between subjects factor, such as Sex (Male, Female). The participants (either Psychology or Engineering Students, and either Male or Female) have to try to recognise shapes (Triangles, Squares, and Rectangles).

In **Variable View**, it will now be necessary to define two grouping variables, *Sex* and *Category*, and the three levels (*Triangle*, *Square* and *Rectangle*) of the within subjects factor *Shape*. The top of **Data View** might appear as in Figure 6.

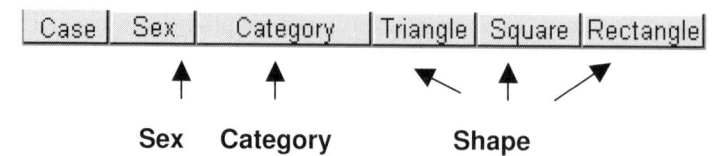

Figure 6. The variable names for a three-factor mixed factorial experiment with one within subjects factor and two between subjects factors

The completed **Repeated Measures ANOVA** dialog box would then appear as in Figure 7.

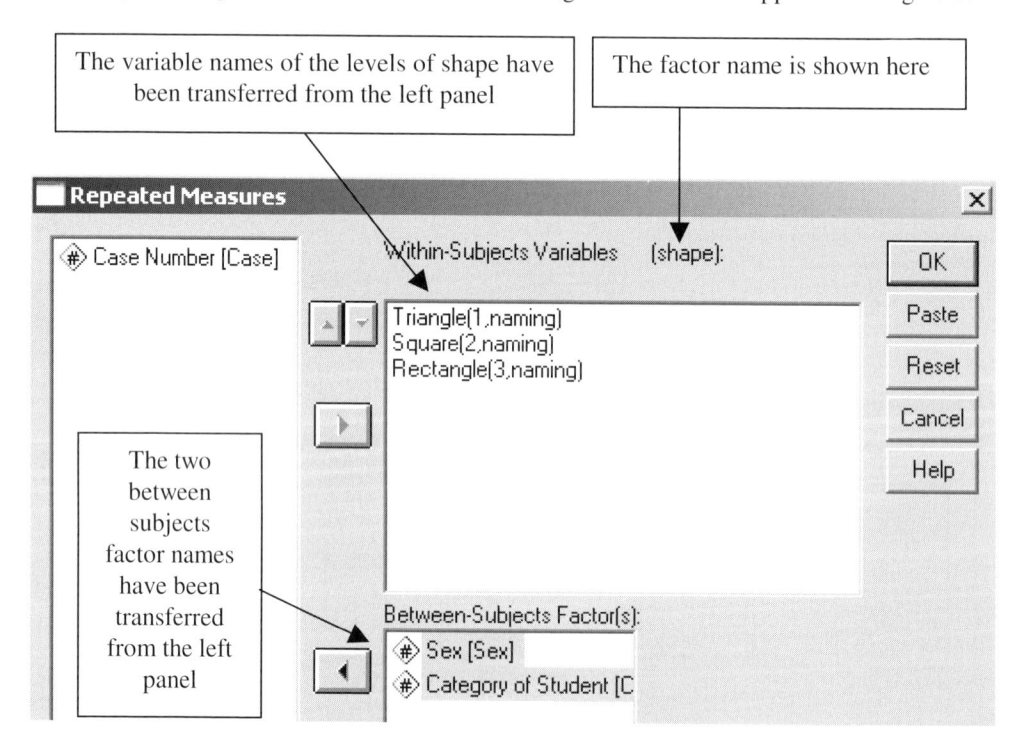

Figure 7. The upper part of the **Repeated Measures** dialog box for a three-factor mixed factorial experiment with one within subjects factor and two between subjects factors

10.4 FURTHER ANALYSIS: SIMPLE EFFECTS AND MULTIPLE COMPARISONS

The analysis of variance is a large topic in statistics, and there are available many more techniques than we can mention in this book. For example, when an interaction is significant, it is often useful to follow up the initial ANOVA with additional tests of the effects of one factor at specific levels of another. Such analysis of **simple effects** can be combined with both planned and unplanned multiple comparisons. We urge the reader who is unfamiliar with such methods to read the relevant chapters in a lucid textbook such as Howell (2002).

At this point, it may be worth reminding the reader that the dangers of committing a **Type I error** in unplanned multiple comparisons increase enormously with the complexity of the experiment. Accordingly, the user must take precautions to control the *per family* **Type I error** rate (the probability of at least one **Type I error**). The use of simple effects tests may justify the specification of a smaller subgroup of treatment means as the 'family', increasing the power of each test.

In a three-factor experiment, for example, the significance of the three-way interaction implies that the interactions between two of the factors are not homogeneous across all levels of the third factor. Should there be a significant two-factor interaction at one particular level of the third factor (i.e. a significant **simple interaction**), one might define the comparison 'family' as the performance means at that level only. The user could then proceed to make pairwise multiple comparisons among this smaller set of means.

EXERCISE 15

Mixed ANOVA (experiments with between and within subjects factors)

Before you start

Readers should study Chapter 10 carefully before proceeding with this Exercise.

Effects of ambient hue and sound on vigilance

In an experiment investigating the effect of the colour of the ambient light upon the performance of a vigilance task, participants were asked to press a button when they thought they could discern a signal against a background of random noise. The experimenter expected that the detection of different kinds of sound would differ depending on the ambient colour. Three types of signal were used: a horn, a whistle and a bell. Each signal was presented 30 times in the course of a one-hour monitoring session, during which the participant sat in a cubicle lit by either red or blue light. The dependent variable was the number of correct presses of the button. For theoretical purposes, it was necessary to use different participants for the different colour conditions. It was considered that there would be advantages in testing each individual with all three kinds of signal. In this experiment, therefore, the factor of Colour was between subjects; whereas the other factor, Signal, was within subjects.

The results are shown in Table 1.

Table 1. The results of a two-factor mixed factorial experiment

Colour	Participant	Horn	Signal Whistle	Bell
Red	1	25	18	22
	2	22	16	21
	3	26	19	26
	4	23	21	20
	5	19	18	19
	6	27	23	27
Blue	7	19	12	23
	8	21	15	19
	9	23	14	24
	10	20	16	21
	11	17	16	20
	12	21	17	19

Mixed factorial experiments

Preparing the SPSS data set

Rearrange the data of Table 1 into a form suitable for entry into SPSS. In **Variable View**, after naming a variable *Case*, you will need to have a grouping variable *Colour* and three variables for the scores: *Horn*, *Whistle*, and *Bell*. The last three variables will be the three levels of the within-subjects factor *Signal*, which is not defined until the ANOVA command is actually being run. Follow the procedure described in Section 10.2.1. Save the data with a suitable file name.

Exploring the data set

Draw boxplots as described in Section 10.2.2.

- What do the plots tell us about the distributions? (Comment on the position of the median bar in the box.)
- Are there any markedly deviant scores, as shown by * or 0?

Running the two-factor mixed ANOVA

Run the ANOVA as described in Section 10.2.3, remembering to request **Descriptive Statistics**, a **Profile Plot** and **Bonferroni Pairwise Comparisons** for the factor *Signal* (see Chapter 9, Figure 16 for details of how to request **Bonferroni pairwise comparisons**).

Output for the two-factor mixed ANOVA

The main features of the output are explained in Section 10.2.4. After tables listing the **Within-Subjects Factors** and **Between-Subjects Factors**, look at the table of **Descriptive Statistics** and the **Profile Plot**.

- Can you discern any pattern in the means for each level of colour across the three signals?

The next table, **Multivariate Tests**, can be deleted by highlighting its icon in the left-hand pane of **SPSS Viewer** and pressing the **Delete** key. Next, comes the table showing the results of **Mauchly's Test of Sphericity**, followed by the **Tests of Within-Subjects Effects**. If the Mauchly's Test is not significant, read the rows labelled **Sphericity Assumed** and delete the conservative test rows by double-clicking anywhere in the table, highlighting the material to be deleted and then pressing the **Delete** key. Delete the **Tests of Within-Subjects Contrasts** table.

- For the Signal factor, write down the value of F and its associated p-value. Do the same with the interaction between Signal and Colour.
- Next there is a table of Tests of Between-Subjects Effects. For the Colour factor, write down the value of F and its associated p-value.

Finally look again at the **Profile Plot**. Does the graph show a pattern consistent with the results of the ANOVA?

- Has the experimenter's hypothesis been confirmed?

Finishing the session

Close down SPSS and any other windows before logging out.

EXERCISE 16

Mixed ANOVA: Three-factor experiment

Before you start

Before proceeding with this Exercise, you should study Section 10.3. From the procedural point of view, the analysis of mixed experiments with three factors is a fairly simple extension of the command for two-factor mixed experiments. In general, however, the interpretation of data from factorial experiments becomes increasingly problematic as more factors are added. In particular, where there is a complex experiment with repeated measures on some factors but not on others, the naming of the factors must be carried out with special care.

A three-factor mixed factorial experiment with two within subjects factors and one between subjects factor

Imagine an experiment investigating the recognition of shapes under sub-optimal conditions on a monitor screen. The experimenter is interested in whether the different shapes are more readily recognised if they are filled rather than merely outlines, and whether Engineering students are more adept at recognising shapes than Psychology students. There are three shapes (Shape1, Shape2, Shape3), each of which can be either Open (merely an outline) or Filled. Each participant in the experiment is tested under all six combinations of these two treatment factors, which can be labelled *Shape* and *Shade*. The between subjects factor *Category* is the observer group: one group consists of Psychology students, the other of Engineering students. The dependent variable is the number of correct identifications over a fixed series of trials. The results are shown in Table 1.

Table 1. Three-factor mixed factorial experiment with two within subjects treatment factors

Participant	Category	Shape 1 Open	Shape 1 Filled	Shape 2 Open	Shape 2 Filled	Shape 3 Open	Shape 3 Filled
1	Psychology	2	12	3	1	4	5
2	Psychology	13	22	5	9	6	8
3	Psychology	14	20	8	7	5	7
4	Engineering	12	1	3	9	6	10
5	Engineering	11	2	8	10	5	9
6	Engineering	12	7	2	4	4	10

Preparing the SPSS data set

In **Variable View**, in addition to a case variable, it will be necessary to name one grouping variable *Category* and six other variables (one for each combination of the *Shape* and *Shade* factors) to contain the results. We suggest that you name the variables in the systematic fashion described in Section 10.3.1.

The ANOVA

The command for running the **Repeated Measures ANOVA** is outlined in Section 10.3.1. The procedure is a straightforward extension of the routine for the two-factor mixed experiment. Name and specify the numbers of levels of two within subjects factors (*Shape* and *Shade*). Transfer the between subjects variable *Category* to the **Between-Subjects Factor(s):** box. To request the profile plots, click the **Plots...** button to open the **Repeated Measures: Profile Plots** dialog box. Enter *Shape* in the **Horizontal Axis:** box, *Shade* in the **Separate Lines:** box and *Category* in the **Separate Plots:** box. Click **Add** and then **Continue**, to return to the original dialog box. Select **Options...** to request **Descriptive Statistics** and **Bonferroni Pairwise Comparisons** for the factor *Shape*. Click **Continue** and **OK** to run the analysis.

The output

Check the **Within-Subjects Factors** table and **Between-Subjects Factors** table for accuracy. Inspect the table of **Descriptive Statistics** to see if you can discern a pattern of means. Delete the table of **Multivariate Tests**. The **Mauchly** tests will appear in the table **Mauchly's Test of Sphericity**. The Mauchly test only arises with factors that have more than two levels. In this case, there will be Mauchly tests for the *Shape* factor and the *Shape* × *Shade* interaction. Check that the p-values are greater than 0.05.

The within subjects tests are given in the table **Tests of Within-Subjects Effects**. If the relevant Mauchly test is not significant, you need study only the rows in the ANOVA table labelled **Sphericity Assumed** and you can delete the rows for the conservative tests. Delete the **Tests of Within-Subjects Contrasts** table. The next table is **Tests of Between-Subjects Effects** for the factor *Category*.

- Write down the F ratios (and p-values) for the three factors, their two-way interactions and the three-way interaction. Do the values of F confirm the patterns among the treatment means you have observed in the table of Descriptive Statistics and the Profile Plots?

Look at the table of **Pairwise Comparisons**.

- Are any of the pairs significantly different? If not, why not, considering that the factor Shape is significant in the ANOVA?

Finally inspect the **Profile Plots** again. Compare the pattern of lines in both plots.

- Does the ANOVA confirm the appearance of the graphs? Why was the triple interaction significant?
- Has the experimenter's hypothesis been confirmed? In your answer, refer to the relevant features of the results.

Finishing the session

Close down SPSS and any other windows before logging out.

CHAPTER 11

Measuring statistical association

11.1   Introduction

11.2   Correlational analysis with SPSS

11.3   Other measures of association

11.1   INTRODUCTION

11.1.1   Statistical association between quantitative variables

So far, this book has been concerned with statistical methods devised for the purpose of comparing averages between or among samples of data that might be expected to differ in general level: for example, right-handed people might be compared with left-handed people; the trained might be compared with the untrained; males might be compared with females.

Consider, however, a set of paired data of the sort that might be produced if one were to weigh each of a sample of one hundred men before and after they had taken a fitness course. Previously, our concern would have been with the **comparison** of the men's average weight before the course with their average weight afterwards. We would certainly expect these averages to be different. A bivariate data set such as this, however, is likely to have another striking characteristic. The person who was heaviest before the course is likely to be among the heaviest in the group afterwards; the lightest person before the course should be among the lightest afterwards; and one with an intermediate score before the course is likely to be in the middle of the group afterwards. In other words, there should be a statistical **association** or **correlation** between people's weights before and after taking the course.

Depicting an association: The scatterplot

The existence of a statistical association between two variables is most apparent in the appearance of a diagram called a **scatterplot** (see Chapter 5, Section 5.6) which, in the foregoing example, would be constructed by representing each person as a point on a graph, using as co-ordinates that person's weights before and after taking the course. The cloud of points would take the shape of an ellipse (see bottom right scatterplot in Figure 1 on the next page), whose longer axis slopes upwards from left to right across the page. An elliptical scatterplot indicates the existence of a

See Section 5.6

Measuring statistical association

linear (straight line) relationship between two variables. If the slope of the major axis is positive, the variables are said to be **positively correlated**; if it is negative, they are **negatively correlated**. The thinner the ellipse, the stronger the degree of linear relationship; the fatter the ellipse, the weaker the relationship. A circular scatterplot indicates the absence of any relationship between the two variables.

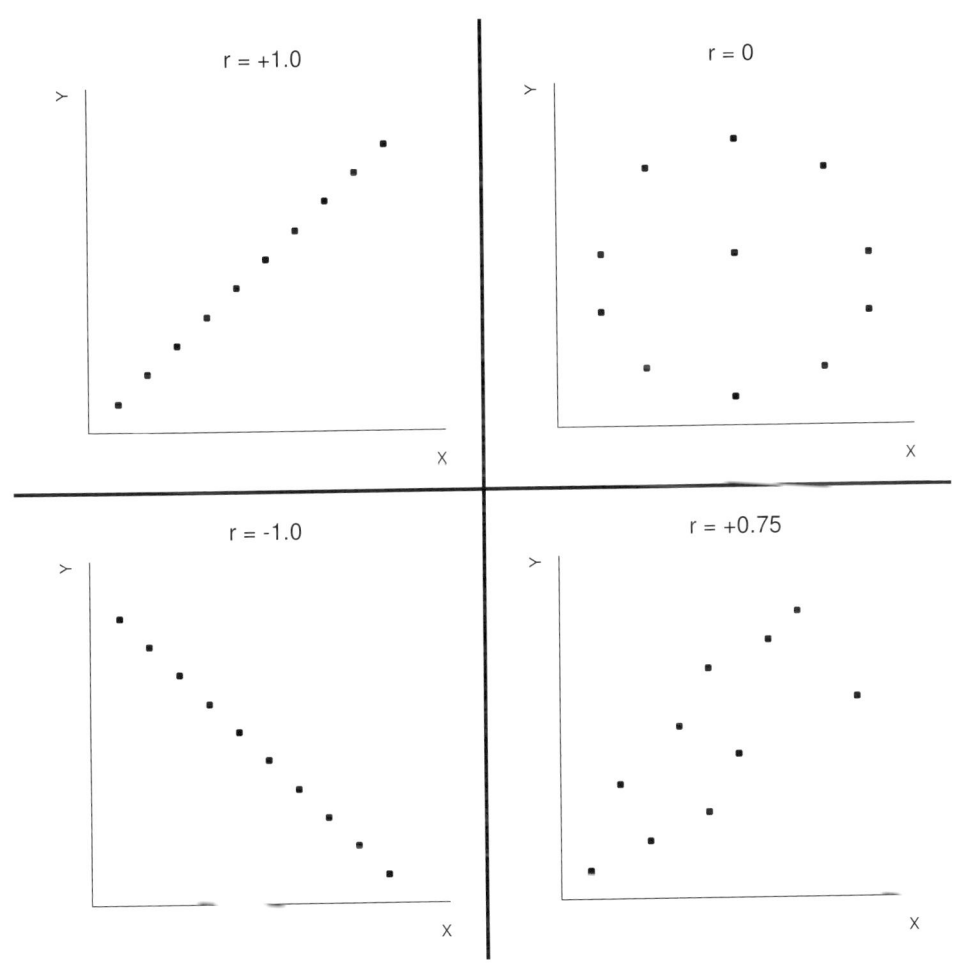

Figure 1. The scatterplots of sets of data showing varying degrees of linear association

Linear association

The term **linear** means 'of the nature of a straight line'. In our current example, a straight line (known as a **regression line**) can be drawn through the points in the elliptical scatterplot so that it is as close to as many of the points as possible (though there may be one or two outliers). We can use the regression line to make quite a good **estimate** of a particular man's weight after the course from a knowledge of his weight before the course: if we have Weight Before on the horizontal axis and Weight After on the vertical axis, we need only move up to the point on the regression line vertically above his first weight, and then move across to the vertical scale to estimate his second weight. If we do that, we shall probably be in error, the difference between his true weight after the course and his estimated weight from the regression line being known as a **residual.** The value of the residual, however, is likely to be small in comparison with the man's true weight after the course.

Measuring the strength of a linear association: The Pearson correlation

A **correlation coefficient** is a statistic devised for the purpose of measuring the strength, or degree, of a supposed linear association between two variables, each of which has been measured on a scale with units. The most familiar correlation coefficient is the **Pearson correlation (r)**. The Pearson correlation is so defined that it can take values only within the range from −1 to +1, inclusive. The larger the absolute value (i.e. ignoring the sign), the narrower the ellipse, and the closer to the regression line the points in the scatterplot will fall. A perfect correlation arises when the values of one variable are exactly predictable from those of the other and the Pearson correlation takes a value of ± 1, in which case all the points in the scatterplot lie on the regression line. In other cases, the narrower the elliptical cloud of points, the stronger the association, and the greater the absolute value of the Pearson correlation. When there is no association whatever between two variables, their scatterplot should be a roughly circular cloud, in which case the Pearson correlation will be about zero (top right in Figure 1).

A word of warning

It is quite possible, from inspection of a scatterplot, to do two useful things:
1. See whether there is indeed a linear relationship between the variables, in which case the Pearson correlation would be a meaningful statistic to use;
2. Guess fairly accurately what the value of the Pearson correlation would be if calculated.

In other words, from inspection of the scatterplot alone, one can discern the most important features of the true relationship (if any) between two variables. So if we reason from the scatterplot to the statistics, we shall not go seriously wrong.

The converse, however, is not true: **given only the value of a Pearson correlation, one can say nothing whatsoever about the relationship between two variables**. Many years ago, in a famous paper, the statistician Anscombe (1973) presented some bivariate data sets which illustrate how misleading the value of the Pearson correlation can be. In one set, for instance, the correlation was high, yet the scatterplot showed no association whatsoever; in another, the correlation was zero, but the scatterplot showed a perfect, but nonlinear, association. The moral of this cautionary tale is clear: when studying the association between two variables, always construct a scatterplot, and interpret (or disregard) the Pearson correlation accordingly. In the same paper, Anscombe gave us a useful rule for deciding whether there really is a robust linear relationship between two variables: should the shape of the scatterplot be unaltered by the removal of a few observations at random, there is probably a real relationship between the two variables.

Measuring statistical association

To sum up, the **Pearson correlation** is a measure of a **supposed** linear relationship between two variables; but the supposition of linearity must always be confirmed by inspection of the scatterplot.

11.1.2 Significance of a correlation coefficient and effect size

As with any other statistic, a correlation describes a characteristic of a sample of data from a population of possible data. Therefore, as with statistics such as t, F or chi-square, it is necessary to confirm a correlation with a test of significance. We have also seen, however, that the mere fact of statistical significance can fall far short of telling us what we really need to know about our results.

Unlike t, F or chi-square, the value of a correlation is, in itself, a measure of 'effect size', bearing in mind that correlation does not imply causation. However, for the purposes of comparison with other measures of effect size, the **square** of the correlation r^2, which is known as the **coefficient of determination**, is often used instead. Earlier, we observed that by drawing a **regression line** through the points in a scatterplot, we could make serviceable predictions of the real values of one variable from knowledge of those of another. If there is a linear association, the errors we would make are usually smaller than if we were to simply guess the average of the target variable each time. In this sense, we can 'account for' some of the variance in the target variable in terms of its association with the predictor variable (or **regressor**, as it is often termed). The **coefficient of determination** measures the proportion of the variance of the target variable that can be predicted from regression. So, if we have a correlation of .6 between two variables in a linear association, we can account for .36 (36%) of the variance of one variable in terms of the variance that it shares with the other.

In the coefficient of determination (r^2), we have a measure of effect strength which is comparable to those we have met in the context of t tests and ANOVA. The ANOVA eta squared η^2 statistics are actually coefficients of determination: they represent the proportion of the variance of the scores on the dependent variable that can be predicted from knowledge of the treatment categories.

We suggest the following categorisation of effect size:

Effect size (r^2)	Size of Effect
<0.01 (<1%)	Small
0.01 to 0.10 (1-10%)	Medium
>0.10 (>10%)	Large

11.2 CORRELATIONAL ANALYSIS WITH SPSS

The principal of a tennis coaching school considers that tennis proficiency depends partly upon general hand-eye co-ordination. To confirm this view, she measures the hand-eye co-ordination (Initial Co-ordination) of some pupils who are beginning the course and their proficiency in tennis at the end of the course (Final Proficiency). The data are shown in Table 1.

Table 1. Measures of Initial Co-ordination and Final Proficiency in ten pupils at a tennis school

Pupil	Initial Co-ordination	Final Proficiency	Pupil	Initial Co-ordination	Final Proficiency
1	4	4	6	4	2
2	4	5	7	7	5
3	5	6	8	8	6
4	2	2	9	9	9
5	10	6	10	5	3

Preparing the SPSS data set

Using the techniques described in Chapter 2, Section 2.3, open **Variable View** and name the variables *Pupil*, *Coordination* and *Proficiency*. Use **Label** to assign more meaningful variable names such as *Pupil Number*, *Initial Co-ordination* and *Final Tennis Proficiency*. Switch to **Data View** and enter the data. Save the data set.

See Section 2.3

Obtaining a scatterplot

To obtain the scatterplot of *Final Tennis Proficiency* against *Initial Co-ordination*,
- Choose
  Graphs
  Scatter...
  to open the **Scatterplot** dialog box (Figure 2).

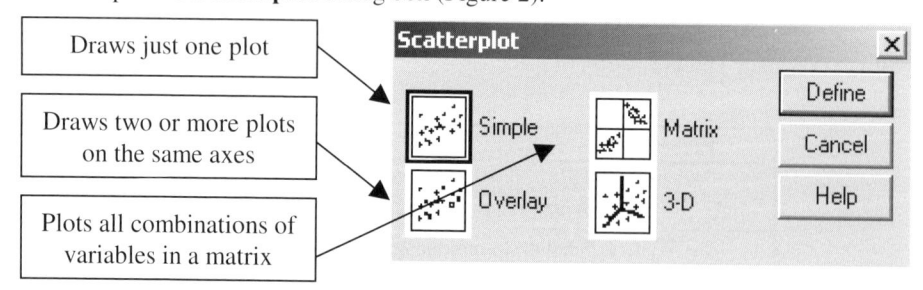

Draws just one plot

Draws two or more plots on the same axes

Plots all combinations of variables in a matrix

Figure 2. The **Scatterplot** dialog box

- Since the default scatterplot is **Simple**, click **Define** to open the **Simple Scatterplot** dialog box. The completed version is shown in Figure 3.
- Transfer the variable names *Coordination* and *Proficiency* to the **X Axis:** box and the **Y Axis:** box, respectively, as shown in Figure 3.
- Click **OK**.

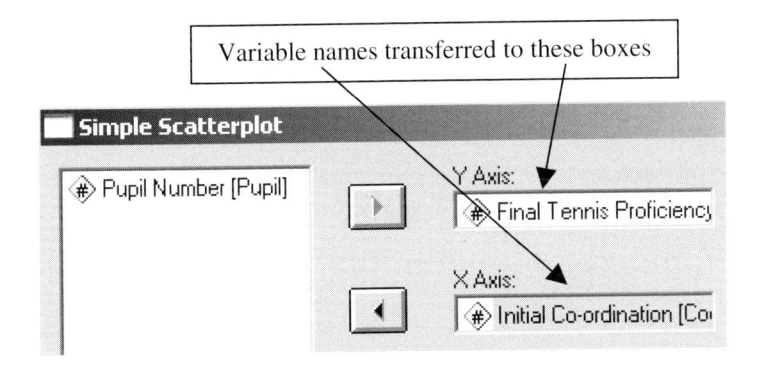

Figure 3. The upper part of the completed **Simple Scatterplot** dialog box

The edited version of the scatterplot is shown in Output 1. The changes included centring the axis labels and making the point markers black and white. The plot shows a consistent linear trend, with no outliers.

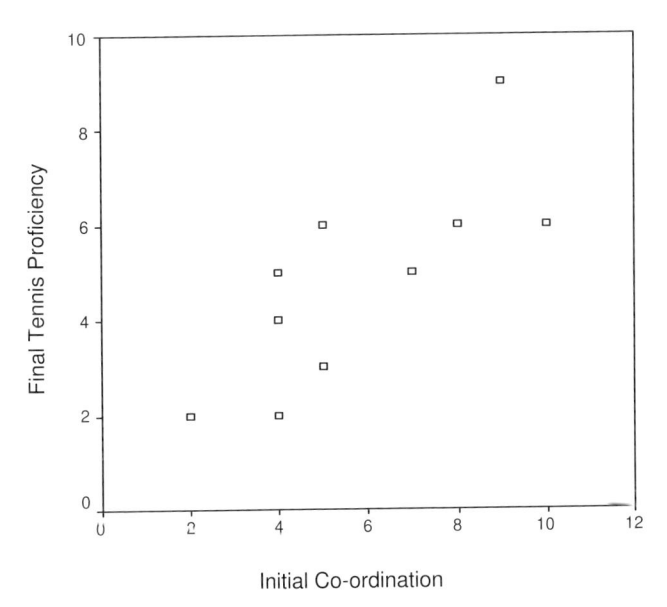

Output 1. Scatterplot of Final Tennis Proficiency against Initial Co-ordination

It is possible to categorise points on a scatterplot by the levels of a grouping variable (e.g. sex) by inserting the grouping variable name in the **Set Markers by** box in the **Simple Scatterplot** dialog box. The points for males and females will be plotted in different colours. (For black-and-white reproduction, simply use different shapes for the male and female plots.)

11.2.1 Procedure for the Pearson correlation

- Choose
  Analyze
    Correlate (see Figure 4)
      Bivariate...
  to open the **Bivariate Correlations** dialog box (the completed version is shown in Figure 5).

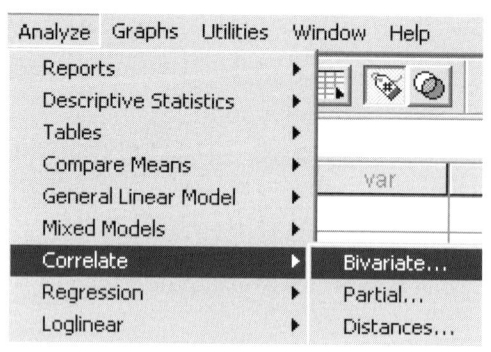

Figure 4. The **Correlate** menu

- Highlight both variables and click ▶ to transfer the names to the **Variables** box.

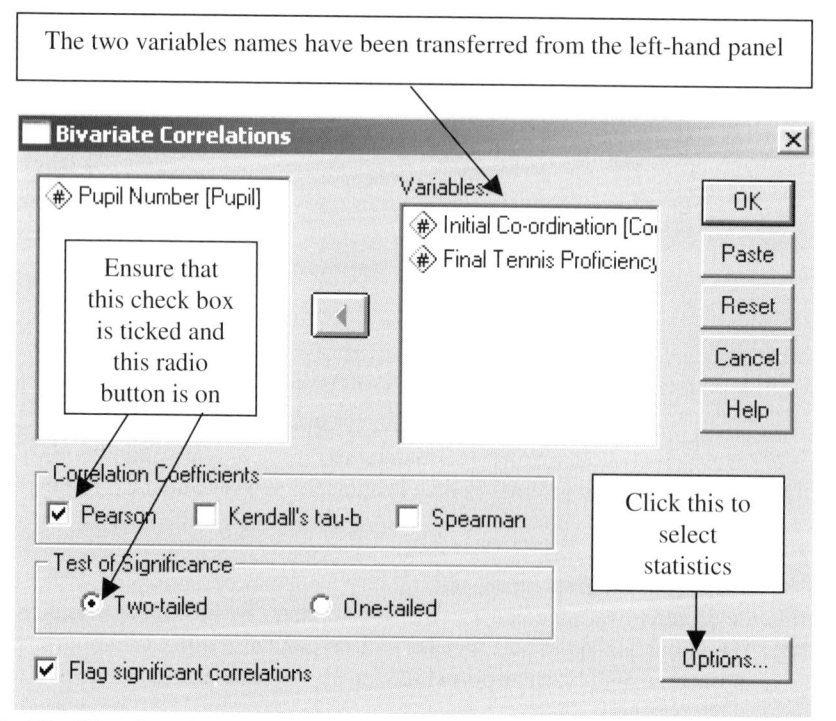

Figure 5. The **Bivariate Correlations** dialog box for Initial Co-ordination and Final Tennis Proficiency

Measuring statistical association

- To tabulate means and standard deviations, click the **Options** button to open the **Bivariate Correlations: Options** dialog box. Click the **Means and Standard Deviations** check box and then **Continue** to return to the **Bivariate Correlations** dialog box.
- Ensure that the check boxes for **Pearson** and for **Two-tailed** are ticked.
- Click **OK** to obtain the correlation coefficient and the additional statistics.

11.2.2 Output for the Pearson correlation

The output begins with a tabulation of the means and standard deviations of the two variables, as requested with **Options** (Output 2).

Descriptive Statistics

	Mean	Std. Deviation	N
Initial Co-ordination	5.80	2.57	10
Final Tennis Proficiency	4.80	2.15	10

Output 2. The Descriptive Statistics table

Output 3 tabulates the Pearson correlation, with its p-value. With a value for r of 0.775 and a two-tailed p-value of 0.008, it can be concluded that the correlation coefficient is significant beyond the 1 per cent level. This is written as:

$r = 0.78; n = 10; p = .008. \ r^2 = 0.60$ representing a large effect.

Correlations

		Initial Co-ordination	Final Tennis Proficiency
Initial Co-ordination	Pearson Correlation	1	.775**
	Sig. (2-tailed)	.	.008
	N	10	10
Final Tennis Proficiency	Pearson Correlation	.775**	1
	Sig. (2-tailed)	.008	.
	N	10	10

**. Correlation is significant at the 0.01 level (2 tailed)

The correlation coefficient is 0.775 and its p-value, **Sig. (2-tailed)**, is 0.008 (r is significant beyond the 1% level)

Output 3. The Pearson correlation table

Notice that in Output 3, all the information we need (the value of r, the number of pairs of data and the p-value) is contained in the upper right cell or in the lower left cell of the table. This occurs because the correlation of A with B is the same as the correlation of B with A. Thus we can delete one of the rows and one of the columns if the table is going to be copied to a document.

Were we to have more than two variables, the results would have appeared in the form of a square matrix with results from above the principal diagonal being duplicated below the diagonal. When there are more than two variables, SPSS can be commanded to construct this **correlation matrix** by simply entering as many variable names as required into the **Variables** box (Figure 5).

11.3 OTHER MEASURES OF ASSOCIATION

The Pearson correlation is suitable only for data in the form of measurements on quantitative variables. With ordinal or nominal data, other statistics must be used.

11.3.1 Measures of association strength for ordinal data

The term **ordinal data** includes both ranks and assignments to ordered categories. When, as in the case of the same objects ranked independently by two judges, ordinal data are paired, the question arises as to the extent to which the two sets of ranks agree. This is a question about the strength of association between two variables which, although quantitative, are measured at the ordinal level.

The Spearman rank correlation (r_S or ρ)

Suppose that the ranks assigned to ten paintings by two judges are as in Table 2.

Table 2. Ranks assigned by two judges to each of ten paintings

Painting	A	B	C	D	E	F	G	H	I	J
First Judge	1	2	3	4	5	6	7	8	9	10
Second Judge	1	3	2	4	6	5	8	7	10	9

It is obvious that the judges generally agree closely in their rankings: at most, the ranks they assign to a painting differ by a single rank. One way of measuring the level of agreement between the two judges is by calculating the Pearson correlation between the two sets of ranks. This correlation is known as the **Spearman rank correlation r_S** (or as **Spearman's rho ρ**, not to be confused with the use of rho to represent the population correlation coefficient). The Spearman rank correlation is usually presented in terms of a formula which, although it looks very different from that of the Pearson correlation, is actually equivalent, provided that no ties are allowed.

The use of the Spearman rank correlation is not confined to ordinal data. Should a scatterplot show that the Pearson correlation is unsuitable as a measure of the strength of association between two measured quantitative variables, the scores on both variables can be converted to ranks and the Spearman rank correlation calculated instead.

Kendall's tau (τ) statistics

Kendall's tau statistics, represented by the Greek letter τ, provide an alternative to the Spearman rank correlation as measures of agreement between rankings, or assignments to ordered categories. The basic idea is that one set of ranks can be converted into another by a succession of reversals of pairs of ranks in one set: the fewer the reversals needed (in relation to the total number of possible reversals), the larger the value of tau. The numerator of **Kendall's tau** is the difference between the number of pairs of objects whose ranks are concordant (i.e. they go in the same direction) and the number of discordant pairs. If the former predominate, the sign of tau is positive; if the latter predominate, tau is negative.

There are three different versions of Kendall's tau: **tau-a**, **tau-b** and **tau-c**. All three measures have the same numerator, the difference between the numbers of concordant and discordant pairs. It is in their denominators that they differ, the difference being in the way they handle tied observations.

The denominator of the correlation **tau-a** is simply the total number of pairs. The problem with tau-a is that when there are ties, its range quickly becomes restricted, to the point where it becomes difficult to interpret.

The correlation **tau-b** has terms in the denominator that consider, in either variable, pairs that are tied on one variable but not on the other. (When there are no ties, the values of tau-a and tau-b are identical.)

The correlation **tau-c** was designed for situations where one wishes to measure agreement between assignments to unequal-sized sets of ordered categories. Provided the data meet certain requirements, the appropriate tau correlation can vary throughout the complete range from −1 to +1.

Note that the calculation of Kendall's statistics with **ordinal** data, in the form of assignments of target objects to ordered categories, is best handled by the **Crosstabs** procedure (see next section); indeed, **tau-c** (which is appropriate when the two variables have different numbers of categories) can only be obtained in **Crosstabs**.

Procedures for obtaining the Spearman and Kendall rank correlations

In **Variable View**, name two variables, *Judge1* and *Judge2*. Click the **Data View** tab to switch to **Data View** and, from Table 2, enter the ranks assigned by the first judge into the *Judge1* column and those assigned by the second judge into the *Judge2* column.
- Choose
  Analyze
    Correlate
      Bivariate…
  to obtain the **Bivariate Correlations** dialog box (the completed version is shown in Figure 6).
- By default, the **Pearson** check box will be marked. Click off the **Pearson** check box and click the **Kendall's tau-b** and the **Spearman** check boxes.
- Transfer the variable names *Judge1* and *Judge2* to the **Variables:** box.
- Click **OK** to obtain the correlations shown in Output 4.

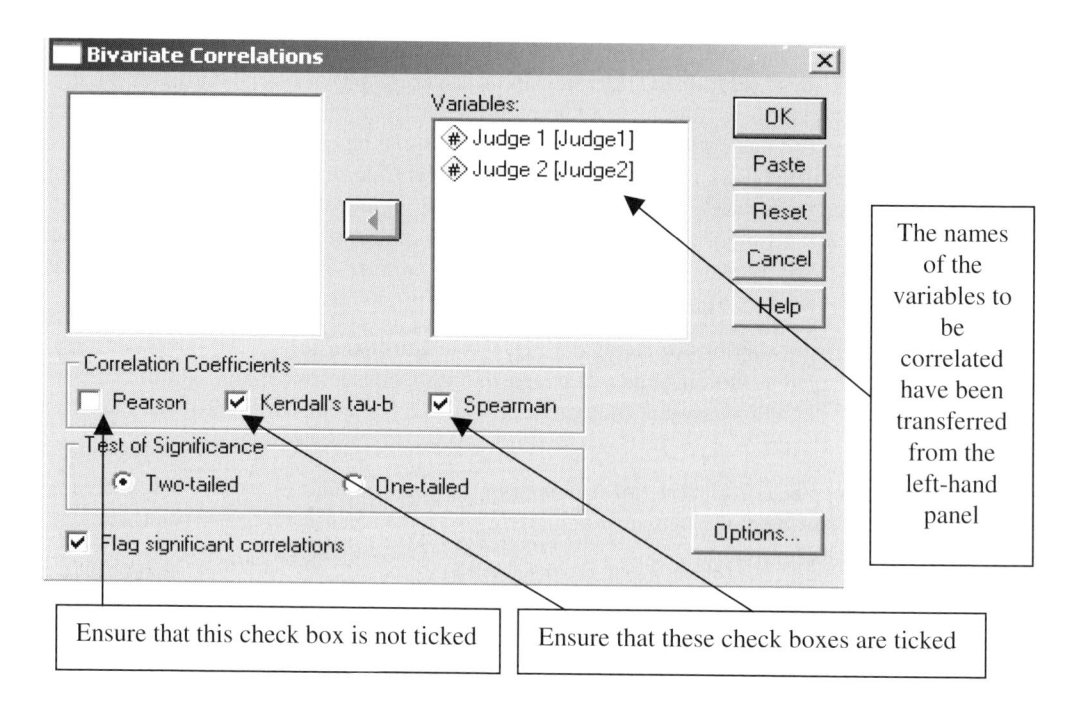

Figure 6. The completed **Bivariate Correlations** box for computing **Kendall's tau-b** and **Spearman**'s coefficient

Nonparametric Correlations

Correlations

			judge1	judge2
Kendall's tau_b	judge1	Correlation Coefficient	1.000	.822**
		Sig. (2-tailed)	.	.001
		N	10	10
	judge2	Correlation Coefficient	.822**	1.000
		Sig. (2-tailed)	.001	.
		N	10	10
Spearman's rho	judge1	Correlation Coefficient	1.000	.952**
		Sig. (2-tailed)	.	.000
		N	10	10
	judge2	Correlation Coefficient	.952**	1.000
		Sig. (2-tailed)	.000	.
		N	10	10

**. Correlation is significant at the 0.01 level (2-tailed).

Spearman's correlation coefficient, with p-value, for the two judges

Kendall's tau-b correlation coefficient, with p-value, for the two judges

Output 4. Correlations between two sets of ranks

Output 4 shows that the **Kendall correlation** is *0.82* and the **Spearman correlation** is *0.95*. These values differ, but there is nothing untoward in this. The two statistics are based on quite different theoretical foundations and often take noticeably different values when calculated from the same data set. (Incidentally, the Pearson option would have given the same value as the Spearman: *0.95*.) These results would be written thus:

$\tau = 0.82$; n = 10; p = .001. $r^2 = .68$ representing a large effect.

$r_S = 0.95$; n = 10; p < 0.0005. $r^2 = .91$ representing a large effect.

11.3.2 Measures of association strength for nominal data: The Crosstabs procedure

When people's membership of two sets of mutually exclusive and exhaustive categories (such as sex or blood group) is recorded, it is possible to construct a **crosstabulation**, or **contingency table** (see Chapter 4, Section 4.3.1). In the analysis of **categorical data** (that is nominal assignments or assignments to ordered categories), the crosstabulation is the equivalent of the scatterplot. Note that the categories of each variable must be mutually exclusive: no individual or case can be in more than one combination of categories.

See Section 4.3.1

In SPSS, crosstabulations are handled by the **Crosstabs** procedure, which is found in **Descriptive Statistics**, in the **Analyze** drop-down menu. In the **Crosstabs** dialog box, there is a **Statistics** sub-dialog box containing check boxes for several measures of association (Figure 10 on p. 310). The correct choice from the available statistics depends upon whether the data in the table are nominal or ordinal. We have seen that for ordinal categorical data, Kendall's statistics are applicable. For nominal data, there are statistics based on the familiar **chi-square** statistic χ^2, which is used for determining the presence of an association between two qualitative variables. The rejection of H_0, however, only establishes the **existence** of a statistical association: it does not measure its **strength**. In fact, the chi-square statistic is unsuitable as a **measure** of association, because its value is partly determined by the total frequency of the observations in the contingency table.

A word of warning about the misuse of chi-square should be given here. It is important to realise that the calculated statistic is only **approximately** distributed as the theoretical chi-square distribution: the greater the expected frequencies, the better the approximation, hence the rule about minimum expected frequencies, which is stated later in this Section. SPSS, however, provides exact p-values, which should be reported when the data are scarce. It is also important to note that the use of the chi-square statistic requires that **each individual studied contributes to the count in only one cell in the crosstabulation**. There are several other potential problems the user should be aware of. A lucid account of the rationale and assumptions of the chi-square test is given by Howell (2002).

Several measures of strength of association for nominal data have been proposed. An ideal measure should mimic the correlation coefficient by having a maximum absolute value of 1 for perfect association, and a value of 0 for no association. The choice of the appropriate statistic depends on whether the contingency table is 2×2 (each variable has two categories) or larger. Guidance can be found by clicking the SPSS **Help** box in the **Crosstabs: Statistics** dialog box. One measure of association strength, for example, is the **phi coefficient** φ, obtained by dividing the value of chi-square by the total frequency and taking the square root. For two-way contingency tables involving variables with more than two categories, another statistic, known as **Cramér's V**, is preferred because with more complex tables, Cramér's measure, unlike the phi coefficient, can still, as in the 2×2 case, achieve its maximum value of unity. Other measures of association, such as **Goodman & Kruskal's lambda**, measure the proportional reduction in error achieved when membership of a category on one attribute is used to predict category membership on the other.

A 2×2 contingency table

Suppose that 100 children (50 boys and 50 girls) are individually asked to select toys from a cupboard. The available toys have previously been categorised as mechanical or non-mechanical. The hypothesis is that boys prefer mechanical toys, whereas girls prefer non-mechanical toys. There are two grouping variables here: *Group* (*Boys* or *Girls*); and *Children's Choice* (*Mechanical* or *Non-Mechanical*). The null hypothesis (H_0) is that there is no association between the variables. Table 3 shows the children's choices.

Table 3. Children's choice of toys

Group	Children's Choice Mechanical	Non-Mechanical	Total
Boys	30	20	50
Girls	15	35	50
Total	45	55	100

From inspection of this 2×2 contingency table, it would appear that there is an association between the *Group* and *Choice* variables: the majority of the boys did, in fact, choose mechanical toys, whereas the majority of the girls chose non-mechanical toys. Notice the predominance of counts in the diagonal cells (Boys, Mechanical; Girls, Non-Mechanical) of the table.

Procedure for crosstabulation and associated statistics (chi-square, phi and Cramér's V)

The SPSS data set for a contingency table must include two grouping variables to identify the various cell counts, one representing the rows (*Group*), the other the columns (*Choice*). In this example, since the data have already been counted within the grouping variables, a third variable for the cell counts (*Count*) is needed.
- In **Variable View**, name the variables *Group*, *Choice*, and *Count*.
- In the **Values** column, define the numerical values and their labels for the two grouping variables. For the *Group* variable, assign the code numbers *1* and *2* to *Boys* and *Girls*, respectively. For the *Choice* variable, assign the numbers *1* and *2* to *Mechanical* and *Non-Mechanical* toys, respectively.
- Click the **Data View** tab to switch to **Data View** and enter the data into the three columns, as shown in Figure 7.

Group	Choice	Count
Boys	Mechanical	30
Boys	Non-mechanical	20
Girls	Mechanical	15
Girls	Non-mechanical	35

Figure 7. **Data View** showing the two grouping variables and the count of the children's choices

For this example, the next step is essential. Since the data in the *Count* column represent cell frequencies of a variable (not values), SPSS must be informed of this by means of the **Weight Cases** item in the **Data** menu.
- Choose
    Data
        Weight Cases…
    to open the **Weight Cases** dialog box.
- Click the name of the variable that contains the weightings, *Count*. Now click **Weight Cases by**, thus cancelling the default item **Do not weight cases**. Finally click ▶ to transfer *Count* to the **Frequency Variable** box.
- Click **OK**.

Note that if the data had been recorded case by case in the data file (i.e. not collated), then there would be no need to use the **Weight Cases** procedure because the **Crosstabs** procedure would count up the cases automatically.

To analyse the contingency table data, proceed as follows:
- Choose
    Analyze
        Descriptive Statistics (see Figure 8)
            Crosstabs…
    to open the **Crosstabs** dialog box. The completed version is shown in Figure 9.

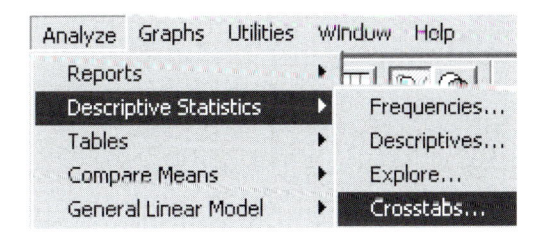

Figure 8. Finding **Crosstabs** in the **Analyze** menu

- Transfer the variable names, as shown in Figure 9.

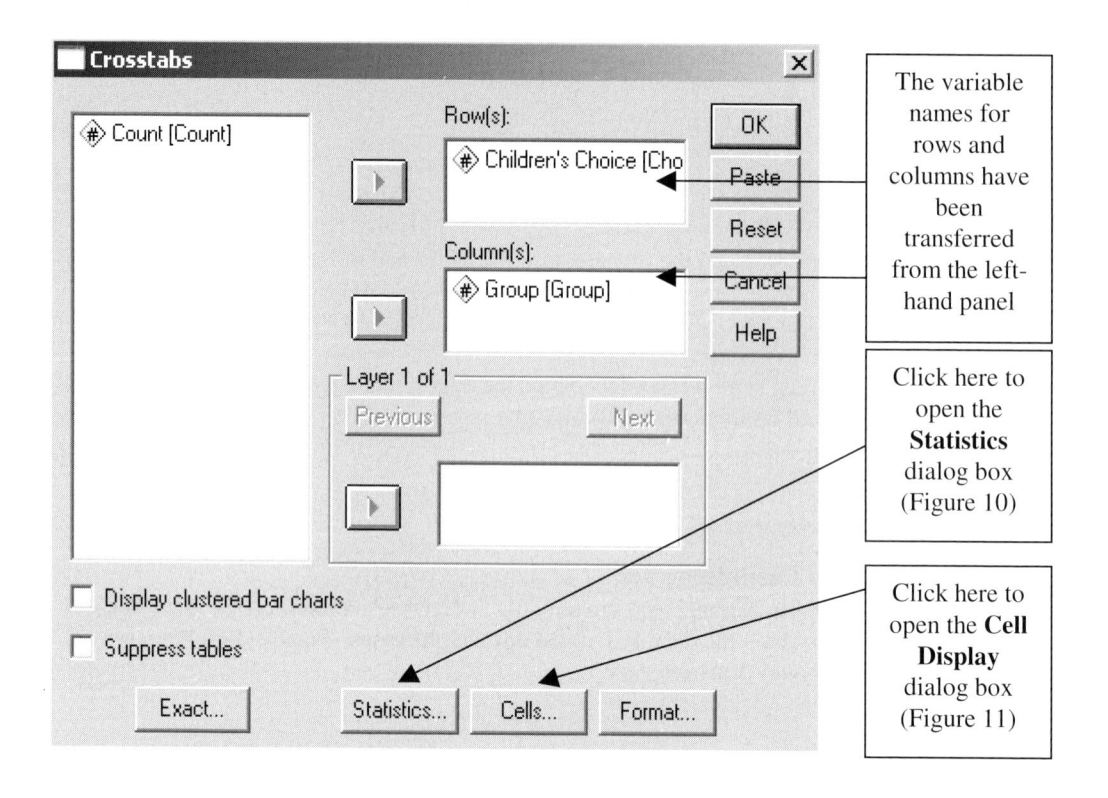

Figure 9. The **Crosstabs** dialog box for group in the rows and choice in the columns

- Click **Statistics...** to open the **Crosstabs: Statistics** dialog box (Figure 10) and select the statistics shown. Click **Continue**.

Figure 10. The **Statistics** dialog box with **Chi-square** and **Phi and Cramér's V** selected

Measuring statistical association

We recommend an additional option for computing the expected cell frequencies. This enables the user to check that the prescribed minimum requirements for the valid use of chi-square have been fulfilled. Although there has been much debate about these, some leading authorities have proscribed the use of chi-square when:
1. In 2 × 2 tables, any of the expected frequencies is less than 5;
2. In larger tables, any of the expected frequencies is less than 1 or more than 20% are less than 5.

- Click **Cells…** to open the **Crosstabs: Cell Display** selection box (Figure 11). Select the **Expected** in **Counts** box to display the expected frequencies in the output. Click **Continue**.
- Finally click **OK**.

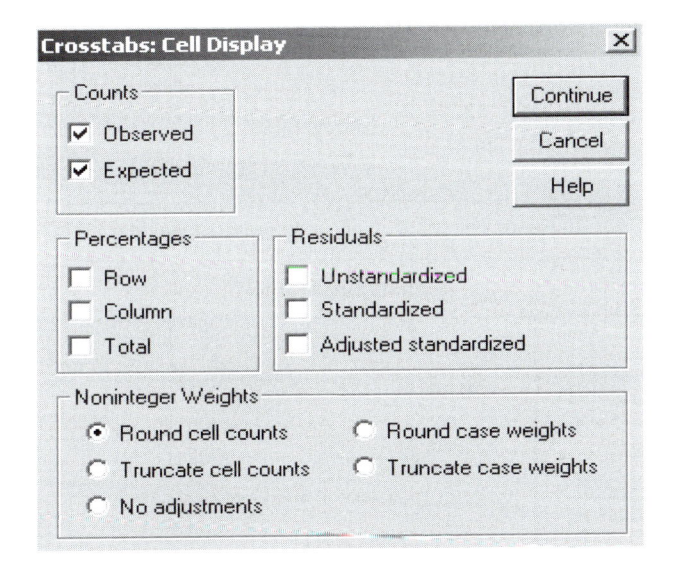

Figure 11. The **Cell Display** dialog box with **Observed** and **Expected** selected

Output for **Crosstabs** *and associated statistics (chi-square, phi and Cramér's V)*

In the **SPSS Viewer**, the output begins with a **Case Processing Summary** (which is not reproduced here) showing the number of valid cases used in the computation.

Output 5 displays the cross-tabulation (contingency) table, with the observed and expected frequencies, as requested in the **Crosstabs: Cell Display** dialog box. None of the expected frequencies is less than 5. This means that we can accept the 'asymptotic' p-values; otherwise, we should place our reliance upon the exact p-values.

Crosstabs

Group * Children's Choice Crosstabulation

			Children's Choice		Total
			Mechanical	Non-mechanical	
Group	Boys	Count	30	20	50
		Expected Count	22.5	27.5	50.0
	Girls	Count	15	35	50
		Expected Count	22.5	27.5	50.0
Total		Count	45	55	100
		Expected Count	45.0	55.0	100.0

Output 5. The contingency table including the optional expected values

Output 6 shows the requested chi-square statistic, together with other statistics similar in purpose to the basic Pearson chi-square.

Chi-Square Tests

Value of chi-square and its associated p-value

	Value	df	Asymp. Sig. (2-sided)	Exact Sig. (2-sided)	Exact Sig. (1-sided)
Pearson Chi-Square	9.09[b]	1	.003		
Continuity Correction[a]	7.92	1	.005		
Likelihood Ratio	9.24	1	.002		
Fisher's Exact Test				.005	.002
Linear-by-Linear Association	9.00	1	.003		
N of Valid Cases	100				

a. Computed only for a 2x2 table

b. 0 cells (.0%) have expected count less than 5. The minimum expected count is 22.50.

Output 6. Statistics of a contingency table

The row labelled **Pearson Chi-Square** contains the conventional chi-square statistic, with its tail probability under H_0, **Asymp. Sig. (2-sided)**. It can be concluded from the smallness of the p-value, that there is a significant association between the variables *Group* and *Choice*: chi-square is significant beyond the .01 level. This is written as:

$$\chi^2 = 9.09; df = 1; p = .003.$$

In Output 6, Note b tells the user how many cells have an expected frequency of less than 5; but in this example, there is no such cell. In the special case of a 2×2 table, **Fisher's Exact Test** can be used instead of chi-square when the expected frequencies are small.

Measuring statistical association

The last item is a table (Output 7) giving the values of the **Phi coefficient** and **Cramér's V**. These provide a measure of the strength of the association rather like that of the Pearson correlation coefficient. These are written as:

$$\phi = 0.30;\ p = .003.\quad \phi^2 = 0.09 \text{ representing a medium effect.}$$

$$\text{Cramér's V} = 0.30;\ p = .003$$

Here in the case of a 2×2 table, the **Phi (φ) coefficient** is an appropriate measure.

Symmetric Measures

		Value	Approx. Sig.
Nominal by Nominal	Phi	.30	.003
	Cramer's V	.30	.003
N of Valid Cases		100	

a. Not assuming the null hypothesis.

b. Using the asymptotic standard error assuming the null hypothesis.

Output 7. The Phi and Cramér's V statistics for the contingency table

11.3.3 Finding the meaning of statistics in output tables

A table such as those in Output 6 may include items that are unfamiliar to you. SPSS supplies notes explaining such items. Suppose, for example, that you want to learn more about **Fisher's Exact Test**. Double-click anywhere in the table to open the **SPSS Output Editor**. Now follow the steps below.

Chi-Square Tests

	Value	df	Asymp. Sig. (2-sided)	Exact Sig. (2-sided)	Exact Sig. (1-sided)
Pearson Chi-Square	9.09[b]	1	.003		
Continuity Correction[a]	7.92	1	.005		
Likelihood Ratio	9.24	1	.002		
Fisher's Exact Test				.005	.002
Linear-by-Linear Association	9.00	1	.003		
N of Valid Cases	100				

a. Computed only for a 2x2 table

b. 0 cells (.0%) have expected count less than 5. The minimum expected count is 22.50.

Output 8. Double-clicking on an item of output causes its outline box to become hashed

	Value	df
Pearson Chi-Square	9.09[b]	1
Continuity Correction[a]	7.92	1
Likelihood Ratio	9.24	1
Fisher's Exact Test		
Linear-by-Linear Association		
N of Valid Cases		

(right-click menu: What's This?, Cut Ctrl+X, Copy Ctrl+C)

Output 9. Click on item and then the **right-hand** mouse button to open a selection box

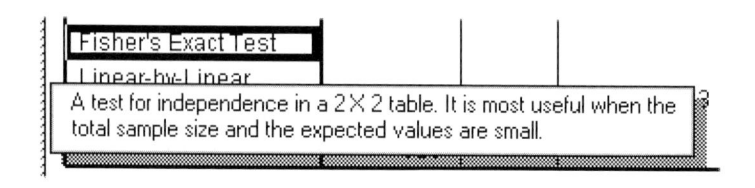

Fisher's Exact Test
Linear-by-Linear
A test for independence in a 2 X 2 table. It is most useful when the total sample size and the expected values are small.

Output 10. Click on **What's This?** to open an explanation of Fisher's Exact Test

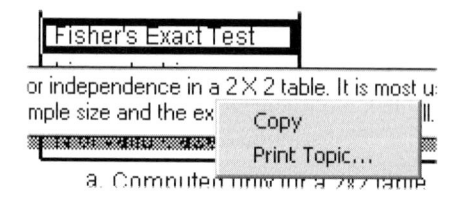

Fisher's Exact Test
or independence in a 2 X 2 table. It is most u:
mple size and the ex   Copy
                       Print Topic...
a. Computed only for a 2x2 table

Output 11. If desired, the explanation can be copied or printed by moving the cursor into the box, clicking the **right-hand** mouse button and selecting **Copy** or **Print Topic...**

EXERCISE 17

The Pearson correlation

Before you start

Before starting to work through this practical exercise, we recommend that you read Chapter 11. The **Pearson correlation r** is one of the most widely used (and abused) of statistics. Despite its apparent simplicity and versatility, it is only too easy to misinterpret a correlation. The purpose of the present Exercise is not only to show you how to use SPSS to obtain correlations, but also to illustrate how a given value for *r* can sometimes be misleading.

A famous data set

This exercise involves the analysis of four sets of paired data, which were constructed many years ago by Anscombe (1973), in order to make some important points about correlations. Each set yields exactly the same value for the **Pearson correlation**. The scatterplots, however, will show that in only one case are the data suitable for a Pearson correlation; in the others, the Pearson correlation gives a highly misleading impression of the relationship between the two variables. Ideally a scatterplot should indicate a **linear relationship** between the variables i.e. that all the points on the scatterplot should lie along or near to a diagonal straight line as shown in the two left-hand plots in Chapter 11, Figure 1. Vertical or horizontal lines are not examples of linear relationships; moreover, the Pearson correlation is not defined when a data set comprises only one value of one variable in combination with various values of another.

Table 1. Anscombe's four data sets

Participant	X1	Y1	Y2	Y3	X2	Y4
1	10.0	8.04	9.14	7.46	8.0	6.58
2	8.0	6.95	8.14	6.77	8.0	5.76
3	13.0	7.58	8.74	12.74	8.0	7.71
4	9.0	8.81	8.77	7.11	8.0	8.84
5	11.0	8.33	9.26	7.81	8.0	8.47
6	14.0	9.96	8.10	8.84	8.0	7.04
7	6.0	7.24	6.13	6.08	8.0	5.25
8	4.0	4.26	3.10	5.39	19.0	12.50
9	12.0	10.84	9.13	8.15	8.0	5.56
10	7.0	4.82	7.26	6.42	8.0	7.91
11	5.0	5.68	4.74	5.73	8.0	6.89

The data are presented in Table 1. The four sets we shall examine are variable *X1* with each of the variables *Y1*, *Y2*, and *Y3*, and finally variable *X2* with variable *Y4*.

Preparing the SPSS data set

After naming the first variable in **Variable View** as *Case*, name the remaining variables as shown in the data table above. Ensure that the value in the **Decimals** column is 2. Switch to **Data View**, enter the data and save the set to a file called *Anscombe*. (This file will be used again in Exercise 19.)

Exploring the data

Obtain scatterplots of the four data sets, as described in Section 11.2. These plots can be produced either one at a time by choosing **Simple** within the **Scatterplot** dialog box or, more dramatically, by selecting **Matrix**, which obtains a grid of scatterplots made up of all pairwise combinations of several variables. In the present Exercise, however, we only want the plots of variables *Y1*, *Y2* and *Y3* against variable *X1*, and of variable *Y4* against variable *X2*. Thus it is better to use **Matrix** for the plots with *X1* and **Simple** for the plot of *Y4* against X2.

If the matrix scatterplot is selected and variables *X1*, *Y1*, *Y2* and *Y3* are transferred to the **Matrix Variables** box, only the first column of plots, (those with *X1* on the horizontal axis), will be of interest.

- **What do you notice about the scatterplots in the first column? Which one is (in its present state) suitable for a subsequent calculation of a Pearson correlation? Describe what is wrong with each of the others.**

Return to the **Graphs** menu, select **Scatter...** and **Simple**, and prepare a simple scatterplot of variable *Y4* against variable *X2* (see Section 11.2).

- **Is the plot suitable for a Pearson correlation?**

The plot of *Y1* against *X1* shows a substantial linear relationship between the variables. The thinness of the imaginary ellipse of points indicates that the **Pearson correlation** is likely to be high. This is the kind of data set for which the Pearson correlation gives an informative and accurate statement of the strength of the linear association between two variables. The other plots, however, are very different: that of *Y2* against *X1* shows a perfect, but clearly non-linear, relationship; *Y3* against *X1* shows a basically linear relationship, which is marred by a glaring outlier; *Y4* against *X2* shows a column of points with a single outlier up in the top right corner.

Pearson correlations for the four scatterplots

Using the procedure described in Section 11.2.1, obtain the correlations between *X* and *Y* for the four sets of paired data. This is most easily done by entering the variables *X1*, *Y1*, *Y2*, *Y3* in the first run of the procedure so as to get a correlation matrix, and then *X2* and *Y4* in the second run.

- **What do you notice about the value of *r* for each of the correlations?**

Anscombe's data strikingly illustrate the need to inspect the data carefully to ascertain the suitability of statistics such as the Pearson correlation.

Removing the outliers

It is instructive to recalculate the **Pearson correlation** for the data set (*X1*, *Y3*) when the values for Participant 3 have been removed. The outlier is the value *12.74* on the variable *Y3*. Use the **Select Cases...** procedure to select all participants except Participant 3.

Return to the **Scatterplot** and **Bivariate Correlations** dialog boxes for *X1* and *Y3* (ignore the other variables) to re-run these procedures using the selected cases. Check that in the listing, only 10 rather than 11 cases have been used. You should find that the Pearson correlation for *X1* and *Y3* is now +1, which is what we would expect from the appearance of the scatterplot.

Conclusion

This Exercise has demonstrated the value of exploring the data first before calculating statistics such as the **Pearson correlation**. While it is true that Anscombe's data were specially constructed to give his message greater force, there have been many misuses of the Pearson correlation with real data sets, where the problems created by the presence of outliers and by basically non-linear relationships are quite common.

Finishing the session

Close down SPSS and any other windows before logging out.

318   Chapter 11

EXERCISE 18

Other measures of association

Before you start

Please read Section 11.3 before proceeding with this Exercise. The **Pearson correlation** was devised to measure a supposed linear association between quantitative variables. There are other kinds of data (ordinal and nominal), to which the Pearson correlation is inapplicable. Moreover, even with data in the form of measurements, there may be considerations which render the use of the Pearson correlation inappropriate. Fortunately, other statistical measures of strength of association have been devised and in this Exercise, we shall consider some statistics that are applicable to ordinal and nominal data.

ORDINAL DATA

The Spearman rank correlation

Suppose that two judges each rank ten paintings, A, B, ..., J. Their decisions are shown in Table 1.

Table 1. The ranks assigned to the same ten objects by two judges

	Best									Worst
First Judge	C	E	F	G	H	J	I	B	D	A
Second Judge	C	E	G	F	J	H	I	A	D	B

It is obvious from this table that the judges generally agree closely in their rankings: at most, the ranks they assign to a painting differ by two ranks. But how can their level of agreement be measured?

Table 2. A numerical representation of the orderings by the two judges in Table 1

Painting	C	E	F	G	H	J	I	B	D	A
First Judge	1	2	3	4	5	6	7	8	9	10
Second Judge	1	2	4	3	6	5	7	10	9	8

The information in this table can be expressed in terms of numerical ranks by assigning the counting numbers from 1 to 10 to the paintings in their order of ranking by one judge, and

Measuring statistical association

pairing each of these ranks with the rank that the same painting received from the other judge, as shown in Table 2.

This is not the only way of representing the judgements numerically. It is also possible to list the objects (in any order) and pair the ranks assigned by the two judges to each object, entering two sets of ranks as before. Where the measurement of agreement is concerned, however, the two methods give exactly the same result.

Preparing the SPSS data set

In **Variable View**, name two variables, *Judge1* and *Judge2* (remembering not to put a space before the digit), and set the value in the **Decimals** column to *0*. Switch to **Data View** and enter the ranks assigned by the judges into the two columns. Save the data, because they will be used again later.

Obtaining the Spearman correlation coefficient

Select **Correlate** and then **Bivariate...** from the **Analyze** menu to open the **Bivariate Correlations** dialog box. Transfer the variables to the **Variables** box and select the **Spearman** check box (leave the default **Pearson** check box active). Click **OK** to obtain the **Pearson correlation** and the **Spearman correlation**.

- How closely do the judges agree (state the value of the Spearman correlation coefficient)?
- What do you notice about the values of the two coefficients? Explain.

Use of the Spearman rank correlation where there is a monotonic, but non-linear, relationship

Table 3 shows a set of paired interval data. On inspecting the scatterplot, we see that there is a **monotonic relationship** between the two variables: that is, as X increases, so does Y. On the other hand, the relationship between X and Y is clearly non-linear (in fact, $Y = \log_2 X$), and the **Pearson correlation** would belie that perfect association between the two variables.

Table 3. A set of paired interval data showing a monotonic, but non-linear, relationship

Y	1.00	1.58	2.00	2.32	2.58	2.81	3.00
X	2.00	3.00	4.00	5.00	6.00	7.00	8.00

Save the data from Table 2 (they will be needed later). To prepare a new data set (from Table 3) in a fresh file, enter the **File** drop-down menu, select **New** and then **Data** from the rightmost menu. Name the new variables in **Variable View** and enter the values into **Data View**. Obtain the **scatterplot** and compute the **Pearson** and **Spearman** correlation coefficients.

- Describe the shape of the scatterplot and write down the values of the two correlation coefficients. Since there is a perfect (but non-linear) relationship between *X* and *Y*, the degree of association is understated by the Pearson correlation coefficient.

- Which value of *r* is the truer expression of the strength of the relationship between *X* and *Y* ? Explain.

Kendall's correlation coefficients

The association between variables in paired ordinal data sets (or in paired measurements) can also be investigated by using one of **Kendall's correlation** coefficients, **tau-a**, **tau-b** or **tau-c** (see Section 11.3.1). (When there are no tied observations, **tau-a** and **tau-b** have the same value.) With large data sets, **Kendall's** and **Pearson's** coefficients give rather similar values and tail probabilities. With a given data set, however, their two values will not be identical. This is because the two statistics have quite different rationales and different sampling distributions. Their p-values, however, will usually be very similar. When the data are scarce, however, Kendall's statistics are better behaved, especially when there are tied observations, and more reliance can be placed upon the Kendall tail probability. Kendall's correlations really come into their own when the data are assignments to predetermined ordered categories (rating scales and so on).

There are two ways of obtaining **Kendall's correlations** in SPSS:
1. In the **Bivariate Correlations** dialog box, mark the **Kendall's tau-b** checkbox.
2. Use the **Crosstabs** procedure (see Section 11.3.2).

Use the **Bivariate Correlations** procedure to obtain **Kendall's tau-b** (there are no ties) for the data in Table 3. Now do the same with the data set saved from Table 2.

- Write down the values of tau-b and compare them with your previously obtained coefficient values.

With the restored Table 2 data set, use the **Crosstabs** procedure to obtain Kendall's correlations. Note that in this application, there is no variable such as *Count* and hence no need for **Weight Cases...** Enter *Judge1* in **Row(s):** and *Judge2* in **Column(s):**. Click the **Statistics...** button to open the **Crosstabs: Statistics** dialog box and select the checkboxes for **Correlations**, **Kendall's tau-b** and **Kendall's tau-c**. Click **Continue** and **OK** to run the correlations procedure.

- Write down the values of all the coefficients in the output and comment on any similarities and differences.

Finishing the session

Close down SPSS and any other windows before logging out of the computer.

EXERCISE 19

The analysis of nominal data

Before you start

Before proceeding with this practical, we strongly recommend you to read Section 11.3.2 (measures of association strength for nominal data) in Chapter 11.

THE CHI-SQUARE TEST OF GOODNESS-OF-FIT

Some nominal data on one qualitative variable

Suppose that a researcher, interested in children's preferences, expects a spatial response bias towards the right-hand side. Thirty children enter a room containing three identically-marked doors: one to the right; another to the left; and a third straight ahead. They are told they can go through any of the three doors. Their choices are shown in Table 1.

Table 1. The choices of one of three exit doors by thirty children

Door		
Left	Centre	Right
5	8	17

It looks as if there is indeed a preference for the rightmost door, at least among the children sampled. Had the children been choosing at random, we should have expected about 10 in each category: that is, the theoretical, or expected distribution (E), of the tallies is **uniform**. The observed frequencies (O), on the other hand, have a distribution which is far from uniform.

Pearson's chi-square test can be used to test the goodness-of-fit of the expected to the observed distribution. Its rationale is lucidly discussed in any good statistics textbook (e.g. Howell, 2002). Here, we shall merely describe the SPSS procedure.

Preparing the data set

In **Variable View**, name the grouping variable *Position* for the three positional categories and a second variable *Count* for the numbers of children in the different categories. To the three categories, assign the values *1*, *2*, and *3* and in the **Labels** column, enter the respective labels *Left*, *Centre*, and *Right*. Check that the values in the **Decimals** column are *0*. Click the **Data View** tab and enter the data.

Weight cases

To ensure that SPSS treats the entries in *Count* as frequencies rather than scores, follow the procedure described in Section 11.3.2.

Run the Chi-square test

To obtain the correct dialog box, select
Analyze
> **Nonparametric Tests**
>> **Chi-Square…**

to open the **Chi-Square Test** dialog box. Click *Position* (not on *Count*) and on ▶ to transfer *Position* to the **Test Variable List:** box. Click **OK** to run the procedure.

- Write down the value of the chi-square statistic and its p-value. Is chi-square significant?
- Write down the implications for the experimenter's research hypothesis. When considering the implications, be clear about the precise null hypothesis being tested. Is the experimental hypothesis the simple negation of the null hypothesis? Can you suggest any further tests that might be useful here?

Running the goodness-of-fit test on a set of raw data

When the researcher carried out the experiment, the door that each child chose was noted at the time. In terms of the code numbers, their choices might have been recorded as:

$$1\ 1\ 3\ 2\ 1\ 1\ 3\ 3\ 3\ ,\ ...,\ \text{and so on.}$$

If the user defines the variable *Position*, and enters the 30 (coded) choices that the children made, the chi-square test is then run directly: there is no need to use the **Weight Cases** procedure since there is no variable for count or frequency.

THE CHI-SQUARE TEST OF ASSOCIATION BETWEEN TWO QUALITATIVE VARIABLES

An experiment on children's choices

Suppose that a researcher, having watched a number of children enter a room and recorded each child's choice between two objects, wants to know whether there is a tendency for boys and girls to choose different objects. This question concerns two variables: *Sex* and *Choice*. In statistical terms, the researcher is asking whether they are associated: do more girls than boys choose one of the objects and more boys than girls choose the other object? Suppose that the children's choices are as in Table 2.

Table 2. Choices by 50 children of one of two objects		
Object	Boys	Girls
A	20	5
B	6	19

Procedure for the chi-square test of association between two variables

Prepare a new data set from Table 2. In **Variable View**, create the variables *Object* and *Sex*, assigning code numbers and explanatory labels in the usual way. Create a third variable *Count*. The use of the **Crosstabs** procedure is fully described in Section 11.3.2. We recommend the inclusion of expected frequencies (using the **Cells...** option) so that you can check for the presence of cells with unacceptably low expected frequencies (see Section 11.3.2 for details).

Output for the chi-square test of association

The output is discussed in Section 11.3.2. Three tables are presented: the first is a **Case Processing Summary** table showing how many valid cases have been processed; the second is a **Crosstabulation** table with the observed and expected frequencies in each cell, along with row and column totals; and the third is a table (headed **Chi-square Tests**) listing various statistics, together with their associated significance levels.

- Write down the value of the Pearson chi-square and its associated tail probability (p-value). Is it significant?

- In terms of the experimental hypothesis, what has this test shown?

MEASURES OF ASSOCIATION STRENGTH FOR NOMINAL DATA

So far we have considered the use of the **chi-square statistic** to test for the presence of an association between two qualitative variables. Recall that, provided that the data are suitable, the **Pearson correlation** measures the strength of a linear association between two interval variables. In that case, therefore, the same statistic serves both as a test for the presence of an association and as a measure of associative strength. It might be thought that, with nominal data, the chi-square statistic would serve the same dual function. The chi-square statistic, however, cannot serve as a satisfactory measure of associative strength, because its value depends partly upon the total frequency.

To illustrate the calculation of measures of association for two-way contingency tables, we shall use again the data of choice of objects by children. Run the **Crosstabs** procedure again but this time deselect **Chi-square** and select instead **Phi and Cramér's V** within the **Nominal** box of the **Crosstabs: Statistics** dialog box.

The output consists of three tables: the first is a **Case Processing Summary** table, the second is a **Crosstabulation** table, and the third is a table called **Symmetric Measures** listing the values of **Phi** and **Cramér's V** together with their associated significance levels.

- Write down the value of Phi for the strength of the association between the qualitative variables of Gender and Object. Has a strong association been demonstrated?

Finishing the session

Close down SPSS and any other windows before logging out of the computer.

CHAPTER 12

Regression

12.1   Introduction

12.2   Simple regression

12.3   Multiple regression

12.4   Scatterplots and regression lines

12.1   INTRODUCTION

Much of Chapter 11 was devoted to the use of the **Pearson correlation** to measure the strength of the association between two measured quantitative variables.

But the associative coin has two sides. On the one hand, a single number can be calculated (a correlation coefficient) which expresses the **strength** of the association. On the other, however, there is a set of techniques, known as **regression methods**, which utilise the presence of an association between two variables to predict the values of one (the dependent, target or criterion variable) from those of another (the independent variable, or regressor). It is with this predictive aspect that the present chapter is concerned.

12.1.1   Simple, two-variable regression

In **simple, two-variable regression**, the values of one variable (the dependent variable, y) are estimated from those of another (the independent variable, x) by a linear (straight line) **regression equation** of the general form

$$y' = b_0 + b_1(x)$$

where y' is the estimated value of y, b_1 is the slope (known as the **regression coefficient**), and b_0 is the intercept (known as the **regression constant**). A measure of **effect size** is the **coefficient of determination r^2**. We suggest the following categorisation of effect size:

Effect size (r^2)	Size of Effect
<0.01 (<1%)	Small
0.01 to 0.10 (1-10%)	Medium
>0.10 (>10%)	Large

12.1.2 Multiple regression

In **multiple regression**, the values of one variable (the dependent variable y) are estimated from those of two or more other variables (the independent variables $x_1, x_2, \ldots, x_p$).

This is achieved by the construction of a linear **multiple regression equation** of the general form

$$y' = b_0 + b_1(x_1) + b_2(x_2) + \ldots + b_p(x_p)$$

where the parameters $b_1, b_2, \ldots, b_p$ are the partial **regression coefficients** and the intercept b_0 is the **regression constant**. This equation is known as the **multiple linear regression equation of y upon $x_1, \ldots, x_p$**.

12.1.3 Residuals

When a regression equation is used to estimate the values of a variable y from those of one or more independent variables x, the estimates y' will usually fall short of complete accuracy. Geometrically speaking, the data points will not fall precisely upon the straight line, plane or hyperplane specified by the regression equation. The discrepancies ($y - y'$) on the predicted variable are known as **residuals**. When using regression methods, the study of the residuals is of great importance, because they form the basis for measures of the accuracy of the estimates and of the extent to which the **regression model** gives a good account of the data in question. (See Tabachnick & Fidell, 2001, for advice on **regression diagnostics**.)

12.1.4 The multiple correlation coefficient

One simple (though rather limited) measure of the efficacy of regression for the prediction of y is the Pearson correlation between the true values of the target variable y and the estimates y' obtained by substituting the corresponding values of x into the regression equation. The correlation between y and y' is known as the **multiple correlation coefficient R**. Notice that the upper case is used for the multiple correlation coefficient, to distinguish it from the correlation between the target variable and any one independent variable considered separately. It can be shown algebraically that the multiple correlation coefficient cannot have a negative value, even if there is only one independent variable correlating negatively with the dependent variable, in which case R has the absolute value of r.

An estimate of **effect size** is **R Squared (R^2)** which, by analogy with the coefficient of determination in bivariate regression (and eta-squared in ANOVA), is the proportion of variance in the dependent variable that can be accounted for by the variance in the independent variables.

12.2 SIMPLE REGRESSION

Among North American university authorities, there is much concern about the efficacy of the methods used to select students for entry. How closely are scores on the entrance tests and exam results associated? If there is an association, how accurately can one predict university performance from students' marks on the entrance tests?

Given data on students' final exam marks and their performance on the entrance test, a Pearson correlation can be used to measure the degree of statistical association between the two. It is also possible to use simple regression to predict exam performance at university from marks in the entrance test. It can be shown by mathematical proof, however, that when two or more independent variables are used to predict the target variable y, the predictions will, on average, be **at least as accurate** as when any one of the same independent variables is used. In other words, the multiple correlation coefficient R must be at least as great as any single Pearson correlation r. For the moment, however, we shall be considering the simple regression of university exam results upon the marks in one entrance test alone.

12.2.1 Procedure for simple regression

In Table 1, the score *Fin* is a student's mark in the Final University Exam, and the score *Ent* is the same student's mark in the Entrance Exam. Table 1 contains the marks of 34 students: Student 1 (whose data are in the first row of the first two columns from the left) got 44 in the Entrance Exam and 38 in the Final University Exam. Student 34, on the other hand, (whose data are shown in the seventh row of the last two columns on the right), got 49 in the Entrance Exam and 195 in the Final University Exam.

Table 1. Table of the Final University Exam (Fin) and the Entrance Exam (Ent) scores

Case	Fin	Ent	Case	Fin	Ent	Case	Fin	Ent	Case	Fin	Ent
1	38	44	10	81	53	19	105	43	28	142	56
2	49	40	11	86	47	20	106	55	29	145	60
3	61	43	12	91	45	21	107	48	30	150	55
4	65	42	13	94	41	22	112	49	31	152	54
5	69	44	14	95	39	23	114	46	32	164	58
6	73	46	15	98	40	24	114	41	33	169	62
7	74	34	16	100	37	25	117	49	34	195	49
8	76	37	17	100	48	26	125	63			
9	78	41	18	103	48	27	140	52			

Preparing the SPSS data set

Using the techniques described in Chapter 2, Section 2.3, enter **Variable View** and name the variables *Case*, *FinalExam* and *EntranceExam*. In the **Label** column, add more informative names such as Case Number, Final University Exam and Entrance Exam. In **Data View**, enter the data in the labelled columns.

See Section 2.3

Exploring the data

Usually the user would explore the data for incorrect transcriptions and detect any outliers by examining the scatterplot. Here, in the interests of brevity, we shall proceed directly with the regression analysis and let the regression procedure itself find any problem cases.

Running simple regression
- Choose
  Analyze
    Regression (see Figure 1)
  and click **Linear** to open the **Linear Regression** dialog box (the completed dialog box is shown in Figure 2).

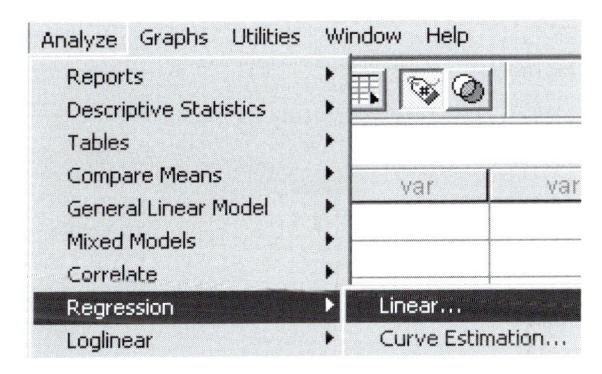

Figure 1. Finding the **Linear Regression** procedure

- Transfer the variable names as shown in Figure 2, taking care to select the appropriate variable names for the dependent and independent variables.
- Request additional descriptive statistics and a residuals analysis. Click **Statistics...** to open the **Linear Regression: Statistics** dialog box (Figure 3) and click the **Descriptives** checkbox. Analysis of the residuals gives a measure of how good the prediction is and whether there are any cases that are so discrepant as to be considered outliers and dropped from the analysis. Click the **Casewise diagnostics** checkbox to obtain a listing of any exceptionally large residuals. Click **Continue** to return to the **Linear Regression** dialog box.
- Since systematic patterns between the predicted values and the residuals can indicate violations of the assumption of linearity, we recommend that a plot of the standardised residuals (*ZRESID) against the standardised predicted values (*ZPRED) also be requested. Click **Plots...** to open the **Linear Regression: Plots** dialog box (Figure 4) and transfer *ZRESID to the **Y:** box and *ZPRED to the **X:** box. Click **Continue** to return to the **Linear Regression** dialog box.
- Values of statistics such as predicted values or residuals can be saved to **Data View** by clicking **Save...** and selecting the desired statistics from the dialog box. Click **Continue** to return to the **Linear Regression** dialog box. For example, having computed the regression equation from one set of data, predicted values for other (later) cases can then be calculated and saved.
- Click **OK**.

The name of the dependent variable (i.e. what is being predicted) has been transferred from the left-hand panel

The name of the independent variable (i.e. the predictor) has been transferred from the left-hand panel

Linear Regression

- Case Number [Case]
- Entrance Exam [Entrar

Dependent:
- Final University Exam [

Block 1 of 1
Previous | Next

Independent(s):
- Entrance Exam [EntranceEx

Method: Enter

Selection Variable: | Rule...

Case Labels:

WLS Weight:

Statistics... | Plots... | Save... | Options...

OK | Paste | Reset | Cancel | Help

Click here to select various statistics such as **Descriptives**; also **Casewise diagnostics** (Figure 3)

Click here to request plots such as standardised predicted residuals against standardised predicted values (Figure 4)

Click here to select statistics such as predicted values and residuals to be saved to **Data View**

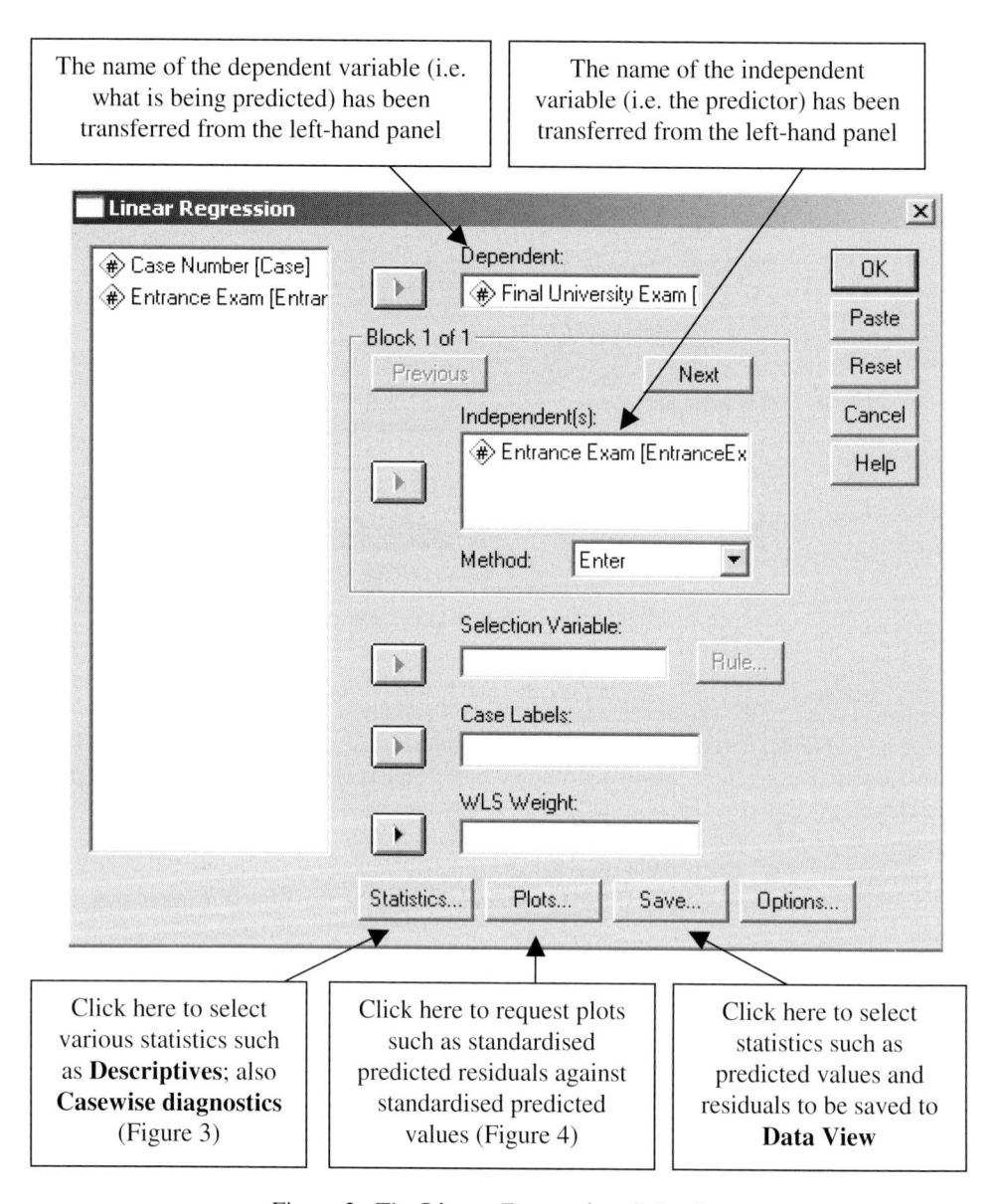

Figure 2. The **Linear Regression** dialog box

Regression

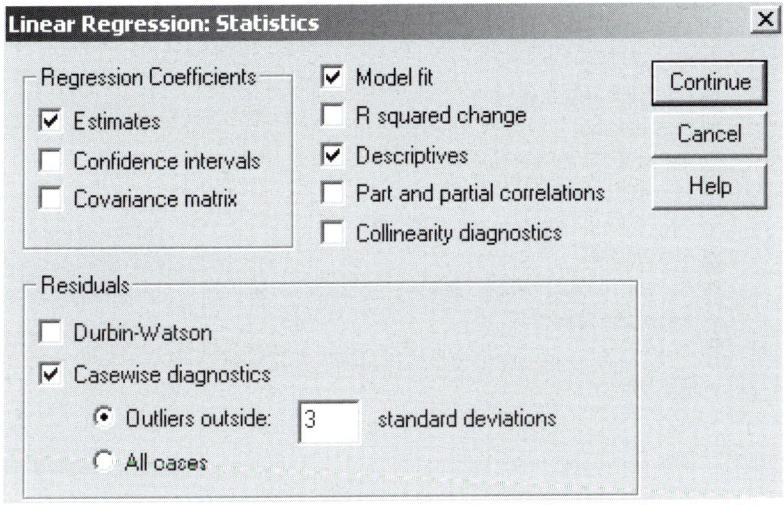

Figure 3. The **Statistics** dialog box with extra options of **Descriptives** and **Casewise diagnostics** selected

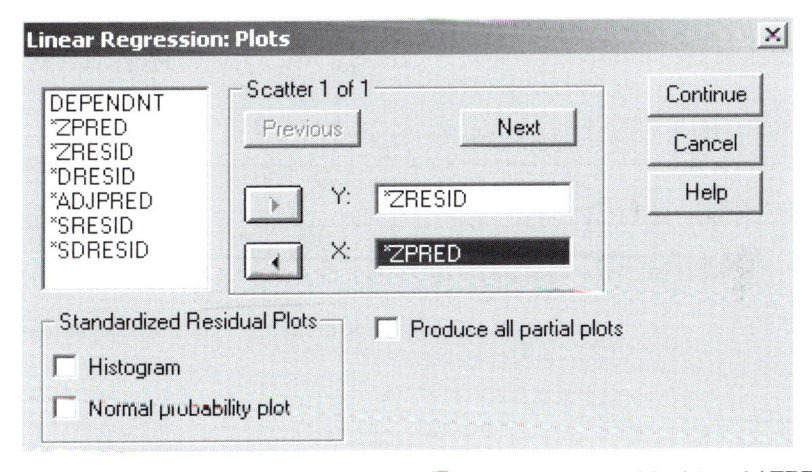

Figure 4. The **Plots** dialog box with ***ZRESID** (standardised residuals) and ***ZPRED** (standardised predicted scores) selected for the axes of the plot

12.2.2 Output for simple regression

The various tables and charts in the output are listed in the left-hand pane of **SPSS Viewer**, as shown in Output 1. After tables of descriptive statistics and correlations (as requested) and several other tables, the first table to scrutinise is **Casewise Diagnostics**. The information it contains may indicate that the regression analysis should be aborted and re-run after outliers have been removed from the data set. The table can be selected directly by moving the cursor to **Casewise Diagnostics** in the left-hand pane and clicking the left-hand mouse button.

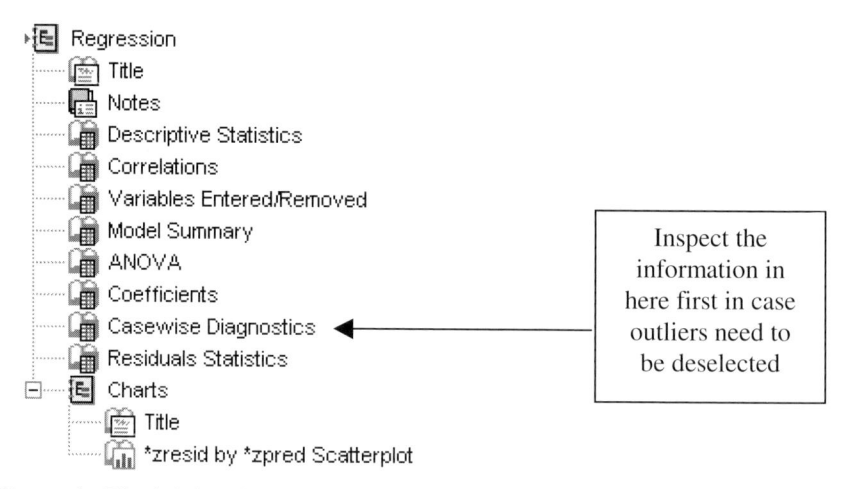

```
▸ⒺRegression
  ├─ Title
  ├─ Notes
  ├─ Descriptive Statistics
  ├─ Correlations
  ├─ Variables Entered/Removed
  ├─ Model Summary
  ├─ ANOVA
  ├─ Coefficients
  ├─ Casewise Diagnostics  ◀──── Inspect the information in here first in case outliers need to be deselected
  ├─ Residuals Statistics
  └─Ⓔ Charts
      ├─ Title
      └─ *zresid by *zpred Scatterplot
```

Output 1. The left-hand pane listing the tables and charts in the right-hand pane

Indication of residual outliers

The table of cases (**Casewise Diagnostics**) in Output 2 shows only one outlier with an absolute standardised residual greater than 3. This is Case 34, with a score of *195* for *Final University Exam*. The next section describes how to eliminate this outlier and re-run the regression analysis.

Casewise Diagnostics [a]

Case Number	Std. Residual	Final University Exam	Predicted Value	Residual
34	3.12	195	110.95	84.05

a. Dependent Variable: Final University Exam

Output 2. A list of cases with residuals greater than ± 3 standard deviations

Elimination of outliers

A more reliable regression analysis can be obtained by eliminating outliers using the **Select Cases** procedure described in Section 3.3.1.

See Section 3.3.1

- Choose
  Data
    Select Cases…
  to open the **Select Cases** dialog box.
- Click the **If condition is satisfied** radio button and define the condition as *Case ~=34* (the symbol ~= means 'not equal to'.)
- Click **Continue** and then **OK** to deselect this case.

If there are several outliers, it might be simpler to deselect using a cut-off value for one of the variables (e.g. defining the condition with an inequality operator such as *FinalExam < 190*). Sometimes, in order to see what value to use in the inequality, it is convenient to arrange scores in order of value by entering the **Data** menu and choosing **Sort Cases…** .

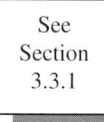

Regression

Output for simple regression after elimination of the outliers

When the regression analysis is re-run after deleting the original output, there will be no table of **Casewise Diagnostics**, since no cases will now have outlying residuals. We can therefore begin with the various tables and plots in the output. In Output 3, are the tables of descriptive statistics and the correlation coefficient for the 33 cases remaining in the data set.

Descriptive Statistics

	Mean	Std. Deviation	N
Final University Exam	102.82	32.633	33
Entrance Exam	47.27	7.539	33

Correlations

		Final University Exam	Entrance Exam
Pearson Correlation	Final University Exam	1.00	.73
	Entrance Exam	.73	1.00
Sig. (1-tailed)	Final University Exam	.	.00
	Entrance Exam	.00	.
N	Final University Exam	33	33
	Entrance Exam	33	33

Output 3. The Descriptive Statistics and Correlations tables for the data set without the outlier

Output 4 gives the value for **Multiple R** which, in the case of just one independent variable, has the same value as the correlation coefficient *r* listed in Output 3. (Had r been negative, R would have had the same value, minus the sign.)

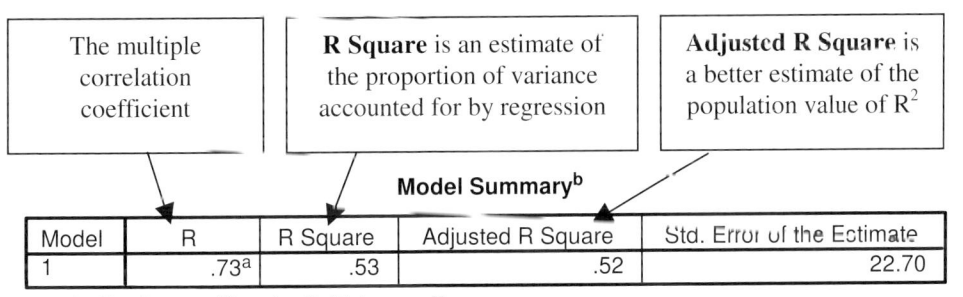

The multiple correlation coefficient

R Square is an estimate of the proportion of variance accounted for by regression

Adjusted R Square is a better estimate of the population value of R^2

Model Summary[b]

Model	R	R Square	Adjusted R Square	Std. Error of the Estimate
1	.73[a]	.53	.52	22.70

a. Predictors: (Constant), Entrance Exam
b. Dependent Variable: Final University Exam

Output 4. The values of the multiple correlation coefficient R and other statistics

The other statistics listed are **R Square** (a positively biased estimate of the proportion of the variance of the dependent variable accounted for by regression), **Adjusted R Square** (which corrects this bias and therefore has a lower value), and the **Standard Error** (the standard deviation of the residuals). The **effect size** estimated by R^2 is 0.53 (53%) and is therefore a large effect.

Output 5 shows the regression ANOVA, which tests for a linear relationship between the variables. The F statistic is the ratio of the mean square for regression to the residual mean square. In this example, the value of F in the ANOVA Table is significant beyond the .01 level. **It should be noted, however, that only an examination of their scatterplot can confirm that the relationship between two variables is genuinely linear.**

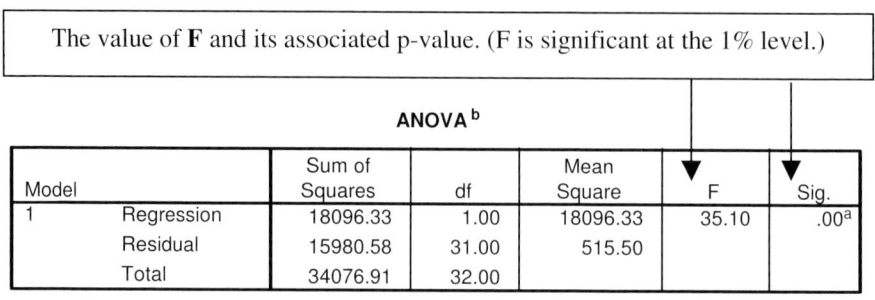

The value of **F** and its associated p-value. (F is significant at the 1% level.)

ANOVA [b]

Model		Sum of Squares	df	Mean Square	F	Sig.
1	Regression	18096.33	1.00	18096.33	35.10	.00 [a]
	Residual	15980.58	31.00	515.50		
	Total	34076.91	32.00			

a. Predictors: (Constant), Entrance Exam
b. Dependent Variable: University Exam

Output 5. The ANOVA for the regression

Output 6 presents the kernel of the regression analysis, the regression equation. The values of the **regression coefficient** and **constant** are given in column **B** of the table.

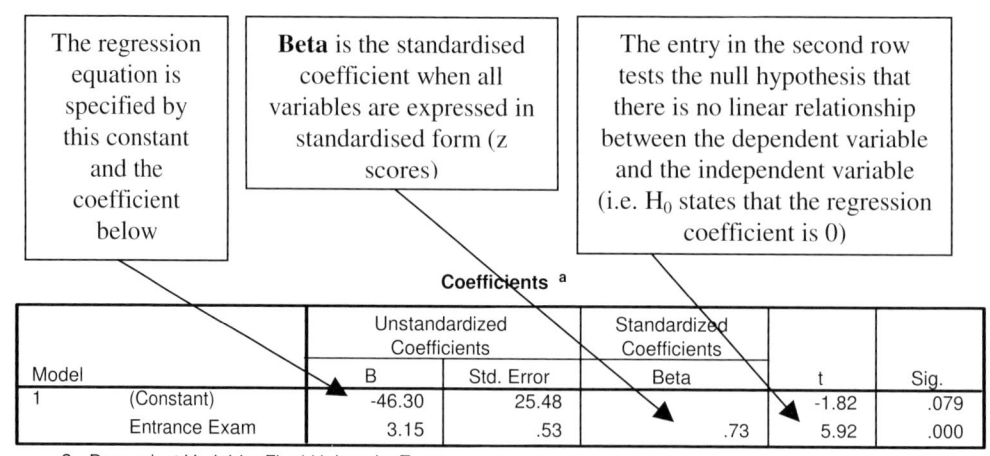

The regression equation is specified by this constant and the coefficient below

Beta is the standardised coefficient when all variables are expressed in standardised form (z scores)

The entry in the second row tests the null hypothesis that there is no linear relationship between the dependent variable and the independent variable (i.e. H_0 states that the regression coefficient is 0)

Coefficients [a]

Model		Unstandardized Coefficients B	Std. Error	Standardized Coefficients Beta	t	Sig.
1	(Constant)	-46.30	25.48		-1.82	.079
	Entrance Exam	3.15	.53	.73	5.92	.000

a. Dependent Variable: Final University Exam

Output 6. The regression equation and associated statistics

The equation is, therefore,

$$(\text{Final University Exam})' = -46.30 + 3.15 \times (\text{Entrance Exam})$$

where (Final University Exam)′ is the predicted value of (Final University Exam). Thus a person with an *Entrance Exam* mark of 60 would be predicted to score
$$-46.30 + 3.15 \times 60 = 142.7 \quad (\text{i.e. } 143).$$

Notice from the data that the person who scored *60* on the *Entrance Exam* actually scored *145* on the *Final University Exam*. So $y = 145$ and $y' = 143$. The residual $(y - y')$ is, therefore, $145 - 143 = +2$.

Other statistics are also listed. The **Std. Error** is the standard error of the regression coefficient, **B**. **Beta** is the beta coefficient, which is the change in the dependent variable (expressed in standard deviation units) that would be produced by a positive increment of one standard deviation in the independent variable. (In multiple regression, beta coefficients are more comparable across independent variables, since they are all in the same units.) The **t** statistic tests the regression coefficient for significance, and **Sig.** is the p-value of **t**. (Here .00 means <0.005, i.e. t is significant beyond the 0.01 level for the variable Entrance Exam.)

Output 7 is a table of statistics relating to the residuals. The variable *Predicted Value* contains the unstandardised predicted values. The variable *Residual* contains the unstandardised residuals. The variable *Std. Predicted Value* (identified as *ZPRED in the **Plots** dialog box in Figure 4) contains the standardised predicted values (i.e. Predicted Value transformed to a scale with mean *0* and SD *1*); the empirical value for the SD of .98 is very close to 1. The variable *Std. Residual* (identified as *ZRESID in the **Plots** dialog box in Figure 4) contains the standardised residuals (i.e. residuals standardised to a scale with mean *0* and SD *1*).

Residuals Statistics [a]

	Minimum	Maximum	Mean	Std. Deviation	N
Predicted Value	60.95	152.43	102.82	23.780	33
Residual	-54.49	30.97	.00	22.35	33
Std. Predicted Value	-1.76	2.09	.00	1.00	33
Std. Residual	-2.40	1.36	.00	.98	33

a. Dependent Variable: Final University Exam

Output 7. Table of statistics relating to the residuals

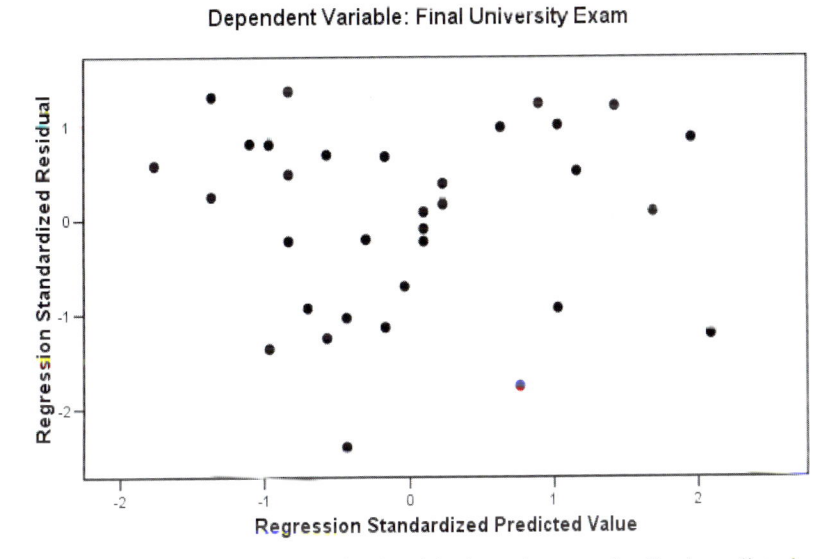

Output 8. Scatterplot of standardised residuals against standardised predicted scores

Output 8 is the scatterplot of the standardised residuals (*ZRESID*) against the standardised predicted values (*ZPRED*). The plot shows no obvious pattern, thereby confirming that the assumptions of linearity and homogeneity of variance have been met. If the cloud of points had been crescent-shaped or funnel-shaped, further screening of the data (or abandonment of the analysis) would have been necessary.

Other diagnostic plots such as a histogram of the standardised residuals (ideally they should be distributed normally) and a cumulative normal probability plot (ideally the points should lie along or adjacent to the diagonal) could have been selected from within the **Standardized Residual Plots** box in Figure 4.

12.3 MULTIPLE REGRESSION

The process of constructing a linear equation predicting the values of a target (dependent) variable from knowledge of specified values of a regressor (independent variable) can readily be extended to situations where we have data on two or more independent variables. The construction of a linear regression equation with two or more independent variables on the right-hand side of the equation is known as **multiple regression**.

In Table 2, three extra variables, the subject's *Age*, the score obtained on a relevant academic *Project*, and *IQ* have been added to the original variables in Table 1. The outlier that was detected in the preliminary regression analysis, however, has been removed.

Table 2. An extension of Table 1, with data on three additional independent variables

Case	Fin	Ent	Age	Pro	IQ	Case	Fin	Ent	Age	Pro	IQ
1	38	44	21.9	50	110	18	103	48	22.3	53	134
2	49	40	22.6	75	120	19	105	43	21.8	72	140
3	61	43	21.8	54	119	20	106	55	21.4	69	127
4	65	42	22.5	60	125	21	107	48	21.6	50	135
5	69	44	21.9	82	121	22	112	49	22.8	68	132
6	73	46	21.8	65	140	23	114	46	22.1	72	135
7	74	34	22.2	61	122	24	114	41	21.9	60	135
8	76	37	22.5	68	123	25	117	49	22.5	74	129
9	78	41	21.5	60	133	26	125	63	21.9	70	140
10	81	53	22.4	69	100	27	140	52	22.2	77	134
11	86	47	21.9	64	120	28	142	56	21.4	79	134
12	91	45	22.0	78	115	29	145	60	21.6	84	132
13	94	41	22.2	68	124	30	150	55	22.1	60	135
14	95	39	21.7	70	135	31	152	54	21.9	76	135
15	98	40	22.2	65	132	32	164	58	23.0	84	149
16	100	37	39.3	75	130	33	169	62	21.2	65	135
17	100	48	21.0	65	128						

In the following discussion, we shall be concerned with two main questions:

1. Does the addition of more independent variables improve the accuracy of predictions of the value of *Final University Exam*?
2. Of these new variables, are some more useful than others for prediction of the dependent variable?

We shall see that the answer to the first question is 'Yes, up to a point'. The second question, however, is problematic, and none of the available approaches to it is entirely satisfactory (see, for example, Howell, 2002). Essentially, the problem is this: **Correlation does not imply causation**. In a situation where everything correlates with everything else, it is impossible to attribute variance in the dependent variable unequivocally to any one independent variable.

In a multiple regression equation, the coefficients of the independent variables are known as **partial regression coefficients**. A partial regression coefficient is the increase in the dependent variable that would be produced by a positive increase of one unit in the independent variable, the effects of the other independent variables, both on the independent variable and the dependent variable, being supposedly held constant. Such **statistical control**, however, is no substitute for true **experimental** control, where the independent variable, having been manipulated by the experimenter, really is independent of the dependent variable.

In this section, we shall consider two approaches to multiple regression, neither of which is entirely satisfactory. In **simultaneous** multiple regression, all the available independent variables are entered in the equation directly. In **stepwise** multiple regression, the independent variables are added to (or taken away from) the equation one at a time, the order of entry (or removal) being determined by statistical considerations. Despite the appeal of the second approach, there is the disconcerting fact that the addition of another 'independent' variable to those already in the study can completely change the apparent contributions of the other predictors to the variance of scores on the dependent variable. Statistical considerations, it would appear, are insufficient to resolve some of the most pressing research questions.

Constructing the SPSS data set

Using the techniques described in Section 3.5, restore the original data set (minus the outliers) to **Data View**. In **Variable View**, name the three new variables (e.g. *Age*, *Project* and *IQ*). Use the **Label** column to assign a variable label such as *Project Mark*. Now enter the scores in **Data View**. The first three cases are shown in Figure 5.

Case	FinalExam	EntranceExam	Age	Project	IQ
1	38	44	21.9	50	110
2	49	40	22.6	75	120
3	61	43	21.8	54	119

Figure 5. The first three cases in **Data View**

12.3.1 Procedure for simultaneous multiple regression

- In the **Linear Regression** dialog box, transfer the variable name *Final University Exam* into the **Dependent Variable:** and *Entrance Exam*, *Age*, *Project Mark* and *IQ* into the **Independent Variables:** box.
- Select the other optional items as in Section 12.2.1. and then click **OK**.

Output for simultaneous multiple regression

The first table in the output is a table of the requested descriptive statistics for each variable (Output 9).

Descriptive Statistics

	Mean	Std. Deviation	N
University Exam	102.82	32.63	33
Entrance Exam	47.27	7.54	33
Age	22.518	3.046	33
Project Mark	67.94	9.14	33
IQ	129.03	9.66	33

Output 9. The Descriptive Statistics table

The next item is an edited table of correlations (Output 10) showing that the dependent variable *Final University Exam* correlates significantly with three of the independent variables but not with the fourth (*Age*).

Correlations

		University Exam
Pearson Correlation	University Exam	1.00
	Entrance Exam	.73
	Age	-.03
	Project Mark	.40
	IQ	.65
Sig. (1-tailed)	University Exam	.
	Entrance Exam	.00
	Age	.43
	Project Mark	.01
	IQ	.00

Output 10. Edited table of Correlations

Output 11 lists the variables entered.

Variables Entered/Removed[b]

Model	Variables Entered	Variables Removed	Method
1	IQ, Age, Project Mark, Entrance Exam [a]	.	Enter

a. All requested variables entered.

b. Dependent Variable: Final University Exam

Output 11. List of variables entered, the dependent variable and the method of analysis

Output 12 shows that the multiple correlation coefficient (**R**) is 0.87 and the **Adjusted R Square** is 0.73. The effect size represented by R^2 is 76% i.e. a **large effect size**.

Model Summary [b]

Model	R	R Square	Adjusted R Square	Std. Error of the Estimate
1	.87[a]	.76	.73	16.92

a. Predictors: (Constant), IQ, Age, Project Mark, Entrance Exam
b. Dependent Variable: Final University Exam

Output 12. Value of R and other statistics

Recall that when one independent variable (*Entrance Exam*) was used to predict *Final University Exam*, the value of **R** was 0.73 and **Adjusted R Square** (the estimate of the proportion of variance accounted for by regression) was 0.52 (52%). With **R** now at 0.87 and **Adjusted R Square** up from 52% to 73%, we see that the answer to the question of whether adding more independent variables improves the predictive power of the regression equation is definitely 'Yes'.

Not surprisingly, the ANOVA (Output 13) shows that the regression is still significant beyond the .01 level: ($p < 0.0005$).

ANOVA [b]

Model		Sum of Squares	df	Mean Square	F	Sig.
1	Regression	26059.63	4	6514.91	22.75	.000[a]
	Residual	8017.28	28	286.33		
	Total	34076.91	32			

a. Predictors: (Constant), IQ, Age, Project Mark, Entrance Exam
b. Dependent Variable: Final University Exam

Output 13. The ANOVA for regression

From column **B** in Output 14, we see that the multiple regression equation of *Final University Exam* upon *Entrance Exam*, *Age*, *Project Mark* and *IQ* is:

(Final University Exam)' = $-272.13 + 2.49 \times$ (Entrance Exam) $+ 1.24 \times$ Age $+ .50 \times$ (Project Mark) $+ 1.51 \times$ IQ

where (Final University Exam)' is the predicted *Final University Exam* mark.

Thus a person with *Age 21.6* and scoring *60* on the *Entrance Exam*, *84* on the *Project* and having an *IQ* of *132* would have an estimated score of

$-272.13 + 2.49 \times (60) + 1.24 \times (21.6) + 0.50 \times (84) + 1.51 \times (132) = 145.37$

Notice that case 29, who meets these specifications, actually scored 145 in the *Final University Exam*. However, not all cases have estimates so close to the actual values: for case 6, the estimate is 113.34, but the actual value is 73.

But what about the second question? Do all the new variables contribute substantially to the predictive power of the regression equation, or is one or more a passenger in the equation? We can learn little about the relative importance of the variables from the sizes of their regression coefficients (**B**), because the **values of the partial regression coefficients reflect the original units in which the variables were measured**. For this reason, although the coefficient for *Age* is larger than that for *Project*, we cannot thereby conclude that *Age* is the more important predictor.

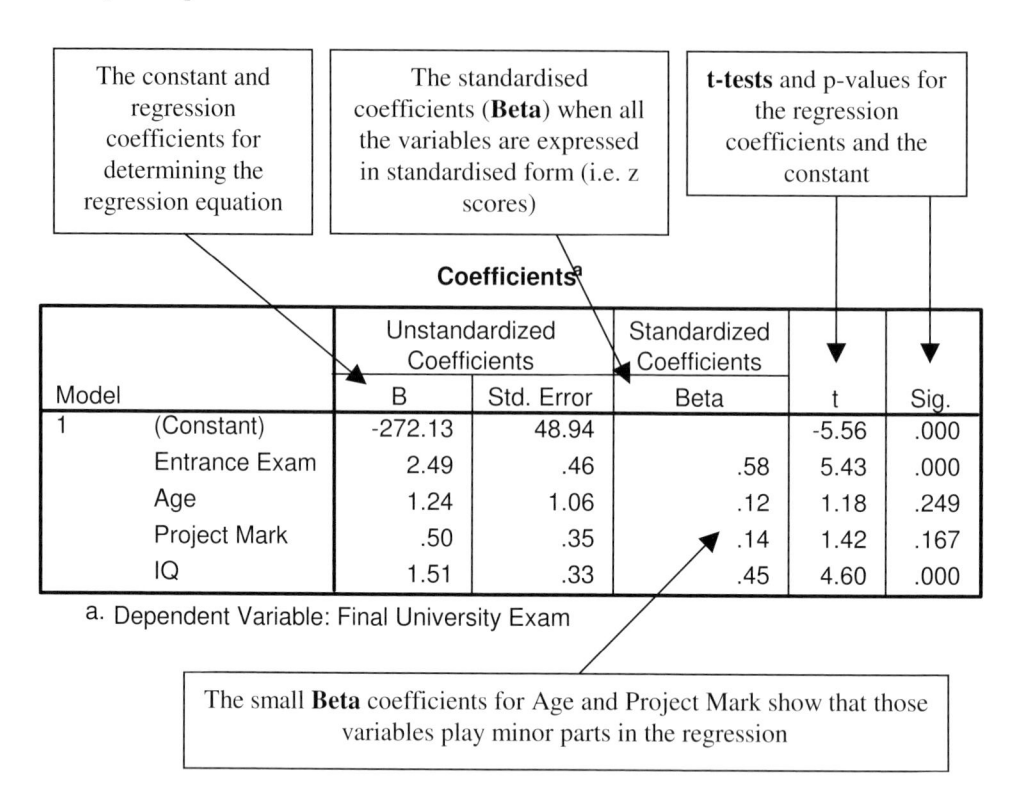

| | The constant and regression coefficients for determining the regression equation | The standardised coefficients (**Beta**) when all the variables are expressed in standardised form (i.e. z scores) | **t-tests** and p-values for the regression coefficients and the constant |

Coefficients[a]

Model		Unstandardized Coefficients B	Std. Error	Standardized Coefficients Beta	t	Sig.
1	(Constant)	-272.13	48.94		-5.56	.000
	Entrance Exam	2.49	.46	.58	5.43	.000
	Age	1.24	1.06	.12	1.18	.249
	Project Mark	.50	.35	.14	1.42	.167
	IQ	1.51	.33	.45	4.60	.000

a. Dependent Variable: Final University Exam

The small **Beta** coefficients for Age and Project Mark show that those variables play minor parts in the regression

Output 14. The regression equation and associated statistics

The **beta coefficients** (in the column headed **Beta**) tell us rather more, because each gives the number of standard deviations change on the dependent variable that will be produced by a change of one standard deviation on the independent variable concerned. On this count, *Entrance Exam* still makes by far the greatest contribution, because a change of one standard deviation on that variable produces a change of 0.58 standard deviations on *Final University Exam*. Next is *IQ* with a change of 0.45, but *Project Mark* produces a change of only 0.14 and *Age* a change of 0.12 of a standard deviation on *Final University Exam*. This ordering of the standardised beta coefficients is supported by consideration of the correlations between the dependent variable and each of the three predictors (Output 10). The predictor with the largest beta coefficient also has the largest correlation with the dependent variable.

The remaining items of output (the table of **Residual Statistics** and the scatterplot of standardised predicted values against standardised residuals) are not shown here. There were no residual outliers.

Regression

12.3.2 Procedure for stepwise multiple regression

If, in the **Linear Regression** dialog box, the choice of **Method** is changed to **Stepwise**, rather than **Enter**, a stepwise regression will be run, whereby predictors are added to (or subtracted from) the equation one at a time. In **Forward selection**, predictors are added one a time, provided they meet an entry criterion. In **Backward deletion**, the predictors are all present initially and are removed one at a time if they do not meet a retention criterion. The SPSS **Stepwise regression** routine is a combination of these two processes: a variable, having been added at an early stage, may subsequently be removed. Selected portions of the results of a **Stepwise regression** analysis are shown in Outputs 15-19.

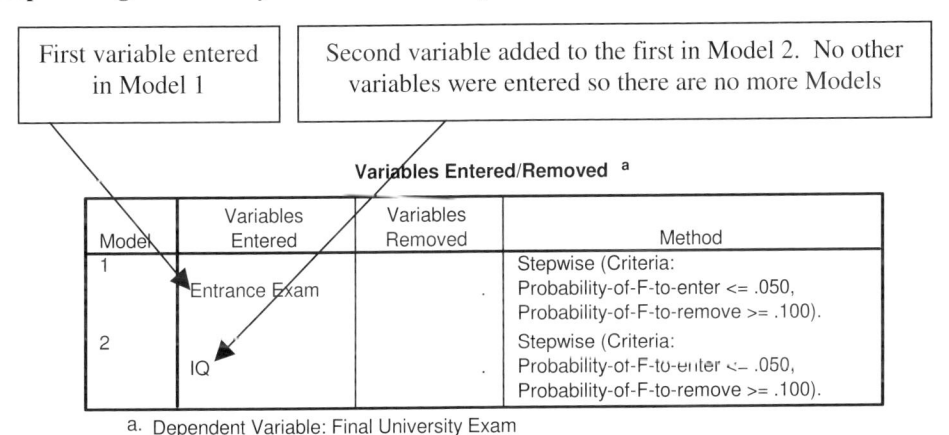

First variable entered in Model 1

Second variable added to the first in Model 2. No other variables were entered so there are no more Models

Variables Entered/Removed a

Model	Variables Entered	Variables Removed	Method
1	Entrance Exam	.	Stepwise (Criteria: Probability-of-F-to-enter <= .050, Probability-of-F-to-remove >= .100).
2	IQ	.	Stepwise (Criteria: Probability-of-F-to-enter <= .050, Probability-of-F-to-remove >= .100).

a. Dependent Variable: Final University Exam

Output 15. List of variables entered (only two achieved entry in the stepwise regression)

The value of R for Model 2 is smaller than the value (0.87) given for simultaneous regression of *Final University Exam* upon *Entrance Exam*, *Project Mark*, *Age* and *IQ* but only slightly so. This shows the lack of predictive value of the two excluded variables (*Age* and *Project Mark*). The values of R^2 for Model 1 and Model 2 are large (53% & 73%, respectively) so the **effect sizes** are large.

Model Summary c

Model	R	R Square	Adjusted R Square	Std. Error of the Estimate
1	.73[a]	.53	.52	22.70
2	.85[b]	.73	.71	17.62

a. Predictors: (Constant), Entrance Exam
b. Predictors: (Constant), Entrance Exam, IQ
c. Dependent Variable: Final University Exam

Notice the increase in the value of **R** after the addition of a second variable

Output 16. Value of R and associated statistics for each Model

The ANOVA (Output 17) for each regression Model is significant.

ANOVA[c]

Model		Sum of Squares	df	Mean Square	F	Sig.
1	Regression	18096.33	1	18096.33	35.10	.000[a]
	Residual	15980.58	31	515.50		
	Total	34076.91	32			
2	Regression	24757.87	2	12378.93	39.85	.000[b]
	Residual	9319.04	30	310.63		
	Total	34076.91	32			

a. Predictors: (Constant), Entrance Exam
b. Predictors: (Constant), Entrance Exam, IQ
c. Dependent Variable: Final University Exam

Output 17. The ANOVA for each regression Model

The decision of the stepwise program is that, since the increment in **R** with the inclusion of either of the remaining variables (*Project Mark* and *Age*) does not reach the necessary statistical criterion, these variables are excluded from the final equation (Output 18).

From column **B** in Output 18, we see that the multiple regression equation of *Final University Exam* upon *Entrance Exam* and *IQ* is:

$$(\text{Final University Exam})' = -219.07 + 2.51 \times (\text{Entrance Exam}) + 1.58 \times IQ$$

where $(\text{Final University Exam})'$ is the predicted value of the *Final University Exam*. Thus the estimated score of a person with *Age 21.6* scoring *60* on the *Entrance Exam* and having an *IQ* of *132* is

$$-219.07 + 2.51 \times (60) + 1.58 \times (132) = 140.09$$

Notice that case 29, who meets these specifications, scored 145 in the *Final University Exam*. In this case the simultaneous regression equation provides a better estimate than the stepwise regression equation; but there are other cases for which the opposite is true.

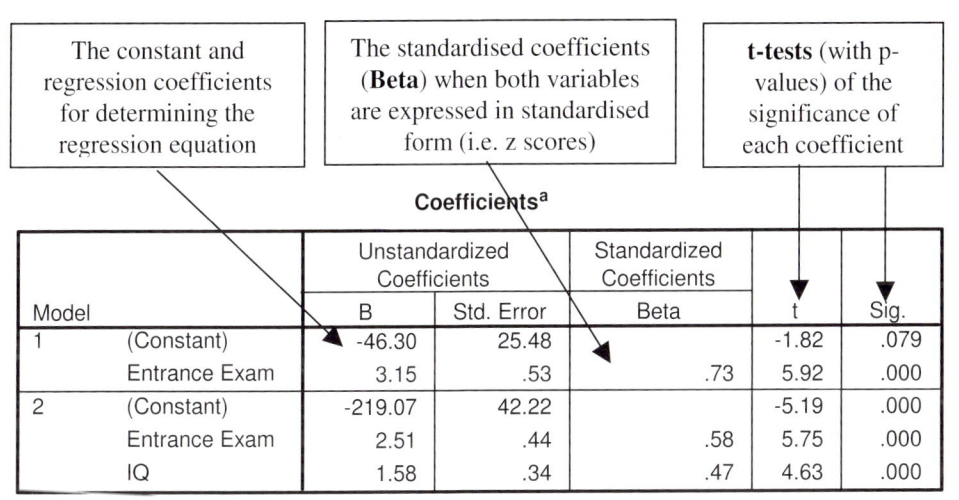

Regression

| | The constant and regression coefficients for determining the regression equation | | The standardised coefficients (**Beta**) when both variables are expressed in standardised form (i.e. z scores) | | **t-tests** (with p-values) of the significance of each coefficient | |

Coefficients[a]

		Unstandardized Coefficients		Standardized Coefficients		
Model		B	Std. Error	Beta	t	Sig.
1	(Constant)	-46.30	25.48		-1.82	.079
	Entrance Exam	3.15	.53	.73	5.92	.000
2	(Constant)	-219.07	42.22		-5.19	.000
	Entrance Exam	2.51	.44	.58	5.75	.000
	IQ	1.58	.34	.47	4.63	.000

a. Dependent Variable: Final University Exam

Output 18. The regression coefficients tables for the single variable (Model 1) and the two variables (Model 2) remaining in the stepwise regression analysis

Output 19 lists the statistics for the excluded variables. Note the low values of t and their correspondingly high (i.e. > 0.05) p-values.

Excluded Variables[c]

					Partial	Collinearity Statistics
Model		Beta In	t	Sig.	Correlation	Tolerance
1	Age	.18[a]	1.42	.167	.25	.93
	Project Mark	.21[a]	1.69	.102	.29	.92
	IQ	.47[a]	4.63	.000	.65	.90
2	Age	.15[b]	1.56	.129	.28	.92
	Project Mark	.17[b]	1.77	.088	.31	.91

a. Predictors in the Model: (Constant), Entrance Exam
b. Predictors in the Model: (Constant), Entrance Exam, IQ
c. Dependent Variable: Final University Exam

Output 19. The variables excluded from the stepwise regression analysis

In the table in Output 19, **Beta In** is the standardised regression coefficient that would result if the variable were entered into the equation at the next step. The **t** test is the usual test of significance of the regression coefficient. Partial correlation is the correlation that remains between two variables after removing the correlation that is due to their mutual association with the other variables. **Collinearity** is the undesirable situation where the correlations among the independent variables are high. Collinearity can be detected by the **Tolerance** statistic, which is the proportion of a variable's variance not accounted for by other independent variables in the equation. A variable with very low tolerance contributes little information to a model, and can cause computational problems.

In conclusion, the **stepwise regression** confirms the conclusion from the beta coefficients in the simultaneous regression that only the variables *Entrance Exam* and *IQ* are useful for predicting *Final University Exam* marks. The other two variables can be dropped from the analysis.

12.3.3 The need for a substantive model of causation

These results highlight an important consideration for the use of multiple regression as a research tool. The addition of new predictors can sometimes affect the relative contributions of those variables already in the equation. Therefore, when planning a multiple regression and selecting predictors, the researcher must be guided by a sound theoretical rationale. A *statistical* model alone cannot yield an unequivocal interpretation of regression results: the user also requires the guidance of a *substantive* model of causation.

12.4　SCATTERPLOTS AND REGRESSION LINES

It is often useful to add a regression line to a scatterplot such as Output 1 in Chapter 11 (see page 301).

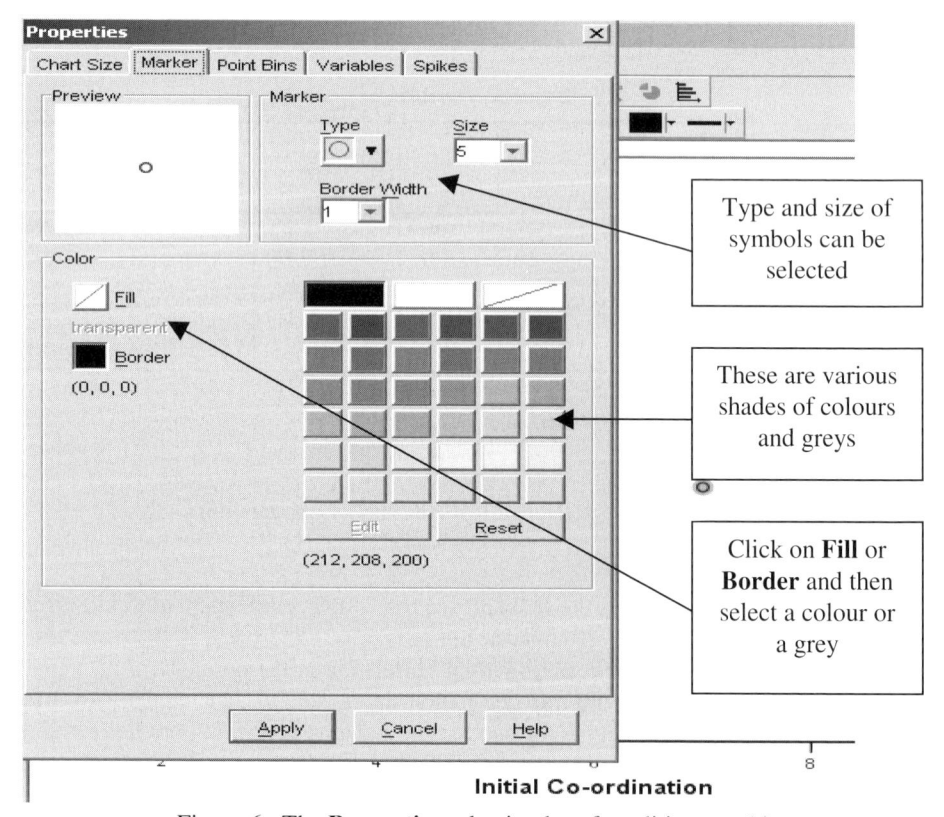

Figure 6. The **Properties** selection box for editing graphics

Regression 343

Proceed as follows.
- After plotting the scatterplot in the usual way by completing the **Simple Scatterplot** dialog box, double-click anywhere on the scatterplot in **SPSS Viewer** to open the **Chart Editor**.
- Edit the scatterplot as desired (e.g. change the coloured points to black by double-clicking any of the points to open a **Properties** selection box (see Figure 6).
- To add the regression line, click on any of the points in the scatterplot so that they are all highlighted, enter the **Chart** menu, select **Add Chart Element** and select **Fit Line at Total** (Figure 7).

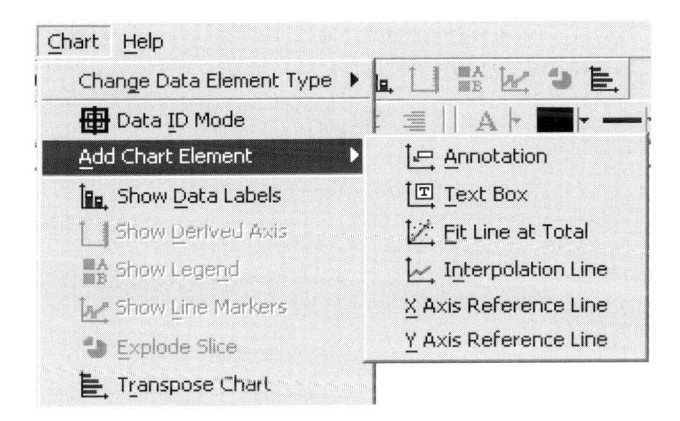

Figure 7. Finding the **Fit Line at Total** site for drawing the regression line

- Another dialog box will appear (Figure 8) with the **Linear** radio button highlighted as the default setting. Click on **Linear** and then on the **Apply** button at the foot of the box (not shown in Figure 8). The regression line will then appear on the scatterplot after a few moments (Output 20).

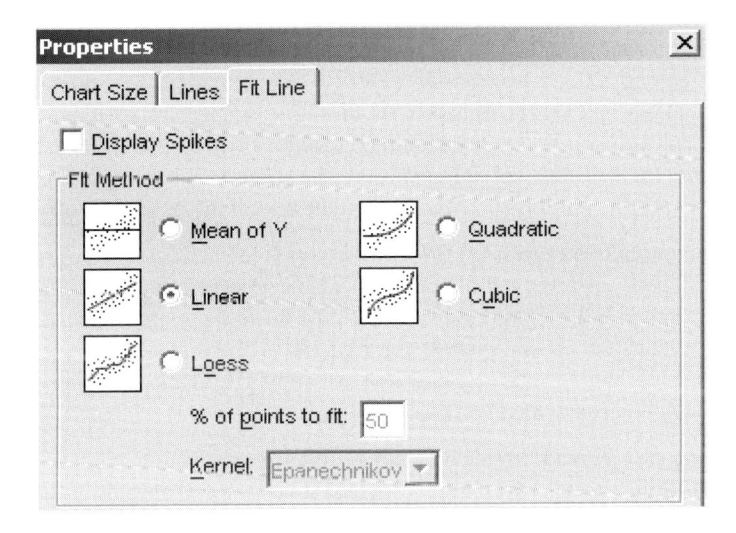

Figure 8. Selecting the line fitting method – **Linear** is the default setting

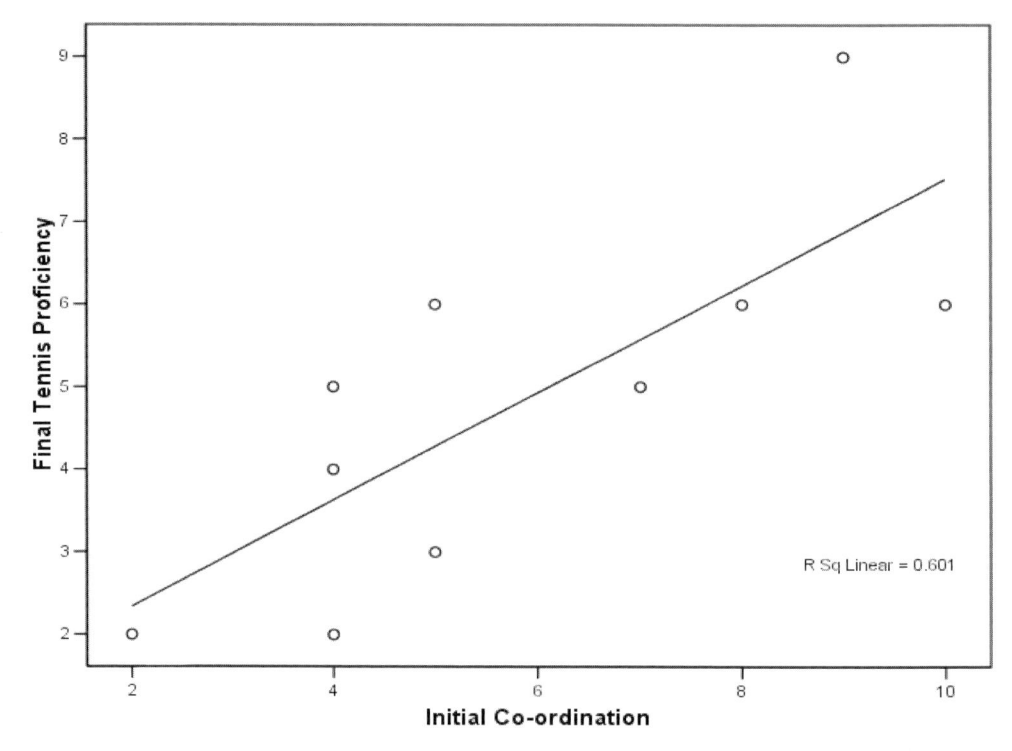

Output 20. Scatterplot with linear regression line added

Clustered scatterplots

It is possible to draw scatterplots and their regression lines for data that have been subdivided into clusters (e.g. sex). In Chapter 4, for example, a data set was introduced which consisted of observations on four variables: height, weight, sex and blood group. A scatterplot of weight against height can be refined by entering sex as a category variable. Some of the points will now represent males and others females. A clustered scatterplot is drawn by accessing the **Simple Scatterplot** dialog box and including a category variable in the **Set Markers by** box. (In this example, the category variable is *Sex*.) The result will be a scatterplot in which some of the points denote one participant category and the remaining points the other.

It is also possible to plot a regression line for the points in each category. To plot a regression line for *Males*, click on the symbol for *Male* in the legend box to highlight just the *Male* points. Then proceed as described above to plot the *Male* regression line. Repeat the process for *Females* by clicking on the symbol for *Female* in the legend box. For greater clarity, change the type of line by clicking the line to highlight it, clicking the **Lines** tab in the **Properties** dialog box and selecting a dashed line.

You might wish also to add annotations to the lines (e.g. 'Males', 'Females'). Do this by selecting **Annotation** in the **Add Chart Element** item of the **Chart** drop-down menu. A box will appear in the middle of the chart into which you can type your annotation (e.g. Males). Its position can then be changed by entering values in the X and Y co-ordinate variables boxes within the adjacent **Properties** dialog box. Repeat the procedure for Females. The final edited scatterplot is shown in Output 21.

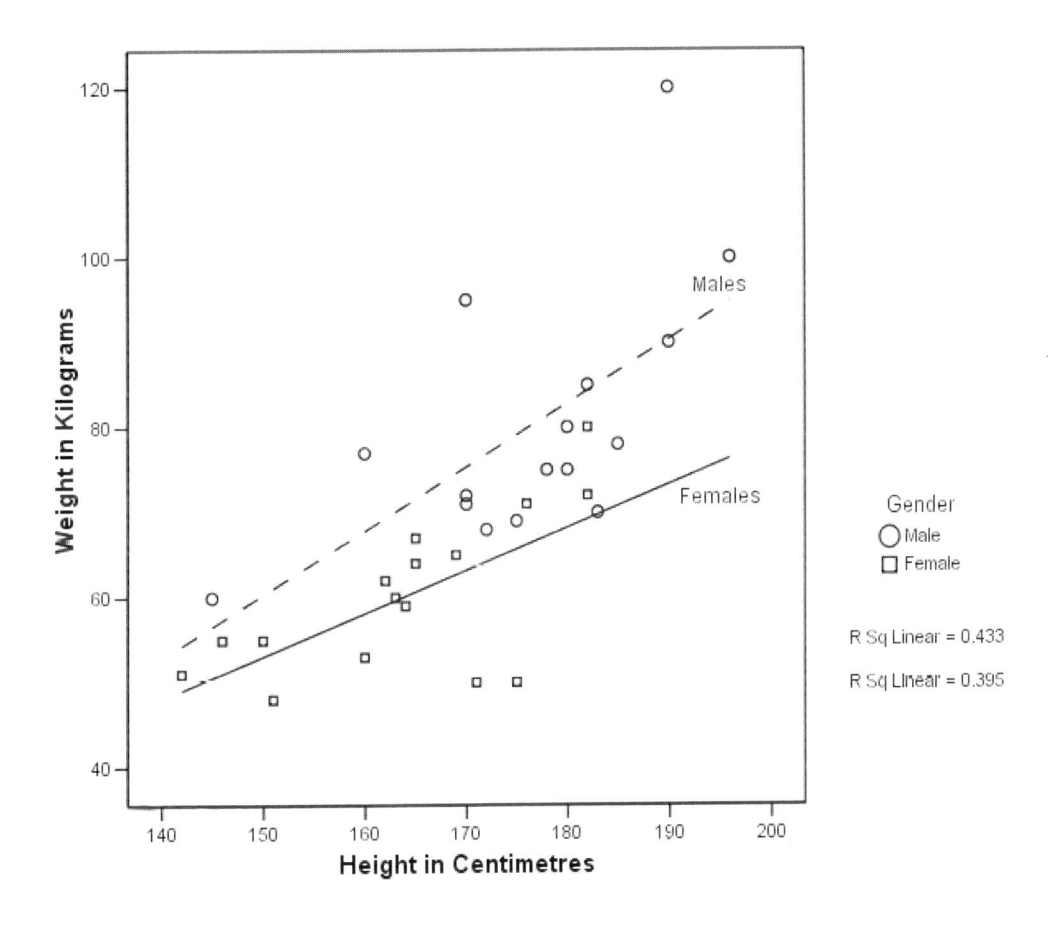

Output 21. Clustered scatterplot with two linear regression lines

When a scatterplot has dense clusters of points, it is possible to clarify them by replacing the densest clusters with either points of varying diameter or points of varying intensity of colour. Here we will illustrate the first approach. Output 22 shows a scatterplot for the heights and weights of the cases in the Questionnaire data used in Exercise 3. Output 23 shows the same scatterplot with varying diameter points.

To vary the diameter points, proceed as follows:
- Highlight the points by clicking on them in the **Chart Editor**.
- **Right-click** the mouse to open the **Properties** dialog box.
- Click the **Point Bins** tab and select the **Bins** radio button.
- Marker size is the default selection. Click **Apply** and **Close**.

The result is shown in Output 23.

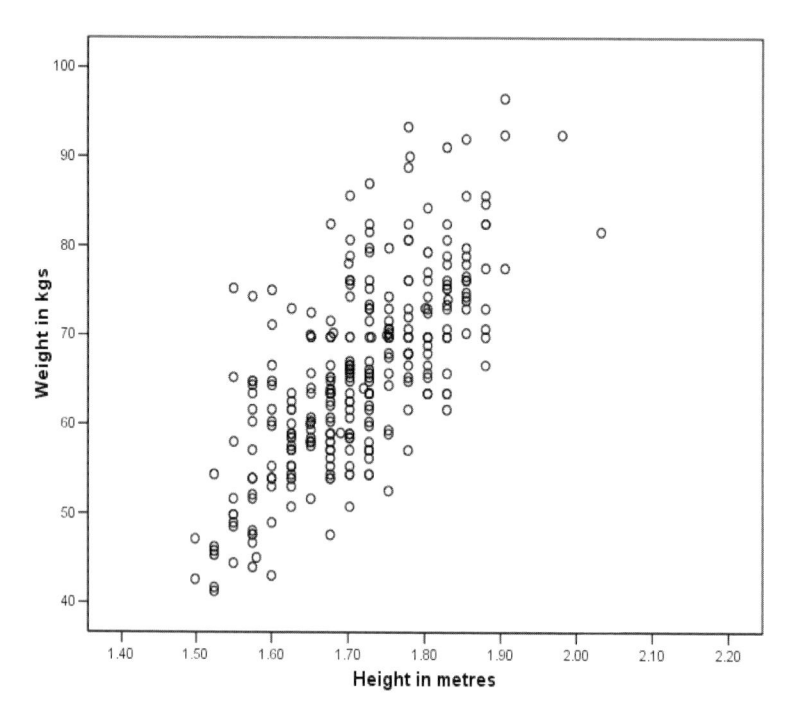

Output 22. The scatterplot of height and weight of over 300 cases

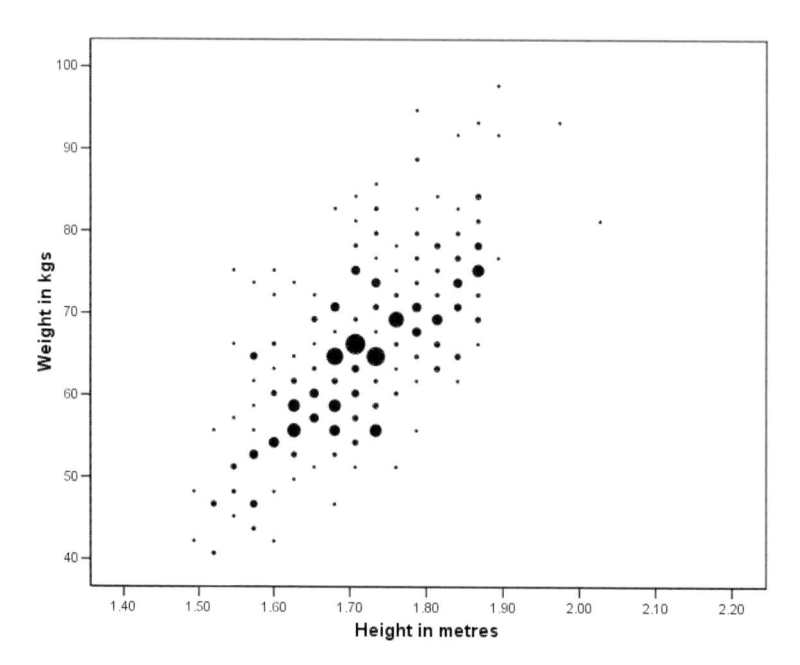

Output 23. The same scatterplot with varying diameter spots to show density of clusters

Regression 347

EXERCISE 20

Simple, two-variable regression

Before you start

Before proceeding with this Exercise, please read Chapter 12.

Purpose of the project

In this Exercise, we shall look at some of the pitfalls that await the unwary user of regression techniques; in fact, as we shall see, all the cautions and caveats about the **Pearson correlation** apply with equal force to regression.

In Exercise 17, Anscombe's specially devised data set (whose columns were named $X1$, $X2$, $Y1$, $Y2$, $Y3$, $Y4$) was saved in a file named **Anscombe**. Scatterplots and correlation coefficients were obtained for the pairings $(X1, Y1)$, $(X1, Y2)$, $(X1, Y3)$ and $(X2, Y4)$. All sets yielded exactly the same value for the Pearson correlation. When the scatterplots were inspected, however, it was seen that the Pearson correlation was appropriate for only one data set: in the other sets, it would give the unwary user a highly misleading impression of a strong linear association between X and Y. One problem with the Pearson correlation is that it is very vulnerable to the leverage exerted by atypical data points, or **outliers** as they are termed. The Pearson correlation can also have large values with monotonic but non-linear relationships. All this is equally true of the parameters of the regression equation. In this Exercise, we return to Anscombe's data to investigate the statistics of the regression lines for the four sets of paired data.

Opening SPSS

Open SPSS and select the data file *Anscombe* from the opening window. This was the file saved from Exercise 17.

Running the simple regression procedure

Following the procedure described in Section 12.2.1, obtain the regression statistics of $Y1$, $Y2$ and $Y3$ upon $X1$ and of $Y4$ upon $X2$. Remember that the dependent variable is Y, and the independent variable is X. For present purposes, the plotting of the scatterplot of *ZRESID (**y-axis** box) against *ZPRED (**x-axis** box) should provide illuminating tests of the credibility of the assumption that the data are linear. Full details of preparing the **Linear Regression** dialog box are given in Section 12.2.1.

Since we want to carry out regression upon all four (X,Y) data sets, it will be necessary to prepare the **Regression** dialog box for the first pair to include a scatterplot of *ZRESID against *ZPRED, and then change the variable names on subsequent runs for the remaining three pairs. To return to the **Regression** dialog box after inspecting the scatterplot, click the

Analyze drop-down menu at the top of the **SPSS Viewer** window and select **Regression** and **Linear** again. Change *Y1* to *Y2* in the **Dependent** box and click **OK**. Follow this procedure for each pair of variables (i.e. *Y3* upon *X1* and then *Y4* upon *X2* – here you need to substitute *X2* for *X1* in the **Independent(s)** box). After each run, you should record the value of **R Squared** and the regression equation, and note the appearance of the scatterplot.

Output for the simple regression analyses

The main features of the Output of a simple regression analysis are fully explained in Chapter 12.

- Compare the regression statistics and scatterplots for all four bivariate data sets. What do you notice about the values of R Squared and the appearances of the scatterplots? What is the 'take-home' message here?

Another example

A researcher interested in the relationship between blood alcohol level and road accidents examined the accident rates for various levels of blood alcohol from 5 to 35 mg/100 ml. The data are shown in Table 1:

Table 1. Blood alcohol level and number of accidents

Alcohol level	5	10	15	20	25	30	35
No of accidents ($\times 10^3$)	10	17	26	30	32	38	42

Find the regression of the number of accidents upon blood alcohol level and predict the number of accidents for a blood alcohol level of 40mg/100ml. Draw the scatterplot with SPSS and fit the regression line.

Preparing the data set

Prepare the data set in the usual manner with two variables.

Running the regression and inspecting the output

Run the regression command as described in Section 12.2.1, but omit the optional extras Descriptives, Casewise diagnostics, and the plot. Use either a calculator or SPSS to calculate the number of predicted accidents for an alcohol level of 40 mg/100 ml. In SPSS, insert the value of 40 in the *blood* column of **Data View** and then complete a **Compute** command by entering the appropriate coefficients and variable name to calculate predicted values for a new variable with a name such as *Predicted*.

- Write down the regression equation.
- What is the predicted number of accidents for a blood alcohol level of 40 mg/100 ml?

Drawing the regression line

Use the procedure described in Section 12.4 to draw the scatterplot and insert the regression line.

- **Does the value calculated for 40 mg/100 ml correspond with what you can see in the scatterplot with its fitted regression line? In your answer, comment on the size of the residual, in relation to the difference between the true accident rate for a level of 40 mg/100 ml and the mean accident rate for the entire sample.**

Finishing the session

Close down SPSS and any other windows before logging out of the computer.

EXERCISE 21

Multiple regression

Before you start

The reader should study Section 12.3 before proceeding with this Exercise.

A problem in reading research

Reading comprises many different component skills. A reading researcher hypothesises that certain specific kinds of pre-reading abilities and behaviour can predict later progress in reading, as measured by performance on reading tests taken some years after the child's first formal lessons. Let us, therefore, label the dependent variable (DV) in this study *Progress*. While they are still very young indeed, many children show a considerable grasp of English syntax in their speech. Our researcher devises a measure of their syntactic knowledge, *Syntax*, based upon the average length of their uttered sentences. Some researchers, however, argue that an infant's prelinguistic babbling (which we shall label *Vocal*) also plays a key role in their later reading performance. At the pre-reading stage, some very young children can acquire a sight vocabulary of several hundreds of words. The ability to pronounce these words on seeing them written down is known as logographic reading; but many authorities do not accept that this is true reading. Our researcher, who views the logographic strategy as important, includes a measure of this skill, *Logo*, in the study.

Preparing the data set

Fifty children are studied over a period beginning in infancy and extending through their school years. Their scores on the four measures, the DV *Progress* (P), and the three IVs *Logo* (L), *Vocal* (V) and *Syntax* (S), are listed in the appendix to this Exercise. Since it would be very laborious for you to type in all the data during the exercise, we must hope that you already have them available in an accessible file, with a name such as **Reading**. The data are also available on the Internet as ***Ex21 Reading data for multiple regression*** at:

http://www.abdn.ac.uk/psychology/materials/spss.shtml

Exploring the data

The distributions of the variables are most easily explored by using the **Boxplot** option in the **Graphs** drop-down menu. Select **Boxplot**, click the **Summaries of separate variables** button, and then click **Define**. Transfer the variable names to the **Boxes Represent** box and click **OK**. This will plot four boxes side-by-side for easy comparison.

Regression is most effective when each IV is strongly correlated with the DV but uncorrelated with the other IVs. Although the correlation matrix can be listed from within the regression procedure, it is often more useful to scrutinise the matrix before proceeding with a regression analysis in order to make judgements about which variables might be retained and which dropped from the analysis. For example, it might be advisable to make a choice between two variables that are highly correlated with one another.

Use the **Bivariate Correlations** procedure to compute the correlation matrix. The same procedure is also useful for tabulating the means and standard deviations, which are available as an option. After transferring the variable names to the **Variables** box, click **Options** and (within the **Statistics** choice box) select **Means and standard deviations**. Click **Continue** and **OK**. Notice that the DV *Progress* shows substantial correlations with both *Logo* and *Syntax*. On the other hand, there is no appreciable correlation between *Logo* and *Syntax*. The remaining variable (*Vocal*) shows little association with any of the other variables, although there is a hint of a negative correlation with *logo*.

Running the multiple regression analysis

Run the multiple regression of *Progress* upon the three predictors, by following the procedure in Section 12.3. Remember that the **Dependent** variable is what you are predicting (*Progress*) and the **Independent** variables are the predictors (*Logo, Vocal, Syntax*). On the first run, use the **Method** *Enter* (this enters all the variables simultaneously) and on the second run the **Method** *Stepwise* (this is a forward stepwise selection procedure).

Output for the multiple regression

The main features of a multiple regression output, both for the simultaneous and stepwise methods, are explained in Section 12.3.

- **Do the decisions of the multiple regression procedure about which variables are important agree with your informal observations during the exploratory phase of the data analysis?**

- **Write out the regression equation that you would use to predict progress from a participant's scores on Logo, Vocal and Syntax.**

Finishing the session

Close down SPSS and any other windows before logging out of the computer.

Appendix to Exercise 21 – The data

P	L	V	S	P	L	V	S	P	L	V	S	P	L	V	S
65	75	34	48	46	55	75	32	65	50	75	68	34	32	42	27
58	29	18	67	51	31	50	66	71	65	23	64	54	64	55	32
42	40	43	38	61	69	59	46	60	56	52	44	81	82	60	69
55	55	9	48	45	19	71	59	17	10	64	20	77	66	50	79
68	81	41	54	53	48	44	45	55	41	41	55	57	30	20	54
59	28	72	68	46	45	29	45	69	51	14	62	80	82	65	58
50	39	31	42	25	28	58	28	47	49	46	59	89	51	52	48
50	26	78	56	71	70	51	54	53	14	53	77	50	34	45	60
71	84	46	50	30	55	42	25	50	40	51	31	69	49	72	72
65	71	30	52	62	53	52	57	80	45	59	90	71	69	57	60
34	30	30	20	47	20	78	69	51	18	22	61	39	25	81	49
44	71	79	22	60	46	80	67	79	58	13	82				
47	62	26	30	70	66	40	61	51	43	31	50				

CHAPTER 13

Multiway frequency analysis

13.1   Introduction

13.2   Two examples of loglinear analyses

13.1   INTRODUCTION

The starting point for the analysis of nominal data on two or more attributes is a **contingency table**, each cell of which is the frequency of occurrence of individuals in various combinations of categories. In an earlier chapter (Chapter 11), we described the use of the chi-square test to test for the presence of an association between qualitative variables in a two-way contingency table.

In a two-way contingency table, the presence (or absence) of an association between the attributes is often apparent from inspection alone: a predominance of tallies in the diagonal cells of the table suggests an association between the variables; on the other hand, comparable frequencies in the off diagonal cells suggest the absence of an association. The formal chi-square test merely confirms what is evident from the table. In more complex contingency tables, however, in which individuals are classified with respect to three or more qualitative variables, patterns can be considerably more difficult to discern.

The familiar Pearson chi-square statistic can easily by applied to multi-way contingency tables, from which the expected frequencies on the basis of total independence can be found from the marginal and total frequencies in a manner analogous to two-way contingency tables. All that this chi-square test will tell you, however, is that there is an unspecified dependency among the variables **somewhere**, which is of very little use. The Pearson chi-square test is still sometimes used with multi-way contingency tables in which the number of dimensions has been reduced to two by **collapsing** across the other dimensions. That approach, however, is decidedly risky; moreover, the researcher may have questions that require a test for the presence of a three-way interaction.

Recent years have seen great advances in the analysis of multi-way contingency tables, and these new methods, collectively known as **loglinear analysis**, are now available in computing packages such as SPSS. (See Howell, 2002, for a readable introduction to the basic principles. Tabachnick & Fidell, 2001, have an extensive chapter on loglinear analysis with computing packages.) These techniques allow the user to do much more than merely reject the total independence model, which is often very unlikely to be true anyway. With loglinear analysis, the precise loci of any associations can be pinpointed and incorporated into a precise model of the data.

13.1.1 Comparison of loglinear analysis with ANOVA

To understand how loglinear analysis works, it may be helpful to recall some aspects of the completely randomised factorial analysis of variance, because there are some striking parallels between the two sets of techniques. In the factorial ANOVA, it is possible to test for **main effects** and for **interactions**. The former are estimated from the marginal means; the latter are estimated partly from the cell means. In multi-way tables, similarly, there are also 'main effects', reflected in the marginal frequencies, and interactions, which are partly reflected in the patterns of the cell frequencies. Loglinear analysis, like the factorial ANOVA, offers tests of both main effects and interactions.

There are other similarities between loglinear analysis and the between subjects factorial ANOVA. The models upon which the two techniques are based both interpret the data as the sum of main effect and interaction terms. There is also another similarity. The ANOVA model is **hierarchical**, in the sense that together with each interaction term, the model also contains the main effects of its component factors. In hierarchical log-linear analysis, which we shall consider in this chapter, a model containing an interaction must also contain terms for the main effects; and models with higher-order interaction terms must also contain terms for lower order interactions involving their component factors.

On the other hand, there are important differences between loglinear analysis and ANOVA. In ANOVA, the focus of interest is the cell mean, the average of several measurements on an independent scale with units. In loglinear analysis, the focus is on cell frequencies, each datum being simply a nominal assignment, not a true measurement. Often, the marginal cell frequencies are of no interest at all in themselves, and must only be taken into consideration in order to test for the presence of an interaction. If we want to know whether there is a gender difference in agreement (yes or no) to legitimised violence, for example, neither the numbers of men and women in the study nor the numbers of individuals saying yes and no (the analogues of ANOVA main effects) are of special interest in their own right. Their main effects, however, must be included in a loglinear model containing the interaction term.

A loglinear model that contains all the possible effect terms is known as a **saturated model**. It can be shown that a saturated model will always predict the cell frequencies (actually, the natural logs of the cell frequencies) perfectly. The purpose of a loglinear analysis is to see whether the cell frequencies can be adequately approximated by a model that contains **fewer** than the full set of possible treatment effects, subject to the hierarchical constraint that if a model includes an interaction, it must also include terms for the main effects of its component factors.

13.1.2 Building a loglinear model

When we carry out a traditional Pearson chi-square test on a two-way contingency table (or, indeed, a multi-way contingency table), we are testing the null hypothesis of complete independence between (or among) the dimensions of the table. A large value of chi-square means that the null hypothesis of independence gives a poor account of the data: that is, there are substantial differences from the frequencies expected (E) on the basis of no association and the observed (O) frequencies. Since the null hypothesis of no association is rejected by the test, we conclude that there is evidence for an association (the alternative or scientific hypothesis). With the traditional chi-square test, therefore, as far as the researcher is concerned, the bigger the value of chi-square, the better.

The process of building a loglinear model of the frequencies in a contingency table works rather differently. In the **backward hierarchical** approach to model-building, we begin with a saturated model containing all possible effects, which we know in advance will predict the cell frequencies perfectly. Next, we remove the most complex interaction term from the model. The effect of this removal will be to increase the value of chi-square from zero. This increment in chi-square can be tested, to see if it 'makes a difference'. If not, we remove the term from the model. While the reduced model will now no longer predict the cell frequencies perfectly, the differences (O-E) between the observed frequencies (O) and the expected frequencies (E) on the basis of the reduced model are likely to be much smaller than they would be with a traditional chi-square test of total independence. The reduced model shows closer goodness-of-fit to the data. We continue removing further terms and testing the increment in chi-square for significance until the removal of a term results in no significant increment, in which case, we retain the term in the model. (If the term is an interaction, we also retain any lower order interactions and the main effects.) Here we see an obvious difference between traditional hypothesis-testing and model-building: in the former, as far as chi-square is concerned, the bigger the better; in the latter, a model is a good fit if chi-square is small and insignificant.

In the foregoing account, we have spoken of the 'chi-square' statistic. Rather than the **Pearson chi-square** statistic, however, the testing of a loglinear model employs what is known as a **'maximum likelihood chi-square'**, which SPSS calls **L.R. (Likelihood Ratio) Chisq**. This is because the **L.R. chi-square** has certain properties not shared by the Pearson statistic. In particular, it has an additive property, whereby its total value can be apportioned among the different models being tested. We can thus see whether the removal of any term from the model makes a significant difference to the total value of chi-square.

As in regression analysis, it is also advisable to examine the distribution of **residuals** (the differences between the observed and expected frequencies) or, more conveniently, the **standardised residuals** (residuals expressed in standardised form). Such regression diagnostics can cast further light on the model's goodness-of-fit for the data.

13.2 TWO EXAMPLES OF LOGLINEAR ANALYSES

13.2.1 First example: Exam success

A Director of Teaching at a School of Psychology is interested in the factors determining whether students can pass the Psychology statistics examination. Researchers have collected a body of information on 176 students, including whether they had taken an advanced mathematics course at school and whether they passed a data-processing examination in their first year at University. On each student's record, it was also noted whether he or she passed the second year Psychology statistics examination. The data are presented in Table 1, which is a **three-way contingency table**.

Table 1. A three-way contingency table showing the levels of success (Pass or Fail) in the Psychology Statistics Exam and the first year Data Processing Exam, and whether students had taken a course at school in Advanced Maths

		Psychology Statistics Exam		
Advanced Maths Course	Data Processing Exam	Pass	Fail	Total
Yes	Pass	47	10	57
Yes	Fail	4	10	14
No	Pass	58	17	75
No	Fail	10	20	30

The predominance of frequencies in the diagonal cells of Table 1 (e.g. 47 and 10; 58 and 20) suggest an association between success in the Data Processing Exam and success in the Psychology Statistics Exam. On the other hand, the pattern is similar whether or not the student had taken an Advanced Mathematics Course at school. Thus there is little sign of a three-way interaction.

Output 1 shows the two-way (Data Processing × Psych Stats) contingency table, in which it is evident that students who had passed the Data Processing Exam were much more likely to pass the Psychology Statistics Exam. This pattern is even more evident in the bar chart alongside the table. The pattern is statistically significant beyond the .01 level: Fisher's Exact $p < .0005$.

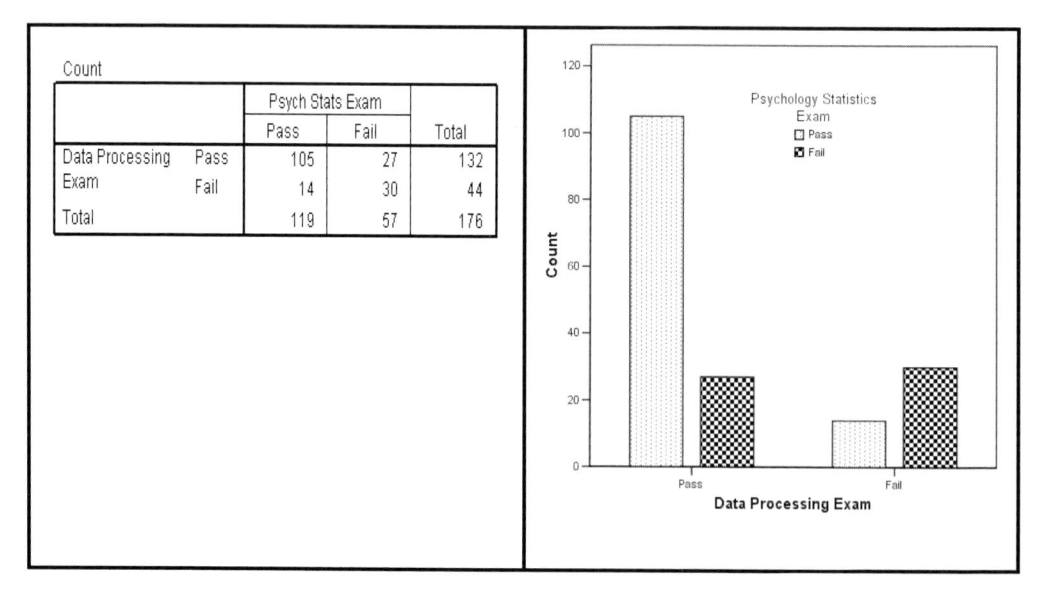

Count

		Psych Stats Exam		Total
		Pass	Fail	
Data Processing Exam	Pass	105	27	132
	Fail	14	30	44
Total		119	57	176

Output 1. Two-way Psych Stats × Data Processing contingency table and bar graph

Multiway frequency analysis

13.2.2 Running a loglinear analysis for the Exam success data

To run a loglinear analysis, do the following:
- In **Variable View**, name three grouping variables: *Maths*, *DataProcessing* and *PsychStats*. In the **Label** column, add suitable expanded names such as *Advanced Maths Course*, *Data Processing Exam* and *Psych Stats Exam*. In the **Values** column, label the code values: for *Maths*, 1 is Yes, 2 is No; for *DataProcessing* and *PsychStats*, 1 is Pass, 2 is Fail. Name a fourth variable *Count* for the cell frequencies. Click the **Data View** tab and enter the data. Finally, save the data set to a file in the usual way. The complete SPSS data set is shown in Figure 1.

Maths	DataProcessing	PsychStats	Count
Yes	Pass	Pass	47
Yes	Pass	Fail	10
Yes	Fail	Pass	4
Yes	Fail	Fail	10
No	Pass	Pass	58
No	Pass	Fail	17
No	Fail	Pass	10
No	Fail	Fail	20

Figure 1. **Data View** showing the data set

- It is now necessary for this example to inform SPSS that the variable *Count* contains frequencies and not simply scores. Note that this step is not needed if the data set consists of individual cases. Choose
Data
  Weight Cases…
to open the **Weight Cases** dialog box and transfer the variable *Count* to the **Frequency Variable** box. Click **OK**.

The next stage is to confirm (by using the **Crosstabs** command in Chapter 11, Section 11.3.2) that the expected frequencies are sufficiently large. Just as in the case of the traditional chi-square test, loglinear analysis requires the **expected** cell frequencies (E) to meet certain requirements. Tabachnick and Fidell (2001) recommend examining the expected cell frequencies for all **two-way associations** to ensure that all **expected frequencies** are greater than 1 and that no more than 20% are less than 5.

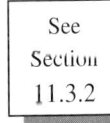

See Section 11.3.2

- Choose
Analyze
  Summarize
    Crosstabs…
and then complete the **Crosstabs** dialog box (Figure 2) by transferring *Data Processing Exam* to the **Row(s)** box, *Psych Stats Exam* to the **Column(s)** box, and *Advanced Maths Course* to the lowest (Layer) box.
- Click **Cells…** to bring to access the **Cell Display** dialog box (See Chapter 11, Figure 11). Within the **Counts** box, tick the **Expected** check box, click **Continue** and then **OK**.

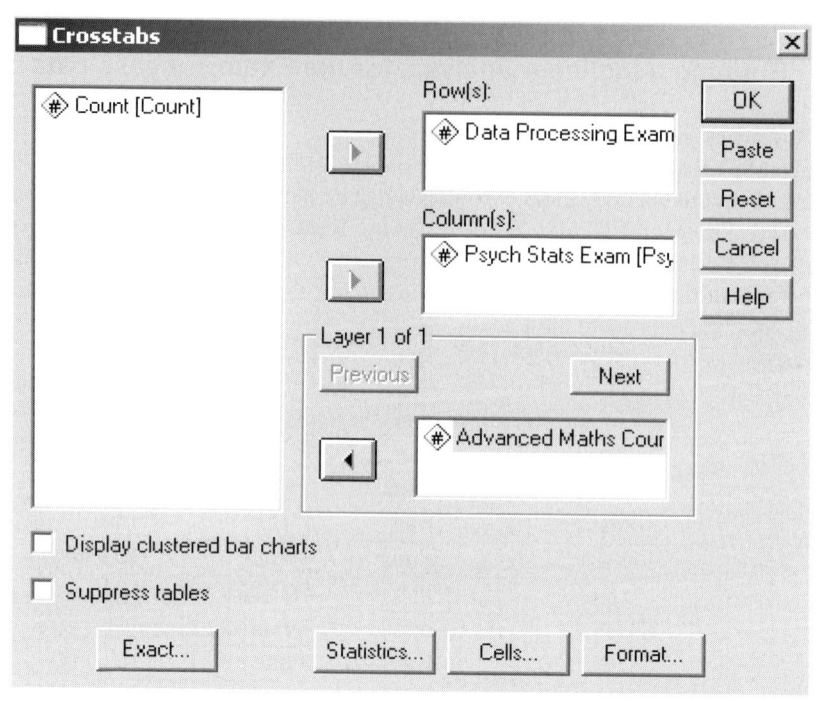

Figure 2. The completed **Crosstabs** dialog box

The **Crosstabs** command presents two-way contingency tables for each layer of *Advanced Maths Course*, because that was chosen as the layering variable. The table (Output 2) shows that no cell has an expected frequency of less than 1 and only one cell has one of less than 5. There is no problem with low expected frequencies.

Data Processing Exam * Psych Stats Exam * Advanced Maths Course Crosstabulation

Advanced Maths Course					Psych Stats Exam		Total
					Pass	Fail	
Yes	Data Processing Exam	Pass		Count	47	10	57
				Expected Count	40.9	16.1	57.0
		Fail		Count	4	10	14
				Expected Count	10.1	3.9	14.0
	Total			Count	51	20	71
				Expected Count	51.0	20.0	71.0
No	Data Processing Exam	Pass		Count	58	17	75
				Expected Count	48.6	26.4	75.0
		Fail		Count	10	20	30
				Expected Count	19.4	10.6	30.0
	Total			Count	68	37	105
				Expected Count	68.0	37.0	105.0

The only expected frequency less than 5

Output 2. Observed and expected frequencies for a three-way contingency table

Multiway frequency analysis

The hierarchical loglinear command is run as follows:
- Select
  Analyze
    Loglinear
      Model Selection...
  to open the **Model Selection Loglinear Analysis** dialog box (the completed version is shown in Figure 3).
- Transfer the three grouping variable names *Maths*, *DataProcessing* and *PsychStats* to the **Factor(s)** box.

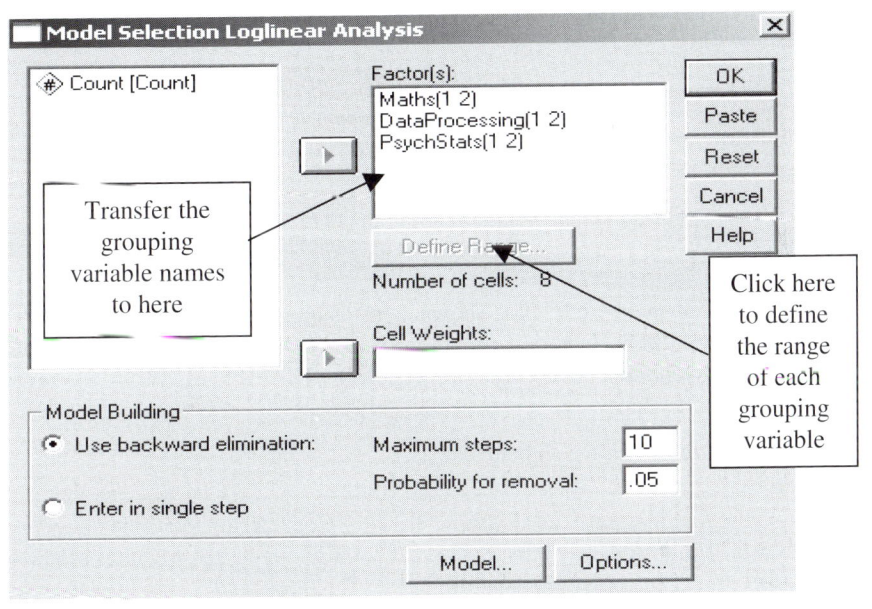

Figure 3. The completed **Model Selection Loglinear Analysis** dialog box for three factors

- Click **Define Range** and enter *1* into the **Minimum** box and *2* into the **Maximum** box. Click **Continue** and the names will appear with [1 2] after each of them. If some of the variables had different numbers of categories, it would have been necessary to enter the ranges separately for each variable.
- The default model is **backward elimination**. Makes sure its radio button is on.
- Click **OK**.

13.2.3 Output for the Exam success loglinear analysis

The output in **SPSS Viewer** is not in the tabulated form encountered in previous Chapters. A red triangle at the foot of the output (on the left-hand side of the right-hand pane) means that there is more output to be viewed. To view the additional material, double-click the output. The surrounding box will then become a window, which can be explored by moving the cursor or by using the **Page Up** and **Page Down** keys.

Output 3 contains information about the data and the factors. Although our variable names contained more than eight characters (e.g. *DataProcessing*), the output limits the names to eight characters (e.g. *DataProc*).

```
* * * *  H I E R A R C H I C A L   L O G   L I N E A R  * * * *

DATA    Information

        8 unweighted cases accepted.
        0 cases rejected because of out-of-range factor values.
        0 cases rejected because of missing data.
        176 weighted cases will be used in the analysis.

FACTOR Information

    Factor   Level   Label
    Maths      2     Advanced Maths Course
    DataProc   2     Data Processing Exam
    PsychSta   2     Psych Stats Exam
```

Output 3. Information about the data and the factors

Output 3 is followed by a table (not shown here) listing the counts (OBS count) for the combinations of the three factors. At this stage, SPSS is fitting a **saturated model**, Maths*DataProc*PsychStats, to the cell frequencies. The table is useful for checking the accuracy of the data transcription.

Output 4 shows the results of the statistical tests.

> The p-value for chi-square for 3-way effects is > 0.05 but for 2-way plus 3-way effects p < 0.05. Thus only effects at the third level fail to reach significance

> Considering the three effect levels individually, the p-values of chi-square for 1-way and 2-way effects are < 0.05 but for the 3-way effect, p > 0.05.

```
Tests that K-way and higher order effects are zero.

 K   DF    L.R. Chisq    Prob    Pearson Chisq    Prob    Iteration
 3    1         .431    .5115            .425    .5143        4
 2    4       35.310    .0000          37.077    .0000        2
 1    7      110.282    .0000         123.000    .0000        0

- - - - - - - - - - - - - - - - - - - - - - - - - - - - - - - - -

Tests that K-way effects are zero.

 K   DF    L.R. Chisq    Prob    Pearson Chisq    Prob    Iteration
 1    3       74.972    .0000          85.923    .0000        0
 2    3       34.879    .0000          36.651    .0000        0
 3    1         .431    .5115            .425    .5143        0
```

Output 4. Tests of effects

Multiway frequency analysis

The upper table in Output 4 shows the chi-squares and p-values for effects at a specified level (K) **and above**. The lower table gives the chi-squares and p-values of effects **at specified levels only**. That is why the chi-squares for K = 1 and K = 2 are smaller in the lower table. We can see that there are significant effects at levels 1 and 2, but not at level 3 (K = 3). The fact that there are significant effects at level 2, however, does not imply that **all** two-way interactions are significant.

Outputs 5-9 show the most interesting part of the output, which is headed:

'Backward Elimination (p = .050) for Design 1 with generating class . . .'

The purpose of the analysis was to find the unsaturated model that gives the best fit to the observed data. This is achieved by checking that the model currently being tested does not give a significantly worse fit than the next most complex in the hierarchy. Recall that hierarchical backward elimination begins with the most complex model (which in the present case contains all three factors, together with all their possible interactions). Testing progresses down the hierarchy of complexity, eliminating each effect from the model in turn and determining which decrement in accuracy is less than the **least-significant change in the chi-square value**. At each step, such an effect would be eliminated, leaving the remaining effects for inclusion, as specified by the heading:

'The best model has generating class . . .'

The procedure continues until no elimination produces a decrement with a probability greater than 0.05. The model containing the remaining effects is then adopted as 'The final model'. In this example, the final model is reached after four steps.

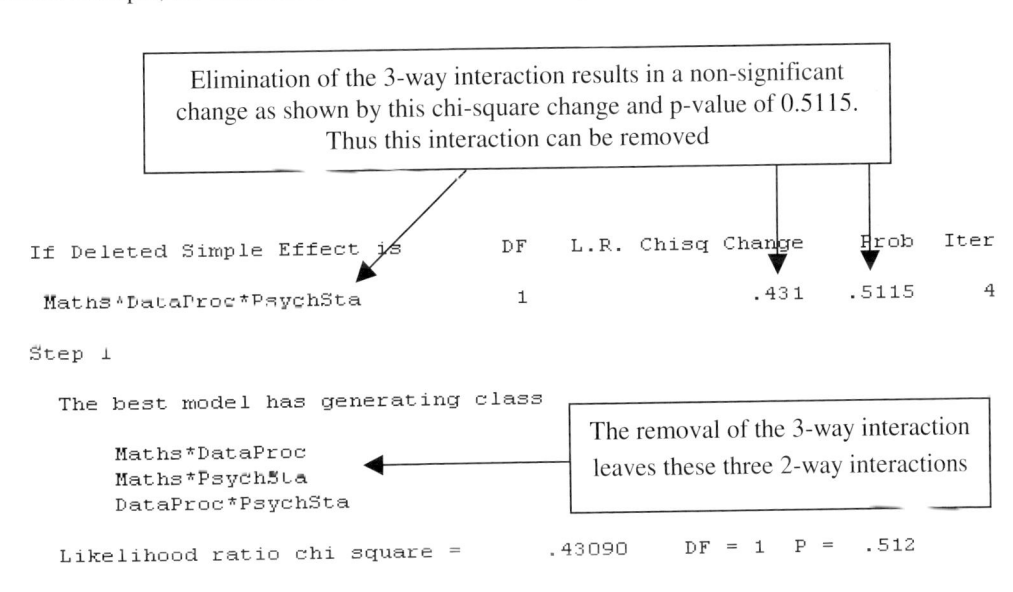

```
                                            DF    L.R. Chisq Change    Prob    Iter
If Deleted Simple Effect is
  Maths*DataProc*PsychSta                    1              .431       .5115     4

Step 1

  The best model has generating class

    Maths*DataProc
    Maths*PsychSta
    DataProc*PsychSta

  Likelihood ratio chi square =           .43090        DF = 1    P =   .512
```

Elimination of the 3-way interaction results in a non-significant change as shown by this chi-square change and p-value of 0.5115. Thus this interaction can be removed

The removal of the 3-way interaction leaves these three 2-way interactions

Output 5. Step 1 of the loglinear analysis

At Step 2, *Maths*Psystats* is eliminated, because it has the largest probability (.6564).

> The 2-way interaction with the least effect (i.e. smallest chi-square change and largest p-value) is eliminated

```
If Deleted Simple Effect is      DF    L.R. Chisq Change    Prob    Iter

Maths*DataProc                    1           1.029         .3104     2
Maths*PsychSta                    1            .198         .6564     2
DataProc*PsychSta                 1          32.098         .0000     2

Step 2

  The best model has generating class

      Maths*DataProc
      DataProc*PsychSta

  Likelihood ratio chi square =       .62884    DF = 2   P =  .730
```

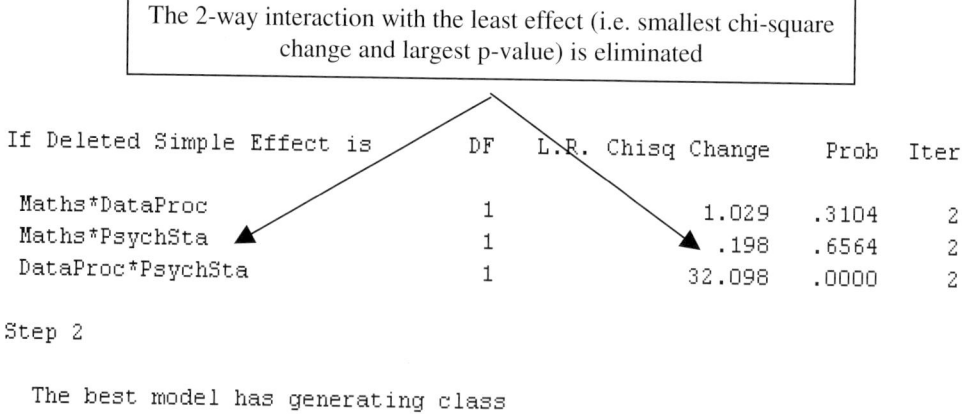

Output 6. Step 2 of the loglinear analysis

At Step 3, *Maths*DataProc* is eliminated, because it has the larger probability (which is greater than the criterion level of 0.05). The remaining interaction, *DataProc*PsychSta* cannot be eliminated, because the p-value is less than .05. All the interactions now having been processed, it remains for any main effect that is **not part of the remaining 2-way interaction** to be tested for inclusion. In this case, only *Maths* qualifies.

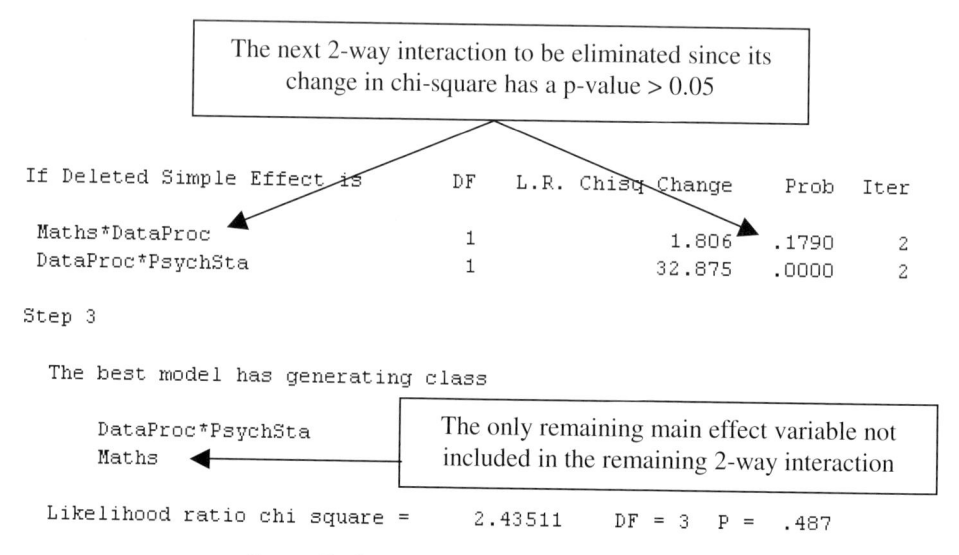

> The next 2-way interaction to be eliminated since its change in chi-square has a p-value > 0.05

```
If Deleted Simple Effect is      DF    L.R. Chisq Change    Prob    Iter

Maths*DataProc                    1           1.806         .1790     2
DataProc*PsychSta                 1          32.875         .0000     2

Step 3

  The best model has generating class

      DataProc*PsychSta
      Maths
```

> The only remaining main effect variable not included in the remaining 2-way interaction

```
  Likelihood ratio chi square =      2.43511    DF = 3   P =  .487
```

Output 7. Step 3 of the loglinear analysis

At Step 4, neither of these effects can be eliminated, because both probabilities are less than 0.05. Both effects, therefore, must be included in the final model.

> Both the one remaining 2-way interaction DataProc*PsychSta and the main effect Maths have p-values < 0.05 and therefore remain in the model

```
If Deleted Simple Effect is       DF    L.R. Chisq Change     Prob    Iter

DataProc*PsychSta                 1               32.875      .0000    2
Maths                             1                6.610      .0101    2

Step 4

  The best model has generating class

       DataProc*PsychSta
       Maths

  Likelihood ratio chi square =    2.43511     DF = 3    P =   .487

The final model has generating class

       DataProc*PsychSta
       Maths
```

> The Step 4 model is therefore adopted as the final model

Output 8. The final step of the loglinear analysis

The final model includes the interaction between the variables representing the Data Processing Exam and the Psychology Statistics Exam, plus a main effect of Maths. Note that there are no interactions involving the Maths variable. Thus the most interesting finding is the interaction between the two examinations.

Finally, the computer lists the table of observed frequencies and the expected frequencies **as estimated by the final model** (Output 9). The **Goodness-of-fit chi-square test** shows that these expected frequencies do **not** differ significantly from the observed frequencies (the p-value for chi-square is not significant since it is much greater than 0.05). Thus the final model based on the interaction of the *Data Processing Exam* and the *Psychology Statistics Exam*, together with the main effect of the *Advanced Maths Course*, provides an excellent fit to the data. The analysis has shown that whereas the results of the *Data Processing Exam* and the *Psychology Statistics Exam* are associated, it makes no difference whether the *Advanced Maths Course* had been taken.

```
Observed, Expected Frequencies and Residuals.

    Factor        Code      OBS count   EXP count   Residual   Std Resid

    Maths         Yes
     DataProc      Pass
      PsychSta      Pass       47.0        42.4        4.64        .71
      PsychSta      Fail       10.0        10.9        -.89       -.27
     DataProc      Fail
      PsychSta      Pass        4.0         5.6       -1.65       -.69
      PsychSta      Fail       10.0        12.1       -2.10       -.60

    Maths         No
     DataProc      Pass
      PsychSta      Pass       58.0        62.6       -4.64       -.59
      PsychSta      Fail       17.0        16.1         .89        .22
     DataProc      Fail
      PsychSta      Pass       10.0         8.4        1.65        .57
      PsychSta      Fail       20.0        17.9        2.10        .50

Goodness-of-fit test statistics

    Likelihood ratio chi square =    2.43511    DF = 3    P = .487
              Pearson chi square =    2.39308    DF = 3    P = .495
```

> The final goodness-of-fit chi-square test. If there is a good fit, the test should not be significant (i.e. p-value should be > 0.05)

Output 9. Observed frequencies (OBS), expected frequencies (EXP) and residuals estimated by the final model

13.2.4 Comparison with the total independence model

The reader might wish to use the loglinear command to confirm the expected frequencies which are predicted by the total independence model.

- After inserting the factor names and values in the **Factor(s)** box as before, click the **Model** box to open the **Model** dialog box.
- In the **Specify Model** box, select the **Custom** radio button. Enter the three factor names into the **Generating Class** box by highlighting each name and clicking on the arrow under **Build Term(s)**. Within the **Build Term(s)** box, click **Interaction** and select **All 3-way**. Part of the completed dialog box is shown in Figure 4.
- Click **Continue** to return to the **Model Selection Loglinear Analysis** dialog box.
- Within the **Model Building** box, click the **Enter in single step** radio button.
- Click **OK**.

The expected frequencies for the three-way interaction (involving all the factors) will appear in a table similar to the one in Output 9. The goodness-of-fit chi-square has a value of 37.08 and a p-value less than 0.01, showing that the correspondence between these expected frequencies and the observed frequencies is very poor.

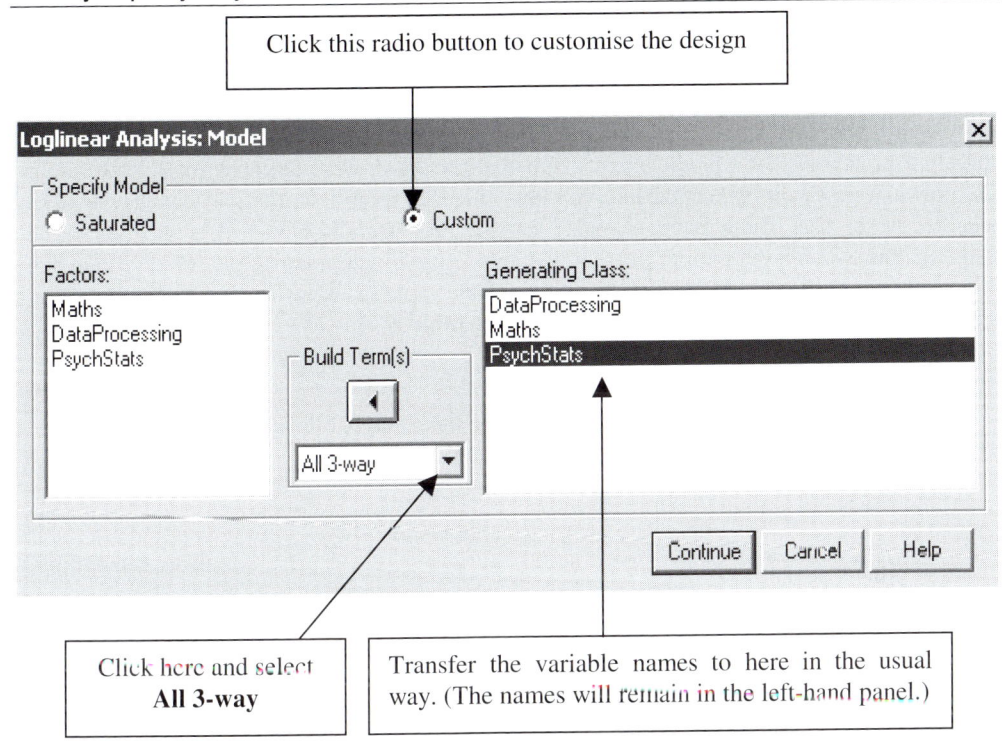

Figure 4. Part of the completed dialog box for determining the expected frequencies from the total independence model (i.e. All 3-way)

Table 2 contrasts the observed and expected cell frequencies under the assumptions of the 'best model' generated by the hierarchical loglinear command with the corresponding discrepancies under the total independence model. Clearly, the correspondence with the loglinear model is much closer. The superiority of the loglinear analysis over the traditional Pearson chi-square approach in producing a convincing interpretation of the data has been amply demonstrated.

Table 2. Observed frequencies and expected frequencies under the final loglinear model E(final) and the total independence model E(indep)

Advanced Maths	Yes				No			
Data Processing	Pass		Fail		Pass		Fail	
Psychology Statistics	Pass	Fail	Pass	Fail	Pass	Fail	Pass	Fail
Cell Freq:								
Observed	47	10	4	10	58	17	10	20
E(final)	42.4	10.9	5.6	12.1	62.6	16.1	8.4	17.9
E(indep)	36.0	17.2	12.0	5.7	53.2	25.5	17.7	8.5

13.2.5 Second example: Gender and professed helpfulness

In a study of gender and professed helpfulness, a researcher arranges for fifty men and fifty women to be presented with a scenario in which the observer would have had the opportunity to help a protagonist in a predicament. Half the interviews were taken by male interviewers, the others were taken by female interviewers. At each interview, the participant was asked whether he or she would have provided help in the circumstances. The purpose of the investigation was to determine whether the incidence of reported helping was affected by whether the interviewer and interviewee were of the same or opposite sexes. The results are shown Table 3, which is a **three-way contingency table**.

Table 3. Three-way contingency table showing the results of the gender and professed helpfulness experiment

Sex of Interviewer	Sex of Participant	Would you help? Yes	No	Total
Male	Male	4	21	25
Male	Female	16	9	25
Female	Male	11	14	25
Female	Female	11	14	25
	Total	42	68	100

Before embarking upon a loglinear analysis, it is instructive to use the **Crosstabs** procedure to explore this set of data (see Section 3.2.2). Output 10 shows the incidence of helping in male and in female participants and with male and female interviewers. It is clear from this output (and especially from the bar charts alongside) that the female participants were more inclined to help (Fisher's Exact two-tailed probability = .025) and that the incidence of helping was comparable with male and female interviewers (Fisher's Exact two-tailed probability = .840).

See Section 3.2.2

Neither of the foregoing observations, however, bears directly upon the experimenter's hypothesis, which predicted a higher incidence of helping when the participants and the interviewers were of opposite sex. This hypothesis implies an **interaction** between the factors of *Sex of Participant* and *Sex of Interviewer*; whereas, so far, we have been considering only main effects. Output 11 shows clearly that the difference between the incidence of helping in male and female participants is markedly less when the interviewer is female. Moreover, superimposed upon the general tendency for female participants to be more helpful, there is also an evident tendency for both males and females to be more helpful when the interviewer is of the opposite sex.

So far, the approach we have been taking, although affording some appreciation of the results of the experiment, has afforded no direct statistical test that would support the experimental hypothesis. Loglinear analysis, however, can provide such a test.

Multiway frequency analysis

Helpfulness in male and female participants: p = .025

Count

		Would you help?		Total
		Yes	No	
Sex of Participant	Male	15	35	50
	Female	27	23	50
Total		42	58	100

Helpfulness with male and female interviewers: p = .840

Count

		Would you help?		Total
		Yes	No	
Sex of Interviewer	Male	20	30	50
	Female	22	28	50
Total		42	58	100

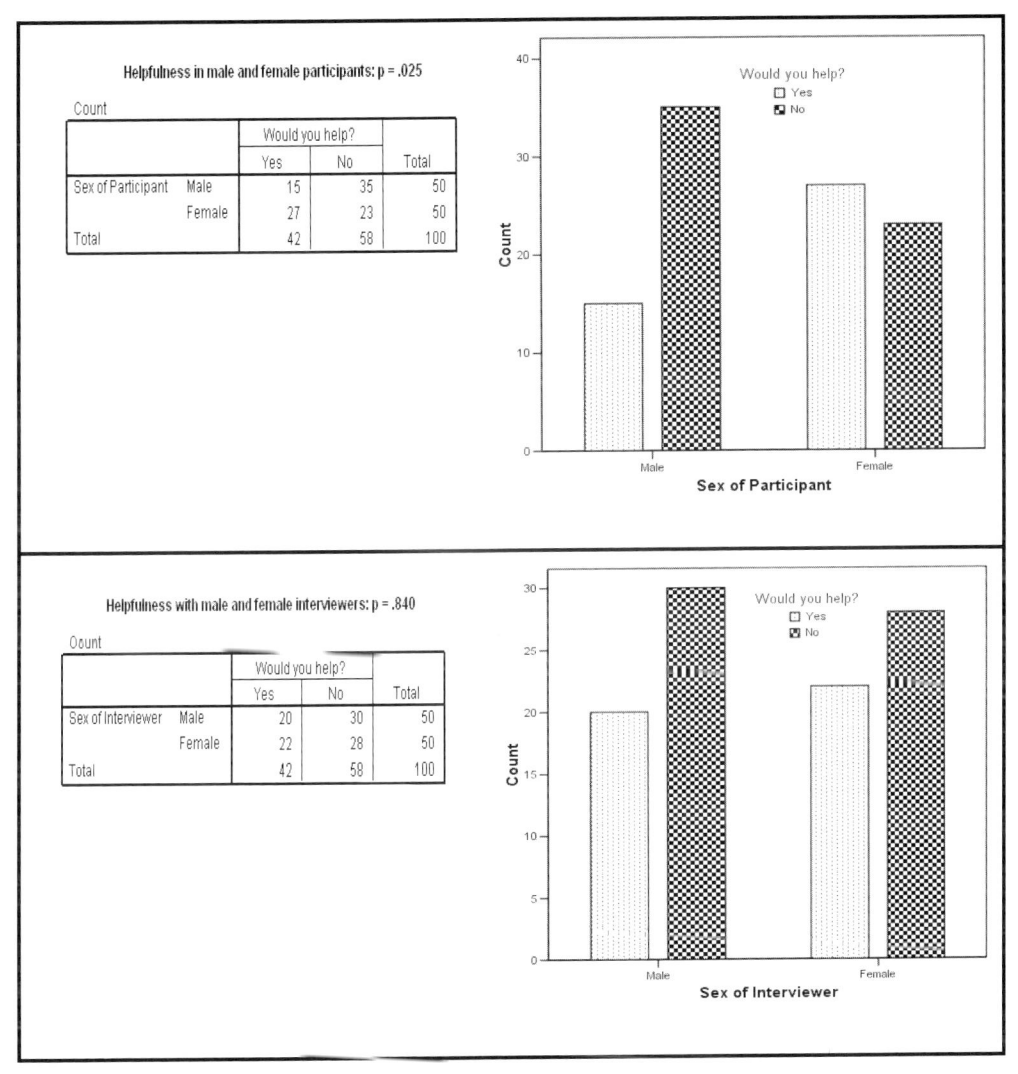

Output 10. Levels of helpfulness in male and female participants (upper row) and in male and female interviewers (lower row)

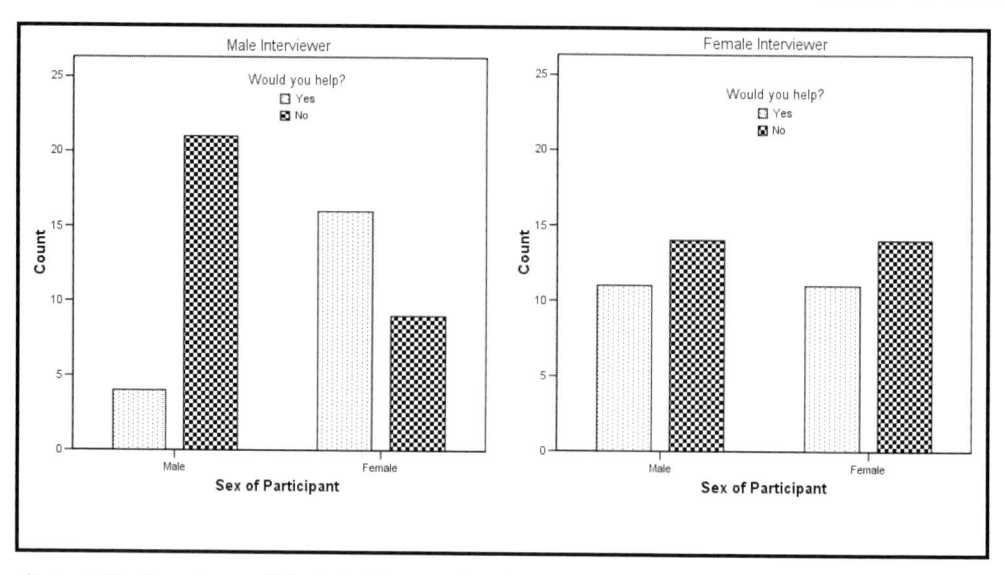

Output 11. Bar charts of the helpfulness of male and female participants with male and female interviewers showing an interaction pattern

13.2.6 Running a loglinear analysis for the Gender data

The loglinear analysis is run as follows:

- In **Variable View**, create three grouping variables: *Participant (Sex of Participant), Interviewer (Sex of Interviewer), Help (Would you help?)* and a fourth variable, *Frequency*, for the cell counts. Use the **Values** column to assign values to the code numbers, such as, for the *Help* variable, *1 = Yes, 2 = No*. The complete SPSS data set is shown in Figure 5.

	Participant	Interviewer	Help	Frequency
1	Male	Male	Yes	4
2	Male	Male	No	21
3	Male	Female	Yes	11
4	Male	Female	No	14
5	Female	Male	Yes	16
6	Female	Male	No	9
7	Female	Female	Yes	11
8	Female	Female	No	14

Figure 5. **Data View** showing the Gender data set

Multiway frequency analysis 369

- It is now necessary for this example to inform SPSS that the variable *Count* contains frequencies and not simply scores. Note that this step is not needed if the data set consists of individual cases. Choose
  Data
     Weight Cases...
  to open the **Weight Cases** dialog box and transfer the variable *Frequency* to the **Frequency Variable** box. Click **OK**.
- The next stage is to confirm that the expected frequencies are sufficiently large using the **Crosstabs** procedure as in Section 13.2.2. The output table (which we have omitted) shows that no cell has an expected frequency of less than 1, so there is no problem with low expected frequencies.

  See Section 13.2.2
- Select
  Analyze
     Loglinear
        Model Selection...
  to open the **Model Selection Loglinear Analysis** dialog box (the completed version is shown in Figure 6).

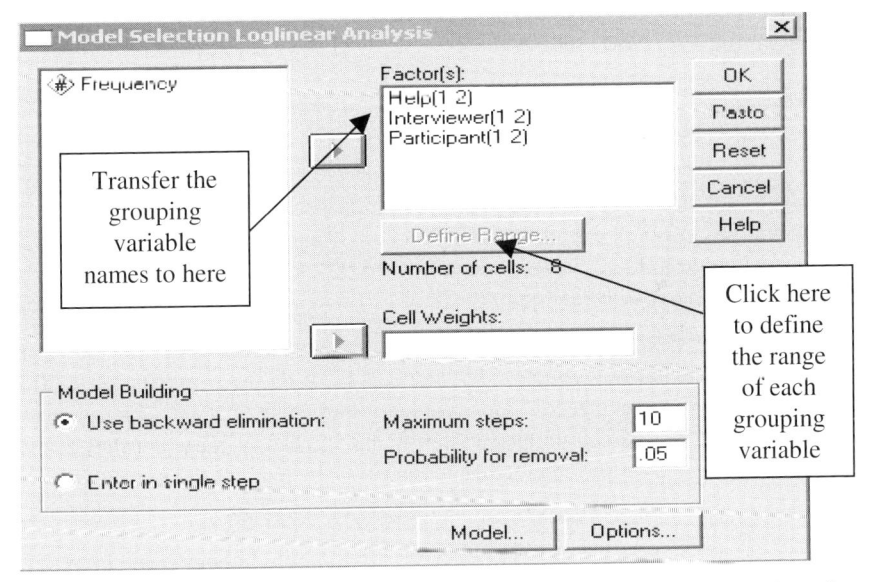

Figure 6. The completed **Model Selection Loglinear Analysis** dialog box for three factors

- Transfer the three grouping variable names *Sex of Participant*, *Sex of Interviewer* and *Would you help?* to the **Factor(s)** box (see Figure 6).
- Click **Define Range** and enter *1* into the **Minimum** box and *2* into the **Maximum** box. Click **Continue** and the names will appear with [1 2] after each of them. If some of the variables had different numbers of categories, it would have been necessary to enter the ranges separately for each variable.
- The default model is **backward elimination**. Makes sure its radio button is on.
- Click **OK**.

13.2.7 Output for the Gender loglinear analysis

The output in **SPSS Viewer** is not in the tabulated form encountered in previous Chapters. A red triangle at the foot of the output (on the left-hand side of the right-hand pane) means that there is more output to be viewed. To view the additional material, double-click the output. The surrounding box will then become a window, which can be explored by moving the cursor or by using the **Page Up** and **Page Down** keys.

The first item in the output (not shown here) contains information about the FACTORS in the experiment. Make sure that the information is consistent with the design of the experiment as we have described it: in this example, there should be three factors, each having two levels.

The next item is a table (not shown here) listing the counts (OBS count) for the combinations of the three factors. At this stage, SPSS is fitting a **saturated model**, *Sex of Interviewer × Sex of Participant × Would you help?* to the cell frequencies. This is why, in this section of the output, the observed and expected frequencies have the same values. The table, however, is useful for checking the accuracy of the data transcription.

Notice the following item.

```
Goodness-of-fit test statistics

    Likelihood ratio chi square =     .00000    DF = 0   P =  .
             Pearson chi square =     .00000    DF = 0   P =  .
```

Since the saturated model predicts the cell frequencies perfectly, the statistics have no degrees of freedom and no statistical testing is possible. Only when terms are removed from the model and residual differences (O-E) between the observed (O) and expected (E) frequencies begin to appear, can we begin to make chi-square tests.

The third item (see Output 12) is of central importance, because it lists the results of the statistical tests for the various effects. The upper part of the section lists '**Tests that K-way and higher order effects are zero**'. Here we learn that, as the pattern of frequencies graphed in Output 12 indicates, there is indeed a significant three-way (*Sex of Interviewer × Sex of Participant × Would you help?*) interaction in the row labelled 3 in the K column:

$$\text{L.R. Chisq (1)} = 6.659; p = .0099.$$

Loglinear analysis, therefore, has given us something that the traditional approach of collapsing the three-way table cannot offer: a direct test for a three-way interaction.

The lower part of the output lists the changes in **L.R. Chisq** (and **Pearson Chisq**) for effects at each level considered separately. Here, in addition to the fact that the three-way interaction term is significant, we learn that no other effect (e.g. in rows labelled 1 and 2 in column K) makes a significant contribution to the total **Likelihood Ratio Chi-Square**.

Multiway frequency analysis

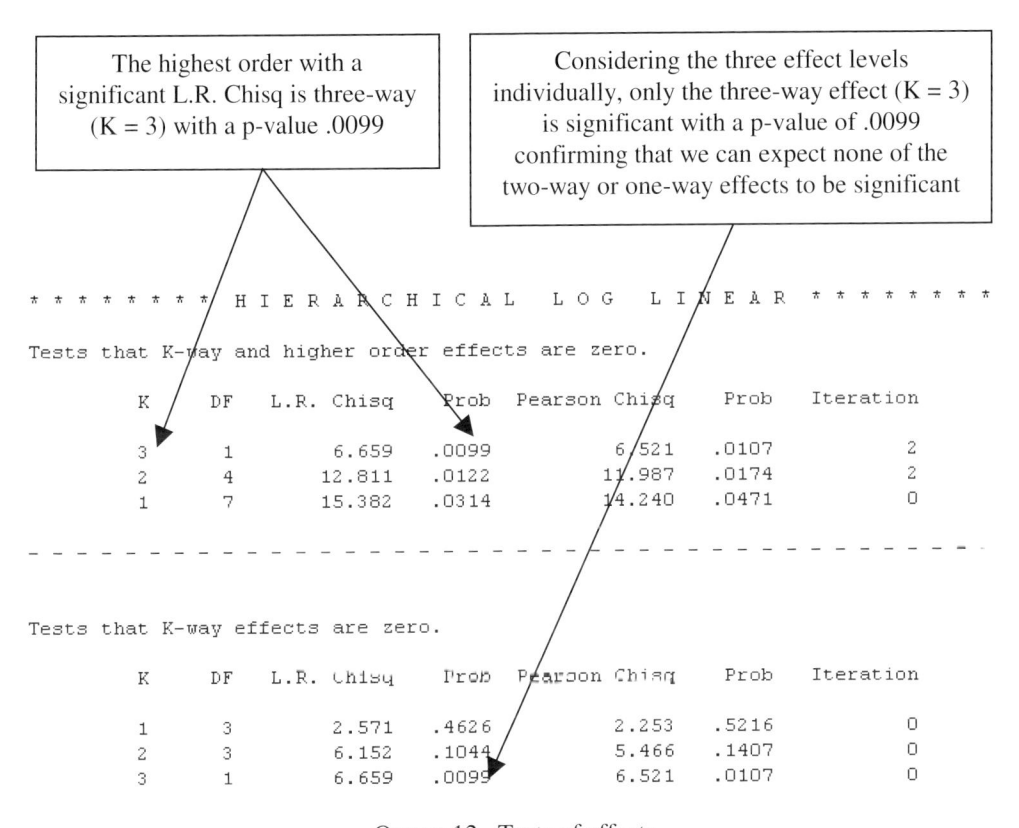

> The highest order with a significant L.R. Chisq is three-way (K = 3) with a p-value .0099

> Considering the three effect levels individually, only the three-way effect (K = 3) is significant with a p-value of .0099 confirming that we can expect none of the two-way or one-way effects to be significant

```
* * * * * * * *  H I E R A R C H I C A L   L O G   L I N E A R  * * * * * * * *

Tests that K-way and higher order effects are zero.

    K      DF    L.R. Chisq    Prob    Pearson Chisq    Prob    Iteration

    3      1        6.659     .0099        6.521       .0107        2
    2      4       12.811     .0122       11.987       .0174        2
    1      7       15.382     .0314       14.240       .0471        0

- - - - - - - - - - - - - - - - - - - - - - - - - - - - - - - - - - - - - - -

Tests that K-way effects are zero.

    K      DF    L.R. Chisq    Prob    Pearson Chisq    Prob    Iteration

    1      3        2.571     .4626        2.253       .5216        0
    2      3        6.152     .1044        5.466       .1407        0
    3      1        6.659     .0099        6.521       .0107        0
```

Output 12. Tests of effects

The fourth part of the SPSS output (Output 13) concludes that the saturated model (i.e. the three-way interaction) after just one step is the best one for the data, because removal of the interaction term would result in a significant increase in LR chi-square. This is therefore adopted as the final model.

```
Step 1

    The best model has generating class

        Particip*Intervie*Help

    Likelihood ratio chi square =    .00000    DF = 0    P = .

    The final model has generating class

        Particip*Intervie*Help
```

Output 13. The final model for the Gender and professed helpfulness data

This confirms the hypothesis that the difference between the incidence of helping in male and female participants is markedly less when the interviewer is female and that there is a tendency for both males and females to be more helpful when the interviewer is of the opposite sex.

EXERCISE 22

Loglinear analysis

Before you start

Before you proceed with this practical, please read Chapter 13.

Helping behaviour: The opposite-sex dyadic hypothesis

In the literature on helping behaviour by (and towards) men and women, there is much interest in three questions:
1. Are women more likely to receive help?
2. Are women more likely to give help?
3. Are people more likely to help members of the opposite sex?
   (This is known as the **opposite-sex dyadic hypothesis**.)

A male or female confederate of the experimenter approached male and female students who were entering a university library and asked them to participate in a survey. Table 1 shows the incidence of helping in relation to the sex of the confederate and that of the participant.

Table 1. Results of an experiment to test the opposite-sex dyadic hypothesis

Sex of Confederate	Sex of Participant	Help Yes	Help No
Male	Male	52	35
	Female	21	43
Female	Male	39	40
	Female	23	75

Preparing the SPSS data set

Prepare the data set as in Section 13.2.1 with three coding variables Confederate's Sex (*ConfedSex*), Participant's Sex (*ParticSex*), and Participant's Response (*Help*), complete with appropriately defined value labels. There will be a fourth variable (*Count*) for the cell frequencies. Remember to use the **Weight Cases** command for the cell frequency variable *count*.

Exploring the data

Before carrying out any formal analysis, a brief inspection of the contingency table (Table 1) may prove informative. First of all, we notice that, on the whole, help was more likely to be refused than given; moreover, the females helped less than did the males. In view of the generally lower rate of helping in the female participants, therefore, there seems to be little support for the hypothesis that females help more. Finally, turning to the third question, although the male participants did help the male confederate more often, the female participants tended to be more helpful towards the male confederate. This provides some support for the opposite-sex dyadic hypothesis.

Procedure for a loglinear analysis

To answer the three research questions, we shall use a **hierarchical loglinear analysis** (following the **backward elimination** strategy), with a view to fitting the most parsimonious **unsaturated model**. Run the loglinear command (ignoring the preliminary Crosstabs operation) as described in Section 13.2.2 by selecting

Analyze
> **Loglinear**
>> **Model Selection…**

to open the **Model Selection Loglinear Analysis** dialog box.

Enter the coding variables in the **Factor(s)** box and the **Range** values for each factor. In the **Model Building** box, select **Use backward elimination** (the default radio button). Click **OK**.

Output for the loglinear analysis

The main features of the output for a hierarchical loglinear analysis are described in Section 13.2.3.

Look at the table of Tests that K-way and higher order effects are zero.
- Up to what level of complexity do you expect the effects to be significant?

Now look for the effects retained in the **final model**.
- List the effects in the final model. Does the highest order of complexity correspond with what you noted in the previous bullet point question?

Finally look at the table of **Observed, Expected Frequencies and Residuals**. Compare the magnitudes of the observed (OBS) count and the expected (EXP) count assuming the final model.
- Write down the value of chi-square for the Goodness-of-fit test and its associated p-value. Does this p-value suggest a good or a bad fit?

Finally, test the hypothesis of total independence of all three variables, using the procedure described in Section 13.2.4.
- Write down the value of chi-square for the Goodness-of-fit test and its associated p-value? Does this p-value suggest a good or a bad fit?

Conclusion

It should be quite clear from the foregoing comparisons that the final loglinear model is a very considerable improvement upon the model of total independence. Loglinear models provide a powerful tool for teasing out the relationships among the variables in multi-way contingency tables.

CHAPTER 14

Discriminant analysis and logistic regression

14.1   Introduction

14.2   Discriminant analysis with SPSS

14.3   Binary logistic regression

14.4   Multinomial logistic regression

14.5   Some general points

14.1   INTRODUCTION

In Chapter 12, it was shown how the methods of regression could be used to predict scores on one dependent (or **criterion**) variable from knowledge of scores on dependent variables (known also as **regressors**). In the situations we discussed, both the dependent variable and the independent variables were always quantitative and the data were always in the form of measurements. There are circumstances, however, in which one might wish to predict, not scores on a quantitative dependent variable, but category membership.

Suppose that a premorbid blood condition has been discovered, which is suspected to arise in middle life partly because of smoking and drinking. A hundred people are tested for the presence of the condition and a record made of their smoking and alcohol consumption. Can people's levels of smoking and drinking be used to predict whether they have the blood condition?

Here, although the independent variables (smoking and alcohol consumption) are *quantitative*, the dependent variable is *qualitative*, comprising the categories *Yes* and *No*. Could we assign arbitrary code numbers to the categories (e.g. *1 = No; 2 = Yes*) and carry out a regression in the usual way? There are many problems with that approach, and it is not recommended (see, for example, Tabachnick & Fidell, 2001). The techniques that we shall describe have been specially designed to overcome these problems.

In this Chapter, we shall discuss two regression techniques that have been devised for the purpose of making predictions of category membership:
    1.   Discriminant analysis;
    2.   Logistic regression.

14.1.1 Discriminant analysis

Discriminant analysis is a technique for combining the independent variables into a single new variable, on which each participant in the study gets a score. This new variable, known as a **discriminant function**, is constructed in such a way that the participants' scores on it, to the greatest possible extent, separate, or discriminate among, those people in the different categories of the dependent variable. Ideally, if a one-way ANOVA were then to be carried out on the new scores there would be significant differences among the category means. In discriminant analysis, however, a statistic called **Wilks' lambda (Λ)** is used to test the efficacy of the discriminant function in producing significant differences among the target groups.

To express this idea a little more formally, let DV be the dependent variable, and $IV_1, IV_2, \ldots, IV_p$ be p independent variables. The purpose of discriminant analysis is to find a linear function D of the independent variables, that is, a function of the type

$$D = A + B_1(IV_1) + B_2(IV_2) + \ldots + B_p(IV_p)$$

such that people's scores on D are spread out as much as possible over the categories of the dependent variable. The function D is a **discriminant function**.

If, as in the blood condition example, the dependent variable consists of just two categories, you can imagine two overlapping bell-shaped normal distributions, each being a distribution of D for one of the categories. Each distribution of D will be centred on the mean score on D for that particular group. The discriminant function D has been constructed in such a way (by finding just the right values for the coefficients $A, B_1, \ldots, B_p$) that the two distributions are as far apart as possible.

As in multiple regression, techniques are available to help the researcher to identify those independent variables that make the greatest contributions to the prediction of the dependent variable. There are many other parallels between multiple regression and discriminant analysis.

14.1.2 Types of discriminant analysis

There are three types of discriminant analysis (DA): **direct**, **hierarchical**, and **stepwise**. In **direct DA**, all the variables enter the equations at once; in **hierarchical DA**, they enter according to a schedule set by the researcher; and in **stepwise DA**, statistical criteria alone determine the order of entry. Since in most analyses, the researcher has no reason for giving some predictors higher priority than others, the third (**stepwise**) method is the most generally used. While this approach is understandable, however, it can lead to difficulties in interpreting the results of the analysis.

14.1.3 Stepwise discriminant analysis

The statistical procedure for stepwise discriminant analysis is similar to multiple regression, in that the effect of the addition or removal of an IV is monitored by a statistical test and the result used as a basis for the inclusion of that IV in the final analysis. When there are only two groups, there is just one discriminant function. With more than two groups, however, there can be several functions (one fewer than the number of groups), although it is unusual for more than the first three discriminant functions to be statistically robust.

Various statistics are available for weighing up the addition or removal of variables from the analysis, but the most commonly used is **Wilks' Lambda (Λ)**. The significance of the change in Λ when a variable is entered or removed is obtained from an **F test**. At each step of adding a variable to the analysis, the variable with the largest F (**F TO ENTER**) is included. This process is repeated until there are no further variables with an F value greater than the critical minimum threshold value. Sometimes a variable, having been included at one point, is removed later when its F value (**F TO REMOVE**) falls below a critical level. (This can happen with the stepwise regression procedure as well – see Section 12.3.2.)

Eventually, the process of adding and subtracting variables is completed, and a summary table is shown indicating which variables were added or subtracted at each step. The variables remaining in the analysis are those used in the discriminant function(s). The next table shows which functions are statistically reliable. The first function provides the best means of predicting group membership. Later functions may or may not contribute reliably to the prediction process. Additional tables displaying the functions and their success rates for correct prediction can be requested. Plots can also be specified.

14.1.4 Restrictive assumptions of discriminant analysis

While it is assumed that the independent variables will usually be quantitative, it is also possible to include some qualitative independent variables (e.g. sex, marital status) just as it is in multiple regression.

The use of discriminant analysis, however, carries several restrictive assumptions. It is assumed, for example, that the data are **multivariate normal** (i.e. that the sampling distribution of any linear combination of predictors is normally distributed). The procedure is sufficiently robust to cope with some skewness, provided the samples are not too small. The problem of outliers, however, is more serious. It is best to remove extreme values if that can be justified. In addition, there is the usual assumption of **homogeneity of variance-covariance matrices**. It is also important to avoid **multicollinearity** (high correlations among the independent variables). In particular, no variable must be an exact linear function of any of the others, a condition known as **singularity**.

14.2 DISCRIMINANT ANALYSIS WITH SPSS

A school's vocational guidance officer would like to be able to help senior pupils to choose which subjects to study at university. Fortunately, some data are available from a project on the background interests and school-leaving examination results of architectural, engineering and psychology students. The students also filled in a questionnaire about their extra-curricular interests, including outdoor pursuits, drawing, painting, computing, and kit construction. The problem is this: can knowledge of the pupils' scores on a number of variables be used to predict their subject category at university? In this study, subject category at university (psychologists, architects or engineers) is the dependent variable, and all the others are independent variables.

14.2.1 Preparing the data set

Since the data for this example are the scores of 118 participants on ten variables, it would be extremely tedious for readers to type the data into **Data View**. The data are available on WWW at:

http://www.abdn.ac.uk/psychology/materials/spss.shtml

Select ***Ch14 Vocational guidance data*** and save it to the hard disk (or a floppy) for easier access.

A section of the data set in **Data View** is shown in Figure 1.

Case	StudySubject	Sex	ConKit	ModelKit	Drawing	Painting	Outdoor	Computing	VisModel	Quals
32	Architect	Male	4	2	7	4	2	2	4	9
33	Architect	Female	4	10	7	3	5	1	6	7
34	Psychologist	Male	2	2	0	0	1	1	2	9
35	Psychologist	Female	2	4	3	1	1	1	6	9

Figure 1. Some cases in the Vocational Guidance data set

14.2.2 Exploring the data

Before embarking on the discriminant analysis, the user should probe the data for possible violations of the underlying assumptions. A full treatment of this topic is beyond the scope of this book, but the interested reader should consult a statistical text such as Tabachnick & Fidell (2001) for more details.

Here we suggest you check for extreme scores and outliers by using the **Explore** command (see Chapter 4, Section 4.3.2) to examine the distributions of the variables within the different categories of the grouping factor (*StudySubject*)

> See Section 4.3.2

- In the **Explore** dialog box, click the **Plots** radio button in the **Display** options, and transfer the variable names of all the predictors except *Sex* into the **Dependent List** box. Transfer the variable name *Study Subject* into the **Factor List** box, and the variable name *Case Number* into the **Label Cases by** box.
- Click **OK** to plot all the boxplots and stem-and-leaf displays.

Most of the **boxplots** are satisfactory except for *Interest in Painting* (see Output 1). Here one box is much larger than the others; moreover, in the Engineers' box, the median line is positioned close to the lower side of the box, rather than centrally. There are also some outliers. (See Table 2 in Section 4.3.2 for a reminder of the layout of a boxplot.) The corresponding **stem-and-leaf** displays also show discrepancies among the distributions. Should the first run of the discriminant procedure indicate that there are problems with the data, it might be advisable to omit the independent variable *Interest in Painting*.

> See Section 4.3.2

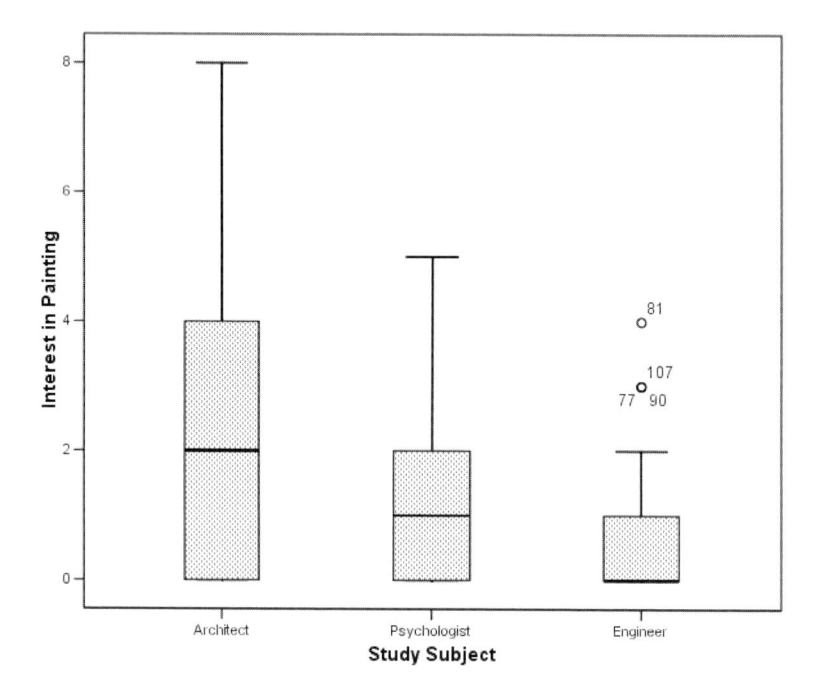

Output 1. The boxplots of *Interest in Painting* for the three subject categories

14.2.3 Running discriminant analysis

- Choose
    Analyze
       Classify (see Figure 2)
           Discriminant...
    to open the **Discriminant Analysis** dialog box, the completed version of which is shown in Figure 3.

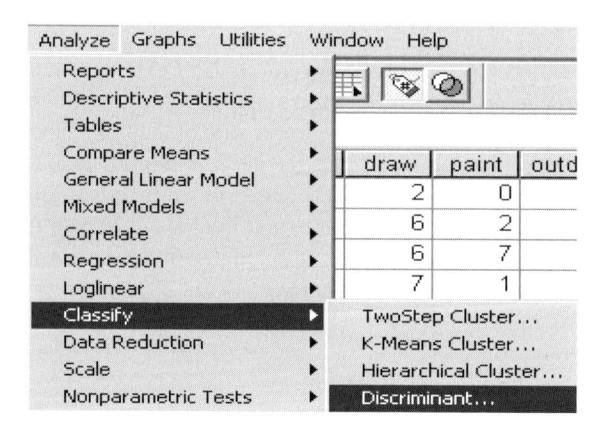

Figure 2. Finding the **Discriminant...** procedure

Discriminant analysis and logistic regression

- Transfer the dependent variable name (here it is *StudySubject*, the subject of study) to the **Grouping Variable** box. Click **Define Range** and type *1* into the **Minimum** box and *3* into the **Maximum** box.
- Drag the cursor down the names of the independent variables to highlight them and transfer them all to the **Independents** box.
- Since a stepwise analysis is going to be used, click the radio button for **Use stepwise method**.

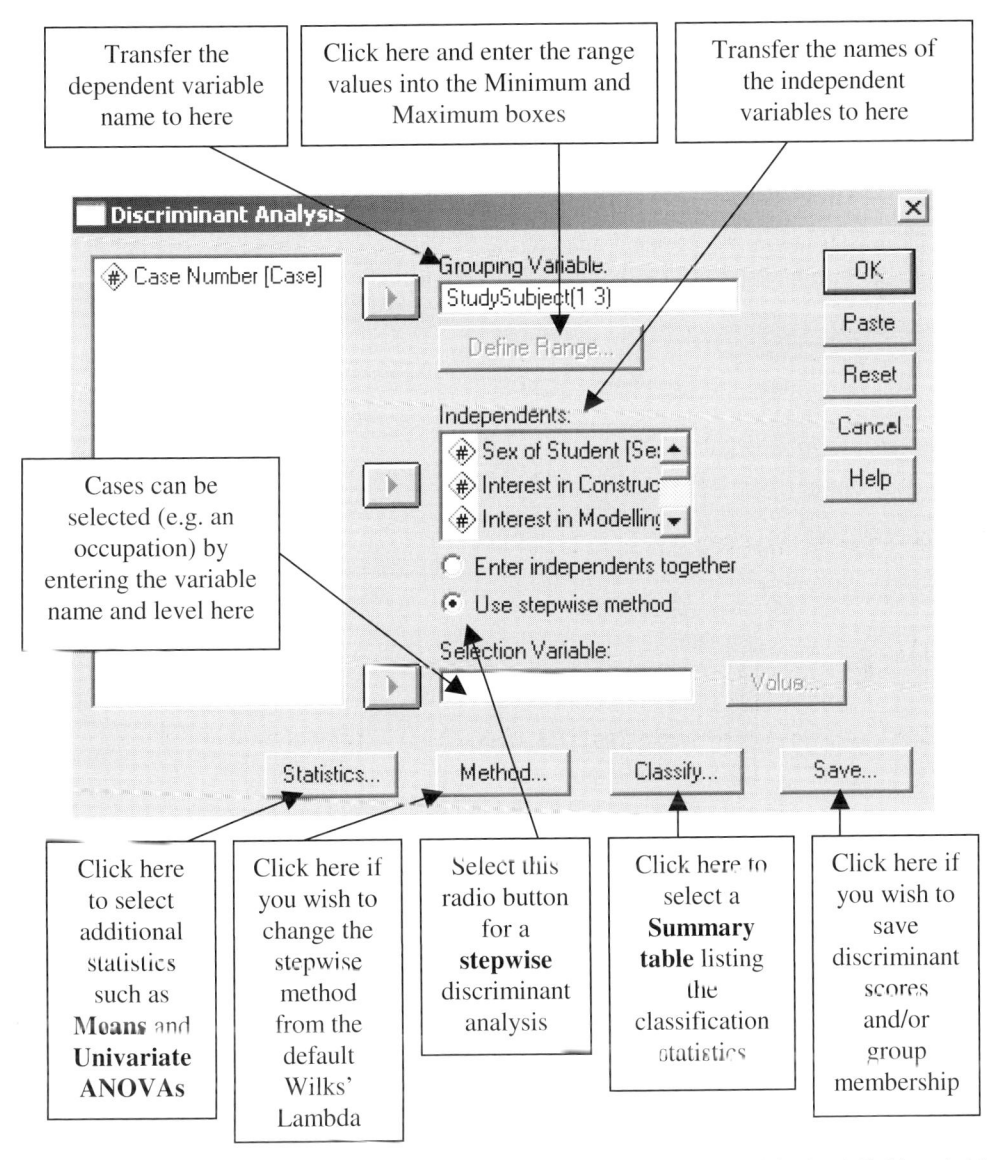

Figure 3. The **Discriminant Analysis** dialog box for the grouping variable *StudySubject* (with three levels) and several independent variables, using the **stepwise method**

- Recommended options include the means and one-way ANOVAs for each of the variables across the three levels of the independent variable. To obtain these options, click **Statistics...** and select **Means** and **Univariate ANOVAs**. Click **Continue** to return to the original dialog box.
- Another recommended option is a final summary table showing the success or failure of the analysis. Click **Classify...** and select **Summary table**. Click **Continue** to return to the original dialog box.
- In some analyses there may be a grouping variable for which just one level is of interest. It can be selected by entering the variable name and level value in the **Selection Variable** box.
- Click **OK** to run the **Discriminant Analysis**.

14.2.4 Output for discriminant analysis

The output, as listed in the left-hand pane of the **SPSS Viewer** (Output 2), is rather daunting. Fortunately, as with the regression output, not all of it is required.

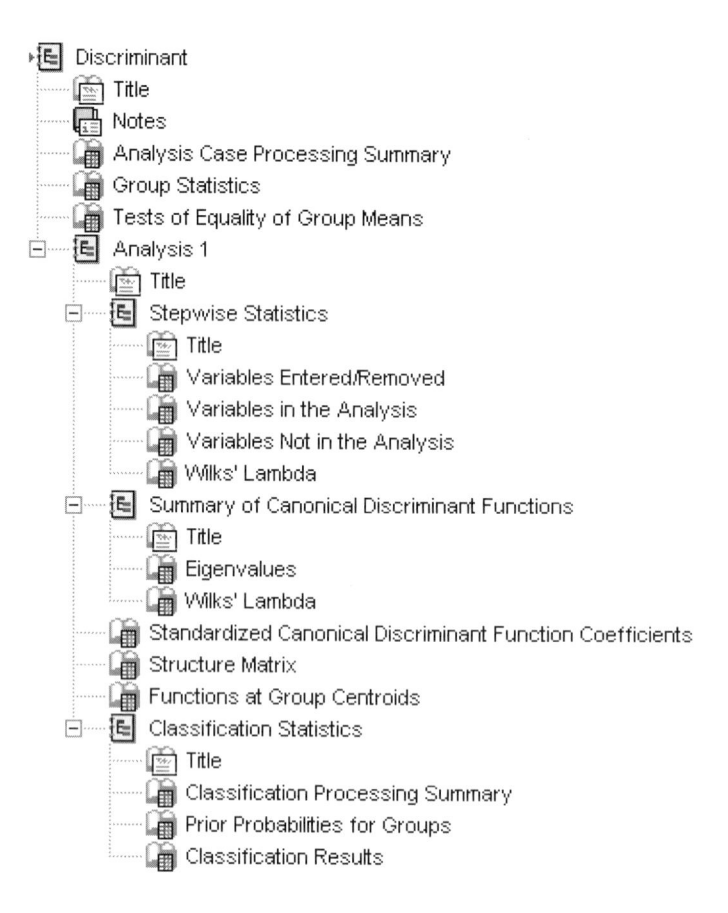

```
Discriminant
    Title
    Notes
    Analysis Case Processing Summary
    Group Statistics
    Tests of Equality of Group Means
    Analysis 1
        Title
        Stepwise Statistics
            Title
            Variables Entered/Removed
            Variables in the Analysis
            Variables Not in the Analysis
            Wilks' Lambda
        Summary of Canonical Discriminant Functions
            Title
            Eigenvalues
            Wilks' Lambda
            Standardized Canonical Discriminant Function Coefficients
            Structure Matrix
            Functions at Group Centroids
        Classification Statistics
            Title
            Classification Processing Summary
            Prior Probabilities for Groups
            Classification Results
```

Output 2. The left-hand pane of the SPSS Viewer

Discriminant analysis and logistic regression

Information about the data and the number of cases in each category of the grouping variable

Output 3 shows how many valid cases were used in the analysis. Ten cases, which were missing a score on one or more of the independent variables, have been excluded.

Analysis Case Processing Summary

Unweighted Cases		N	Percent
Valid		108	91.5
Excluded	Missing or out-of-range group codes	0	.0
	At least one missing discriminating variable	10	8.5
	Both missing or out-of-range group codes and at least one missing discriminating variable	0	.0
	Total	10	8.5
Total		118	100.0

Output 3. Information about the number of valid cases

Statistics

The next table (Output 4) is part of the **Group Statistics** table, which shows the optional statistics and the number of cases for each independent variable at each level of the grouping variable and all of them together (here only those for *Architect* are shown).

Group Statistics

Study Subject		Mean	Std. Deviation	Valid N (listwise) Unweighted
Architect	Sex of Student	1.27	.45	30
	Interest in Construction Kits	3.33	1.58	30
	Interest in Modelling Kits	3.97	2.68	30
	Interest in Drawing	5.10	2.29	30
	Interest in Painting	2.50	2.18	30
	Interest in Outdoor Pursuits	2.30	2.07	30
	Interest in Computing	1.77	1.45	30
	Ability to Visualise Model	5.53	1.25	30
	School Qualifications	6.63	2.86	30

Output 4. An edited table showing part of the optional statistics and the number of cases for each independent variable at each level of the grouping variable Study Subject

The **Univariate ANOVAs** (Output 5) show whether there is a statistically significant difference among the three grouping variable means (*StudySubject*) for each independent variable. All these differences are significant (as shown in the column **Sig.**), except *Interest in Computing* and *Interest in Modelling Kits*.

Tests of Equality of Group Means

	Wilks' Lambda	F	df1	df2	Sig.
Sex of Student	.77	15.99	2	105	.00
Interest in Construction Kits	.84	9.71	2	105	.00
Interest in Modelling Kits	.96	2.11	2	105	.13
Interest in Drawing	.90	6.09	2	105	.00
Interest in Painting	.83	10.41	2	105	.00
Interest in Outdoor Pursuits	.94	3.24	2	105	.04
Interest in Computing	1.00	.00	2	105	1.00
Ability to Visualise Model	.84	9.74	2	105	.00
School Qualifications	.88	7.38	2	105	.00

All ANOVAs are significant except those with p-value > 0.05

Output 5. Univariate ANOVAs

The summary table

The **Stepwise Statistics** section begins with a summary table (Output 6) showing which variables were entered and removed (though in this analysis none was removed), along with values of **Wilks' Lambda** and the associated probability levels. Notice the values of **F to Enter** and **F to remove** in footnotes b and c. These are the default criteria, which can be changed in the **Stepwise Method** dialog box.

Variables Entered/Removed [a,b,c,d]

		Wilks' Lambda				Exact F			
Step	Entered	Statistic	df1	df2	df3	Statistic	df1	df2	Sig.
1	Sex of Student	.77	1	2	105	16.0	2	105	.00
2	Interest in Painting	.64	2	2	105	16.0	4	208	.00
3	School Qualifications	.54	3	2	105	12.4	6	206	.00
4	Ability to Visualise Model	.48	4	2	105	11.3	8	204	.00
5	Interest in Outdoor Pursuits	.44	5	2	105	10.3	10	202	.00
6	Interest in Construction Kits	.40	6	2	105	9.59	12	200	.00
7	Interest in Computing	.37	7	2	105	8.99	14	198	.00

At each step, the variable that minimizes the overall Wilks' Lambda is entered.
a. Maximum number of steps is 18.
b. Minimum partial F to enter is 3.84.
c. Maximum partial F to remove is 2.71.
d. F level, tolerance, or VIN insufficient for further computation.

Output 6. Summary table of variables entered and removed

Discriminant analysis and logistic regression

Entering and removing variables step by step

The next table, **Variables in the Analysis**, lists the variables in the analysis at each step. Output 7 shows only Steps 1-3 and the final stage, Step 7.

Variables in the Analysis

Step		Tolerance	F to Remove	Wilks' Lambda
1	Sex of Student	1.00	15.99	
2	Sex of Student	.88	15.71	.83
	Interest in Painting	.88	10.19	.77
3	Sex of Student	.88	15.26	.70
	Interest in Painting	.85	12.34	.67
	School Qualifications	.95	9.78	.64
7	Sex of Student	.59	7.47	.43
	Interest in Painting	.73	10.92	.46
	School Qualifications	.91	10.83	.46
	Ability to Visualise Model	.90	7.96	.43
	Interest in Outdoor Pursuits	.84	3.96	.40
	Interest in Construction Kits	.80	4.33	.41
	Interest in Computing	.70	3.85	.40

Output 7. Variables in the analysis at Steps 1 to 3, and finally at Step 7

In Output 7, the column labelled **Tolerance** lists the tolerance for a variable not yet selected and is one minus the square of the multiple correlation coefficient between that variable and all the other variables already entered. Very small values suggest that a variable can contribute little to the analysis. The column **F to remove** tests the significance of the decrease in discrimination should that variable be removed. But since no F-ratio is less than the criterion of 2.71, none of the variables entered has been removed.

The table, **Variables not in the Analysis**, tabulates the variables not in the analysis at the start and at each step thereafter until the final step (Output 8 shows only Steps 0 & 1, then Step 7). It can be seen that *Sex of Student* had the highest **F to Enter** value initially (and the lowest **Wilks' Lambda**) and is, therefore, selected as the first variable to enter at Step 1 (Output 7).

At Step 1, the variable with the next highest **F to Enter** value is *Interest in Painting*, which is then entered at Step 2 as shown in Output 7. Finally at Step 7, the variables *Interest in Modelling Kits* and *Interest in Drawing* are never entered because their **F to Enter** values are smaller than the criterion of 3.84.

Variables Not in the Analysis

Step		Tolerance	Min. Tolerance	F to Enter	Wilks' Lambda	
0	Sex of Student	1.00	1.00	15.99	.77	This variable is entered at Step 1 (Output 7) with the largest **F to Enter** value
	Interest in Construction Kits	1.00	1.00	9.71	.84	
	Interest in Modelling Kits	1.00	1.00	2.11	.96	
	Interest in Drawing	1.00	1.00	6.09	.90	
	Interest in Painting	1.00	1.00	10.41	.83	
	Interest in Outdoor Pursuits	1.00	1.00	3.24	.94	
	Interest in Computing	1.00	1.00	.00	1.00	
	Ability to Visualise Model	1.00	1.00	9.74	.84	
	School Qualifications	1.00	1.00	7.38	.88	
1	Interest in Construction Kits	.93	.93	3.43	.72	This variable is entered at Step 2 (Output 7) with the largest **F to Enter** value
	Interest in Modelling Kits	.94	.94	2.20	.74	
	Interest in Drawing	1.00	1.00	6.04	.69	
	Interest in Painting	.88	.88	10.19	.64	
	Interest in Outdoor Pursuits	.98	.98	1.49	.75	
	Interest in Computing	.75	.75	4.20	.71	
	Ability to Visualise Model	1.00	1.00	8.83	.66	
	School Qualifications	.98	.98	7.69	.67	
7	Interest in Modelling Kits	.72	.57	.36	.37	
	Interest in Drawing	.63	.52	.91	.37	

These variables at Step 7 are excluded because their **F to Enter** values are < 3.84

Output 8. Part of the table of variables not in the analysis at Steps 0, 1 and 7

The next table in the output, **Wilks' Lambda**, is a repeat of the table given in Output 5 and is not reproduced.

Statistics of the discriminant functions

Output 9 shows the percentage (**% of Variance**) of the variance accounted for by each discriminant function and how many of them (if any) are significant (see the **Sig.** column in the **Wilks' Lambda** table). Here we see that both functions are highly significant.

Summary of Canonical Discriminant Functions

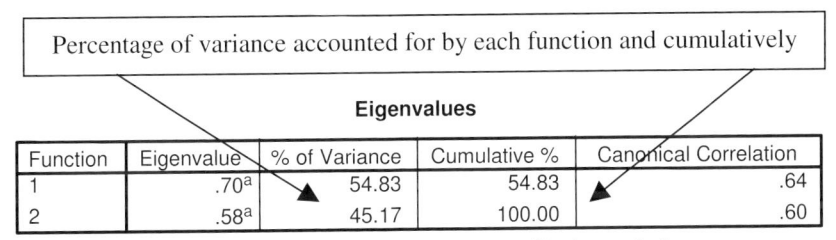

Percentage of variance accounted for by each function and cumulatively

Eigenvalues

Function	Eigenvalue	% of Variance	Cumulative %	Canonical Correlation
1	.70[a]	54.83	54.83	.64
2	.58[a]	45.17	100.00	.60

a. First 2 canonical discriminant functions were used in the analysis.

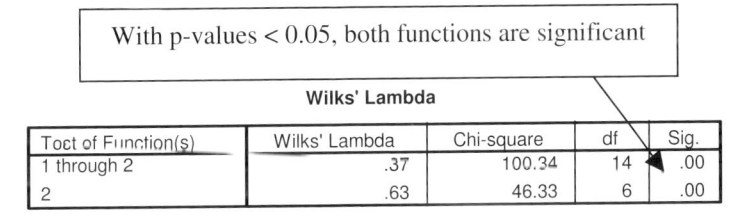

With p-values < 0.05, both functions are significant

Wilks' Lambda

Test of Function(s)	Wilks' Lambda	Chi-square	df	Sig.
1 through 2	.37	100.34	14	.00
2	.63	46.33	6	.00

Output 9. Statistics of the discriminant functions

Standardised coefficients and within groups correlations with discriminants

Two tables follow in the listing, the first (not reproduced here) being the **Standardized Canonical Discriminant Function Coefficients**, and the second (Output 10) the **Structure Matrix**, which is a table of pooled within groups correlations between the independent variables and the discriminant functions.

Structure Matrix

	Function 1	Function 2
Ability to Visualise Model	-.51*	-.10
School Qualifications	.43*	-.16
Interest in Painting	-.42*	.36
Interest in Drawing [a]	-.22*	.12
Interest in Modelling Kits [a]	-.12*	.07
Interest in Computing	.01*	.00
Sex of Student	.19	.70*
Interest in Construction Kits	-.15	-.54*
Interest in Outdoor Pursuits	.19	.25*

Pooled within-groups correlations between discriminating variables and standardized canonical discriminant functions
Variables ordered by absolute size of correlation within function.

* Largest absolute correlation between each variable and any discriminant function

a. This variable not used in the analysis.

Output 10. The structure matrix

It is clear from the information in Output 10 that the first function is contributed to positively by participants' school qualifications and their interest in painting, and negatively by their ability to visualise models. The second function is contributed to positively by sex and negatively by interest in construction kits, and in outdoor pursuits. The asterisks mark the correlations with the higher value for each variable.

The next table in the output (not reproduced), **Functions at Group Centroids**, lists the within-group means for each canonical variable by group (i.e. Architect, Psychologist, Engineer).

Success of predictions of group membership

The optional selection of **Summary table** from the **Classify** options in the **Discriminant Analysis** dialog box provides an indication of the success rate for predictions of membership of the criterion grouping variable's categories using the discriminant functions developed in the analysis (see Output 11). The footnote to the table indicates that the overall success rate is 72.2%.

Classification Results[a]

	Study Subject	Architect	Psychologist	Engineer	Total
Count	Architect	22	2	6	30
	Psychologist	4	25	8	37
	Engineer	5	5	31	41
%	Architect	73.3	6.7	20.0	100.0
	Psychologist	10.8	67.6	21.6	100.0
	Engineer	12.2	12.2	75.6	100.0

a. 72.2% of original grouped cases correctly classified.

Output 11. Classification results

Output 11 also shows that the *Engineers* were the most accurately classified, with 75.6% of the cases correct. The *Architects* were next with 73.3%. The *Psychologists* were the least accurately classed, with a success rate of 67.6%. Notice also that incorrectly classified *Architects* were more likely to be classified as *Engineers* than as *Psychologists*, and that incorrectly classified *Psychologists* are more likely to be classified as *Engineers* than as *Architects*!

14.2.5 Predicting group membership

Section 14.2 posed the question of whether knowledge of pupils' scores on a number of variables could be used to predict their subjects of study at university. The analysis has demonstrated that two discriminant functions can be generated using all the variables except *Interest in Modelling Kits* and *Interest in Drawing*, and that these functions can predict 72.2% of the cases correctly. So far, however, we have not seen what the predicted subject of study was for any particular individual. Moreover, the vocational guidance officer in our example wants to make predictions of the subjects that future students will eventually take, given knowledge of their scores on the same independent variables. It is easy to do either or both of these things with the **Discriminant** procedure.

To compare the actual subject of study with the predicted subject of study, proceed as follows:
- Complete the **Discriminant Analysis** dialog box as before but, in addition, click **Save...** and then click the radio button for **Predicted group membership**. Click **Continue** and **OK**.
- The predicted group membership will appear in a new column labelled **Dis_1** in **Data View**, along with the predictions for all the other cases.
- We suggest that you actually try this and, once **Dis_1** appears in **Data View**, switch to **Variable View** and rename the variable *PredictDiscrim*. Figure 4 is a section from **Data View** showing some of the predictions of choice of subject from the discriminant analysis.

To predict the subject of study for a future student, proceed as follows:
- Enter the data for the potential students at the end of the data in **Data View**. Leave the grouping variable (*StudySubject*) blank or enter an out-of-range number so that the analysis does not include these cases when it is computing the discriminant functions.
- Then after completing the steps described above, the predicted group membership will appear in a new column labelled *PredictDiscrim* in **Data View**, along with the predictions for all the other cases.

Case	StudySubject	Sex	ConKit	ModelKit	Drawing	Painting	Outdoor	Computing	VicModel	Quals	PredictDiscrim
96	Engineer	Male	4	2	4	0	2	1	4	7	Engineer
97	Engineer	Male	3	2	2	0	0	2	4	0	Architect
98	Engineer	Male	4	1	5	1	0	2	7	7	Architect
99	Engineer	Female	1	0	0	0	6	0	2	6	Psychologist
100	Engineer	Male	6	2	2	0	4	2	4	7	Engineer
101	Engineer	Female	4	2	5	1	4	1	4	9	Psychologist

Figure 4. Section of **Data View** showing the predictions from discriminant analysis of choice of main university subject

14.3 BINARY LOGISTIC REGRESSION

14.3.1 Introduction

Logistic regression is another approach to category prediction, which carries fewer assumptions than does discriminant analysis. Moreover, with logistic regression, any number of qualitative predictors such as gender can be included in the regression. For these reasons, it is fast overtaking discriminant analysis as the preferred technique for this kind of research problem. Returning to the example of the premorbid blood condition mentioned at the start of this Chapter, suppose that of the hundred people studied, forty-four people have the condition and fifty-six do not. Let us assign code numbers to the two categories: to those who have the condition, we assign 1; and to those who do not, we assign 0. In this section, we shall outline the use of logistic regression to predict category membership.

On the basis of the foregoing information, a prediction of category membership can be made without doing any regression at all. Since the probability that a person selected at random having the condition is 44/100 = .44 (44%) and not having the condition is 56/100 = .56

(56%), our best prediction of category membership for any particular person is to assign them to the 'condition absent' category. If we do that, we shall be right in 100% of the cases in which the condition was absent, but wrong in the 44% of cases in which the condition was present, giving us a net success rate of 56% over the hundred assignments. The purpose of logistic regression is to improve upon this success rate by exploiting any association between the dependent and independent variables to predict category membership (the dependent variable) with the greatest possible accuracy.

It is not an unreasonable assumption that, although an individual may or may not have the premorbid blood condition, certain variables such as number of cigarettes smoked and amount of drink consumed actually increase the probability of developing the condition **continuously** throughout the range of consumption. This probability, however, cannot be expected to be a linear function of the independent variables. In fact, the probability of the condition is likely to rise more rapidly as scores on the independent variable begin to increase and less rapidly at a later stage, so that the probability graph would be rather like a flattened S (See Figure 5).

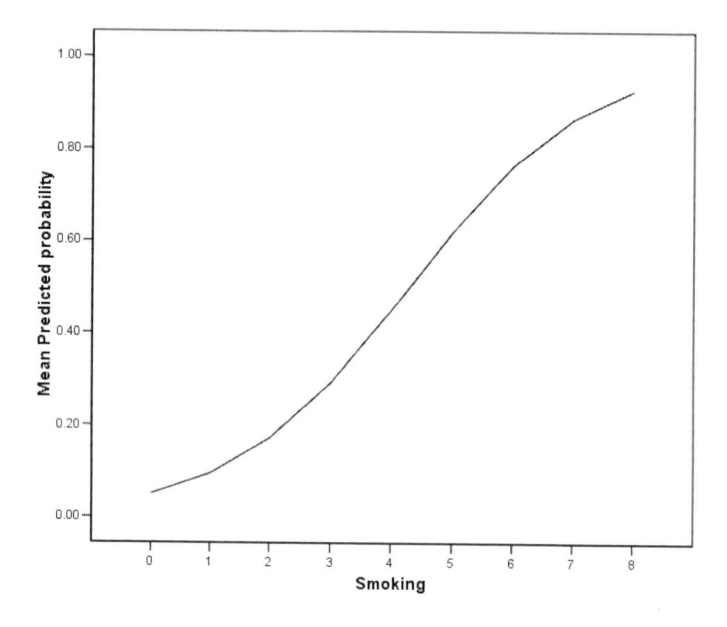

Figure 5. A logistic regression function, giving the estimated probability of a person smoking a certain number of cigarettes having the premorbid blood condition

An estimate of this curve is called the **logistic regression function**, which expresses the probability of the premorbid blood condition in terms of the number of cigarettes smoked and alcohol consumption. On the basis of the number of cigarettes that a person smokes and the amount that they drink, that person is assigned a probability by the logistic regression function.

These probability estimates can be used to assign individuals to either of the two categories of the dependent variable. First, a criterion probability is set, above which an individual will be assigned to the condition-present category. When the value of the probability estimate (from the logistic regression function) for a particular participant exceeds .5, that participant is

Discriminant analysis and logistic regression 389

assigned to the group with the premorbid blood condition; if the probability is less than .5, the participant is assigned to the other category.

Recall that in **multiple regression**, the dependent variable Y is predicted from the p independent variables $X_1, X_2, \ldots, X_p$ by means of the regression equation

$$Y' = B_0 + B_1 X_1 + B_2 X_2 + \ldots + B_p X_p$$

where B_0 is the regression constant and $B_1, B_2, \ldots$ are the regression coefficients.

The logistic regression function, although itself nonlinear, also involves a linear function Z of the independent variables, where

$$Z = B_0 + B_1 X_1 + B_2 X_2 + \ldots + B_p X_p \quad \text{-----} \quad (1)$$

The logistic regression function itself is

$$p = \frac{e^Z}{1 + e^Z}$$

where p is the probability that a person will have the premorbid blood condition and Z is the function defined in (1).

In logistic regression, as in ordinary multiple regression, the values of the parameters B_0, B_1, ..., B_p are chosen so that the logistic regression equation predicts the independent variable (in this case category membership) as accurately as possible.

Binary and multinomial logistic regression

When the dependent variable consists of only two categories, the technique known as **binary logistic regression** is applicable; when there are three or more categories, **multinomial logistic regression** is the appropriate choice (see Section 14.4).

14.3.2 An example of a binary logistic regression with quantitative independent variables

For our first example, we return to the data set on the premorbid blood condition, smoking and drinking. In this data set, both independent variables (IVs) are quantitative and in the form of measurements. Later, we shall consider examples with qualitative, categorical independent variables. While both binary and multinomial logistical regression can cope happily with categorical independent variables, such IVs must be clearly identified as such; moreover, the manner in which this is done is somewhat different in the two procedures.

Table 1 shows the first eight cases from some data on the incidence of a premorbid blood condition in 100 people, together with their average daily smoking levels and alcohol consumption. (The complete data set is given at the end of this Chapter.) The units have been selected to cover the entire range of consumption for each variable: one smoking unit is five cigarettes; one drinking unit is the equivalent of half a glass of wine or a quarter-pint of beer.

Table 1. The first eight cases in a hypothetical set of data showing the presence or absence of a blood condition along with their smoking and drinking habits

Case	Blood	Smoke	Alcohol	Case	Blood	Smoke	Alcohol
1	Yes	8	17	5	Yes	8	15
2	Yes	8	15	6	Yes	8	18
3	Yes	8	16	7	Yes	8	18
4	Yes	8	16	8	No	8	15

14.3.3 The importance of exploring the data

As usual, we recommend a thorough exploration of the data set with familiar statistics (e.g. correlations – see Section 11.2) before embarking upon any sophisticated multivariate method. For example, the correlation procedure will show that while category membership correlates substantially and significantly with the smoking variable, it does not correlate with the level of alcohol consumption. Moreover, smoking and alcohol consumption turn out not to be significantly correlated.

See Section 11.2

Correlations

		Blood Condition	Smoking	Alcohol
Blood Condition	Pearson Correlation	1	.622**	-.188
	Sig. (2-tailed)		.000	.062
	N	100	100	100
Smoking	Pearson Correlation	.622**	1	.140
	Sig. (2-tailed)	.000		.164
	N	100	100	100
Alcohol	Pearson Correlation	-.188	.140	1
	Sig. (2-tailed)	.062	.164	
	N	100	100	100

**. Correlation is significant at the 0.01 level (2-tailed).

Output 12. Correlations among category membership (presence or absence of the premorbid blood condition), amount of smoking and level of alcohol consumption

As with any other multiple regression procedure, logistic regression is most likely to be successful if there are low or insignificant correlations among the regressors or IVs.

14.3.4 Preparing the data set

The data set for this example is large, and it would be extremely tedious to type it into **Data View**. The set *Ch14 Blood, smoking & alcohol data* is available on WWW at:

http://www.abdn.ac.uk/psychology/materials/spss.shtml

Discriminant analysis and logistic regression

14.3.5 Running binary logistic regression

In its logistic regression dialog box, SPSS uses the term **covariate** for independent variables in the form of quantitative measurements. In this example, both IVs are quantitative.

- Choose
  Analyze
     Regression
        Binary Logistic ...
  to open the **Logistic Regression dialog box** (Figure 6).

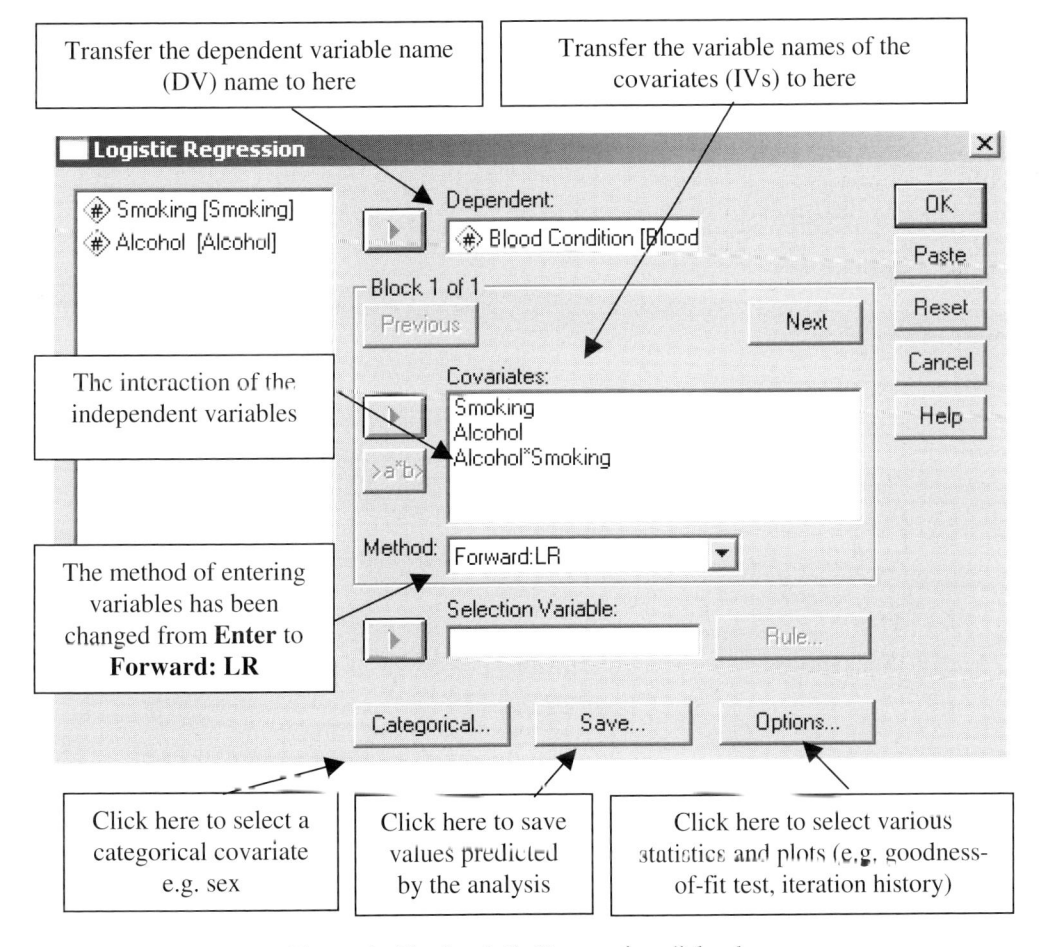

Figure 6. The **Logistic Regression** dialog box

- Transfer the dependent variable name *Blood Condition* to the **Dependent** box, and the covariate (i.e. independent variable IV) names *Smoking* and *Alcohol* to the **Covariate** box.

Notice the button labelled >a*b> underneath the transfer arrow outside the **Covariates** box. This is the **interaction button**. It is worth exploring whether the effects of one IV are compounded by the effects of the other IV, so we shall include an interaction term in the model.

- Click *Smoking* again from the left-hand box (not the **Covariates** box), press the keyboard's **Ctrl** key and, keeping the **Ctrl** key held down, click *Alcohol*. The interaction button will now be enabled. Click the interaction button to transfer the interaction term to the **Covariates** box, where it will now appear as **Alcohol*Smoking**.
- The default **Method** is **Enter** but we recommend using **Forward: LR**. Click the arrow on the right of the **Method** box and select **Forward: LR**. This method will show clearly which variables are entered into the analysis and which are finally excluded.
- We recommend selecting some optional statistics and displays. Click **Options...** to obtain the **Options** dialog box (Figure 7). Select **Hosmer-Lemeshow goodness-of-fit** and **Iteration history**. Click **Continue** to return to the **Logistic Regression** dialog box.
- Click **OK**.

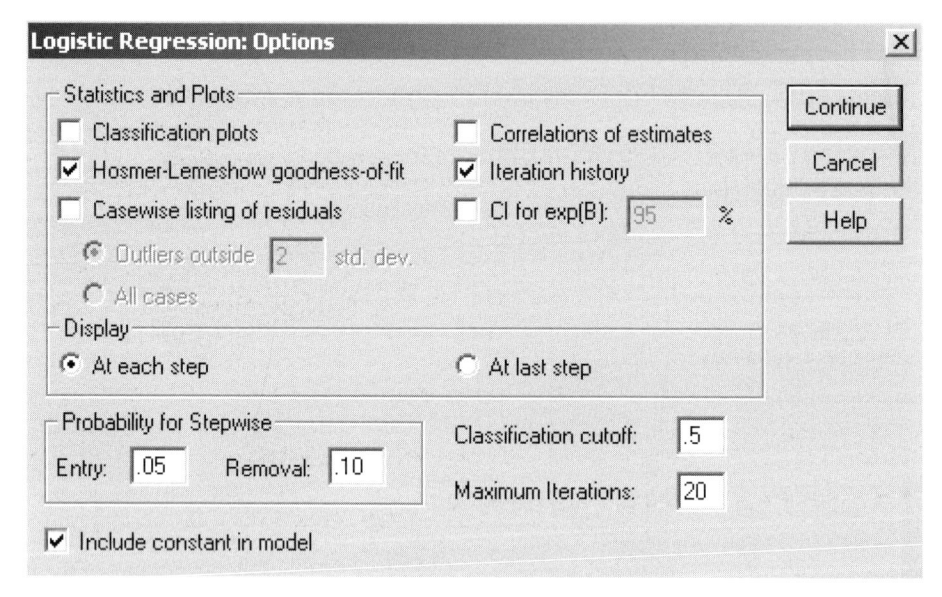

Figure 7. The **Options** dialog box with **Hosmer-Lemeshow goodness-of-fit** and **Iteration history** selected

The logistic regression procedure maximises its predictions of category membership by a highly computer-intensive process of successive approximations called **iterations**. If all goes well, the estimates converge (i.e. become progressively closer) to constant values, which are taken to be the best estimates. By choosing the item **Iteration history** in the **Options**, you can check that the successive iterations really did converge. Beware that an analysis of a data set with many variables may take some time to complete. Failure to converge may occur if some of the variables are highly correlated (the **multicollinearity** problem); the solution is to delete one or more redundant variables from the analysis.

In the **Logistic Regression** dialog box, there is another button labelled **Save...** which accesses the **Save New Variables** dialog box (not shown). Selecting items from this box will add several new variables to those already in **Data View**, including **Probabilities** and **Group membership** from the **Predicted Values** selection section, and **Standardized** and

Discriminant analysis and logistic regression 393

Studentized from the **Residuals** selection section. We suggest that, for the present, the reader should focus on the basic regression and experiment with the **Save...** button options later.

14.3.6 Output for binary logistic regression

The output for logistic regression is extensive, even if no options are selected. In this section, we shall describe some of the most useful items. First, however, some preliminary points are in order.

In logistic regression, pivotal use is made of a statistic called **log likelihood** which is written variously as **−2 log(likelihood)**, **−2LL**, or **−2LogL**. This statistic behaves as chi-square, and has a large value when a model fits poorly, and a small value when the model fits well. The **log likelihood** statistic is analogous to the error sum of squares in multiple regression: the larger its value, the more the variance that remains to be accounted for.

In the introduction, we saw that the best bet of a person's category membership was the more frequently occurring category (i.e. not having the premorbid blood condition). The first two tables (not shown here) are a **Case Processing Summary** table specifying how many cases were selected and a **Dependent Variable Encoding** table tabulating the two levels of the dependent variable (here they are *No* and *Yes*).

Next there is a block of tables called **Block 0: Beginning Block** in which the logistic regression procedure begins with a model with neither of the dependent variables present (i.e. a 'no regression' model). This guessing stage is called **Step 0** by SPSS. Included in this block is a **Classification Table** (see Output 13) in which the Observed and Predicted values of *Blood Condition* are the same. There are no surprises here: we already knew that the success rate without any regression is 56%. Three other tables in Block 0 (not shown here) tabulate the **Iteration history**, **Variables in the Equation** and the **Variables not in the Equation**.

Classification Table [a,b]

			Predicted		
			Blood Condition		
	Observed		No	Yes	Percentage Correct
Step 0	Blood Condition	No	56	0	100.0
		Yes	44	0	.0
	Overall Percentage				56.0

a. Constant is included in the model.
b. The cut value is .500

Output 13. The 'no regression' classification table

The next block of tables of output is headed **Block 1: Method = Forward Stepwise (Likelihood Ratio)** confirming our choice of method selected in the **Logistic Regression** dialog box (Figure 6). This block contains some very interesting information. The first item is the **Iteration history** (this is provided because **Iteration history** was selected as an option in Figure 7), showing convergence of the estimates towards fixed values after five iterations for Step 1 and seven iterations for Step 2 (Output 14). Notice that at **Step 1**, *Smoking* was the first variable selected and then at **Step 2**, *Alcohol* was added. The interaction *Alcohol*Smoking* was never added.

Iteration History[a,b,c,d,e]

Iteration		-2 Log likelihood	Coefficients		
			Constant	Smoking	Alcohol
Step 1	1	94.933	-2.258	.477	
	2	91.805	-3.125	.646	
	3	91.662	-3.364	.691	
	4	91.662	-3.379	.694	
	5	91.662	-3.379	.694	
Step 2	1	84.827	-.915	.507	-.135
	2	75.184	-.964	.799	-.262
	3	71.727	-.812	1.079	-.400
	4	70.934	-.713	1.287	-.504
	5	70.884	-.691	1.356	-.537
	6	70.883	-.689	1.361	-.540
	7	70.883	-.689	1.361	-.540

a. Method: Forward Stepwise (Likelihood Ratio)

b. Constant is included in the model.

c. Initial -2 Log Likelihood: 137.186

d. Estimation terminated at iteration number 5 because parameter estimates changed by less than .001.

e. Estimation terminated at iteration number 7 because parameter estimates changed by less than .001.

Output 14. The Iteration History table showing that *Smoking* was the first variable to be included at Step 1 and then *Alcohol* at Step 2

The **Model Summary** table (Output 15) includes two statistics which are similar to the coefficient of determination (R^2) in ordinary least-squares regression. The **Cox & Snell R Square** is based on the log likelihood for the model compared with the log likelihood for a baseline model. The **Nagelkerke R Square** is an adjusted version of the Cox & Snell R^2. It adjusts the scale of the statistic to cover the full range from 0 to 1. The size of R^2 (65% after Step 2) indicates that the model contributes powerfully to the prediction of the presence or absence of the blood condition.

Model Summary

Step	-2 Log likelihood	Cox & Snell R Square	Nagelkerke R Square
1	91.662[a]	.366	.490
2	70.883[b]	.485	.649

a. Estimation terminated at iteration number 5 because parameter estimates changed by less than .001.

b. Estimation terminated at iteration number 7 because parameter estimates changed by less than .001.

Output 15. The Model Summary table showing various measures of R Square

Output 16 shows the **Hosmer and Lemeshow Test** of the model's goodness-of-fit. The small value of chi-square and high p-value mean that the model fits the data well. Remember that for a good fit, you want a low, insignificant value for chi-square.

Hosmer and Lemeshow Test

Step	Chi-square	df	Sig.
1	3.295	7	.856
2	7.016	8	.535

Output 16. The Hosmer and Lemeshow Test of the model's goodness-of-fit

This table is followed by a **Contingency Table for Hosmer and Lemeshow Test** (not shown here).

Next is the **Classification Table** (Output 17). When the full model is applied, the success rate increases from 56% to 81%, which is an enormous improvement on the 'no regression' predictions.

Classification Table[a]

			Predicted		
			Blood Condition		Percentage Correct
Observed			No	Yes	
Step 1	Blood Condition	No	44	12	78.6
		Yes	10	34	77.3
	Overall Percentage				78.0
Step 2	Blood Condition	No	45	11	80.4
		Yes	8	36	81.8
	Overall Percentage				81.0

a. The cut value is .500

Output 17. The Classification Table showing that after Step 2, the rate for predicting the premorbid blood condition rises to 81%

Testing the individual components of the model

Output 18 shows the increases in the **log likelihood** statistic as the variables *Smoking* and then *Alcohol* are removed from the model. It is clear that each would have a significant effect if they were to be removed. Note that the interaction *Alcohol*Smoking* is not included since this interaction was never included in the model.

Model if Term Removed

Variable		Model Log Likelihood	Change in -2 Log Likelihood	df	Sig. of the Change
Step 1	Smoking	-68.593	45.524	1	.000
Step 2	Smoking	-66.824	62.765	1	.000
	Alcohol	-45.831	20.778	1	.000

Output 18. Tests of the significance of the model's individual components

The remaining tables (not shown here) include **Variables in the Equation** and **Variables not in the Equation** for each **Step**, the latter showing that the interaction *Alcohol by Smoking* was never included.

We can conclude on the basis of the results of this binary logistic regression that smoking and alcohol consumption both independently increase the incidence of the premorbid blood condition and that 81% of the premorbid conditions (yes or no) could have been predicted using the equation of the model.

14.3.7 Binary logistic regression with categorical independent variables

Neither binary nor multinomial regression has any problems with categorical independent variables: in fact, all the independent variables can be qualitative, as the following example will illustrate.

In Chapter 13, we described an experiment on gender and professed helpfulness, in which participants were asked by a male or female interviewer whether they would be prepared to help in a certain situation. The results are reproduced in Table 2.

Incidence of helping by male and female participants with male and female interviewers

Count

Sex of Interviewer			Would you help? Yes	Would you help? No	Total
Male	Sex of Participant	Male	4	21	25
		Female	16	9	25
	Total		20	30	50
Female	Sex of Participant	Male	11	14	25
		Female	11	14	25
	Total		22	28	50

Table 2. Three-way contingency table showing the results of the Gender and professed helpfulness experiment

Discriminant analysis and logistic regression

In Chapter 13, we saw that a **loglinear analysis** of these data confirmed the presence of a three-way interaction of all three dimensions of the contingency table: *Sex of Participant*; *Sex of Interviewer* and *Would you help?* The same research question can also be approached by using binary logistic regression. Since the purpose of the present analysis is to test the components of the model of significance, we shall not concern ourselves with the accuracy with which the final model predicts whether help will be given. For present purposes, we are only interested in the tests for the significance of the various factors.

With the file *Ch13 Helping* in the **Data Editor**, proceed as follows.
- Choose
   Analyze
      Regression
         Binary Logistic ...
   to open the **Logistic Regression** dialog box (the completed box is shown in Figure 8).

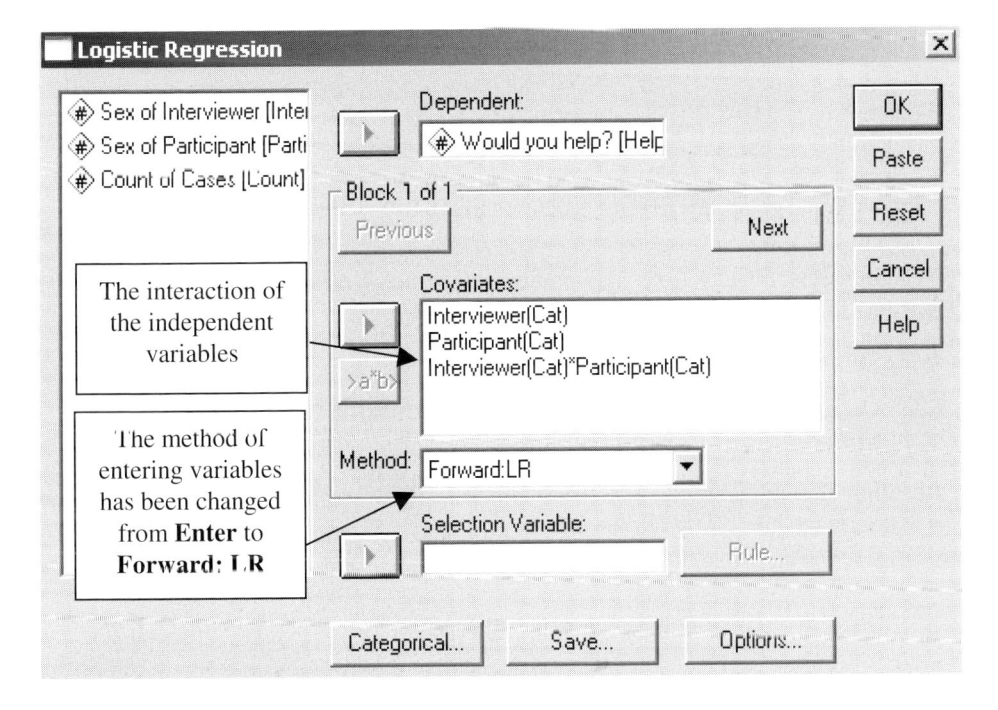

Figure 8. The **Logistic Regression** dialog box showing that the independent variables have been registered as categorical (they have **Cat** in brackets) which occurs after defining them as categorical in the **Define Categorical Variables** dialog box (see Figure 9)

- Transfer the dependent variable name *Would you help?* to the **Dependent** box, and the independent variables (covariates) *Sex of Participant* and *Sex of Interviewer* to the **Covariate** box. Use the **Ctrl** key to select both variables and press the interaction button >a*b> to transfer the *Interviewer×Participant* interaction to the **Covariates** box.
- Click the arrow on the right of the **Method** box and select **Forward: LR**.
- At this point the **Categorical...** will have become active. Press it to see a dialog box labelled **Define Categorical Variables** (see Figure 9). Transfer the names *Participant* and

Interviewer to the **Categorical Covariates:** box. The default type of **Contrast** is **Indicator** which is a contrast registering the presence or absence of a category membership (here it would be *Female* and *Not Female*). Click **Continue** to return to the **Logistic Regression** dialog box. You will see that, in the **Covariates** box in Figure 8, the variable names are now marked as categorical with **Cat** in brackets after the variable names.

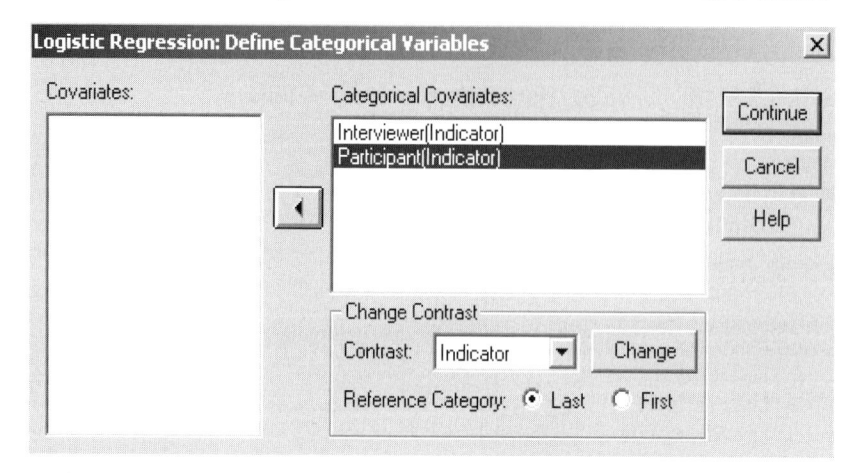

Figure 9. The completed dialog box for **Define Categorical Variables**

- Select **Iteration history** from the options (see Figure 7 in the previous example). Click **Continue** to return to the **Logistic Regression** dialog box.
- Click **OK**.

14.3.8 Output of binary logistic regression with categorical independent variables

The **Iteration History** table (Output 19) in **Block 1: Forward Stepwise (Likelihood Ratio)** shows that only the interaction of the two categorical variables *Interviewer by Participant* was entered in the model and that the values converged after just four iterations.

Iteration History[a,b,c,d]

Iteration		-2 Log likelihood	Coefficients	
			Constant	Interviewer(1) by Participant(1)
Step 1	1	126.262	-.027	1.387
	2	125.945	-.027	1.659
	3	125.942	-.027	1.685
	4	125.942	-.027	1.685

a. Method: Forward Stepwise (Likelihood Ratio)
b. Constant is included in the model.
c. Initial -2 Log Likelihood: 136.058
d. Estimation terminated at iteration number 4 because parameter estimates changed by less than .001.

Output 19. The Iteration History showing that only the *Interviewer by Participant* interaction was entered in the model

Discriminant analysis and logistic regression 399

The Classification Table (Output 20) shows that the model predicted 59% of the *Would you help?* results correctly using just the interaction of *Interviewer and Participant*.

Classification Table[a]

			Predicted		
			Would you help?		Percentage
	Observed		Yes	No	Correct
Step 1	Would you help?	Yes	38	4	90.5
		No	37	21	36.2
	Overall Percentage				59.0

a. The cut value is .500

Output 20. The Classification Table showing a 59% success rate for predicting whether someone would help

The **Model if Term Removed** table (Output 21) shows that if the interaction were to be removed, it would have a significant effect on the model. The Table of **Variables not in the Equation** (not shown here) shows that the variables *Interviewer* and *Participant* were not entered into the model.

Model if Term Removed

Variable	Model Log Likelihood	Change in -2 Log Likelihood	df	Sig. of the Change
Step 1 Interviewer * Participant	-68.029	10.116	1	.001

Output 21. Only the Sex of Interviewer × Sex of Participant interaction is significant.

This binary logistic regression, therefore, confirms the interaction that was explored in Chapter 13 with **loglinear analysis**, namely that there is a tendency for both males and females to be more helpful when the interviewer is of the opposite sex.

14.4 MULTINOMIAL LOGISTIC REGRESSION

14.4.1 Introduction

In Section 14.2, **discriminant analysis** was used to predict the university subject chosen by students on the basis of several independent variables. In Section 14.3, we introduced you to **logistic regression** which has fewer assumptions than **discriminant analysis** but SPSS's logistic regression procedure can only be used for predicting a two-category dependent variable. If there are more than two categories, then a different procedure needs to be used. Here we shall illustrate the **multinomial logistic regression** procedure applied to the data used in Section 14.2 which consisted of a three-category dependent variable (Psychologists,

Architects and Engineers). The purpose of the following illustration is to see whether **multinomial logistic regression** can predict choice of Subject at University with the same level of accuracy as can **discriminant analysis**. In multinomial logistic regression, the independent variables can be factors or covariates. In general, factors should be categorical variables (e.g. *Sex of Student*) and covariates should be continuous variables (e.g. all the remaining variables in our example).

14.4.2 Running multinomial logistic regression

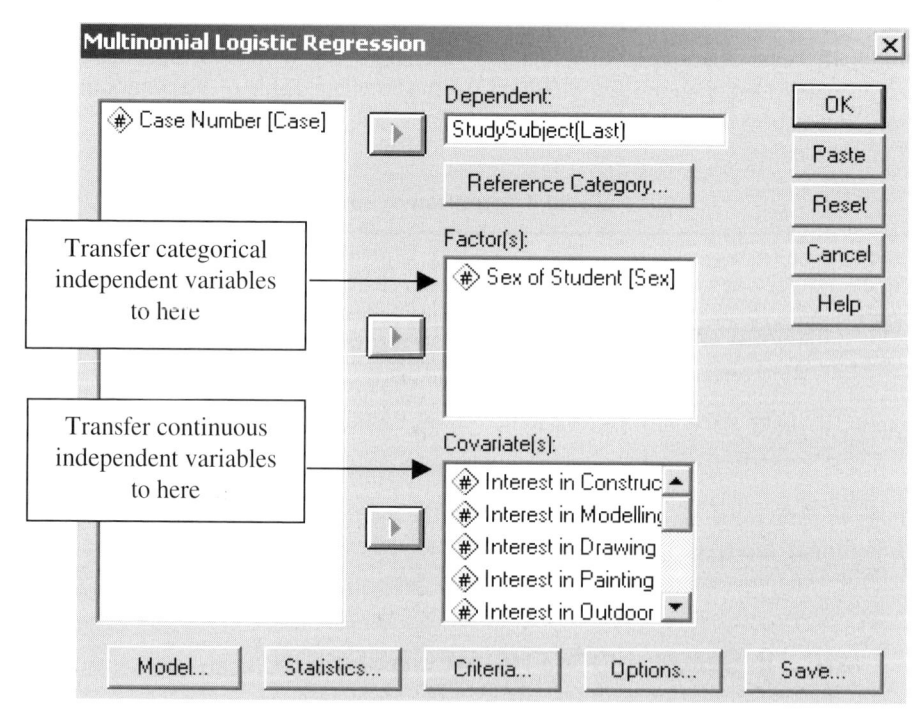

To run the multinomial logistic regression procedure with the choice of subject data, choose:
- **Analyze**
    Regression
        Multinomial Logistic…
    to open the **Multinomial Logistic Regression** dialog box (Figure 10).
- Transfer *StudySubject* to the **Dependent** box, *Sex of Student* to the **Factor(s)** box and the remaining quantitative independent variables into the **Covariate(s)** box.

Figure 10. The **Multinomial Logistic Regression** dialog box

- Click **Model…** at the bottom of the **Multinomial Logistic Regression** dialog box to open the **Model** dialog box (Figure 11). Activate the **Custom/Stepwise** radio button, transfer the variables to the **Stepwise Terms:** panel and choose **Forward entry** as the **Stepwise Method**. Click the downward arrow to the left of the **Stepwise Terms** box and select **Main effects** instead of **Interaction**. Click **Continue** to return to the main dialog box.

Discriminant analysis and logistic regression

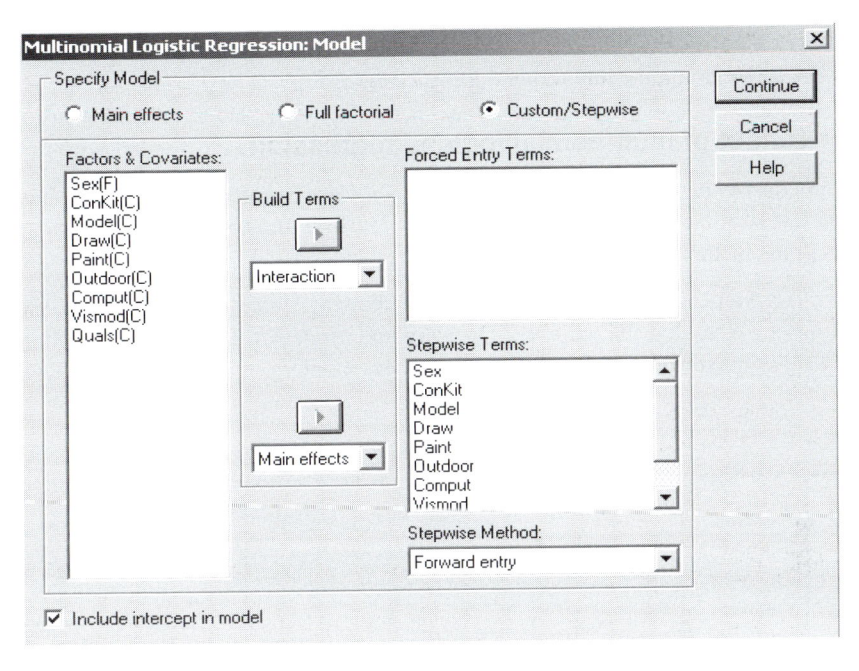

Figure 11. The **Model** dialog box with **Forward entry** selected

- Click **Statistics** to see a dialog box labelled **Multinomial Logistic Regression: Statistics**. Check the boxes as in Figure 12.

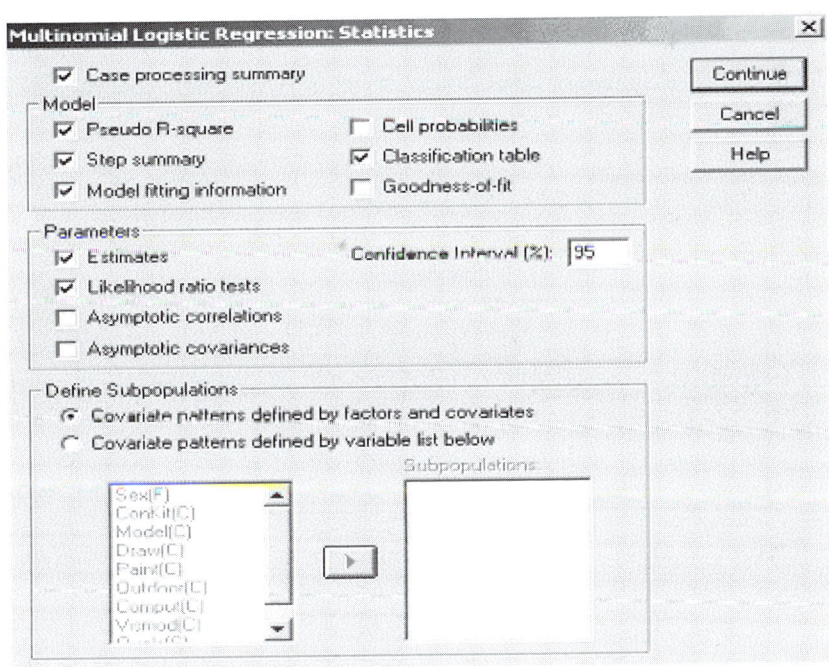

Figure 12. The **Statistics** dialog box with **Classification table** selected

- Click **Continue** to return to the **Multinomial Logistic Regression** dialog box.
- Click **OK** to run the multinomial logistic regression.

14.4.3 Output of multinomial logistic regression

The output consists of several tables. First there is a **Case Summary Table** (not shown here) listing the levels of the dependent variable (*Study Subject*) and the numbers of each, and also the levels of the factor *Sex* and the numbers of males and females.

Next there is a **Step Summary** table (Output 22) showing which covariates were entered and in which order. Note that the variables *Drawing* and *ModelKit* were never entered, the same two that were omitted from the **discriminant analysis** model.

Step Summary

Model	Action	Effect(s)	-2 Log Likelihood	Chi-Square	df	Sig.
0	Entered	Intercept	235.548			
1	Entered	Sex	208.820	26.727	2	.000
2	Entered	Painting	191.144	17.677	2	.000
3	Entered	Quals	171.760	19.384	2	.000
4	Entered	VisModel	159.182	12.578	2	.002
5	Entered	Computing	146.761	12.422	2	.002
6	Entered	Outdoor	140.055	6.705	2	.035
7	Entered	ConKit	133.221	6.834	2	.033

Stepwise Method: Forward Entry

Output 22. The **Step Summary** table showing which covariates were entered in the model

Finally after several other tables not shown here, there is the **Classification** table (Output 23) showing that 72.2% of the cases were correctly predicted using the final model.

Classification

Observed	Predicted Architect	Predicted Psychologist	Predicted Engineer	Percent Correct
Architect	20	2	8	66.7%
Psychologist	2	28	7	75.7%
Engineer	5	6	30	73.2%
Overall Percentage	25.0%	33.3%	41.7%	72.2%

Output 23. Predictions of category membership by multinomial logistic regression

Recall that a level of 72.2% accuracy of category assignment was also achieved by using **discriminant analysis** but the numbers correctly predicted for the three Study Subjects differed slightly. **Multinomial logistic regression** has been more successful at predicting

Psychologists and slightly less successful at predicting Architects. Engineers differ by just one case.

Although the general level of accuracy of assignment is the same with the two procedures, you will find, if you use the **Save** button to obtain the assignments by both techniques in **Data View**, that there is some disagreement between the category assignments by the two procedures in individual cases.

14.5 SOME GENERAL POINTS

As with multiple regression, there are three different kinds of logistic regression:
1. Direct (or simultaneous) usually called "Enter".
2. Sequential (not illustrated in this book).
3. Stepwise (forward or backward).

As with linear regression, these techniques have their limitations. Multiple regression is always least problematic when
1. Some independent variables correlate substantially with the dependent variables *and*
2. Those independent variables that correlate with one another only do so to a very small extent.

It is when there are substantial correlations among the independent variables that problems arise. These problems, which are serious for any kind of regression, intensify when one is following a stepwise regression strategy. One obvious solution to the problem of a high correlation between two independent variables is to remove one of them. But which one should be removed? There may be no clear-cut statistical answer to this question (cf. Field, 2000; pp. 203 – 204).

The need for a substantive, as well as a statistical, model

When independent variables are correlated, there is always doubt about which (if any) is the cause of the other. Earlier, in the context of multiple regression (Section 12.3.3), we made the point that decisions about such matters require a **sound substantive theoretical rationale**, as well as a statistical model that applies to the data. They cannot be made on the basis of any automatic statistical testing procedure.

The point would be trivial with the sequential approach (when the researcher specifies the order of variables to be entered into the analysis), which obviously requires a strong rationale for imposing a specific *a priori* (i.e. theoretically-driven) order on the independent variables. That happy situation, however, is rather rare in multivariate correlational research. Even the direct or simultaneous method is not without its risks. It is true that each independent variable is treated as if it had been entered into the equation last. But there is no guarantee that if a new variable were to be added, the picture would remain the same. The safe use of any multiple regression method requires not only a sound statistical model, but also a cogent **causal model**. See Howell (2002), Tabachnick & Fidell (2001) and Field (2000), each of which has its special merits and emphases, and all of which are highly readable.

Appendix

The data for logistic regression

Blood	Smoke	Alcohol	Blood	Smoke	Alcohol	Blood	Smoke	Alcohol
Yes	8	17	No	5	14	No	3	13
Yes	8	15	Yes	5	9	No	2	14
Yes	8	16	No	5	12	No	2	13
Yes	8	16	Yes	5	10	No	2	12
Yes	8	15	Yes	5	10	No	2	12
Yes	8	18	Yes	5	11	No	2	9
Yes	8	15	Yes	5	12	No	2	5
No	8	15	No	5	11	Yes	2	5
Yes	8	17	Yes	5	5	No	2	14
Yes	8	17	No	5	14	No	2	13
No	8	16	No	5	10	No	2	12
Yes	8	3	Yes	5	10	No	1	14
Yes	7	15	No	4	10	No	1	13
No	7	14	Yes	4	10	No	1	4
Yes	7	3	No	4	10	No	1	3
Yes	7	15	No	4	9	No	1	14
No	7	14	Yes	4	9	No	1	13
Yes	7	3	Yes	4	9	No	1	12
Yes	7	15	Yes	4	9	No	1	12
Yes	7	3	Yes	4	9	No	1	11
No	7	14	No	4	14	No	1	12
Yes	7	1	Yes	4	8	No	1	13
No	7	14	No	4	12	No	0	13
Yes	7	13	No	4	12	No	0	12
Yes	7	13	No	4	13	No	0	2
Yes	7	18	No	4	8	No	0	14
Yes	7	15	No	4	12	No	0	12
Yes	7	2	Yes	4	7	No	0	13
Yes	6	13	No	4	13	No	0	12
Yes	6	2	Yes	4	8	No	0	10
Yes	6	10	No	4	13	No	0	12
Yes	6	2	Yes	3	6	No	0	8
Yes	6	3	No	3	12			
No	6	13	No	3	5			

EXERCISE 23

Predicting category membership: Discriminant analysis and binary logistic regression

Before you start

Before proceeding with this practical, please read Chapter 14.

Prediction of reading success at the school-leaving stage

Just before they leave school, students in the most senior class of a school are regularly tested on their comprehension of a difficult reading passage. Typically, only 50% of students can perform the task. We shall also suppose that, for a substantial number of past pupils, we have available data not only on their performance on the comprehension passage but also on the very same variables that were investigated in the exercise on multiple regression, namely, the reading-related measures that we have referred to in Table 1 below as *Logo*, *Syntax* and *Vocal*, all of which were taken in the very earliest stages of the children's education.

The full data set is given in the appendix of this Exercise. As with the multiple regression example, we hope that the data have already been stored for you in a file with a name such as **discrim**, the contents of which you can access by using the **Open** procedure. The data (*Ex23 Reading data for discriminant analysis*) are also available from WWW in the website

http://www.abdn.ac.uk/psychology/materials/spss.shtml

Table 1 shows the first and the last two lines of the data set.

Table 1 Part of the data set

Logo	Syntax	Vocal	Comprehension
10	20	64	1
28	28	58	1
...	...	...	...
82	69	60	2
51	48	52	2

The rightmost variable is a coding variable whose values, *1* and *2*, denote, respectively, *failure* and *success* on the comprehension task.

Exploring the data set

Before moving on to the main analysis, a preliminary exploration of the data will bring out at least some of their important features. For example, if a particular variable is going to be useful in assigning individuals to categories, one might expect that, if its scores are subdivided by category membership, there should be a substantial difference between the group means. If there is no difference, the variable will probably play a minimal role in the final discriminant function. To investigate these differences, **one-way ANOVAs** can be used to compare the group means on the various independent variables. These tests, however, are requested by options in the **Discriminant** procedure. We shall therefore return to the descriptive statistics when we come to prepare the dialog box.

Since discriminant analysis assumes that the distribution of the independent variables is multivariate normal, we shall also need to look at their distributions.

In the **Graphs** drop-down menu choose **Boxplot...** (see Section 14.2.2). Choose the **Summaries of Separate Variables** option and define the variables as *Logo, Syntax* and *Vocal*.

- Study the output and note whether the boxplots reveal any outliers. Do the side-by-side boxplots show anything of interest?

DISCRIMINANT ANALYSIS

Procedure for discriminant analysis

Run the discriminant analysis as described in Section 14.2.3. There, however, we recommended the **Stepwise** method of minimisation of **Wilks' Lambda**. In the present example, because of its simplicity, it is better to use the default method known as **Enter**, in which all the variables are entered simultaneously. Since **Enter** is the default method, there is no need to specify it. In the **Discriminant Analysis** dialog box, click **Statistics** to open the **Discriminant Analysis: Statistics** dialog box. Select **Univariate ANOVAs** and click **Continue**. In the **Discriminant Analysis** dialog box, click **Classify** to open the **Discriminant Analysis: Classification** dialog box and (in **Display**) select **Summary table**. Click **Continue**, then **OK**.

Output for discriminant analysis

The main features of the output for a discriminant analysis are explained in Section 14.2.4, which you should review. In the present example, the table labelled Group Statistics shows the number of cases in each of the categories of the variable *Comp*. The next table, headed Tests of Equality of Group Means lists **Wilks' Lambda** and **F-ratios** (with their associated p-values in the column **Sig.**) for the comparisons between the groups on each of the three independent variables.

- Which variables have significant F ratios and which do not?

There now follows the first of the tables labelled **Eigenvalues**, which show the output of the discriminant analysis proper. Because there are only two groups, there is only one function. The next table, **Wilks' Lambda**, tabulates the statistic **lambda**, its **chi-square value** and the associated p-value (**Sig.**). You will notice immediately that the value of lambda is smaller than the value for any of the three IVs considered separately. That is well and good: the discriminant function *D*, which uses the information in all the IVs should do a better job than any one IV alone. Here there is an obvious parallel with multiple regression, in which the predictive ability of the multiple regression equation cannot (provided there is no multicollinearity) be less than the simple regressions of the target variable on any one predictor alone. In the case of the variable *Vocal*, however, the improvement is negligible. Since, however, two of the IVs can each discriminate reliably between the groups, the result of the chi-square test of lambda in the discriminant analysis table is a foregone conclusion. As expected, the p-value is very small. The discriminant function D can indeed discriminate reliably between the two groups on the basis of performance on the independent variables.

Ignore the table labelled Standardized Canonical Discriminant Function Coefficients. A more useful table is the next one, labelled **Structure Matrix**, which lists the pooled-within-groups correlations between discriminating variables and the standardized canonical discriminant function.

- **Are the correlations as you expected?**

Ignore the table Functions at Group Centroids.

The next set of tables relate to the classification of cases. We have shown that the discriminant function D discriminates between the two groups; but how effectively does it do this? This is shown under the heading: 'Classification Results'.

- **Write down the percentage of grouped cases correctly classified, the percentage of correct group 1 (failure) predictions and the percentage of correct group 2 (success) predictions.**

Now try out the discriminant function on some fresh data by adding them at the end of the data file (e.g. enter in the columns for *Logo*, *Syntax*, *Vocal*, the values 50, 50, 50; 10, 10, 10; 80, 80, 80 and any others you wish). Leave the column blank for *Compreh*. Then re-run the analysis after selecting **Save** in the **Discriminant Analysis** dialog box, clicking the radio button for **Predicted group membership**, and then clicking **Continue** and **OK**. The predicted memberships will appear in the variable called **dis_1**.

- **Would someone with Logo, Syntax and Vocal scores of 50, 50, 50 respectively be expected to pass or fail the comprehension test?**

Conclusion

This Exercise is intended to be an introduction to the use of a complex and sophisticated statistical technique. Accordingly, we chose an example of the simplest possible application, in which the dependent variable comprises only two categories. The simplicity of our interpretation of a number of statistics such as **Wilks' lambda** breaks down when there are more than two categories in the dependent variable. For a treatment of such cases, see Tabachnick & Fidell (2001).

BINARY LOGISTIC REGRESSION

Procedure for binary logistic regression

We shall use the same data set for the binary logistic regression analysis at the start of this Exercise. Use the procedure described in Section 14.3.5 except for **Method** which should be left at the default method **Enter**.

Output for binary logistic regression

The main features of the output for binary logistic regression are explained in Section 14.3.6, which you should review.
Examine the tables in Block 1.
- What is the value of R^2 as calculated by the Nagelkerke formula? What is the meaning of this value?
- What is the value of chi-square for the Hosmer and Lemeshow test and is it significant? What do you conclude about the fit of the model?
- What is the overall percentage of correct predictions? How does this compare with the success rate of the discriminant analysis?

Conclusion

In this example, the results of the **discriminant analysis** and **binary logistic regression** are similar but where there are several binary predictors, logistic regression would be the preferred analysis.

Appendix to Exercise 23 – The data

L is Logo; S is Syntax; V is Vocal; C is Comprehension

L	S	V	C	L	S	V	C	L	S	V	C	L	S	V	C
10	20	64	1	49	59	46	1	41	55	41	2	49	72	72	2
28	28	58	1	39	42	31	1	30	54	20	2	66	61	40	2
55	25	42	1	26	56	78	1	29	67	18	2	84	50	46	2
30	20	30	1	40	31	51	1	28	68	72	2	70	54	51	2
32	27	42	1	34	60	45	1	46	67	80	2	65	64	23	2
25	49	81	1	31	66	50	1	56	44	52	2	69	60	57	2
40	38	43	1	18	61	22	1	69	46	59	2	66	79	50	2
71	22	79	1	43	50	31	1	53	57	52	2	58	82	13	2
19	59	71	1	48	45	44	1	75	48	34	2	45	90	59	2
55	32	75	1	14	77	53	1	71	52	30	2	82	58	65	2
45	45	29	1	64	32	55	1	50	68	75	2	82	69	60	2
62	30	26	1	55	48	9	1	81	54	41	2	51	48	52	2
20	69	78	1					51	62	14	2				

CHAPTER 15

Exploratory factor analysis

15.1   Introduction
15.2   A factor analysis of data on six variables
15.3   Using SPSS control language

15.1   INTRODUCTION

15.1.1   What are the 'factors' in factor analysis?

Suppose that a sample of pupils is tested on several variables, perhaps an assortment of school subjects such as foreign languages, music, mathematics, mapwork and so on. The correlations of performance on each test with every other test in the battery can be arranged in a rectangular array known as a **correlation matrix**, or **R-matrix** (Table 1).

Correlation Matrix

		French	German	Latin	Music	Maths	Mapwork
Correlation	French	1.000	.933	.977	-.351	-.335	-.456
	German	.933	1.000	.928	-.468	-.516	-.612
	Latin	.977	.928	1.000	-.366	-.310	-.448
	Music	-.351	-.468	-.366	1.000	.908	.962
	Maths	-.335	-.516	-.310	.908	1.000	.939
	Mapwork	-.456	-.612	-.448	.962	.939	1.000

Table 1.   A correlation matrix (as output by SPSS) showing, in each row or column, the correlations of one test with each of the other tests

In its basic form, a correlation matrix is **square**, that is, there are as many rows as there are columns. The diagonal of cells running from top left to bottom right is known as the **principal diagonal** of the matrix. The correlations in the off-diagonal cells are the same above and below the principal diagonal (e.g. the correlation of *French* with *German* is the same as that of *German* with *French*). Each row (or column) of the **R-matrix** contains all the correlations involving one particular test in the battery. Since the variables are labelled in the same order in the rows and columns of the **R-matrix**, each of the cells along the principal diagonal contains the correlation of one of the variables with itself (i.e. *1*). The **R-matrix** can be the starting point for a variety of multivariate statistical procedures, but in this chapter we shall consider just one technique: **factor analysis.**

The presence in the **R-matrix** of clusters of sizeable correlations among subsets of the tests in the battery (e.g. Music and Maths; French and German) would suggest that these subset tests may be tapping the same underlying intellectual dimension or ability. If the traditional British theories of the psychology of intelligence are correct, there should be fewer (indeed, far fewer) dimensions than there are tests in the battery. The purpose of factor analysis is to identify and to quantify the dimensions supposed to underlie performance on a variety of tasks.

The **factors** produced by factor analysis are mathematical entities, which can be thought of as classificatory axes for plotting the results of the tests. The greater the value of a test's co-ordinate, or **loading**, on a factor, the more important that factor is in accounting for the correlations between that test and the others in the battery. A **factor**, then, has a geometric interpretation as a classificatory axis in an axial reference system with respect to which the tests in the battery are represented as points in space.

The term **factor** also has an equivalent algebraic, or arithmetical interpretation as a linear function of the observed scores that people achieve on the tests in a battery. If a battery comprises eight tests, and each person tested were also to be assigned a ninth score consisting of the sum of the eight test scores, that ninth, artificial, score would be a **factor score**, and it would make sense to speak of correlations between the factor and the real test scores. We have seen that the loading of a test on a factor is, geometrically speaking, the co-ordinate of the test point on the factor axis. But that axis represents a 'factor' in the second, algebraic sense, and the loading is the correlation between the test scores and those on the factor.

In factor analysis, a major assumption is that the mathematical factors represent **latent variables** (i.e. psychological dimensions), the nature of which can only be guessed at by examining the nature of tests that have sizeable co-ordinates on any particular axis. It should perhaps be said at the outset that this claim is controversial, and there are those who insist that the factors of factor analysis are statistical realities, but psychological fictions.

The topic of factor analysis is not elementary, and the SPSS output bristles with highly technical terms. If you are unfamiliar with factor analysis, we suggest you read the lucid texts by Kim and Mueller (1978a, 1978b) and by Tabachnick and Fidell (2001), which contain relatively painless introductions.

15.1.2   Stages in a factor analysis

A factor analysis usually takes place in three stages:
1. A **matrix of correlation coefficients** is generated for all possible pairings of the variables (i.e. the tests).
2. From the correlation matrix, **factors** are extracted. The most common method is called **principal factors** (often wrongly referred to as **principal components** extraction, hence the abbreviation **PC**).
3. The factors (axes) are **rotated** to maximise the relationships between the variables and some of the factors and minimise their association with others. The most common method is **varimax**, a rotation method which maintains

independence among the mathematical factors. Geometrically, this means that during rotation, the axes remain **orthogonal** (i.e. they are kept at right angles).

A fourth stage can be added at which the scores of each participant on each of the factors emerging from the analysis are calculated. It should be stressed that these **factor scores** are not the results of any actual test taken by the participants: they are estimates of the participants' standing on the **supposed** latent variables that have emerged as mathematical axes from the factor analysis of the data set. Factor scores can be very useful, however, because they can subsequently be used as input for further statistical analysis.

It is advisable to carry out only Stage 1 initially, in order to be able to inspect the correlation coefficients in the correlation matrix R. Since the purpose of the analysis is to link variables together into factors, those variables must be related to one another and therefore have correlation coefficients larger than about 0.3. Should any variables show no substantial correlation with any of the others, they would be removed from R in subsequent analysis. It is also advisable to check that the correlation matrix does not possess the highly undesirable properties of **multicollinearity** and **singularity**. The former is the condition where the variables are very highly correlated, which can arise when two tests are measuring essentially the same thing. The latter, an extreme case of the former, would obtain in the unlikely event of some of the variables being exact linear functions of others in the battery. Should the matrix show multicollinearity, some of the variables must be omitted from the analysis.

15.1.3 The extraction of factors

The factors (or axes) in a factor analysis are **extracted** (or, pursuing the geometric analogy, **constructed**) one at a time. The process is repeated until it is possible, from the loadings of the tests on the factors so far extracted, to generate good approximations to the correlations in the original **R matrix**. Factor analysis tells us how many factors (or axes) are necessary to achieve a reconstruction of R that is sufficiently good to account satisfactorily for the correlations that R contains.

15.1.4 The rationale of rotation

If we think of the tests in the battery and the origin of the axis (factor) set as stationary points and rotate the axes around the origin, the values of all the loadings will change. Nevertheless, the new set of loadings on the axes, *whatever their new position*, can still be used to produce exactly the same values as the estimates of the correlations in the R-matrix. In this sense, the position of the axes is arbitrary: the factor matrix (or **F-matrix**) only tells us *how many* axes are necessary to classify the data adequately: it does not thereby establish that the initial position of the axes is the appropriate one.

In **rotation**, the factor axes are rotated around the fixed origin until the loadings meet certain criteria. The set of loadings that satisfies the criteria is known as the **rotated factor matrix**. The purpose of rotation is to arrive at a factor matrix with a pattern of loadings that is easier to interpret than the original factor matrix. More technically, the aim is to achieve a configuration of loadings with a rather elusive quality known as **simple structure**, which means that most tests are loaded on a minimum number of factors. The fewer the factors that are involved in accounting for the correlations among a group of tests, the easier it is to invest those factors with meaning. In fact, simple structure is an ideal never achieved in practice, partly because the concept, in its original form, is actually rather vague and embodies contradictory properties. Modern computing packages such as SPSS offer a selection of rotation methods, each based upon a different (but reasonable) interpretation of simple structure.

15.1.5 Confirmatory factor analysis and structural equation modelling

So far, we have considered the use of factor analysis to ascertain the minimum number of classificatory variables (or axes) we need to account for the shared variance among a set of tests. While the researcher will almost certainly have expectations about how many factors are likely to emerge, the process of factor extraction proceeds automatically until the criterion is reached, after which the process terminates. In several fields, such as human abilities and intelligence, 'factor invariance' has been found with those factors accounting for the greatest amounts of variance, such as the general intelligence (g) factor and the major group factors.

There are, nevertheless, some problems and issues associated with factor analysis. Even when the same battery of tests is used, the precise number of factors extracted has been found to vary from study to study. Moreover, the pattern shown by the loadings in the final rotated factor matrix depends upon the method of rotation used: some methods (such as **varimax**) keep the factor axes at right angles; but others (such as **quartimax**) allow **oblique** (correlated) factors. There has been much argument about which method of rotation is best, and the preferred method tends to reflect the theoretical views of the user. In the circumstances, traditional factor analytic methods seem ill-suited to the testing of specific hypotheses, and many hold the view that they are appropriate only in the early, exploratory stages of research.

The methods we have been describing are known as **exploratory factor analysis**. In **confirmatory factor analysis**, the user hypothesises that there should be a predetermined number of factors, on which the tests in the battery should show specified patterns of loadings. Such a model can then be put to the test by gathering data. Recent years have seen dramatic developments in what is known as **structural equation modelling** (for example, see Tabachnick & Fidell, 2001, Chapter 14) of which confirmatory factor analysis is just one aspect.

At present, SPSS for Windows does not include a procedure for confirmatory factor analysis.

15.2 A FACTOR ANALYSIS OF DATA ON SIX VARIABLES

Suppose a researcher has available the marks of 10 children in six tests: **French, German, Latin, Music, Mathematics** and **Mapwork** as shown in Table 2. In order to identify the psychological dimensions tapped by these six tests, it is decided to carry out a factor analysis.

Exploratory factor analysis

	Table 2. Scores of 10 children on six variables					
Case	French	German	Latin	Music	Maths	Mapwork
1	72	69	81	45	53	51
2	41	32	40	78	91	81
3	47	54	46	50	47	49
4	33	34	40	56	65	63
5	75	76	91	46	54	47
6	41	46	48	92	88	90
7	67	72	68	56	45	47
8	32	41	35	32	36	37
9	84	76	92	44	51	43
10	45	36	45	72	67	79

15.2.1 Some technical terms

To understand the SPSS output, you must have at least an intuitive grasp of some factor analytic terminology.

- The **loading** of a test on a factor is the correlation between the test and the factor.

- The **communality** of a test is the total proportion of its variance that is accounted for by the extracted factors. The communality is the squared multiple correlation (R^2) between the test and the factors emerging from the factor analysis. If the factors are independent (as they will be in the example we shall consider), the communality is given by the sum of the squares of the loadings of the test on the extracted factors. The communality of a test is related to its reliability: an unreliable test cannot have a high communality.

- The **eigenvalue** (or **latent root**) of a factor is the total variance accounted for by the factor. If the eigenvalue is divided by the number of tests in the battery, the quotient is the **proportion of the total test variance** that is accounted for by the factor. The first factor extracted has the largest eigenvalue, the second the next largest eigenvalue, and so on. The process of extraction continues until the factors extracted account for negligible proportions of the total variance.

- If the eigenvalues of successive factors are plotted against the ordinal numbers of the factors, the curve eventually flattens out and has been likened to the rubble or scree on a mountainside. This is known as a **scree plot**. There is general agreement that the factorial litter or 'scree' begins when the eigenvalues fall below one.

- The process of **rotation** changes the eigenvalues of the factors that have been extracted, so that the common factor variance accounted for by the extraction is more evenly distributed among the factors after rotation. The communalities, on the other hand, are unchanged by rotation.

15.2.2 Entering the data for a factor analysis

Enter the data using the procedures described in Section 2.3. In **Variable View**, name the six variables for the factor analysis. Include an extra variable for the case number. Ensure that there are no decimals by changing the **Decimals** column value to 0. Click the **Data View** tab at the foot of **Variable View** and enter the data in **Data View**.

Note that there are no grouping variables in this data set. This is a purely correlational (as opposed to experimental) study. Inasmuch as there can be said to be an 'independent' variable, it is one whose existence must be inferred from whatever patterns may exist in the correlation matrix. It is the *raison d'être* of factor analysis to make such an inference credible. The first three cases in **Data View** are shown in Figure 1.

Case	French	German	Latin	Music	Maths	Mapwork
1	72	69	81	45	53	51
2	41	32	40	78	91	81
3	47	54	46	50	47	49

Figure 1. **Data View**, showing the scores of the first three children on six variables

15.2.3 The factor analysis procedure

To run the factor analysis procedure:
- Choose
  Analyze
      Data Reduction
          Factor… (see Figure 2)
  to open the **Factor Analysis** dialog box (Figure 3).

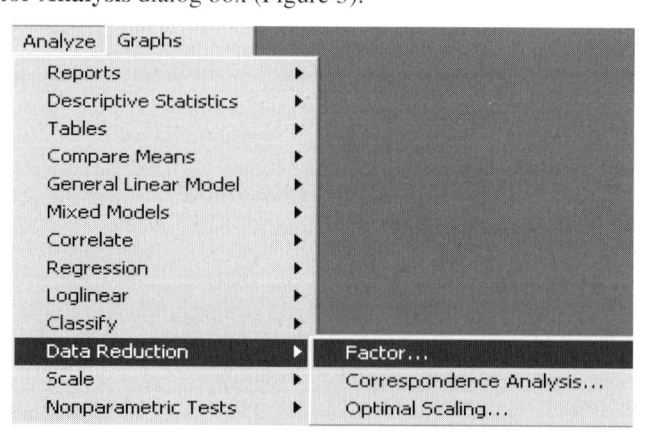

Figure 2. Finding the **Factor** dialog box

- Transfer all the variable names except *Case Number* to the **Variables** box.

Exploratory factor analysis

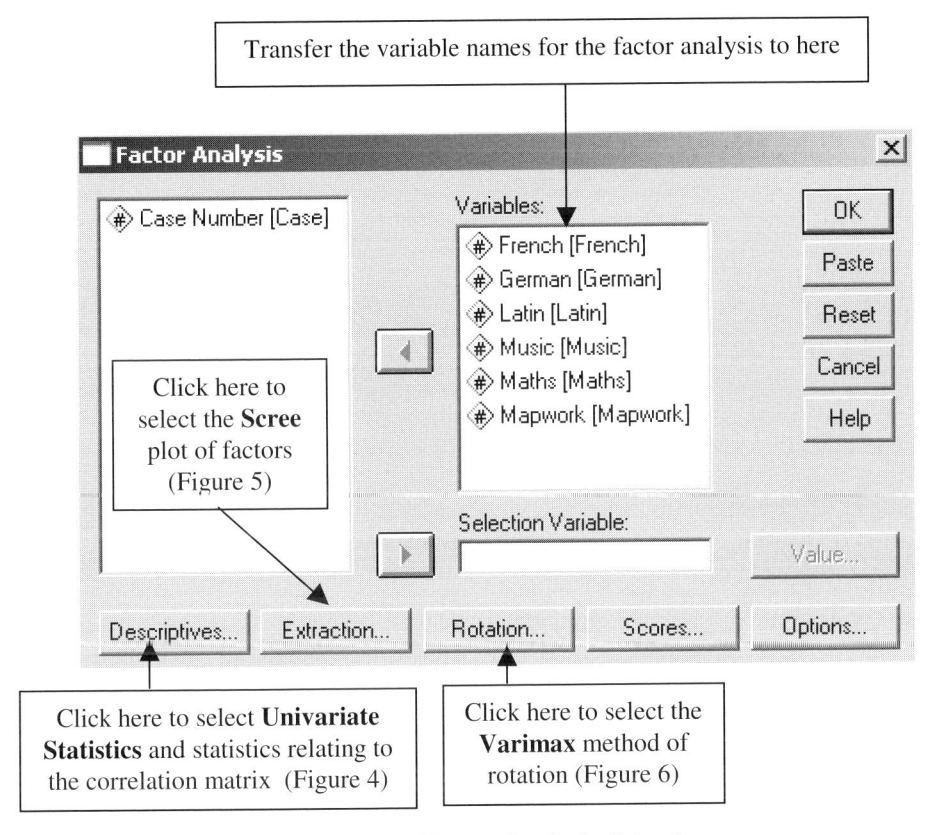

Figure 3. The **Factor Analysis** dialog box

Before running the analysis, it is necessary to select some options that regulate the manner in which the analysis takes place and to add some useful extra items to the output.
- Click **Descriptives...** to open the **Descriptives** dialog box (Figure 4). Click the following check boxes: **Univariate descriptives**, to tabulate descriptive statistics, **Initial solution**, to display the original communalities, eigenvalues and the percentage of variance explained; **Coefficients**, to tabulate the R-matrix; and **Reproduced**, to obtain an approximation of the R-matrix from the loadings of the factors extracted by the analysis. The **Reproduced** option will also obtain communalities and the residual differences between the observed and reproduced correlations.
- Click **Continue** to return to the **Factor Analysis** dialog box.

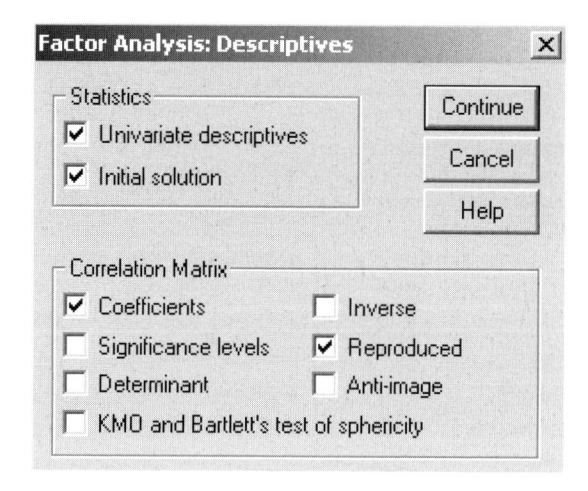

Figure 4. The **Descriptives** dialog box with **Univariate descriptives**, **Initial solution**, **Coefficients** and **Reproduced** selected

- Click **Extraction…** to open the **Extraction** dialog box (Figure 5). Click the **Scree plot** check box. The scree plot is a useful display showing the relative importance of the factors extracted.
- Click **Continue** to return to the **Factor Analysis** dialog box.

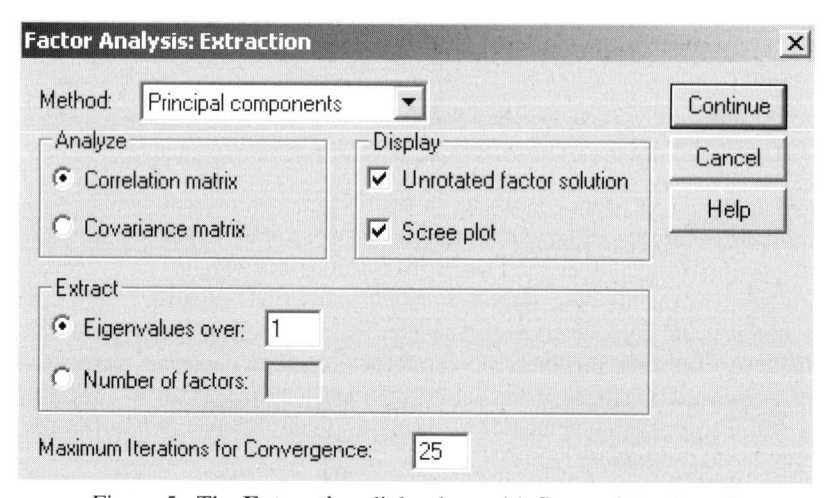

Figure 5. The **Extraction** dialog box with **Scree plot** selected

- To obtain the rotated F-matrix, click **Rotation…** to obtain the **Rotation** dialog box (Figure 6). In the **Method** box, click the **Varimax** radio button.
- Click **Continue** and then **OK**.

Exploratory factor analysis

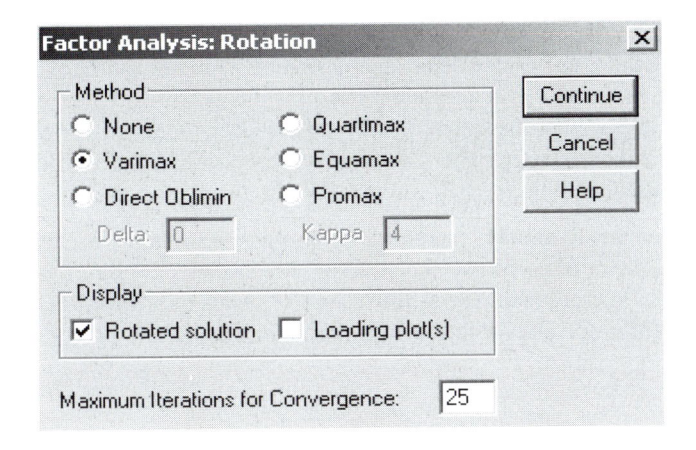

Figure 6. The **Rotation** dialog box with **Varimax** selected

15.2.4 Output for factor analysis

Descriptive statistics

Output 1 shows the specially requested descriptive statistics for the variables.

Descriptive Statistics

	Mean	Std. Deviation	Analysis N
French	53.70	18.933	10
German	53.60	18.124	10
Latin	58.60	22.262	10
Music	57.10	18.260	10
Maths	59.70	18.117	10
Mapwork	58.70	18.415	10

Output 1. Descriptive statistics for the variables

The correlation matrix (R-matrix)

The correlation matrix (edited by adding additional shading) is shown in Output 2.

		French	German	Latin	Music	Maths	Mapwork
Correlation	French	1.000	.933	.977	-.351	-.335	-.456
	German	.933	1.000	.928	-.468	-.516	-.612
	Latin	.977	.928	1.000	-.366	-.310	-.448
	Music	-.351	-.468	-.366	1.000	.908	.962
	Maths	-.335	-.516	-.310	.908	1.000	.939
	Mapwork	-.456	-.612	-.448	.962	.939	1.000

Output 2. The correlation matrix (R-matrix) with additional shading

Inspection of the correlation matrix in Output 2 reveals that there are two clusters of high correlations among the tests (shaded): one among *French, German* and *Latin*, the other among *Music, Maths* and *Mapwork*. Another interesting feature is that in either cluster, each test, while correlating highly with the others in the same cluster, does not correlate substantially with the tests in the other cluster. This pattern is what we should expect if the two groups of tests are tapping different abilities.

From inspection of the **R-matrix**, therefore, it would appear that we can account for the pattern of correlations in terms of two independent dimensions of ability. Presently, we shall see whether such an interpretation is confirmed by the results of a formal factor analysis. Are two factors sufficient to account for the correlations among the tests?

Communalities

Output 3 is a table of communalities assigned to the variables by the factor analysis.

Communalities

	Initial	Extraction
French	1.000	.981
German	1.000	.957
Latin	1.000	.979
Music	1.000	.952
Maths	1.000	.947
Mapwork	1.000	.984

Extraction Method: Principal Component Analysis.

Output 3. Table of variable communalities

The communality, as we have seen, is the proportion of the variance of the test that has been accounted for by the factors extracted. For example, we see that 98% of the variance of the scores on French is accounted for by the factors.

The next table (Output 4) displays information about the factors (SPSS calls them 'components') that have been extracted. Earlier, we saw that an **eigenvalue** is the total test variance accounted for by a particular factor, the total variance for each test being unity.

The first block of three columns, labelled **Initial Eigenvalues**, comprises the eigenvalues and the contributions they make to the total variance. The eigenvalues determine which factors (components) remain in the analysis: following Kaiser's criterion, factors with an eigenvalue of less than 1 (i.e. factors 3-6) are excluded. From the eigenvalues, the proportions of the total test variance accounted for by the factors are readily obtained. For example, the eigenvalue of the first factor is 4.18. Since the total test variance that could possibly be accounted for by a factor is 6, the proportion of the total test variance accounted for by the first factor is 4.18 ÷ 6 = 69.65 %, the figure given in the **% of Variance** column. In this analysis, the two factors that meet the Kaiser criterion account for nearly 97% of the variance (see column labelled **Cumulative %**).

The second block of three columns (**Extraction Sums of Squared Loadings**) repeats the output of the first block for the two factors that have met Kaiser's criterion.

Exploratory factor analysis

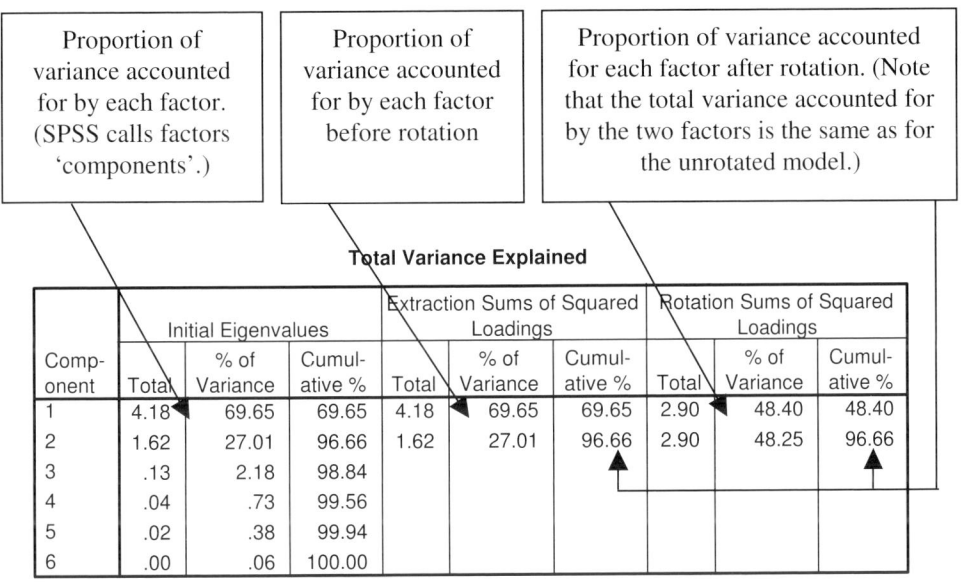

Total Variance Explained

Component	Initial Eigenvalues Total	% of Variance	Cumulative %	Extraction Sums of Squared Loadings Total	% of Variance	Cumulative %	Rotation Sums of Squared Loadings Total	% of Variance	Cumulative %
1	4.18	69.65	69.65	4.18	69.65	69.65	2.90	48.40	48.40
2	1.62	27.01	96.66	1.62	27.01	96.66	2.90	48.25	96.66
3	.13	2.18	98.84						
4	.04	.73	99.56						
5	.02	.38	99.94						
6	.00	.06	100.00						

- Proportion of variance accounted for by each factor. (SPSS calls factors 'components'.) → Initial Eigenvalues
- Proportion of variance accounted for by each factor before rotation → Extraction Sums of Squared Loadings
- Proportion of variance accounted for each factor after rotation. (Note that the total variance accounted for by the two factors is the same as for the unrotated model.) → Rotation Sums of Squared Loadings

Extraction Method: Principal Component Analysis.

Output 4. Edited table of statistics relating to the two components extracted

The third block (**Rotation Sums of Squared Loadings**) tabulates the output for the rotated factor solution. Notice that the proportions of variance explained by the two factors are similar in the rotated solution, in contrast with the unrotated solution, in which the first factor accounts for a much greater percentage of the variance. Notice also that the accumulated proportion of variance from the two components is the same for the unrotated and unrotated solutions.

Note that the communality for each test, i.e., the total proportion of the variance of the test accounted for by the factor analysis, has not been changed by rotation.

Scree plot

Figure 7 shows the **scree plot**, which was specially requested in the **Factor Analysis: Extraction** dialog box. The plot provides a graphic image of the eigenvalue for each component extracted. The amount of variance accounted for (the eigenvalue) by successive components initially plunges sharply as successive factors (components) are extracted.

The point of interest is where the curve connecting the points begins to flatten out, a region which has been fancifully likened to the rubble or scree on a mountain-side. It can be seen that the 'scree' begins to appear between the second and third factors. Notice also that Component 3 has an eigenvalue of less than 1, so only the first two components have been retained.

Scree Plot

[Scree plot showing eigenvalues decreasing from ~4.2 at component 1, ~1.6 at component 2, then dropping near 0 for components 3-6, with annotation: "Only the first two components (factors) with an eigenvalue > 1 are retained in the analysis"]

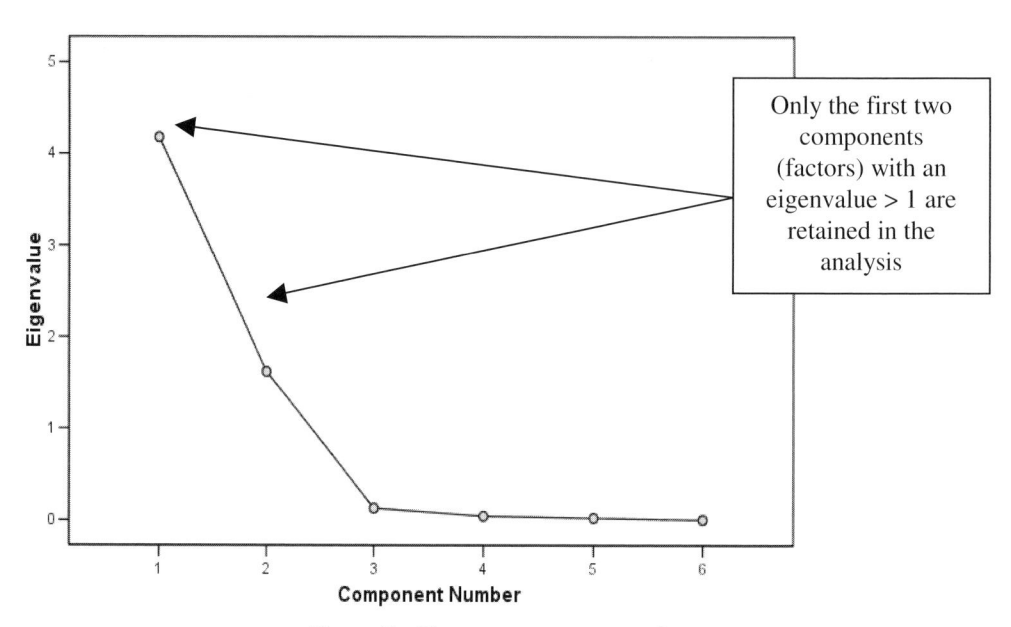

Figure 7. The component scree plot

The component matrix (unrotated factor matrix)

Output 5 shows the component (factor) matrix containing the loadings (partial correlations) of the six tests on the two factors extracted.

Component Matrix [a]

	Component 1	Component 2
French	.810	.570
German	.892	.401
Latin	.805	.574
Music	-.810	.545
Maths	-.801	.552
Mapwork	-.883	.451

Extraction Method: Principal Component Analysis.
a. 2 components extracted.

Output 5. The component matrix (correlations between the variables and the unrotated components)

When the factors (or 'components') are **orthogonal** (i.e. uncorrelated with each other), the factor loadings are the partial correlation coefficients between the variables and the factors.

Exploratory factor analysis

Thus the higher the absolute value of the loading (which can never exceed a maximum of 1), the more the factor accounts for the total variance of scores on the variable concerned.

It can be seen that the factor analysis has extracted two factors, in agreement with the impression given by the correlation matrix. On the other hand, it is not particularly easy to interpret the unrotated factor matrix. Both groups of tests show substantial loadings on both factors, which is not in accord with the obvious psychological interpretation of the original R-matrix.

Reproduced correlation matrix and residuals

Output 6 shows the **reproduced correlation matrix** of coefficients, computed from the extracted factors (components).

> If the factor analysis is correct, these correlations should match the original ones in Output 2

> The loadings labelled b are the communalities listed in Output 3 (i.e. the proportion of the variance of the test that is accounted for by the two factors extracted in the analysis)

Reproduced Correlations

		French	German	Latin	Music	Maths	Mapwork
Reproduced Correlation	French	.981[b]	.951	.980	-.346	-.334	-.459
	German	.951	.957[b]	.949	-.504	-.493	-.608
	Latin	.980	.949	.979[b]	-.339	-.328	-.452
	Music	-.346	-.504	-.339	.952[b]	.949	.961
	Maths	-.334	-.493	-.328	.949	.947[b]	.957
	Mapwork	-.459	-.608	-.452	.961	.957	.984[b]
Residual[a]	French		-.018	-.002	-.006	.000	.003
	German	-.018		-.021	.037	-.023	-.005
	Latin	-.002	-.021		-.027	.018	.004
	Music	-.006	.037	-.027		-.041	.001
	Maths	.000	-.023	.018	-.041		-.018
	Mapwork	.003	-.005	.004	.001	-.018	

Extraction Method: Principal Component Analysis.

a. Residuals are computed between observed and reproduced correlations. There are 0 (.0%) nonredundant residuals with absolute values greater than 0.05.

b. Reproduced communalities

> The residuals show the differences between the reproduced correlations and the original correlations: the smaller the residuals, the better the fit

Output 6. The reproduced correlation matrix and residuals

Each reproduced correlation between two tests is the sum of the products of their loadings on the factors emerging from the analysis. For example, the sum of the products of the loadings of *French* and *German* on the two factors extracted is, from the loadings in the unrotated F-matrix in Output 6, $[(0.81 \times 0.89) + (0.57 \times (0.40))] = 0.95$, which is the value given for the reproduced correlation between *French* and *German* in Output 6. The diagonal values labelled b are the reproduced communalities listed in Output 3.

The residuals are the differences between the actual and reproduced correlations. For example, the original correlation between *French* and *German* was 0.93 (Output 2) and the reproduced correlation is 0.95 so the difference is –0.02 which is the residual shown in the lower half of Output 6. Footnote *a* states the number and proportion of residuals (i.e. the differences) that are greater than 0.05. There are none. Thus in the present case, all the residuals are very small, showing that the two-component model accounts for the covariance among the six tests very well indeed. Had the residuals been large, there would have been reason to doubt the two-component interpretation of the correlation matrix.

The values in Output 6 labelled with the superscript *b* are the communalities, previously shown in Output 3. Notice that they are all large – at least 90%.

The rotated factor (component) matrix

Output 7 shows the rotated factor (component) matrix, which should be compared with the unrotated matrix in Output 5.

The purpose of rotation is not to change the number of components extracted, but to try to arrive at a new position for the axes (components) which is easier to interpret in psychological terms. In fact, the rotated component matrix is much easier to interpret than the unrotated matrix in Output 5. The three language tests now have high loadings on one factor alone (Component 2); whereas *Mapwork*, *Mathematics* and *Music* have high loadings on the other (Component 1). These factors are uncorrelated. This is quite consistent with what we gleaned from our inspection of the original R-matrix, namely, that the correlations among the six tests in our battery could be accounted for in terms of two independent psychological dimensions of ability.

Rotated Component Matrix [a]

	Component 1	Component 2
French	-.172	.975
German	-.349	.914
Latin	-.165	.975
Music	.958	-.185
Maths	.957	-.174
Mapwork	.944	-.304

Extraction Method: Principal Component Analysis.
Rotation Method: Varimax with Kaiser Normalization.
a. Rotation converged in 3 iterations.

Output 7. The rotated component matrix

15.3 USING SPSS CONTROL LANGUAGE

Throughout this book so far, the statistics provided by SPSS have been accessed by exploiting the advantages of the graphics environment that the **Windows** operating system provides. Although this is by far the most painless way of familiarising oneself with SPSS, there is an alternative approach which, for some purposes, has considerable advantages.

It is also possible to run SPSS procedures and analyses by writing instructions in SPSS **control language**. This is done in a special **syntax window**, either by typing in commands from the keyboard or by pasting them in. Commands are then executed by selecting (emboldening) them and pressing the **Run** button (see below).

For many users, SPSS syntax is daunting, to say the least. It is possible to appeal to **SPSS Help** and obtain what is known as a **syntax map**, but at first sight a syntax map seems even more opaque than the written commands themselves. There are, nevertheless, great advantages in learning how to use SPSS syntax, because for some analyses there are more options available than those accessible via dialog boxes. Moreover, the syntax for a particular analysis (even one set up initially from dialog boxes) can be saved as a syntax file and re-used later. If an analysis has been set up from dialog boxes, pressing **Paste** (instead of **OK**) in the final dialog box will paste the hitherto hidden syntax into the **syntax window** from which it can be saved to a file in the usual way.

We believe that the most efficient way of learning SPSS syntax is by working from the dialog boxes in this way, rather than ploughing through the available texts on SPSS syntax, which are better left until one has already acquired a working knowledge of the language.

15.3.1 The power of SPSS syntax: An example

With the children's scores in **Data View**, access the **Factor Analysis** dialog box in the usual way. Make the selections as before, remembering to select the buttons at the bottom of the dialog box to specify the rotation, order a scree test, request a correlation matrix and so on. Now click **Paste**. When this is done, a window with the title **!untitled syntax 1** will appear on the screen. This is the **syntax window**, which will contain the commands written in SPSS control language that have just been specified by your choices from the dialog boxes, (see Figure 8).

Some **commands** (the **data commands**) control the entry of data into SPSS. Others select and direct the statistical analysis. **In SPSS syntax, a command always ends in a full stop.** In the statement in the syntax window, there is only one full stop at the very end. This is because there is only a single command: the FACTOR command. The statement, nevertheless, is not a short one. Notice the terms /PLOT EIGEN, /ROTATION VARIMAX and so on. A phrase that begins with / is a **subcommand**. Subcommands are requests for optional extras. They are the written equivalent of pressing those special buttons at the bottom of the original dialog box.

Now select the whole of the written FACTOR command by emboldening the entire contents of the syntax window. Click the **Run** button ▶ in the toolbar above the syntax window. This has the effect of re-running the entire factor analysis. Inspect the contents of the output window to confirm that the output is the same as before.

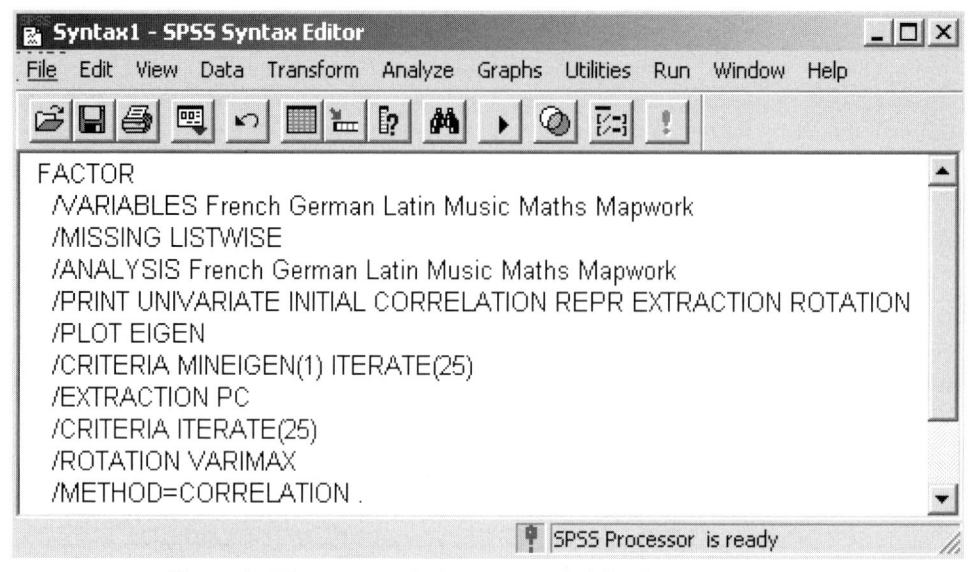

Figure 8. The syntax window and the **FACTOR** command

Saving the contents of a syntax window

To save this syntax file, select
File
    Save
and select a suitable disk drive and/or folder where the file is to be saved. The file will automatically be saved with an **.sps** extension to show that it is a syntax file (see Figure 9).

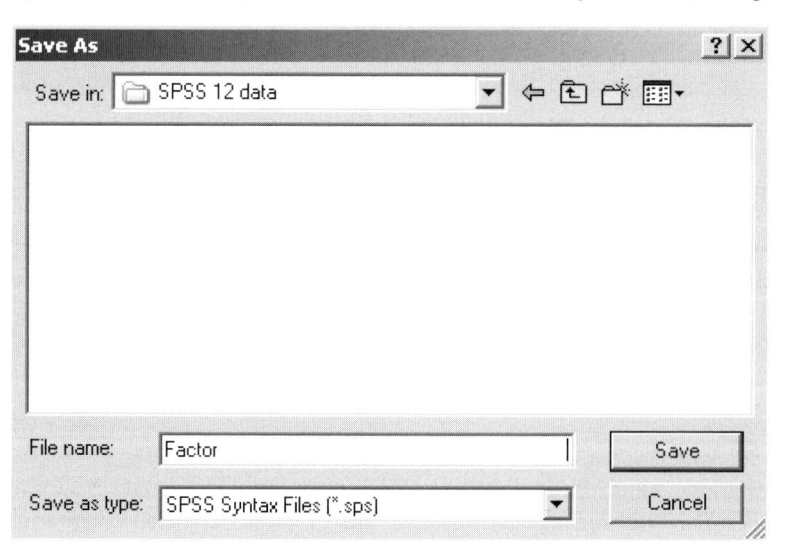

Figure 9. Saving a syntax file

Exploratory factor analysis 425

Running SPSS from a syntax file

After opening a saved data file or entering new data into **Data View**, it is a very simple matter to run a routine from a saved syntax file.

- Select
  File
    Open
      Syntax…
  to open the **Open File** dialog box (Figure 10).

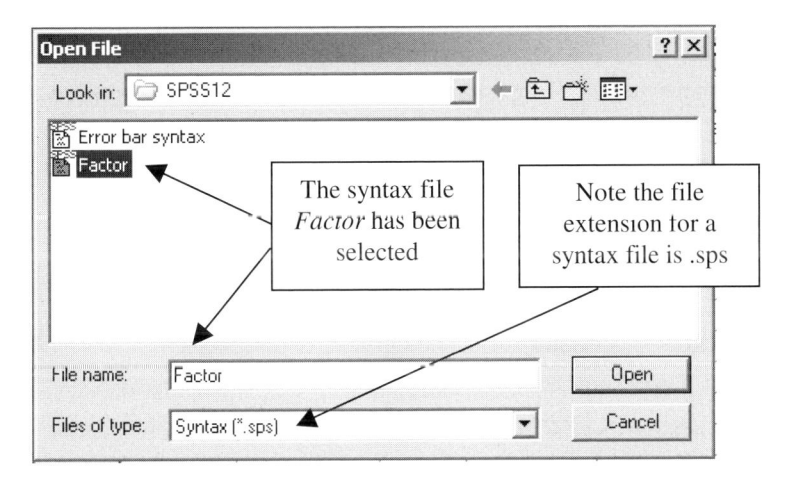

Figure 10. The **Open File** dialog box with the syntax file *Factor* selected

- It may be necessary to change the folder specified in **Look in** so that the required folder appears in the slot.
- Select the appropriate file name (here it is *Factor*).
- Click **Open** to open the syntax file factor in the **SPSS Syntax Editor** window.
- Now, you need only embolden the command in the window and click the **Run** button in the toolbar above the syntax window to re-run the complete factor analysis.

It is easy to see that with another data set comprising scores on a different battery of tests, it would be easy to edit the **FACTOR** command by changing the variable names and other specifications to match the new data in **Data View**. Inevitably, the experienced user of SPSS builds up a library of written commands, because it is quicker to carry out the analysis by editing the display in the **SPSS Syntax Editor** than to go through all the dialog and subdialog boxes again.

15.3.2 Using a correlation matrix as input for factor analysis

The graphical interface using dialog boxes is a comparatively recent development. SPSS (like several other major statistical packages) was originally designed to respond to the user's syntax commands. The translation to dialog boxes, moreover, is as yet incomplete: there are some statistical procedures that cannot yet be accessed in the graphical interface. Ultimately, to harness the full power of SPSS, you sometimes still need to use syntax commands.

Factor analysis from a correlation matrix

So far we have been considering the statistical analysis of **raw scores**, that is, data sets comprising original measurements or observations, upon which no statistical manipulations have yet been carried out. In the present factor analytic context, for example, our starting point has been a data set comprising the participants' scores on a set of tests.

Sometimes, however, it may be more convenient to use correlations (rather than raw scores) as the input for a factor analysis. The user may already have an **R-matrix** and wish to start at that point, rather than going back to the raw data. Unfortunately, since this cannot be done with dialog boxes, the user must turn to **SPSS syntax**. The procedure has two stages:
1. Preparing the correlation matrix in a suitable format;
2. Commanding SPSS to read in the matrix and run the factor analysis.

Preparation of the correlation matrix
- Choose
  File
    New
      Syntax
  to open the **SPSS Syntax Editor** window.

The procedures must be of a specific form, but help with the matrix data command syntax is available by entering **MATRIX DATA** in the **Syntax Editor** and clicking [icon] in the toolbar to open a window showing the structure of the syntax. Figure 11 shows the correct syntax of the commands needed for the entry of the **R-matrix** shown in Output 2. Note that it is immaterial whether upper or lower case text is used.

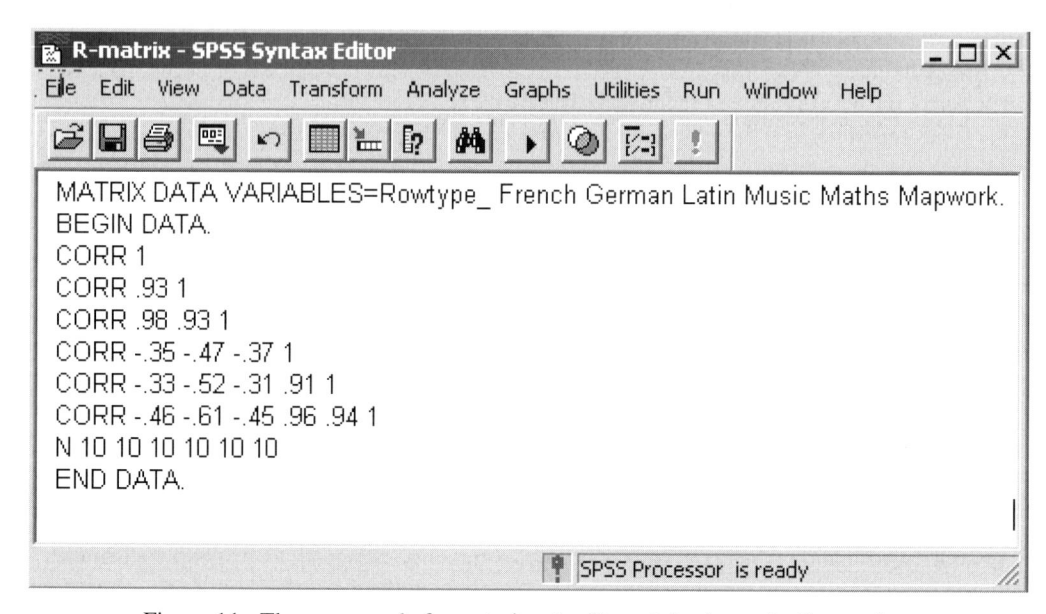

```
MATRIX DATA VARIABLES=Rowtype_ French German Latin Music Maths Mapwork.
BEGIN DATA.
CORR 1
CORR .93 1
CORR .98 .93 1
CORR -.35 -.47 -.37 1
CORR -.33 -.52 -.31 .91 1
CORR -.46 -.61 -.45 .96 .94 1
N 10 10 10 10 10 10
END DATA.
```

Figure 11. The commands for entering the **R-matrix** shown in Output 2

Exploratory factor analysis

The first command is **MATRIX DATA** followed by **VARIABLES=** and a list of variable names. This command warns SPSS to prepare to receive data in the form of a matrix whose dimensions are specified by the number of variables in the list. Like all commands, it must end in a full stop. Note the compulsory variable name **Rowtype_**, which is a special string variable used to identify the type of data for each record (row).

Next comes the data commands. First there is **BEGIN DATA** then the data themselves and finally the **END DATA** command. **Note the compulsory full stops after BEGIN DATA and END DATA.**

The first six rows of the data begin with the word **CORR**, which tells SPSS that the data are in the form of correlation coefficients. The final (7th) row begins with **N**, which is a count of the number of data points in each column. The terms **CORR** and **N** are instances of the generic term **Rowtype_** which appeared in the matrix data command.

The default structure of a correlation matrix is a lower triangular matrix. This is a square matrix with all entries above the principal diagonal omitted. If an upper triangular or rectangular matrix were to be input, an additional **/FORMAT** subcommand would be required. The value of **N** is not needed for a basic factor analysis, but it is required for tests of significance and for assessing the sampling adequacy of the data. The correlation matrix and value of **N** are then entered (preceded in each row with **CORR** or **N**, as appropriate) between the usual **BEGIN DATA** and **END DATA** commands.

To run this syntax file, do the following:
- Drag the cursor over all the syntax in Figure 11 to highlight it all.
- Click the **Run** button in the toolbar above the syntax window.
- The matrix will appear in **Data View** (Figure 12), not in **SPSS Viewer**.
- If there are any errors in the syntax, they will be flagged in the **SPSS Viewer**.

ROWTYPE	VARNAME	French	German	Latin	Music	Maths	Mapwork
N		10.00	10.00	10.00	10.00	10.00	10.00
CORR	French	1.00	.93	.98	-.35	-.33	-.46
CORR	German	.93	1.00	.93	-.47	-.52	-.61
CORR	Latin	.98	.93	1.00	-.37	-.31	-.45
CORR	Music	-.35	-.47	-.37	1.00	.91	.96
CORR	Maths	-.33	-.52	-.31	.91	1.00	.94
CORR	Mapwork	-.46	-.61	-.45	.96	.94	1.00

Figure 12. The data set after running the **MATRIX DATA** command

Preparation of the FACTOR command

Return to the syntax window and type the **FACTOR** command below the previous syntax as shown in Figure 13. Notice that the identification of the source of the matrix in the **/MATRIX =IN** subcommand is given as (**CORR=***). This shows that it is a correlation matrix (and not, say, a factor matrix), and that it is in the current data file (represented by *), as shown in **Data View** window. The **/PRINT** options are those selected in the **Descriptives** dialog box and the

/PLOT option is that selected in the **Extraction** dialog box. It is not necessary to enter /ROTATION VARIMAX because this is the default choice if none is specified. **Again note the full stop at the end of the command: it is absolutely essential.**
- Run the **FACTOR** command by highlighting the whole command with the cursor and then clicking the ▶ icon in the toolbar at the top of the syntax window. The output for the factor analysis will be identical with that previously described in Section 15.2.4.

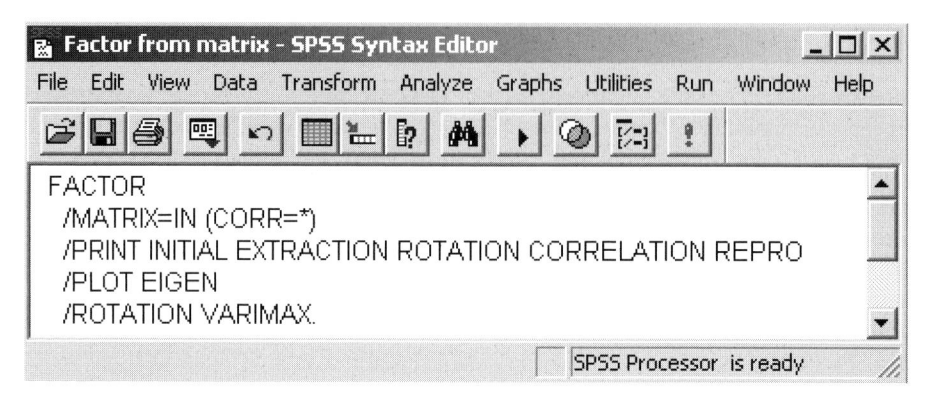

```
FACTOR
  /MATRIX=IN (CORR=*)
  /PRINT INITIAL EXTRACTION ROTATION CORRELATION REPRO
  /PLOT EIGEN
  /ROTATION VARIMAX.
```

Figure 13. The **FACTOR** command for running a factor analysis from a correlation matrix in **Data View** with various options as chosen in Section 15.2.3

15.3.3 Progressing with SPSS syntax

We believe that the best way of learning SPSS syntax is by pasting the minimal basic commands into the **syntax window** from the appropriate dialog boxes in the usual way, and observing how the syntax becomes more elaborate when extra options are chosen from the subdialog boxes.

The more experienced user will find it helpful, when writing a command in SPSS control language, to access the **Syntax Help** window by writing the command in the syntax window and clicking 🖹 in the toolbar to open a window showing the structure of the syntax, as mentioned in the previous Section. Optional subcommands are shown in square brackets. Relevant parts can be typed in the syntax window. Alternatively, the whole block of syntax can be copied over for editing from the **Syntax Help** window to the **Syntax** window by using **Copy** and **Paste** in the usual way. (These are in the **Options** menu of the **Syntax Help** window.) We do not recommend that you follow this procedure until you have already acquired some experience with SPSS syntax in the way we have described.

EXERCISE 24

Factor analysis

Before you start

Before proceeding with this practical, please read Chapter 15.

A personality study

Ten participants are given a battery of personality tests, comprising the following items: Anxiety; Agoraphobia; Arachnophobia; Extraversion; Adventure; Sociability. The purpose of this project is to ascertain whether the correlations among the six variables can be accounted for in terms of comparatively few latent variables, or factors (see Chapter 15).

Preparing the data set

The data are shown in Table 1. Name the variables in **Variable View** and assign longer names in the **Label** column. Ensure that the values in the **Decimals** column are *0*. Click the **Data View** tab to open **Data View** and enter the data.

Table 1. The questionnaire data

Participant	Anxiety	Agora	Arachno	Advent	Extrav	Sociab
1	71	68	80	44	54	52
2	39	30	41	77	90	80
3	46	55	45	50	46	48
4	33	33	39	57	64	62
5	74	75	90	45	55	48
6	39	47	48	91	87	91
7	66	70	69	54	44	48
8	33	40	36	31	37	36
9	85	75	93	45	50	42
10	45	35	44	70	66	78

Procedure for the factor analysis of the raw data

Follow the procedure described in Section 15.2.3, requesting the **Univariate descriptives**, **Initial solution**, **Coefficients**, **Reproduced**, **Scree plot**, and **Varimax** options.

Interpretation of the results

After a table of descriptive statistics, there is a table labelled **Correlation Matrix**. Is there any evident pattern that would suggest that the R-matrix might be accounted for in terms of relatively few factors (components)? Examine the remainder of the output in the manner outlined in Section 15.2.4, considering the **scree plot**, the table labelled **Component** (factor) **Matrix** listing the unrotated loadings for each factor, the residuals and the final rotated matrix in the table labelled **Rotated Component Matrix**.

- **How might the patterns among the correlations in the R-matrix be explained psychologically? Look at the table Rotated Component Matrix and make a list of the loadings that are greater than about 0.5 on each factor (component).**

Procedure for the factor analysis of the correlation matrix

Sometimes (e.g., after a large psychometric study) it is convenient to run a factor analysis from a table of correlation coefficients rather than from raw scores. Following the procedure described in Section 15.3.3, type the appropriate commands and the lower triangular version of the R-matrix (the correlation matrix in the **SPSS Viewer**) into the syntax window. Include the following items.

- The MATRIX DATA command with the appropriate variable names (including *rowtype_*).
- A BEGIN DATA command.
- Rows of correlation coefficients (each preceded by CORR).
- A row indicating the size of N (preceded by N and then the size of N repeated for as many variables as you have).
- An END DATA command concluding with a period (.).

When the data syntax is complete, run the factor analysis by dragging the cursor over all the syntax and clicking ▶. **Data View** should now appear similar to that shown in Chapter 15, Figure 12.

If all is well, proceed to prepare the FACTOR command by studying the model shown in Chapter 15, Figure 13. Run the factor analysis by selecting the command and clicking the **Run** button, as described above. Confirm that the results of the analysis are the same as those obtained when you began with the raw scores.

Revision Exercises

The revision exercises are designed to challenge the reader as to what is the most appropriate exploratory data analysis (EDA) and/or statistical test to employ given the experimental situation presented and, where appropriate, the experimental hypothesis specified. For this reason, no help is given.

It is strongly recommended that an EDA is conducted initially in case any extreme values need to be deselected or the distribution of values makes certain statistical tests unsuitable. If necessary, deselect extreme values before conducting the appropriate statistical test.

The bullet points after each Exercise are provided in case your tutor wants to know what you have done.

Revision Exercise 1

In order to test the hypothesis that, when presented with lists of words, younger children process more information than do older children, a psychologist asked groups of older and younger children to inspect and commit to memory the same list of words and then recall the words in the list. The results were as follows:

Number of words recalled by younger and older children								
Case	Younger	Case	Younger	Case	Older	Case	Older
1	16	6	16	11	12	16	4
2	223	7	21	12	20	17	16
3	20	8	20	13	10	18	9
4	23	9	18	14	13	19	11
5	17	10	20	15	15	20	9

- **Do the data confirm the hypothesis?**
- **Describe how you reached your conclusion.**
- **Name the statistical test and express the result in the usual manner.**

Revision Exercise 2

To test the hypothesis that, in families with two female children, the second-born child is more sociable than the first-born, a researcher selected twenty two-child families. In order to ensure, in each family, the comparability of the social backgrounds of the children, only families with children of Primary School age were selected. The children were tested for sociability, each child receiving a score in the range from 0 (very unsociable) to 10 (very sociable). The scores the children obtained are shown in the table below.

| Sociability scores of the first- and second-born children from twenty families ||||||
Family	First-born	Second-born	Family	First-born	Second-born
1	4	7	11	1	5
2	1	5	12	5	8
3	8	6	13	8	9
4	2	4	14	9	9
5	0	2	15	1	4
6	8	8	16	5	7
7	9	8	17	3	4
8	2	7	18	3	6
9	4	6	19	4	5
10	6	8	20	6	7

- **Do the data confirm the hypothesis?**
- **Describe how you reached your conclusion.**
- **Name the statistical test and express the result in the usual manner.**

Revision Exercise 3

A clinician has carried out a study on the efficacy of a type of cognitive therapy, in which the aim is to reduce the number of negative, self-destructive thoughts, as recorded by the patient in a special diary. The Table shows the numbers of negative thoughts recorded by 9 patients over five days, the first two days before therapy and the remaining three days after therapy. The therapy did not begin until the third day, because the therapist wanted to establish a baseline rate with which subsequent frequencies during therapy could be compared.

Numbers of negative thoughts recorded during a course in cognitive therapy					
Patient	First day	Second day	Third day	Fourth day	Fifth day
1	22	22	9	7	6
2	20	20	10	4	4
3	18	15	6	4	5
4	25	30	13	12	16
5	31	26	13	8	6
6	19	27	8	7	4
7	25	16	5	2	5
8	17	18	8	1	5
9	25	24	14	8	10

- Was the cognitive therapy effective?
- Describe how you reached your conclusion.
- Name the statistical test and express the result in the usual manner.
- A boxplot would show extreme scores for the fifth day. Would you deselect them from the data? Explain your decision.

Revision Exercise 4

For some years there was, in social psychology in the US, much emphasis upon the advantages of a 'democratic', as opposed to an 'authoritarian' leadership style in enhancing group performance. It was suspected by some, however, that the efficacy of leadership style might depend upon the nature of the task. Perhaps, for some tasks, an authoritarian (i.e. instructional) style might actually be more effective than a democratic one (i.e. one encouraging questions and discussion)? This is the hypothesis under test.

In a project designed to test the efficacy of leadership style on group performance, groups of soldiers were trained under democratic or authoritarian leadership styles. Later, groups who had been trained under each regime were tested on one of two tasks:

1. A Structured Task, namely, the assembly of a field gun;
2. A Group Problem, in which, given equipment such as barrels and ropes, the group was required to construct a bridge across a fast-flowing river.

On the basis of their performance, each group was awarded a mark on the scale from 1 (low efficacy) to 20 (high efficacy). The results are shown in the Table:

Scores achieved on a criterion group task by twenty groups of soldiers trained under democratic or authoritarian leadership styles

Criterion Task	Leadership Style — Authoritarian	Leadership Style — Democratic
Structured Task (Gun Assembly)	13 13 17 15 18	5 5 8 11 10
Group Problem (Bridge Construction)	9 2 5 12 7	19 15 18 13 14

- **Is the hypothesis supported?**
- **Describe how you reached your conclusion.**
- **Name the statistical test and express the result in the usual manner.**

Revision Exercise 5

There is a widespread belief (supported by actuarial evidence) that, in tests of decision-making in driving, those between the ages of fifty-five and sixty-five should outperform those in their twenties, despite the inevitable slowing of reaction speed that occurs as a person gets older. To investigate this claim, ten volunteers, five in their twenties and five in their late fifties and early sixties, were recruited to take part in a driving-simulation study.

Driving was assessed under simulated conditions of light and heavy road traffic in both daytime and in night-time illumination. Each driver received a score between 1 (poor) and 100 (excellent) for their performance in each of the four conditions.

The results are shown below:

Performance of drivers in two age groups, driving under simulated conditions of light and heavy traffic, and of daytime and night-time illumination

Group	Light Traffic Day	Light Traffic Night	Heavy Traffic Day	Heavy Traffic Night
Older	74	55	75	15
	72	70	70	10
	70	60	60	10
	68	50	50	10
	66	65	45	5
Younger	40	15	30	30
	25	20	20	20
	30	30	10	10
	25	40	15	15
	10	45	25	25

- **Is the hypothesis supported?**
- **Describe how you reached your conclusion.**
- **Name the statistical test and express the result in the usual manner.**

Revision Exercise 6

A researcher investigated people's ratings of their state of happiness and whether they considered life to be exciting or dull in relation to whether they were white or non-white and whether they were male or female. Is there any evidence of differences among the races and sexes for their ratings of happiness and lifestyle? Is there a relationship between happiness and lifestyle?

The data were as follows:

		Very Happy		Fairly Happy		Not Very Happy	
Race	Sex	Exciting	Dull	Exciting	Dull	Exciting	Dull
White	Male	84	33	92	129	5	20
White	Female	88	52	96	162	6	44
Non-White	Male	8	4	10	14	7	2
Non-White	Female	10	8	14	36	2	15
	TOTAL	190	97	212	341	20	81

Number of white and non-white males and females rating themselves for happiness and lifestyle

- Describe how you reached your conclusions about the researcher's questions.
- Name the statistical tests and express the results in the usual manner.

References

American Psychological Association. (2001). Publication manual of the American Psychological Association (5th ed.). Washington, D. C.: American Psychological Association.

Anscombe, F. J. (1973). Graphs in statistical analysis. American Statistician, 27, 17 - 21.

Clark-Carter, D. (1997). Doing quantitative psychological research: From design to report. Hove, East Sussex: Taylor & Francis: Psychology Press.

Cohen, J. (1962). The statistical power of abnormal-social psychological research: A review. Journal of Abnormal and Social Psychology, 65, 145 - 153.

Cohen, J. (1988). Statistical power analysis for the behavioral sciences (2nd ed.). Hillsdale, N.J.: Lawrence Erlbaum Associates.

Erdfelder, E., Faul, F., & Buchner, A. (1996). GPOWER: A general power analysis program. Behavior Research Methods, Instruments, and Computers, 28, 1 - 11.

Field, A. (2000). Discovering statistics using SPSS for Windows. London: Sage.

Gravetter, F., & Wallnau, L. (2000). Statistics for the behavioral sciences (5th ed.). Belmont, CA: Wadsworth.

Howell, D. (2002). Statistical methods for psychology (5th ed.). Pacific Grove, CA: Duxbury Press.

Keppel, G., & Wickens, T. (2004). Design and analysis: A researcher's handbook (4th ed.). Upper Saddle River, NJ: Pearson Prentice Hall.

Kim, J., & Mueller, C. W. (1978a). Factor analysis: Statistical methods and practical issues. Newbury Park, CA: Sage.

Kim, J., & Mueller, C. W. (1978b). Introduction to factor analysis: What it is and how to do it. Newbury Park, CA: Sage.

Siegel, S., & Castellan, N. J. (1988). Nonparametric statistics for the behavioral sciences (2nd ed.). New York: McGraw-Hill.

Tabachnick, B. G., & Fidell, L. S. (2001). Using multivariate statistics (4th ed.). Boston: Allyn and Bacon.

Welkowitz, J., Ewen, R., & Cohen, J. (1982). Introductory statistics for the behavioral sciences. New York: Academic Press.

Winer, B. J., Brown, D. R., & Michels, K. M. (1991). Statistical principles in experimental design (3rd ed.). New York: McGraw-Hill.

Index

A

Adding new cases in Data View *57*
Adjusted R Squared *331, 336*
Aggregating data *67*
Align in Variable View *55*
Alpha (α) *176*
Alternative hypothesis *176*
Analysis of variance - see ANOVA
Analyze menu *96*
ANOVA:
    completely randomised factorial *226*
    covariate *232*
    designs *10*
    flow chart *13*
    mixed *278*
    in regression *332*
    repeated measures (within subjects) *248*
    two-way (within subjects) *264*
ANOVA (menu items):
    One-Way ANOVA *207, 210*
    GLM – Univariate for factorial *231*
    GLM – Repeated Measures *252, 281*
Anscombe data *315*
A priori comparisons *208*
Association:
    between variables *15, 296*
    flow chart *15*
Asymptotic p-values *179*
Averages flow-chart *8*

B

Backward hierarchical method (loglinear analysis) *355, 369*
Bar graph (or bar chart):
    clustered *136*
    editing *139*
    interactive *141*

simple *102, 111, 136*
with error bars *141*
Basic tables *103*
Bernoulli trials *188*
Beta (β) *176*
Beta coefficients – see Regression
Between subjects:
experimental designs *11, 226*
factors *10*
t test *164*
Binary logistic regression *387, 389*
procedure *391, 397*
Binomial test *19, 188*
Bivariate
correlation – see Correlation
data *3*
Blocking in Data View *33*
Bonferroni method *256, 259, 261, 269, 273, 282, 287*
Boxplot *110, 211, 230, 251, 280*
Boxplot structure *115*

C
Case summaries *87*
Cases in Variable View:
adding additional cases *57*
selection – see Selecting cases
weighting of – see Weighting cases
Casewise diagnostics – see Regression
Categorical data *3*
Cell editor in Data View *32*
Chart Aspect Ratio *135*
Chart Editor *135*
Charts – see Graphs
Chi-square see also Likelihood Ratio (L.R.) Chi-square
cautions and caveats *311*
test for association *9, 14, 15, 310*
test for goodness-of-fit *19, 190, 221, 363*
Class intervals *110*
Closing SPSS *40*
Clustered bar charts – see Bar charts
Cochran's Q test *14, 263*
Coefficient of determination – see R square & r-square

Collinearity & multicollinearity (in regression) *341, 377, 392*
Columns column in Variable View *30*
Communality *413, 418*
Compare Means procedure *36, 108*
Compare Means submenu *96, 167, 173*
Complete eta squared *240*
Complete omega squared *240*
Compute
    conditional *119*
    for numbering cases *50*
    procedure *50, 116*
Confidence interval *161, 169, 174, 192, 193, 217*
Confirmatory factor analysis *21, 412*
Confounded variable *4*
Conservative F test – see Greenhouse-Geisser
Contingency table *16, 308, 353*
Control group *3*
Control language *423, 428*
Copying data or output to other applications *78*
Copying in the Data Editor *31, 33*
Correlation *296*
    coefficient *298*
    matrix (R-matrix) *304, 409*
    matrix as input for factor analysis *425*
    procedure *302, 305*
    rank – see Spearman
    ratio *208*
Correlational (versus experimental) research *4*
Counterbalancing *249*
Covariance, heterogeneity of – see Mauchly
Covariate *17*
    in ANOVA *232*
Cox & Snell R Square *394*
Cramér's V *15, 308, 310*
Creating new folder *35*
Creating short-cut icon *33*
Critical difference (CD) *218*
Critical region *161*
Crosstabulation *308*
Crosstabs procedure *97, 102, 307, 309, 357*

D

d statistic *163, 194*

Data: measurements, ordinal and nominal *2, 3, 9*

Data Editor *22, 26, 48*
    window *48*

Data View *26, 31, 48, 55*

Decimals:
    setting with Options *28*
    in Variable View *27, 28*

Deleting:
    columns & rows from the Data Editor *59*
    from the Viewer *59, 81*

Dependent and independent variables *3, 17*

Descriptives procedure *100, 104*
    Statistics submenu *96*

Directional hypothesis *162*

Discriminant analysis: *17, 18, 374*
    assumptions *376*
    procedure *378*

Discriminant function: *375*
    coefficients *385*

Distribution-free tests *9*

Drop-down menus *22*

DV (Dependent Variable) *3*

E

EDA (Exploratory Data Analysis) *44*

Editing:
    data – see Data View
    graph or bar chart *135, 139*
    SPSS output (with SPSS Viewer) *39, 58*

Effect size: *163, 170, 175, 194, 208, 233, 235, 240, 249, 256, 269, 282, 303, 324, 325, 331, 336*
    – see also d statistic, estimated eta squared, estimated omega squared, eta squared, partial eta squared, partial omega squared

Eigenvalue *413, 418*

Entering data into SPSS *22, 32*
    between subjects *164*
    within subjects *172*

Error bar charts *140*

Error bars in bar charts *141*

Estimated eta squared *163*

Estimated omega squared *163, 209, 217*
Estimates of parameters *2*
Eta squared (η^2) *163, 208, 240*
Exact p-values *179*
EXCEL spreadsheet *76, 78*
Expected frequencies *311, 357*
Experiment *3*
Experimental group *3*
Experimental hypothesis *162*
Experimental (versus correlational) research *4*
Exploratory data analysis (EDA) *44*
Exploratory factor analysis *21, 95, 409*
Explore procedure *110, 111*
Exporting data *76*
Extreme value in boxplot *115*

F
F ratio *207*
F to Enter *376*
F to Remove *376*
Factor in experimental design *10*
Factor (in ANOVA):
    between subjects *207, 226, 227, 229*
    repeated measures (within subjects) *252, 267, 281, 289*
Factor (in factor analysis): *21, 409*
    communalities *413, 418*
    eigenvalue *413, 418*
    extraction *411*
    loading *410, 413*
    rotation *410, 413, 419*
    scree plot *413, 419*
    with correlations as input *425*
Factor analysis:
    command syntax *425, 427*
    meaning *21, 409*
    procedure *414*
Factorial ANOVA *11, 226, 229*
Factor matrix - see F-matrix
File name *26*
Find procedure *129*
Fisher's Exact Test *312*
Fixed effects – cf. Random effects *232*

Index 443

Flow chart:
    ANOVA *13*
    Difference between averages *8*
    Measures of association *15*
    One-sample tests *19*
    Procedures for prediction *17*
F-matrix (factor matrix):
    rotated *411*
    unrotated *411, 420*
Frequencies:
    procedure *100, 105*
    table *98*
Frequency distribution *110*
Friedman test *14, 261*

G

General Linear Model (GLM) *231, 252, 281*
General Tables procedure *98*
Global default *50*
Goodman & Kruskal's Lambda *308*
Goodness-of-fit *18, 19, 184*
Graphs and charts *134,*
Graphs menu *96*
Graphs:
    bar – see Bar graph
    boxplot – see Boxplot
    editing – see Editing
    histogram – see Histograms
    line – see Line graph
    pie – see Pie chart
    scatterplot – see Scatterplot
Greenhouse-Geisser test *249, 259*
Grouping variable *29*

H

Help drop-down menu in SPSS *53, 78*
Hierarchical loglinear model *354*
Histograms *106, 110, 111*
Homogeneity of covariance *249, 258, 270, 285*
Homogeneity of variance *168*
Homogeneity of variance-covariance matrices *376*
Hosmer-Lemeshow goodness-of-fit test in logistic regression *392, 395*

Huynh-Feldt test *249, 259*
Hypothesis, scientific *3*
Hypothesis: alternative & null *176*

I
Importing and exporting data *76*
Independent and related samples *6*
Independent samples *t* test *164*
Independent variable *3, 17*
Inserting additional cases and variables *48, 57, 58*
Interaction in ANOVA *227, 228*
Interaction graph *228*
Interactive Graph *134, 141*
Interval data *2*
Interval estimate *2*
Iteration history in logistic regression *392, 398*
IV (independent variable) *3*

K
Kendall's tau correlations (tau-a tau-b tau-c) *15, 305*
Kolmogorov-Smirnov test *18, 19, 185*
Kruskal-Wallis test *14, 219*

L
-2LL in logistic regression *393*
Label in Variable View *27*
Lambda, Wilks' *375, 382*
Latent root – see Eigenvalue
Latent variables *21, 410*
Layering in Compare Means *109*
Level (of a factor in ANOVA) *10*
Levene's test of homogeneity of variance *168, 174*
Likelihood ratio (L.R.) chi-square *355, 370*
Linear association *298*
Line graph *149*
Listing data *87*
Loading (in factor analysis) *410, 413*
Log(likelihood) *393, 395*
Logistic regression – see also Binary LR and Multinomial LR *17, 18, 374, 387*
Logistic regression coefficient *389*
Logistic regression function *388*
Loglinear analysis *15, 16, 353*

comparison with ANOVA *354*
procedure *359, 369*
saturated model *354, 360, 370*
small expected frequencies *357*
total independence model *364*

M

Main effect in ANOVA *227*
Mann-Whitney test *9, 179*
Matrix data command syntax *427*
Mauchly sphericity test (homogeneity of covariance) *249, 258, 270, 285*
McNemar test *9, 184*
Means procedure *108*
    – see also Compare Means, Descriptive Statistics and Explore
Measure type in Variable View *55*
Merging files:
    to add cases *70*
    to add variables *72*
Meta-analysis *103*
Missing values in Variable View *54*
Mixed (split-plot) experiments *12, 278*
Model *21, 159, 249, 325, 339, 342, 354, 394, 412*
Multicollinearity *376, 411*
Multinomial logistic regression *389, 399*
    procedure *400*
Multiple comparisons   see Post-hoc comparisons
Multiple correlation coefficient R *325, 331*
Multiple regression *17, 18, 325, 334*
    ANOVA *340*
    beta coefficients *338, 341*
    collinearity *341*
    equation *340*
    procedure *335*
    simultaneous *335*
    stepwise *339*
    tolerance *341*
Multivariate data *3*
Multivariate-normal assumption *376*
Multiway contingency tables *353*

N

Nagelkerke R Square *394*
Naming variables *27*
Nominal data *3, 9*
Nonparametric tests *9, 159, 179*
    – see also Binomial test, Chi-square test, Cochran's Q test, Friedman test, Kolmogorov-Smirnov test, Kruskal-Wallis test, Mann-Whitney test, McNemar test, Sign test, Wilcoxon test
Null hypothesis *161, 176*
Numbering cases *50*

O

OLAP Cubes *96*
Omega squared (ω^2) *163, 209*
One-factor ANOVA *210*
One-factor experiment:
    between subjects *13*
    within subjects (repeated measures) *13, 250*
One-sample tests *18, 184*
    binomial procedure *188*
    chi-square procedure – see Chi-square
    flow chart *19*
    Kolmogorov-Smirnov *185*
    t test 20, 193
    t test procedure *193*
One-tailed and two-tailed tests *162*
One-way ANOVA *210*
Opening SPSS *25*
Options menu *51, 135*
Ordinal data *3*
Orthogonal factors (in factor analysis) *411, 420*
Outlier in boxplot *115*
Outliers, effect of *96*
Output listing (SPSS Viewer) *37*

P

Page breaks *82*
Page Setup *83*
Paired data (related samples) *7*
Paired-Samples T Test procedure *159, 171*
Parameter *2*
Parametric and nonparametric tests *159* (see also Nonparametric tests)

Partial eta squared (η_p^2) *217, 235, 240, 249, 258, 271, 286*
Partial omega squared (ω_p^2) *240*
Partial regression coefficients *325, 335, 338*
Paste button *423*
Pasting in Data Editor *33*
Pearson correlation *15, 298,*
Percentiles *105, 114, 127*
Per family type error rate *261*
Phi coefficient (φ) *15, 307, 310*
Pie chart *146*
Pivot menu *39, 60*
Pivoting trays *61*
Plots (in ANOVA) – see Profile plot
Plots (in regression) *327, 333, 343*
Point estimate *2*
Pooled *t* test (cf. separate-variance *t* test) *164*
Population *1*
Post hoc comparisons *208, 213, 234, 282*
Power *175, 176, 240*
Predicting category membership *374, 387, 392*
Predicting scores *334, 343*
Prediction flow chart *17*
Predictors *17, 335, 338, 343*
Preparing data for SPSS *24*
Principal components *410*
Principal diagonal *409*
Print preview *81*
Printing in SPSS *79, 86*
Profile plot in ANOVA *214, 233, 238, 255, 260, 268, 272, 288*
p-value (tail probability) *161,*
p-value for a one-tail test *169*

Q
q (Studentized range statistic) *219*
Qualitative & quantitative variables *2*
Quartiles *105, 114*
Quasi-experiment *4*
Quitting SPSS *40*

R
R – see Multiple correlation coefficient
Random assignment *4*

Random effects – cf. Fixed effects *232*
Rank correlation (see Kendall's tau and Spearman's rho) *15, 16*
Reading in SPSS files *55*
Rearranging variables:
    in Data View *57*
    in Variable View *49*
Recode procedure *122*
Regression:
    ANOVA *332*
    Beta coefficient *332, 333*
    casewise diagnostics *325, 327, 329, 331*
    coefficient *324, 325*
    constant *324, 325*
    equation *324, 332, 337*
    line *343*
    plots *327, 342*
    procedures *327, 334*
    residuals *298, 325, 330, 333*
    simple *17, 18, 324*
    multiple *334*
    standardized predicted value *333*
    standardized residual *333*
Regressors *17, 374*
Related samples *7, 159*
Repeated measures *7*
Reports submenu *96*
Reproduced correlation matrix (in factor analysis) *421*
Research question *5*
Residuals (in loglinear) *355*
Residuals (in regression) – see Regression
Resuming work on a saved data file *41*
R-matrix *409, 417*
Robust *21*
Rotated factor matrix *422*
Rotation (of factors) *413, 419*
r square (r^2) *299, 303, 324*
R square (R^2) *325, 331, 336*
    see also Cox & Snell R Square;
        Nagelkerke R Square
Run button (for syntax) *425, 428*

S

Sample *1*
    independent and related samples *6*
Sampling variability *1*
Saturated model (loglinear) *354, 360, 370*
Save a file *36*
Scatterplot: *150*
    clustered *300, 344*
    importance of *172, 296*
    procedure *151, 300, 342*
    with regression line *342*
Scree plot *413, 419*
Selecting cases *65, 330*
Separate-variance *t* test (cf. pooled variance *t* test) *164*
Setting decimal places – see Decimals
Sign test *9, 172, 179, 184, 264*
Significance: *161*
    correlation coefficient *299*
    level *161*
Simple main effects (ANOVA) *239, 273, 290*
Simple regression – see Regression
Simple structure (in factor analysis) *411*
Singularity (of R-matrix) *376, 411*
Size of sample *175, 210, 240*
Sort Cases procedure *69*
Spearman's rho (rank correlation) *15, 16, 304, 305*
Sphericity - see Mauchly
Split-plot (mixed) factorial designs *12, 278*
SPSS command language (syntax) *423*
SPSS Data Editor – see Data Editor
SPSS tutorials *36*
SPSS Viewer *23, 38, 58*
Statistic *2*
Statistical association – see Association
Statistical hypothesis *160*
Statistical inference *2*
Statistical model *159* (see also Model)
Stem-and-leaf display *110*
Stepwise method in discriminant analysis *375*
Stepwise method in multiple regression – see Multiple regression
String variable *52*
Structure matrix (in discriminant analysis) *385*

Structural equation modelling *412*
Studentized range statistic (q) *219*
Substantive model of causation (in regression) *343*
Syntax *423*
Syntax window *423*

T
Tables submenu *97, 98*
Tail probability - see p-value
Task bar *40*
Tau-a, tau-b, tau-c *305*
Three-factor factorial ANOVA *241*
Three-factor mixed ANOVA *288*
Tolerance (in discriminant analysis) *383*
Tolerance (in regression) *341*
Total independence model – see Loglinear analysis
Transform submenu *96*
Transposing data *61*
Transposing rows and columns *61, 74*
t test:
    assumptions *159, 164, 179*
    flow chart *8*
    independent samples *8, 164*
    one-sample *8, 193*
    paired samples *171*
    pooled variance *8, 169*
    related samples *8, 171*
    separate variance *8, 164*
Tutorials *36, 64, 139*
Two-factor mixed ANOVA *279*
Two-factor within subjects ANOVA *264*
Two-sample tests *159*
Two-tailed tests *162*
Tukey's HSD test *217, 234, 237, 282*
Type I and Type II errors *176, 291*
Type of variable in Variable View *52*

U
Univariate data *3*
Univariate menu *212, 232*
Unplanned multiple comparisons – see Post
    hoc comparisons

Unrotated factor matrix *420*
User-missing values *54*

V

Value labels *29, 34*
Values of variable in Variable View *29*
Variable *2*
    rules for naming *27*
    entering variable name in Variable View *27*
Variable Type dialog box *53*
Variable View *26, 27, 48*
Variance, homogeneity of – see Levene's test
Varimax method of factor rotation *410, 416*
Viewer (SPSS) *23, 38, 58*
Visual Bander *122, 124*

W

Weighting of cases *188, 309, 357, 369*
Width column in Variable View *29*
Wilcoxon paired samples test *9, 172, 179, 182*
Wilks' Lambda statistic *375*
Within subjects experiments *7, 9, 11, 248*
    advantages and disadvantages *248*
Within subjects:
    assumptions *249*
    designs *11, 248*
    factors *10*
    factorial experiments *12, 264, 279*
    t test *171*